Checklists and Boxes

ESL Highlights

Prentice Hall
Handbook for Writers

12th Edition

Melinda G. Kramer
Prince George's Communtiy College

Glenn Leggett
Professor Emeritus, Grinnell College

C. David Mead
Michigan State University

Prentice Hall, Englewood Cliffs, New Jersey 07632

Library of Congress Cataloging-in-Publication Data

KRAMER, MELINDA G. (date)
    Prentice-Hall handbook for writers / Melinda G. Kramer, Glenn
Leggett, C. David Mead. — 12th ed.
      p. cm.
    Prev. ed. cataloged under: Leggett, Glenn H.
    Includes index.
    ISBN 0–13–037425–3. — ISBN 0–13–149618–2 (pbk.)
    1. English language—Rhetoric—Handbooks, manuals, etc.
    2. English language—Grammar—Handbooks, manuals, etc. I. Leggett,
Glenn H. (date). II. Mead, C. David (Carl David) (date).
III. Leggett, Glenn H. (date) Prentice-Hall handbook for writers.
IV. Title.
PE1408.K699 1995
808'.042—dc20
                                        94–32494
                                        CIP

Acquisitions editor: Alison Reeves
Editorial production/supervision: F. Hubert
Development editor: Leslie Taggart
Design: Douglass Scott, Cathleen Damplo, WGBH Design
Manufacturing buyers: Tricia Kenny and Mary Ann Gloriande

Cover credit: Patrick Henry Bruce, *Composition III.*
Yale University Art Gallery, Gift of Collection Societe Anonyme.

Credits begin on page xxxiv, which constitutes
a continuation of the copyright page.

 © 1995 by Prentice-Hall, Inc.
A Simon & Schuster Company
Englewood Cliffs, New Jersey 07632

Printed in the United States of America

10 9 8 7 6 5 4 3 2 1

ISBN 0-13-149618-2

Prentice-Hall International (UK) Limited, *London*
Prentice-Hall of Australia Pty. Limited, *Sydney*
Prentice-Hall Canada Inc., *Toronto*
Prentice-Hall Hispanoamericana, S.A., *Mexico*
Prentice-Hall of India Private Limited, *New Delhi*
Prentice-Hall of Japan, Inc., *Tokyo*
Simon & Schuster Pte. Ltd., *Singapore*
Editora Prentice-Hall do Brasil, Ltda., *Rio de Janeiro*

Contents

Preface

This edition of the *Prentice Hall Handbook for Writers* is virtually a new text. Seeking the advice of many current, past, and potential users of the handbook, we have provided what they told us they most desired in an English composition handbook while retaining the best of what advisors told us they valued in previous editions. And, of course, we had one or two ideas of our own.

New in this edition are the following features:

- organization beginning with the writing process and emphasizing critical thinking throughout the book. Students learn to analyze writing tasks to see what kinds of thinking and writing they are being asked to do. They are also encouraged to consider audience and context as they make choices about their writing.

- entirely reworked chapters on the writing process (1-5), featuring one student's essays as she developed them during an English composition course. By presenting several essays written by the same student, we are able to show not only how her writing progressed but also how she used a single topic for different writing purposes. This case study will help English composition students see possibilities for shaping their own experiences and ideas into essays.

- emphasis on research (gathering and evaluating information) as a process fundamental to critical thinking and writing—from personal experience essays through documented, secondary-source research papers. The writing process chapters (1-5) show Kara, the English composition student, determining whether she needs additional evidence to support her personal experience and observations. The argumentation chapter (7) explores Kara's research, thinking, and writing processes for a short argumentative essay. Her work illustrates that use of external sources is not a matter solely for term papers and may involve types of research other than library reading.

These research processes are explored in further detail in the research writing chapters (46-48). The new MLA research paper, on corporate responsibility and the environment, follows another student writer from topic generation to final editing, illustrating how pursuing a research path frequently requires adjustments in thesis and organization as new evidence confirms or confounds original notions. Our exploration of researched writing concludes in the chapters dealing with writing in different disciplines (49-52), where research goals, tasks, methods, formats, and documentation styles (Modern Language Association, American Psychological Association, Council of Biology Editors, and Chicago Manual of Style) are compared across four disciplines.

- English-as-a-second-language aids highlighted within chapters, as well as a full chapter on ESL verb problems (30). These additions to the handbook will benefit not only ESL students but can also provide helpful insights for other students having difficulty with a particular aspect of written English.

- exercises—approximately two-thirds new—and examples that draw upon the strengths and interests of the United States' diverse population. We want as many readers as possible to find themselves or their interests among the people and subjects appearing in our text. We also want to broaden readers' awareness and understanding. We think the topics and quotations we have chosen for this edition will accomplish those goals.

- "In Your Own Words" exercises that focus on writing rather than error recognition. We continue to believe that connected discourse exercises most closely replicate students' experience editing their own prose, and thus we have used connected discourse wherever possible. But because the ability to recognize errors in someone else's prose does not always transfer to one's own writing, we have added "In Your Own Words" exercises to provide more writing practice and self-study.

- chapters on writing in the humanities, social sciences, natural and applied sciences, and business, with examples and explanations of MLA, APA, CBE, and CMS documentation styles. Sample papers include a literary analysis, a history research paper, a psychology laboratory report, a geography case study, a chemistry literature review, a biology field report, and an analytical business report.

- a fresh and functional design created to give this edition the most attractive and easy-to-use format of any handbook on the market. Charts, diagrams, boxes, and checklists aid readers in understanding and retaining information. We are extremely pleased with the work of our graphic design team, who admirably met the challenge of integrating the numerous elements of a handbook into an elegant, functional whole.

We have maintained the features that have supported the *Prentice Hall Handbook*'s long-standing popularity:

- concise but thorough treatment of the topics of most frequent concern to writers

- a point of view that addresses students as writers developing their craft

- emphasis on revision, using the "Writers Revising" feature to show several drafts of a writer's work, along with an analysis of his or her choices

- sentence and paragraph exercises representing the most typical as well as the widest possible range of writing problems

An unparalleled supplements package provides outstanding support for both new and experienced writing instructors. These supplements include:

- An *Annotated Instructors Edition* (013–148933–X) updated and revised by Linda Julian, Furman University; Teresa Purvis, Lansing Community College; and Betty Dillard, Sul Ross State University. The annotations, located in the text's margins, provide Teaching Suggestions, Extra Examples, Answers to Exercises in the handbook, Extra Exercises, and Collaborative Writing Activities.

- An *Answer Key* (013–435926–7) to the handbook provides all the AIE marginal annotations in a separate booklet for those instructors who prefer to use the student text, rather than the AIE, as their desk copy.

- A *Resource Guide* (013–149022-2) which pulls together under one spiral-bound cover a *Teachers Guide* written by Meg Morgan, University of North Carolina @ Charlotte, and extensive special sections on the following issues in and approaches to teaching writing: *Collaborative Writing* by Teresa Purvis, Lansing Community College; *Portfolios for Writing Instructors* by Kathleen Blake Yancey, University of North Carolina @ Charlotte; *ESL Writing* by Melinda Reichelt, Purdue University; *Computers and Writing* by Dawn Rodrigues, Kennesaw State College; and *Writing Across the Curriculum* by Sylvia Gamboa, College of Charleston. The section on *Writing Across the Curriculum* has been broken out as a separate booklet (013–435959 –3) for professors in other departments who have students using the handbook as part of a discipline-specific writing course.

- A *Test Bank with Diagnostic Tests* (013–149048–6) prepared by Harold Nelson, Minot State University. The test bank contains seven diagnostic tests, two of which are ESL diagnostic tests, and a section test for each chapter in the *Prentice Hall Handbook*. It is available in a computerized format called *Test Manager* (IBM 3.5-inch: 013–149055–9; IBM 5.25-inch: 013–149063–X).

- *A Basic Workbook for Writers* (013–149154–7) by Thomas Beery, Lima Technical College. This workbook condenses information in the text and provides all new exercises in a workbook format for each of the writing process and grammar chapters. A separate answer key (013–435975–5) is available.

- *The Prentice Hall Guide to Research and Documentation* (013–149147–4) by Josephine Tarvers, In-Scribe Communications. This handy guide reprints the documentation material from the *Prentice Hall Handbook for Writers* along with an overview of the research process.

- *Preparing for TASP* (013–149188–1) by Lane Johnson, North Harris College, and *Preparing for CLAST* (013–149170–9) by Kay Smith and Mailin Barlow, Valencia Community College, are available free to professors and may be copied free of charge for students using the *Prentice Hall Handbook for Writers*. These are also available for student purchase at minimal cost.

- An *On-Line Handbook* available in three formats: IBM (3.5-inch: 013–149113–X or 5.25-inch: 013–150616–1), Macintosh (013–150624–2), and Windows (013–435967–4).

- *Blue Pencil* editing activities software by Bob Bator and Mitsura Yamada, available in IBM (3.5-inch: 013–149089–3 or 5.25-inch: 013–149097–4) and Macintosh (013–149105–9) formats.

In addition to the above text-specific supplements we also provide the following Prentice Hall Resources for Composition:

Teaching Writing (013–435942–9) by Phyllis Hastings of Saginaw Valley State University. This manual provides guidelines on teaching writing for both new and experienced teachers. Topics include student–teacher interaction, class dynamics, course plans, and evaluating student works.

Computers and Writing (013–435934–8) by Dawn Rodrigues of Kennesaw State College provides an overview of the possibilities for computer use in English departments. It is aimed not only at faculty who are currently using technology in teaching, but also those who are just beginning to consider it and/or those who merely want to learn about the possibilities. (This booklet is also provided as part of the *Resource Guide* and so need not be ordered separately from the *Resource Guide*.)

The Research Organizer (013–813957–1) by Sue D. Hopke of Broward Community College. This handy booklet offers guidance on the research paper and provides space for the students to record their research strategy, notes, citations, outlines, and drafts all in one place. May be copied free for students upon adoption of the *Prentice Hall Handbook for Writers* or purchased by students at a minimal cost.

Model Research Papers for Writers (013–101338–6) by Janette S. Lewis of the University of California @ Los Angeles. This collection of reproducible student-written research papers in fields ranging from biology and political science to art history and English literature serves as a model of documentation, stylistic conventions, and formal requirements for various disciplines.

Supplementary Essays for Writers (013–101388–6) by Gary Schmidt of Calvin College. A rhetorically arranged collection of thirty-one classic essays accompanied by questions for discussion and writing suggestions. It is free to instructors upon adoption of the handbook. Individual essays may be photocopied free of charge or students may purchase the entire book at a minimal cost.

Prentice Hall/Simon & Schuster Transparencies for Writers (013–703209–9) by Duncan Carter of Portland State University. This set of 100 two- and four-color transparencies features exercises, examples, and suggestions for student writing that focus on all aspects of the writing process—from generating ideas and shaping an outline to preparing a draft and revising, editing, and documenting the final paper. These transparencies also cover grammar, punctuation, and mechanics via overlays that show how sentence and paragraph errors can be corrected most effectively. Each section contains a transparency of a work of fine art which is intended to serve as a springboard for student writing.

Prentice Hall Critical Thinking Audio Study Cassette (013–678335–X). This 60-minute cassette helps students develop their critical thinking skills—from asking the right questions about material they are reading or hearing to helpful tips on how to study, take effective notes, and become more efficient learners.

Bibliotech (013–008583–0). Using this computerized bibliography generator, students follow prompts to format their bibliography in either MLA, APA, or CBE documentation style. The students can print the bibliography directly from the program or save it to an ASCII file which can then be converted to a word processing file of their choice.

Websters Dictionary Offers. Websters New World Dictionary, Third Edition, or *Websters New World Compact School & Office Dictionary* may be shrinkwrapped to the *Prentice Hall Handbook for Writers* at a discounted price.

As always we have drawn upon the best theory and practice our profession has to offer, in the knowledge that good writing permeates daily life. We who teach rhetoric and writing owe it to our students—and to ourselves—to hold those fine examples to the light at least as often as we call attention to those that fall short.

Melinda G. Kramer
Glenn Leggett
C. David Mead

Acknowledgments

A project of the magnitude of a handbook reaches its audience only with the assistance of many talented people. Chief among them for this edition of the *Prentice Hall Handbook for Writers* is Leslie Taggart, our development editor in Amherst, Massachusetts, whose expertise, good judgment, and general bonhomie have improved every page of this textbook. We also wish to thank Frank Hubert, our production editor, who so efficiently managed the legions who turned the manuscript into a book. Special thanks go to Linda Julian, Furman University, for providing fresh and plentiful exercises and examples. We are indebted to Stephanie Demma, Prince George's Community College, for her excellent work on the research paper chapters and to Mary Boyd, Indiana University–Purdue University at Indianapolis, for her assistance with the English-as-a-second-language highlights.

This edition of the handbook is rich in student writing. We would particularly like to thank the following student writers: at Prince George's Community College, Letitia Anderson, Matthew Bates, Stephanie Blue, Frank C. Brown, Christine Frechette, Lara Lardizabal, Regina Mills, Ann Wallas, and Stephanie Whitlington; at the University of Maryland-College Park, Christopher A. Coleman; at College of Charleston, Keith Bannis, Maria Carter, Brett Nachman, and Leigh Truett; at Earlham College, Emily Boone. Faculty and staff members at these institutions also deserve our thanks for helping us locate student papers and for supplying field-specific expertise: Sherman Silverman, Meg Ryan, and Susan Roth at Prince George's Community College; Sylvia Gamboa at College of Charleston; and Jeff Hansen, Jerry Bakker, and Evan Farber at Earlham College.

Conscientious reviewers are the invisible hand behind a successful textbook and, in the case of this twelfth edition, they have been crucial in determining its new direction. Our reviewers are Janet H. Carr, Northeastern University; Suzanne Clepper, Tarrant County Junior College; Colleen Corless, St. Peters College; Sarah E. Cummings, St. Michael's College; Joseph K. Davis, Memphis State University; Robert W. Funk, Eastern Illinois University; Linda Julian, Furman University; Walter Levy, Pace University; Hugh W. Paschal, Hillsborough Community College; Leigh Ryan, University of Maryland; John W. Taylor, South Dakota State University; and Robert Wiltsonberg, Washington University.

Our families have aided our endeavors in ways too numerous to list, but Gary Kramer's expert technical knowledge and computer support, H. Samuel Gamble III's amusing writing samples, and Devona E. Gamble's proofreading and editorial assistance deserve special mention.

Finally, we are particularly fortunate in our superb editorial team at Prentice Hall: Philip Miller, president of the humanities and social science division; Alison Reeves, executive editor, English; Joyce Perkins, development editor, English; and Gina Sluss, marketing manager. Their knowledge of the marketplace and enthusiasm for the project, as well as the respect and trust we have developed during our years of working together, are certainly an important part of the *Prentice Hall Handbook's* success.

Throughout the *Handbook* we have quoted from copyrighted material, and we are grateful to the copyright holders acknowledged below for their permission.

"Abandoned Disciplines" (excerpt), special advertising section "Fighting for Our Business Future: Part 2" from *Business Week,* November 25, 1991. Copyright © 1991 McGraw-Hill, Inc. Reprinted by permission of Business Week.

John M. Allswang, *Macintosh: The Definitive Users Guide.* Bowie: Brady Communications Company, Inc. A Prentice-Hall Publishing Company, 1985.

Maya Angelou, *I Know Why the Caged Bird Sings.* New York: Random House, Inc., 1969. By permission of Random House, Inc.

W. H. Auden, *Tales of Grimm and Andersen.* Copyright © 1952 by Random House, Inc.

Newman and Genevieve Birk, *Understanding and Using English.* By permission of the Odyssey Press, Inc.

Lawrence Block, "Fiction: Huffing and Puffing," *Writer's Digest,* August 1982, p. 11.

Douglas H. Chadwick, "The American Prairie: Roots of the Sky" from *National Geographic Magazine,* October 1993. Reprinted by permission of National Geographic Magazine.

Sucheng Chan, "You're Short, Besides!" from *Making Waves* by Asian Women United of California. Copyright © 1989 by Asian Women United. Reprinted by permission of Beacon Press.

Kim Chernin, "The Tyranny of Slenderness" from *The Obsession* by Kim Chernin. Copyright © 1981 by Kim Chernin. Reprinted by permission of HarperCollins Publishers.

Don Colburn and Abigail Trafford, "Guns at Home" from *The Washington Post Health,* October 12, 1993. Copyright © 1993 The Washington Post. Reprinted with permission.

Peter Davis, "The Game" from *Hometown.* Copyright © 1982 by Peter Davis. Reprinted by permission of Simon & Schuster, Inc.

Robert A. Day, *How to Write and Publish a Scientific Paper* (4th ed.). Copyright 1944 by Robert A. Day. Published by The Oryx Press. Reprinted with permission from Robert A. Day and The Oryx Press, (800) 279–6799.

Joan Didion, excerpt from "On Keeping a Notebook" from *Slouching Towards Bethlehem.* Copyright © 1966, 1968 by Joan Didion. Reprinted by permission of Farrar, Straus & Giroux, Inc. and Andre Deutsch Ltd.

Michael Dolan, "Looking for America, Potholes and All" from "Book World Review," *The Washington Post,* August 23, 1993. Copyright © 1993, Washington Post Writers Group. Reprinted with permission.

Maureen Dowd, "Rape: The Sexual Weapon," copyright © 1983 Time Inc. All rights reserved. Reprinted by permission of *Time.*

Loren Eiseley, excerpts from "Instruments of Darkness," in *The Night Country.* Copyright © 1972 by Loren Eiseley. Reprinted with permission of Charles Scribner's Sons.

Electronic index title screen and full record screen from users manual for ABI/INFORM Ondisc: Express Edition, Fig. 14-15. Reprinted by permission of University Microfilms, Inc.

Leonid Fridman, "Voices of the New Generation: America Needs Its Nerds" from *The New York Times,* January 11, 1990. Copyright © 1990 by The New York Times Company. Reprinted by permission.

Mike Gauert, "The Abandoned Car Told the Tale: Everglades Mosquitoes Had Struck" from *Chicago Tribune,* August 7, 1988. Reprinted by permission of the author and The Sun-Sentinel, Fort Lauderdale, Florida.

Charles J. Gelso and Bruce R. Fretz, *Counseling Psychology*. Copyright © 1992 by Holt, Rinehart and Winston, Inc. Reprinted by permission of the publisher.

Edward T. Hall, "Private Space" from *The Hidden Dimension* by Edward T. Hall. Copyright © 1966 by Edward T. Hall. Reprinted by permission of Doubleday, a division of Bantam Doubleday Dell Publishing Group, Inc.

S. I. Hayakawa, from *Language in Thought and Action*, Fourth Edition. Copyright © 1978 by Harcourt Brace Jovanovich, Inc. Reprinted by permission of the publisher.

William A. Henry III, "Only 2,500 Miles from Broadway," *Time*, August 4, 1986.

Cathy Horyn, "Fashion Notes" ("Man Thing") from *The Washington Post*, September 19, 1993. Copyright © 1993 The Washington Post. Reprinted by permission.

Jane Howard, *Families*. Copyright 1978 by Jane Howard. By permission of Simon & Schuster, Inc. Reprinted by permission of A. D. Peters & Co. Ltd.

Rachel Jones, "What's Wrong With Black English" from *Multitude: Cross-Cultural Readings for Writers*, ed. Chitra B. Divakaruni, 1993. Reprinted by permission of the author.

Howard A. Karten, "Making the Most of Dow Jones News/Retrieval: Technical Considerations" from *How to Profit from Dow Jones News/Retrieval* by Howard A. Karten. Copyright © 1986 by Howard A. Karten. Reprinted by permission of the author.

Tracy Kidder, *The Soul of a New Machine*. Copyright © 1980 by John Tracy Kidder. By permission of Little, Brown and Company in association with the Atlantic Monthly Press.

Clyde Kluckhohn, "The Gift of Tongues" from *Mirror for Man* by Clyde Kluckhohn, 1949 McGraw-Hill, Inc. Reprinted by permission of George E. Taylor.

Conrad Phillip Kottak, "Swimming in Cross-Cultural Currents" from *Natural History*, May 1985. Copyright © 1985 the American Museum of Natural History. With permission from *Natural History*, May 1985.

George Laycock, "Games Otters Play" from *Audubon*, January, 1981. By permission of the National Audubon Society.

Robert Levine and Ellen Wolff, "Social Time: The Heartbeat of Culture" from *Psychology Today*, March 1985. Copyright © 1985 Sussex Publishers, Inc. Reprinted with permission of Psychology Today.

Kenneth Lincoln, "Old Like Hills, Like Stars" from *Native American Renaissance* by Kenneth Lincoln. Copyright © 1983 the Regents of the University of California. Reprinted by permission of the Regents of the University of California and the University of California Press and by permission of the author.

William H. Macleish, "The Year of the Coast" from *Smithsonian*, Sept. 1980.

Judith Martin, "Weapons for the Dessert Wars" from *The Washington Post*, September 23, 1990.

Robert K. Massie, *Peter the Great: His Life and World*. New York: Knopf, 1980.

David Mills, "The West Alternative" from *The Washington Post Magazine*, August 8, 1993. Copyright © 1994 The Washington Post Magazine. Reprinted by permission.

Joan Mills, excerpted with permission from "The One, the Only…Joanie!" by Joan Mills, *Reader's Digest*, July 1983. Copyright © 1983 by The Reader's Digest Assn., Inc.

Toni Morrison, "The Site of Memory." Copyright © 1986 by Toni Morrison. Reprinted by permission of International Creative Management, Inc.

Lance Morrow, excerpt from "A Dying Art: The Classy Exit Line." Copyright 1984 Time Inc. All rights reserved. Reprinted by permission from *Time*.

J. Madeleine Nash, "How Did Life Begin?" from *Time*, October 11, 1993. Reprinted by permission of Time, Inc.

Father Frank O'Loughlin, excerpt from *New Americans: An Oral History* by Al Santoli. Copyright © 1988 by Al Santoli. Used by permission of Viking Penguin, a division of Penguin Books USA Inc.

Luke O'Neill, Michael Murphy, and Richard B. Gallagher, "What Are We? Where Do We Come From? Where Are We Going?" from *Science*, January 14, 1994, Vol. 263. Copyright © 1994 by the AAAS. Reprinted by permission of *Science* and Luke O'Neill Ph.D., Biochemistry Dept., Trinity College, Dublin, Ireland, Dr. Michael P. Murphy, and Richard B. Gallagher.

Michael Omi and Harold Winant, "Racial Formation" from *Racial Formation in the United States* by Michael Omi and Harold Winant, 1994. Reprinted by permission of the publisher, Routledge, New York.

Part 1

The Writing Process

Authors arrive at text and subtext in thousands of ways, learning each time they begin anew how to recognize a valuable idea and how to render the texture that accompanies, reveals, or displays it to its best advantage. The process by which this is accomplished is endlessly fascinating to me.

–Toni Morrison, "The Site of Memory"

Critical Thinking, Purposeful Writing

All writing conveys a message, or tries to. Its general goal is to communicate. The purpose of this handbook is to help you do the best possible job of communicating in writing to an audience, whether that audience is yourself or someone else. To communicate well, you will need to make a series of decisions about

- the nature of the writing task,
- the nature of your readers,
- the selection and arrangement of the information that you include in the message, and
- the context in which your message will be read.

Working through these decisions involves critical thinking skills ranging from gathering information to analyzing and interpreting that information. Each writing task and audience require a new combination of information and critical thinking. Some writing tasks and audiences call for complex thinking; others are fairly simple and straightforward. Part of becoming an effective writer is learning to identify and apply the critical thinking and writing skills necessary to a particular task and readership.

Writing for Oneself, Writing for Others

Why do people write? Broadly, we can say that people write to accomplish something. People write to express themselves, to think through problems and emotions, to communicate ideas to others. Sometimes they write just to please themselves: a diary entry or a personal poem, for instance. Sometimes they write as a necessary means to get a task accomplished: a homework assignment at school or a business letter at work. Obviously people write for many reasons and situations. In fact, most people are surprised by how much and how often they do write in the normal course of a week's activities.

"Am I writing this message for myself or for others?" You should ask yourself this question early and often. It can provide you with direction and serve as a way of checking your progress along the way. The answer will depend not only on your reason for writing but also on where you are in the process of completing the writing task. The following table illustrates the relationships among purposes, audiences, and functions of writing.

Who Benefits?	Why Write?	Function?
Writing for myself	To explore feelings To see what I know or don't know	Writing to express Writing to learn

Who Benefits?	Why Write?	Function?

Writing for others	To supply information
	To get something done
	To change someone's mind
	   or behavior
		Writing to inform or instruct
		Writing to transact
		Writing to convince or
		   persuade

These categories may overlap. You might write to express your feelings to others, as in a love letter. Poets, novelists, and dramatists hope to touch the emotions of others with their writing. Similarly, you might write solely for yourself about the pros and cons of two job offers to help yourself decide which job to accept. Or you might begin writing a memo to your supervisor by first jotting notes to yourself: "How do I feel about the issues? What facts support my feelings?" These inward notes can help you focus your ideas and emotions before you consider outward factors—the needs and perceptions of the other person you will ultimately address in the memo. Thus, inward writing can be a stage in the process of developing an effective, outwardly directed communication for others to read.

Your writing will undergo changes as you broaden its scope beyond yourself toward a wider audience. As you move from writing that is personal to writing intended for a wider public, your writing should become less writer oriented and more reader oriented. The following chart illustrates the progression from writer orientation to reader orientation.

Writer Oriented	Reader Oriented

self-centered
   (writer/"I" most important)
narrative, chronological structure
focus on what writer has learned
	reader centered
	   (reader/"you" most important)
	main idea, supporting points structure
	focus on what reader needs to know

For an example of how one college student's writing developed from a self-centered orientation to a reader-centered orientation, look at the "Writers Revising" section at the end of this chapter. The student, Kara Lardizabal, wrote the passage as part of a semester-long project in her English composition class. Throughout Part 1 of the *Prentice Hall Handbook*, you will see other examples of Kara's writing as she explored the subject "working as a waitress."

Exercise 1.1

Chart the frequency and types of writing you do in the course of a week. First make a grid like the one that follows, listing the seven days of the week along one side and types of writing across the top. Brainstorm for a few minutes to develop your own categories for types of writing. Here are just a few possibilities: to-do lists, notes written in classes, tests or quizzes, homework assignments, essays, personal diary or journal writing, lab reports, postcards to friends, letters to family, letters to businesspeople, notes to roommates, telephone messages, grocery lists, checks to pay bills, instructions for the babysitter, and crossword puzzles. Once you have finished the grid, make a mark on the relevant day for every time you engage in a particular writing task. The marks will graphically illustrate your writing activities. Do you write more often or less often during the week than you would have guessed? Write a message to your instructor *summarizing* what the chart revealed to you about your writing.

Writing Types and Frequency

	Class Notes	To-do List	English Paper	Letter Home	Biology Lab Notes	Phone Messages	Quizzes and Tests	Other
Mon.								
Tues.								
Wed.								
Thur.								
Fri.								
Sat.								
Sun.								

Exercise 1.2

Refer to your writing frequency chart from Exercise 1.1. Using two different colors of ink, color code the chart to show how much of your writing for the week is inwardly directed (yourself as principal audience) and how much is outwardly directed (others as principal audience). Use one color to highlight the categories relating to writing tasks that you performed for your own personal information or satisfaction (class notes, diary entry, poem, grocery list) and a second color to highlight those writing tasks you performed for someone else to read and understand (telephone message, essay test, memo to business colleague, instructions to babysitter). If a task served both yourself and others, mark it with both colors. Look at the distribution of colored highlights and note the proportion of writing that is self-directed and the proportion that is other directed.

For five minutes, brainstorm: List on paper all the differences you can think of between writing for yourself as audience and writing for others as audience. Use the list to write a message to your instructor *summarizing* what you have learned about writing from this color-coding and brainstorming exercise.

In Your Own Words

Choose a familiar activity that you strongly like or dislike (a sport, hobby, job, household chore, or extracurricular activity, for example). Spend ten minutes writing a note to yourself, explaining why you especially like or dislike the activity. Go into some detail. Then let a day pass. The next day, without reading the note you wrote to yourself, spend ten minutes writing a note to a person you know who is less familiar than you are with the activity. Explain to that person why you especially like or dislike the activity. Go into some detail, keeping in mind your reader's degree of familiarity with the activity. Then compare that note with the one you wrote to yourself the previous day. Do you see any differences? Finally, in a brief written message to your instructor, *summarize* and *analyze* the differences between the two notes. In other words, summarize the differences and explain why they have occurred.

Writers Revising

For her English composition class, Kara Lardizabal drafted the following paragraph on why customers should tip their waitresses or waiters. The class instructor asked students to revise their drafts to make them more reader oriented. He said, "Ask yourself, 'What is the most important thing my reader needs to understand from the passage?' Could your audience summarize your main idea after reading the passage? Revise with those goals in mind." Kara framed the main idea she wanted to get across: "Customers should tip their servers a minimum of 15 percent for good service." Following her instructor's advice, revise Kara's paragraph to make it reader oriented and focused on her main idea. Add or delete words as necessary. Then compare your version with her retyped revision.

Draft

```
    Many people do not have the slightest idea of
what goes on behind the scenes of waiting tables. I
```

work at the Grill in Bradford two nights a week and
on weekends. On my shift, I may have as many as ten
tables at a time. The first thing I do is go over to
the table and ask my customers how they are. Next, I
tell them my name and ask them if I can get them
something to drink. Then, I have to go to the bartender to get the drinks and take them over to the
table. When the customers are ready, I take their
food order and ring it into the register. While I
wait for their order to be cooked, I have to keep
looking after that table to make sure their drinks
are always full. Finally, I pick up the food in the
kitchen and bring it to the table. I have to bring
condiments and any other items they may need. Keep in
mind that I may have nine other tables, and I have to
do the same procedures for those tables at the same
time. After the diners are through and ready to pay
their checks, I anxiously wait to see how good they
thought my service was, as indicated by the amount of
my tip. On some nights I stand on my feet for eight
hours nonstop looking after my tables until the
restaurant closes at 11:00 p.m.

Revision

If people knew what really goes on behind the
scenes at a restaurant, they would understand that
good service merits at least a 15 percent tip. My
after-school job as a waitress at the Grill in
Bradford is a good illustration. Customers at each of
my tables receive a minimum of ten separate acts of
service during their visit to the restaurant. First I
go to the table and greet the customers, asking how
they are. Then I ask them if I can get them something
to drink, take the order to the bartender, and bring
it back to the table. Next I take food orders and
then ring the orders into the register. While their
food is being cooked, I look after the table to make
sure the customers' drinks are always full. When
their food is ready, I pick it up in the kitchen,
bring it to the table, and then get the customers any
condiments or other items they may need. When the

diners are through, I bring them their check and thank them for coming. Keep in mind that I may have nine other tables to serve, and I have to do the same procedures for those tables at the same time. The innumerable steps, friendly smile, and courteous conversation are carried out not just once but over and over during the course of an evening. Some nights I stand on my feet for eight hours nonstop looking after my tables until the restaurant closes at 11:00 p.m. With each table of customers, I anxiously wait to see how good they thought my service was, as indicated by the amount of my tip. A pleasant dining experience at a restaurant has as much to do with good service as with good food. People should show their appreciation for the hard work that goes into good service by thanking the server with a good tip.

Analysis

Kara maintains a chronological organization in her revision because she wants her readers to understand the sequence of activities that servers must go through for every table of customers. Consequently, she narrates all the steps from start to finish. However, she has combined some steps in the revision so that the narrative moves a bit faster. More importantly, she has strengthened the focus on her main idea, "good service merits good tips," by adding language at the opening and closing of the paragraph to emphasize that main idea. The first draft ends with the restaurant's closing at 11:00 P.M., an ending that focuses on Kara's personal experience, not on the reader's awareness of what that long day means in terms of customer service. The ending of the revision focuses less on Kara (writer orientation) and more on the connection between hard work, good service, and customers' appreciation as signified by good tips. This shift to an emphasis on the customers (her potential audience) shows that Kara is developing a reader orientation.

2　The Process of Writing: Planning

By studying what writers think about and do when they write, researchers have learned that writing involves a number of interrelated activities. These activities occur *recursively*. That is, writers repeat the activities as needed, in whatever order best helps them accomplish their writing task. Very few writers sit down in front of a clean sheet of paper or blank computer screen and write an essay, newspaper article, or book chapter just the way they want it the first time through. Even those people who appear to dash off "first-time final" drafts have spent considerable time planning what they are going to say. The manuscripts of numerous authors show that many famous novels and poems went through multiple revisions—sometimes dozens of them—before the authors were satisfied.

The activities involved in writing fall into categories we can term **planning, organizing, drafting, revising,** and **editing/proofreading.** Taken together, these activities are called the **writing process.** The remaining chapters in this section of the *Prentice Hall Handbook* explore the parts of the writing process in detail. For now, we can summarize the activities in each category as follows:

Planning: identify the writing task and its requirements
                      identify the audience(s)
                      decide what information will be needed
                      account for constraints
Organizing: take a stance on the topic
                      turn the stance into a thesis statement
                      arrange ideas to support the thesis statement
Drafting: use information in body paragraphs to support the thesis
                      write an effective beginning and ending
Revising: make changes for meaning
Editing/Proofing: make changes for correctness

The following diagram is part of Kara Lardizabal's writing process for her essay on working as a waitress. Notice how she moves recursively among the various activities.

One Writer's Process for an Essay

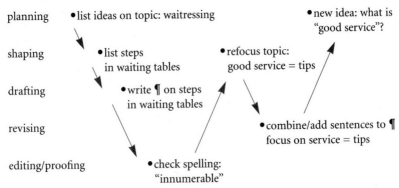

planning   • list ideas on topic: waitressing   • new idea: what is "good service"?

shaping   • list steps in waiting tables   • refocus topic: good service = tips

drafting   • write ¶ on steps in waiting tables

revising   • combine/add sentences to ¶ focus on service = tips

editing/proofing   • check spelling: "innumerable"

It is natural to begin a writing task with planning and finish it with a final proofreading for correctness. But, as Kara's process illustrates, writers also move between activities as the need arises. Although you should lay initial plans for an entire writing task and shape the broad outline of the whole piece, you should also feel free to revise your plans to include new ideas as the document develops. It is perfectly all right to throw out sections you had planned if they don't seem to work.

Also, be aware that you can improve the efficiency and success of your writing process. One of the differences between expert writers and novices is the extent to which experts capitalize on the strengths of their own process and try to minimize the weaknesses. Similarly, you can analyze your own writing behavior with the goal of improving it: Observe which activities seem easier for you, which more difficult. Notice what you are doing when a part of the writing process goes well or when it goes badly. Then try to practice the more productive habits and activities. For example, Kara has learned that ten minutes spent preparing a scratch outline early in the writing process saves her hours of aimless drafting later. Another writer has learned from self-observation that when he is stuck he tends to fritter away minutes editing the sentences he has already written rather than looking for ways to push ahead with his ideas. The editing gives the impression that he is making progress, when he is really just tinkering with words. To get past these writer's blocks, he now shifts from drafting to planning and shaping: He draws idea trees (see page Section **3e**) to visualize his thoughts and get the sentences flowing again.

2 a Identify the writing task.

As you begin planning for your writing, you should consider the nature of the writing task: What is it that you are being asked (or you are asking yourself) to do? The answer to this question determines the kinds of critical thinking skills you should employ and the kinds of writing that are possible.

● **1 Types of critical thinking.** Does the writing task require that you
- report or summarize information?
- synthesize information by drawing together facts and ideas from several sources?
- analyze information and ideas to determine what they mean, and draw conclusions about them?
- evaluate and interpret information and ideas to state your position or recommend a course of action?

Some writing tasks require one of these types of thinking; others require several or all of them.

The complexity and difficulty of the tasks increase as you move from reporting through analysis to evaluating and interpreting. Summarizing information from a single source is easier than merging information from multiple sources. Evaluating information from many sources and explaining its meaning is hardest of all. When your elementary school teacher assigned a book report ("Tell me about what you read. What happened?"), that task was appropriate for the skill level of someone just learning to recollect information and repeat it for an audience. Later, teachers asked you to complete more complex thinking and writing tasks, such as research reports in which you recorded scientific experiments and drew conclusions about the results. Such assignments require the analysis of data and explanations of cause and effect, which are much more difficult tasks than simple reporting.

More difficult still is the creation of new knowledge. New knowledge results when you analyze information for patterns and relationships and then use the information you have gathered and the conclusions you have drawn to prove the correctness of your interpretation. Consider the following essay test question: "Discuss immigration patterns to the United States in the last third of the nineteenth century and the last third of the twentieth century. What are the probable long-term effects on U.S. society? Defend your conclusions."

This question sets a complex task for the writer. It calls for an analysis using comparison and contrast (similarities and differences between two periods of immigration), conclusions about and evaluations of the similarities and differences (what they mean in terms of the changing make-up of the U.S. population), and interpretation of these similarities and differences (probable long-term effects resulting from differences in immigrant groups and U.S. society existing at each time). Finally, the writer must back up all conclusions and interpretations with factual evidence and logical thinking. A successful essay answer to this test question will show that the writer is capable not just of repeating information but of using it to create new meaning.

A person skilled at critical thinking will take any writing task apart to see just what kinds of thinking and writing he or she is being asked to do. In this case the task involves much more than simply reporting facts about immigration patterns. It requires a combination of analysis, synthesis, evaluation, and interpretation to create a well-supported argument about the long-term effects of two waves of immigration to the United States.

● **2 Types of writing.** As the foregoing discussion on critical thinking suggests, certain types of critical thinking problems pair naturally with certain types of writing. For example, writing that compares or contrasts is a logical result of analytical thinking that examines similarities or differences.

The following chart shows critical thinking skills paired with types of writing that often result.

Thinking and Writing Counterparts

Critical Thinking Skill	Type of Writing
summarizing	description, narration
synthesizing	exposition
analyzing	comparison/contrast
drawing conclusions	definition and classification
interpreting	cause and effect
advancing solutions	argument
defending/countering	

Description, narration. Writing that **describes** tells how something looks, acts, sounds, feels, smells, or tastes. Writing that **narrates** tells what happened over time (chronology)—who did what to whom in what order. An accident report about a fender bender, the minutes of a business meeting, and a postcard to a friend about your vacation in Florida use combinations of description and narration to summarize what occurred in a particular setting, to "sum it all up."

Exposition. The core of the word **exposition** is *expose*—to lay open or set forth, displaying to view. The main purpose of expository writing is to explain something, to make it clear to the reader's understanding. An automobile owner's manual, a recipe for Southern fried chicken, a physics textbook, and a newspaper article about presidential candidates use exposition to explain their subjects.

Exposition relies on the thinking skill of synthesis, drawing together and blending information from several sources, merging it into a single explanation. For example, a news article about the campaign appearance of a presidential candidate will likely report factual information, give observations from people in the crowd and from political commentators, and quote the candidate. In the hands of a skilled and objective journalist, this synthesis of information will give the reading public a reasonably accurate and balanced representation of the campaign appearance. Of course, description (how the candidate looked and sounded) and narration (the order in which events occurred) will probably be involved, but these types of writing are subordinated to the main goal, to explain.

Comparison and contrast. Writing that **compares** looks at similarities between or among people, ideas, or things. Writing that **contrasts** looks at their differences. Comparing and contrasting rely on the thinking skill of analysis, the ability to take things apart and accurately present the characteristics of the components. The essay question about United States immigration patterns in the nineteenth and twentieth centuries (p. 10) requires such an analysis. The writer must break "immigration patterns" into individual components: the countries from which immigrants came during each period, the number of immigrants from each country, where each group settled in the United States, their average level of education or vocational skill, the economic and social conditions in the United States at the time, and so forth. Once the information has been categorized, the categories must be compared between the two periods and their similarities and differences noted. This analysis then provides the basis for thinking about the crux of the question, the long-term effects of immigration patterns.

Definition and classification. Types of comparison and contrast, definition and classification analyze people, ideas, and things by sorting and grouping them. Classification puts things into **classes** or categories based on their similarities. Stools, chairs, tables, and beds are all classified as furniture, for example. Definition sets **limits** on things and puts them in classes distinguished first by similarities (a stool is a piece of furniture for seating a single person, like a chair) and then by differences (but unlike a chair, a stool has no back or arms). For further discussion of definition, see Section **7d**.

Cause and effect. Writing that discusses causes and effects relies on thinking that both analyzes and interprets information. When you write about what causes something, two lines of analysis are possible. You can either reason from results back to their causes. Or you can predict what will happen if certain conditions continue or events occur, reasoning from causes forward to results. In either case, you must analyze the facts. But because there arguably may be several causes contributing to an effect, your writing task will involve mentally sorting information, weighing it, and judging which causes are most likely. This reasoning calls for an interpretation of the facts based on your own judgment. Persuasive writing shows readers that your analysis and interpretation are supported by the evidence.

For example, a student answering the immigration essay question might state that current immigrants to the United States will find success more difficult to achieve than nineteenth-century immigrants did because there are fewer low-skill and manual labor jobs available in today's technological society. Such an answer requires the writer to compare the skill levels of immigrant populations to the requirements of available jobs and conclude whether a match exists. Then the writer must interpret the conclusion, determining the probability for the immigrants' success and projecting the likely effect on U.S. society as a whole (possibly greater unemployment, increased welfare rolls). In short, the writer must interpret the facts, following a cause-and-effect chain of reasoning.

Argument. A detailed discussion of argumentative writing appears in Chapter 7. But here we can note that argumentation draws on all the critical thinking skills already mentioned, particularly analysis, evaluation, and interpretation. An argument puts forth a proposition, a statement the writer offers as true but which readers may disbelieve. The writer's task, then, is to supply sufficient, reliable evidence to prove the truth of the proposition. A strong argument also anticipates opposing viewpoints and presents counterarguments in defense of the writer's viewpoint.

Arguments may contain cause-and-effect analysis, comparisons and contrasts, and definitions of terms as well as exposition, description, and narration. In fact, complex arguments are likely to draw on many types of writing as they strive to persuade their audiences. Clearly, successful argumentative writing requires well-researched information, sharp thinking, and careful planning.

Task Checklist

If you are asked to …	*your task is to …*
• explain what occurred or how something/someone looked, behaved, felt, etc.	summarize information
• explain, merging information from several sources	synthesize information
• discuss similarities and differences	analyze by comparing and contrasting
• identify problems or propose solutions, give reasons why something occurred	analyze and interpret information to identify probable causes and effects
• agree or disagree with a statement, take a stand, or defend a point of view	argue logically with convincing evidence and rebut counterarguments

Exercise 2.1

Following are writing assignments people have encountered in college classes and on the job. After each, write the number(s) of the predominant thinking/writing tasks listed at the end of this exercise. Some assignments may require more than one thinking/writing task.

a Find out why the office keeps running out of copy paper and propose what we should do about it.

b If "greenhouse gases" continue to be produced at current rates for the next twenty-five years, what is likely to happen to the environment?

c What symptoms does a patient exhibit if he or she is going into shock?

d Using the following statements by Alexander Hamilton and Patrick Henry, explain how they represent the debate over federalism versus state sovereignty that occurred during the writing and ratification of the U.S. Constitution in 1787–1788.

e What advice would you give a person preparing for an important job interview?

1. summary/description
2. summary/narration
3. synthesis/exposition
4. analysis/comparison and contrast
5. analysis/definition
6. analysis/classification
7. interpretation/cause and effect
8. interpretation/argument

Exercise 2.2

Following are an assignment and one student's written response. The student received a low grade. What had she been asked to do that she did not do?

Assignment

Read the following statement by a drug dealer and then write a brief analysis of the reasoning you find there.

> "Take the case of a jeweler. He's a business man, and he's in the game to make money. OK, so I'm a businessman too, and I'm also out to make money. We just use different methods. The jeweler makes a profit—and very often a big profit—out of what he sells. On top of that he cheats on his income tax, the sales tax, and even the customs duty as well if he can get away with it. That's considered all right by him and others like him, and if he makes enough to buy himself a big house and a posh car everyone looks up to him as a clever fellow, a shrewd business man. But how's he got his money? By rooking people, taking advantage of soft young couples getting engaged to sell them a more expensive ring than they can afford. . . . The jeweler takes care of his family, pays his employees a living wage, and puts money into the economy. So do I. In fact, my business supports people who wouldn't have the money to eat, if they didn't work for me. Let's face it, if American society weren't so racist, these guys wouldn't have to work for me."
>
> —adapted from "A Criminal Justifies Himself" in
> Annette T. Rottenberg, *Elements of Argument*

Student Answer

In this statement, the drug dealer is pointing out facts about himself and the jeweler—that both are businessmen but that they just use different methods, such as when the drug dealer discusses how the jeweler cheats customers and cheats on his taxes. The drug dealer is denying that what he is doing by selling drugs is against the law, no matter how he distributes his money to people or family members for bills and so forth. Although some businessmen are not honest in how they run their businesses, society accepts their way of surviving. If the drug dealer doesn't like how the jeweler runs his business, why doesn't he get involved in trying to do things the right way?

In Your Own Words

In a paragraph analyze the skills you have that would persuade an employer to offer you a part-time job that you would really like. Then imagine that you have been hired by this employer for the part-time job, and write a two-paragraph summary description of your duties on the new job. This description is to be included in a letter you are writing to your best friend, who is a thousand miles away for a month.

Essay in Progress

Making Plans

Kara challenged herself to write about being a waitress from several different angles before she decided on the approach she would take for her final paper. Her first task was to explain what a waitress or waiter does, since many restaurant customers are not aware of the amount of work involved in food service. The narrative summarizing Kara's typical evening on the job appears in "Writers Revising" at the end of Chapter 1. Her preliminary plan for this writing assignment was to make a list of the steps involved in waiting on a table, from greeting the customers to wishing them goodnight.

The next part of Kara's writing project grew from a comment by a classmate during peer review. "OK, so I should leave a good tip. But what if the service has been poor? What then?" Kara decided to tackle this subject for her next paper. She recognized that her main task would be to analyze good service and poor service so that customers would have criteria for judging the difference and tipping accordingly. Here is a paragraph of contrast that resulted:

> When service has been poor and you feel like not tipping the waiter, ask yourself if the reason is circumstances beyond the waiter's control. For example, if you notice that your waiter is standing around talking to friends while your food gets cold at the pass-through window, then give him a smaller tip. However, if you see that the restaurant is crowded, that your waiter is always on the go, and that customers arriving after you are not being served their meals ahead of you, then you can assume the cooks have their hands full and your waiter is not at fault.

Later Kara decided to investigate a controversial alternative to voluntary tipping: mandatory service charges automatically added to cus-

tomers' bills. She hoped to explore the effects service charges might have on the food service industry, on service personnel, and on customers. In planning, she saw that her overall task was complex: Research the issue, analyze and evaluate the pros and cons, and take a stand for or against mandatory service charges. Here is one of the cause-and-effect paragraphs for her paper:

> My poll of twenty-eight service staff at the Grill showed that 70 percent favor mandatory service charges as long as the charge is at least 15 percent of the bill. Those in favor believe that 20 percent is not necessary because a 15 percent tip would make up for those customers who undertip on the current voluntary system. The 30 percent of waiters and waitresses who are against a mandatory service charge think that many customers will boycott restaurants with service charges and take their business where tipping is still voluntary. They also believe mandatory charges will actually reduce their income because they usually make tips of more than 15 percent.

2b Identify the audience.

If you want your readers to feel what you feel, see what you see, or believe as you believe, you must establish a relationship with them. To develop such a relationship, search for the common ground you and your audience may share: assumptions, points of view, experiences, knowledge, and background. You can then use that commonality as a bridge to experiences or beliefs you do not share.

As you think about your audience's characteristics, see if you can categorize readers according to how much they know about your subject and their probable attitude toward it.

● 1 **General readers.** Writing aimed at a general readership assumes no special degree of knowledge about a subject or issue. This audience may work in highly specialized professions and have any number of particular interests, but when these readers turn to general-interest publications such as *Ebony, Newsweek, People, Psychology Today, Sports Illustrated,* or *National Geographic,* they expect to find articles that are written in standard, nontechnical language that can be easily understood, with definitions and explanations supplied for unfamiliar terms. These are readers like you; they wish to be informed without having to become experts in a subject. Kara

Lardizabal assumed a general audience of people who eat restaurant meals and sometimes ponder what amount of money to leave for a tip. Kara explained all the steps involved in serving a table of customers because she assumed few of her readers had shared her experience of being a waitress.

● **2 Specialized readers.** Writers can take for granted this audience's interest in the subject matter as well as a certain level of knowledge about it. Such an audience will be able to make sense of information, ideas, and specialized language, or jargon, that would be inappropriate for general readers. Today, numerous publications exist for readers who have highly specialized interests: *Antique Monthly, Chemical and Engineering News, The Chronicle of Higher Education, Model Railroader, Industrial Marketing, Journal of American History,* and *Indiana Farmer,* to name a few.

What is true for authors writing for specialized journals and magazines is true for you: The professor reading your political science paper and the insurance agent reading your letter questioning a medical bill have expertise that makes them specialized readers of the information you are presenting.

● **3 Novice and expert readers.** One of your tasks as a writer is to estimate your readers' level of expertise. Even among specialized audiences, there may be a fairly wide range of expertise. One reader of an essay on personal computers may be a first-time computer purchaser; another may have owned a PC for years. Naturally it is more difficult to write for a broad range of readers because you must define more terms and provide more explanations than experts would need. When planning your writing, try to determine how much breadth and depth of knowledge your audience possesses about your subject.

● **4 Convinced, neutral, or skeptical readers.** If your audience is likely to accept your ideas, your writing task is easier than if your audience requires convincing. Establishing common ground between you and your readers can help defuse hostility and lay the foundation for agreement. Of course, even an audience that is likely to be interested in your topic and agree with what you have to say about it deserves the best information and writing skills you have to offer. But a skeptical audience calls for particularly careful thinking and writing. You will, for instance, need to supply a skeptical audience with more evidence in support of your viewpoint than a less skeptical audience would require.

Audience Checklist

- What is the *common ground*? What characteristics do I share with my readers?
  - education, age, income level, occupation, family circumstances, geographical location
  - beliefs and attitudes (political, social, religious, ethical)
  - level of knowledge about and interest in the subject

- What are the crucial *differences* between my readers and me?
- Are my readers likely to be *sympathetic, hostile, or indifferent*?
- What *steps will I need to take* to overcome or minimize the effects of differences between me and my audience?
  - define terms, use analogies?
  - include more explanations, examples, and background information?
  - provide more evidence?
  - use a special tone?

During the planning stages of your writing task, a chart like the one that follows can be helpful in identifying important reader characteristics. This grid shows Kara's analysis of the readers of her essay about tipping.

Audience Analysis

Types of Readers	classmates	professor
Educational Level	college freshmen	Ph. D.
Typical Age	18–24 average	about 40
Job or Training	variety of entry-level jobs	college professor but has waited tables
Other Factors	money-conscious paying for school	traveled widely, including Europe
Knowledge of Subject	not much, but eat out fairly often	fairly expert
Attitude toward Subject	probably skeptical	probably neutral, perhaps positive
Relationship to Writer	peers	instructor to student

Exercise 2.3

Review the assignment in the Chapter 1 "In Your Own Words" exercise. Prepare an audience analysis grid for the reader who knows less than you about the activity you chose.

In Your Own Words

Whether you live in a dormitory room, an apartment, or a house, assume that you must write a note to your neighbor about the loudness of the stereo that is keeping you awake at night. Analyze the neighbor using the Audience Checklist on page 18 and then write a note of two paragraphs explaining the problem and asking for help in solving it.

Exercise 2.4

Assume you are planning to write an essay that will be read by your instructor and classmates. Prepare an audience analysis grid for these readers.

2 c Think about information sources.

Every writing task requires research, whether the source is as close as your own memory or as distant as the Library of Congress or the jungles of the Amazon. The questions of what information to use and how to obtain it should be considered very early in your planning because the availability of information may ultimately influence your choice of subject matter. You will need to revisit these questions throughout the writing process as drafting and revising necessitate gathering additional information. But in the initial planning stages you should concern yourself with determining how much you can rely on your personal experience and how much you will need to supplement it with information from other sources.

These decisions are closely related to the nature of the writing task and the characteristics of your audience. For instance, if Kara Lardizabal wants to persuade the skeptical owner of the Grill restaurant that the addition of a 15 percent service charge is a good idea, she knows that her personal experience alone will not be convincing. She is a part-time waitress, not a marketing expert. The owner fears that patronage will drop because customers dislike extra charges. If Kara wants her audience to consider her point of view seriously, she will have to provide solid evidence from several sources that restaurant patrons are willing to accept a service charge.

Source Checklist

- What do I already know about the subject?
- What useful information does my own personal experience offer?
- How does my experience compare with that of others?
- What do I need to find out?
- Where (or from whom) can I find more information?

Even when a writing task requires information from other sources, it is always appropriate to begin with what you know. Your own experiences can often serve as a primary source of information for your writing. A **primary source** of information is the basic source: the data collected in a survey, questionnaire, or interview; the laboratory notes or research article resulting from a chemistry experiment, environmental study, or archeological dig; a work of art or literature; someone's recollected experiences; an expert reporting his or her know-how. Primary sources also include original documents or recordings of things such as court cases and legal proceedings, speeches, eyewitness accounts, diaries, letters, historical documents (such as the U.S. Constitution, the Magna Carta, or the Gettysburg Address), and statistical databases in print or electronic form.

A **secondary source** is other people's commentary on primary sources. Evaluations, interpretations, and critiques of primary materials are considered secondary sources: for instance, a newspaper story by a journalist reporting on the latest AIDS research, an economist in *Business Week* explaining the meaning of the latest balance of trade figures, a scholarly journal article written by a literature professor about Caribbean poetry, a review in *Rolling Stone* of a new rap album, a television documentary on farm labor leader Caesar Chavez. The AIDS research, the balance of trade numbers, the Caribbean poems, the rap music, and the words and deeds of Caesar Chavez's life are the primary sources.

● **1 Firsthand information: Self as primary source.** For many subjects, you are your own best resource. But you need to discover what you know, to probe your mind for knowledge you already possess. Useful discovery techniques include journal writing, free association, brainstorming and note jotting, free writing, journalistic questions, and Aristotle's topic exploration.

Journal writing. The habit of writing in a journal, day book, or commonplace book is an honorable tradition dating back centuries. People from all walks of life—from Roman senators and Chinese poets to American schoolchildren—have kept notebooks in which they recorded the activities of the day, thought-provoking quotations, ideas to explore later, books to read, shopping lists, whatever they wanted to save or recall. If you are working on a writing assignment, a journal provides a good place to jot down ideas and observations so that you can return to them later, perhaps even drafting some short passages in the journal pages.

Free association. Free association means letting the mind range freely over a subject to see what bubbles up from the memory. Free association can help you find a subject to write about when a writing assignment allows you to choose your own subject, or it can help you discover what you know about a subject. It also can be helpful if you are experiencing writer's block and need to stop trying to compose sentences. Instead of trying to impose order on your ideas prematurely, wait to see what percolates from your thoughts.

Brainstorming and note jotting. At this stage of the planning process, you are merely trying to uncover mental material for possible use. Jotting does not involve a mental censor. Concentrate on your subject or an aspect of it, and then write down what comes to mind in the form of key words, a list, or whatever will help you recall ideas later. This technique can be a good step to follow free association—when your mind is generating enough potentially useful information that you want to get some of it down on paper.

Free writing. Like free association, free writing can to help you generate ideas by simply writing for five or ten minutes without stopping to censor yourself. Do not worry about spelling or punctuation, grammar or paragraphing. Just start writing everything you think about your subject.

Free writing can be helpful when you can choose your own subject. It can also help when you are overwhelmed by too much information about a subject. Rather than struggling to bring order out of chaos, try free writing about the subject for a while. Useful groupings and relationships among bits of information may emerge. If not, give yourself a break and return to the writing task when you are refreshed.

Journalistic questions. When you are trying to discover what you know about a topic and what you need to find out, try asking the questions Who, What, When, Where, Why, and How. Journalists use these questions to collect the information they need to report news events and to make sure they haven't omitted important details.

> Who is involved?
> What is involved? What happened? What is the issue?
> When did it happen? When did it begin? When did it end?
> Where did it happen?
> Why did it occur? Why is it an issue? Why is it important?
> How did it occur?

Aristotle's topic exploration. The ancient Greek philosopher Aristotle identified four common topics as keys for exploring a subject: definition, chronology, comparison and contrast, cause and effect.

> Definition: What are this subject's characteristics? What are its parts? What is it a part of?
> Chronology: What happened concerning this subject?
> Comparison/contrast: How is this subject similar to or different from other things in its class?

Cause/effect: What are the reasons and the results related to this subject?

Kara used Aristotle's topic exploration in planning her essay about mandatory service charges:

> Exactly what is a mandatory service charge? How would I explain it to a customer?
>
> What has happened in the restaurant business that makes service charges an option?
>
> How is a service charge different from tipping? How is it similar?
>
> What reasons can I offer for a service charge? What are the reasons against it?

Thinking about these questions showed her what she already knew about the subject and what information she would have to obtain from other sources.

● 2 Firsthand information: Direct observation and field work.

Although your own experiences are a rich source of information for many writing tasks, frequently they will need to be confirmed by further research. Systematic observation is one method of collecting additional evidence. Scientists, for instance, carefully test their hypotheses and generalizations to see if their initial observations are supported by repeated occurrences. Primatologist Jane Goodall spent years in the wild observing families of chimpanzees to confirm her theories about chimpanzee behavior.

Direct observation and field work are not limited to scientists, however. These tools may be appropriate for your own information gathering. For example, you might observe people in the cafeteria for a week for a paper on nonverbal communication. A student who wanted to write a paper on welfare fraud jotted notes after work each day about instances of food stamp abuse that he witnessed as a clerk at a convenience store. He also obtained a food stamp application form so that he could learn how people qualified for assistance. A business major who had chosen franchising as the subject for a writing project spent a day at a franchise fast-food restaurant and a day at a franchise muffler shop, talking to the managers and employees and observing customers and operations.

● 3 Secondhand information: Self-reports and direct observations by others.

One way to confirm your own observations is to check them against the observations of others. If your writing task requires synthesis or analysis and interpretation of information from several sources, don't overlook interviews, questionnaires, and surveys as means of collecting information. Family, friends, and colleagues at work or school may be useful sources of information.

Naturally, you should select as sources people who have expertise on the subject—unless you only need "person-on-the-street" reactions. The student who wanted to write about food stamp abuse conducted a brief telephone survey of other convenience store clerks whom he knew. He also arranged to interview a social worker at the local welfare office to help him understand how people qualified for food stamps and how the government defined abuse or fraud. For her paper on tipping, Kara prepared questions to ask fellow Grill employees about their definitions of good or bad service.

● **4 Secondhand information: Secondary sources.** Besides speaking or writing directly to people who have information about your subject, your writing task may require that you consult print or electronic secondary sources—books, newspapers, magazines, journals, recordings, microfilm, and so forth. Keep in mind that a secondary source means information has already been filtered at least once. Whenever you are getting information second- or thirdhand, you must be aware that the information may have been colored by the point of view of the reporter. Even direct quotations from primary sources can be affected this way. The very acts of selecting and arranging information to communicate it have an effect on what is communicated.

When consulting any source, be sure to differentiate between summaries or reports of information and analyses and interpretations of it. Is the source delivering unvarnished facts or offering opinions and interpretations—explaining (or trying to convince you about) what the facts mean? Don't confuse fact and opinion. Both can be useful in your writing, but they do not carry the same weight. (See Section **4b**, "Use Supporting Points to Build Body Paragraphs," and Chapter 7, "Critical Thinking and Argument.")

Essay in Progress

Gathering Information

Following are examples of Kara Lardizabal's planning for three different writing assignments on restaurant service.

Brainstorming for Personal Experience Narrative on Waitressing

```
stand on feet all night
be pleasant to all customers (even nasty ones)
know how to make every step count
must be able to do several things at once
order of service: greet, drink order, menus, take
     food order, give order to kitchen, refresh drinks,
     serve food, condiments, add up check and deliver
     it to table
keep uniform neat
```

```
set up tables before and after rush
remember who ordered what
deal with unusual requests for food
handle harassers and drunks politely
be able to describe menu items, what's in them,
   how large, etc.
keep track of up to 10 tables at one time
deal with slow kitchen
```

**Interview Questions for Definition
of Good Service versus Bad Service**

```
1. What are the characteristics of "good" restau-
   rant service?
2. Of those characteristics, which ones would you
   rank 1 and 2 in importance?
3. What are the characteristics of "bad" restaurant
   service?
4. Which two characteristics are the worst?
5. What complaints do you hear most often from
   customers?
6. Do customers make unreasonable demands? How often?
   Give examples.
7. What can be done to improve service?
```

**Possible Sources for Paper on Potential Consequences
of Mandatory Service Charge**

```
Grill manager (her opinion of consequences):
   secondary source
Roberto (friend who was waiter in Italy where they
   have service charge): primary source
articles in restaurant trade magazines (college
   library): secondary sources
survey of Grill customers' preferences (will manager
   give permission?): primary source
```

Exercise 2.5

Write down two subjects about which you have some knowledge but are not an expert. For each, use different discovery techniques to generate ideas about each subject: journal entries, free association, brainstorming and note jotting, free writing, journalistic questions, or Aristotle's topic exploration. Then make a list of possible primary and secondary sources of information.

In Your Own Words

Imagine that you have decided to write an essay about possible solutions to a problem at your school (for example, lack of parking spaces for students or the need to streamline the registration process), and write a two-paragraph note to your instructor explaining what kinds of information and sources you will use in your essay. Be specific about the kinds of details you hope to gain from each source.

2 d Recognize constraints.

Planning a paper should include an assessment of any constraints that might affect the writing process. The three most common constraints are time, length, and availability of resources. Frequently these constraints are interdependent.

● **1 Time.** Most writers must face a deadline, either self-imposed or imposed by others. Most writers procrastinate. Drawing up a schedule by working backward from the final due date can be a good defense against procrastination and give you a realistic picture of the progress that will be necessary to turn the final draft in on time. Take into account not only writing and revision time but also research time. Try to provide a cushion for the unexpected: interviews that must be rescheduled, computer disks that crash, and dogs that eat your homework.

A realistic schedule, even for a modest writing task such as a 500-word personal experience essay, can help you avoid all-nighters and late papers. It can also help you see where to scale back a project if there clearly is not enough time to implement your original plan. For instance, scheduling may reveal that you can manage to cover only two aspects of a subject rather than the three you had planned. Kara's schedule for a writing assignment appears at the end of Section **2d.**

● **2 Length.** The length of your paper may be a matter of choice, or it may be imposed as part of the assignment. Sometimes length is determined by the subject; a more complex subject requires more pages of explanation or analysis. Length is also related to time. The more time you have to research and write, the longer your final draft can be.

But learn to take length constraints seriously. If a professor says she wants an essay of 500 words, she will lower your grade if you write only half that. If your supervisor at work asks for a five-page report, you can be sure he will resent the extra time it takes to read anything longer than that. The employment advertisement that specifies a one-page résumé is quite serious: Résumés exceeding that limit will be thrown away unread.

● **3 Availability of resources.** If the library books you need are checked out, the person you want to interview is on vacation, the magazine you want to consult is missing from the stacks, or the census bureau has not yet published the statistics you need, you will have to adjust your plans. Sometimes you can substitute other sources, but you will have to adjust your subject or perhaps even abandon it. Early and thorough planning can help you anticipate and uncover potential problems and develop alternatives in time to complete the task satisfactorily.

Kara's Writing Schedule

Week	1	2	3	4	5
Mon.		in class, discuss idea with peer review group	interview manager at work	first draft for peer review	paper due at class time!
Tues.		schedule interview with restaurant manager	summarize interview results		
Wed.		library—background reading	do first mind map of ideas		
Thurs.		write survey for servers	develop working thesis		
Fri.	English paper assigned	try out questions on peer group	questionnaire for my customers	have friend read revised draft	
Sat.		survey servers at work			
Sun.	brainstorm ideas and possible sources	summarize survey results	tabulate and summarize quest. results write first draft	final revisions edit and proofread	

Exercise 2.6

Prepare a schedule for a writing assignment of your own. Use Kara's grid as a model.

The Process of Writing: Shaping Ideas

Whether the purpose of your writing is to explain how to prepare for a job interview, to inform dormitory residents of an important meeting, to convince the dry cleaner to reimburse you for a ruined suit, or to show your American literature professor that you understand characterization in Toni Morrison's novel *Beloved*, the writing must be governed by a **controlling idea.** The controlling idea provides the focus of the paper. All the other ideas and information you present should be related in some evident way to the controlling idea. Without a controlling idea, the paper will run off on tangents and split apart into fragments with no clear theme. Your audience will be left wondering what main point you wanted to make.

In most cases, the controlling idea, or **thesis,** tells the reader not only the subject of the paper but also your stance—your viewpoint on the subject. Even fairly neutral narrative or expository writing—explaining how to make a positive impression at an employment interview or informing residents of a dorm meeting, for instance—often has an implied viewpoint: This is a good way to approach your interview; Tuesday's meeting is important (be there!). At the college level, most writing tasks require that you formulate a stance: "What do I think, based on the available information? What conclusions can I reasonably draw? What position do I take on this subject?" A point of view results naturally from thinking critically about information.

A writer's stance generally emerges during the planning stages of the writing process. As they collect information from various sources, writers begin to discover what they think about a subject, if they did not already have a point of view. As a writer, one of your tasks is to communicate you point of view as well as the reasoning that led you to take that stance. A shapeless shopping bag of ideas will not do. You must organize your ideas and information into a coherent, meaningful whole that your audience can understand. A controlling idea well expressed as a thesis statement plays a major role in shaping the whole.

Think of your thesis statement as a promise to the reader.

A thesis statement is not simply an announcement of the paper's subject. "This essay is about the effects of industrialization on developing nations" is not a thesis statement. "Aboutness" does not qualify as a controlling idea for a paper; it offers no direction.

A thesis statement is an **assertion**: It answers the questions *What point does this paper make? What opinion does it offer? What stand does the*

writer take? What does the writer want us to focus on as we read this paper? A carefully stated thesis introduces and summarizes the entire paper—puts into a nutshell the central idea, which the rest of the paper explores and develops. We speak of the thesis as a statement, implying that it is a single sentence. Typically, a short paper's thesis can be stated in one or two sentences; however, a lengthy paper with a complex thesis may require several sentences to express the controlling idea.

Think of your thesis statement as a promise to the reader. Consider the following thesis: "Industrialization has been both a blessing and a curse for developing nations. It has been a blessing because it has brought improvements in standards of living, and it has been a curse because it has often destroyed important social customs and relationships." The thesis promises readers that the paper will do at least two things, and do them in a particular order. First, the paper will show the positive aspects of industrialization, specifically improvements in living standards. Second, it will show negative aspects, specifically how (1) social customs and (2) social relationships have suffered. If the paper addresses the negative side of industrialization first, or omits a discussion of social relationships, the reader's expectations will have been violated and the writer will have broken the promise made in the thesis.

Keep in mind that as you collect information for your paper you may need to adjust your point of view, requiring a change in thesis and a reshaping of ideas. That is perfectly all right. In fact, it is to be expected. What's the point of reading and writing if you can't discover something new along the way? Just remember to check the thesis against the point of view and organization of ideas in your final draft to be sure that you have actually fulfilled its promise to the reader. The "Writers Revising" at the end of this chapter will give you some practice in comparing the promises in a thesis statement to their fulfillment in the essay itself.

3 b Develop a working thesis statement: A subject and a predicate.

Because the thesis statement indicates the shape your ideas will take in the rest of the paper, it can be a helpful initial focus and guide in the early stages of your writing process. So try to develop a working thesis as soon as you have gathered enough information to have some notion of the direction of your ideas.

Like any other statement, a thesis statement consists of a subject and a predicate. The main topic is the subject. Writing a predicate is a matter of stating the assertion you wish to make about the subject. For her first essay about her part-time restaurant job, Kara Lardizabal used the following working thesis:

subject	predicate

Restaurant customers should tip at least 15 percent to show appreciation for the server's hard work.

This thesis promises that the paper will show why a server's hard work merits a 15 percent tip. Thus one of Kara's writing tasks is to support her stance by summarizing the things she must do to serve a table of customers to show that she deserves to be tipped well in return. Her working thesis thus not only provides a focus for her ideas but also a rough organization (chronological narration) for the essay.

When drafting a working thesis, be wary of statements containing *is* verbs and predicate adjectives or predicate nouns that rename the subject:

> Waiting on tables <u>is</u> *difficult and tiring.*
>
> Fernando Valenzuela and Barry Bonds <u>are</u> *talented athletes.*
>
> The industrialization of developing nations <u>is</u> both *a blessing and a curse.*

In each of these cases the thesis requires a definition of terms: Just what do the writers mean by "difficult and tiring," "talented athletes," "a blessing and a curse"? Even if terms are defined, the question "why" remains: Why is waiting on tables difficult and tiring, why do Valenzuela and Bonds fulfill the definition of "talented," why is industrialization both a blessing and a curse? To function successfully as thesis statements, each must be paired with another sentence or clause that answers the question "why": "*because* [industrialization] has brought improvements in the standard of living, and ... *because* it has often destroyed important social customs and relationships."

You need not automatically reject statements with *is* verbs. Write whatever expresses the controlling idea of your paper best. But do make sure that your thesis indicates the reasons or other supporting points you will develop in the paper.

3 c Write a thesis statement that is unified, focused, structured, and interesting.

A well-formed thesis statement has four main characteristics:

Unity. The thesis states *a single controlling idea.* The idea may be complex and have several parts, but it should be one idea nevertheless.

Focus. The thesis should be restricted and specific enough for the reader to gain a clear idea of the subject and the direction of your paper. Your stance on the subject may also be indicated.

Structure. If the thesis is sufficiently focused, it will provide a basis for decisions about which information to include and which to exclude from the paper. As a result, it will help you organize your ideas. In fact, the thesis statement can indicate the structure of your paper by stating the aspects of the subject you intend to discuss in the order that you plan to address them.

Interest. The thesis should sharpen the reader's interest in the subject. Although the thesis statement need not be shocking or sensational, neither do you want readers to yawn and say "So what?"

Weak thesis statements usually suffer from lack of unity and/or lack of focus.

LACK OF UNITY AND FOCUS
My difficulties in philosophy class are unbelievable, but I'm doing OK in biology.

REVISION
Because I seem to be more comfortable with concrete things like frogs than with abstract concepts like existence, I am getting better grades in biology than in philosophy.

LACK OF FOCUS
Kids face a lot of problems today and need help.

REVISION
Increasingly, teenagers face problems such as drug use, street violence, suicide, parental divorce, AIDS, and unwanted pregnancy. Consequently, we need many more counseling programs than are currently available to teens.

The first example fails the test for unity because it contains two separate ideas with no indication of how, or if, they will be brought together. A paper using this thesis is likely to break into two unconnected halves—one half devoted to biology class, one half to philosophy class. The revision corrects this problem by establishing a cause-and-effect relationship that connects the two subjects.

Both the first and second examples fail the test for focus because they use vague generalities such as "are unbelievable," "doing OK," and "a lot of problems." The territory opened by "a lot of problems" and "need help" is vast and unmanageable. The focus must be restricted to something the writer can reasonably tackle within the constraints of time and length.

The territory staked out by the second revision is still too ambitious for a 500-word essay. The writer would do better to focus on one or two related problems—AIDS and unwanted pregnancy, for instance—or the two the writer thinks are most prevalent among teens.

As mentioned in Section **3b**, predicates that consist of an *is* verb plus a vague modifying phrase or complements such as *good, interesting,* or *a serious problem* are usually too imprecise to be useful to either writer or reader. The writer will likely flounder around, ending up with an essay that offers little beyond obvious generalities. The reader will lose interest and patience waiting for the writer to come to the point and say something concrete. Readers want a thesis assertion that supplies a specific subject and clear direction as quickly as possible—as does the second revision.

The first example, poor as it is, provides more organizing structure for an essay than the second does. At least we assume the writer will first address the difficulties of philosophy class (whatever they are) and then the positive aspects of biology class. The second example provides virtually no clues beyond the general subject areas "problems" and "help." However, the second revised thesis leads readers to expect a review of available counseling programs for teen problems in support of the assertion that they are insufficient. The direction that the paper will take is clear.

Not every kind of writing needs an explicit thesis statement. Business or technical writing may have a clearly stated purpose and overall controlling idea, but no single sentence that functions as the thesis. Similarly, in a novel or short story the theme may emerge gradually rather than being stated explicitly in one or two sentences. Nevertheless, especially in essays that explain or argue a point, a clear thesis sentence—the promise you make to your readers—greatly aids readers' understanding.

3 **d** Place the thesis statement early in your paper.

Where you put a thesis statement depends on your goals, your audience, your purpose, and your paper's organization. The most common position for the thesis sentence in short expository and argumentative essays is in the opening paragraph. It may appear early in the opening paragraph, followed by sentences that further define or explain the assertion the thesis makes. Or the thesis sentence may be positioned near the end of the opening paragraph, after an introduction of the subject and some background information or scene setting.

Although other locations for the thesis statement can work, remember that readers like a clear sense of what is going on. Be sure that your controlling idea is indeed controlling the paper, wherever the thesis is located. The principal argument for its early appearance in an essay is that readers will understand the relevance of your discussion better if you first tell them the main idea that governs it.

Exercise 3.1

For practice in writing unified, focused thesis statements, revise the following thesis sentences. If any of them are satisfactory as written, explain why.

1 Underage drinking is out of control.

2 There aren't enough computers available for student use on campus, and the library doesn't stay open late enough either.

3 The incredible scenery and the good food are what made my vacation so memorable.

4 Hosting an exchange student from Japan not only broadened our knowledge of another culture but gave us a new outlook on the United States.

5 Participating in sports can be a big influence in a person's life.

Exercise 3.2

Draft at least *two* working thesis statements for an essay on *one* of the subjects you used in Exercise 2.5 (or another subject of your choice). Revise these statements so that they are unified and focused. Strive to develop thesis statements that would result in very different essays.

Exercise 3.3

Working with two classmates, test each other's thesis statements from Exercise 3.2 for unity, focus, and direction. Next discuss an appropriate audience for an essay each of you might write using one of your thesis statements. According to your group analysis of each audience, together revise each thesis statement for maximum interest and appeal to its audience.

In Your Own Words

In a paragraph, critique a classmate's thesis in terms of its unity, focus, structure, and implied audience. Include suggestions for revision if you think the thesis needs further work.

3 **e** Begin shaping your ideas.

Once you have gathered information and constructed a preliminary thesis to provide some focus and direction for your paper, you can apply additional techniques that will help you shape your essay. Mind mapping, idea trees, and scratch outlines are three such techniques.

● **1 Mind mapping.** Mind mapping encourages the free flow of ideas, but it also allows you to define relationships among ideas. Thus, without forcing a predetermined organizational scheme, you can discover connections that may suggest a possible shape for your paper.

Start by writing the subject in the center of a piece of paper or computer screen. Then, as you think of other ideas or bits of information, write them down in new circles that radiate outward from the central idea. Don't censor your ideas: Write down whatever occurs to you about your subject. If ideas are related to one another, draw overlapping circles, or connect the circles with lines. Later you can cross out information that ultimately remains unrelated to the emerging direction of the paper. Your mind map can be as simple or as detailed as you choose.

Mind mapping can be especially helpful if you want to collect ideas about aspects of a subject but find yourself troubled by the best order in which to present them. Seeing the ideas without a superimposed structure but in relationship to one another can help postpone the need to organize them until you have finished collecting information and are ready to think productively about an organizational scheme.

The following mind map resulted from the collaborative work of student writers exploring the first thesis statement in Exercise 3.1.

Mind map

● **2 Idea trees.** An idea tree invites somewhat more structure than mind mapping. It represents ideas not only in relation to each other but also in hierarchical arrangements. Various arrangements could be from greater to lesser, general to specific, most important to least important, main idea to supporting idea, and so forth, depending on the subject and the nature of the writing task. Kara Lardizabal drew the following idea tree to shape her ideas for an essay about people who stop by the bar at the Grill restaurant. (See the "Writer's Revising" at the end of Chapter 5 for the finished essay.) As Kara's example illustrates, idea trees are useful for exploring the parts of a subject and for organizing the presentation of ideas. Drawn in some detail, an idea tree will reveal the potential shape of your essay. It can show how much information you have on various aspects of the subject, where you may need more information, where you may have too much material, and where you may have wandered away from the controlling idea.

Idea tree

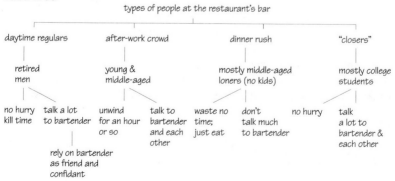

As Kara worked on the preceding idea tree, what had begun as an essay classifying (contrasting) different types of bar patrons emerged as an essay about the social role of the bartender. She thought, "So different types of people sit at the bar. So what? That's not new or particularly interesting. What's more interesting here is how the different types relate to the bartender." After a bit more planning and research (interviewing the restaurant's bartenders, further observing the customers), Kara's original idea took a new direction and a new shape—one she found more satisfying. In writing to inform others, she had learned something new herself.

● **3 Scratch outlines.** Formal outlining will be discussed as part of Chapter 5 on revision. For now, let's focus on how informal outlines can assist you in shaping your writing. An informal, or scratch, outline can be especially valuable when you must write against a deadline—an in-class essay or exam, for instance. It can keep you from discovering too late that you have confused issues, wandered from the main line of argument, left out important points, or maybe even failed to understand the question.

Begin by writing your working thesis at the top of a clean sheet of paper or blank computer screen. If you are working with an assigned subject or essay exam question, write the assignment at the top. Immediately under it, put the thinking and writing task(s) you need to perform: analyze, compare or contrast, explain a procedure, discuss causes and/or their consequences. Next, list the major topic divisions you want to address to fulfill the writing task. Under each major division, list two or three supporting points or key facts. Finally, restate the thesis, assignment, or question, in different words if possible.

Review your outline to see if the progression is orderly and logical, if your information is accurate, and if the points you have listed respond fully to the task. If not, reorganize, add or delete information. When you are satisfied, turn the outline into an essay using complete sentences and paragraphs.

For a situation other than an in-class essay or exam, your scratch outline acts as a guide for information from your own experience and observation and a guide to information you need to obtain from other sources. In fact, you can jot notes about sources next to points on your outline. Kara's scratch outline shows how she created the basic structure for her paper on tipping without yet knowing which stance she would take in her thesis. Because she still lacked some crucial information, she reserved that decision for later, but the outline helped her to plan the overall shape of the essay.

Scratch outline

Working thesis: Voluntary tipping should (should not?) be replaced by a mandatory service charge added to customers' restaurant bills. (Task: Analyze and evaluate pros and cons of each, draw conclusion.)

Mandatory service charge: what is it? (define)
Where has it been used successfully?
    Europe
    Groups of six or more in many U.S. restaurants
    Other places? (research)
Advantages
    No cheapskates or "stiffs"
    Reliable income
    Fair to everybody
    Simple: already calculated for customer
Disadvantages
    Customers not used to it
    Customer boycott
    Exceptional service unrewarded
    Possible decline in level of service
    Other? (research)
Advantages compared to disadvantages
Mandatory service charge is (is not) the best way of rewarding service staff.

Although a scratch outline does not need the parallel headings and careful construction of a formal outline, use key words or phrases that are as specific and concrete as possible. If you merely write vague words such as *introduction* or *conclusion*, you aren't getting much mileage from your minutes spent planning. What do you intend to put in the introduction or the conclusion? The answer to that question will give you the key words for the headings.

Exercise 3.4

Using your subject and working thesis statement from Exercise 3.3 (or another subject and thesis statement, if you prefer), create a mind map for an essay. Then try developing an idea tree or scratch outline for the same subject and thesis. Which shaping technique did you find most helpful? Why? As evidence of your own writing process, make a mental note or journal entry about your choice and reasons.

In Your Own Words
Write a paragraph explaining the advantages and disadvantages of each of the shaping techniques—mind-mapping, idea tree, and scratch outline.

Writers Revising

Read the first paragraph of the following early draft that Kara Lardizabal wrote for one of her English assignments, and underline the sentence you think is the thesis statement. Then read the rest of the draft. When you have finished, decide if the draft fulfills the promise made in the thesis. Be prepared to explain your decision.

Draft

Students need to have some type of income while attending school. Restaurants provide many opportunities to earn extra money. I work at a restaurant near campus. While working there I have been able to meet many different types of people.

The restaurant work schedule is made up of two shifts, a day shift and a night shift. The restaurant is a different place during the daytime compared to the night. The daytime business is fairly slow. The staff has time to sit around and complain about their job. Most of the waitresses and bartenders talk about getting a new job. The night shift is extremely busy, which makes the night go by quickly.

At the bar, the daytime crowd is mostly retired men. Most of them have gone home by 5:00 p.m. The older daytime crowd is replaced by a younger group of people who stop in for a drink or two on their way home from work. These people come in several nights a week to relax and talk with their friends. The conversations at the bar range from the weather to sports, which is the most popular topic. Two of the regular customers are Toby and Al. Toby works at the college and is one of those guys who still lives with his mother at age fifty-eight. He is always the butt of practical jokes. Al is a nice guy, but he thinks that he knows everything. He reminds us of Cliff on the television show Cheers. We call him the Cliff Clavin of the Grill bar. I think every bar has one or two Cliffs.

The dinner rush, which begins at 5:30, is usually busy and will last about three hours. Several people will eat at the bar to avoid the wait in line for a table in the dining room. These people usually eat, talk with a few people, and then go home.

Our youngest group of customers arrives at 9:00 p.m. Most of these people are friends and classmates of the night staff. I enjoy waiting on these people because they are easy to deal with and I have a lot in common with them. This group hangs out at the bar until last call at 11:30 p.m. The words "last

call" are the most loved by bartenders and hated by
customers. Clean-up begins after last call. The bartenders begin by wiping down the liquor bottles and
cleaning off the bar. At the end of the shift one bartender makes a bank for the next shift while the others restock the beer that was used throughout the day.
The bank is a small amount of money that we leave in
the register so the next shift can make change for
customers. The last task of the night for the bartenders is splitting the tips. The tips range from a
few pennies to several dollars, depending on the customers' moods and the type of service they receive.

I have worked various types of part-time jobs
while attending college. Working in a restaurant
offers the most flexibility for a student's schedule.

Now suggest revisions for Kara's draft by crossing out sentences that do
not fit with her thesis statement: *While working there I have been able to
meet many different types of people.* Then compare your revision with
Kara's, which follows.

Revision

~~Students need to have some type of income while
attending school. Restaurants provide many opportunities to earn extra money~~. I work at a restaurant near
campus. While working there I have been able to meet
many different types of people.

The restaurant work schedule is made up of two
shifts, a day shift and a night shift. The restaurant
is a different place during the daytime compared to
the night. The daytime business is fairly slow. ~~The
staff has time to sit around and complain about their
job. Most of the waitresses and bartenders talk about
getting a new job~~. The night shift is extremely busy,
~~which makes the night go by quickly~~.

At the bar, the daytime crowd is mostly retired
men. Most of them have gone home by 5:00 p.m. The
older daytime crowd is replaced by a younger group of
people who stop in for a drink or two on their way
home from work. These people come in several nights a
week to relax and talk with their friends. The conversations at the bar range from the weather to sports,

which is the most popular topic. Two of the regular customers are Toby and Al. Toby works at the college and is one of those guys who still lives with his mother at age fifty-eight. He is always the butt of practical jokes. Al is a nice guy, but he thinks that he knows everything. He reminds us of Cliff on the television show <u>Cheers.</u> We call him the Cliff Clavin of the Grill. I think every bar has one or two Cliffs.

The dinner rush, which begins at 5:30, is usually busy and will last about three hours. Several people will eat at the bar to avoid the wait in line for a table in the dining room. These people usually eat, talk with a few people, and then go home.

Our youngest group of customers arrives at 9:00 p.m. Most of these people are friends and class-mates of the night staff. I enjoy waiting on these people because they are easy to deal with and I have a lot in common with them. This group hangs out at the bar until last call at 11:30 p.m. The words "last call" are the most loved by bartenders and hated by customers. ~~Clean up begins after last call. The bar-tenders begin by wiping down the liquor bottles and cleaning off the bar. At the end of the shift one bar-tender makes a bank for the next shift while the oth-ers restock the beer that was used throughout the day. The bank is a small amount of money that we leave in the register so the next shift can make change for customers. The last task of the night for the bar-tenders is splitting the tips. The tips range from a few pennies to several dollars, depending on the cus-tomers' moods and the type of service they receive.~~

~~I have worked various types of part-time jobs while attending college. Working in a restaurant offers the most flexibility for a student's schedule.~~

Analysis

If you had trouble deciding which sentence in Kara's opening para-graph was intended as the thesis, you weren't alone. The opening paragraph is not unified; it introduces several subjects (students' need for income, restaurants as an opportunity for earning income, meet-ing various types of people at restaurants), any one of which could be the essay's main idea. Since most of the following essay paragraphs discuss various types of characters who frequent the restaurant bar, the last sentence in the opening paragraph is the most logical choice for the working thesis statement. It seems to exert the most control over the rest of the essay.

When Kara reread the final paragraph, she saw that it violates the audience's expectations by introducing a subject that has not been discussed previously in the essay: the compatibility of restaurant work with a college student's schedule. She has not kept the promise her apparent thesis makes to readers.

Other sentences in the essay (for example, those having to do with closing the bar) are unrelated to the apparent main idea, so Kara crossed them out. The remainder provides the material for Kara's next step. By comparing all the sentences in the draft to the emerging thesis, she saw that she needed to return to the planning phase of the writing process and gather more information to describe various types of people who frequent the restaurant bar. Two possibilities for further development are the dinner rush customers, about whom she has said very little, and the after-nine crowd, who are obviously college students but whom she has left faceless in her first draft.

4 The Process of Writing: Drafting the Paper

If your planning has been productive, you will have much material with which to begin drafting your paper. In fact, in the process of gathering information and beginning to shape your ideas, you may already have written some portions of the paper, at least in rough form. Every jotted note, mind map, or scrap of an outline gives you tangible material for the first draft. What do you do next? Following are two approaches you can try. Choose the one that best seems to fit your personal writing process.

 Experiment with drafting all at once or a bit at a time.

● **1 All at once.** Some writers find success by quickly drafting the whole paper in rough form. Somewhat like free writing, the principle here is first to capture as much material as possible, going back later to revise as necessary, sometimes extensively. Just dive in, writing down your ideas according to the structure suggested by your working thesis statement and scratch outline (or other planning techniques). Keep writing until you have "used up" your outline or notes. If you get stuck along the way, write a note to yourself in brackets to capture the gist of what you might say at that point, and move on. For example, you might write: [need an additional example here] or [don't like transition—work on this].

This approach can be particularly helpful when you face a deadline and have to get maximum results from limited time. It is also a good choice both when ideas are flowing well and when they are flowing slowly. If ideas are flowing quickly, you don't want to risk losing your train of thought by interrupting it with grammar or word choice decisions. When ideas are flowing slowly, it is tempting to take a side road into editing or revising when it really might be more productive to resist that temptation and just push on with the next idea, even if you aren't very satisfied with the result.

One advantage to this approach is that at the end of the drafting session you will have a good amount of material to show for your efforts— plenty of words on the page. That is satisfying. Another advantage is that you have a clear task ahead: revising. Even if you aren't satisfied with the draft, at least you can see the present shape of all your ideas and have enough material to begin making substantial changes. For many writers, an extremely rough first draft is preferable to stopping with only a few paragraphs written.

A disadvantage of the all-at-once approach is that you may not have enough time available at one sitting to complete a draft, or you might become too tired or distracted to continue. So before you begin, you may want to divide your general organizing scheme into several large chunks. Then you can write as many chunks as time allows.

Another disadvantage for some writers is that once their words appear on paper, they look good enough to leave as is. The temptation to be satisfied with a first-time-final draft can be very strong. It takes discipline to return to a draft and revise it. One way to overcome this temptation is to make revision (discussed in Chapter 5) an integral part of your writing process, allowing plenty of time for it in your schedule. Assume that every first draft is just that—the first of several—and always a rough draft, not one that is polished enough to submit to your audience.

Even an essay test answer written in the classroom can be considered a first draft. Although you should not use valuable time copying it over, certainly you should not turn your test answer in until you have read it over for correctness, drawn through bits that need eliminating, and neatly inserted the necessary changes in information, spelling, grammar, or wording. In a testing situation, always watch your time to allow a few minutes at the end of the test period for necessary revisions.

● **2 A bit at a time.** As its name suggests, this method of drafting works well for writers who prefer to get one section in good shape before moving on to the next. When you are trying to communicate complex thoughts, as in an analytical or argumentative essay, you may have to work hard to show the relationships among your ideas. This kind of painstaking thinking and writing can consume a lot of time and energy. Consequently, it may be necessary to tackle drafting in small bits, not moving to the next piece until you are reasonably satisfied with the groundwork you have laid.

One advantage of this approach is that you are likely to achieve a fairly tight and well-unified first draft because you have been rewriting and revising throughout the drafting of each section of the paper. A disadvantage is that you may become discouraged because your progress seems slow. Ask yourself whether you are the sort of person who can be satisfied with progress measured in what seem to be small steps or whether you need to experience great leaps forward.

The amount of drafting time available for one sitting may dictate that you use the bit-at-a-time approach. If so, set realistic short-term goals, dividing the writing task into manageable portions (e.g., "I'll spend this fifteen minutes before I have to go to chemistry lab sketching out an example that supports this point on my idea tree."). At each sitting, just before you stop drafting, jot down a sentence or some key words to remind you of where you left off. When you return, you'll find it much easier to pick up your train of thought.

In Your Own Words

Choose either your instructor or a classmate as your audience and write a two-paragraph discussion of the all-at-once and the a-bit-at-a-time methods of drafting an essay. In your discussion explain which method works best for you and why.

Use supporting points to build body paragraphs.

Your paper's thesis presents your audience with an assertion that requires proof. In so many words, you have said to your readers, "I think thus-and-so is true." They respond, "What makes you think so? Why should I take your word for it? Show me why I should agree with you." Your responsibility as a writer, then, is to support your assertion with evidence the audience will find convincing. Presenting these supporting points is the function of the body paragraphs. Common types of proof include facts, explanations, examples, illustrations, and testimony. Each type has strengths and weaknesses.

● **1 Facts.** A fact is something that people accept as true because it is verifiable. That is, the truth of a fact can be established through repeated observation or experimentation. The sun comes up in the east; in the northern hemisphere water runs clockwise down the drain; blue and yellow make green; people who were abused as children are more likely to be child

abusers themselves. If your thesis states that underage drinking is increasing, you will need to supply such facts as the number of American teenagers who drink alcohol and the frequency of their drinking as well as facts about these behaviors in the past. Your paper might include a body paragraph on each statistical category as evidence supporting your thesis.

Facts provide strong support for a thesis. Difficulties arise when an essay contains insufficient supporting facts or when facts have been presented selectively (i.e., facts supporting the writer's stance are presented but those in conflict with the writer's stance are omitted). However, most disputes over facts arise because people interpret them differently and disagree about what they mean.

● **2 Explanations.** When we explain an event or phenomenon, we offer reasons to account for what has happened. The purpose of an explanation is to make clear to readers what is going on and why or how something has come about. If Kara Lardizabal wants readers to understand why waiting on tables is difficult work, she must develop body paragraphs that explain the things employees do to provide restaurant customers with good service.

Explanations are especially important when the audience has less expertise or knowledge about a subject than the writer. Remember that reader-based writing brings the reader into the picture as quickly as possible. Two common hazards of explanation are that a writer may supply more details than readers require or may become so involved in an explanation that the focus and unity of the essay are destroyed. So think carefully about your audience when drafting explanatory portions of your paper. Concentrate on what the reader needs to know to understand your main point rather than on what you have learned.

● **3 Examples and illustrations.** A generalization offers a broad statement. An example or illustration is a concrete and particular instance of a generalization. To be accepted as true, a generalization must be based on enough particular instances that people are willing to say, "Yes, that is generally the case." Thesis statements are often generalizations—for instance, "Freshmen often get into academic trouble because of poor study habits."

In writing, we frequently use examples and illustrations as part of an explanation to help readers understand precisely what we mean. The unspoken conversation between reader and writer goes something like this: "Freshmen often get into academic trouble because of poor study habits." "What do you mean by 'poor study habits'?" "Well, look at Amiee. She spends most of the evening talking on the phone or watching TV. By the time she finally opens a book, she's too sleepy to do her homework."

Examples and illustrations do more than clarify: They also help to convince readers of the truth of a generalization or stance. For example, if Kara wishes to convince readers that customers will accept mandatory service charges, she will need to provide several examples of restaurants where service charges have been successfully substituted for tipping. Kara would include in the body of her essay a paragraph citing these successful instances.

Several strengths of examples and illustrations have already been mentioned. Their very concreteness is appealing, and therefore they can also be emotionally compelling. A newspaper story describing starving refugee children will move people to support foreign aid much faster than any government policy statement about American interests abroad. But the concreteness and emotional impact of examples and illustrations also contain a potential weakness. If readers suspect that their emotions are being manipulated at the expense of their reason, they will distrust the writer and discount what he or she has to say.

● **4 Testimony.** The body paragraphs of a paper may include testimony that supports the thesis statement. The word *testimony* comes from a Latin word meaning "witness." When you use testimony in your writing, you are telling what you or someone else has witnessed. The previous example concerning freshman study habits takes the form of testimony—one person observes another person's behavior and then states what he or she has seen. Frequently, testimony appears in writing as a paraphrase or direct quotation of the observer's words.

Testimony can be a very effective form of support. However, you should scrutinize it carefully to avoid the charge that it is mere opinion. Just as in a courtroom trial, ask yourself whether the witness is reliable. Is the emotional impact of powerfully told testimony masking weak factual content? Is the witness expert enough to report accurately or interpret correctly what he or she saw? Do you need additional factors or other kinds of evidence to supplement or balance someone's testimony? These questions are equally important when you are the observer providing the testimony. In the body of her essay on restaurant service charges, Kara used the observations of Roberto, who had been a waiter in Italy where such charges are the norm. Since her readers would probably point out that Italian customers are used to service charges whereas U.S. customers are used to tipping, Kara knew she could not rely solely on Roberto's testimony to persuade her audience.

As you plan and draft a piece of writing, you will be deciding what kinds of supporting evidence to use in the body paragraphs. Your choices will depend on the writing tasks you have undertaken—whether you are summarizing or synthesizing information, reporting and explaining, analyzing by comparing and contrasting or by identifying causes and effects, agreeing or disagreeing with a point of view, or trying to convince readers or simply inform them. The content of your body paragraphs will also depend on your audience's knowledge and experience. Given their background, do your readers require more or fewer explanations and examples? Will readers be skeptical, neutral, or readily in agreement with the ideas and testimony you bring to your subject and thus require more, or fewer, facts?

Essay in Progress

Drafting Supporting Paragraphs

To write her essay on the pros and cons of mandatory service charges, Kara Lardizabal gathered information from people she knew and worked with as well as from several newspaper and magazine articles. Following are three body paragraphs from an early draft of her paper. See if you can identify the types of supporting evidence she used.

It used to be that how much a restaurant employee earned in tips was a private matter between server and customer. Since 1982, however, the issue of tips is of concern not just to the person leaving the tip and the person receiving it. Because of changes in federal tax laws, restaurant owners now must keep records and report employees' tips to the IRS. In addition, owners must pay Social Security and unemployment taxes on their employees' tips. The government wanted to close a tax loophole on billions of dollars in unreported income from tips. But the result has been a bookkeeping nightmare and major expenses for restaurant owners.

Service charges are widely used in Europe. For example, most hotels and restaurants automatically add 10 to 20 percent to the bill. My friend Roberto Rosanova, who worked as a waiter in his uncle's restaurant in Milan, Italy, says that is the case in all nice restaurants in Italy. At his uncle's restaurant, for instance, the bill has servizio compreso (service included) written on it. Some restaurants, especially those with a sidewalk cafe in front, also add a coperta or cover charge. Because sidewalk cafe customers tend to order coffee or drinks, their total bill (and service charge) will be relatively small. Roberto says the coperta helps make up for the fact that the waiter has given as much service as if the customer had ordered a whole meal. In addition to the

<u>servizio</u> and the <u>coperta</u>, Italians usually still leave a small tip for the waiter (<u>cameriere</u>).

There is disagreement over whether American customers prefer mandatory service charges or voluntary tipping. Barry Wine, who owns the Quilted Giraffe in New York City, and Michael Fawcett of the Rattlesnake Club in Denver say that customers like the service charge system used at their restaurants. Fawcett believes people like it because with the service charge they don't have to figure out how much to leave the server. On the other hand, in a poll taken for <u>Time</u> magazine 77 percent of the people polled said they did not favor a service charge of 15 percent to 18 percent added to their bill. A poll of my customers at the Grill restaurant showed that 54 percent of them would not mind a 15 percent service charge-- as long as the service was good.

The first paragraph is primarily an **explanation** of the impact federal tax laws have had on the way tips are reported. Kara uses **facts** about the laws as part of the explanation. The second paragraph offers Italian custom as an extended **example** of how services charges are applied in Europe. It also includes the **testimony** of Kara's friend Roberto. The first half of the third paragraph relies primarily on **testimony** from restaurant owners. The second half of the paragraph presents statistical **facts** derived from two polls, a formal scientific one by a professional pollster and an informal one by Kara.

Exercise 4.1

An eighteen-year-old in his first semester of college wrote the following thesis for an English composition on after-school jobs: "Working more than about fifteen hours a week is harmful to adolescents because it reduces their involvement in school, encourages a materialistic and expensive lifestyle, and increases the chance of having problems with drugs and alcohol." He identified his primary audience to be the other members of his English class, the majority of whom were eighteen to twenty years old and many of whom held part-time jobs. Read the following sample body paragraphs and then rate each one from 1 to 5 (1 = weak; 5 = strong) according to how well you think it supports the student's thesis statement. You may use the same number more than once if you think two paragraphs are equally effective. Be prepared to defend your choices.

a Teenagers who work long hours do not get the benefits of schoolwork and extracurricular activities. High school teachers I talked to said they are facing increasing difficulty keeping the attention of tired pupils and giving homework to students who simply don't have time to do it. These students' grades predictably slip as the school year progresses. In addition, educators have noticed less involvement in extracurricular events. In the past five years, the number of students trying out for the band and athletic teams has dropped 30 percent, according to the dean at my high school. Attendance at sports events has fallen 20 percent. She blames after-school jobs for this decrease. No one has the time anymore.

b Most teenagers don't really need the money they earn in part-time jobs. They aren't saving it for college or to help out with the family budget. They are using their money to buy luxury items such as CD players, tickets to rock concerts, expensive clothing, and cars. I agree with my dad, who says these kids aren't learning to spend their money wisely. They are becoming accustomed to a materialistic lifestyle that they won't be able to support a few years down the road when their parents aren't paying for food and shelter, car insurance, and other necessities.

c Teenagers who work a lot are more likely than others to get involved with alcohol and drugs because they may seek a quick release from stress, just like the adults who need to drink a couple of martinis after a hard day at work. Stress is probably greater in our society today than it has been at any time in the past. Also, teens who have money are more likely, for various reasons, to get involved with drugs.

d Those teenagers who try to do it all—homework, extracurricular activities, after-school job—may find themselves exhausted and ill. A recent newspaper story, for example, described a girl in California who came down with mononucleosis as a result of aiming for good grades, playing on two school athletic teams, and working thirty hours a week. She is not an isolated case. Young people are much more likely to get sick if they are tired and run-down. The school nurse at my old high school used to make an announcement toward the end of every semester when students were driving hard toward exams, end-of-term concerts, tournaments, and so forth, warning us to get enough sleep and eat right. Of course we pretty much ignored her, but this advice was based on the fact that the number of students visiting her office with colds, mono, and other complaints always increased at these times of year.

4 c Begin the paper effectively.

The beginning of a paper serves as a springboard into its subject and the assertion being made about that subject. Journalists strive to write a "hook" that will attract readers' attention and draw them into the story. Businesspeople, on the other hand, write to get things done. For business readers an effective beginning is one that clearly announces the subject and purpose of a document. Whereas an entertaining anecdote might be a good beginning for a magazine article, it probably would not be an appropriate opening for a progress report from a production manager to corporate headquarters. Consider the needs of your audience, the goal you want the writing to accomplish, and the nature of your subject when evaluating the merits of a particular beginning.

● **1 Effective beginnings.** Important as a good beginning is, do not be overly concerned about it in your rough draft. If you think of a strong beginning, fine. But you may find that your purpose is clearer and the opening is easier to write after at least one rough draft. Some people habitually compose the opening paragraph last, with good results. At least be prepared to perform major surgery on your opening. One of the following types of beginnings may prove useful.

Statement of fact, startling statement, or unusual detail

FACTUAL STATEMENT
Ninety-two percent of the students at State College live at home and commute.

STARTLING STATEMENT
There's a fine line between cheap and sleazy. I know. I recently drove right along it. Let me explain.
—Carrie Dolan, "'Little Lady' Suffers a Lapse of Luxury to Prove Boss Right"

UNUSUAL DETAIL
We knew there was trouble ahead when we saw the cans of mosquito repellent, littering the roadside like spent cartridges.
—Mark Gauert, "The Abandoned Car Told the Tale: Everglades Mosquitoes Had Struck"

Firm statement of opinion or directly stated proposition

OPINION
It begins with a bow. It ends with a bow. In between are the screams and blows of kendo. The Japanese sport of kendo is not new to the United States, just unknown to most people in this country. That's unfortunate.
—Frank Brown (student), "Do You Know Kendo?"

DIRECTLY STATED PROPOSITION
Global warming is much less of a problem than painted by the extremists.
—Glenn T. Wilson, "Hot Air in the Greenhouse Debate"

Brief anecdote or incident leading directly to subject

BRIEF ANECDOTE
"My name is Mr. George Louise. First, I'd like to welcome you to Canada. Secondly, I don't mean to discourage you so soon, but an American has not

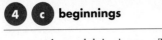

made my club in six years. There's hockey, and then there's Canadian hockey. It's just a fact that Canadian hockey is superior to American hockey." This was my introduction to the general manager of the Milton (Ontario) Merchants hockey team when I arrived at Toronto International Airport. I learned quite a bit about Canadian hockey during my try-out for the Merchants. I also learned about prejudice.

—"A Level Playing Field," student essay

● **2 Ineffective beginnings.** A weak beginning that bores, confuses, or otherwise alienates readers will cause them to lose patience and quit reading before you have even begun to discuss your subject. The following are some types of beginnings to avoid.

Vague openings that cannot be understood without referring to the title

Everyone is against it. People worry that a serious accident will occur like the one that caused the evacuation and illness of hundreds of people in Russia several years ago.

—"Nuclear Energy," student essay

The first thing to do is lay all the parts on the table. Then compare them with the parts list to be sure you have everything.

—"Parents' Guide to Surviving Christmas Eve," student essay

Openings that start too far back

Remember the difference between writing that is reader oriented and writing that is writer oriented (Chapter 1). Openings that start too far back try to force-feed the audience with unnecessary background information, such as in the following introductory paragraph.

Father Knows Best

You're probably wondering from my title what I am going to write about. Well, it's a long story. It started when I was born. The doctor announced to my parents that I was a boy. "We're going to send him to State University!" my father exclaimed. So here I am at State, a member of the freshman class.

It was my father's idea from the first that I should come to State. He was a sophomore here when he met my mother....

Openings that complain or apologize

COMPLAINT
Describing a building accurately is a very difficult task. Though it is a good assignment because it makes you look closely and observe details you would not otherwise notice, it takes considerable time and does not leave the student enough time to write the actual paper. I discovered this when I tried to observe and describe the college chapel.

APOLOGY
After trying unsuccessfully to write an essay describing my roommate, and then attempting to gather some ideas on books I had read during the

summer, I gave up and decided to write on my experience in reading *The Joy Luck Club* by Amy Tan. I hope this fits the assignment.

4 **d** Provide readers with a sense of completion at the end.

A decisive ending lends your paper a finished, polished note. It echoes your introduction and brings your paper to a logical, satisfying conclusion.

Just as the nature of the opening depends on the length and complexity of the paper, so too does the conclusion. An essay of 500 words may require a concluding paragraph of just a few sentences, whereas a paper of two or three times that length will probably need a final paragraph of perhaps half a dozen sentences to summarize its contents. Long, analytical essays and research reports often have multiple-paragraph concluding sections to bring the various threads of the paper together and present the final results.

● **1 Effective endings.** The following are several types of effective endings that you may wish to adapt to your essays.

Restatement of thesis or a quotation that clearly illustrates the thesis

Keep in mind that a restatement of the thesis does not mean a word-for-word repetition of it—which will bore readers and make them wonder at your lack of originality.

> THESIS RESTATED
>
> Now that I have been here and have seen the school for myself, I am convinced that Father *does* know best. I have decided to enroll at State next fall.

> QUOTATION
>
> I realize the image of chemistry is in such disrepair that it would take a major effort on all our parts to turn this round. . . . Most important, surely, is that we reach the general public and the politicians with the message that chemistry is absolutely essential to our modern way of life. Let's revive the spirit once contained in the slogan, "Better things for better living though chemistry."
>
> —Fred Basolo, "Let's Be Positive about Chemistry"

Summary of major ideas developed in the paper

> SUMMARY
>
> So how can you guarantee that your Christmas Eve will be spent relaxing in front of the fireplace instead of tearing your hair out trying to put your kid's new bike together? As I have shown, if you make sure you have all the necessary parts and tools, read the directions FIRST, and start far enough ahead to give yourself plenty of time, assembling Christmas toys does not have to be traumatic.

Conclusion drawn from the facts
presented in the paper

CONCLUSION BASED ON PRESENTED FACTS

The fact that a state judge could seem almost casual about rape shows that beneath the new surface sensitivity, many of the cultural prejudices linger. "What we do in our society, whether it's in photography, films, or language, is devalue sex," says Psychologist Groth, "and that gives the message that sex can become a weapon to degrade somebody." Such moral carelessness is what has made the U.S. violent in private, as well as in public.

—Maureen Dowd, "Rape: The Sexual Weapon"

Ending with a punch line, surprise,
or ironic twist

A punch-line ending provides a surprising or humorous twist that can be appealing, especially if it is consistent with the tone of the rest of the paper. The following ending effectively concludes an essay that argues for exercise as a good remedy for writer's block.

PUNCH LINE

Give it a fair trial—three months, say, long enough for the novelty to wear off and for it to become a part of your routine. You may find, as I have, that exercise helps create a climate for the solution of writing problems. You may find only that it makes you feel better. On the other hand, it may be that all you get for your troubles is better health and longer life.

Listen, you can't win 'em all.

—Lawrence Block, "Fiction: Huffing and Puffing"

● **2 Ineffective endings.** A weak ending can spoil the momentum and interest you have worked so hard to create in the body of the paper. The following are three of the most common weak endings.

Bringing up a new aspect of the subject
or introducing a new subject

UNEXPLORED NEW ASPECT OF SUBJECT

To summarize, I really enjoyed working at Busch Gardens last summer. Not only did I earn money for college, I met people from all over the United States and foreign countries and made many new friends. On the other hand, I don't think I'd work there again.

INTRODUCTION OF NEW, UNRELATED SUBJECT

As we have seen, global warming represents a tremendous threat to life as we know it on earth. Climactic changes could affect everything from crop production to the frequency of deadly hurricanes. Out-of-control population growth is another problem that will need serious attention in the next century.

For another example of a weak ending that brings up a new subject, review Kara Lardizabal's concluding paragraph in "Writers Revising" at the end of Chapter 3.

Leaving the paper hanging in midair

Readers need a sense of closure. Papers that just quit leave the audience with an uneasy feeling of unfinished business, as is the case with the magazine article closing that follows. The subject of the article is the battle between the Coast Guard and shrimpers over the use of TEDs (Turtle Extruder Devices) on shrimp nets.

> ENDING LEFT HANGING
> One shrimper spoke angrily at a meeting with the Coast Guard: "It's the on-again, off-again, on-again stuff we can't stand. If they'd have made us put on TEDs—and leave us alone—we'd either get by, starve, or go bankrupt, but there wouldn't be this misery of jerking us around." "This whole thing is terrible," agreed one woman.

Ending with an apology or disclaimer

> APOLOGY
> In this paper I may not have been able to persuade you to my point of view, but after looking at the pros and cons, I do not think Dr. Jack Kevorkian should be prosecuted for helping suffering, terminally ill people to commit suicide.

> DISCLAIMER
> Of course, I'm no expert, and everybody is entitled to their own opinion.

4 e Write an informative, effective title for your essay.

First, the title of any piece of writing should indicate its subject matter. Your primary objective should be to inform your readers. Second, a title arouses interest by provoking, entertaining, or intriguing readers. A clever title can be an attention-getting way to draw readers to your essay. On the other hand, don't overdo the cleverness at the expense of clarity. A "cute" title serves no one if it puzzles readers or patronizes them.

Sometimes writers think of a good title early in the writing process. More often, however, the title emerges gradually after several drafts have clarified the writer's thinking about subject and viewpoint. *Do* spend time on the title. It is the first thing your audience sees and consequently will shape their expectations about your essay, influencing their decision to read it or not.

Exercise 4.2

Look at articles in at least two different magazines (only one may be a news magazine). Do the titles of the articles attract your attention? Which titles are the most appealing, the least appealing, and why? Do the titles tell you anything about the types of people who read these magazines? What sorts of beginnings and endings do you find in the articles? Do any of them fit the types discussed in Sections **4c** and **4d**? Look at the beginning and ending of Kara Lardizabal's first draft in the "Writers Revising" that follows. Do they fit any of the types discussed in Sections **4c** and **4d**?

In Your Own Words

Using your subject and working thesis statement from the exercises in Chapter 3 (or another subject and thesis statement, if you prefer), write a rough draft of an essay. Try to notice the times when you stop drafting to do more planning or to reread and revise. In other words, try to become conscious of your own writing process—what you are doing when the writing goes well and what is happening when it does not. Do not polish too much. Leave the essay as a rough draft at this point, to be revised after you have read Chapter 5.

Writers Revising

Kara Lardizabal's first draft comparing different types of bar patrons at the Grill needed substantial changes. The following revised first draft shows how she eliminated first-draft sentences having nothing to do with her working thesis. After she spent more time shaping her ideas with the help of an idea tree (see Section **3e**), Kara decided to revise her thesis statement, too. The new thesis statement is underlined in the first paragraph.

Using her new thesis statement as a guide, look at each of Kara's body paragraphs, circle information she should keep, and write suggestions for other information that would support the new thesis. Then suggest new opening and closing paragraphs. Compare your suggestions with Kara's second draft.

Revised First Draft

I work at a restaurant near campus. While working there I have been able to meet many different types of people. One of the most interesting things about the people who come into the Grill's bar is the different ways they relate to the bartender. It's clear to me that some of these people really depend upon the bartender. For some types of customers the bartender is just a person who makes their drink, but for others the bartender is a friend, a confessor, an audience, and maybe even a lifeline to the rest of the world.

The restaurant work schedule is made up of two shifts, a day shift and a night shift. The restaurant is a different place during the daytime compared to

the night. The daytime business is fairly slow. At the
bar, the daytime crowd is mostly retired men. Most of
them have gone home by 5:00 p.m. The older daytime
crowd is replaced by a younger group of people who
stop in for a drink or two on their way home from
work. These people come in several nights a week to
relax and talk with their friends. The conversations
at the bar range from the weather to sports, which is
the most popular topic. Two of the regular customers
are Toby and Al. Toby works at the college and is one
of those guys who still lives with his mother at age
fifty-eight. He is always the butt of practical jokes.
Al is a nice guy, but he thinks that he knows everything. He reminds us of Cliff on the television show
<u>Cheers</u>. We call him the Cliff Clavin of the Grill bar.
I think every bar has one or two Cliffs.

The dinner rush, which begins at 5:30, is usually
busy and will last about three hours. Several people
will eat at the bar to avoid the wait in line for a
table in the dining room. These people usually eat,
talk with a few people, and then go home.

Our youngest group of customers arrives at
9:00 p.m. Most of these people are friends and classmates of the night staff. I enjoy waiting on these
people because they are easy to deal with and I have a
lot in common with them. This group hangs out at the
bar until last call at 11:30 p.m. The words "last
call" are the most loved by bartenders and hated by
customers.

Second Draft Revision

At three o'clock in the afternoon, a heavy-set
widower sits on a bar stool at the Grill restaurant
where I work at a restaurant near campus. He tells
Patty the day bartender about the cruise he and his
wife took on their last wedding anniversary together,
ten years ago today. By 5:15 p.m. the same stool is
occupied by Al, a computer programmer who explains to
anyone who will listen just how last night's football
game should have been coached. At 6:30 p.m. a young
woman occupies the stool. She looks tired. The only

words she utters are to give Phil, the night bartender, her order for a club sandwich and a beer. By
nine o'clock, all the stools are filled with college
students. While working at the Grill, I have been able
to meet many different types of people. One of the
most interesting things is the different ways customers relate to the bartenders. It's clear to me that
some of these people really depend upon the bartender.
For some customers the bartender is just a person who
makes their drink, but for others the bartender is a
friend, a confessor, an audience, and maybe even a
lifeline to the rest of the world.

The daytime business at the bar is fairly slow.
The crowd is mostly retired men who apparently come in
to pass the time talking to the bartender. Some of
them nurse a beer for an hour, talking about their
wives, bragging about their grandchildren, and telling
how they would solve the world's problems. Usually
they don't converse a lot with each other, but direct
their comments mainly to the bartender. Some of these
guys come to the bar for awhile nearly every day. You
get feeling they have nothing much to do and nobody
else to talk to. Patty manages to smile, comment, and
look interested in their conversation while she pours
their beer and washes glassware.

By 5:00 p.m., the older daytime crowd is replaced
by a younger group of people who stop in for a drink
or two on their way home from work. These people come
in several nights a week to relax and talk with their
friends. The conversations at the bar range from the
weather to sports, which is the most popular topic.
Two of the regular customers are Toby and Al. Toby
works at the college and is one of those guys who
still lives with his mother at age fifty-eight. He is
always the butt of practical jokes. Al is a nice guy
but he thinks that he knows everything. He seems to
regard the bartender as his personal audience. If Phil
is busy, he addresses anyone who will listen. He
reminds us of Cliff on the television show Cheers. We
call him the Cliff Clavin of the Grill bar. I think
every bar has one or two Cliffs.

The dinner rush, which begins at 5:30, is usually busy and will last about three hours. Several people will eat at the bar to avoid the wait in line for a table in the dining room. These people usually eat, maybe talk with the person sitting next to them, and then go home. For this group, the bartender might as well be invisible. Phil is just a pair of hands that serve food and drink. Once in a while someone strikes up a little conversation, but usually the people at the bar look like they just want to be left alone to eat and then hurry on their way. Bartenders must find the dinner rush busy but boring.

Our youngest group of customers arrives at 9:00 p.m. Most of these people are friends and classmates of the night staff. I enjoy waiting on these people because they are usually easy to deal with and I have a lot in common with them. This group hangs out at the bar until last call at 11:30 p.m. The words "last call" are the most loved by bartenders and hated by customers. These late evening hours are a purely social time for both the customers and bartender. The only major difference between the two is which side of the bar they are on. Everybody is catching up on what's happening at school, with their friends, and the usual topics college students talk about.

If you always go to a bar at about the same time of day and with the same people, you probably have never seen the variety of people and purposes a bar really serves. A bar can be a place to be strictly alone or a place to be companionibly with others. The bartender provides a substitute family, a therapist's couch, a performance stage, or a fraternity lounge-- and changes roles to suit the "scene" the customers want to play. Obviously a good bartender is skilled at alot more than mixing drinks.

Analysis

Kara has preserved a good deal of the first draft (for instance, the basic descriptions of the four types of customer groups). She sticks to her original organization, introducing the customers narratively according to a chronological structure (order by time of day).

However, she has expanded and refocused some of her descriptions with more detail. She provides the example of the retired man who misses his wife and needs to talk to Patty, the bartender, about it. She develops the original paragraph about the evening rush diners from three sentences to seven and also focuses on the bartender's role. In most instances Kara has used revision to shift the paper's emphasis to include the bartender, consistent with her new controlling idea.

The opening paragraph also contributes to the shift in emphasis. It uses an anecdote to set the scene for the thesis—the types of customers and their various types of relationships with the bartender. Kara's new closing paragraph works toward the same goal by summarizing the gist of the essay and restating the thesis in the final two sentences.

5 The Process of Writing: Revising the Paper

If you review the "Writers Revising" sections at the ends of Chapters 3 and 4, you will see the extensive revisions that Kara Lardizabal's essay underwent as she progressed toward the final draft. Most people believe that good writers do not need to rework their writing—just a little polishing here and there, a check for spelling mistakes, and they're finished. Nothing could be farther from the truth. Consider Theodor Geisel, for example.

Better known as Dr. Seuss, Ted Geisel published forty-eight books between 1937 and 1990, including his most famous, *The Cat in the Hat,* and his most popular, *Green Eggs and Ham.* Following his death in 1991, Geisel's widow Audrey donated to the library of the University of California at San Diego drawings and manuscripts for all but one of the Seuss books published after 1968. The collection includes everything from first drafts and preliminary sketches to final texts and finished drawings. These works-in-progress show that even for writing that appears as simple and spontaneous as the Dr. Seuss books, Geisel revised extensively—sometimes over 100 different versions of lines in a text only a few hundred words long. An early draft of *The Butter Battle Book* (1984) begins, "When I was a young Yook and not very tall." The final manuscript reads, "On the last day of summer, ten hours before fall." Geisel was never afraid to throw something away and start afresh. The vast majority of professional writers work this way. You should, too.

Schedule a cooling-off period.

The key to revising is being able to see your paper critically. To **revise** means "to see again." You may need a few hours, or even a few days, away from your paper to be able to review it effectively. Being involved too closely with what you are writing can be a disadvantage to reading your work critically and finding the weak spots.

At other times, you may recognize the nagging sensation of something being wrong while you are writing and may find that stopping right then and puzzling out the problem is the most effective method. If you are afraid that stopping will cause you to lose your train of thought, put a check mark, a key word, or a brief note in the margin as a reminder for later revision, and go on with your writing.

But when you have arrived at what you believe to be the final draft stage, be sure to allow sufficient time for that crucial cooling-off period, which will enable you to see your paper with fresh eyes for final revising. Your goal is to see the paper as your audience will see and react to it.

Work with a trusted reviewer.

Professional authors commonly work with reviewers. When they submit a manuscript to a magazine, a book publisher, or a scholarly journal, the manuscript is reviewed not only by the editorial staff but frequently by outside reviewers as well, people who are experts in the field. These reviewers read the manuscript for accuracy of content and for organization, unity, coherence, clarity of expression, audience appropriateness, and so forth. People who write on the job often use the buddy system to accomplish the same ends. They pair with a colleague so that each can serve as a reviewer and editor of the other's work when the need arises. Similarly, you have probably asked a friend, roommate, or family member to look over your writing and see if it makes sense or has any mistakes. Perhaps your English composition class provides an opportunity for class members to evaluate and critique one another's rough drafts. Besides your own careful reading, a good reviewer can be your most valuable writing aid.

Professional reviewers work from a set of guidelines, specifications, or questions as they respond to manuscripts. Likewise, you will benefit the most if your reviewer uses a thoughtful approach and a specific set of guidelines rather than just responding off the cuff to the vague request "read this and tell me what you think." Here are some tips for reviewers.

1 **Read the paper carefully several times, and do not respond before you have thought about what to say.** It is important to get the big picture and try to determine the writer's purpose, audience, and role. You should also be sure you understand the task or assignment to which the writer is responding.

2 Be honest but fair and tactful. It is important to say what you think and not mislead the writer about the paper's strengths or weaknesses. On the other hand, remember that writers tend to take criticism personally, so talk about the writing, not about the writer. Say "This thought doesn't follow from the previous one" rather than "You don't make sense here."

3 Be as specific as possible about problems, and suggest priorities for revision. Are some problems bigger or more important than others? Which one should be tackled first? Which one is the key to others? If you are being critical, you should also try to suggest alternatives if you can.

4 Point out strengths as well as weaknesses. It is important to build a writer's confidence. Nearly everybody's paper has something admirable in it, even if there are many poor spots. How will writers know where their text works well if no one tells them?

5 Remember that peer review is not the same as editing or rewriting another person's paper for him or her. You should not be asked, nor should you volunteer, to act as another person's ghost writer. Authors may expect a thoughtful critique, but they must not expect someone to fix their writing when the assignment calls for independent, individual work. Such editing, when carried too far, amounts to plagiarism—submitting the writing of another instead of one's own. It is dishonest and can result in such academic penalties as a failing grade.

The evaluation form on the next page can be used as a model for providing advice about another person's writing.

5 c Global search: Revise for meaning changes.

Your first concern when revising should not be with spelling and grammar. These sentence-level matters are important, but they can be cleared up later with careful editing and proofreading. Your first concern should be with meaning. Does your paper respond to the writing assignment you were given or you set for yourself: Have you fulfilled the task? Does your paper convey your ideas clearly? Does it adequately develop and support the thesis you have stated? These are some of the questions that you alone, or with the help of a peer reviewer, must answer as you work toward the final draft. As Kara Lardizabal discovered (see Chapters 3 and 4), substantial portions of the essay may need to be discarded and others added to achieve the meaning you desire. The following checkpoints will help you decide if your essay meets your goals.

● 1 Check the organizational structure against your purpose and task. If your goal has been to compare or contrast, to discuss cause and effect, to prove a point, or to accomplish another task, does the structure of the essay reflect that goal? One good tool for checking structure is a formal outline. Such an outline will show whether you have compared or

Evaluative Critique
Reader Response Form

Author's name: *Reader's name:*

1 Read the first paragraph and then pause. Write down what you expect will be the subject, purpose, and audience of this paper.

2 Now finish reading the paper. Were your expectations for the paper's subject, purpose, and audience fulfilled? If not, what do you now think the subject, purpose, and audience are?

3 What do you think the controlling idea, or thesis, of the paper is? Can you find a sentence that expresses this controlling idea? Should there be one?

4 What sort of evidence is used to develop or support this controlling idea? Is it convincing? Is it the right kind? Is there enough of it?

5 Summarize the paper, devoting one sentence to each paragraph. Does each relate clearly to the paper's apparent controlling idea?

6 What did you like best about the paper?

7 Did anything in the paper surprise you?

8 Now look at the sentences. Do any sentences confuse you? If so, try to describe your confusion or ask the author questions about the sentence.

9 Are there any punctuation, mechanical, or grammatical mistakes in the paper? If so, point them out to the author, but do not correct them.

10 Decide what the paper's most important strengths are (at least two). Point these out to the author, and write them below.

11 What features of the paper most need improvement? (Indicate at least two.)

contrasted the same points and issues, whether there are sections sufficiently explaining causes and results, if the point-to-point order is logical, and so forth. A well-developed outline reveals the skeleton of a paper so that the structure emerges clearly from the verbiage and details.

Some writers construct a formal outline as a blueprint for the paper they will write. A detailed sentence outline can virtually serve as a first draft. On the other hand, many writers use an outline as part of their revision process, preparing it after writing their paper as a means of testing the structure and development of their ideas. A partial outline of Kara's early draft reveals that her goal of comparing types of bar patrons was not carried out by the structure of the paper.

Main idea: Meet different types of people.
- I. Comparison of day shift and night shift.
  - A. Day
    1. Business fairly slow
    2. Staff sits around
  - B. Night
    1. Fairly busy
    2. Time passes quickly for staff
- II. Daytime crowd
  - A. Retired men
    1. Gone home by 5 o'clock
  - B. After-work crowd
    1. Younger men and women
    2. Relax and talk with friends
       a. Weather
       b. Sports
       c. Tony and Al

Whereas the second half of the outline clearly pertains to the types of customers, the first half does not. Although the first half is a comparison (day shift versus night shift), the focus is on how the staff spends its time rather than on types of customers. The outline helped Kara see that to support her goal, the first part of her draft needed revising.

Some assignments, such as research papers or long reports, require that a formal outline be submitted as part of the document. The conventions of formal outlining are as follows:

a Number and indent headings and subheadings consistently; do not use single headings or subheadings. Follow the rule "for every I, there must be a II; for every A, there must be a B." Any category of heading or subheading must have at least two parts. The foregoing partial outline contains an incorrect heading: "1. Gone home by 5 o'clock." This single heading indicates poor organization or incorrect partition. You cannot logically divide something into just one part. A single subheading should be incorporated into the heading of which it is logically a part, or it should be divided in two.

Note also that the preceding outline contains same-level headings that do not represent the same classification principle. Items II.B.2.a, b, and c are not of the same class. The patrons talk about the weather and about sports; they do not talk about Toby and Al. Toby and Al are, in fact, patrons Kara refers to as examples of the after-work crowd. Consequently, the discussion of Toby and Al should be labeled II.B.3, the same level as II.B.2.

b Follow either topic, sentence, or paragraph style throughout an outline, and use parallel grammatical structure. A topic outline may use either a noun (or noun substitute) and its modifiers or a verb phrase for each heading. There is no punctuation at the end of the headings in a topic outline. A sentence outline uses a complete sentence for each heading, with corresponding end punctuation. For an example of a sentence outline, see the sample research paper in Chapter 48. A paragraph outline gives a summary sentence for each paragraph of the paper and does not divide and subdivide headings into subordinate parts. The first word of each heading is capitalized in all three types of outlines.

Do not mix types in the same outline, as Kara does in the preceding outline. I.A.2 and I.B.2 are complete sentences, whereas the other entries are phrases more appropriate to a topic outline. Also remember to make all parts within the same level or degree of the outline parallel in grammatical structure. Using consistent grammatical form emphasizes the logic of the outline and provides clarity and smoothness. The grammatical form of II.B.1 and 2 in Kara's outline is inconsistent: Part 1 contains a noun phrase, whereas 2 contains a verb phrase. They should be in the same grammatical form.

c Avoid vague outline headings such as Introduction, Body, and Conclusion. These headings will not help you or your readers because they do not contain content information. Indicate in the outline what the introduction will include. If your paper is to have a formal conclusion, show in the outline what conclusion you will draw. Think of a formal outline as a table of contents for the reader, a preview of important information and its organization. Because it does provide such an overview, a formal outline often begins with a statement of the paper's thesis, as does the outline for the research paper in Chapter 48.

The following is a correctly constructed topic outline for a subsequent draft of Kara's comparison/contrast essay.

I. Daytime regulars
   A. Retired men
      1. Old guys
      2. Time on their hands
      3. Extended conversation with bartender
         a. Bartender as friend
         b. Bartender as confidant
   B. After-work happy hour crowd
      1. Young and middle-aged professionals (men and women)
      2. Hour or so to unwind
      3. Conversations with each other and bartender
         a. Bartender as friend
         b. Bartender as audience
II. Evening customers
   A. Dinner rush
      1. Middle-aged loners
      2. Quick eaters
      3. Little conversation; no relationship with bartender
   B. Late evening "closers"
      1. College students
      2. Relaxed, unhurried socializers
      3. Noisy conversation
         a. Bartender as college buddy
         b. Little difference between bartender and customers

● **2 Check each paragraph against the thesis statement.** An essay whose paragraphs wander from the main point will lack unity and coherence. The essay will seem to go in several directions at once, losing readers along the way. Checking each paragraph to be sure that it pertains to the thesis will reveal those that either should be omitted or that need rewriting to strengthen and clarify their connection to the essay's controlling idea.

In her revision, Kara deleted a paragraph and a half from the end of her first draft (compare the revisions in the "Writers Revising" at the ends of Chapters 3 and 4). She saw that the discussion of procedures for closing the bar and splitting the tips had nothing to do with her central theme, types of customers.

● **3 Tighten or change the thesis if necessary.** As you revise your essay, you may find that your thesis needs to be adjusted to fit new directions your thoughts have taken. After some initial revisions, Kara decided that she needed to change her thesis. From a very muddled opening paragraph in her first draft, she gradually extracted the core idea that exerted the most control over her essay: "While working there [at the Grill restaurant and bar] I have been able to meet many different types of people." In subsequent revisions, this statement evolved along with Kara's ideas about customers. By the time she had settled on the relationship between customers and the bartender for her core subject, she had developed a new thesis as well: "For some types of customers the bartender is just a person who makes their drink, but for others the bartender is a friend, a confessor, an audience, and maybe even a lifeline to the rest of the world." Notice that by now she has replaced the vague and fuzzy "meet different types of people" with a much more specific and focused central idea. Even so, the thesis was to undergo further revision. To see the final changes, read the "Writers Revising" at the end of this chapter.

● **4 Note paragraphs in which additional information or further research is necessary.** Remember that what seems obvious or well supported to you may need further proof to be convincing to your audience. As noted in Sections **2b** and **4b** (in Chapters 2 and 4, respectively), readers who share less common ground with the writer are likely to be more skeptical and require more evidence. Have you provided enough facts, explanations, examples and illustrations, and credible testimony to support all assertions throughout your essay as well as the primary assertion that functions as your thesis? Often a peer reviewer, reading as a devil's advocate, can alert you to spots where additional evidence may be needed.

● **5 Delete redundant or superfluous information.** As you compare the contents of each paragraph with the thesis, you will notice information that does not develop the essay's central idea. Be ruthless and eliminate things that really don't add to the discussion. Also search for places where you have repeated ideas to no purpose. A peer reviewer can be helpful in spotting these kinds of redundancies because it is often difficult for authors to see them. Ask your reviewer to point out sentences where you "said that already." Then ask yourself if there is any real reason for repeating the idea. There may be a good reason, but you need to check the effectiveness of such repetitions.

● **6 Check tone against stance and audience.** The attitude your writing expresses about both your subject and your readers can have an enormous effect on whether your audience ends up agreeing with you. A sarcastic tone will alienate readers who do not already agree with your point of view, although it might entertain readers who are sympathetic from the start.

Consider the case of the lawyer who wrote an essay for a newsletter aimed at politically liberal readers of moderate income living a comfortable lifestyle. His subject was the rights of homeless people, and his purpose was to point out that the homeless have the same Constitutional rights as people who own homes. His ideas were legally and socially sound. Unfortunately, while trying to make his point, the tone of his essay began to criticize people who could afford to own homes. He used words such as *obscene wealth* and *luxurious* to contrast homeowners' neighborhoods to the streets and park benches where the homeless lived. Wealth is relative; compared to the situation of a homeless person, even a modest house may seem like a mansion. However, the tone that emerged in the essay appeared to attack the middle-class readers, suggesting that their lifestyle was excessive and perhaps even evil. This tone would surely undermine the writer's purpose by making the audience defensive and thus destroying whatever sympathy they might feel for the plight of the homeless.

Local search: Revise for surface changes.

Surface changes involve sentence-level matters of correctness, convention, and style. Spelling, grammar, punctuation, sentence construction, word and sentence order, and vocabulary choice are types of surface changes.

Sometimes revisions for surface changes are referred to as editing (changing sentence construction, word choice, and word order) and proofreading (spelling, grammar, and punctuation correctness). The term *revision* may be reserved for activities involving meaning changes. However, sentence-level surface changes can certainly result in meaning changes.

> The average American child who attends public school receives a poor education in science and math.
>
> The average American child, who attends public school, receives a poor education in science and math.

As the foregoing example shows, the addition of a pair of commas that changes a restrictive modifier to a nonrestrictive one can substantially alter the meaning of a sentence (from *some average American children* to *all average American children*) and thus the whole focus of a paragraph. For this reason, *revision* in the *Prentice Hall Handbook for Writers* refers to any and all changes that result from reviewing and evaluating text. Use Chapters 8 through 45 in this handbook as a resource for checking surface changes suggested by your reading and that of your peer reviewers.

Revision Checklist

Meaning Changes

- **Subject.** Is the subject clear? Are the ideas in the paper all related to the subject?
- **Focus.** In addition to the subject, does the paper have a clear controlling idea? Are all the paragraphs in the paper related to the controlling idea?

- **Thesis.** Is there a thesis statement that expresses the controlling idea? If not, should there be one?
- **Development.** Are all the thoughts in the paper explained adequately for the audience being addressed?
- **Organization.** Do the ideas and the paragraphs in the paper progress in an organized fashion?
- **Logic.** Are the assertions supported adequately with evidence? Are ideas presented fairly without being one-sided? Is credit given to others where credit is due?
- **Audience.** Does the paper show sufficient awareness of the audience's background, knowledge, interest, and other characteristics?
- **Opening and closing.** Does the paper have an effective beginning and a strong conclusion?
- **Purpose.** Does the paper have an apparent aim? Has it fulfilled that aim?
- **Title.** Does the paper have a title that captures the reader's interest and indicates clearly what the paper is about?

Surface Changes
- **Grammar, punctuation, spelling.** Has proofreading for these errors been thorough? Have mistakes been corrected? (See Chapters 12 through 20 and 25 through 42.)
- **Mechanics.** Have the conventions of capitalization, use of abbreviations, numbers, and so forth that are appropriate for the subject and audience been observed? (See Chapters 43 through 45.)
- **Level of language.** Is word choice precise and appropriate for the subject and audience? (See Chapters 22 and 23.)
- **Wordiness.** Have words been used economically and effectively, avoiding wordiness, unnecessary jargon, and vagueness? (See Chapter 24.)
- **Sentence structure.** Are sentences logical, well constructed, and effective in their use of subordination, variety, parallelism, and emphasis? (See Chapters 9 through 11.)

ESL Highlight

Editing Tips
1 Underline subjects and circle verbs. Check for subject-verb agreement.
2 Check verbs for tense consistency and correct form.
3 Check for correct use of verbs.
4 Use brackets to identify sentence boundaries. Does each sentence have a subject and a verb?
5 Do you have many simple sentences in your essay? Are any of the sentences closely related in meaning? Could the sentences be combined with coordinating or subordinating conjunctions?

6 Circle all the commas in your sentences. What are the functions of the commas? Eliminate any single commas between subjects and verbs.

7 Cover each comma and determine if you have complete sentences on both sides of the comma. If you do, are the sentences joined with a comma and a conjunction? If not, should you use a semicolon? Would a period be the best choice?

8 Find the pronouns in your sentences and draw lines to the nouns or noun phrases that they represent.

9 Circle all the expletives (*there is, there are, it is*) and rewrite the sentences if possible, using action verbs.

10 Read your paper sentence by sentence backward to identify sentence fragments.

11 Circle all the transitional words and phrases in your essay. Do they provide logical, meaningful connections between your sentences and paragraphs?

Exercise 5.1

Give the rough draft you wrote in Chapter 4 to a peer reviewer for an evaluation and critique. Revise your paper using those suggestions you feel are appropriate, creating a new draft.

Exercise 5.2

To check the structure of your draft, construct a formal topic outline of it. Write the headings so that they conform to the rules of outlining (Section **5c**). Adjust your draft's organization if the outline indicates you should do so.

Exercise 5.3

Revise your draft a final time, using the checklist at the end of Section **5d**.

In Your Own Words

Review the changes you made in revising your first draft and write a one-paragraph summary of the kinds of problems you solved in revising and the techniques you used to solve them.

Writers Revising

After she had finished the second draft revision, Kara Lardizabal exchanged papers with a classmate for peer review. The reviewer's comments are written on the draft. Following that is Kara's final draft as she submitted it to her English professor for grading.

Peer Review of Draft

                                    title?   sp
      At three o'clock in the afternoon, a heavy-set

widower sits on a bar stool at the Grill restaurant
                   repetition
where I work at a restaurant near campus. He tells
           punct.
Patty the day bartender about the cruise he and his
                                          sp
wife took on their last wedding anniversery together,

ten years ago today. By 5:15 p.m. the same stool is

occupied by Al, a computer programmer who explains to

anyone who will listen just how last night's football

game should have been coached. At 6:30 p.m. a young

woman occupies the stool. She looks tired. The only

words she utters are to give Phil, the night bar-

tender, her order for a club sandwich and a beer. By
I like this intro.
nine o'clock, all the stools are filled with college

students. While working at the Grill, I have been able

to meet many different types of people. One of the

most interesting things is the different ways cus-

tomers relate to the bartenders. It's clear to me that

some of these people really depend upon the bartender.

For some customers the bartender is just a person who

makes their drink, but for others the bartender is a
                                promises more than you deliver
friend, a confessor, an audience, and maybe even a

lifeline to the rest of the world.

      The daytime business at the bar is fairly slow.

The crowd is mostly retired men who apparently come in

to pass the time talking to the bartender. Some of

them nurse a beer for an hour, talking about their

wives, bragging about their grandchildren, and telling

how they would solve the world's problems. Usually
they don't converse a lot with each other, but direct
some ideas seem redundant
their comments mainly to the bartender. Some of these
sp
guys come to the bar for awhile nearly every day. You
get the feeling they have nothing much to do and
nobody else to talk to. Patty manages to smile, comment, and look interested in their conversation while
she pours their beer and washes glassware.

By 5:00 p.m., the older daytime crowd is replaced
by a younger group of people who stop in for a drink
or two on their way home from work. These people come
in several nights a week to relax and talk with their
friends. The conversations at the bar range from the
weather to sports, which is the most popular topic.
Two of the regular customers are Toby and Al. Toby
works at the college and is one of those guys who
still lives with his mother at age fifty-eight.
He is always the butt of practical jokes. Al is a nice
punct.
guy but he thinks that he knows everything. He seems
to regard the bartender as his personal audience. If
Phil is busy, he addresses anyone who will listen. He
reminds us of Cliff on the television show Cheers. We
call him the Cliff Clavin of the Grill bar. I think
every bar has one or two Cliffs.

The dinner rush, which begins at 5:30, is usually
verb tense shift
busy and will last about three hours. Several people
will eat at the bar to avoid the wait in line for a
usually: word repet.
table in the dining room. These people usually eat,

maybe talk with the person sitting next to them, and

then go home. For this group, the bartender might as

agree error (but neat metaphor)
well be invisible. Phil is <u>just a pair of hands that</u>

<u>serve</u> food and drink. Once in a while someone strikes

word repet.
up a little conversation, but <u>usually</u> the people at

the bar look like they just want to be left alone to

eat and then hurry on their way. [Bartenders must find

the dinner rush busy but boring.] *seems off subject*

Our youngest group of customers arrives at

9:00 P.M. Most of these people are friends and class-

mates of the night staff. [I enjoy waiting on these

idea not relevant
people because they are usually easy to deal with and

I have a lot in common with them.] This group hangs

out at the bar until last call at 11:30 p.m. The words

"last call" are the most loved by bartenders and hated

by customers. These late evening hours are a purely

social time for both the customers and bartender. The

only major difference between the two is which side of

you're right!
the bar they are on. <u>Everybody</u> is catching up on

agree error
what's happening at school, with <u>their</u> friends, and

the usual topics college students talk about.

point of view shift
If <u>you</u> always go to a bar at about the same time

of day and with the same people, you probably have

never seen the variety of people and purposes a bar

really serves. A bar can be a place to be strictly

sp
alone or a place to be <u>companionibly</u> with others. The

bartender provides a substitute family, a therapist's

couch, a performance stage, or a fraternity lounge--

and changes roles to suit the "scene" the customers

want to play. [Obviously a good bartender is skilled

at <u>alot</u> more than mixing drinks.] new subject introduced?

sp (above alot)

Final Draft

More Than Just a Pair of Hands

At three o'clock in the afternoon, a heavyset widower sits on a bar stool at the Grill restaurant where
I work near campus. He tells Patty, the day bartender,
about the cruise he and his wife took on their last
wedding anniversary together, ten years ago today. By
5:15 p.m. the same stool is occupied by Al, a computer
programmer who explains to anyone who will listen just
how last night's football game should have been
coached. At 6:30 p.m. a young woman occupies the stool.
She looks tired. The only words she utters are to give
Phil, the night bartender, her order for a club sandwich and a beer. By nine o'clock, all the stools are
filled with college students. While working at the
Grill, I have been able to meet many different types
of people. One of the most interesting things is the
different ways customers relate to the bartenders. It's
clear to me that some of the people really depend upon
the bartender. For some customers the bartender is just
a person who makes their drink, but for others the
bartender is a counselor, an audience, and a friend.

The daytime business at the bar is fairly slow.
The crowd is mostly retired men who come in nearly
every day to pass the time talking to the bartender.
Some of them nurse a beer for an hour, talking about
their wives, bragging about their grandchildren, and
telling how they would solve the world's problems. You
get the feeling they have nothing much to do and
nobody else to talk to. Patty manages to smile, comment, and look interested in their conversation while
she pours their beer and washes glassware.

By 5:00 p.m., the older daytime crowd is replaced
by a younger group of people who stop in for a drink
or two on their way home from work. These people come
in several nights a week to relax and talk with their

friends. The conversations at the bar range from the weather to sports, which is the most popular topic. Two of the regular customers are Toby and Al. Toby works at the college and is one of those guys who still lives with his mother at age fifty-eight. He is always the butt of practical jokes. Al is a nice guy, but he thinks that he knows everything. He seems to regard the bartender as his personal audience. If Phil is busy, he addresses anyone who will listen. He reminds us of Cliff on the television show <u>Cheers</u>. We call him the Cliff Clavin of the Grill bar. I think every bar has one or two Cliffs.

The dinner rush, which begins at 5:30, is busy and lasts about three hours. Several people may eat at the bar to avoid the wait in line for a table in the dining room. These people usually eat, perhaps exchange a few words with the person sitting next to them, and then go home. For this group, the bartender might as well be invisible. Phil is just a pair of hands that serves food and drink. Once in a while someone strikes up a little conversation, but mostly the people at the bar look like they just want to be left alone to eat and then hurry on their way.

Our youngest group of customers arrives at 9:00 p.m. Most of these people are friends and class- mates of the night staff. This group hangs out at the bar until "last call" (the words most loved by bar- tenders and hated by customers) at 11:30 p.m. These late evening hours are a purely social time for both the customers and bartender. The only major difference between the two is which side of the bar they are on. People catch up on what's happening at school, with their friends, and the usual topics college students talk about.

If you always go to a bar at about the same time of day and with the same people, you probably have never seen the variety of people and purposes a bar really serves. A bar can be a place to be strictly alone or a place to be companionably with others. The bartender provides a substitute family, a therapist's couch, a performance stage, or a fraternity lounge--

```
and changes roles to suit the "scene" the customers
want to play. Obviously a good bartender is skilled at
a lot more than mixing drinks.
```

Analysis

Kara took the advice of her peer reviewer in most cases, correcting grammar, spelling, and punctuation. She also removed redundancies in the first and second paragraphs, inserting some of the information into other sentences.

The reviewer's comment about the thesis sentence showed Kara that she had developed only three of the four aspects of the bartender's role in the essay. Thus she eliminated the "lifeline to the rest of the world" portion, changed "confessor" to "counselor" (which more accurately reflected later description), and reordered the three aspects to follow the actual organization of the essay.

The peer reviewer correctly challenged Kara's use of future tense verbs in the fourth paragraph. She had been narrating in the present tense, to give readers a sense of being present as witnesses throughout the day. Changing to future tense disrupted this sense of immediacy.

At the end of the fourth paragraph and at several points in the fifth paragraph, the reviewer noted sentences that were not relevant to the essay's main idea. The point of the essay is the needs of the customers (what they seem to want from the bartender, and hence how they relate to the bartender). Observations about how the bartender may feel (paragraph 4) or how Kara feels about waiting on certain customers (paragraph 5) are beside the point and should be eliminated. Nevertheless, Kara couldn't resist keeping the comment about "last call." But she placed the information in parentheses to de-emphasize it somewhat.

The reviewer questioned the point-of-view shift (from third-person "they" to second-person "you") in the final paragraph. It is an important issue: Ordinarily such a shift in point of view throws readers off balance. However, Kara wanted to generalize her observations and draw the audience even further into her essay at the conclusion, so she felt that "you" ("you, the reader") was an appropriate choice.

The reviewer also questioned the final sentence in the essay, wondering if it introduced a new topic. As you may do with your own peer reviewers, Kara chose not to take the reviewer's advice in this case. She explained that the last sentence echoed the title of the essay—that a good bartender's skill extends beyond the hands that mix the drinks to the heart that responds to customers' emotional needs.

6 Writing Paragraphs

When you first draft a paragraph, your major concern is probably getting your ideas on paper before you forget them. In fact, you may even write your paper without being especially conscious of where or why you have placed paragraph indentions. But when we read paragraphs, we have definite expectations about how they should function based on our understanding of paragraphing conventions. For example, as readers we have learned that paragraphs "package" meaning, that paragraph indention signals the introduction of a new topic, a new aspect of a current topic, or perhaps a change of speakers in dialogue.

Readers expect the following from paragraph "packages":

- **unity** that derives from a **controlling idea** around which the paragraph is organized;
- **coherence** (from a Latin word meaning "to hang together") that links the thoughts within a paragraph and relates the paragraph to those that precede and follow it;
- **development** sufficient to explain and illustrate the controlling idea and any other subordinate ideas the paragraph may contain.

Research studies have shown conclusively that unity, coherence, and development are important to readers' ability to perceive and understand meaning. But what do these abstract terms mean? Consider the following paragraph.

Paragraph lacking unity, coherence, and development

The week I spent in Mayville, New York, unfortunately did not give me much time to see things. The weather was not in our favor. Everyone was kind, respectful, and helpful. In order to go to stores, movies, and restaurants, you have to drive thirty to forty-five minutes to Jamestown, New York. Mayville is a small town. It is located between Buffalo, Niagara Falls, Panama Rocks, and a wine vineyard. The small town also has an old-fashioned steamboat (the *Chautauqua Belle*) that was not operating on the day we were going to ride it. It rained most of the time. I bought postcards of the scenic places we had planned to visit. What I liked best about Mayville was its peacefulness.

Unity. A paragraph that lacks unity jumps from idea to idea, topic to topic, with no clear sense of goal or purpose. In the preceding paragraph, what have the weather, the kind and respectful people, the location of Mayville, and the steamboat to do with each other? Because the writer has not provided a controlling idea to unite the sentences and give them focus, we will never know. Methods for achieving paragraph unity are discussed in Section **6a**.

Coherence. Ideas that are connected in the writer's mind may not seem obviously connected to the reader. Consequently, it is important to provide language that makes plain any relationships between sentences and ideas. In the sample paragraph, it is possible that the author intended for readers to see a connection between the bad weather and the fact that the steamboat was not running. However, without connecting language the ideas in the paragraph won't "stick together." Ways of achieving paragraph coherence are discussed in Section **6b**.

Development. A paragraph that lacks development is one that introduces a topic but fails to provide enough information to explain it to readers. If readers are to understand the controlling idea, or even be interested in it, it must be explained and supported sufficiently. Frequently, paragraphs that lack development simply need more details or examples to explain a generalization the writer has stated baldly and assumed readers will understand. The final sentence of the preceding example paragraph illustrates how lack of development can frustrate readers. The idea of the town's peacefulness receives no elaboration or explanation and leaves readers trying to guess what the writer's intentions might have been. A discussion of paragraph development appears in Section **6c**.

In the "Writers Revising" at the end of this chapter, you will find a revised version that improves the unity, coherence, and development of the preceding example paragraph.

6 a Use a controlling idea to achieve paragraph unity.

A unified paragraph has a single controlling idea. The **topic sentence** of a paragraph expresses the focus of the paragraph, just as a thesis statement expresses the focus of an essay. All the sentences in a paragraph should be related to the focus specified by the topic sentence. Those that seem unrelated to the controlling idea spoil the paragraph's unity, as in the example that follows.

Paragraph lacking unity

Upper Marlboro, my hometown, is more urban than rural, which means it is not as peaceful or relaxing as Mayville. Even the woods are different. In the Upper Marlboro woods, there are honeysuckles, battered old trees, dried up leaves and underbrush, and sometimes even trash. Mayville, on the other hand, is far from any urban area, which makes it more peaceful. People don't seem to be in as much of a hurry. They stop on the street for leisurely conversation. The woods are filled with tall, healthy-looking trees, wild ferns, raspberries along the paths, and streams you can swim in.

The controlling idea expressed in the topic sentence of this paragraph leads the reader to expect an explanation contrasting the urban and rural features of the two towns to show why Mayville is more peaceful and relaxing than Upper Marlboro. Consequently, the sentences describing the woods seem out of place and cause the paragraph to break apart.

● **1 Topic sentence: loose control or tight control.** Some paragraphs are meant to deliver information without making a particularly forceful assertion about the information. A paragraph about parent-child bonding might have as its topic sentence "Touching is one of the main ways bonding occurs between a mother and her newborn" and then go on to describe additional types of bonding behavior without the reader feeling that the paragraph has become disunified. This topic sentence has rather loose control over its paragraph.

Other topic sentences present stronger assertions, going beyond statements of fact to make arguable propositions. Such topic sentences exert strong control, defining more sharply what ideas are and are not relevant to the paragraph. The topic sentence "Some of the problems of psychologically disturbed children can be traced to a lack of bonding in infancy" allows for no digressions if the paragraph is to fulfill readers' expectations about unity. This paragraph will show cause-and-effect relationships between parent-child bonding and psychological problems.

Paragraphs perform a variety of functions—from introducing a subject to providing transitions between events in a narrative to summarizing the points of an argument. Thus, either tight control or loose control may be appropriate depending on the purpose and context of the paragraph. Your responsibility is to be sure that your paragraphs fulfill their intended functions and are clearly focused. When you revise your writing, supply a controlling topic sentence and either eliminate unrelated ideas or rewrite sentences so that relationships among ideas are clear.

● **2 Placement of the topic sentence.** Readers' understanding will be quicker and more complete if they first have a general idea of the subject and the direction the writer intends to go with it. Topic sentences provide this information. But you may have observed that many satisfactory paragraphs do not position the topic sentence first. The controlling idea may come last, in the middle, or be implied rather than stated.

Even so, readers need an initial sentence that provides an appropriate frame of reference so they can relate the information that follows to what they already know. This orienting sentence need not be the topic sentence.

The emphatic positions in paragraphs are the same as in sentences: first and last. As readers, we expect to find the key information first. If it is not delivered in the form of a topic sentence, then other orienting words must be supplied. When they are not, we will make our own inferences and build our own meanings—a time-consuming and risky business because we are apt to create meanings quite different from the writer's intention.

The following paragraphs illustrate various placements for topic sentences. Topic sentences appear in italics. When the topic sentence is not positioned first in a paragraph, note how the writer initially orients the reader.

Topic sentence first

The main idea is expressed at the beginning, sometimes as a generalization. The rest of the sentences provide supporting evidence, concrete examples, and explanatory detail.

> *What Indians gave in the exchanges between immigrants and natives is not so much remembered as what was taken from them,* primarily the richest lands—fertile valleys for farming, mountains rifted with minerals, grazing lands for stock, coastal fishing shores, river passages, forests of game. The Indians' intimate knowledge of American ecology rescued many pilgrims and pioneers from hardship, or even death, in a continent the newcomers viewed as "wilderness." Indian cultivations such as beans, maize, squash, hickory, pecan, pumpkin, and sweet potatoes fed the new Americans; Indian skills in gathering native foods saved settlers from their own agricultural failures (the first Thanksgiving of 1621, for example, where Indians and pilgrims ate, among other foods, corn and eel). Indian expertise in hunting secured the bounty of the animal food pack of America—turkey, deer, buffalo, rabbit, salmon, sturgeon, shellfish, among hundreds of other game. Indians contributed over a third of the medicines we now use synthetically, 220 drugs in the National Formulary, according to Virgil Vogel's native pharmacopoeia—astringents, cathartics, childbirth medicines, febrifuges, vermifuges, emetics, poisons, antibiotics, diabetes remedies, and contraceptives, including quinine, cocaine, tobacco, and techniques of birth control.
>
> —Kenneth Lincoln, "Old Like Hills, Like Stars"

Transitional topic sentence

A paragraph's first sentence may combine a transition from the preceding paragraph with the topic statement of the new paragraph. The following example refers to previous information before continuing the explanation of brain development.

> Actually, brain development is even more complicated than this. During pregnancy and early infancy, brain cells branch out with abandon, creating more interconnections than will be needed in adulthood—a condition that many neurologists believe is responsible for the phenomenally rapid learning rates of young children. This explosion of synaptic connections reaches its maximum density by about age 2, after which the brain begins pruning connections that aren't being used. In a very real sense, then, neural pathways that aren't exercised *do* "wither away."
>
> —"The Abandoned Disciplines," magazine advertising supplement

Topic sentence last

Some paragraphs give details or explanations first, leading up to the main point in the final sentence.

Even within our own country, of course, ideas of time and punctuality vary considerably from place to place. Different regions and even cities have their own distinct rhythms and rules. Seemingly simple words like "now," snapped out by an impatient New Yorker, and "later," said by a relaxed Californian, suggest a world of difference. Despite our familiarity with these homegrown differences in tempo, problems with time present a major stumbling block to Americans abroad. Peace Corps volunteers told researchers James Spradley of Macalester College and Mark Phillips of the University of Washington that their greatest difficulties with other people, after language problems, were the general pace of life and the punctuality of others. *Formal "clock time" may be a standard on which the world agrees, but "social time," the heartbeat of society, is something else again.*

— Robert Levine and Ellen Wolff, "Social Time: The Heartbeat of Culture"

Topic sentence first and last

In some paragraphs, the last sentence repeats the idea introduced in the first sentence, frequently restating it with some amplification or a slightly different emphasis in light of the intervening details or discussion.

A *metal garbage can lid has many uses*. In the spring it can be used to catch rainwater in which a small boy can create a world of his own, a world of dead leaves and twigs inhabited by salamanders, small frogs, and worms. In the summer it can be turned on its top, the inside lined with aluminum foil, and used to hold charcoal for a barbecue. In the fall it can be used, with a similar lid, to frighten unsuspecting Halloween "trick-or-treaters." In the winter, if the handle is removed or flattened, the lid can be used by children to speed down snow-packed hills. *A garbage can lid covers garbage most of the time, but with a little imagination, one can uncover new uses for it.*

— Student paragraph

Implied topic sentence

Sometimes a writer may decide not to use an explicitly stated topic sentence. This is frequently the case in narrative and descriptive paragraphs, but it can also be appropriate in other types of writing. Implied topic sentences carry risks, however. Omit a topic sentence only if you are sure that your readers can state the controlling idea if asked to do so. In the following paragraph by Joan Didion, the controlling idea might be stated thus: "Though the sources of one's childhood imaginings are long lost, the record of those imaginings can reveal lifelong habits of mind."

My first notebook was a Big Five tablet, given to me by my mother with the sensible suggestion that I stop whining and learn to amuse myself by writing down my thoughts. She returned the tablet to me a few years ago; the first entry is an account of a woman who believed herself to be freezing to death in the Arctic night, only to find, when day broke, that she had stumbled onto the Sahara Desert, where she would die of the heat before lunch. I have no idea what turn of a five-year-old's mind could have prompted so insistently "ironic" and exotic a story, but it does reveal a certain predilection for the

extreme which has dogged me into adult life; perhaps if I were analytically inclined I would find it a truer story than any I might have told about Donald Johnson's birthday party or the day my cousin Brenda put Kitty Litter in the aquarium.

—Joan Didion, "On Keeping a Notebook"

Exercise 6.1

The following two topic sentences are each accompanied by a set of statements. Some of the statements are relevant to the topic, some are not. Eliminate the irrelevant ones. Organize the others into two separate, unified paragraphs.

1. **Topic sentence:** Good nutrition is about 75 to 85 percent of the bodybuilding or powerlifting regimen.

- A high-protein, high-carbohydrate, low-fat diet is required if you want your body to make muscle gains.
- Powerlifting deals with muscle mass, which leads to strength and very large muscles.
- On a powerlifter's body, some muscles will be much larger and more developed than others because the lifter has exercised them more.
- Bodybuilding deals with the size, shape, and symmetry of muscle.
- It is also good to have a set eating pattern.
- Whether you want to gain weight or lose weight, you should divide your eating pattern into five or six smaller meals rather than rely on two or three big meals.
- The goal is to maintain a flow of nutrients throughout the day.
- You should try to steer clear of deep-fried foods, sugar-loaded foods, and fast food, which is high in fat and salt.
- Also avoid alcoholic drinks.

Topic sentence: Hispanics will replace blacks as the largest U.S. minority group around 2010.

- According to the Census Bureau, the non-Hispanic white portion of the population in the United States will be 67.7 percent by 2010, down from 75.7 percent in 1990.
- By 2050, non-Hispanic whites will account for 52.5 percent of the population.
- In 1990 blacks made up 11.8 percent of the U.S. population.
- Hispanics accounted for 9 percent of the population in 1990.
- By 2010, Hispanics are projected to be at 13.5 percent.
- The number of blacks in the U.S. population by 2010 is projected to be 12.6 percent.
- By 2050, Hispanics will outnumber blacks—22.5 percent (Hispanic) to 14.4 percent (blacks).
- The ability to communicate effectively with people from many cultural backgrounds will be vital in the twenty-first century.

Exercise 6.2

What is the topic sentence, expressed or implied, in each of the following paragraphs?

1 If the business of an immigrant is to learn to function in a new society, the business of [the Kanjobal Indians from Guatemala] is to worry. When you talk to them, they are very stoic. Like rural people I knew in Ireland, they never express their best hopes or their worst fears. When we look at an American child, we say, "What a beautiful little girl." They would never say a thing like that. They wouldn't want to burden a kid with their hopes. And they never express their fear. It's a trait of people whose whole lives are at the mercy of nature, which is very fickle and unpredictable.

—Father Frank O'Loughlin, in *New Americans: An Oral History*

2 The social sciences have come to reject biologistic notions of race in favor of an approach which regards race as a *social* concept. Beginning in the eighteenth century, this trend has been slow and uneven, but its direction clear. In the nineteenth century Max Weber discounted biological explanations for racial conflict and instead highlighted the social and political factors which engendered such conflict. The work of pioneering cultural anthropologist Franz Boas was crucial in refuting the scientific racism of the early twentieth century by rejecting the connection between race and culture, and the assumption of a continuum of "higher" and "lower" cultural groups. Within the contemporary social science literature, race is assumed to be a variable which is shaped by broader social forces.

—Michael Omi and Harold Winant, "Racial Formations"

3 The little witch Halloween costume may look cute to you, but don't be surprised if your two-year-old throws a tearful fit rather than wear it. "The younger the child, the thinner the membrane between fascination and fear and the thinner the boundary between fantasy and reality," says Kyle Pruett, clinical professor of psychiatry at the Yale Child Study Center. Toddlers may be afraid that they could become the thing they are pretending to be. "Two-year-olds aren't entirely sure who they are and who other people are," explains child psychologist Joan Kinlan. Very young children may refuse to wear any costume at all, Kinlan says, "even a benign pumpkin or ice cream cone, that is not like their regular clothes"; their feelings are saying "'That's not me.'"

—Melinda Kramer, "If That Were My Child ..."

4 Yet here sits not a formal man, some dull dealer in ideas. His bony fingers are holding a pencil-thin British cigar. A watch chain glints against his vest, a vest belonging to a sharp three-piece suit, a suit of the sort that tightly wraps his lean body whenever you see him. Chunky ornaments hold together his wide white shirt cuffs. His ample Afro belongs in a memory. His beard is Malcolm's. It all seems part of a proudly cultivated personal style: Cornel West, the Sporty Intellectual.

—David Mills, "The West Alternative"

5   An atmosphere that is a strange mixture of bleakness, tranquility, and expectancy pervades the downstairs hall of the old gym early in the morning. As I walk from the chilly dawn outdoors into the basement of the old gym, I feel the dry heat on my face; although I assume that I am alone, I am surrounded by the impersonal noises of an antiquated steam-heating system. All the doors, which stand like sentries along the walls of the hallway, are locked, so that the deserted nature of that place and that hour are apparent; pipes hang from above, making the ceiling resemble the ugly, rarely viewed underside of a bizarre animal. I feel peaceful, however, in this lonely place, because of the silence. I know, moreover, that the desert-like heat is a sign that preparation has been made for my arrival and a signal that the day of work is about to begin.

—Student paragraph

In Your Own Words

Think about your own habits as a writer. Is it better for you to begin with a topic sentence and then use it as a springboard to help generate details, or is more effective to start with details and have a topic sentence grow out of them? Look at several drafts of your earlier paragraphs and essays and write a paragraph explaining which method works better for you and why.

6 b Organize ideas to achieve paragraph coherence.

A coherent paragraph moves logically from thought to thought, knitting the thoughts together in an orderly way. The sentences should flow into one another so that their relation to one another and to the paragraph's main point is clear. Building a paragraph according to an organizational structure that is both familiar to your readers and appropriate to the development of the paragraph's controlling idea will help achieve this coherence.

The following are familiar patterns that can be used to organize not only paragraphs but essays or parts of essays as well.

● **1 Time.** Narrative paragraphs naturally arrange themselves in **chronological order,** the order in which events occur. Paragraphs organized chronologically are frequently controlled loosely by a topic sentence; or they may have no topic sentence at all, instead using natural breaks in the action or time sequence to guide the reader. In the following example, italics indicate some of the time cues used to achieve coherence in the paragraph.

During dinner, I found that I was coaching myself through the proposal, reciting in my head what I was going to say when I asked her to be my wife. Heather finished her dinner very quickly, which was rare for her. Were things happening faster or had I taken more time to eat than usual? I began to feel rushed, adding to the tension I was already experiencing. I started fidgeting with everything in reach, from the salt and pepper shakers to the little sugar packets. *Before I knew it,* the waitress had brought us the two glasses of wine I had secretly ordered beforehand for the presentation of the engagement ring.

Why did everything seem to happen so quickly? I just needed a little more time to get my nerve up to "pop the question" (I was beginning to understand the truth behind that expression). *Suddenly* I realized Heather had finished her wine. There went the toast! *In the meantime*, the waitress dropped off the check. How could I have let that happen? My fingers started feeling sticky before I figured out that I had perspired through the sugar packet I was holding. *By now* I was thinking I should do this at another time. "No!" I thought, "I need to finish what I've started. Now! Okay, I'll pretend that I'm reaching for money, but instead I'll slip the ring to her while asking her to marry me."

—Chris Coleman (student), "The Art of Proposing"

● **2 Space.** Many descriptive paragraphs arrange themselves easily according to some **spatial order,** from east to west, top to bottom, far to near, center to edges, and the like. Spatial cues include such words as *over, above, below, on each side, in front, behind, next to,* and so forth. The words that provide spatial coherence in the following paragraph have been italicized.

When *I walked through the doors into the lobby,* I saw disfigured elderly people slumped over in wheelchairs. Some were shuffling across the floor not going anywhere particular. Others were propped in front of the 32-inch color television watching *Good Morning America. I crossed the lobby into the dimly lit hallway. Throughout the hallway* was an offensive stench of stale urine and bowel elimination. *As I passed each resident's room,* I peeked in. *In each room* were two to four hospital beds with bright yellow spreads, bedside stands with telephones and water cups *on the top,* a couple of straight-back chairs, and televisions. Some of the rooms were empty, others occupied. Some of the residents lay in bed with their heads slightly elevated, gazing at the off-white walls *in front of them.* Some were chanting, murmuring, and singing to themselves as if they were in their own worlds.

—Letitia Anderson (student), "A Look Inside"

● **3 General to particular or particular to general.** Many paragraphs begin with a topic sentence that makes a general statement, followed by sentences supporting the generalization with details, examples, and evidence. Also known as **deductive organization** (from a Latin word meaning "lead away from"), this order presents the main idea first and follows it with reasons. The reverse may also be effective. Particular-to-general order, **inductive organization** (from a Latin word meaning "lead into"), presents details, explanations, or reasons first and concludes with a general statement.

The following paragraph begins with a general statement—that teenage rejection in love is tormenting—followed by the specific behavior that exemplifies the generalization.

Rejection-in-love is one of the most tormenting aspects of teenage life you will ever be forced to witness. Because it's like this: The first time a teenage boy ever gets serious about a girl, he realizes that she is a very highly evolved

creature. That unlike his two best friends, Chuck and Ernie, she is actually able to carry on a conversation without bugging her eyes, belching, swearing, or kicking parking meters. So he tells this girl some *very important junk* about his innermost psyche, and if it works, great. If it doesn't well, it doesn't become the end of the world; but the end of the world will certainly be visible from where he's sitting.

—Stephanie Brush, "Understanding Teenage Boys"

The following paragraph follows an inductive pattern, moving from particular items of evidence to a general statement about fashion trends.

"Sartorial slovenliness—worn trousers, crumpled corduroy, dirty shirts, torn sweaters, sagging socks, unshined shoes—became a part of street-level existentialism" after World War II, Farid Chenoune writes in his new book, *A History of Men's Fashion.* French fashion designer Pierre Cardin "thought that this dilapidated wardrobe was simply a by-product of war, whereas Roger Vadim felt it represented a refusal to enter normal society, and Anne-Marie Cazalis saw it as a type of poor-man's snobbery." It will come as both a surprise and a disappointment (to 14-year-olds, at least) that grunge is hardly new.

—Cathy Horyn, "Fashion Notes"

● **4 Climax.** Some paragraphs can be made coherent by arranging details or examples in order of increasing importance. Arranging evidence from least important to most important is a strategy used routinely in arguments and debates. Because climactic order, like a well-constructed play, achieves its big moment at the end, it also works well when you want to create drama or suspense.

The molecule was not alive, at least not in any conventional sense. Yet its behavior was astonishingly lifelike. When it appeared last April at the Scripps Research Institute in La Jolla, California, scientists thought it had spoiled their experiment. But this snippet of synthetic RNA—one of the master molecules in the nuclei of all cells—proved unusually talented. Within an hour of its formation, it had commandeered the organic material in a thimble-size test tube and started to make copies of itself. Then the copies made copies. Before long, the copies began to evolve, developing the ability to perform new and unexpected chemical tricks. Surprised and excited, the scientists who witnessed the event found themselves wondering, Is *this* how life got started?

—J. Madeleine Nash, "How Did Life Begin?"

● **5 Comparison and contrast.** Writing that points out similarities compares; writing that notes differences contrasts. Frequently, paragraphs of comparison and contrast coexist in the same paper. When you remember that the principal way our minds process new information is to attach it to old information, it makes sense that writers naturally rely a good deal on comparison and contrast to communicate their ideas. We learn about the unknown by viewing it in terms of what we already know: How is it the same as (compared to) or different from (contrasted with) our previous experience? The following paragraph compares American and Asian adults (both are inept at interacting with people with disabilities) as well as contrasting them (adult Americans and Asians think about and react to disabled people in different ways, which are, in turn, different from children's reactions).

> Americans, for the most part, do not believe as Asians do that physically handicapped persons are morally flawed. But they are equally inept at interacting with those of us who are not able-bodied. Cultural differences in the perception and treatment of handicapped people are most clearly expressed by adults. Children, regardless of where they are, tend to be openly curious about people who do not look "normal." Adults in Asia have no hesitation in asking visibly handicapped people what is wrong with them, often expressing their sympathy with looks of pity, whereas adults in the United States try desperately to be polite by pretending not to notice.
>
> —Sucheng Chan, "You're Short, Besides!"

Extended comparisons usually use one of two organizational patterns: either point-by-point or parallel order. In point-by-point organization, the things being compared are discussed one point at a time: first point of *A* followed by first point of *B* and so on. Parallel order requires that all points of *A* be discussed, followed by all points of *B*, with the points of each in the same order.

Point-by-Point Organization		Parallel Order Organization
A	*B*	*A*
first point	first point	first point
second point	second point	second point
third point	third point	third point
etc.	etc.	etc.
		B
		first point
		second point
		third point
		etc.

The following paragraph is arranged in point-by-point order, first discussing German preferences and then American preferences.

> The open-door policy of American business and the closed-door patterns of German business culture cause clashes in the branches and subsidiaries of American firms in Germany. The point seems to be quite simple, yet failure to grasp it has caused considerable friction and misunderstanding between American and German managers overseas. I was once called in to advise a firm that has operations all over the world. One of the first questions asked was, "How do you get the Germans to keep their doors open?" In this compa-

ny the open doors were making the Germans feel exposed and gave the whole operation an unusually relaxed and unbusinesslike air. Closed doors, on the other hand, gave the Americans the feeling that there was a conspiratorial air about the place and that they were being left out. The point is that whether the door is open or shut, it is not going to mean the same thing in the two countries.

—Edward T. Hall, "Private Space"

● **6 Analogy.** A special kind of comparison, analogy draws a parallel between two things that have some resemblance, using that resemblance as a basis for implying further similarity. The comparison in an analogy is between things of different classes, things that are not normally categorized together. The point is to compare the unfamiliar with the familiar or point up striking or unusual resemblances between familiar things. Although they may be inexact in many respects, parallels of this sort enable readers to visualize ideas or relationships and therefore to understand them better— for instance, the following illustration of the impact of the personal computer on information systems management.

> We technical people pride ourselves on being scientific and coolly rational about our profession. But it seems to me that, in the field of computers, we're unconsciously reenacting a religious drama: the Protestant reformation. In this scientific drama, the computer is God and many people want this God to take care of them. Until the late 1970's there was a standard way to get taken care of by the computer. The user would implore his local programmer (priest) to intercede for him with the machine to get his accounting, bookkeeping, or other such problems solved on the computer. If a litany of prayers (programming) in a dead language (ALGOL, COBOL, Fortran, etc.) were recited flawlessly, and if the user obeyed the 1010 commandments of the machine when he entered data...and if the user tithed to the programmer and the machine for the rest of his life...then the machine might take care of him. In this world IBM was seen as the Roman Catholic church...benevolently setting the standards and working through data processing managers (local bishops) to see that the faithful were well taken care of.... In the late 70s a reformist (Steve Jobs) arose and staked a thesis on the pink slip of his Volkswagen that every man should talk directly to his own computer.
>
> —Ed Lee, "The Computer as God"

Analogies occur in all types of writing, including argumentation. In an argument by analogy, the proof is only as strong as the number of points of similarity between the two things being compared. In fact, a logical fallacy (type of invalid reasoning) called false analogy occurs when someone tries to win an argument by declaring two things analogous (similar) when in fact they have crucial points of difference. The following analogy is part of an argument that violence, particularly violence involving guns, is not just a law-and-order issue between police and criminals but is really a public health issue that threatens society as a whole.

For the medical community, firearms are increasingly analogous to the deadly microbes that carry infectious diseases. A growing medical specialty tracks trauma the way its predecessors tracked smallpox or tuberculosis, searching for preventive strategies that can contain the epidemics and prevent further outbreaks.

—Don Colburn and Abigail Trafford, "Guns at Home"

● **7 Analysis and classification.** Analysis takes things apart. Classification groups things together on the basis of their differences or similarities. You break your days into morning, noon, and night; in the supermarket you look for pepper among the spices and chicken in the meat department because you know that's the way they are classified. Similarly, in both individual paragraphs and entire essays, analysis and classification can serve as guides to organization. The first of the following paragraphs analyzes a kiss according the variety of purposes it may serve. The second paragraph groups the grasslands of the American Great Plains into classes.

Among cultures of the West, the number of nonsexual uses of the kiss is staggering. The simple kiss has served any or all of several purposes: greeting and farewell, affection, religious or ceremonial symbolism, deference to a person of higher status. (People also kiss icons, dice, and other objects, of course, in prayer, for luck, or as part of a ritual.) Kisses make the hurt go away, bless sacred vestments, seal a bargain. In story and legend a kiss has started wars and ended them, and awakened Sleeping Beauty and put Brunhilde to sleep.

—Leonore Tiefer, "The Kiss"

Three distinct belts of prairie developed. In the immediate rain shadow of the Rockies lies the shortgrass prairie, scraped by wind and dominated by the most drought tolerant of prairie grasses, buffalo grass and blue grama; they rise little more than six to twelve inches high. The easternmost third of the Great Plains, watered by an average of 30 inches of rain annually, yields tallgrass prairie characterized by Indian grass, switchgrass, and above all, big bluestem; in a good year they tower six to twelve feet high, growing half an inch or more a day. Between is the mixed-grass prairie, with elements of both the shortgrass and tallgrass belts, combined with midsize grasses such as little bluestem, needlegrass, side oats grama, and wheatgrass.

Together they once formed the greatest grasslands on earth....

—Douglas H. Chadwick, "The American Prairie: Roots of the Sky"

Classifying a person or group without systematic and valid analysis is called **stereotyping** and results in prejudice directed toward members of ethnic, political, sexual, racial, or religious groups. An argument that offers stereotypes for evidence is invalid because such sweeping generalizations are never true. Before you put people or things into categories, be sure that you have fully and fairly examined the components that make up those people or things and have drawn valid conclusions about them.

● **8 Definition.** When you wish to explain an abstract concept or something

unfamiliar to your readers, definition may be an appropriate paragraph structure. If definition provides the structure for most of the paper, you are writing **extended definition.** Paragraphs of definition may use details and examples, comparison and contrast, and restatement in familiar terms.

Definition is a form of comparison, beginning with the thing to be defined (the unfamiliar or unknown term) and describing it in terms of things with which the reader is familiar. In addition, definition uses classification, first placing the thing to be defined within a broad category (*genus*) and then within narrower and narrower categories (*differentiation*) which establish its differences from other items in the category.

Term	Genus	Differentiation
A crumpet is	a light, soft bread similar to a muffin	baked on a griddle, often toasted and served with tea.

The following definition first states the two basic elements of the fairy story—"a human hero and a happy ending." The author develops the paragraph by describing the kind of hero and the kind of story pattern that are the special marks of the fairy tale. Italics show the movement of the paragraph, following the progress of the hero from beginning to end of the tale.

Definition

A *fairy story*, as distinct from a merry tale, or an animal story, *is a serious tale with a human hero and a happy ending. The progression of its hero is the reverse of the tragic hero's: at the beginning* he is either socially obscure or despised as being stupid or untalented, lacking in the heroic virtues, *but at the end*, he has surprised everyone by demonstrating his heroism and winning fame, riches, and love. *Though ultimately he succeeds, he does not do so without a struggle* in which his success is in doubt, for opposed to him are not only natural difficulties like glass mountains, or barriers of flame, but also hostile wicked powers, stepmothers, jealous brothers, and witches. *In many cases indeed, he would fail were he not* assisted by friendly powers who give him instructions or perform tasks for him which he cannot do himself; that is, in addition to his own powers, he needs luck, but this luck is not fortuitous but dependent upon his character and his actions. *The tale ends with the establishment of justice;* not only are the good rewarded but also the evil are punished.
—W. H. Auden, Introduction to *Tales of Grimm and Andersen*

Chapter 7, "Critical Thinking and Argument," contains a full discussion of various types of definition.

● **9 Cause and effect.** When your writing task involves trying to determine why something has occurred or analyzing the results of some action, you examine causes and effects. If your English instructor asks you to write a paper on why you selected the college you attend, you will be expected to develop the paper using an effect-to-cause relationship. The decision is the effect or result, an already accomplished action; the reasons for your decision are the causes.

Cause-and-effect organization naturally falls into the pattern of (1) stating causes and describing or arguing what their consequences will be, or (2) identifying a problem or consequence and then explaining the causes. Cause-and-effect reasoning typically involves complex relationships, chains of multiple reasons and results. Pollution and poverty exist. What causes them? What are their effects? The following paragraph analyzes the complex reasons that prompt women to lose weight and argues that the result is political as well as personal.

> When all other personal motives for losing weight are stripped away—the desire to be popular, to be loved, to be successful, to be acceptable, to be in control, to be admired, to admire one's self—what unites the women who seek to reduce their weight is the fact that they look for an answer to their life's problems in the control of their bodies and appetites. A woman who walks through the doors of a weight-watching organization and enters the women's reduction movement has allowed her culture to persuade her that significant relief from her personal and cultural dilemma is to be found in the reduction of her body. Thus, her decision, although she may not be aware of it, enters the domain of the body politic and becomes symbolically a political act.
>
> —Kim Chernin, "The Tyranny of Slenderness"

In Your Own Words

Assume you are writing an essay on the subject "out of sight, out of mind." Write a paragraph with the topic sentence first. Then revise the paragraph, making the necessary changes so that the topic sentence comes last. Which organizational structure did your first paragraph follow? Which organizational structure resulted from placing the topic sentence last?

Exercise 6.3

Name appropriate organizational structures for paragraphs based on the following topic sentences. Explain your choices. Then write coherent paragraphs on three of the topic sentences. Try writing at least one of the paragraphs with the topic sentence last. Did your paragraphs develop according to your original notion?

1 When you are waiting for someone who is late, time bears no relation to reality.
2 Slang is a puzzle to the uninitiated.
3 A detective looking around my room would find important clues to my personality.
4 Lack of exercise can result in psychological as well as physical problems.
5 Knowing the Latin or Greek root of a word may help you figure out the word's meaning.
6 A cat is more suited to apartment living than a dog is.

7 The way teenagers dress sends a messages about which group they want to be identified with.

8 Some people refuse to learn that their actions have consequences.

9 Home, after the children have gone, is like an empty nest.

10 Painting and photography have a lot in common.

6 c Check the arrangement of major points and supporting points.

In addition to the organizational superstructures that shape ideas into coherent paragraphs, hierarchical structures can be employed within paragraphs to achieve unity as well as flow. If the topic sentence or controlling idea appears at the top of the hierarchy (level 1) in the first sentence, then all the other sentences in the paragraph should relate to it as parallel or subordinate ideas. For example,

1. A good vacation means different things to different people.
    2. For some, the best vacation is the one that takes them away from home.
        3. They crave new sights, new sensations.
            4. A tip to the beach or the mountains refreshes the city dweller,
            4. while a trip to the city excites the country dweller.
    2. For others, a chance to stay at home is the best vacation.
        3. These folks want the ease and restfulness of familiar surroundings.
            4. They like lying around the house in old clothes.
            4. They enjoy puttering in the garden and talking to the neighbors.
        3. For them, the "new sight" or "new sensation" of not having to face the world or go to work in the morning is vacation enough.

You'll notice that the indentation technique used to examine the preceding paragraph (known as the Christensen method, named for Francis Christensen, author of *Notes Toward a New Rhetoric*) looks very much like an outline. Like an outline, it reveals the relationships between main ideas and subordinate ideas. Thus, it reveals their interconnecting logic. The paragraph is well knit, unified, and coherent, as can be seen from its structure of parallel and subordinate ideas. Each generality is supported by at least one level of specificity. You might want to check the relationships between elements in your own paragraphs by comparing sentence levels in this way.

Another option for visualizing paragraph structures is to construct an idea tree (see Section **3e**). By using a tree diagram to chart the organization of your paragraph, you will be able to see not only its hierarchical arrangement but also the spatial relationship among ideas. For some people, this spatial representation makes it easier to see whether ideas are satisfactorily arranged and connected. Following is a tree diagram of the paragraph previously outlined using the indentation method.

"good" vacation

best to go away from home   best to stay home

crave new sights   crave ease &   crave "newness"
& sensations   restfulness   of not having
                          of familiar   to go to work

beach or   city trip   lying around   puttering in
mountains   for country   house in old   garden;
for city   dweller   clothes   talking to
dweller   neighbors

Exercise 6.4

Outline the following paragraphs using the Christensen indentation method or the tree diagram method illustrated in Section **6c**. How do the levels of generality and specificity and the relationships among major ideas and subordinate ideas contribute to each paragraph's coherence? Do they help develop the paragraph's topic? Do you see any similarities in the structure of the two paragraphs that increase the coherence of the two taken together?

> There was a time when the deathbed was a kind of proscenium, from which the personage could issue one last dramatic utterance, full of the compacted significance of his life. Last words were to sound as if all of the individual's earthly time had been sharpened to that point: he could now etch the grand summation. "More light" the great Goethe of the Enlightenment is said to have cried as he expired. There is some opinion, however, that what he actually said was "Little wife, give me your little paw."
>
> In any case, the genre of great last words died quite a few years ago. There are those who think the last genuinely memorable last words were spoken in 1900, when, according to one version, the dying Oscar Wilde said, "Either that wallpaper goes, or I do."
>
> —Lance Morrow, "A Dying Art: The Classy Exit Line"

In Your Own Words

Using the Christensen method, outline one of the paragraphs you wrote for Exercise 6.3. Then use a tree diagram to outline another of the paragraphs you wrote. Revise the paragraphs, incorporating changes the outlines suggest for improving coherence.

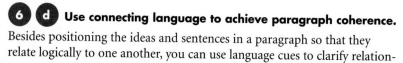

6 **d** Use connecting language to achieve paragraph coherence.

Besides positioning the ideas and sentences in a paragraph so that they relate logically to one another, you can use language cues to clarify relation-

ships for readers. The most obvious ones are repeated key words and phrases, parallel grammatical structures, and transitional markers. Less obvious but equally helpful is using old information to introduce new information.

● **1 Repeated key words and phrases.** Many well-constructed paragraphs rely on the repetition of key words and phrases, often with slight modification, to emphasize major ideas and carry the thought from sentence to sentence. Pronouns referring to clearly established antecedents in the previous sentence function in the same way. In the following paragraph the words and phrases that are repeated to provide clear links from sentence to sentence and produce a closely integrated whole are in italics.

> *Nostalgia* is a recurrent theme in Chinese poetry. An American reader of translated Chinese poems may well be taken aback—even put off—by the frequency, as well as the *sentimentality* of the lament for *home*. To understand the strength of this *sentiment*, we need to know that the Chinese desire for *stability* and *rootedness* in *place* is prompted by the constant threat of war, exile, and the natural disasters of flood and drought. Forcible *removal* makes the Chinese keenly aware of their loss. By contrast, the Americans *move*, for the most part, voluntarily. Their *nostalgia* for *home* town is really longing for childhood to which they cannot return: in the meantime the *future* beckons and the *future* is "out there," in open *space*. *When we criticise American rootlessness* we tend to *forget* that it is a result of ideals we admire, namely, social mobility and optimism about the *future*. *When we admire Chinese rootedness*, we *forget* that the word "*place*" means both location in *space* and position in society: to be tied to *place* is also to be bound to one's station in life, with little *hope* of betterment. *Space* symbolizes *hope*; *place*, achievement and *stability*.
>
> —Yi-Fu-Tan, "American Space, Chinese Place"

● **2 Parallel grammatical structure.** Using parallel grammatical structure in successive sentences is one of the most important ways of connecting them. Just as parallel grammatical form in coordinate parts of a single sentence emphasizes the coordinate relationship of the ideas, so parallel structure from sentence to sentence within a paragraph emphasizes the relationship of these sentences to the single idea of the paragraph (see also Section **9a**). The author of the following paragraph develops three streams of parallelism: one for subjects, a second for predicates, and a third for introductory subordinate clauses. These are indicated by underlining, italics, and bold face type, respectively.

> For a guy, learning to cook can pay rich dividends. <u>A teenage boy who can whip up lasagna and Caesar salad</u> *will never be at a loss for friends, although he may take a little ribbing at first.* <u>A teenage boy who can roast a chicken, sauté fresh vegetables, and concoct a chocolate mousse</u> *will be the apple of his mother's eye, though his father may joke a bit about "my son 'Cookie.'"* **If he is a bachelor,** <u>the twenty-five-year-old who can make veal scalloppine or leg of</u>

lamb *will be the toast of his social circle*. <u>His paté</u> *will be his entrée to* the most stimulating of cliques, and <u>his perfect technique with sauces</u> *will win him invitations from* beautiful, intelligent women who want to learn his ways. **If he should marry,** <u>the twenty-five-year-old husband who can produce fresh blueberry muffins for breakfast, fresh clam chowder for lunch, and fresh chicken fricasee for dinner</u> *will be the mate of a lifetime*. <u>His nouvelle cuisine</u> *will keep* his wife coming back for more, and <u>his pastries</u> *will seduce* her happily from her diets. And, of course, a guy who cooks never has to do the dishes!

● **3 Transitional markers.** A transitional marker is a word or a phrase placed at or near the beginning of a sentence to indicate its relation to the preceding sentence. The coordinating conjunctions *and, but, or, nor, so,* and *yet* are often used this way, particularly in informal writing, for they provide easy bridges from one sentence to another. But English provides a wide variety of transitional markers, as suggested in the following lists. Good modern writing uses the more formal markers sparingly. Be wary of cluttering your writing with unnecessary *however*'s, *moreover*'s, and *consequently*'s. But you should be equally careful to know them and to use them when they create clarity.

Here is a list of many of the common transitional words and phrases:

TO INDICATE ADDITION
again, also, and, and then, besides, equally important, finally, first, further, furthermore, in addition, last, likewise, moreover, next, second, third, too

TO INDICATE CAUSE AND EFFECT
accordingly, as a result, consequently, hence, in short, otherwise, then, therefore, thus, truly

TO INDICATE COMPARISON
in a like manner, likewise, similarly

TO INDICATE CONCESSION
after all, although this may be true, at the same time, even though, I admit, naturally, of course

TO INDICATE CONTRAST
after all, although true, and yet, at the same time, but, for all that, however, in contrast, in spite of, nevertheless, notwithstanding, on the contrary, on the other hand, still, yet

TO INDICATE SPECIAL FEATURES OR EXAMPLES
for example, for instance, incidentally, indeed, in fact, in other words, in particular, specifically, that is, to illustrate

TO INDICATE SUMMARY
in brief, in conclusion, in short, on the whole, to conclude, to summarize, to sum up

TO INDICATE TIME RELATIONSHIPS

after a short time, afterward, as long as, as soon as, at last, at length, at that time, at the same time, before, earlier, immediately, in the meantime, lately, later, meanwhile, of late, presently, shortly, since, soon, temporarily, thereafter, thereupon, until, when, while

Transitional words and phrases are italicized in the following:

> *As I have remarked,* the pilots' association was now the compactest monopoly in the world, perhaps, and seemed simply indestructible. *And yet* the days of its glory were numbered. *First,* the new railroad stretching up through Mississippi, Tennessee, and Kentucky, to Northern railway-centers, began to divert the passenger travel from the steamboats; *next* the war came and almost entirely annihilated the steamboating industry during several years, leaving most of the pilots idle and the cost of living advancing all the time; *then* the treasurer of the St. Louis association put his hand into the till and walked off with every dollar of the ample fund; *and finally,* the railroads intruding everywhere, there was little for steamers to do, when the war was over, but carry freights; *so straightway* some genius from the Atlantic coast introduced the plan of towing a dozen steamer cargoes down to New Orleans at the tail of a vulgar little tugboat; and behold, in the twinkling of an eye, *as it were,* the association and the noble science of piloting were things of the dead and pathetic past!
>
> —Mark Twain, *Life on the Mississippi*

● **4 Old information introducing new information.** Like repeated key words or parallel grammatical structures, this technique builds on readers' expectations by using repetition. People appreciate receiving new information by way of known information, so sentences that begin with the known (or previously mentioned) and then tie it to the unknown (newly mentioned) meet readers' expectations and replicate a familiar mental process. The following paragraph indicates this process with italic type for old information and boldface type for new information.

> What's happening when you are hooked up to Dow Jones News/Retrieval, **sending requests to the computer and in turn receiving financial and other information?** No matter what kind of computer and modem (or terminal) you're using, no matter which communications service you've used to dial in to the…system, what's happening is fundamentally identical in all cases. *Musical tones are traveling over the telephone lines;* and just as *"scary" music on a movie soundtrack conveys certain information to the viewer (consider, for example, the "shark's theme" in the movie* Jaws), so, too, **the data transmitted over the telephone line is contained in the "music."**
>
> —Howard A. Karten, "Making the Most of Dow Jones News/Retrieval: Technical Considerations"

To explain how data are sent and received by computers over phone lines, the author here compares music, and specifically movie music that the listener recognizes as notes for danger or suspense, with electronic tones that the computer recognizes as bits of data. The analogy relates the unknown to the known.

Thinking carefully about readers' needs is important when you build new information on old information. Use this piggyback technique of paragraph development only where readers require this assistance to understand meaning, not where it merely slows comprehension and makes the reader impatient.

Exercise 6.5

Make a coherent paragraph of the following statements. First, use the Christensen method or a tree diagram (Section **6c**) to help determine an appropriate order for the sentences. Then link them smoothly with connecting language to achieve coherence.

(1) This attitude shows a naive faith in the competency of secretaries. (2) Practicing engineers and scientists say they spend half their time writing letters and reports. (3) Many students foolishly object to taking courses in writing. (4) College students going into business think their secretaries will do their writing for them. (5) Students going into technical or scientific fields may think that writing is something they will seldom have to do. (6) Young businesspeople seldom have private secretaries. (7) Their notion that only poets, novelists, and newspaper reporters have to know how to write is unrealistic. (8) Other things being equal, people in any field who can express themselves effectively are sure to succeed more rapidly than those whose command of the language is poor.

Exercise 6.6

Review the paragraphs you wrote for Exercise 6.3 and revised for the previous "In Your Own Words" exercise, adding any necessary connecting language to improve coherence.

In Your Own Words

Write a paragraph about fast-food and nutrition and rely on repetition of key words and phrases to achieve coherence. Then revise the paragraph using transitional markers, parallel structure, or new information from old information to make the paragraph cohesive.

6 e Develop paragraphs by supplying details readers need.

Readers want details—they *need* details. Consider, for example, the following paragraph from a letter written by an Alaskan to a friend in the Midwest whom he had not seen in several years.

During the same summer you and Nancy were here, in August Faye and I were severely mauled by a grizzly bear on the Yukon River about 22 miles

below Dawson. We spent three weeks in the Whitehorse hospital, and when we got home Faye was in and out of hospitals in Fairbanks and Anchorage all the rest of the winter and spring. It was kind of rough going there for awhile, but we're back in shape and back on the river again this winter.

You can imagine the reader's reaction. Details, man, details! The problem here is a misalignment of goals. The writer's goal was to reassure his friend that he and his wife are now all right by deemphasizing the mauling incident. Although this goal is also important to his friend, the friend's goal is to learn the details of the incident. The writer has focused on effects; the reader wants to know about causes.

Compare the following paragraphs built on the same topic sentence:

It is not always true that a good picture is worth a thousand words. Often writing is much clearer than a picture. It is sometimes difficult to figure out what a picture means, but a careful writer can almost always explain it.

It is not always true that a picture is worth a thousand words. Sometimes, in fact, pictures are pretty useless things. Far from being worth more than words, they can be downright frustrating. If you buy a new typewriter, would you rather have a glossy picture of it, or a 1,000-word booklet explaining how it works? If your carburetor is clogged, do you need a picture of the carburetor, or an explanation of how to unclog it? If you can't swim and you fall in the river and start gulping water, will you be better off to hold up a picture of yourself drowning, or start screaming "Help!"?

The first paragraph has given us no details that explain why it is not true that pictures are worth more than words, or any reasons for believing the topic sentence. The second sentence merely restates the topic sentence, and the final sentence does very little more.

In contrast, the second paragraph has given us three concrete examples of how words may in fact be worth more than pictures. We may object that pictures of both the typewriter and the clogged carburetor would be helpful along with the words. But we understand what the writer means, and we've been kept interested.

Exercise 6.7

Choose two of the following topic sentences and develop each into a meaningful paragraph by supporting it with details, examples, evidence, and reasons.

1 No news is good news.
2 High ACT scores do not necessarily mean a student will do well in college.
3 It is a mistake to try to work forty hours a week and go to school, too.
4 This season should show everyone we need a new coach.
5 A good man is hard to find.
6 A first impression is not always a reliable basis for judgment.

7 Good news seldom makes the headlines.
8 Keeping a detailed budget is more trouble than it's worth.
9 People tend to fear the new or the unfamiliar.
10 Fashions in clothes (books, slang, hairstyles, music, etc.) change from one year to the next.

In Your Own Words

Write a paragraph explaining how you wrote one of the paragraphs in Exercise 6.7. What made you choose the topic you did? Did you begin with a particular detail and then try to think of other details like it? Did you use a mind-map or an idea tree? Did you outline the paragraph? How did you decide what kinds of transitional devices to use to make the paragraph coherent?

  Think about paragraph length.

A paragraph can *look* long enough and still not be developed adequately. Conversely, a paragraph can be too long for a reader to digest easily, even though it discusses a single topic. No magic number of sentences will predictably give you just the right paragraph length for every writing task. However, the following guidelines are helpful.

● **1 Reader expectations.** From experience, readers expect that paragraphs in novels or history books will be longer than paragraphs in newspaper articles or business letters. Readers' expectations also grow from their experience with content: A philosophical argument, for example, is likely to require longer paragraphs to accommodate extended explanations of complex ideas; an instruction manual, on the other hand, will use short paragraphs to mark off each step in a process.

● **2 Visual appeal.** The narrowness of a newspaper column makes lengthy paragraphs difficult to read. The undifferentiated letters and wide type blocks of a typescript need the white space of frequent paragraphing to provide a visual and a mental resting place for the reader. In the case of an instruction manual, the reader knows by simply observing the visual paragraph cues where the steps in the procedure are located.

Remember that where you mark a paragraph has a definite effect on meaning. Because readers expect the first sentence in a paragraph to be an orienting sentence, their specific interpretation of the paragraph will be shaped by that sentence, whatever it is. Thus you should not think of indenting to signal the start of a paragraph as an arbitrary act. Paragraphing defines a unit of coherent thought for your reader.

● **3 Dividing paragraphs that are too long.** A useful strategy is to think about paragraphs not only in terms of topics but also in terms of *aspects* of topics. If your development of a topic needs to be fairly lengthy to

provide adequate support, divide it into manageable chunks—aspects or subtopics that will be easier for the reader to handle.

For example, Section **6e**'s grizzly bear paragraph would have been much more satisfying if divided in two: the first paragraph developing the details of the mauling, the second paragraph discussing the hospitalization and recuperation and ending with the reassurance that the couple was all right.

It is especially important to apply the techniques for achieving coherence when you divide a paragraph. The reader needs connecting language such as that described in Section **6d** to be able to see relationships between as well as within paragraphs.

● **4 Revising paragraphs that are too short.** Short, insufficiently developed paragraphs usually show a lack of attention to detail and an imperfect grasp of the full idea of the paragraph. When you want to revise short, choppy paragraphs, look for a controlling idea that might direct them. What is the overall point you want to make? Can several short paragraphs be combined and refocused under a single controlling idea? Or you might outline each paragraph by the Christensen indentation method (**6c**), looking for omissions in the paragraph's levels of supporting detail.

Exercise 6.8

Revise the following paragraphs on drunk driving so that each is adequately developed, unified, coherent, and so that together they comprise a brief essay on the topic. Be advised that simply stitching these fragmentary ideas together will not produce satisfactory paragraphs. The material needs be thought through again and rewritten.

> I am in favor of tightening the drunk driving laws in this state. Too many people are getting killed on the highway.
>
> For one thing, the legal drinking age is too low. For another, the legal blood alcohol limit is too high.
>
> The penalties are not stiff enough either. We ought to throw the book at people arrested for drunk driving.
>
> A light sentence or a suspended sentence doesn't save lives.

Exercise 6.9

Group the following sentences into two paragraphs. Provide transitional markers for the sentences, and, when possible, combine sentences.

> Martin Luther King was an ordained minister from Atlanta, Georgia. He gained prominence as a civil-rights leader during the 1950s and 1960s. In 1956 he led a boycott by Montgomery, Alabama, blacks against segregated city bus lines. After his success in Montgomery, he founded the Southern Christian Leadership Conference. This gave him a base to expand the civil-

rights movement in the South and throughout the nation. In 1963 he organized a massive civil-rights march on Washington, D.C., which brought
together more than 200,000 people. It was there that he delivered his famous
"I Have a Dream" speech. In the years that followed, King broadened his
political involvement. He continued to work for civil rights, but he also
became an outspoken critic of the Vietnam war. His criticism of the war was
based on his belief that the war was contributing to poverty in America. He
argued that our valuable national resources were being used to finance the
war rather than to fight poverty at home. In 1968 he planned another large-
scale march to Washington. It was to be called the Poor People's March. He
never fulfilled his wish though. In April of 1968 he went to Memphis,
Tennessee, to help settle a strike by sanitation workers. While there he was
assassinated.

In Your Own Words

Read the following paragraphs and write a paragraph explaining why you
think the writer divided them into two paragraphs instead of using one
long paragraph. Explain also how unity and coherence have been maintained between the two paragraphs, and explain what you believe is the
controlling idea.

> Many people find New York an unattractive city to inhabit because of the
> physical filth, and while, God knows, the city is filthy, I doubt that that ele-
> ment plays an important role in our decision to leave. Naples is far dirtier,
> and so are Bombay and countless other cities, but a tolerance for dirt seems
> to grow where some fondness exists. Tangiers is one of the dirtiest cities in
> the world, yet a friend of mine who possesses flawless taste lives in a casbah
> there and would live nowhere else. A few days ago in Central Park, I saw a
> man leaning on a litter can drinking a carton of orange juice, and when he
> finished he tossed the container not in the receptacle but on the ground.
>
> I don't understand this, but there is a lot about New York I don't under-
> stand. Mainly, I don't understand why the city has no soul, no detectable
> heartbeat, why the chief element in the city's emotional economy is indiffer-
> ence. I think that's what sent me on my way. Vienna almost suffocates the
> Viennese with care. Paris manages to imbue her own with an obsession for
> their fulfillment, San Francisco exudes a pride that even gathers to her heart
> total strangers; but the key to New York's character is that it really doesn't
> care about anything.
>
> —Caskie Stinnett, from "Farewell, My Unlovely"

6 **g** **Check paragraphs for consistent point of view and tone.**

Readers dislike conflicting cues. For example, if information is being
reported from the writer's point of view, readers expect that point of view
will continue throughout the paragraph. If the tone is friendly, readers get
upset if the author attacks them without warning. A unified, developed, and
coherent paragraph can still fail if it is not consistent within itself and consistent with paragraphs in the essay.

● **1 Consistent point of view.** Unnecessary shifts in person, tense, or number within a paragraph leave readers wondering who is speaking and to whom (person), what the time sequence is (tense), and how many are being discussed (number). (See also Chapter 16.)

Unnecessary shifts in person

A pleasant and quiet place to live is essential for a serious-minded college student. If possible, you should rent a room from a landlady with a reputation for keeping order and discipline among her renters. Moreover, a student ought to pick a roommate with a similar temperament. Then you can agree to and keep a schedule of study hours.

Unnecessary shift in tense

Every time I have seen one of Clint Eastwood's Dirty Harry movies, I suffered conflicting reactions. Harry Callahan, Dirty Harry, was a policeman who follows his own code of justice rather than the code of the law. Harry's justice amounts to vigilante action which he carried out by excessively violent means—usually with a handgun as big as a bazooka. These movies' brutal violence repulses me, but I can sympathize with Harry's feelings. Although reason tells us vigilante justice is wrong, especially in a law-enforcement officer, these films replaced audiences' reason with emotions that make such violence at least momentarily acceptable.

Unnecessary shift in number

Of great currency at the moment is the notion that education should prepare students for "life." A college graduate no longer goes out into the world as a cultivated individual. Instead students feel obligated to prepare themselves for places in the business world. Consequently, we are establishing courses on how to get and keep a mate, how to budget an income, and how to win friends and influence people—that is, how to sell yourself and your product. The study of things not obviously practical to a businessperson is coming to be looked upon as unnecessary.

Be aware that in writing about works of literature, drama, film, or the like it is customary to use the present tense to describe occurrences in the "present" of the narrative. For example, the foregoing description of Dirty Harry should read: "Harry Callahan...*is* a policeman who *follows* his own code of justice....Harry's justice amounts to vigilante action which he *carries* out by excessively violent means...." (See also Section **29d1**.)

● **2 Consistent tone.** In its usual sense **tone** means the quality of sound—the pitch, the duration. In writing, tone has to do with the "sound" of the text, the attitude about subject and audience that the writer projects. Tone can be variously described as the manner of expression (*she affected a breezy tone in her letter to hide her disappointment*), general atmosphere (*Poe's short story "The Fall of the House of Usher" has the most somber tone, full of darkness and foreboding*), or dominant impression (*didn't you think* *the retraction printed in today's newspaper sounded patronizing rather than apologetic?).*

Sentence structure and length, word choice, methods of organization and development, the kinds of examples, illustrations, and details, as well as other factors combine to create the "tone of voice" that reveals a writer's stance toward his or her subject and audience. Even punctuation or the use of sentence fragments can influence a reader's perception of a writer's tone. Ranging from impersonal to personal, formal to informal, literal to ironic, sentimental to sarcastic, enthusiastic to indifferent, dogmatic to doubtful, hostile to friendly, flippant to respectful, modest to authoritative, serious to humorous, the tone a writer creates should suit his or her purposes. For example, in some situations a hostile tone will put readers off—not what the writer intended; in other situations, it may rouse them to action—just what the writer intended. The key is to choose an appropriate tone.

An **appropriate tone** reflects the writer's understanding of and respect for the needs and feelings of the readers. Although generalizations about tone are risky, the following tactics will probably offend your readers: talking down to them by repeating the obvious; talking over your audience's heads, merely to impress them, by using words, allusions, or examples they don't understand; being excessively dogmatic or sarcastic; being excessively or falsely enthusiastic. It is hard to imagine situations in which such tones would be appropriate. Consider the following opening from a student paper:

Inappropriate tone

No one can tell me that people who vote for the slimeballs on the Republican ticket aren't putting their own selfish interests ahead of the true good of the country.

Whatever readers may think of this thesis, the writer's dogmatic attitude and inappropriately hostile tone make any sort of balanced or reasoned discussion of the topic seem unlikely.

Consistent tone requires maintaining a particular tone once you have established it. A jarring tone can ruin the effect of a paragraph, as the following excerpt from a student essay illustrates:

Jarring shift in tone

Jim woke up, but the cold air in his room pushed him back toward the warmth of sleep. Gradually, he noticed the light flickering through his closed eyelids. He opened his eyes. He looked out the window next to his bed, and his mind was, like, totally blown away. Everything that could be seen by the human eye was covered by snow. He prayed that school would be cancelled.

The shift to conversational slang ("like, totally blown away") is completely at odds with the fairly formal tone in the rest of the paragraph.

When used deliberately to achieve effects such as humor or irony,

shifts of tone can be appropriate. Notice how Judith Martin, who writes an etiquette column under the pen name "Miss Manners," mixes humor and seriousness to educate readers while keeping her subject (and herself) from sounding too stuffy.

> But for the super-fastidious, or let us say those like Miss Manners who have nothing better to do with their time, there is special flatware expressly designed for different kinds of dessert. If you are going to laugh yourself silly at Miss Manners over this, you had better not let her see your collection of useless and expensive electronic gadgets....
>
> Berries may be eaten with the generic berry spoon, which has a berry design done in relief in the bowl as a reminder to those whose powers for making distinctions are all fuddled by dessert time. But strawberries also have their own fork, some of them offering a kind of hint in the form of a carving of a strawberry on the handle, but some not. You just have to know that the miniature fork with the long tines is not there to pick your teeth with. It's for spearing a strawberry, dipping it in sugar and popping it down.
>
> —Judith Martin, "Weapons for the Dessert Wars"

Exercise 6.10

The following paragraphs and paragraph parts are marred by inconsistent point of view (person, tense, number). Revise them to ensure consistency.

1   Many children are injured every day because of carelessness in the home. Some of these injuries include electrical shock and ingestion of poisonous chemicals. Most people have stored cleaning solutions, pesticides, and other chemicals under the sink where these were in perfect reach for a small child. Electrical outlets draw a child's attention because it's at their eye level.

2   "Battle Royal," by Ralph Ellison, tells of an incident in a young black man's life when he comes face to face with the arrogant attitude that "the town's leading white citizens" have toward the blacks. After giving an impressive speech at his graduation, the boy was invited to give the same speech at a gathering of prominent white citizens. At this gathering, where most of the white men were drunk, the boy and group of nine other black men were put through a series of humiliating circumstances for the entertainment of the white men. After he gave his speech, during which he is ridiculed and taunted by the men, the boy is given a scholarship to a state college for Negroes as a reward.

3   One of the books I read in high school English was Dickens's *Tale of Two Cities*. In it the author tells of some of the horrors of the French Revolution. Her spent several pages telling us about how the French aristocrats suffered. The climax part of the book tells how a ne'er-do-well who failed in life sacrifices himself for another. He took his place in a prison and went stoically to the guillotine for him.

Exercise 6.11

Study the following paragraphs. Describe the tone of each and discuss the factors that contribute to it.

1   I got the call just last night. One of my best male friends was hysterically crying and mumbling into the receiver. Although I could not understand what he was saying, I knew exactly what he meant—another one of our friends had been killed. You see, getting these calls is becoming commonplace.

I am eighteen years old, and over the past two years this story has been replayed ten times. Always the call, always similar details. What is happening to us? Are we caught up in a vortex of senseless crime and self-annihilation that will one day kill us all? When will it ever end? Why does it just keep happening to US?

—Stephanie Blue (student), "Why Are All My Friends Dying?"

2   After a night of noisy sex, heavy breathing, snarling spats and much scampering to and fro, the couple upstairs settles into a sunrise slumber as our bleary-eyed homeowner is roused from a fitful sleep by a smell that isn't fresh-brewed coffee.

Enough already! It's time to call Peter the Possum Man, a point guard in Melbourne's ongoing marsupial mayhem. But Peter's six trucks are already out this morning, responding to other complaints. Competitors, including Paul the Possum Catcher, Shield Pest & Weed Control's "Possum Removal Specialists," and an outfit called Possoff, are also at work.

—James P. Sterba,
"Urban Aussies Have this Little Problem Living with Possums"

3   Even though large tracts of Europe and many old and famous States have fallen or may fall into the grip of the Gestapo and all the odious apparatus of Nazi rule, we shall not flag or fail. We shall go on to the end. We shall fight in France, we shall fight in the seas and oceans, we shall fight with growing confidence and growing strength in the air; we shall defend our Island, whatever the cost may be. We shall fight on the beaches, we shall fight on the landing grounds, we shall fight in the field and in the streets, we shall fight in the hills; we shall never surrender; and even if, which I do not for a moment believe, this Island or a large part of it were subjugated and starving, then our Empire beyond the seas, armed and guarded by the British Fleet, would carry on the struggle, until, in God's good time, the New World, with all its power and might, steps forth to the rescue and liberation of the Old.

—Winston Churchill, *Speech at Dunkerque*

4   My education and that of my Black associates were quite different from the education of our white schoolmates. In the classroom we all learned past participles, but in the streets and in our homes the Blacks learned to drop *s*'s from plurals and suffixes from past-tense verbs. We were alert to the gap separating the written word from the colloquial. We learned to slide out of one language and into another without being conscious of the effort. At school, in a given situation, we might respond with "That's not unusual." But in the street, meeting the same situation, we easily said, "It be's like that sometimes."

—Maya Angelou, *I Know Why the Caged Bird Sings*

In Your Own Words

Write down five advertising slogans from television or magazines. To experiment with tone, rewrite them by substituting a single word for a single word two places in each. Your substitutions might be more formal than the rest of the slogan—or less formal. You might use substitutions that seem falsely enthusiastic, patronizing, or overly intellectual. How do these small changes affect the tone? Share your versions of the ads with your classmates. Are any of the revisions more effective than the original ads?

Paragraph Checklist

- Is the paragraph focused on a single topic or aspect of a topic?
- Is there an expressed or clearly implied controlling idea, a topic sentence, that governs the paragraph?
- Do all the sentences in the paragraph explain or relate to the controlling idea?
- Is the paragraph organized according to some logical pattern such as time, space, general to particular, particular to general, climax, comparison, contrast, definition, cause and effect?
- Are the major points in the paragraph supported sufficiently by subordinate points?
- Is there enough connecting language to make relationships among ideas and sentences clear and coherent?
- Is the paragraph sufficiently developed, containing enough details, examples, reasons, and explanations to provide readers with what they need to know?
- Are there any shifts in tone or point of view that are unnecessary or possibly confusing to the reader?
- Is the paragraph an appropriate length? Does it need to be divided according to different aspects or subtopics? Does it need to be developed with additional explanation and detail?

Paragraphs for Study

There is no substitute for writing if you want to learn to do it well. However, reading is an integral part of this learning process. Research shows what many people have suspected for years: Those who read widely, attentively, and often are usually better writers than those who do not. The reason is that frequent readers are more comfortable with language and familiar with a wider range of options and techniques for using language. Reading and analyzing what you read to understand how it is written can add to your own writing skills. Test your understanding of the principles of good paragraphs by studying the samples that follow. Analyze each to determine the controlling idea, the topic sentence if one is provided, the transitional markers and other means of achieving coherence, the organizational patterns, the level of development, and the tone. Identify what you believe to be the author's goal in each paragraph: What is it that he or she wants to accomplish?

Then write a paragraph explaining how one of the writers tries to accomplish his or her goal. Your paragraph should not be a summary of the paragraph's contents. It should be a discussion of the writing techniques the author has used and how successful these techniques are in accomplishing the goal.

1   Going to work for the Eclipse [computer] Group could be a rough way to start out in your profession. You set out for your first real [engineering] job with all the loneliness and fear that attend new beginnings, drive east from Purdue or Northwestern or Wisconsin, up from Missouri or west from MIT, and before you've learned to find your way to work without a road map, you're sitting in a tiny cubicle or, even worse, in an office like the one dubbed the Micropit, along with three other new recruits, your knees practically touching theirs; and though lacking all privacy and quiet, though it's a job you've never really done before, you are told that you have almost no time at all in which to master a virtual encyclopedia of technical detail and to start producing crucial pieces of a crucial machine. And you want to make a good impression. So you don't have any time to meet women, to help your wife buy furniture for your apartment, or to explore the unfamiliar countryside. You work. You're told, "Don't even mention the name Eagle outside the group." "Don't talk outside the group," you're told. You're working at a place that looks like something psychologists build for testing the fortitude of small animals, and your boss won't even say hello to you.

—Tracy Kidder, *The Soul of a New Machine*

2   Just opening or closing the screen door behind me was an important experience. I'd rarely leave home all alone or without feeling reluctance. Walking down the sidewalk, under the canopy of tall trees, I'd warily notice the (suddenly) silent neighborhood kids who stood warily watching me. Nervously, I'd arrive at the grocery store to hear there the sounds of the gringo, reminding me that in this so-big world I was a foreigner. But if leaving home was never routine, neither was coming back. Walking toward our house, climbing the steps from the sidewalk, in summer when the front door was open, I'd hear voices beyond the screen door talking in Spanish. For a second or two I'd stay, linger there listening. Smiling, I'd hear my mother call out, saying in Spanish, "Is that you, Richard?" Those were her words, but all the while her sounds would assure me: *You are home now. Come closer inside. With us.* "*Sí*," I'd reply.

—Richard Rodriguez, "Aira: A Memoir of a Bilingual Childhood"

3   Often at my desk, now, I sit contemplating the fish. Nor does it have to be a fish. It could be the long-horned Alaskan bison on my wall. For the point is, you see, that the fish is extinct and gone, just as those great heavy-headed beasts are gone, just as our massive-faced and shambling forebears of the Ice [Age] have vanished. The chemicals still about me here took a shape that will never be seen again so long as grass grows or the sun shines. Just once out of all time there was a pattern that we call *Bison regius*, a fish called *Diplomystus humilis*, and, at this present moment, a primate who knows, or thinks he knows, the entire score.

—Loren Eiseley, *The Night Country*

4   The gym detonates, fifteen hundred throats in peril of rupture. The town's best game in years has ended in a tie, Hamilton equalling Hamilton. The crowd owes the night to Robbie Hodge, and no one begrudges him the credit. From the Garfield side comes "Hodge! Hodge! Hodge!" and the Taft side echoes. The sound builds until no words at all can be heard. It is almost like silence, the gym roaring for a performance that on Broadway gets a ten-minute curtain call and in Madrid two ears and a tail.

—Peter Davis, *Hometown*

5   The pluralist approach to multiculturalism promotes a broader inter-pretation of the common American culture and seeks due recognition for the ways that the nation's many racial, ethnic, and cultural groups have transformed the national culture. The pluralists say, in effect, "American culture belongs to us, all of us; the U.S. is us, and we remake it in every generation." But particularists have no interest in extending or revising American culture; indeed, they deny that a common culture exists. Particularists reject any accommodation among groups, any interactions that blur the distinct lines between them. The brand of history that they espouse is one in which everyone is either a descendant of victims or oppressors. By doing so, ancient hatreds are fanned and re-created in each new generation. Particularism has its intellectual roots in the ideology of ethnic separatism and in the black nationalist movement. In the particularist analysis, the nation has five cultures: African American, Asian American, European American, Latino-Hispanic, and Native American. The huge cultural, historical, religious, and linguistic differences within these categories are ignored, as is the consider-able intermarriage among these groups, as are the linkages (like gender, class, sexual orientation, and religion) that cut across these five groups. No serious scholar would claim that all Europeans and white Americans are part of the same culture, or that all Asians are part of the same culture, or that all people of Latin-American descent are of the same culture, or that all people of African descent are of the same culture. Any categorization this broad is essentially meaningless and useless.

—Diane Ravitch, "Multiculturalism: *E Pluribus Plures*"

6   An American swimming meet closely mirrors the larger society in that most people have good and bad moments, strong and weak performances, and despite disappointments, generally find rewards. Swimming is a particu-larly appropriate sport for a competitive, achievement-oriented society in which lines of social class are not clearly and rigidly drawn. Status within the American swimmer's world is like the form of social organization that anthropologists call the chiefdom, common a century ago in the Polynesian islands. In the chiefdom, slight gradations in prestige and power, rather than demarcated social classes, meant that everyone had a distinctive social status, just a bit higher or lower than anyone else's. A swimmer's unique status is the end result of a complex scoring process that takes into account a series of constantly changing times in different events. Like a Polynesian, every swimmer has a social status slightly different from everyone else's.

—Conrad Phillip Kottak, "Swimming in Cross-Cultural Currents"

Writers Revising

The following are the first few paragraphs of an essay written by a student named Charlene for an English composition assignment that asked students to describe a location they had visited, focusing on what had impressed them about it. During the class's peer view of rough drafts, Charlene's reviewer remarked that the paragraphs seemed "jumpy" and without a clear focus. He said, "The ideas are all over the place. Just when I thought you were going to pursue a thought, you switched to something else."

Review Charlene's draft and provide detailed comments about what you think she should do to improve unity, coherence, and development of the paragraphs. Then read her revision and see if it follows your suggestions.

Draft

```
    Believe it or not, there is a place in New York
that I found to be peaceful, quiet, and relaxing. My
neighbor, along with her children, invited me to spend
a week with them in Mayville, New York. The time spent
driving was well worth it for the peaceful vacation of
getting away from the noises of Maryland. The week I
spent in Mayville unfortunately did not give me much
time to see things. The weather was not in our favor.
Everyone was kind, respectful, and helpful. In order
to go to stores, movies, and restaurants, you have to
drive thirty to forty-five minutes to Jamestown, New
York. Mayville is a small town. It is located between
Buffalo, Niagara Falls, Panama Rocks, and a wine vine-
yard. The small town also has an old-fashioned steam-
boat (the Chautauqua Belle) that was not operating on
the day we were going to ride it. It rained most of
the time. I bought postcards of the scenic places we
had planned to visit. What I liked best about Mayville
was its peacefulness.
```

Upper Marlboro, my hometown, is more urban than rural, which means it is not as peaceful or relaxing as Mayville. Even the woods are different. In the Upper Marlboro woods, there are honeysuckles, battered old trees, dried up leaves and underbrush, and sometimes even trash. Mayville is far from any urban area, which makes it more peaceful. People don't seem to be in as much of a hurry. They stop on the street for leisurely conversation. The woods are filled with tall, healthy-looking trees, wild ferns, raspberries along the paths, and streams you can swim in.

Revision

When I hear the words "New York," I think of the hustle of Wall Street, the bustle of Broadway, and the rude honking of taxis. But believe it or not, there is a place in New York that I found to be peaceful and quiet--the opposite of the stereotype. Last summer my neighbor, along with her children, invited me to spend a week with them in Mayville, New York. Compared to my suburban hometown of Upper Marlboro, Maryland, Mayville was peaceful, quiet, relaxing, and friendly.

Mayville is a small town located between Buffalo, Niagara Falls, Panama Rocks, and a wine vineyard in upstate New York. It is in a rural setting far from any urban area, which makes it peaceful and quiet. There just isn't much going on in Mayville. In order to go to stores, movies, and restaurants, a person has to drive thirty to forty-five minutes to Jamestown, New York. In contrast, Upper Marlboro, although about the same in population as Mayville, has become a suburb of Washington, D.C., as the city has grown outward over the years. Where there were once pastures and tobacco fields, today there are shopping malls, gas stations, and rush-hour traffic.

For entertainment in Mayville, people can enjoy the beautiful scenery or a ride on the old-fashioned steamboat, the <u>Chautauqua Belle</u>. It rained most of the time we were there, so we didn't have much time to see things. However, I bought postcards of the many scenic places in the area.

It did stop raining long enough for us to enjoy several walks in the woods. Even the woods in Mayville are different from those in Upper Marlboro. Mayville's woods are filled with tall, healthy-looking trees, wild ferns, raspberries along the paths, and streams you could swim in. Upper Marlboro's woods, on the other hand, look tired and brown instead of fresh and green. Our woods are filled with tangled honeysuckles, battered old tires, dried up leaves and underbrush, and sometimes even trash. You wouldn't even want to dip your hand in the brown water running through the drainage ditch that serves as the stream in our woods.

Mayville's rural setting and slower pace seem to affect the people who live there. They don't appear to be in as much of a hurry as people are in Upper Marlboro. Mayville folks stop on the street for leisurely conversation. When people pass each other one the sidewalk, they automatically say "hi" to one another. We were surprised that the townspeople always smiled and said hello to us, even though they didn't know us. Everyone was kind, respectful, and helpful, giving us advice about sights to see and trails to hike. The considerate behavior left us with the impression that Mayville is a very friendly town.

Analysis

First, Charlene realized that readers had no reason not to believe that she found New York state peaceful—unless she told them that she had previously always thought of New York City. Consequently, she revised the opening paragraph to clarify that assumption. With the help of her peer reviewer, she also sharpened the focus of the paper. The reviewer had underlined the several sentences that mentioned peace, quiet, and friendliness, asking if these might be the true focus of her ideas. Charlene then developed paragraphs that explained what contributed to the feeling of peaceful relaxation in Mayville. Making sure that all the information in the paragraphs related in some way to this main idea improved the unity of each paragraph and of the paper as a whole. Charlene contrasted Mayville with her own hometown to illustrate further the source of her feelings.

Charlene improved the coherence of the paragraphs by repeating key words and phrases and by adding transition words (*in con-*

trast, on the other hand, however). She also used parallel grammatical structures (in paragraph 4, describing the woods in Mayville and Upper Marlboro, for example).

You may have noticed that paragraph 3 is the least developed of the paragraphs in the revised draft. Although it ends with a transition sentence that links it to the following paragraph, the third paragraph contains insufficient information for readers to understand how it relates to the controlling idea of the essay. Charlene needs to develop this paragraph with concrete details about specific scenic spots in the Mayville area and tie them to the theme of peace and friendliness.

Critical Thinking and Argument

People argue to settle differences of opinion. Using intelligence and reasoning in an exchange of words rather than blows, arguers strive to convince their audience to accept an idea, course of action, or point of view. In his book *The Elements of Reasoning*, Professor Edward Corbett has written, "When we argue informally with friends and acquaintances, many of us resort to arguing by vigorous assertion rather than by reasoned demonstration": Reliable evidence and logical presentation sometimes take a back seat to shouting and emotion. However, sound and fury rarely persuade people as successfully as a convincing presentation of well-marshaled facts.

The familiar process of gathering information, deciding what it means, and using it to shape someone else's thoughts or actions occurs repeatedly in your own life. Your history exam requires that you write a short essay answering the question, "What caused the end of the Cold War?" Your boss asks you to prepare a report comparing two computer software packages and recommending the one that seems better. To cut costs, the school board is thinking of closing your child's school, sending him or her to a more distant one. You decide to write a letter to the local newspaper in protest.

Each of these tasks requires the complex skills of critical thinking and argumentative writing—more than just reporting facts and summarizing information. As Chapters 1 and 2 explained, argumentative writing draws on the most complex of the critical thinking skills. Each writing task mentioned in the preceding paragraph will have as its focus a central thesis, an assertion of the writer's position on the subject: "The primary causes of the end of the Cold War were a, b, and c"; "The Digital Dynamite software will best serve our needs"; "The school board should not close our neighborhood elementary school because of y and z." Convincing readers of the truth of these assertions requires analysis, evaluation, and interpretation of the facts to transform the information into a well-reasoned point of view, a persuasive case, an adequately supported stand.

Analysis and interpretation go beyond summarizing and synthesizing facts, beyond asking "What are the main ideas?" Higher-level thinking seeks to answer the question, "What does it all mean?" Critical thinkers take information apart and put it back together in new combinations, looking for patterns and relationships. In argumentation, information becomes evidence to prove a point, to make a decision, to convince people to think or act in certain ways. The following chart shows how different parts of the aforementioned writing tasks draw on different critical thinking skills.

Critical Thinking and Writing Counterparts

Activity	Level of Critical Thinking	Type of Writing
Repeating the sequence of events that led to the end of the Cold War	Summary	Narrative
Explaining why certain events resulted in the end of the Cold War	Analysis and interpretation	Argument
Presenting features of two computer software packages	Synthesis	Exposition
Weighing the pros and cons of two software packages and recommending one for purchase	Analysis and interpretation	Argument
Insisting that local elementary school must not be closed	Emotional reaction	Unsupported opinion
Presenting workable ways to keep local school open	Analysis and interpretation	Argument

Drawing conclusions about information involves two fundamental logical processes: induction and deduction.

Inductive reasoning proceeds from the particular to the general. *If* particular facts are shown to be true time after time or *if* a laboratory experiment yields the same result whenever it is run or *if* people in a wide and varied sampling respond the same way to a given question, *then* a general conclusion may be drawn. Thus, repeated experimentation and testing led to the conclusion that the Sabin vaccine would prevent polio. Scientists use induction when they test and retest a hypothesis before stating it as a general truth. The scientific method proceeds by inductive reasoning.

Deductive reasoning proceeds from the general to the particular. From a general conclusion other facts are deduced. The validity of the deduction depends on the truth of the initial conclusion. Because you know that penicillin is an effective weapon against infection, seeking a doctor to administer it to you if you have an infection is valid deductive reasoning.

Induction and deduction may occur in the same argument, with conclusions from one serving as the basis for the other. For example, based on data from its years of careful recordkeeping of the occurrence and circumstances of highway accidents, the National Safety Council has concluded that the proportion of automobile accidents on holiday weekends is the same as the proportion on weekends that are not holidays. From this conclusion, arrived at inductively, you may deduce that you can travel as safely by car to a Memorial Day celebration as you can to the mall on Saturdays.

 **Decide whether an issue is arguable.**

The novelist Joseph Conrad wrote, "Every sort of shouting is a transitory thing, after which the grim silence of facts remains." A corollary to Conrad's statement is that some things simply cannot be debated from factual evidence. Learn to distinguish those things that are arguable from those that are not.

Things That Are Arguable
- Matters of opinion about which reasonable people disagree
    - that present alternative possibilities for which a believable case can be made,
    - for which sufficient proof can be assembled to establish a likelihood of truth, and
    - for which absolute proof has not yet been established.

Things That Are Not Arguable
- A priori premises
- Matters of taste
- Matters of fact
- Unverifiable facts
- Insufficient facts

Disagreement about issues has resulted in solutions to difficult problems, important scientific breakthroughs, and new ways of thinking and behaving. Argument about matters for which evidence exists (or can be discovered, as in scientific research) is, in fact, the basis for much of your college education. When choosing a topic for an argumentative essay, ask yourself the following questions:
- Does the topic involve an identifiable controversy?
- Can the sides of the controversy be argued from evidence?
- Is reliable information available about the sides of the controversy?
- Is there enough information to construct a stand on the controversy that can be defended?

If you answer yes to all four questions, you can probably write a successful argument on the topic.

It is impossible to argue successfully about subjects that do not contain controversial issues or statements that cannot be supported with evidence. For example, matters of taste and matters of faith are basically inarguable. The following discussion will help you identify inarguable subjects.

A priori premises. *A priori* is a term of logic meaning, roughly, "before examination." A statement based on an a priori premise cannot be argued because such a premise can be neither proved nor disproved: People are simply convinced of its truth or untruth. A priori premises have the force of fact because they are so deeply held, even though they cannot be supported by factual evidence.

Many deeply held and widely shared assumptions about human nature are a priori premises with cultural, racial, social, or religious roots. If you argue from an a priori premise with someone who does not share it, you will find yourself arguing in circles or along parallel lines—but never toward resolution—because legitimate proof is not possible. For instance, many arguments about the value of one social system or government versus another are futile because they are based on different a priori premises. Or if one person believes, a priori, that human beings are basically good, altruistic, and trustworthy, whereas another person believes human nature is essentially wicked, selfish, and dishonest, then the two can never agree about human nature—no matter how many examples each person cites.

A priori premises may change or be replaced over time, as attitudes toward gender roles in American society show. A priori assumptions about the unsuitability of women for the workplace or men for child-care roles are not widely shared today, as they once were.

Subjective expressions of taste and nonrational reactions. The Latin phrase *de gustibus non disputandum est,* "there is no disputing about tastes," is another way of saying that subjective reactions do not lend themselves to reasoning. Some people prefer green; others prefer purple. Similarly, no matter how sound your logic that there is plenty of oxygen in the stalled elevator, to a claustrophobic the sense of suffocation can be very real.

Matters of fact. If a fact is verifiable, there is no point debating it. It can either be true (a bona fide fact) or false (not a fact), but in neither case is it a matter for argument because the record can be checked. The earth is round, or nearly so. This fact was verified by fifteenth-century explorers and more recently by means of space flights.

Unverifiable facts. Although it is interesting to speculate about whether there is life after death, we simply cannot know. Various types of proof may be offered for theories as yet unverified. For instance, theories such as

Einstein's theory of relativity may be proved mathematically before they can be verified through physical observation. Although scientists were willing to grant the mathematical validity of Einstein's theory, they searched for other forms of verification. Be aware of the need to differentiate between fact and theory, even widely accepted theory. Whereas it is possible to argue from theory, it is not possible to argue conclusively.

Insufficient facts. Statements based on insufficient facts cannot be argued conclusively. For instance, people enjoy arguing that life exists on other planets. Statistically, the odds favor the existence of extraterrestrial life forms, but we have no hard evidence to prove this assertion. If information pointing one way or the other comes to light, a conclusion may eventually be reached. In the meantime, logical reasoning on the topic won't carry us very far.

Keep in mind that facts are slippery and not necessarily static. What may be accepted as verifiably true this year may be proven false by next year. Before sailors circled the globe, the populace accepted as fact that the world was flat. During the Middle Ages, the plagues that killed millions were attributed to God's wrath; Europeans had no knowledge that fleas could transmit microorganisms from rats to humans and thus infect the population. What was once the fact of God's wrath is today regarded as a problem of hygiene. Correspondingly, what serves as fact today may be tomorrow's quaint, ignorant notion. Time and scientific inquiry have taught us that very little is absolutely certain. The best we can do is draw conclusions from available data, deciding to formulate an argument when the supporting data warrant it.

Exercise 7.1

Decide which of the following statements are arguable and which are not. Be prepared to explain your reasons.

1 Those romance novels you see at the supermarket check-out counter are cheap, trashy, and not worth reading.
2 Smoking is harmful.
3 People should practice safe sex.
4 Condoms should be available in high schools.
5 All people are created equal.
6 Capital punishment is murder.
7 Navy blue is a more businesslike color than brown.
8 Drinking and driving don't mix.
9 John F. Kennedy would have been a truly great president if he had lived to finish his term in office.
10 Homosexuality is learned behavior, not a genetically influenced trait.

7 b Analyze your audience.

Section **2b** discusses the importance of identifying audience characteristics (such as education, age, knowledge of and probable attitude toward a subject) and provides a grid for analyzing an audience. Because argumentative writing seeks to change readers' views or move them to action, analyzing your readers is as important as thinking about the points you want to make.

As you consider the audience for your argumentative paper, you should understand that three outcomes are possible:

- You will change your reader's point of view from opposition to agreement. This outcome is ideal, but also the most unlikely.
- You will be able to modify your reader's point of view, bringing it closer to your own. If not total agreement, you may be able to gain some acceptance for your point of view and establish a basis for greater understanding between you and your audience.
- You will not change your audience's mind at all. Even in the face of faultless logic, readers can reject your argument.

In her argumentative essay, student Kara Lardizabal hoped to persuade readers toward acceptance of mandatory restaurant service charges. The ideal outcome would have been to convince customers to prefer restaurant service charges over voluntary tipping, but, given her audience of money-conscious fellow students, Kara believed this goal to be unrealistic. Drafts of Kara's essay appear at the end of this chapter.

The outcome of your argument depends in part on how well you understand your audience and accordingly shape your material to make it convincing. The audience's level of expertise and its preexisting point of view are two important components of this understanding.

Expert versus novice readers. As Chapter 2 notes, specialized or expert readers will require a different approach than general or novice readers. Someone who knows little about the subject will need more background information. Someone who is already familiar with the facts and various points of view on the subject will probably demand greater detail, more evidence and expert testimony, and a more sophisticated analysis.

Convinced, neutral, or skeptical readers. If your audience already agrees with you, clearly you do not have to persuade them further. Rather, your goal is get them to act. When Thoreau wrote "Civil Disobedience," he knew his audience was already opposed to slavery; his task was to inspire them to act on behalf of the antislavery cause. Given their preexisting viewpoint, he did not need to compile catalogs of factual evidence. Instead, Thoreau's essay, full of emotionally charged language, calls for action passionately.

If readers are neutral or skeptical, you must convince them at least to consider your position. Establishing common ground will help you get a hearing for your point of view: What characteristics do you share? What points can be agreed on? Identifying common ground, acknowledging opposing points of view, even admitting the strength of some of those arguments shows respect for readers' convictions. If you suggest that your readers are uninformed, ignorant, stupid, or ridiculous for believing as they do, you will only antagonize them. You will never persuade them.

Skeptical audiences are likely to be very exacting readers—highly critical of misused facts, weak evidence, insufficient proof, biased testimony, faulty logic, and slanted or emotional language. These readers require the most rigorous arguments and counterarguments to refute opposing viewpoints.

Emotional versus rational appeals. Audience analysis can help you decide whether readers are likely to be swayed by examples, anecdotes, and language that appeals to the emotions. Some expert or skeptical readers may insist on factual evidence and reject emotional appeals as manipulative. In contrast, a reader who is familiar with a subject may respond positively to emotional language that reinforces his or her agreement with the point of view being expressed.

How much emotion is too much in argumentative writing? There are no easy rules of thumb. Emotion has had a legitimate place in argumentation since ancient times. The following diagram shows a traditional representation of the relationship between the message, the writer (or speaker), and the audience. Each element in the diagram is associated with a particular argumentative appeal.

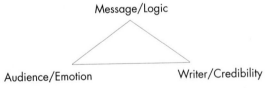

Message/Logic

Audience/Emotion   Writer/Credibility

The message focuses on the clarity of the point of view being advocated: the logic of the reasons, the validity of the supporting evidence, and the structure of the presentation. This element of an argument is called the logical appeal (from the Greek word *logos*, meaning "word"). The writer's relationship to the argument involves credibility and trustworthiness. Should we believe what the writer says? This element is called the ethical appeal (from the Greek word *ethos*, meaning "character"). The audience's role in the argument concerns feelings and imagination. How can readers be engaged and motivated to think or act in a certain way? This element is called the appeal to emotions (from the Greek word *pathos*, meaning "emotion"). Successful arguments balance the three elements. Too much *pathos*, and the argument becomes propaganda; too little, and the argument will fail to engage its audience's interest.

Exercise 7.2

Rate the listed audiences as (1) novice or expert and (2) convinced, neutral, or skeptical about the following assertions.

> *Assertion:* Reintroducing wolves to the mountains and prairies of the American west is a good idea.
> *Audiences:* Wyoming rancher, contributor to World Wildlife Fund, seventh graders in Philadelphia, Pennsylvania

> *Assertion:* The United States needs stricter gun control laws.
> *Audiences:* An emergency room nurse in Cincinnati, a grandmother from the public housing projects of Chicago, a street gang member in Washington, D.C., a migrant laborer in Homestead, Florida

> *Assertion:* Extreme life-saving procedures and organ transplants should not be used for the terminally ill.
> *Audiences:* Thirty-five-year-old accountant, sixty-eight-year-old cardiac patient, father of a nine-year-old cancer victim, twenty-three-year-old medical student, eighty-four-year-old nursing home resident

In Your Own Words

Assume that you and your roommate have decided to make a major investment together in a stereo system. Since your roommate works more hours than you do, you have volunteered to do some comparison shopping of stereo systems so that you two can make a good decision. List the characteristics of your roommate that you would take into consideration when making the argument for the system you believe is best to buy. Then write a persuasive paragraph attempting to "sell" your roommate on the system, taking into consideration the attitudes and thought patterns of your roommate.

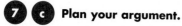 **Plan your argument.**

Once you have determined that your topic is arguable and you have researched it enough to know that you will be able to locate supporting material, you can plan your argument. If you have approached the differences of opinion with the idea of learning which side has the most convincing evidence, you may not want to frame your final thesis until you have investigated the different sides of the controversy. However, you should write a working thesis statement fairly early in the planning stages so that you have established a focus to guide further research and drafting (see Sections **3a** through **3c**). In addition to writing a working thesis, early planning involves compiling a list of the supporting points you will need to prove your thesis and thinking carefully about the logical connections

between the thesis and the supporting points. These three elements of argumentative writing are termed the assertion, the evidence, and the warrant.

● **1 Assertion.** In an argumentative essay, the thesis expresses the position you are taking on the controversy. It asserts your belief and stakes out your claim to the argumentative territory. In fact, the words *assertion* and *claim* are synonyms for an argumentative thesis. An assertion along with reasons forms the core of an argumentative thesis:

ASSERTION	Schools should place more emphasis on math and science because
REASON	American students lag far behind students from other industrialized countries on math and science test scores.
ASSERTION	Voluntary tipping at restaurants should be replaced by a mandatory 15 percent service charge
REASONS	because a service charge would be fairer to servers and make owners' bookkeeping simpler.
REASONS	Neither drug and alcohol abuse, mental illness, nor crime, but
ASSERTION	a severe shortage of low-income housing, causes the majority of homelessness in the United States.

● **2 Evidence.** The reasons rest on evidence. Your essay must supply evidence to support your assertion and to show that the reasons you offer are valid. Evidence is the part of an argument the reader is willing to accept as true without further proof.

Common Types of Supporting Evidence

Facts	Verifiable occurrences or experiences; statistics compiled from systematic observation
Testimony	Reliable reports of events, experiences, or observations
Informed Opinion	Judgment believed reliable because the source is highly knowledgeable about the subject, prestigious, and authoritative
Examples and Illustrations	Particular instances of generalizations

As you plan your argument, you will need to think about the type and quantity of evidence needed to convince your audience (see also Sections **4b** and **6e**). Although most people respond to emotional appeals, they are unlikely to be convinced unless you also offer solid evidence. Of the types of evidence in the preceding list, which ones are most convincing? The more factual your evidence, the more your audience is likely to believe it. The more prone to bias or the farther from the original source the evidence is, the less credibility it will have with your audience. As a general rule, facts carry the most weight as evidence in an argument, followed by testimony from reliable observers, informed opinion from experts, and finally examples and illustrations. As the evidence moves farther from hard fact, it becomes more and more open to error, emotion, and manipulation (see Section **7g** for a discussion of logical fallacies).

When Kara Lardizabal asserts that mandatory service charges should replace voluntary tipping in restaurants (see Chapter 2 and "Writers Revising" at the end of this chapter), she must offer more than her personal experience as a waitress. She is, after all, just one person and certainly not impartial. Even the testimony of restaurant owners and employees will not be enough to convince skeptical readers. A restaurant owner claiming that his customers prefer a service charge to tipping does not carry the same weight of evidence as a scientifically conducted customer survey that shows the majority prefers a service charge to tipping. If possible, Kara should supply such facts to support her case.

Evidence often comprises a major portion of an argument, especially if the issues are complex. How much evidence is enough depends on the nature of the subject and the characteristics of the audience—on how likely the readers are to agree or disagree with you. The more widely shared or commonly acknowledged an experience, the less evidence you need to convince readers. If, for example, you state that traffic accidents are a leading cause of death among teenagers, most people will agree with you. Numerous news reports have verified the statement. Statistics comparing traffic deaths to other leading causes of death for this age group would simply strengthen the validity of the assertion. If, on the other hand, in a paper on the value of home remedies you offer as truth the statement that mustard plasters are good for curing colds, you will need plenty of evidence. Most readers would view your statement not as fact but as an assertion needing proof. To convince your audience, you will have to cite a wide and representative sampling of incidents as well as testimony from respected medical authorities who have studied the effect of mustard plasters on colds.

Evidence is only as good as its accuracy and your audience's willingness to accept it. Consequently, persuading the reader means looking at the evidence from the reader's point of view and then supplying statistics, illustrations, specific examples, personal experience, and occurrences reported by authorities to validate the evidence in your reader's eyes.

The evidence you cite in your writing should always be attributed. That is, you should tell readers what sources you are using. Chapters 46 through 52, on writing formal research papers and reports, illustrate the documentation methods appropriate for lengthy papers in English, humanities, sciences, and other disciplines. For a short argumentative paper such as Kara's, the instructor did not require formal citations or a list of references. Still, as a responsible author, Kara carefully attributed supporting

information to the proper sources by giving the name of the source person, organization, or group. Note that she identifies her sources by position or affiliation as well as by name. Thus, readers will understand that Michael Fawcett's opinion should be considered informed because he is a restaurant manager. Such attributions not only show the care Kara has taken not to plagiarize information or misrepresent her own expertise but they also add to the credibility of her argument.

● **3 Warrant.** The third element in an argument, the warrant shows the connection between the truth of the supporting evidence and the truth of the assertion. It represents the *because* or *therefore* in the assertion + reasons core of the argument. Sometimes the warrant is implied rather than stated.

ASSERTION	You should reduce the amount of fried food you eat.
EVIDENCE	Research has connected cholesterol to heart disease.
WARRANT	Fried foods often contain high amounts of cholesterol.

Using an implied warrant and a different order of presentation, the same argument might be written as follows:

EVIDENCE	Because research has connected cholesterol to heart disease,
ASSERTION	you should reduce the amount of fried food you eat.

The word *because* serves as the warrant, clearly implying the reason why or connection between the truth of the evidence and the truth of the assertion.

Sometimes your audience will accept the warrant; other times you will have to prove its truth, just as you would the assertion. For instance, few people will dispute that fried foods are often high in cholesterol. This warrant rests on well-verified fact. However, the argument "You should increase the amount of red wine you drink because research has connected red wine to lower incidence of heart attack" will probably not be accepted as readily. Most people will want to see scientific evidence for the warrant that "red wine contains heart-attack-reducing agents."

Exercise 7.3

Find the assertion, evidence, and warrant in each of the following passages. If any of the parts is implied, point out the words that indicate the implied part or supply the missing words.

1 If so many mental institutions had not been closed in the past, there would not be so many homeless people on the streets today.

2 Professor Smith is a bad teacher. Some students fall asleep in class while others look out the window.

3 Marcia should be promoted to district manager because she gets along with many different types of people.

4 Just as movies are rated with R, PG, and so forth, television programs should also be rated for violent and sexually explicit content.

5 If you don't behave yourself, Santa Claus won't bring you any presents.

6 Pregnant women should not drink alcoholic beverages.

7 I have a terrible sinus headache. Whenever the weather changes, I get one of these headaches, so we can expect rain later today.

8 Some acreage in California's San Joaquin Valley is suffering from a build-up of salt deposits, the result of irrigation without adequate drainage. Irrigation can bring life to crop lands, but it can also bring slow death.

9 The freeze on faculty hiring is preventing some students from completing their programs of study and graduating on time.

10 Our state should pass a law requiring all motorcyclists to wear helmets.

Exercise 7.4

Choose one or two of the assertions in Exercise 7.2. For each of the audiences given for an assertion, write a brief list of evidence that you believe would be convincing. Rank order the evidence from most convincing to least convincing. Then label each item of evidence by type (fact, example or illustration, testimony, etc.). Do you see any correlation between type of evidence and type of audience?

In Your Own Words

Assume that you and your friend, visiting the local museum of art, find yourselves standing in front of a striking modern painting. Your friend says it's the most beautiful recent painting she's ever seen; you tell her that it's the most worthless piece of canvas ever to insult the walls of a museum. Write a paragraph explaining whether or not one of you can win this argument and how that might happen.

7 d Define terms in your argument.

As you plan your argument, identify terms your audience may not understand or may define differently than you do. Much senseless argument arises because people do not agree on meanings. Readers must understand your terms before they can follow your reasoning. Proving the assertion "The end of the Cold War signaled the failure of communism" requires careful definition of not only the term *communism* but also what the writer means by *failure*. Both words are abstractions, and abstract terms are among the most difficult to define.

There are three principal methods of defining terms. Which you choose will depend to some extent on whether your readers require a brief definition or a lengthy one. Word substitution is the shortest type of definition; formal definition (also called sentence definition) is somewhat longer; extended definitions may be quite long.

● **1 Definition by word substitution.** Many terms can be defined satisfactorily by offering a synonym the reader is likely to know. Often an

appositive—another noun or a group of words used as a noun—placed immediately after the term will define it sufficiently.

> aerobic (oxygen-requiring) bacteria
> aquifer, a natural underground water reservoir
> layette, clothing or equipment for a newborn child

● **2 Formal definition.** We learn about something new first by discovering that it resembles things we already know and then by noting how it differs from them. Following the same steps, formal definition also relies on comparison and contrast. First, we explain the class of things (its *genus*) to which a term belongs, and then we show how it differs from other things in that class (its *differentiation*). Formal definition characteristically takes the form "x is a y that...," which is why it is sometimes called a sentence definition. The following steps are important in creating a good formal definition.

Classify the term by putting it with other items of its kind. In general, the narrower the classification, the clearer the eventual definition.

	Term		Class
	A carpet	is	a floor covering.
	A rifle	is	a firearm.
NOT	A rifle	is	a weapon.

Although *weapon* is a legitimate classification for *rifle*, the class is broader than necessary (including knives, spears, clubs, and so on).

Differentiate the term from other members of its class.

Term		Class	Differentiation
A carpet	is	a floor covering	of woven or felted fabric usually tacked to a floor.
A rifle	is	a firearm	with a spiral-grooved bore, designed to be fired from the shoulder.

Use parallel form in stating the term and its definition. Do not use the phrases *is when* or *is where* in definitions (see also Section **20a2**).

NOT A debate *is when* two people or sides argue a given proposition in a regulated discussion.

BUT A debate is a regulated discussion of a given proposition between two matched sides.

Avoid circular definition. Definitions are circular when words are defined in terms themselves.

NOT A rifle is a firearm with *rifling* inside its barrel to impart rotary motion to its projectile.

BUT A rifle is a firearm with spiral grooves inside its barrel to impart a rotary motion to its projectile.

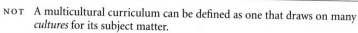

NOT   A multicultural curriculum can be defined as one that draws on many *cultures* for its subject matter.

BUT   A multicultural curriculum can be defined as a course of study that draws on people and events from many ethnic, racial, national, geographic, and gender backgrounds for its subject matter.

Define a term in words that are familiar to the reader. It doesn't do much good to describe a truffle as a "fleshy, subterranean fungus, chiefly of the genus *Tuber,* often esteemed as food" if your readers won't know the meaning of *subterranean, fungus,* or *genus.* "An edible, lumpy plant that grows underground and is related to the mushroom" may be a much more understandable definition, depending on your audience. As always, analyze the audience to determine which terms need defining and which synonyms to use.

● **3 Extended definition.** Abstract words like *propaganda, democracy, happiness, religion, justice,* and *harassment* may require more than word substitution or a formal sentence definition to make their meaning clear. Extended definitions usually include a formal definition but expand it using examples, analogies, descriptions, and various other explanations to show the reader precisely what is meant. Depending on the complexity of the term being defined, the audience's background, and the importance of the term in the argument, an extended definition might be a single paragraph or many pages long.

The following extended definition of the term *induction* first puts the term into a class of things ("reasoning") and then differentiates it as the kind of reasoning that examines particulars to draw conclusions. This general definition is then developed in two parts: (1) by explaining the kind of scientific reasoning that is inductive, and (2) by explaining, through a series of examples, how our everyday reasoning is inductive.

Induction is the kind of reasoning by which we examine a number of particulars or specific instances and on the basis of them arrive at a conclusion. The scientific method is inductive when the scientist observes a recurrent phenomenon and arrives at the conclusion or hypothesis that under certain conditions this phenomenon will always take place; if in the course of time further observation supports his hypothesis and if no exceptions are observed, his conclusion is generally accepted as truth and is sometimes called a law. In everyday living, too, we arrive at conclusions by induction. Every cat we encounter has claws; we conclude that all cats have claws. Every rose we smell is fragrant; we conclude that all roses are fragrant. An acquaintance has, on various occasions, paid back money he has borrowed; we conclude that he is frequently out of funds but that he pays his debts. Every Saturday morning for six weeks the newspaper boy is late in delivering the paper; we conclude that he sleeps on Saturday mornings and we no longer look for the paper before nine o'clock. In each case we have reasoned induc-

tively from a number of instances; we have moved from an observation of some things to a generalization about all things in the same category.

—Newman and Genevieve Birk, *Understanding and Using English*

Extended definition can be used to clarify terms in an argument, but sometimes it constitutes the whole argument. For example, a charge of sexual harassment may be won or lost in court largely based on whether the alleged behavior meets the legal definition of sexual harassment. The entire case will revolve around definition of terms.

Exercise 7.5

Examine the following definitions below and be prepared to answer these questions about each: Is the class (*genus*) to which the term belongs clearly named? Is the class narrow enough to be satisfactory? Does the definition clearly differentiate the term from other things in the class? Does the definition repeat the term it is defining? Is it stated in parallel form? Rewrite any unsatisfactory definitions.

1 An orange is a fruit.
2 A secretary types, files, and distributes mail.
3 Parched peanuts are when the peanuts have been roasted for about forty minutes at 350 degrees.
4 Gravy is a brown sauce made with meat drippings and flour.
5 Gravy is what slick politicians call fringe benefits.
6 A coaster is a small piece of wood, plastic, or other material placed under a glass to keep watermarks from marring the tabletop.
7 Chaos is when everything gets out of control.
8 A touchdown pass is when the player throws the ball for a touchdown.
9 Skiing is strapping two boards to your feet, pushing yourself off the top of a mountain with two sticks, and praying you will live to see the bottom.
10 A computer manipulates pieces of electronic information. Each single piece of information, called a "bit," exists in electrical form as a high voltage or a low voltage.

Exercise 7.6

Define three of the following terms by word substitution (or by appositive phrases).

1 suitcase
2 Native American
3 condominium
4 sexual harassment
5 athletic scholarship

Now write a formal definition of the same three terms, labeling both the class and the differentiation.

Exercise 7.7

Select one of the following terms (or an abstract term of your own choosing) and write a paragraph of extended definition. Use your first sentence to state a formal definition of the term and then clarify it in the rest of the paragraph. Consult a dictionary for help if necessary.

1 democracy
2 guilt
3 plagiarism
4 recreation
5 maturity

In Your Own Words

Choose a current slang term, one so new that it is not in current dictionaries, and write a one-paragraph extended definition of the term that would educate the reader about both its meaning and the appropriate sentence structure and circumstances for using the term.

7 **e** Anticipate opposing arguments.

Strong arguments anticipate the points that might be raised by the opposition. One good way to prepare for these counterarguments is to do some research; you need to know where, specifically, you and your opponent are likely to disagree. You may be able to find opposing arguments and evidence in books, magazines, journals, and newspapers. If possible, talk to someone who holds an opposing viewpoint to sound out conflicting reasons. You can also ask a friend or classmate to act as devil's advocate and raise as many counterpoints as possible to your assertion and supporting reasons.

From the results of your reading and conversation, make a list of points the opposition may raise. Next to each point, write a counterargument you can use to rebut the opposition. Look for fallacies and weaknesses in the opposition's reasoning; be sure not to include fallacies in your rebuttal points (for a discussion of logical fallacies, see Section **7g**). You probably won't use this list in the order you have written it, but it will help you to remember important points of opposition that you need to take into account when you are drafting your essay.

From such preliminary planning, Kara Lardizabal realized that the strongest argument against her thesis was that U.S. restaurant customers would see no advantage in changing from voluntary tipping to mandatory service charges. Because the present system seems quite satisfactory to most customers, why should they switch to an unfamiliar one? No matter how much fairer a service charge would be for employees or how much simpler for restaurant owners, the bottom line for customers is how the change affects them personally. Thus Kara's analysis of the opposition showed that her counterargument would have to address people's basic distrust of change when they perceive no advantage.

 **Construct your argument.**

Arguments may draw on any of the organizational patterns discussed in earlier chapters. Definition, analogy, cause and effect, comparison and contrast, even narration and description have their place in argumentative writing. Some patterns, such as cause and effect and comparison and contrast, are quite common. Kara's essay in the "Writers Revising" at the end of this chapter relies on comparison and contrast to weigh the pros and cons of mandatory restaurant service charges.

Although the structure of an argument may take a variety of forms, many arguments follow what is called the *standard form*, composed of five basic parts:

Introduction
- Attention-arousing opening (anecdote, example, startling statistic)
- Explanation of issue; definition of terms as necessary
- Other background information as necessary
- Common ground established, if any
- Thesis statement asserting writer's point of view

Summary of opposing viewpoint(s)

Rebuttal of opposing viewpoint(s)
- Weaknesses in opposition's viewpoint attacked
- Strengths in opposition's viewpoint conceded (counterbalanced against strengths in writer's argument)

Explanation of writer's viewpoint
- Writer's claims, evidence, and warrants developed
- Supporting points presented and argued (opposing viewpoints may be reviewed and rebutted here)

Conclusion
- Strengths of writer's argument weighed against opposition
- Thesis assertion shown to be proven

Identifying common ground—issues or points upon which you and the opposition can agree—will strengthen the persuasiveness of your argument. For example, agreeing that everyone wants safe streets can set the stage for a reasoned discussion of how best to achieve that goal.

If you have researched opposing viewpoints, you should be able to summarize them fairly and acknowledge their valid points. In the rebuttal, you may find it more effective to concede the opposition's strengths first and then discuss its weaknesses, rather than the other way around. The subsequent explanation of your viewpoint will benefit from the contrast.

Anticipating opposing viewpoints during the planning stage helps you generate a counterargument that identifies the opposition's weaknesses. Apart from attacking an opponent's reasoning by spotting logical fallacies (see Section **7g**), refuting the evidence is one of the most common ways of revealing weaknesses in an opposing viewpoint. The following are some weaknesses to watch for.

Opinions or interpretations offered as fact. Be alert for incorrect information or opinion that is not validated by sufficient information.

Examples or testimony that can be contradicted or shown to be unrepresentative or insufficient. If you can provide experience, observations, instances, or experts that counter those offered by the opposition, you will cast doubt on your opponent's argument. Showing that there are numerous exceptions to your opponent's representative sample suggests that the opponent is offering atypical cases.

Examples, testimony, or statistics that are irrelevant or not recent enough. Be alert for evidence that is fundamentally unrelated to the issues at hand (red herrings) or that is outdated. Also examine the methods opponents used to collect and interpret data. Were they scientific and careful, or sloppy?

Authorities and experts who lack credibility. Simply because a person is a doctor, he or she may not be an expert in every area of medicine. Gynecologists do not usually make good brain surgeons. Check for relevant expertise on the part of people being offered as authorities. Also look at their objectivity: Are their opinions derived from evidence, or are they the result of biased interpretation?

Exercise 7.8

Find a newspaper or magazine article, or better yet a person, expressing an opinion with which you disagree. Consider the opinion carefully and then restate it in your own words as accurately as you can. Ask another person to read your version and compare it to the original. Then write a counterargument that rebuts the original and supports your own point of view.

7 g Check the logic of your argument.

As you write your argument and look for weaknesses in opposing counterarguments, it is important to check for errors in the logic, called **fallacies**. Most common fallacies can be categorized as either fallacies of oversimplification or fallacies of distortion.

● **1 Fallacies of oversimplification.** Fallacies of oversimplification occur when an arguer draws a conclusion from insufficient evidence, generalizing from too few facts. Generalization is essential to thinking; without it, we could not evaluate experience—only accumulate isolated bits of data. Similarly, generalization is essential to argument. An argument's main assertion may be presented as a generalization: "Most people are indifferent to local politics" or "Assault weapons should be banned." Because arguments of any length or complexity are comprised of clusters or chains of smaller, related arguments whose proof supports the main assertion, writers typically use a number of generalizations in the course of convincing their audiences. But like any claim, generalizations must be supported by sufficient evidence—neither too broad nor too hasty, relying on neither false choices nor false comparisons.

Hasty generalizations. Do not leap to conclusions on the basis of insufficient evidence. It is tempting to generalize from a few striking examples, especially when they agree with what we want to believe. However, unless examples are irrefutably typical, they can lead to fallacies or even absurd assertions.

PARTICULAR A	The newspaper reported that a child was recently mauled by a pit bull dog.
PARTICULAR B	My mother's mail carrier was bitten by a pit bull dog last year.
PARTICULAR C	The gas meter reader said a pit bull chased her from its yard.
HASTY GENERALIZATION	As a breed, pit bull dogs are vicious.

Hasty generalizations rely on unfair **stereotypes**; they make assertions about groups containing thousands of individuals on the basis of a few examples which may not be at all typical of the entire class.

To construct a valid argument and to be fair to your readers, never advance a generalization unless you can support it with sufficient evidence. Two or three examples may be enough when your readers are likely to have encountered evidence elsewhere in their experience, but if readers are likely to be skeptical or unfamiliar with the issue, you will need to analyze the evidence in detail. If you can think of exceptions to the generalization, you can be sure your readers will too. Consequently, you should prepare a counterargument to handle them (see Section **7f**).

Broad generalizations. Be careful about using words such as *always, never, all, none, every, right, wrong* in generalizations. Sweeping statements invite readers to start thinking of exceptions even before you've presented your evidence. Many an otherwise reasonable assertion has foundered for lack of *seldom* instead of *never, usually* instead of *always.*

OVERSTATED	Playing football always results in injury.
	Playing football results in injury.
QUALIFIED	Playing football sometimes results in injury.
	Playing football can result in injury.

Note that an overstated generalization need not specifically state that it applies to *all* people. By not making a qualification it clearly implies *all*, as in the second overstatement in the preceding examples. Similarly, words other than modifiers can act as qualifiers. For example, the verbs *can* and *may* prevent overstatement, as in the second qualification in the preceding example, where *can* implies possibility rather than certainty.

Inadequate cause or *post hoc, ergo propter hoc* ("after this, therefore because of this"). Don't assume that a cause-and-effect relationship exists between two facts simply because one follows the other in time.

> The Navy began allowing women to serve on its ships in the 1970s, and its preparedness has decreased steadily since then. [The newspaper columnist who made this statement ignored other important factors such as cuts in defense spending and a shortage of new vessels and equipment, all of which adversely affected the Navy's military strength.]

False analogy. Don't assume that because two circumstances or ideas are alike in some respects, they are alike in all respects. When one or two points are analogous, it is very tempting to go overboard and claim that two situations or concepts are wholly analogous. Political speeches, for example, are full of oversimplified, faulty analogies.

> I don't believe you can run a major U.S. company from abroad. George III tried to run the United States from Britain, and look what happened to him.
> —Sir Gordon White
> [About the only commonality between the eighteenth-century monarch facing the American Revolution and the head of a twentieth-century multinational corporation is the ocean between continents.]

Analogy can be a useful persuasive tool, but although it can clarify, it can never prove a point. Analogy's value increases in direct proportion to the number of parallels you can cite and decreases with every difference your reader perceives (see Section **6b**).

Either/or fallacy. Don't claim there are only two alternatives if, in fact, there are several. Truth sometimes is an either/or sort of thing: Either you passed the examination, or you failed it. But most things about which we argue are not as clear-cut. During the Vietnam War, some automobiles carried bumper stickers asserting "America. Love it or leave it." Of course, Americans may protest their government's policies without being unpatriotic, although this bumper sticker fallaciously suggested otherwise.

> Students come to college for one of two reasons: either to study or to party. Judging by Mack's attendance at campus mixers, I'd say he didn't come to study. [It's possible Mack studies very little, if at all. It's also possible that he studies very efficiently and thus has free time to go to parties. Many combinations of studying and partying, to say nothing of the endless possibilities that include neither studying nor partying, are available to college students.]

Exercise 7.9

Explain what is wrong with the reasoning in the following statements, and try to identify the fallacies of oversimplification that occur.

1. Alex says he has had more luck getting dates with girls since he stopped working at the computer center. He says that girls obviously thought he was a nerd because he worked there.
2. The best place for a child to live is with his or her biological parents.
3. If you really loved me, you'd spend our anniversary here at home instead of going on that business trip.
4. We have laws that keep stray dogs off the streets. Why can't we pass some that will keep drug dealers off the streets?
5. Either you support antiabortion legislation or you're not a Christian.
6. It doesn't pay to study too hard. Last week I studied all night before the exam, but I flunked it in spite of that.
7. Unless gays are banned from the military, no straight military personnel will be safe.
8. I'd do a lot better in my studies if my parents would buy me a lap-top computer.
9. Making condoms available in high schools is like giving a thief a license to steal.
10. Her repeated failure to find a job indicates that she lacks ambition.

In Your Own Words

Choose a letter to the editor from a daily newspaper and find a magazine advertisement. List the fallacies of oversimplification and distortion in each. Then write a two-paragraph discussion in which you explain which of the two is the weaker argument and why.

● **2 Fallacies of distortion.** If you ignore counterarguments, you will weaken your own position. Worse, if you try to divert attention from counterarguments by appealing to your readers' prejudice and emotions, your argument will be distorted and unfair.

Slanted language. Slanted language distorts meaning by using **connotation** to appeal to emotion and prejudice (see Chapter 23). For example, today words like *radical, permissive,* and *cover-up* produce negative responses from many people, whereas words like *freedom, responsibility,* and *efficiency* produce positive responses. These words evoke emotional rather than reasoned reactions. Ironically, it's not unusual to find diametrically opposed positions described by the same connotative language. "Fiscal responsibility" can mean a tax cut in one politician's campaign and a tax increase in another's. This shows the danger of slanted language: People are persuaded to draw conclusions without learning the facts of the matter.

Transfer. Don't associate a famous name with an idea or cause in the hope that the reputation of the celebrity will persuade people to accept your point of view. Unlike argument from authority, which legitimately uses expert testimony as a form of evidence, transfer relies on the principle of greatness by association. A celebrity often has no more expertise on a subject than the average person. Examples are professional athletes' endorsements of motor oil or coffee makers.

> We are the political party of Franklin D. Roosevelt and John F. Kennedy. Our campaign platform follows in that great democratic tradition.

> If Miss America can get beautiful hair like this using Goo shampoo, you can too.

Argumentum ad hominem (argument to the man). This type of distorted reasoning ignores the point being argued and attacks a person's character instead. An *ad hominem* argument is similar to a red herring because it substitutes a false issue for bona fide proof. Furthermore, even though discredited for one thing, a person may be right about others.

> Why should you believe what Hartwell says about the needs of our schools? He is suspected of taking bribes. [Apart from the fact that Hartwell is only suspected of taking bribes, what he has to say about school needs may be based on extensive study and analysis.]

Argumentum ad populum (argument to the people). This fallacy arouses deeply held emotions about institutions and ideas. When politicians evoke God, country, or motherhood, they are making an argument to the people—as, for example, when candidates say they will protect the interests of the American family.

A slightly different fallacy that uses similar crowd appeal is the *bandwagon* approach. This fallacy says that what is right for the masses is right for the individual: One must go along with the crowd in belief or action. Obviously this is not true, as many incidents of mob behavior have shown. Nevertheless, the bandwagon is a favorite ploy among advertisers (and children) who claim that everyone is buying or doing something.

> But Mom, all the kids are wearing shorts [or rollerskates or green wigs] to the prom!

> The responsible citizens of this state know that a vote for Jenkins is a vote for open and honest government.

Non sequitur. Don't substitute inference for a logically sound conclusion. A non sequitur ("it does not follow") is a fallacy that occurs when a premise requiring proof is put forward as true. A related fallacy is called **circular argument.**

> This insurance policy is a wise purchase. It covers all expenses related to cancer treatment. [Although the policy may pay cancer-related expenses, the

statement assumes the buyer will get cancer. If he or she does not, the policy may not have been a wise purchase.]

His handwriting is hard to read because it is illegible. [This argument does not move from premise to conclusion but merely moves in a circle. *Illegible* means "difficult or impossible to read."]

Red herring. Don't introduce a false issue in the hope of leading your reader away from a real one. A red herring supplies a false scent in an argument, diverting the hounds from their quarry and leading them down an irrelevant trail. Usually the false issue elicits an emotional reaction, sidetracking the reader's attention from the real issue and the proof it needs.

> American tax dollars must not be spent to support medical research and treatment that uses fetal tissue. Such hideous scientific experiments performed with the remains of unborn children simply play into the hands of criminal abortionists who encourage pregnant women to abort their unborn babies for profit. [Any reasoned ethical or scientific debate concerning the role of fetal tissue research is completely obscured by the specter of women being paid to undergo abortions. Here the writer introduces extremely loaded language and a highly emotional issue to short-circuit discussion. Medical advances in the treatment of several fatal diseases and genetic conditions are never mentioned; nor is the fact that the tissue is not purchased from abortion clinics.]

Exercise 7.10

Explain the errors in reasoning in the following statements, and try to identify the fallacies of distortion that occur.

1 My parents taught us that if we did our very best on every job, we would never be without one.
2 If Lee were less scatterbrained, she'd be more organized for her presentation.
3 After his divorce, Mr. Jones left his children with his sister and took a construction job in another state. I don't think he should get custody of his children.
4 Since all my friends have a 1:00 A.M. curfew, I shouldn't have to come in at midnight.
5 Americans who want a better life will support this legislation.
6 Casey's Garage has never done good work on my car, and I think the place should be closed down for good.
7 Bill Swartz, the famous actor, uses the Miracle Quick Weight Loss plan. That's the one you ought to try.
8 Tullia filed for bankruptcy a few years ago. Surely you don't want her to serve as our treasurer.
9 Why shouldn't I be allowed to drive to Florida for spring break with Stacey and Michelle, Dad? Nothing will happen.
10 Since he avoided being drafted during the Vietnam War, he has no right to

be Commander in Chief of the Armed Forces. Therefore, we should not vote for him for President.

Argument Checklist

- Is your thesis assertion arguable?
- What do you want your readers to do after reading your argument? Do you want action, a change in belief, or just a fair hearing?
- Have you defined important terms that readers will find unfamiliar or whose definitions are open to dispute?
- Based on your analysis of the audience (convinced, neutral, or skeptical), have you used the types of evidence (facts, examples, statistics, testimony from eyewitnesses, research results from credible authorities) that will convince readers of your claim?
- Can you argue from your own experience or do you need to do some research? Where can you obtain the evidence you need?
- Will readers accept the warrant in your argument (the connection between claim and evidence) as true, or do you need to prove the truth of the warrant as well?
- Have you balanced logic, emotion, and credibility? How careful should you be about the connotations of the language or examples you use? Are the authorities you cite trustworthy? Will readers perceive them (and you) as trustworthy?
- Have you been able to find any common ground, a shared goal, or one or more points upon which you and your audience can agree? Establishing common goals may help persuade the audience of the relevance of your overall point of view.
- Have you anticipated and answered objections from the opposition? Have you been fair in presenting opposing points of view?
- Have you avoided fallacies of logic or other mistakes in reasoning?

In Your Own Words

Prepare a counterargument for at least one of the following arguments. Be sure your counterargument exposes any fallacious reasoning you find in the statements and does not itself contain fallacies. In addition, anticipate and defuse objections likely to be raised by the opposition.

1 We should not allow women to become police officers. They would have to work long hours with men and would create morale problems for the men's wives.

2 There is no excuse for the large number of homeless people. The jobs are out there if they want them.

3 Since 1964, scores on Scholastic Aptitude Tests have been dropping. What's more, students graduating from high school today can neither read nor write nor do arithmetic at their grade level. Clearly, the minimum competency testing program used in Jacksonville, Florida, should be instituted nation-wide. A student who can't pass these standardized tests shouldn't graduate.

4 My roommate will make a terrific veterinarian. She just loves animals. She's always bringing home stray dogs and cats. It really upsets her to see an animal suffer.

5 If a coat or suit becomes old, ragged, and out of style, we don't continue to wear it. We replace it with a new one. Similarly, employees who reach age sixty-five should be forced to retire to make way for younger people with energy and fresh ideas.

Review Exercise

Argument

Analyze several automobile, alcoholic beverage, cosmetic, or over-the-counter drug advertisements on television or in current magazines. Also analyze several cigarette advertisements in magazines. Use the following questions as your guide:

1 What fallacies can you find?

2 Are all important terms defined clearly?

3 What kinds of generalizations are used or assumed? Are these generalizations supported adequately?

4 Are cause-and-effect relationships clear and indisputable?

5 Is slanted language used? What is the advertiser trying to achieve with the connotative language?

6 Does *logos, ethos,* or *pathos* predominate in the ads? Does one particular type of appeal seem to predominate in the advertising for a particular type of product?

Writers Revising

The following is a draft of the argumentative essay Kara Lardizabal wrote about the pros and cons of voluntary tipping versus mandatory service charges in restaurants. Examine the draft for weaknesses in structure and reasoning. Does it contain any fallacies of oversimplification or distortion? Does the argument show sufficient analysis of the audience (her instructor and classmates)? Does it take counterarguments into account?

After you have critiqued Kara's draft, read her revised argumentative essay to see if she has solved the problems you detected. Has she persuaded you to her point of view? Why or why not?

Draft

A party of six enjoyed a leisurely dinner that began with cocktails, included three courses, and finished with dessert and cappuccino. The waitress

provided friendly, attentive service, making sure the
food was served promptly, keeping glasses filled.
After the diners departed she found a ten-dollar bill
on the table. At 15% per check, her tip should have
been $12. The two dollars the customers "stiffed" her
amounted to less than 35¢ per person at the table,
but to the waitress it represented a loss of nearly
16% on what she should have received for her service.
I am that waitress, and if you were one of those customers you robbed me. You cheated me out of the money
that I need to pay for my rent, my college tuition,
and my groceries.

The few cents an individual customer fails to
leave his or her server can quickly mount up to substantial accumulated losses for the employee. That is
why I think the voluntary tipping policy now in
effect at most restaurants in the United States
should be replaced by a mandatory 15% service charge
added to each check. What's wrong with Americans that
they can't do the civilized thing like the rest of
the world? Europe has had service charges for years.
U.S. restaurants should do the same.

Service charges are widely used in Europe. For
example, most hotels and restaurants automatically
add 10% to 20% to the bill. My friend Roberto
Rosanova, who worked as a waiter in his uncle's
restaurant in Milan, Italy, says that is the case in
all nice restaurants in Italy. At his uncle's restaurant, for instance, the bill has servizio compreso
(service included) written on it. Some restaurants,
especially those with a sidewalk cafe in front, also
add a coperta or cover charge. Because sidewalk cafe
customers tend to order coffee or drinks, their total
bill (and service charge) will be relatively small.
Roberto says the coperta helps make up for the fact
that the waiter has given as much service as if the
customer had ordered a whole meal. In addition to the
servizio and the coperta, Italians usually still
leave a small tip for the waiter (cameriere).

Restaurants now using mandatory service charges
report favorable customer reaction. Michael Fawcett,

manager of the Rattlesnake Club in Denver, says that
customers like the service charge system. Fawcett
believes people like it because with the service
charge they don't have to figure out how much to leave
the server. This information contrasts with a poll
taken for _Time_ magazine in which 77% of those polled
said they did not favor a service charge of 15% to
18% added to their bill. An official at the National
Restaurant Association believes that Americans like
tipping because they can reward or punish good or bad
service. "You just don't take that right away from
people," he says. To sample local opinion, I took a
poll of my customers at the Grill restaurant. My poll
showed that 54% of them would not mind a 15% service
charge.

How do restaurant owners feel about mandatory
service charges? The Grill's manager, Joan Trumble,
thinks a number of owners are seriously considering a
service charge and would adopt it in a minute if customers would accept it. The reason is taxes.

It used to be that how much a restaurant employee
earned in tips was a private matter between server and
customer. Since 1982, however, the issue of tips is of
concern to owners as well. Because of changes in federal tax laws, restaurant owners now must keep records
and report employees' tips to the IRS. In addition,
owners must pay Social Security and unemployment taxes
on their employees' tips. The government's goal was to
close a tax loophole on billions of dollars in unreported income from tips. But the result has been a
bookkeeping nightmare and major expenses for restaurant owners. Eventually these expenses will be passed
along to customers: Either they'll pay through
increased menu prices or they'll pay through a service
charge.

Owners who use a service charge, such as the
Rattlesnake Club's James Schmidt, say it has allowed
them to raise employees' wages and pay them health
benefits, as well as "keep the IRS happy." Employees
say that they are able to get loans and credit more
easily because their wages and the flat service charge

provide a "verifiable income," which was not the case
when tips were involved.

Interestingly, in most restaurants a mandatory
service charge is quite common for parties of six or
more. If customers find it fair and convenient under
these circumstances, would they object under other
circumstances? Probably not. And it would keep them
from cheating their servers out of fair compensation.

Revision

"Try It--You'll Like It":
A Case for Restaurant Service Charges

A party of six enjoyed a leisurely four-course
dinner that began with cocktails and finished with
dessert and cappuccino. The waitress provided friendly, attentive service. She not only took their orders
promptly and made sure the food was served hot, but
she also checked on their needs throughout the meal,
bringing extra rolls and keeping glasses filled. After
the diners departed she found a ten-dollar bill on
the table. At 15% per check, her tip should have been
$12. The two dollars the customers "stiffed" her
amounted to less than 35¢ per person at the table,
but to the waitress it represented a loss of nearly
16% on what she should have received for her service.
The few cents an individual customer fails to leave
his or her server can quickly mount up to substantial
losses for the employee.

I am the waitress who lost the two-dollar tip.
Is my service to those restaurant customers different
from the service provided by the technician who
repairs their television set or the carpenter who
puts the new deck on their house? It is not.
Restaurant service, television repair, and deck
installation are all skilled labor, and people should
be willing to pay fairly for such services. Because
restaurant servers are so frequently short-changed, I
think the voluntary tipping policy now in effect at
most restaurants in the United States should be
replaced by a mandatory 15% service charge added to
each check. True, customers would probably object to

the policy in the beginning. But customer acceptance
in other countries and at restaurants in the U.S.
that have tried service charges suggests that the
public would soon become accustomed to it. Service
charges would also solve some tax problems for
restaurant owners as well as being more fair to
servers.

Service charges are widely used in Europe. For
example, most hotels and restaurants automatically add
10% to 20% to the bill. My friend Roberto Rosanova,
who worked as a waiter in his uncle's restaurant in
Milan, Italy, says service charges are the norm in all
nice restaurants in Italy. At his uncle's restaurant,
for instance, the bill has servizio compreso (service
included) written on it. Italian restaurant checks may
even include additional charges. Some restaurants,
especially those with a sidewalk cafe in front, also
add a coperta or cover charge. Because sidewalk cafe
customers tend to order coffee or drinks, their total
bill (and service charge) will be relatively small.
Roberto says the coperta helps make up for the fact
that the waiter has given nearly as much service as if
the customer had ordered a whole meal. In addition to
the servizio and the coperta, Italians usually still
leave a small tip for the waiter (cameriere).

There is disagreement over how American customers
would react to mandatory service charges. Barry Wine,
who owned the Quilted Giraffe in New York City, and
Michael Fawcett, manager of the Rattlesnake Club in
Denver, say that customers like the service charge system used at their restaurants. Fawcett believes people
like it because with the service charge they don't have
to figure out how much to leave the server. This information contrasts with a poll taken for Time magazine in
which 77% of those polled said they did not favor a
service charge of 15% to 18% added to their bill. An
official at the National Restaurant Association believes
that Americans like tipping because they can reward or
punish good or bad service. "You just don't take that
right away from people," he says. To sample local opinion, I took a poll of my customers at the Grill

restaurant. My poll showed that 54% of them would not mind a 15% service charge--as long as the service was good.

To see what the reaction might be on the other side of the table, I polled the twenty-eight service staff members at the Grill. Seventy percent favored mandatory service charges as long as the charge is at least 15% of the bill. Those in favor believed that 20% is not necessary because a 15% tip would make up for those customers who under-tip on the current voluntary system. The 30% of waiters and waitresses who were against a mandatory service charge thought that many customers will boycott restaurants with service charges and take their business where tipping is still voluntary. They also believe mandatory charges will actually reduce their income because they usually make tips of more than 15%.

How do restaurant owners feel about mandatory service charges? One indicator might be the number of restaurants using it. According to the National Restaurant Association, only about 5% of the restaurants in the United States use a service charge. The Grill's manager, Joan Trumble, says fear of driving away customers is certainly a major reason. Another is the widely held belief that tips are an incentive to work hard and provide good service. However, she thinks a number of owners are seriously considering a service charge and would adopt it in a minute if customers would accept it. The reason is taxes.

It used to be that how much a restaurant employee earned in tips was a private matter between server and customer. Since 1982, however, the issue of tips is of concern to owners as well. Because of changes in federal tax laws, restaurant owners now must keep records and report employees' tips to the IRS. In addition, owners must pay Social Security and unemployment taxes on their employees' tips. The government's goal was to close a tax loophole on billions of dollars in unreported income from tips. But the result has been a bookkeeping nightmare and major expenses for restaurant owners. A flat mandatory ser-

vice charge, which corresponds to the labor charge
people pay to have their car fixed or their house
painted, would simplify bookkeeping and tax reporting
considerably.

As well as keeping the IRS happy, owners who use
a service charge, such as the Rattlesnake Club's James
Schmidt, say it has also allowed them to raise employees' wages and pay them health benefits. Employees say
that they are able to get loans and credit more easily
because their wages now provide a "verifiable income,"
which was not the case when tips were involved.

It appears, then, that the primary reason that
American restaurants have not switched from voluntary
tipping to a mandatory service charge is fear of customer reaction. Mike Hurst, an official at the National
Restaurant Association, doubts that service charges
will ever catch on in the U.S. "Look how quickly the
public has adjusted to the metric system," says Hurst,
drawing an analogy between the two. Although the metric system, like mandatory service charges, is a
European import, the similarity ends there. In fact,
most American restaurants commonly add a flat service
charge of 15% or 20% to the bill for parties of six or
more. The fact that customers find it fair and convenient under these circumstances suggests they are
likely to accept a routine service charge more easily
than the critics suppose. I think it's worth a try.

Analysis

Kara's draft needed substantial work. Three major problems are
immediately apparent. First, Kara was guilty of slanting her argument
by failing to take the opposition's valid points into account. She omitted points that were not in her favor. The revision acknowledges the
opposition in the paragraphs 2, 4, 5, and 6, where Kara mentions
resistance from customers, service staff, and restaurant owners. She
actually strengthens her argument by raising and addressing these
objections. It is quite likely that readers will think of these opposing
points themselves, and Kara's draft would have left them unanswered.

The second major problem is lack of coherence and unity. The
draft delivers information and testimony from various sources but
does not always show the relationship between this evidence and

Kara's point of view. For example, the discussion about IRS reporting in draft paragraph 6 is likely to be fairly murky to anyone not in the restaurant business. When Kara compares the mandatory service charge to labor charges (with which most readers would be familiar), she uses known information to help readers understand new information and see her point.

The third problem in the draft concerns audience awareness and logic. The audience might view her original opening as an attack on them. Kara has introduced the "party of six" who short-change the waitress, and then shifted the point of view to "you" (the reader) and "I" (the waitress). Kara deliberately causes the point of view to move from disinterested third-person pronouns to fully engaged first- and second-person pronouns to draw the reader into the opening scene. But then she must be careful not to insult or anger readers: The slanted language, calling readers robbers and cheats, is likely to alienate them. She wants to induce a little bit of guilt in her readers, but she needs to stop short of a personal attack that would cause them to be defensive rather than sympathetic (or at least willing to listen) to her argumentative stance. In the revision, Kara decided to drop the slanted language and try to establish some common ground instead. She compares restaurant servers to other skilled workers, making the point that the labor of the waitress, the electronics technician, and the carpenter should be compensated in the same way. Since the technician and carpenter add a labor charge to their bills, a restaurant server should be able to do the same thing. Kara reiterates this analogy later in the seventh paragraph.

The argument to the people (bandwagon) fallacy ("like the rest of the world") and the name calling ("what's wrong with Americans") in paragraph 2 have also been eliminated. Paragraph 4, which contained a sweeping generalization (the suggestion that all restaurant owners using service charges had received favorable customer responses—a claim Kara cannot make on the basis of only Fawcett's testimony), has been revised. She also removed the either/or fallacy at the end of draft paragraph 6.

Kara's revision shows that she has recognized the writer's responsibility to play fair with the available information. In paragraph 4 she owns up to the fact that the Grill's customers' acceptance of a mandatory charge is conditional—tied to good service. Paragraph 6 addresses the statistic that few American restaurants actually use a service charge. However, placing Joan Trumble's opinion at the end of the paragraph provides a positive counterpoint and effective transition to the next paragraph, which discusses several points in favor of service charges.

In the revised essay's conclusion, Kara neatly reveals a fallacy used by the opposition. She points out the false analogy between mandatory service charges and the metric system, thus weakening the opposition's argument. Then she turns the tables, arguing by extension that rather than rejecting mandatory service charges, restaurant customers have actually been accepting them quite readily—in the form of flat service charges for groups of six or more. She has transformed a weak ending (a rhetorical question that allows readers to provide an opposing answer, followed by a flabby, negatively worded conclusion) into a strong, positive finish.

Part 2

Effective Sentences

Every people has its own characteristic classes in which individuals pigeonhole their experiences. These classes are established primarily by the language.... The language says, as it were, "notice this," "always consider this separate from that," "such and such things belong together." ...experience is much less an objective absolute than we thought. Every language has an effect upon what the people who use it see, what they feel, how they think....

—Clyde Kluckhohn, "The Gift of Tongues"

8 Coordination and Subordination

9 Parallelism

10 Emphasis

11 Variety

It's one thing to write sentences that are grammatical; it's another to write sentences that not only convey information but also explicitly establish the relationships among the ideas they are intended to express. Writers sometimes think effective sentences are just a matter of style, a concern important in poetry and novels but not vital to everyday writing.

As the following paragraph illustrates, nothing could be farther from the truth. The writer, a manager at a large manufacturing company, forgot that one of his roles is to *make meaning*, to show his reader the connections among the chunks of information he presents. As they stand, his sentences are correct, but they give equal emphasis to everything—and, consequently, to nothing. What's more, when he reviewed this paragraph, the writer discovered he had actually subordinated major ideas and stressed minor details. He concluded that, indeed, sentence structure has a lot to do with how a reader perceives meaning. Compare the original version with the revision that follows it.

> I usually dislike writing. I particularly dislike writing under pressure. My last four written documents were a plant appropriation request, a business letter, and two personal letters. The plant appropriation request was a thirty-five page report. It was prepared for the department staff's review and approval. I was trying to justify a request for funds to purchase a new computer system. The business letter was addressed to a system designer and confirmed a scheduled project review meeting. This letter also contained a list of issues and questions that I wanted discussed during the review. Both the report and the letter had to be written on short notice, and both involved thousands of dollars in business transactions. Thoroughly disliking the task, I really worried about the effect pressure was having on my writing. The two personal letters were written to friends, and I enjoyed writing them because I could relax.

> I usually dislike writing, particularly when under pressure. My last four documents were a plant appropriation request, a business letter, and two personal letters. The plant appropriation request, a thirty-five page report that was prepared for the department staff's review and approval, justified my request for funds to purchase a new computer system. The business letter, addressed to a system designer and confirming a scheduled project review meeting, also contained a list of issues and questions I wanted discussed during the review. Both the report and the letter had to be written on short notice. Because both involved thousands of dollars in business transactions, I really worried about the effect pressure was having on my writing. Consequently, I thoroughly disliked the task. In contrast, because the two personal letters were written to friends, I could relax and enjoy writing them.

Notice that the writer combined some sentences, inserting details previously placed in separate sentences. He also moved some combinations from one sentence to another. For example, instead of leaving the ideas concerning short notice and expensive transactions in a coordinated sentence (the ideas connected by *and*), he decided to develop the cause-and-effect relationship between business responsibility, time pressure, and effective writing. He stressed his dislike of the situation in a short, simple sentence that now varies from the other sentence patterns, thus drawing extra attention to the idea; but he used a connecting word (*consequently*) to show the sentence's relationship to the preceding thought.

Because the ideas are now shaped by sentence structures that clarify meaning, the reader is much more likely to understand what the writer intended. The following sections discuss ways you can use sentence structure effectively.

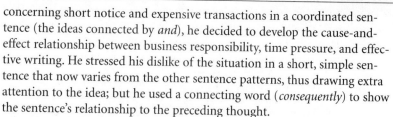

8 Coordination and Subordination

In a broad sense, **coordination** expresses equality: Two things that are coordinate have roughly the same importance, the same rank, the same value. **Subordination** expresses inequality: When one thing is subordinate to or dependent on another, it is of lesser importance, rank, or value. Coordination and subordination allow writers to indicate relationships among ideas by means of grammatical form and placement, without having to say directly "This is equal to that" or "This information is additional, qualifying detail—important, but not as important as the main idea."

8 a Use coordination to connect equal, related ideas.

Coordination allows you to combine separate ideas of equal importance into a single sentence by creating compound subjects, objects, modifiers, whole predicates, or sentences.

● **1 Coordinating conjunctions.** Using coordinating conjunctions to connect words, phrases, and clauses—and putting them in the same grammatical form—you can express clear relationships between ideas without needless repetition. Coordinating conjunctions are the words *and, but, or, nor, so, yet, for.*

> Dogs belong to the Canidae family. Foxes belong to the Canidae family. Jackals belong to the Canidae family.
>
> *Dogs, foxes,* and *jackals* belong to the Canidae family. [coordinate subjects]
>
> Members of the Canidae family possess four legs. They eat meat. They have acute senses of smell.
>
> Members of the Canidae family possess four legs, eat meat, and have acute senses of smell. [coordinate verbs *possess, eat,* and *have*; coordinate objects *legs, meat,* and *senses*]

One of the family's general characteristics is a long muzzle. Another is large canine teeth. Another is a long tail.

The family's general characteristics are a long muzzle, large canine teeth, and a long tail. [coordinate predicate nouns *muzzle, teeth,* and *tail*]

Historians believe that the dog may have been the first animal to be domesticated, that the dog has been domesticated for about 10,000 years, and that the earliest dogs looked like the wild Australian Dingo. [coordinate noun clauses]

Dogs have been bred to herd other animals, they have been trained to track and retrieve game, they have been used for guides, and they have been bred to provide companionship to people. [coordinate independent clauses]

● **2 Correlative conjunctions and conjunctive adverbs.** Correlative conjunctions work in pairs: *both-and, either-or, neither-nor, not-but, not only-but also.* Conjunctive adverbs are words such as *however, consequently, therefore,* and *nonetheless.* Unlike correlative conjunctions, conjunctive adverbs *never* connect words, phrases, or dependent clauses; they coordinate whole sentences only (see also Section **33b**).

The domestic species is characterized by its worldwide distribution in close association with humans. It is also characterized by its enormous amount of genetic variability.

The domestic species is characterized not only by its worldwide distribution in close association with humans but also by its enormous amount of genetic variability. [coordinate adverbial prepositional phrases joined by correlative conjunctions *not only* and *but also*]

The Canidae family is sometimes loosely referred to as the dog family. The term "dog" usually refers only to the domestic species.

The Canidae family is sometimes loosely called the dog family; however, the term "dog" usually refers only to the domestic species. [conjunctive adverb *however* coordinating two sentences]

As these examples illustrate, coordination allows you to combine complex ideas and information from several sentences. When ideas are equal and closely related, you aid your readers if you can bring the ideas together into a single, easy-to-follow sentence that reveals those relationships. Compare the following:

Winter is the season when animals get stripped down to the marrow. Humans also do. Animals can take the winter easy by hibernating. Humans are exposed naked to the currents of elation and depression.

Winter is the season when *both* animals *and* humans get stripped down to the marrow, *but* many animals can hibernate, take the winter easy, as it were; we humans are exposed naked to the currents of elation and depression.

—May Sarton, *Plant Dreaming Deep*

Although the information in both versions is much the same, the first forces the reader to work much harder to discover that animals and humans share the same exposure to winter, but with different effects. May Sarton's single sentence pulls all the relationships tightly and clearly together for the reader by first linking *animals* and *humans* with the coordinating pair *both...and.* Sarton then establishes the idea of contrast between them with *but,* and she carries out the contrast by linking the statements about animals on the one hand and humans on the other with the semicolon, itself a coordinating link.

Exercise 8.1

In the following sentences and paragraph, combine sentences by using coordinating conjunctions either to form compound sentences or to link similar elements to form compound sentences or to link similar elements to form compound subjects, objects, predicates, or modifiers. You may need to make slight changes in wording. If appropriate, use a conjunctive adverb with a semicolon to coordinate two sentences. After you have combined the sentences in items 1 through 5, rewrite them as a paragraph. Revise and recombine sentences as necessary to make a smooth, coherent paragraph.

Sentence Practice

1 The word *wolf* may conjure up childhood visions of horror from "Little Red Riding Hood." It may remind us of the villain in "The Three Little Pigs." The word *shark* may remind us of the terrors in the movie *Jaws.* Such images have conditioned many people to think of wolves and sharks as monsters which live only to terrorize and prey on humans.

2 This fear of sharks and wolves has resulted in the near extermination of some species of each. This fear has made it easy for humans to rationalize killing these species for economic reasons. Wolves have been killed off to protect livestock. Sharks have been killed for their meat. Sharks are killed for their fins. Sometimes sharks are killed only for their highly prized jaws.

3 Like wolves, sharks attack relatively few humans each year. Scientists estimate that sharks kill only five to ten humans worldwide each year. They injure only another sixty or so annually. Many people still believe that sharks are a major threat to humans.

4 Scientists do not know how many sharks are left in the world's oceans. They have been able to estimate more accurately the scant number of wolves that survive.

5 Wolves used to roam over most countries in the northern hemisphere. Today in North America they are found in healthy numbers only in Alaska, Minnesota, and Canada. Now, environmentalists are planning to reintroduce wolves to Yellowstone National Park. Wolves have been restored to the Great Smoky Mountains National Park in Tennessee. They have been reintroduced into Alligator River National Wildlife Refuge in North Carolina.

Paragraph Practice

Reducing the populations of both wolves and sharks has begun to have serious environmental consequences. Scientists believe that even more serious consequences will result from continued killing of wolves and sharks. Some prey of sharks, such as octupuses and stingrays, will reproduce rapidly without the predators. This population explosion will mean that surrounding food chains will become unbalanced. Without wolves to thin the numbers, the elk population in the northwestern United States will continue to overtax the food supply. The loss of natural predators will have more subtle long-term effects. Without such predators as wolves and sharks, the genetically weakest species, previously an easy mark for predators, will be more likely to survive. The weaker species will then breed. Over time, this breeding may weaken the species. Humans must come to terms with their irrational fears of wolves and sharks. If they do not, they may face staggering environmental problems that will result from the extermination of these necessary predators.

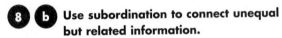

Use subordination to connect unequal but related information.

Put the central idea in the main clause and less important ideas in subordinate constructions. Readers rely on your sentence construction to reveal the meaning you intend. Consequently, the main clause of a sentence should carry your central idea; details, qualifications, and other relevant information that is closely related to but less important than the central idea should be put into subordinate constructions. Deciding which information to subordinate and which to place in the sentence's main clause depends on where you want to focus your reader's attention.

Consider the following sentences as possible topic sentences for a paragraph:

Gorillas have often been killed to permit the capture of their young for zoos, and humans have recently been occupying more and more of their habitat, and gorillas are now threatened with extinction.

Because gorillas have often been killed to permit the capture of their young for zoos, and humans have recently been occupying more and more of their habitat, *gorillas are now threatened with extinction.*

Even though gorillas have often been killed to permit capture of their young for zoos and are now threatened with extinction, *humans have recently been occupying more and more of their habitat.*

The information in the first sentence is perfectly clear. But it is unclear whether the central concern of the paragraph will be the gorillas' threatened extinction or the causes for that threat, because the coordinating conjunction *and* gives equal emphasis to each of the ideas the sentence expresses. (See also Section **8d1**, "Excessive Coordination.")

Either of the other two versions, however, makes the writer's central concern unmistakably clear. In the second sentence, the writer's focus is on the threatened extinction of the gorillas; in the third, the writer's focus is on the current, increasing encroachment on the gorillas' habitat. Neither of these revisions is intrinsically better than the other. Which of them the writer chooses must be determined by the point the writer sees as more important.

● **1 Subordinating conjunctions.** The most important relationships among related ideas, along with the most common subordinating conjunctions expressing them, are as follows:

Cause
because, since

Many animal species are nearing extinction. They are protected by law.

Because many animals species are nearing extinction, they are protected by law.

Condition
if, even if, provided, unless

Some species can be saved. We can protect their habitats.

Some species can be saved *if* we can protect their habitats.

Unless we can protect their habitats, some species cannot be saved.

Concession
although, though, even though

Alligators are protected by law in Florida. Poachers still hunt them for their hide and meat.

Although alligators are protected by law in Florida, poachers still hunt them for their hide and meat.

Purpose
in order that, so that, that

Land has been drained and cleared. It can be used for real-estate development.

Land has been drained and cleared *so that* it can be used for real-state development.

Time
as long as, after, before, when, whenever, while, until

The Florida swamps are drained. The alligators lose more of their natural habitat to human intruders.

Whenever the Florida swamps are drained, the alligators lose more of their natural habitat to human intruders.

Location
where, wherever

New houses now stand on dry ground. Alligators once raised their young amid the sawgrass.

New houses now stand on dry ground *where* alligators once raised their young amid the sawgrass.

● **2 Relative pronouns.** The relative pronouns—*who (whose, whom)*, *which*, and *that*—allow you to use adjective clauses for subordinate information and details about nouns.

Humans have legitimate needs. They have come in conflict with the needs of wildlife.

Humans, *who* have legitimate needs, have come in conflict with the needs of wildlife.

Wildlife has given way. Its needs are equally legitimate.

Wildlife, *whose* needs are equally legitimate, has given way.

Land and wildlife management can help save endangered species. It considers the balance between humans and the rest of nature.

Land and wildlife management, *which* considers the balance between humans and the rest of nature, can help save endangered species.

Exercise 8.2

Sentence Practice
Combine the following pairs of sentences, using subordinating conjunctions that will express the relationships indicated in brackets. You may need to make slight changes in the wording.

1 For many people, fly-fishing is the ultimate sport. It challenges anglers to think subtly and also allows them to enjoy the beauty of gorgeous rivers and streams. [cause]
2 Anglers particularly like fly-fishing for trout during July and August. During these months the caddis flies and mayflies land on the water to lay their eggs, and the trout come to the surface to feast on the flies. [time]
3 The best fly-anglers make their own flies of feathers and hair. The trout mistake these hand-tied flies on the surface of the water for real ones and bite them. [purpose]
4 The most skillfully tied flies and well-cast line will not guarantee success in catching trout. The angler must be able to "read" the surface of the water to see where trout are likely to be. [condition]
5 To some observers, fly-fishing seems tedious. Those who learn the intricacies of the sport find it both exhilarating and soothing. [concession]

Paragraph Practice

Use subordinate conjunctions to combine sentences in this paragraph. In parentheses after each of your combinations, identify the kind of relationship indicated by the subordinate conjunction you have chosen.

> Fly-fishing for trout can benefit the angler in many ways. The angler develops the virtues of patience and diligence. He or she must practice tying flies. Only the most precisely tied flies will lure the trout from deep water or from under rocks or logs. In addition, often the angler must cast and recast the line many times before succeeding in catching a trout. The angler also learns to appreciate the intricate beauty of nature. He or she must stand waist-high in a stream sometimes for hours. During this time the angler may observe the interconnection of insect and plant and water. He or she has the uninterrupted leisure to listen to the music of wind and water, insects, and animals. Fly-fishing may also show the angler how he or she fits into the natural world. Before learning to fish, he or she may have thought that humans were conquerors of nature. Learning fly-fishing may show the angler a more accurate and less grand picture of humans as only a piece of natural splendor. Fly-fishing offers many possibilities for the angler to develop many skills. Many of these skills have little to do with actually catching a fish.

In Your Own Words

Examine the sentences and the paragraph in Exercise 8.1. Where it makes sense to do so, use subordinating conjunctions to combine sentences, placing one idea in the main clause and subordinating those ideas you think are less important. Then compare your new sentences with the ones you wrote using coordinating conjunctions. Write a paragraph to your instructor explaining the differences in meaning that resulted from these changes.

8 c **Use subordinating constructions such as appositives, participial phrases, and absolute phrases to add information to sentences.**

Although subordinate clauses, prepositional phrases, and single-word modifiers are most commonly used for subordinating ideas and details, *appositives*, *participial phrases*, and *absolute phrases* provide good alternatives. With these phrases you can embed information in your sentences to make them more economical and add variety to your writing.

Such constructions are even more important to meaning. Participles, for example, convey action succinctly; absolutes add specific detail to general statements economically; and whole clauses can be reduced to appositives to deliver information quickly. The force and precision of these subordinating constructions help make writing more effective.

● **1 Appositives.** Appositives can replace subordinate clauses or whole sentences. An appositive is a word or word group that renames, clarifies,

identifies, or expands the meaning of another word or phrase: *Sweden, a Scandinavian country, is very beautiful* (see also Sections **27a** and **32c**).

Appositives offer an economical alternative to subordinate clauses or even whole sentences that contain identifying information, as in the following:

TWO SENTENCES	Sven Nilssen has told me much about Sweden. He is my close friend and an accomplished pianist.
RELATIVE CLAUSE	Sven Nilssen, *who is my close friend and an accomplished pianist,* has told me much about Sweden.
APPOSITIVE	Sven Nilssen, *my close friend and an accomplished pianist,* has told me much about Sweden.

Generally, any nonrestrictive clause that consists of *who* or *which* as the subject, some form of the verb *to be*, and a complement can be reduced to an appositive:

My mother, *who was the oldest of seven children,* was born in Lima, Peru.

My mother, *the oldest of seven children,* was born in Lima, Peru.

Often a series of appositives can be used to bring together several details in a single sentence. In the following passage, each of the last three sentences states a separate observation about the way in which keepers of notebooks are a "different breed altogether."

Keepers of private notebooks are a different breed altogether. They are lonely and resistant rearrangers of things. They are anxious malcontents. They are children afflicted at birth with some presentiment of loss.

But in the sentence she wrote, Joan Didion used a series of appositives to combine all these observations into a single smooth, clear sentence packed with information:

Keepers of private notebooks are a different breed altogether, lonely and resistant rearrangers of things, anxious malcontents, children afflicted at birth with some presentiment of loss.

—Joan Didion, *On Keeping a Notebook*

Although appositives are most commonly noun groups, they can function as adjectives, as in the following:

A lovely hand tentatively rose. The hand was almost too thin to be seen.
A lovely hand, almost too thin to be seen, tentatively rose.

—Herbert Kohl, *36 Children*

She was about thirty-five years old. She was dissipated. She was gentle.
She was about thirty-five years old, dissipated and gentle.

—John Cheever, "The Sutton Place Story"

● **2 Participles and participial phrases.** Participles, which can replace longer clauses or sentences, are especially useful for expressing action. Participles cannot serve as main verbs in sentences, but they can help form verb phrases or function as adjectives (see Section **26g**). Like verbs, participles may be regular or irregular in form:

	Regular Verb	*Irregular Verb*
PRESENT PARTICIPLE	liv**ing**	blow**ing,** eat**ing,** cling**ing**
PAST PARTICIPLE	liv**ed**	bl**own,** eat**en,** cl**ung**

Participles can take objects and modifiers to form participial phrases that can be used in place of whole sentences or subordinate clauses to express the same information. Compare the following:

Writing is a slow process. It requires considerable thought and time.

Writing is a slow process, *which requires considerable thought and time.*

Writing is a slow process, *requiring considerable thought and time.*

In contrast to relative clauses, which ordinarily must follow immediately after the nouns they modify, participial phrases can also precede the nouns they modify. Thus, their flexibility of placement often permits you to vary sentence structure to fit a particular purpose in a given paragraph (see also Section **11c**).

The old house, *which was deserted twenty years ago and is said to be haunted,* stood halfway up the hill. [relative clause]

Deserted twenty years ago and said to be haunted, the old house stood halfway up the hill. [participial phrase preceding subject]

The old house, *deserted twenty years ago and said to be haunted,* stood halfway up the hill. [participial phrase following subject]

However, when varying the position of the participial phrase, be careful not to create a misplaced modifier (see Section **18a**).

Participial phrases are particularly useful for conveying action, especially for describing events that occur at the same time as those in the main clause. Compare the following:

The hikers struggled on. They were gasping for breath and nearly exhausted.

The hikers, gasping for breath and nearly exhausted, struggled on.

In the following sentence, notice how author John Updike uses a pair of present participial phrases to suggest that his walking through the yard and his clutching the child's hand both occur at the same time as his thinking that "It was all superstition."

[It was all] superstition, I thought, walking back through my yard, and clutching my child's hand tightly as a good luck token.

—John Updike, "Eclipse"

● **3. Absolute phrases.** Absolute phrases consist of a subject, usually a noun or a pronoun, and a participle, together with any objects or modifiers of the participle. Absolute phrases may be formed from any sentence in which the verb phrase includes a form of the verb *be* followed by a present or past participle by omitting the *be* form. In other sentences they may be formed by changing the main verb into its *-ing* form:

SENTENCE	Her thoughts were wandering
ABSOLUTE	Her thoughts wandering…
SENTENCE	The wind blew with increased fury, and the drifts rose even higher.
ABSOLUTE	The wind blowing with increased fury, and the drifts rising ever higher…

When the participle of an absolute phrase is a form of the verb *be*, the verb is frequently omitted entirely so that the absolute consists simply of a noun followed by adjectives.

The pianist played beautifully. Her technique *was* flawless, and her interpretation *was* sure and sensitive.

The pianist played beautifully, *her technique flawless, her interpretation sure and sensitive.*

Because of its speed and compression, an absolute phrase allows you to add specific, concrete detail to a general statement with greater economy than most alternative constructions. Extremely flexible, it can be placed at the beginning or end of a sentence, or often in the middle:

The rain having stopped, we went to the beach.

Bodies slouched in our seats, we listened to the soothing music, *eyes closed.*

The driver of the wrecked car, *one leg trapped beneath the dashboard, body pinned against the steering wheel,* waited for the rescue squad.

Exercise 8.3

In the following sentences and paragraph, combine the sets of sentences, expressing in the main clause what you consider to be the most important idea and using appositives, participial phrases, or absolute phrases to subordinate other ideas. After you have combined the sentences in items 1 through 5, rearrange, revise, and recombine them to create a smooth, coherent paragraph.

Sentence Practice

1 Mt. Everest is one of the highest mountains in the Himalayas. Its snow-covered peak rises to 29,028 feet.

2 The people of Nepal and Tibet live in the shadow of the mountain. The Nepalese call the mountain "sky head," and the Tibetans call it "goddess mother to the world."

3 The temperatures on Mt. Everest fall much below freezing. The winds on Mt. Everest blow at 150 miles an hour or more. The mountain has long presented the ultimate challenge to climbers.

4 George Leigh Mallory explored the first practical route up Mt. Everest in 1921. Mallory was a British climber. He died in 1924 in an attempt to reach the mountain's summit.

5 The summit was finally reached in 1953 by Tenzing Norgay and Edmund Hillary. Tenzing Norgay was a Sherpa from Nepal. Edmund Hillary was from New Zealand.

Paragraph Practice

Mt. Everest is situated between Nepal and Tibet. Mt. Everest has drawn more and more climbers and tourists each year to those two countries. Nepal is often called "the roof of the world." Nepal was once an isolated mountain kingdom. Today Nepal receives almost a quarter of a million visitors each year. Nepalese authorities have realized that they have to do something to protect their region. They established the Everest National Park in 1976. The park covers 480 square miles. The Tibetan side of the Himalayas is isolated and remote from commercial or tourist centers. Tibet has not suffered quite as badly from the growth of tourism as has Nepal.

8 **d** In revising, check for excessive or faulty coordination and subordination.

Used too often or incorrectly, coordination and subordination can make writing difficult—even unpleasant—to read. Don't force too many chunks of information on the reader at once. Your goal in coordinating and subordinating information should be to clarify meaning.

● **1 Excessive coordination.** Paragraphs composed mainly of short, simple sentences can make writing sound childish. Such sentences are sometimes called "primer" sentences because they resemble those of children's first reading books. Not only are primer sentences monotonous and choppy, but they are also indiscriminate, giving equal weight and importance to all the facts and ideas. Sentences strung together with a series of *and*s and *but*s are just as ineffective. These types of sentences give no clue about which information is more or less important.

PRIMER STYLE   He stood on a street corner. The wind was blowing. He peered into the darkness. The stranger had no place to go.

EXCESSIVE
COORDINATION   He stood on the street corner and the wind was blowing and he peered into the darkness, but he was a stranger so he had no place to go.

Help your readers understand which ideas are important and which are minor by reworking primer sentences into more complex ones that use both coordination and subordination to reflect meaning. The following revisions illustrate two different meanings that emerge from the preceding primer sentences.

REVISED   Standing on a windy street corner and peering into the
               darkness, the stranger had no place to go.
REVISED   Standing on a windy street corner, the stranger peered into the
               darkness. He had no place to go.

Notice the slightly different effects, and thus different meanings, created by the two revisions. The first revision uses the main clause to emphasize the stranger's having no place to go. The second revision gains two points of emphasis by means of the two main clauses *the stranger peered into the darkness* and *He had no place to go.* The concluding short, simple sentence achieves extra impact because its structure differs from the preceding sentence.

● **2 Excessive subordination.** Excessive subordination obscures important information. To avoid confusing your readers, don't include details that are inessential or only loosely related to the main idea of a sentence. Also avoid stringing together dependent clauses that don't have a clear relationship to the main clause. The following sentences show how one writer decided what he really wanted to say and restructured the information to convey that meaning.

EXCESSIVE   My fishing equipment includes a casting rod *which my Uncle*
SUBORDINATION   *Henry gave me many years ago* and which is nearly worn out,
                 and an assortment of lines, hooks, and bass flies, which make
                 good bait *when I can get time off from work to go bass fishing* at
                 Harwood Lake.
REVISED   My fishing equipment includes an old casting rod and an
                 assortment of lines, hooks, and bass flies—which make good
                 bait. When I can get time off from work, I like to go bass fishing
                 at Harwood Lake.

   In the following sentence the successive details are all essential, but the structure of the successive dependent clauses makes their relationship hard to grasp.

EXCESSIVE   We walked down Fifth Avenue, which led us to Washington
SUBORDINATION   Square, where we saw the memorial arch, which resembles the
                 Arc de Triomphe which is in Paris.

   Such a sentence can often be improved by changing some of the clauses to modifying phrases.

REVISED   We walked down Fifth Avenue to Washington Square, where we saw the memorial arch resembling the *Arc de Triomphe* in Paris.

Sometimes effectiveness requires rewriting a sentence as two separate ones. Even when relationships to the main clause are clear, using too many subordinate constructions can overload readers. It may be challenging to see how much information you can pack into a single sentence, but if the meaning becomes too complex many readers will simply stop trying to comprehend it.

● **3 Faulty coordination.** Faulty coordination occurs when you coordinate two or more facts or ideas that have no logical connection.

FAULTY   The poet John Keats wrote "The Eve of St. Agnes," and he died of tuberculosis.

The connection between two such unrelated facts would not be improved even if one were subordinated to the other. Readers will continue to scratch their heads—unless they are given a meaningful context:

> She could remember only two facts about John Keats: He wrote "The Eve of St. Agnes," and he died of tuberculosis.

Sometimes faulty coordination occurs when writers leave out important information that is evident to them but not to the reader.

FAULTY   My uncle was in the army in World War II, but he didn't have enough money to finish college.

REVISED   Although my uncle's service in World War II entitled him to some education under the G.I. bill for veterans, he didn't have enough money to finish college.

A somewhat different kind of faulty coordination occurs when a writer coordinates items from overlapping classes. In the following sentence, the four-item coordinate series makes it appear that there are four different kinds of animals or birds in the pet show. But clearly there are only three: dogs, parrots, and monkeys. The "mangy cocker spaniel" belongs among the dogs.

FAULTY   Entered in the pet show were several dogs, two parrots, three monkeys, and a mangy cocker spaniel.

REVISED   Entered in the pet show were two parrots, three monkeys, and several dogs, one of which was a mangy cocker spaniel.

● **4 Faulty subordination.** If you write *While Lincoln was still President, he was shot,* you emphasize the assassination. If you write *When he was shot, Lincoln was still President,* you emphasize the fact that he was still in office. Your intentions as writer and the demands of a particular context should determine which idea you place in a main clause and which in a subordi-

nate clause. Only these factors make one version preferable over the other.

Even so, remember that readers apply the logic of normal expectation to most sentences. When you contradict the reader's sense of the relative importance of two ideas, the logic will seem to be "upside-down," the subordination faulty. Compare the sentences that follow.

FAULTY
SUBORDINATION
She happened to glance at the sidewalk, noticing a hundred-dollar bill at her feet.

REVISED
Happening to glance at the sidewalk, she noticed a hundred-dollar bill at her feet.

Ordinarily, finding one hundred dollars would be emphasized. Readers would expect the sentence to be constructed to achieve that emphasis, with the finding of the bill in the main clause. If you violate readers' normal expectations, you need to have a good reason for doing so, a reason that your readers will comprehend.

Exercise 8.4

Revise the first passage to eliminate excessive coordination and excessive subordination. Revise the second passage, using both coordination and subordination where appropriate to eliminate choppy, ineffective sentences. Your revisions should create meaningful relationships between ideas.

1   During my first two years of college, I have worked part time as a sales associate for a local department store, where I have earned not only my spending money but also the right to ridicule the peculiar breeds of shoppers I encounter, shoppers who both make me laugh and drive me nearly to the point of homicide. Although all sales personnel are used to the customers who enter the department and ask to see countless items from the stockroom but who have no intention of buying anything at all, I seem to encounter more than my fair share of this breed of shopper, and these shoppers seem to delight in watching my petite body stagger under the weight of boxes containing such heavy items as lamps and cookware. Because I am assigned to whatever department needs help on any given day, I don't know until I enter the store what I'll be selling that day and, therefore, I can never be mentally prepared for the day's work, whether it be selling baby clothes, housewares, perfume, or shoes. One of my most amusing assignments is the men's department, where I meet an unusually high number of people who loathe shopping and who like passing their irritation on to me, although I usually handle them with good humor. Many of these customers are color-blind and genuinely need help shopping, although most of them are reluctant to ask for it but are grateful when I offer to help them match a tie and shirt or when I help them decide whether the alterations person is pinning the hem in the pants at just the right length.

2   Some of the customers really make me crazy. My least favorite is the customer who waltzes into my department at 8:50 P.M. This is ten minutes before the store closes. This customer never knows exactly what he or she is shopping for but is in a panic to buy something. Often he or she has forgotten a birthday or anniversary. This customer doesn't want to go home without a gift. I do my best to help the customer think of good choices. I pull out "hot" items. I match up interesting combinations of items. I pull items out of the stockroom. I point out items that are on sale. I show the customer the unique and expensive items. I suggest a gift certificate. It takes a long time to help this kind of customer. At 9:30, the customer finally decides on something and leaves. I still have to help close the register. I have to help straighten the merchandise for the store's opening the next morning. I finally leave at 10:05, more than an hour late for my date or my studies.

Exercise 8.5

Revise the following passage, eliminating faulty coordination and faulty subordination. Add information as necessary to establish logical, meaningful relationships.

Even though working in a department store has many benefits, it has its problems. One of the major benefits is that I keep up with what's new in fashion and home decor, and I also enjoy the variety of people with whom I work. They are very different from the students I spend most of my time with, so people of all races, ages, and social backgrounds work together, so I really enjoy my job. Another benefit is that we sales associates receive a large discount on any merchandise we buy, and this discount is especially helpful when I buy items that are already marked down, thus getting some goods at almost half price. Although I must admit that the job has taught me a lot about self-discipline because I must be prompt and must often deal with unpleasant customers and situations, still sometimes I have to prod myself into overcoming my natural laziness and going to work. I arrive at the store, and I begin to feel that I am part of a team. Although the customers can occasionally make us sales associates feel really special, we sales associates boost one another's spirits. I arrived at the housewares department one day to find that a customer whom I had helped the day before had brought me a batch of homemade brownies. Customers occasionally take time to write to my supervisor to say that I have been helpful or courteous, and I might get a raise or a faster promotion than I would if I got no compliments. All in all, working in a department store has enriched my life in both tangible and intangible ways, so I plan to continue working there at least until I graduate from college.

Writers Revising

The members of the student council in the business school were asked to nominate a professor for the Outstanding Instructor Award. The nomination was to be presented in writing, with specific discussion of such points as "student evaluations" and "innovations in classroom instruction." Following is a portion of an early draft of their nomination. Revise the draft to eliminate excessive subordination and excessive coordination. Then compare your version with the final draft the business students used to nominate Professor Ashwin Gupta. An analysis of the revision follows the final draft.

Draft

The extraordinary influence that Professor Gupta has had in the professional preparation of his students can be seen by the strong ratings he has received on course evaluations, which frequently place him above the 70th percentile on such questions as "ability to achieve a conceptual understanding of the material" because he creates a close relationship between his class and the students' educational goals, and he is rated above the 80th percentile in the "best course" and "best instructor" categories.

Although the tremendous importance of the personal computer to the accounting profession is now well known, Professor Gupta recognized that importance very early, and his tax accounting course was the school's first undergraduate course to use a personal computer frequently in homework assignments and classroom work, thereby giving business students early and valuable exposure to the computer applications that have since become commonplace in the accounting profession.

Revision

The extraordinary influence that Professor Gupta

has had in the professional preparation of his stu-

dents can be seen by the strong ratings he has

         His course evaluations
received on course evaluations. ~~which~~ frequently

place him above the 70th percentile on such questions

as "ability to achieve a conceptual understanding of

    no doubt
the material," because he creates a close relation-

ship between his class and the students' educational
                    Furthermore,
goals. ~~and~~ he is rated above the 80th percentile in

the "best course" and "best instructor" categories.

Although the tremendous importance of the person-

al computer to the accounting profession is now well

known, Professor Gupta recognized that importance
                              His
very early. ~~and his~~ tax accounting course was the

school's first undergraduate course to use a personal

computer frequently in homework assignments and
                    Thus he gave
classroom work. ~~thereby giving~~ business students

early and valuable exposures to the computer applica-

tions that have since become commonplace in the

accounting profession.

Analysis

The student council members realized that the major flaw in their
first draft was an excessive use of coordinating conjunctions,
particularly *and*. They wanted to focus their readers' attention more
clearly on each distinct idea, but their first-draft sentences did not
emphasize any particular ideas or show the relationships between the
ideas. The first step of their revision was to decide which ideas
seemed most important for the purpose of their nomination. As they
began to revise, they also noticed that each paragraph was only a
single sentence.

   The first sentence in the revision focuses on Gupta's influence
as reflected in course evaluations. The second sentence is constructed
from the *which* dependent clause in the first draft. Thus, rather than
burying the numerical information about Gupta's good ratings in a
subordinate clause, the revision focuses on the ratings (in the main
clause). The reason for these ratings (close relationship between class
and goals) is placed in a dependent clause (*because...*), the writer
having chosen to subordinate the explanation to the numbers. The
third sentence achieves much more emphasis for the 80th percentile
ratings by placing the information in a separate sentence. The con-

nection between this idea and the previous sentence is achieved with the transition *furthermore*.

   The fourth sentence subordinates the importance of the personal computer (*although* dependent clause) to the main clause about Professor Gupta's having *recognized* its importance, thus focusing the reader's attention on the professor rather than the personal computer. However, because the dependent clause occurs first in the sentence, it receives some secondary emphasis. The evidence for the claim stated in the fourth sentence appears in a separate sentence so that both the claim and the evidence will make equally emphatic impressions on the reader's mind. The results—giving students early and valuable exposure to computers—benefit from the focus achieved with a separate sentence. The transition word *Thus* provides the cause-and-effect link to the foregoing sentence.

9   Parallelism

Parallelism is a basic principle of effective writing and speaking. Equal form reinforces equal meaning. By putting equally important parts of a sentence or of successive sentences into equal grammatical constructions, you emphasize their relationship to one another. The parallelism confirms the equal importance of the coordinate parts.

   When you coordinate two or more elements in a sentence, make them **parallel**; that is, state them in the same grammatical form. Noun should be matched with noun, verb with verb, phrase with phrase, and clause with clause.

> A lawyer must be *articulate* and *logical*. [parallel and coordinate adjectives]
>
> She *closed the door*, *opened the window*, and *threw herself* into the chair. [three coordinate and parallel predicates, each consisting of verb plus direct object]
>
> *The otter's fur is dark-chocolate brown,* and *its eyes are small and black.* [two coordinate and parallel independent clauses]

9   a   Use parallelism to make coordinate relationships clear.

● **1 In single sentences.** Putting equal ideas in a sentence in parallel form will help make their coordinate relationship clear to readers. Compare the following sentences:

> If they buy the assigned books, students can usually be successful, but they must read them and careful notes must be taken.

> Students can usually be successful if they *buy the assigned books, read them,* and *take careful notes.*

The first sentence sets three conditions for a student's success: buying the books, reading them, and taking notes. But the sentence muddies this equal relationship by putting the first in an *if* clause separate from the other two; and although the last two conditions—reading the books and taking notes—are coordinated by *and,* the first is active and the second passive, further weakening their coordinate relationship. The revised sentence brings the three conditions clearly together in a single parallel series of predicates.

> The most overworked word in English is the word "set," which has 58 noun uses, 126 verbal uses, and 10 as a participial adjective.
>
> —*Environmental Engineering News*

In this sentence, the rhythm established in the first two items of the series is violated when the expected noun-phrase...*and 10 participial adjective uses* does not occur. Readers may feel annoyed or even cheated on seeing such a sentence, so strong is the desire for parallelism in a series.

● **2 In successive sentences.** Often you can increase the coherence of your writing by combining several successive sentences into a single sentence that uses parallelism carefully (see also Section **6d**).

Suppose you are trying to get together your ideas about the things necessary for good writing and that you have written the following in a first draft:

> Logical thinking is one of the things necessary for good writing. Good writers also have to organize their ideas coherently. And finally, anyone who wants to write well must express his or her ideas clearly.

Look at this draft closely: *thinking, organizing,* and *expressing* are the main related processes here. Parallel structure can help you knit these ideas together tightly and emphasize them clearly. Compare the following single sentences with the three original sentences:

|| Thinking logically,
|| organizing ideas coherently, and
|| expressing ideas clearly } are three requirements of good writing.

or

|| Logical thought,
|| coherent organization, and
|| clear expression. } are the major ingredients of good writing.

or

Anyone who wishes to write well must learn	to think logically, to organize ideas coherently, and to express them clearly.

Each of these revisions pulls the ideas together into a single economical unit and gives emphasis to the three major items.

Notice how parallelism helps to keep the following sentences clear and to emphasize the relationship between the ideas.

Strikes, though sometimes necessary, mean	loss of wages for workers, interference with production for managers, and disruption of services for consumers.

Political language is designed	to make	lies sound truthful and murder respectable
	and to give an appearance of solidity to pure wind.	

● **3 In whole paragraphs.** Just as you can often make single sentences clearer by coordinating equal ideas and putting them in parallel constructions, so you can often use roughly parallel sentences to increase the coherence of an entire paragraph (see also Section **6d**). Study the following paragraph:

> Otters seem to improvise. *When swimming along* in a lake or a stream, *one may push* a leaf or twig ahead of it. Or *it may drop* a pebble, then chase it through the sparkling water, catching it before it touches bottom, only to bring it to the surface and drop it again. *Underwater, it may balance* a rock or mussel on its head as it swims, *or play* cat and mouse games with its prey. *In captivity, it plays* games with every moving object and explores all corners and crevices for string to pull, wires to loosen, latches to open, and new mysteries to solve.
>
> —George Laycock, "Games Otters Play," *Audubon*

The structure of this paragraph is kept unmistakably clear by its careful coordinating and confirming parallelism throughout. The simple topic sentence, *Otters seem to improvise*, is developed by a series of details of their improvisation in three situations: in the water, underwater, and in captivity.

Not only does parallelism provide connecting links between ideas in this paragraph, it also binds information within sentences. An example is the final sentence, which uses parallel prepositional objects: *for string to pull, wires to loosen, latches to open, and new mysteries to solve.*

As is true for all the sentence-writing techniques we have been examining, parallelism can be overdone. While two or three parallel sentences in a paragraph may set up a nice rhythm, nine or ten sentences using the same parallel structures can be overkill. Monotonous repetition of constructions bores readers, blunting their attention to meaning. To write effective sentences, you also need to pay attention to emphasis and variety (see Chapters 10 and 11).

Exercise 9.1

Using parallelism and subordination, revise the following passages, combining sentences as necessary.

1. The tiny hummingbird has always fascinated humans. Hummingbirds are like miniature helicopters. They have incredible ability to stop and hover in their flight. They maneuver easily from flower to flower. They fly fast. It doesn't even look like they move their wings.

2. The hummingbird uses enormous amounts of energy. The hummingbird has a high rate of metabolism. It has to take in enough food to equal more than half its body weight each day. Hummingbirds eat nectar from blooms of plants. They eat insects. They stop in mid-flight and catch insects.

3. Some people want to attract hummingbirds to their yards. These people should put an artificial hummingbird feeder in their garden. The feeder should be filled with a mixture of sugar and water. The mixture should be changed every few days. The feeder should be washed with water. Dishwashing detergent or soap should not be used when washing the feeder. People can also plant flowers that attract hummingbirds. Honeysuckle and fuschia are two flowers that appeal to hummingbirds. Hummingbirds are territorial birds. They will chase other birds away from their area. They will even chase away bigger birds. Hummingbirds do not seem to fear other birds. They don't appear to fear humans. They stay away from bees and wasps.

In Your Own Words

Use parallelism and subordination to write a two-paragraph discussion of the most recent outdoor activity you participated in. Underline the parallel structures in your paragraphs.

9 b Make elements joined by coordinating or correlative conjunctions parallel.

● **1 Coordinating conjunctions.** Parallelism is useful for constructing effective sentences, for combining successive sentences to achieve economy and clarity, and for maintaining coherence throughout an entire paragraph. On the other hand, lack of parallelism can throw a reader off and produce ineffective sentences. To keep your sentences clear, as well as grammatically correct, make sure the structural patterns of the coordinate elements match one another.

FAULTY	As an industrial designer, Pam enjoys *her work* with engineers and *creating* the shape of mass-produced products.
PARALLEL	As an industrial designer, Pam enjoys *working* with engineers and *creating* the shape of mass-produced products.

FAULTY	Industrial designers are *highly trained, with creative ideas,* and *have knowledge* of ergonomics.
PARALLEL	Industrial designers are *highly trained, creative,* and *knowledgeable* in ergonomics.

When you are coordinating prepositional phrases or infinitives, clarity will sometimes require you to point up parallel structure by repeating prepositions.

AMBIGUOUS	A poorly designed telephone may be identified by the trouble it gives you with dialing or holding the receiver. [dialing the receiver?]
CLEAR	A poorly designed telephone may be identified by the trouble it gives you *with* dialing or *with* holding the receiver.

AMBIGUOUS	Industrial designers are trained to study the way people will use a product and then create the most attractive but functional form. [people use and then create?]
CLEAR	Industrial designers are trained *to* study the way people will use a product and then *to* create the most attractive but functional form.

● **2 Correlative conjunctions.** Correlative conjunctions are coordinating pairs: *either...or, neither...nor, both...and, not...but, not only...but also.* Parallelism requires that the structure following the second part of the correlative be the same as that following the first part.

FAULTY	A well-designed office chair *both should be* attractive to look at and *comfortable* to sit in.
PARALLEL	A well-designed office chair should be *both attractive* to look at and *comfortable* to sit in.

FAULTY	Industrial designers work *on not only* office furniture and equipment, bathroom fixtures, kitchen appliances, beds, lamps, and cookware *but also on* cars, camping gear, and cameras.
PARALLEL	Industrial designers work *not only on* office furniture and equipment, bathroom fixtures, kitchen appliances, beds, lamps, and cookware *but also on* cars, camping gear, and cameras.

If you are uncertain of the parallelism with correlative conjunctions, try recasting your sentence as two sentences. Take, for example, the sentence "Not only is Ralph Lauren famous for his fashion designs but also the industrial designs that bear his name." Recast as separate sentences, this becomes

Ralph Lauren is famous for his fashion designs.
Ralph Lauren is famous for the industrial designs that bear his name.

When you combine the common parts of these two sentences to get "Ralph Lauren is famous for," it is clear that the two distinct parts that belong in parallel form are "his fashion designs" and "the industrial designs that bear his name." The correct forms of the sentence are as follows:

> Ralph Lauren is famous for *not only his fashion designs but also the industrial designs* that bear his name.

OR

> Ralph Lauren is famous *not only for* his fashion designs *but also for* the industrial designs that bear his name.

9 **c** Correct faulty parallelism with *and who, and which,* and *that.*

Do not use *and who, and which,* or *and that* to introduce a clause in a sentence unless you have already used a parallel *who, which,* or *that* (so too with *but who, but which,* and *but that*).

FAULTY   We met Abner Fulton, a brilliant biologist and who is also an excellent pianist.

PARALLEL   We met Abner Fulton, who is a brilliant biologist and who is also an excellent pianist.

PARALLEL   We met Abner Fulton, who is both a brilliant biologist and an excellent pianist.

FAULTY   I like a detective novel with exciting action and that keeps me guessing.

PARALLEL   I like a detective novel that has exciting action and that keeps me guessing.

Exercise 9.2

In the following sentences and paragraph, revise and reword as necessary to express coordinate ideas in parallel form.

Sentence Practice

1 Because playing video games is very popular, some parents worry that their children may be spending too much time in front of the video screen and their homework or reading is neglected.

2 Educational experts agree that parents should be concerned if a child sits for hours playing video games, but these experts also point out that video games are valuable in improving hand-eye coordination and for the development of visual-spatial skills.

3 These experts also advise parents who are worried that their children spend too much time playing video games to encourage other activities such as reading a book, to go outside and play with friends, and games like chess and Scrabble®.

4 Educational psychologists warn that parents should screen video games carefully, for children may encounter violence on television but also may see violence in some video games.

5 One contrast that experts make between television and video games is that watching television is a normally passive activity, but to play a video game requires the child to make responses.

Paragraph Practice

Lovers of electronic games can engage in an individual contest with a computer, or a computer game can be played among several people. Games involving finding one's way through a maze, surviving in an adventure world, or how to win a battle in outer space are favorites. Sports games are also popular; in these games either the computer is the opponent or another player. To be successful at maze games, a player needs to have tactical skill and with good hand-eye coordination. In role-playing games in which the player develops a character to participate in an adventure world, the player both needs to be good at strategy and logic.

In Your Own Words

Write at least five sentences, each containing parallel, coordinate elements.

 Emphasis

Effective sentences emphasize main ideas and keep related details in the background. The careful use of coordination, subordination, and parallelism enables you to stress your most important ideas without losing track of less important but related ideas and information. Sentence variety enables you to emphasize important ideas by changing the pace and rhythm of a passage. You can also emphasize ideas within a single sentence by controlling the arrangement of its elements and by using repetition carefully.

As you revise sentences to achieve the emphasis you want, keep in mind that any sentence is part of a paragraph and of a larger whole. To determine what to emphasize in a given sentence, always look at the sentence in relation to its context, your audience, and your overall purpose.

10 a Highlight important ideas in emphatic positions.

The position of a word or idea within a sentence usually determines the emphasis it receives. Generally, the most emphatic place in the sentence is at its end; the next most emphatic, its beginning; the least emphatic, its middle. Consider the following sentence:

> Brunhilda, our Great Dane, loves to play with the neighborhood children, but she is bigger than most of them.

The end position of *bigger than most of them* gives that information the heaviest stress in the sentence. As the topic sentence of a paragraph that contrasts the dog's love of children with their fear of her size, the sentence is effective.

If, however, the sentence introduces a paragraph that focuses on Brunhilda's love of children, it must be revised.

> Brunhilda, our Great Dane, although bigger than most of the neighborhood children, loves to play with them.

In this version, the information about the dog's size is subordinated and placed in the middle of the sentence. Such placement of modifying phrases and clauses delays the predicate, the sentence's action, for the final position in the sentence, thus emphasizing the dog's love of children.

Sometimes you can increase the emphasis on a single-word adverb or a brief adverbial phrase by moving it to the initial position in a sentence.

> Debra reached sleepily for the alarm clock.

> Sleepily, Debra reached for the alarm clock.

On the other hand, don't weaken emphasis by placing minor qualifying phrases before your subject or at the end of the sentence. Be sure any qualifying words or phrases placed at the very beginning or the very end of a sentence are worth emphasizing. Otherwise they may seem distracting, illogical, or tacked on. When such words do not merit emphasis, bury them within the sentence or omit them.

WEAK	Such matters as incorrect spelling and unconventional punctuation can distract a reader's attention even in otherwise good writing.
EMPHATIC	Incorrect spelling and unconventional punctuation can distract a reader's attention even in otherwise good writing.
WEAK	The history of English vocabulary is the history of English civilization, in many ways.
EMPHASIS ON HISTORY	The history of English vocabulary is in many ways the history of English civilization.
EMPHASIS ON QUALIFIER	In many ways, the history of English vocabulary is the history of English civilization.

In Your Own Words

Write ten pairs of sentences using the following phrases and dependent clauses. In the first sentence, place the phrase or clause in an emphatic position. In the second, place it so it receives the least amount of emphasis.

1 Covered in slimy, green muck
2 Unexpectedly
3 Once the smoke cleared

4 Standing on his toes
5 Although she had discovered the formula
6 After the chemistry exam
7 Feeling abandoned
8 By Friday afternoon
9 Almost delirious with joyful anticipation
10 Unless something miraculous happens

10 b Create different emphases by using different sentence structures.

The position of subordinate or modifying material can have a definite impact on where the emphasis falls in a sentence (see Section **10a**). There are four basic sentence structures for handling modifying material: the periodic, or left-branching, sentence; the mid-branching sentence; the balanced sentence; and the loose, or right-branching, sentence.

● **1 Periodic or left-branching sentences.** A periodic or left-branching sentence places a modifying clause at the beginning and holds the main idea until the end. This pattern creates anticipation, first setting up the reader's expectations with background information or qualifying details and then presenting the subject dramatically in the main clause at the end.

PERIODIC, LEFT-
BRANCHING
When her mother was in the hospital for two months and her father was on the edge of a breakdown, Brenda showed great courage.

Because the structure of a periodic sentence contains built-in suspense, it can be extremely effective. However, it also contains inherent risk. The longer readers must wait to discover the subject, the greater the likelihood that they will become impatient or confused. Consequently, the delivery of the subject in the final clause should have a strong clarifying effect and should be worth the reader's wait.

● **2 Mid-branching sentences.** A mid-branching sentence places modifying material between the subject and the verb. Again, you are asking the reader to suspend normal thought patterns and expectations about the way information is delivered. The subordinate information amounts to an interruption, as you imbed detail, before the main idea is carried to completion. This structure can be used to create drama and suspense, or it can be used to de-emphasize information by sandwiching it between the more powerful parts of the sentence—the subject and the verb.

EMPHASIZED
Death Valley—*without a doubt the hottest spot in the country*—comes by its name honestly.

DE-EMPHASIZED Death Valley, *the nation's hot spot,* comes by its name honestly.

Notice in the preceding examples that punctuation and word choice combine with sentence structure to provide additional cues that reinforce the meaning the writer intended.

● **3 Balanced sentences.** A balanced sentence is a compound sentence in which the independent clauses are exactly, or very nearly, parallel in all elements.

> We always like those who admire us; we do not always like those whom we admire.
>
> —La Rochefoucauld, *Maxims*
>
> Grammar maps out the possible; rhetoric narrows the possible down to the desirable and effective.
>
> —Francis Christensen, *Toward a New Rhetoric*
>
> It is as natural to die as to be born; and to a little infant, perhaps, the one is as painful as the other.
>
> —Francis Bacon, "Of Death"

As these three examples illustrate, the balanced sentence is useful for stating contrasts and distinctions. Because it holds two coordinate ideas before the reader, its structure naturally emphasizes meanings involving weighing or choosing.

● **4 Loose or right-branching sentences.** A loose or right-branching sentence, sometimes called a **cumulative sentence**, completes its main statement and then adds subordinate details. This structure follows the most common pattern of human thought, identifying key informational elements (the subject and verb) first and then providing qualifying material.

LOOSE, RIGHT-BRANCHING
> Brenda showed great courage *when her mother was in the hospital for two months and her father was on the edge of a breakdown.*

Because it follows our usual thought patterns, the loose sentence is easy to read and satisfies readers' expectations about normal emphasis in sentences. For the same reason, it does not lend itself to special emphasis and can lead to rambling lists of details that are simply piled on after the subject and verb without regard for effectiveness. Consider the following example, the opening sentence from a newspaper article:

> A bid to set the altitude record for hot-air balloons suffered a setback Saturday when one of the two British crewmen was hurt in a fall and a gust of wind tore the balloon at the Royal Air Force base in Watton, England.

Journalists attempt to include as much pertinent information as possible in the opening sentence of a story: who, what, when, where, why, and how. The foregoing example covers all the bases, but its listlike construction offers little emphasis.

● **5 Loose versus periodic sentences.** Strictly speaking, any sentence consisting of a main clause followed by an adverbial phrase or clause is loose and can be made periodic simply by moving the adverbial modifier to the beginning. Periodic and loose constructions are more or less equally effective. Your choice should be guided by the particular emphasis and effect you want and by the relation of your sentence to those before and after it. In the following passage from a student paper, notice how the writer uses a periodic sentence between two loose, cumulative sentences to emphasize his sense of loss after his mother's death.

> I became aware of myself—who I was and what I was—during the weeks following her funeral. After the relatives had all left and the sympathy cards stopped coming, I was left alone. I had to be independent, find others to shed my tears upon, and look elsewhere for a scolding.

Exercise 10.1

Identify each of the following sentences as periodic (left-branching), mid-branching, balanced, or cumulative (right-branching).

1 Labor-saving devices, taken for granted by most of their users, have increased leisure time dramatically in the last hundred years.

2 Although these devices save hours of labor, they have deprived us of exercise and discipline that probably enhanced the health and well-being of earlier generations.

3 Loading the dishwasher, for example, doesn't take nearly the human effort of scrubbing dishes and drying them by hand, especially now that automatic dishwashers have pot scrubbers and drying elements.

4 Even though vacuuming the floors burns up some calories, it is a much faster and less physically demanding job than sweeping floors with a broom.

5 Washing clothes with a wash board in a tub of scalding water required most of a day and lots of physical exertion; drying clothes by pinning them to a clothesline took much time and muscle power.

6 Instead of rolling her hair around curlers for an overnight set, today's woman can simply heat her electric curlers or curling iron and make curls in five minutes.

7 The modern steam iron, a big improvement over the no-steam, no-temperature-control, heavy irons that had to be heated in a fireplace, offers a wide array of temperatures and wisps of steam appropriate for modern fabrics.

8 Electric can openers and knife sharpeners have removed the upper-arm workout required by manual kinds, and chain saws and log splitters have reduced the once labor-intensive chore of chopping wood almost to child's play.

9 Even the electric range and refrigerator have greatly reduced time and exercise: Cooking over an open fire or old-fashioned cookstove meant tending the fire as well as carefully watching the food, and storing food in ice boxes meant more frequent shopping and cooking because of limited storage space

10 Such modern appliances as blenders, food processors, microwaves, and automatic breadmakers greatly reduce the time cooks must spend in their kitchens while they promote the cooks' flabby muscles and lack of patience and discipline.

In Your Own Words

Write a paragraph describing an accident. Include at least one each of the following sentence structures: periodic, mid-branching, balanced, and loose. Be sure, in each case, that the sentence's structure appropriately reflects the content, meaning, and emphasis you intend.

10 c Use expletives to regulate pace and emphasis.

Expletives such as *there are, there was, it is,* and *it was* (*there* or *it* together with forms of the verb *to be*) can be wordy time-wasters that weaken the emphasis on a sentence's true subject (Section **24a**). In some situations, however, they can add suspense or prepare readers for ideas you want to emphasize.

For example, compare the following two passages, and notice how the expletives in the second add to the suspense by delaying the delivery of information.

> Dead silence prevailed for about a half a minute, during which we might have heard the falling of a leaf, or a feather. A low, but harsh and protracted grating sound which seemed to come at once from every corner of the room interrupted the silence.

> There was a dead silence for about a half a minute, during which the falling of a leaf, or of a feather might have been heard. It was interrupted by a low, but harsh and protracted grating sound which seemed to come at once from every corner of the room.

> —Edgar Allan Poe, "Hop-Frog"

As the preceding example shows, expletives sometimes occur as part of passive voice constructions—verb forms which de-emphasize the actor in a sentence and focus on the receiver of the action or the result (see Section **10f**). By themselves, expletives can also focus the reader's attention on the outcome of some action rather than on the actor. Compare the following:

> You have no excuse for your missing the meeting. You chose to set the time for last night at eight.

> There is no excuse for missing the meeting. It was your choice to set the time for last night at eight.

When you hear expletives in speech, notice that they are often used in preparation for heavier spoken emphasis on the words that follow them—on the grammatical subject of the sentence. Expletives can have a similar effect in writing. They are relatively content-free themselves, but like the wind-up before a pitch, expletives can help readers anticipate and prepare for the delivery of meaning. Thus in some circumstances they can help to achieve emphasis and variety.

Exercise 10.2

Revise the following sentences into sentences which use expletives to delay information. You may need to alter wording slightly.

1 The necessity of balancing the budget means that the company will have unavoidable layoffs.
2 Employees often have the perception that employers have no sympathy for workers when companies must reduce personnel.
3 Rarely today does an executive lay off workers without agonizing over the decision, because management understands the financial impact and personal crisis that layoffs cause.
4 At our firm all employees who are laid off must meet with a special task force set up to help them find new jobs quickly.
5 The president of the company hopes that a rapid increase in sales will make it possible for many workers to be rehired in only a few weeks.

10 d Create cumulative emphasis by using items in parallel series.

When items are arranged in a parallel series, emphasis tends to fall on the last item, simply because it is last. Because readers expect order of increasing importance in parallel series, meaning can be especially enhanced in cumulative series. For example,

> Their lives were brief, pitiable, and tragic.
>
> The life of man [is] solitary, poor, nasty, brutish, and short.
>
> —Thomas Hobbes, *Leviathan*

The first sentence mentions life's brevity but emphasizes its tragic nature, whereas the second sentence puts the full weight of the cumulative effect on the word *short*. In the first sentence, the words and structure combine to emphasize a more sympathetic view of human beings than that of the second sentence.

The arrangement of a series in descending order of importance can sometimes be used for surprise, humor, or irony.

> If once a man indulges himself in murder, very soon he comes to think little of robbery; and from robbing he next comes to drinking and Sabbath-breaking; and from that to incivility and procrastination.
>
> —Thomas De Quincy

In many series some other principle dictates the arrangement: order of events, increasing or decreasing size, spatial order, or some other order that fits the logic of the writer's purpose. In the following paragraph, for example, author Joan Mills uses parallel series effectively in capturing a sense of her childhood:

> Children are spoiled by overindulgence; but never by love. It was a day's work for me to spend 12 hours inside my own littleness: dragging a stool around to see the top of things; living with my daily failures—shoelaces all adraggle again, the peas rolling off the spoon, my sweater on backward; worrying about goblins long past Halloween. But love let me know all was right with the world, and with me.
>
> —Joan Mills, "The One, the *Only…Joanie!*"

Exercise 10.3

Revise the following sentences by arranging parallel items in what seems to you to be a more logical order.

1 Getting stuck in a traffic jam, getting fired when I finally did get to work, and forgetting to take my lunch this morning—nothing went right for me today.
2 My roommate's goals include becoming a partner in an accounting firm, passing her CPA exam on the first try, and earning a bachelor's degree in accounting.
3 The marathon runner finished last in the race and was exhausted after the first ten miles.
4 During vacation, I read a bestseller that had everything I like in a novel: exotic locations, a murder, romance, fast-paced action, and good dialogue.
5 My college basketball team won the NCAA Championship and finished first in our conference.

In Your Own Words

Write sentences containing parallel series of items using the following principles of arrangement:

1 Time order
2 Spatial order
3 Order of increasing importance
4 Order of decreasing importance (for humorous effect)
5 Series arranged for contrasting effect

10 e Repeat key words and ideas for emphasis.

Careless and awkward repetition of words makes sentences weak and flabby (see Section **24a**), but careful, deliberate repetition of key words, when not overdone, can be an effective way of gaining emphasis, as in the following sentences:

> A *moderately* honest man with a *moderately* faithful wife, *moderate* drinkers both, in a *moderately* healthy home: that is the true middle class unit.
>
> —G. B. Shaw

> Don't *join* too many gangs. *Join* few if any. *Join* the United States and *join* a family—but not much else in between, unless a college.
>
> —Robert Frost

It is the *dull* man who is always *sure,* and the *sure* man who is always *dull.*
—H. L. Mencken

As the examples show, repetition and parallel constructions frequently occur together, naturally reinforcing one another. This "sameness" can be used to achieve striking emphasis when parallel words are varied, as in the Mencken example or as in Patrick Henry's exclamation, "…give me *liberty,* or give me *death!*"(For a discussion of ways in which repetition of words and ideas links sentences within a paragraph, see Chapter 6.)

In Your Own Words
Analyze the use of repetition in these sentences. Then write a sentence of your own which imitates the repetition in each of the models.

1 Grandmother was by nature lavish, she loved leisure and calm, she loved luxury, she loved dress and adornment, she loved to sit and talk with friends or listen to music; she did not in the least like pinching or saving and mending and making things do, and she had no patience with the kind of slackness that tried to say second-best was best, or half good enough.
—Katherine Anne Porter

2 Some books are to be tasted, others to be swallowed, and some few to be chewed and digested; that is, some books are to be read only in parts; others to be read, but not curiously; and some few to be read wholly, and with diligence and attention.
—Francis Bacon

3 No one can be perfectly free till all are free; no one can be perfectly moral until all are moral; no one can be perfectly happy until all are happy.
—Herbert Spencer

10 f Create emphasis by using verbs in the active voice.

The **active voice** puts the subject (the actor) first, following it with the active verb, and then the object (the receiver of the action): *The cat killed the rat.* The **passive voice** turns things around, putting the receiver in front, then the verb, and finally the actor: *The rat was killed by the cat.* (See Section **29e**.)

Of the two, the active is almost always more direct, more forceful, and more economical. Therefore, if your goal is to emphasize the actor and the action itself, the active voice is the better choice. If you want to emphasize the receiver or result of the action, downplaying the action and its initiator, the passive voice is usually preferable.

ACTIVE   The firefighter saved the terrified child.
PASSIVE   The terrified child was saved by the firefighter.

The first sentence focuses our attention on the rescue; the second focuses on the object of the rescue, the child. As its name implies, a sentence in the passive voice will always be less forceful than one in the active voice, and longer as well. If your goal is economy and directness, choose active-voice verbs.

PASSIVE   It was voted by the faculty that all students should be required to take mathematics. [15 words]

ACTIVE   The faculty voted to require that all students take mathematics. [10 words]

Exercise 10.4

Revise the following sentences and paragraph so that you make all active verbs passive and all passive verbs active. Make whatever changes in wording are necessary to change the voice. Analyze the changes to see which seem awkward or ineffective.

Sentence Practice

1 Having a dinner party for six or eight friends can be a nerve-wracking experience but one that can ultimately provide rich memories for both guests and hosts.

2 Many people are surprised to learn that the quality of the food does not determine the success of the dinner party; rather, it is the choice of guests that makes a stimulating, memorable evening.

3 The host should invite guests of various ages and backgrounds, but only if they share common interests or compatible personalities: A party of college students can fail just as easily as one for retirees if the guests lack conversational skills or interest in other people.

4 Some hosts give successful dinner parties because the parties are built creatively around a theme, such as the Kentucky Derby or Halloween or the Super Bowl.

5 Exciting dinner parties no longer require stuffy, formal table settings and stodgy, traditional menus; in fact, dinner parties provide a wide range of creative possibilities for talking with stimulating people of all ages.

Paragraph Practice

When my friend Clark decided to give his first dinner party for a group of friends who share his apartment building, he had counted on having his friends Elise and Betsy to do the cooking. Although they offered moral support, they refused to cook the meal, advising him to obtain a cookbook and practice several dishes for the big day. Clark decided to make lasagna, a salad, garlic bread, and German chocolate cake because he could make these dishes ahead and therefore save time at the last minute for cleaning his apartment and setting the table. However, after spending two hours painstakingly assembling lasagna, Clark turned it into a rubberlike, black mass because he did not understand the difference between the "bake" and "broil" settings on his oven. He saved the meal from disaster by doing what many hosts have learned to do: He called a caterer who promised to make lasagna in Clark's own dish so that everyone would assume that Clark had concocted it.

In Your Own Words

1 Write a paragraph in which you use the passive voice effectively at least once for each of these purposes: you don't know the doer of the action, you want to emphasize the action more than the doer of the action, and you don't want to say who the doer is.

2 Write five pairs of sentences, using active and passive voices as appropriate to emphasize the actor in the first sentence and to emphasize the recipient of the action in the second sentence. To get started, try writing a pair of sentences about Congress passing legislation and then a pair about a pilot flying a plane.

11 Variety

A long series of sentences very similar in length and structure is monotonous. But a series of well-written, varied sentences provides more than mere absence of monotony. Varied sentences reflect the writer's careful choice of length and structure to supply the emphasis that creates meaning.

11 a Emphasize meaning by varying sentence structure and length.

Consider the following paragraph by Jane Howard. Notice the variety in length and structure of the eight sentences that make up the paragraph.

> The trouble with the families many of us were born into is not that they consist of meddlesome ogres but that they are too far away. In emergencies we rush across continents and if need be oceans to their sides, as they do to ours. Maybe we even make a habit of seeing them, once or twice a year, for the sheer pleasure of it. But blood ties seldom dictate our addresses. Our blood kin are often too remote to ease us from our Tuesdays to our Wednesdays. For this we must rely on our families of friends. If our relatives are not, do not wish to be, or for whatever reasons cannot be our friends, then by some complex alchemy we must try to transform our friends into our relatives. If blood and roots don't do the job, then we must look to water and branches.
>
> —Jane Howard, *Families*

Such variety of length and structure is by no means accidental. In the paragraph immediately before this one, Howard has set her thesis: All of us need to belong to a clan, a tribe; if our families don't fit that need, we will find a substitute that does. The quoted paragraph develops that thesis. Its pivotal point falls at the cluster of three comparatively short, subject-verb-object sentences—seven, sixteen, and ten words, respectively—that comes at the approximate center of the paragraph: Our blood families often are remote; thus they cannot "ease us from our Tuesdays to our Wednesdays";

for this we need friends. By using shorter, simpler sentences, Howard focus-es the reader's attention, emphasizing those ideas that are in an ordinarily unemphatic, mid-paragraph location.

There is no formula for the "right" variety of length and form among the sentences of a paragraph or a paper. The variety of Jane Howard's para-graph comes from choosing the length and form best suited to the meaning and emphasis she intended to convey to her readers.

Few, if any, writers manage this fitting of form to meaning in a first draft. It is revision that turns early efforts into varied and effective sen-tences. When you begin to revise the early drafts of your writing, be wary if many of your sentences are either short or long or if a single structure seems to recur too often. You will need relatively long and complex sen-tences to relate ideas clearly to one another and to subordinate minor detail; short sentences to give you emphasis where you want it; variety to avoid monotony. Be aware, too, that the kind of sentences that will be appropriate if you are writing a sports column or a set of simple directions will differ from the kind you will need to explain a complex idea.

Most important, always keep in mind that sentence variety is not an end in itself. Your choice of length and structure for any one sentence must always depend on your meaning and on the relationship of that sentence to the sentences before and after it.

11 **b** Enhance meaning by using short, simple sentences and longer, more complex sentences together.

If you are effectively using coordination, subordination, parallelism, and other sentence structures discussed in Chapters 8-10, your writing will already contain a good deal of variety. You will have discovered, for instance, that short sentences are good for introducing a topic or summing up a point and that longer sentences lend themselves to elaboration, detailed explanation, or qualification of a main idea. Notice how the follow-ing passages use this "push, pull" technique to advantage.

> My biology final flopped on my desk. A big, fat *D* stared up at me. Refusing to believe what my eyes had seen, my mind uncomprehending, I scooped up the paper, lunged through the door, and took off across the parking lot. I drove home, cursing the white car that drove so slow I had to pass it and damning the blue truck that drove so fast it had to pass me.
>
> —Student paragraph

> When I was nine, we moved to Boston. I grew up; got my schooling; larked about a while as a reporter; married, and had a little girl of my own. I adored her. . . . Raising three in the baby boom was louder, funnier, messier; more alarming, marvelous, tearful and tender than any prior experience of mine. My children spent emotions and energies over a range I'd never known in my childhood. So did I.
>
> —Joan Mills, "The One, the *Only … Joanie!*"

Both writers take advantage of sentence structure to build details, move their readers forward through the meaning with vigor and energy, and stop them short to make points memorable. The writing is effective not only because the authors have something interesting to say but also because they align the structure of their sentences to the content of those sentences—piling and building, adding and combining, balancing or contrasting, pausing and breaking—in ways that reinforce their thoughts.

11 **c** Change the word order, the sentence pattern, or the sentence type to add variety.

● **1 Word order.** Certain modifiers, called **free modifiers,** can be moved from one position to another in a sentence. Prepositional phrases, clauses, and single words that modify nouns should be placed next to or very close to the nouns they modify; their position is relatively fixed. But adverbs, adverbial phrases and clauses, many participial phrases, and absolute phrases can often be placed at different positions in a sentence; these are free modifiers. Varying the positions of such modifiers can help you place emphasis where you want it and increase sentence variety. As you read the following examples, note the cases in which free modifiers are set off with commas (see also Sections **32c-e**).

ADVERBIAL PHRASES AND CLAUSES

Westerners and Arabs still do not understand each other, *in spite of two thousand years of contact.*
In spite of two thousand years of contact, Westerners and Arabs still do not understand each other.
Westerners and Arabs, *in spite of two thousand years of contact,* still do not understand each other.

The defendant changed his plea to guilty *because the prosecutor had built up such convincing evidence against him.*
Because the prosecutor had built up such convincing evidence against him, the defendant changed his plea to guilty.
The defendant, *because the prosecutor had built up such convincing evidence against him,* changed his plea to guilty.

The bank's vice president kept juggling several customers' large deposits *to cover his own embezzlement.*
To cover his own embezzlement, the bank's vice president kept juggling several customers' large deposits.
The bank's vice president, *to cover his own embezzlement,* kept juggling several customers' large deposits.

PARTICIPIAL PHRASES

The deer, *grazing peacefully in the valley,* were unaware of the approaching hunters.
Grazing peacefully in the valley, the deer were unaware of the approaching hunters.

> [*Being*] *unaware of the approaching hunters*, the deer were grazing peacefully in the valley.

> *Gasping for air*, the diver came to the surface.
> The diver, *gasping for air*, came to the surface.
> The diver came to the surface, *gasping for air*.

In placing participial modifiers, be alert to the possibility of creating a misplaced modifier (see Chapters 17–18). Participial phrases can almost always be placed either before or after the nouns they modify. But whether they can be more widely separated will depend on the sentence. In the preceding examples, *gasping for air* can logically modify only *diver*, not *surface*; and since the sentence is brief, the phrase can comfortably be placed at its end. But in the previous example, if the *grazing* phrase were moved to the end of the sentence, it would modify *hunters* rather than *deer*.

Absolute phrases, since they always modify the entire sentence in which they stand, can usually be moved freely within a sentence.

ABSOLUTE
PHRASES

> *His hair cut close, his arms and legs tanned, his face freckled,* Jonathan seemed the typical country boy in summer.
> Jonathan, *his hair, cut close, his arms and legs tanned, his face freckled,* seemed the typical country boy in summer.
> Jonathan seemed the typical country boy in summer—*his hair cut close, his arms and legs tanned, his face freckled.*

> Sarah settled back for a quiet evening, *the work day over, the bills paid, some letters written.*
> *The work day over, the bills paid, some letters written,* Sarah settled back for a quiet evening.
> Sarah, *the work day over, the bills paid, some letters written,* settled back for a quiet time evening.

● **2 Sentence patterns.** The subject-verb-object pattern of the basic English sentence is so strongly established that any shift in it causes unusually heavy emphasis. Sentences such as "Over the fence jumped Oscar" or "Siamese cats she adores" are rather infrequent in most contemporary writing. But such **inversion,** when context justifies it, can be effective. Consider the following example from a student's essay about his mother's death:

> No longer did I have the security of someone being there to greet me when I arrived home from school—all I had was a high-strung Yorkshire terrier with a bladder problem. What I had to do was fend for myself and take on new responsibilities.

The student might have written "I no longer had the security…," but because he inverted the word order a bit at the opening of his paragraph, its contrast with the parallel "all I had" and "what I had" of the next two independent clauses highlights the change his mother's death brought to his life.

Notice how the next example uses inversion to emphasize the desire for wealth.

> Throughout Dawson's life his great obsession had been to secure wealth, great wealth, wealth that would enable him to indulge his wildest fantasies. Such wealth he constantly dreamed of; and such wealth he was determined to get at all costs.

A more common and much less emphatic inversion occurs when the subject and verb are reversed in a sentence opening with a long adverbial modifier.

> Across the boulevard where a milk truck scurries to more lucrative fields lies the sea and miles of empty beach.
>
> —John J. Rowland, *Spindrift*

● **3 Sentence types.** Except in dialogue, the overwhelming majority of written sentences are statements. But questions, commands, and occasionally even exclamations are useful for achieving emphasis and variety when the context warrants them.

Questions at the beginning of a paragraph can point its direction. The following sentence opens a paragraph in which the author argues that television news coverage is superior to that of all but the best newspapers.

> Why do I think network TV does a better job of informing than [most] newspapers?
>
> —Marya Mannes, "What's Wrong with the Press?"

Or a question may open a paragraph of definition.

> What is a civilized man? By derivation, he is one who lives and thinks in a city.
>
> —Bernard Iddings Bell

Imperative sentences are the staple sentences of writing that gives directions. But occasionally they are useful in other contexts.

> Observations indicate that the different clusters of galaxies are constantly moving apart from one another. To illustrate by a homely analogy, think of a raisin cake baking in an oven.

If not overused, an **exclamation** is a sure attention-getter that will change the flow of a paragraph momentarily. Notice how the following student paragraph mixes exclamations and questions to create an informal, breezy, comic tone.

> Now we all know that college presents many new and exciting experiences to be sampled in the name of education. You want culture and a foreign flavor? There are dozens of international cuisines to be savored, such as *French* fries, *Mexican* tacos, and that all-time breakfast favorite, cold *Italian* pizza. Bon appetit! You want social graces? There are dozens of events to attend where the fine art of genteel behavior can be practiced. Heads up,

water balloons! What about homework? You would ask. Mom, Dad...would a well-brought-up son of yours flunk out of school? Get serious!

Avoid the temptation to vary sentences just for the sake of change. As Sections **10d** and **10e** (on parallelism and effective repetition) explained, sameness can be a strength in your writing, just as variety can be. The important thing is to clarify and reinforce your meaning and aid your reader's understanding. Observe how author William Zinsser uses similar sentence structures to suggest the dreamlike quality of a reverie and then introduces sentence variety to shift from the imaginary to the real.

> Pagination! I have always loved the word and been sorry that it doesn't mean all the things I think it ought to mean. Its sound wafts me to romantic or faraway worlds. I think of the great voyages that paginated the Indies. I watch the moonlight playing across the pagination on the Taj Mahal. I hear glorious music (Lully's pagination for trumpets). I savor gourmet meals (mussels paginated with sage). I see beautiful women—the pagination on their bodice catches my eye—and dream of the nights we will spend in torrid pagination. The wine that we sip will be exquisitely paginated—dry, but not too dry—and as the magical hours slip away we will...
>
> But why torture myself? The fact is that it's a dumb word that means just one thing: the process of arranging pages in their proper sequence and getting them properly numbered.
>
> —William Zinsser, *Writing with a Word Processor*

In Your Own Words

Practice the following techniques for achieving sentence variety.

1 Write two sets of sentences in which a short, simple sentence works together with longer ones that elaborate on the subject of the short sentence and provide details about it.

2 Write two sets of sentences in which several of the sentences use inverted word order effectively.

3 Write pairs of sentences containing free modifiers. In the sentences, move the free modifier to a different position to achieve a change in the meaning of the sentence.

4 Write two sets of sentences in which you vary the second sentence by recasting some declarative statements as questions, commands, and/or exclamations.

5 Write a paragraph that uses at least four of the techniques for varying sentences that are discussed in this chapter. Then write a paragraph explaining why you chose those particular techniques, how you used them, and what effect you wanted to achieve.

Exercise 11.1

Revise the following paragraph by introducing greater sentence variety to enhance meaning.

Mary had been looking forward to her ski trip during Christmas break. She was worn out from a heavy class load and she needed a vacation. She was an experienced skier. She thought a week at a ski resort in Utah would be great. Mary asked two friends to go with her. They arrived at the resort to find the snow melting. The temperatures were in the fifties. The ski lodge manager said the weather was supposed to change, so Mary and her friends decided to stay for the week. They hoped for the best. The weather changed and got even warmer. More snow melted. Mary and her friends swam in the hotel's heated pool. They went to movies. They browsed in every shop in the town. They didn't have enough money to make any purchases. At the end of the week the weather was still warm. Almost no snow remained on the slopes. Mary and her friends had to go back to school. They had spent all their money on their trip to Utah. They hadn't even put on their skis.

Writers Revising

More Effective Sentences

Library users were being asked to share their thoughts on a book that had made a difference in their lives—not just a favorite book, but one that had changed their thinking or their actions. People were being asked to write a page about this book for display in a loose-leaf binder that would be part of a special exhibit during National Library Week. To start the ball rolling, each library staff member had been asked to write a contribution for the binder.

Stacy, who worked part time in the library, drafted several paragraphs, but she wasn't very happy with them. She was challenged by the topic but felt she hadn't effectively conveyed her feeling about it. Her sentences seemed monotonous and uninteresting, without energy and lacking the emotion she felt about the subject.

Although you, of course, cannot bring the same experience to the following draft, experiment with some sentence revisions that help to emphasize the feelings Stacy discusses. Then turn to the revised draft to see what she did in the final version she submitted for the library display. Notice in Stacy's retyped version how her thoughts evolved and how the meaning emerged with the changing sentences.

Draft

```
    A book that has made a difference in my life is
Anne Frank's The Diary of a Young Girl. Actually, two
books have made a difference in my life. One is The
Diary of a Young Girl by Anne Frank and the other is
the diary my Aunt Betty gave me at Christmas when I
was twelve years old. That fall I had read the diary
```

of Anne Frank, the young Jewish girl only a few years older than I who died at Belsen, a Nazi concentration camp, in 1945 during World War II. Then at Christmas, I received my own diary.

I had never kept a diary before, but Anne Frank's diary inspired me and served as a model. Of course my life was very mundane compared to hers and certainly did not contain the tragedies she experienced while hiding from the Nazis, but I understood and appreciated her need to write things down. Writing was the way she came to terms with her life, she tempered suffering by writing about it, and she also kept hope alive through writing. With my own diary, I had the opportunity to use writing as a way of understanding what was happening in my life. I have kept a diary ever since receiving that first one when I was twelve. Anne Frank and Aunt Betty helped me find my voice as a writer, so you can see why I think the two books made a lot of difference.

Revision

Two books--Anne Frank's <u>The Diary of a</u>   8c, 10b
<u>Young Girl</u> and a diary given to me by my aunt--
have made a tremendous difference in my life.
When I was twelve, I read the diary of Anne
Frank, a Jewish girl only a few years older
than I when she wrote her diary. Anne died at   11a, 11b
Belsen, a Nazi concentration camp.   10b

That Christmas, I received a diary of my
own. Although I had never kept a diary before,   10a
Anne Frank's diary provided me with both model
and inspiration. Compared to her life, mine
was very mundane, of course, containing none
of the tragedies she experienced while hiding
from the Nazis. Nevertheless, I did understand
and appreciate her need to write things down.
Writing was the way she came to terms with her
life, the way she tempered suffering, the way
she kept hope alive.

Gradually, writing also became my way of understanding what was happening in my life. Those two

```
books received when I was twelve--one filled, one
blank--helped me find my voice as a writer. I have
kept a diary ever since. It has made all the
difference.
```

Analysis

Most of the information in the first three draft sentences has been compressed into the first revision sentence. Now the paragraph gets off to a faster, smoother start. Stacy decided that, for her readers, her aunt's name was unimportant. She also decided that the information identifying the two books would be more effective in an appositive (8c, 10b) than in separate sentences.

The fourth draft sentence contains a long string of information delivered in prepositional phrases and other modifiers. Some information concerns a comparison between Stacy and Anne Frank; some of it concerns the circumstances of Anne's death. The revision separates the two sets of information, first so that the reader is not confronted by so many unrelated bits and second so that the statement about Anne Frank's death can achieve greater impact (11a-b). The contrast between the periodic sentence ("When I was twelve…") and the loose sentence ("Anne died…") in the revision also helps to emphasize the brutal fact of Anne Frank's death. The relatively short, right-branching sentence that concludes the paragraph makes this information easily accessible (10b). Also for the sake of emphasis, Stacy chose to move the fifth draft sentence to the beginning of the revision's second paragraph, where it would not detract from the starkness of the first paragraph's ending.

Notice that the first sentence of paragraph 2 in the draft is a compound sentence, but in the revision ("Although I had …"), Stacy subordinates the information that previously appeared in an independent clause. This change places full emphasis on the idea of Anne Frank's diary as a model and inspiration for Stacy—emphasis achieved both by situating the main idea in an independent clause and by placing it at the end of the sentence (10a).

Take over the analysis of Stacy's revision. What are the effects of the changes she has made? Also analyze her revision in relation to yours. Which choices do you prefer?

Review Exercise

Effective Sentences

Indicate what you consider to be the principal detraction in the following sentences and paragraph (excessive coordination, faulty subordination, lack of emphasis, lack of parallelism, etc.), and then revise the sentences and paragraph.

Sentence Practice

1 There are usually such unusual items as a waffle iron, a canoe paddle, a collection of unknown cassette tapes, a moth-eaten oriental rug at that all-American institution, the garage sale, and it is also sometimes called a flea market or white elephant sale.

2 Sometimes a garage sale will be held by a single family who are cleaning out their attic and garage. Sometimes such a sale is held by a couple of neighbors. Often several families plan a garage sale. Sometimes a giant garage sale is organized by a charity or arts group.

3 Because garage sales offer great bargains in everything from kitchen utensils to clothing and books, they are considered musts for students setting up apartments and for newlyweds as well as families with small children who often have limited budgets and many needs, but affluent people are also attracted to these sales, expecting the previously unspotted antique piece to be on sale for a pittance or because they simply want to see what other people's castoffs look like.

4 Sometimes broken appliances are bought by some garage sale shoppers who are trying to find a spare part to repair their own broken appliances, and sometimes people buy clothing that is in tatters because it is vintage clothing that is in style.

5 The parade of shoppers pokes through mounds of books and toys and home furnishings, and it includes every age from toddlers to college students, middle-aged shoppers, and retirees, and they are all hoping to find a treasure in the seller's trash.

Paragraph Practice

People who want to have a successful garage sale need to prepare carefully for it, advertising in the newspaper and making signs for the neighborhood, and they need to provide tables for the merchandise. Several days before the sale, price tags need to be taped on all items by the seller, and before the sale the seller needs to get change from the bank, and plastic bags or boxes need to be found so that the buyers can carry their finds away easily. Friends should be found to help the shoppers find what they're looking for, and sellers also need to set up a cash point so that buyers can pay quickly for the goods. There are few buyers who will want to pay the price marked on an item because for many buyers haggling over the price is half of the fun of such a sale, so if an item is priced at fifty cents, many buyers will offer twenty-five cents and finally pay thirty or thirty-five cents if the seller insists. An idea that should be remembered by all sellers, however, is that twenty-five cents for an item is better than nothing, and there is nothing worse than having to put back in the attic or garage all of the stuff that didn't sell because the seller wouldn't bargain with the bargain-hunters.

In Your Own Words

Choose a newspaper or magazine article of at least twenty column inches and analyze in writing the techniques used by the writer to vary sentences and to achieve emphasis. Explain where and why you believe the writer might improve his or her technique for achieving variety and emphasis.

Part 3

Sentence Revision

Will [Strunk] felt that the reader was in serious trouble most of the time, a man foundering in a swamp, and that it was the duty of anyone attempting to write English to drain this swamp quickly and get his man up on dry ground, or at least throw him a rope.

—E. B. White, Introduction to *The Elements of Style*

When you express each of your thoughts in the form of a complete sentence, you allow readers to consider your ideas one at a time. To communicate your meaning clearly, be sure that you maintain the sentence boundaries between one complete thought and the next. Readers expect to find well-defined sentences in English prose, and when your writing does not fulfill this expectation, readers may have great difficulty reconstructing your thoughts.

Sentence Fragments

A complete sentence contains at least one independent clause, which has a subject and a main verb (see Sections **26f** and **26h**). When a group of words lacks one or more of these elements but is punctuated as a sentence with an initial capital letter and end punctuation, a sentence fragment results.

FRAGMENTS After Julia arrived. [prepositional phrase]

Hoping to come to the wedding. [verbal phrase]

Even though she was late. [dependent clause]

Fragments are common in speech, and they are occasionally used for special purposes in writing. But in most writing, sentence fragments create confusion for readers and should be revised. Fragments can be attached to other sentences or rewritten as complete sentences.

Revise most fragments by attaching them to other sentences.

A fragment is usually an improperly punctuated phrase or dependent clause that is part of the sentence that precedes or follows it. Thus the fragment can almost always be revised by joining it to a sentence, although other revisions may be possible and sometimes desirable. The most common types of fragments, together with revisions, are illustrated next.

● **1 Prepositional phrases.** Prepositional phrases consist of a preposition, its object, and any modifiers of the object: *over the mountains, during the long intermission, after eating dinner.* Prepositional phrases usually serve as modifiers (see Sections **26e** and **26g**). The prepositional phrases in the following examples are italicized.

FRAGMENT As long as there have been cities, there have been parks. *For city residents to enjoy.*

REVISED As long as there have been cities, there have been parks *for city residents to enjoy.*

FRAGMENT	Initially parks were for the people in the houses surrounding them. *Not for the city or town as a whole.*
REVISED	Initially parks were for the people in the houses surrounding them, *not for the city or town as a whole.*
	Initially parks were for the people in the houses surrounding them—*not for the city or town as a whole.* [Here both revisions join the prepositional phrase introduced by *for* with the main statement, to which it clearly belongs. The dash gives greater emphasis to the phrase. See Section **35b**.]

● **2 Verbal phrases.** Verbal phrases consist of a verbal (infinitive, participle, or gerund), its object, and any modifiers of the object or verbal (see Section **26g**). The verbal phrases in the following examples are italicized.

FRAGMENT	Architects and developers planned urban parks carefully. *To mix the advantages of city and country living.* [infinitive phrase]
REVISED	Architects and developers planned urban parks carefully *to mix the advantages of city and country living.*
FRAGMENT	Designers borrowed ideas from fashionable country estates. *Featuring elaborate gardens, artificial lakes, and beautiful vistas.* [participial phrase]
REVISED	Designers borrowed ideas from fashionable country estates *featuring elaborate gardens, artificial lakes, and beautiful vistas.*
FRAGMENT	American parks frequently were designed on British models. *Being patterned after famous London parks.* [participial phrase]
REVISED	American parks frequently were designed on British models, *being patterned after famous London parks.*
	American parks frequently were designed on British models; in fact, some were patterned after famous London parks. [This second revision changes the participial phrase (*being patterned* ...) to an independent clause. Consequently, the two sentences could be separated by a period, but the semicolon suggests the close relationship between the ideas expressed by the clauses. See Section **33a**.]

● **3 Subordinate clauses.** Subordinate clauses are usually introduced by such subordinating conjunctions as *after, although, because, when, where, while,* or *until* or by a relative pronoun such as *who, which,* or *that.* Subordinate clauses that occur as fragments are almost always modifiers, which properly belong with the preceding or following sentence (see Section **26h**). Subordinate clauses in the following examples are italicized.

FRAGMENT	Some English landowners preferred planned parks to the natural landscape. *Which was considered too wild and untamed.*
REVISED	Some English landowners preferred planned parks to the natural landscape, *which was considered too wild and untamed.*

FRAGMENT	Regent's Park in London has historical importance. *Because it showed how a large park could be developed within a major city.*
REVISED	Regent's Park in London has historical importance, *because it showed how a large park could be developed within a major city.*
	Regent's Park in London has historical importance; *it showed how a large park could be developed within a major city.* [Here the fragment has been made into an independent clause by dropping the subordinating conjunction *because*, but the close relationship of the second clause to the first is suggested by separating the two with a semicolon rather than a period.]
FRAGMENT	Planners intended New York City's Central Park for everyone's enjoyment. *Although mainly the wealthy used its footpaths and carriageways at first.*
REVISED	*Although mainly the wealthy used its footpaths and carriageways at first,* planners intended New York City's Central Park for everyone's enjoyment.

● **4 Appositives.** Appositives are words or phrases that rename or explain a noun or a pronoun standing immediately before them. The appositives in the following examples are italicized.

FRAGMENT	Central Park was laid out by F. L. Olmsted. *The same landscape architect who later designed the 1893 World Exposition in Chicago.*
REVISED	Central Park was laid out by F. L. Olmsted, *the same landscape architect who later designed the 1893 World Exposition in Chicago.*
	Central Park was laid out by F. L. Olmsted. He was the same landscape architect who later designed the 1893 World Exposition in Chicago. [Here the fragment has been made into an independent clause by adding a subject and a verb. This revision gives greater emphasis to his designing the Chicago exhibition by placing that information in a separate statement.]
FRAGMENT	The Exposition grounds formed one of Chicago's large parks. *Jackson Park along the Lake Michigan shore.*
REVISED	The Exposition grounds formed one of Chicago's large parks, *Jackson Park along the Lake Michigan shore.*
	The Exposition grounds formed one of Chicago's large parks— *Jackson Park along the Lake Michigan shore.* [Here the dash rather than the comma gives greater emphasis to what follows. See Section **35b.**]
FRAGMENT	Both Central Park and Jackson Park were built on seemingly unusable land. *The first being built on garbage-strewn squatters' grounds, the second being dredged from a marshy swamp.*

REVISED   Both Central Park and Jackson Park were built on seemingly
                 unusable land, *the first being built on garbage-strewn squatters'*
                 grounds, the second being dredged from a marshy swamp.

                 Both Central Park and Jackson Park were built on seemingly
                 unusable land. Central Park was built on garbage-strewn
                 squatters' grounds, and Jackson Park was dredged from a
                 marshy swamp.

● **5 Compound predicates.** Fragments beginning with a coordinating
conjunction such as *and* or *but,* followed by a verb and an object or complement can usually be joined to the preceding sentence.

FRAGMENT   New York City's Parks Department has created fifteen "quiet
                 zones" at city parks and beaches. *And declared them off-limits for*
                 radio and compact disc playing.
REVISED   New York City's Parks Department has created fifteen "quiet
                 zones" at city parks and beaches and declared them off-limits
                 for radio and compact disc playing. [Here the fragment is the
                 second half of a compound predicate: *has created...and*
                 declared...]

FRAGMENT   The mayor designated some parts of parks for noisy recreation.
                 But other parts for quiet enjoyment of nature.
REVISED   The mayor designated some parts of parks for noisy recreation
                 but other parts for quiet enjoyment of nature. [Here the fragment
                 is the second part of a compound direct object of the verb
                 designated.]

12 b **When fragments cannot be attached to other sentences,
rewrite them as complete sentences.**

● **1 Phrases.** When a prepositional or verbal phrase cannot logically or
easily be attached to another sentence, make it a complete sentence by
adding a subject, a verb, or both.

FRAGMENT   *Until the beginning of the first quarter of the game.* After all of the
                 players appeared on the field, we knew for certain that Emile
                 would not be allowed to play.
REVISED   *Until the beginning of the first quarter of the game,* no one had
                 any idea whether or not Emile would be allowed to play. After
                 all of the players appeared on the field, we knew for certain that
                 Emile would not be allowed to play.

FRAGMENT   *Cheering wildly and waving orange and white banners in*
                 three- fourths of the stadium. The enthusiasm of the crowd was
                 unsurpassed at any home game in the school's history.
REVISED   *Cheering wildly and waving orange and white banners in three-*
                 fourths of the stadium, the crowd was determined to spur its

team to victory. The enthusiasm of the crowd was unsurpassed at any home game in the school's history.

● **2 Subordinate clauses.** If a subordinate clause fragment does not have a strong relationship with another sentence, revise it to stand alone as a complete sentence by deleting the subordinate conjunction.

FRAGMENT   In the last quarter, the underdogs came to life with a resolve to win that shocked all spectators. *After they resolved to win at any cost.*

REVISED   In the last quarter, the underdogs came to life with a resolve to win that shocked all spectators. *After they resolved to win at any cost,* the underdogs forced the opposing team to make some critical errors.

FRAGMENT   Although the underdogs did not win, they threatened their opponents in an unforgettable blitz. *Because the last quarter of the game was full of nail-biting suspense.*

REVISED   Although the underdogs did not win, they threatened their opponents in an unforgettable blitz. *Because the last quarter of the game was full of nail-biting suspense,* everyone in the stadium stood and screamed wildly during the last ten minutes.

● **3 Appositives.** To emphasize the information in an appositive, revise the fragment to stand alone.

FRAGMENT   The quarterback passed for more than a hundred yards. *An astonishing statistic in the face of a well-practiced and highly acclaimed defensive line.*

REVISED   The quarterback passed for more than a hundred yards. This was *an astonishing statistic in the face of a well-practiced and highly acclaimed defensive line.*

12 c Recognize intentional fragments.

Exclamations, commands, and requests have no expressed subject; the subject *you* is always understood. Such sentences are standard sentence patterns rather than incomplete sentences (see Section **26f**).

Look out!

Please pass the catsup.

Incomplete sentences are common in speech and in written dialogue, which imitates speech.

"Where do you want to go tonight?"

"To the movies."

"When?"

"In about an hour."

Except in exclamations, commands, and reported dialogue, intentionally incomplete sentences appear only in special situations.

● **1 Transitional phrases and familiar expressions.** Sometimes experienced writers conclude one topic and turn to another by using incomplete sentences.

So much for the first argument. Now for the second.

In addition, a few familiar expressions, such as "The quicker, the better" and "The more, the merrier" occur as incomplete sentences.

● **2 Answers to rhetorical questions.** A rhetorical question is one to which the answer is obvious or one that the person asking the question intends to answer. Experienced writers sometimes follow such questions with incomplete sentences.

What does welfare accomplish? Not enough.

● **3 For special effects.** Writers sometimes create intentional fragments to convey emphasis, to give readers the sense that the writer is talking directly to them, or to create effects such as haste, suspense, or anger.

Every day, the farmers raised their eyes to the blazing blue sky. Every day, the same message. No rain.

—Student essay

I had second thoughts as soon as I saw Unkie. He was a nightmare on the hoof. Massive. Shaped like a World War II tank. A head as big as a beer keg. His grunting sounded like thunder in a bucket and his tusks looked like ivory daggers. "Don't worry, he *loves* visitors," the owners assured me.

—James Taylor, *Smithsonian*

Exercise 12.1

In the following sentences and paragraph, eliminate fragments by combining them with a main clause or by making the fragments into complete sentences.

Sentence Practice

1 In the West, slurping down a tall glass of iced tea or jiggling a teabag in a Styrofoam cup of boiling water is not an accurate counterpart to the practice of making and drinking tea in the East. Especially in China, where it originated.

2 Although tea was first brewed as a medicine in China. It quickly became a popular beverage during the T'ang Dynasty (618-907). When it also spread to Japan and Korea.

3 Before the development of kettles and pots, earthenware bottles were used for brewing the tea. Drinking out of small bowls which had no handles. Tea drinkers were unlikely to scald their lips or tongue. Because if the bowls were too hot to hold, the tea was too hot to drink.

4 Tea became available in several forms suitable for different tastes and methods of brewing. In powdered form, coarsely ground, in bricklike cakes, and as loose leaves.

5 Not until the Ming Dynasty (1368-1644) did tea become available to Europeans, who quickly discovered its delights. Both as a drink and as a highly lucrative commodity for trade.

6 In Europe and America, tea was so valuable, in fact, that it was often kept under lock and key. To keep servants from drinking it, because was extremely expensive and often highly taxed.

7 As part of their history, American school children learn about a famous incident involving the taxation of tea. The Boston Tea Party, when citizens dumped tea into Boston Harbor to resist taxation of it by the English. And thus, contributed to the beginning of the American Revolution.

8 In China tea has played many ceremonial roles. For example, in weddings, where it signifies longevity and faithfulness.

9 In the East tea has also served many purposes. For example as a disinfectant, shampoo, and mouthwash. To name only a few of its many uses.

10 The insistence on enjoying tea also led to the development of beautiful porcelain tea caddies, pots, bowls, cups, and plates. These exquisite implements, being the subject of an intricate field of study by art historians today.

Paragraph Practice

The health benefits of drinking tea have been the subject of much research in recent years. Some researchers believe tea aids in blood circulation. Thus increasing alertness and stimulating metabolism. Tea has also been credited with improving digestion. Because of the tannic acid in it, which may help the body digest fatty foods. According to some researchers, tea, stimulating to the general sense of well-being. Some think green tea, not black tea, produces the most beneficial results. Health benefits may be outweighed, however, by the detrimental effects of caffeine in tea. For example, ill effects on the heart and digestive process as well as perhaps contributing to the risk of some kinds of cancer. In addition, herbal teas, which do not have caffeine, may interact detrimentally with drugs or other chemicals in the body. Seriously threatening some people who drink it in large quantities.

Exercise 12.2

In the following paragraph, eliminate fragments by combining them with a main clause or by making the fragments into complete sentences.

The stress associated with our fast-paced and busy lives affects practically everyone. From students to chief executives of large corporations. Stress is not always bad for people, but it can become harmful. If a person isn't able to relax and reduce the negative effects of the stress. People who are experiencing a stressful situation may feel various physical effects. Including headaches, backaches, or stomach aches. To alleviate the negative effects of stress. People should try various methods. Suggested by health experts. One simple stress reliever is to take ten deep breaths. A good way to relax quickly. For those who have to sit at desks or computer terminals all day. Stretching the neck muscles can help relieve stress symptoms. Eating a well-balanced diet and getting plenty of exercise also help to reduce the effects of stress. Although many people overlook these basic but important ways to reduce stress. In addition to a healthy diet and proper exercise. Working at an enjoyable hobby can help to eliminate the symptoms of stress. Finally, people who are feeling tense should remember that a good cry can often help relieve tension. Or a good laugh.

In Your Own Words

Find a magazine or newspaper article in which the writer has used fragments. Write a paragraph explaining whether or not you believe the fragments are effectively used and why.

Comma Splices and Run-On Sentences

Just as a sentence fragment violates readers' expectations because its capital letter and end punctuation signal a complete thought where none exists, a comma splice or run-on sentence violates expectations because it suggests one complete thought where several exist. Readers must interpret beginnings and endings of thoughts and decipher relationships among chunks of information that the writer should have made plain.

A **comma splice** results when two main clauses are joined by only a comma instead of a comma and coordinating conjunction (*and, but, or, for, so, yet*). A **run-on sentence** (also called a **fused sentence**) has two main clauses with no punctuation between them.

COMMA SPLICE   I avoided desserts, I was trying to lose weight.

RUN-ON   I avoided desserts I was trying to lose weight.

 Revise comma splices and run-on sentences.

Comma splices and run-ons can be revised in five ways:

1 Connect the main clauses with a comma and a coordinating conjunction.
2 Connect the main clauses with a semicolon.
3 Make a separate sentence of each main clause.
4 Change one main clause to a subordinate clause.
5 Change one main clause to a phrase.

REVISED   I avoided desserts, *for* I was trying to lose weight.
                I avoided desserts; I was trying to lose weight.
                I avoided desserts. I was trying to lose weight.
                Because I was trying to lose weight, I avoided desserts.
                Trying to lose weight, I avoided desserts.

Revising a comma splice or run-on often entails reworking the sentence rather than just correcting its punctuation. Consider the larger context in which the sentences occur and the shades of meaning you want to convey in deciding how to revise.

13 b Check sentences with conjunctive adverbs and transitional phrases.

Conjunctive adverbs include *accordingly, furthermore, however, therefore,* and *thus* (see Section **26e** for a list). Transitional phrases include *for example, in fact, on the other hand, in conclusion, in the meantime.* When such a word or phrase connects main clauses, it must be preceded by a semicolon or a period. Furthermore, the word or phrase is usually followed by a comma to separate it from the rest of its clause.

COMMA SPLICE	I should drink less coffee, however the caffeine keeps me alert.
REVISED	I should drink less coffee; however, the caffeine keeps me alert.
RUN-ON	First we made coffee then we cooked breakfast.
REVISED	First we made coffee. Then we cooked breakfast.
COMMA SPLICE	Many soft drinks have a high caffeine content, as a result caffeine-free drinks have been developed to respond to consumers' concerns.
REVISED	Many soft drinks have a high caffeine content. As a result, caffeine-free drinks have been developed to respond to consumers' concerns.
RUN-ON	Coffee contains caffeine furthermore, chocolate, tea, and cola also contain significant amounts of caffeine.
REVISED	Coffee contains caffeine; furthermore, chocolate, tea, and cola also contain significant amounts of caffeine.

13 c Know the exceptions.

A comma is sometimes used between main clauses not connected by a coordinating conjunction if two clauses are in balance or in contrast. Commas are also sometimes used between three or more brief and closely related main clauses that have the same pattern.

> Good nutrition is not just smart, it's vital. [balanced main clauses]
>
> Some people eat to live, others live to eat. [contrasting main clauses]
>
> I'm tired, I'm hungry, I'm bored. [main clauses with the same pattern]

Exercise 13.1

Revise the following sentences and paragraph to eliminate comma splices and run-on sentences. Use all five methods of correction.

Sentence Practice

1 Jazz is a uniquely American musical form, however its basic elements of harmony and rhythm are primarily African in origin.

2 Historians trace the beginnings of jazz back to the work songs and spirituals sung by black plantation workers these songs had their roots in the workers' African heritage.

3 New Orleans was an early center of jazz music, there the African elements of jazz came into contact with the varied cultures of that southern city.

4 New Orleans provided a rich mixture of musical cultures, as a result jazz is a blending of the African elements and the French, Creole, and Indian musical influences in the city.

5 By the 1920s, New Orleans had become the center of American jazz music jazz had also become popular throughout the United States and Europe.

6 Classic New Orleans jazz featured the trumpet, the clarinet, and the trombone, although solo playing and improvisation are characteristics of modern jazz, early jazz musicians played together as an ensemble with very little solo playing.

7 Many musical types are related to jazz among these categories of music are the blues and ragtime.

8 The blues, a musical form related to jazz, grew out of the plantation workers' songs, the deep emotion of a blues song and its compact form were influenced by the deep feelings of workers' songs.

9 Ragtime uses fast, syncopated melodies and can be played on various instruments, it is most often performed on the piano.

10 Scott Joplin is the greatest composer of ragtime, he wrote most of his compositions, such as "Maple Leaf Rag," for the piano.

Paragraph Practice

Rock music, the term used to describe a wide range of musical styles that became popular in the 1950s and 1960s, grew out of a variety of musical traditions, among the greatest influences on rock music are the blues, gospel music, and country and western music. In the 1950s singers such as Chuck Berry, Buddy Holly, and Elvis Presley popularized rock music, in the 1960s groups like the Temptations and the Supremes created the Motown sound from Detroit. In 1962 British groups like the Beatles and the Rolling Stones became incredibly popular however American singers like Bob Dylan and Joan Baez were creating their own folk-rock style of music.

Since its beginnings several decades ago, rock music itself has developed into various genres, for instance some fans flock to heavy metal concerts where the extremely loud music emphasizes the sounds of electric guitars and drums. Rap music has many fans the abrasive music of several popular Seattle bands spurred the rise of grunge rock.

Exercise 13.2

Revise the following paragraphs to eliminate comma splices and run-on sentences. Use all four methods of correction.

Duke Ellington, whose real name was Edward Kennedy Ellington, is one of the most famous names in American music, in fact, Ellington was both a musician and a composer. Born in Washington, D.C., in 1899, Ellington began playing the piano as a young boy in 1918 he formed his own band. Ellington was multitalented, in his late teens he worked as a commercial artist during the day and played the piano at night. Ellington went to New York he became nationally famous there while appearing in Harlem nightclubs. Ellington's band played at the famous Cotton Club in Harlem, soon his distinctive jazz sound became familiar to radio listeners all over the country. During the Depression, Ellington and his band toured Europe, that trip was a success, Ellington's music became internationally known.

Duke Ellington liked to experiment in his compositions, for example many of his works used dissonant chords or produced new combinations of sounds. Eventually, Ellington's music combined elements of jazz and symphonic music his long concert work "Black, Brown, and Beige" was performed at Carnegie Hall. Duke Ellington died in 1974, he left a range of music that includes thousands of compositions, among them are his most famous songs such as "Mood Indigo," "Solitude," and "Sophisticated Lady."

In Your Own Words

Review your most recent essay to look for comma splices and run-on sentences. If you find these errors, write a paragraph explaining why you believe you put your thoughts into these structures. In addition, explain which method of correction would be most effective for correcting the error(s).

Writers Revising

Sentence Boundaries

Sentence fragments, comma splices, and run-on sentences all fail to mark clearly for readers the fundamental unit of thought in writing—the sentence.

After revising for overall content and organization, Toni checked the working draft of her sociology research paper to make sure each sentence was grammatically complete: no fragments, run-ons, or comma splices. Revise the following paragraphs from her draft, and then compare your revision to hers to see if you were able to solve the problems caused by lack of clear sentence boundaries.

Draft

```
"Infantilization" is a common stereotype that has
been pinned on a number of minority groups besides
the aged. Including African-American slaves and women
pressed to remain housewives rather than take jobs
```

outside the home (Arluke and Levin 10). This negative
image portrays the minority group member as having
child-like qualities. And as being intellectually,
socially, morally, and/or physically immature. The
members of the minority group are consequently also
portrayed as dependent. In various ways upon the dominant group.

When applied to the elderly. This stereotype usually takes the form of "second childhood" in which
the older person is viewed as unable to cope as an
adult. Arluke and Levin note that the second childhood image has a long history of association with the
elderly they trace it through television and print
advertising to illustrate its prevalence today. Older
people are shown. Throwing tantrums, eating like
children (small portions, bland food), having the
physical problems of children (incontinence or con-
stipation), and being entertained as if they were
children (parties with silly hats). "This dim view of
the elderly suggests that they are losing, or have
lost, the very things a growing child gains. It
implies a backward movement to earlier developmental
stages," they write (8), it denies the lifetime of
experience that separates age from youth.

Revision

"Infantilization" is a common stereotype

that has been pinned on a number of minority

1   groups besides the aged, including African-   12a(2)

American slaves and women pressed to remain

housewives rather than take jobs outside the

home (Arluke and Levin 10). This negative

image portrays the minority group member as

2   having child-like qualities. And as being   12a(2)

intellectually, socially, morally, and/or

physically immature. The members of the

minority group are consequently also por-

3 trayed as dependent. *y* *i* ~~I~~n various ways upon the   12a(1)

dominant group.

4   When applied to the elderly, *t* ~~T~~his stereo-   12a(3)

type usually takes the form of "second child-

hood" in which the older person is viewed as

unable to cope as an adult. Arluke and Levin

note that the second childhood image has a

5 long history of association with the elderly,   13a

and
ₐthey trace it through television and

print advertising to illustrate its preva-

6 lence today. Older people are shown. *y t* ~~T~~hrowing   12a(2)

tantrums, eating like children (small por-

tions, bland food), having the physical prob-

lems of children (incontinence or constipa-

tion), and being entertained as if they were

children (parties with silly hats). "This dim

view of the elderly suggests that they are

losing, or have lost, the very things a grow-

ing child gains. It implies a backward move-

ment to earlier developmental stages," they

and
7 write (8), ^it denies the lifetime of experi-   13a

ence that separates age from youth.

Analysis

Toni assumed that fragment 1 probably resulted because the sentence before the verbal beginning "including" is itself a complete sentence. Looking back through her previous drafts, Toni realized that fragment 2 was the outcome of joining thoughts from two different drafts without reading them together. Fragment 3 resulted when Toni realized she needed a more detailed transition from one paragraph to the next block of paragraphs and added the prepositional phrase that starts "in various ways."

Sentence fragment 4 and run-on sentence 5 were the results of hurried copying from one draft to the next. Fragment 6 occurred when Toni added details from her research to her previous draft, which had read "Older people are shown. (Add examples from Arluke and Levin.)" Finally, comma splice 7 occurred because Toni was focused on incorporating the quotation into her own sentence. After she reread this revised draft, Toni changed the last sentence to read

"It implies a backward movement to earlier developmental stages," they write (8), and denies the lifetime of experience that separates age from youth.

Once *it* is deleted, *denies* becomes part of a compound verb (*implies* and *denies*). The words "they write" become parenthetical in the new sentence and so are set off by commas (see Section **32f**). Another possible revision would be to precede *it* with a semicolon:

...they write (8); it denies the lifetime...

Analyzing the causes of her errors gave Toni insight into how to avoid similar errors in future assignments.

14 Agreement

Grammatical **agreement** helps readers keep straight which actors and actions go together by defining relationships between subjects and verbs, pronouns and their antecedents, and demonstrative adjectives (*this, that, these, those*) and the words they modify. The following passage shows all three kinds of agreement.

> *Ursula K. LeGuin*, author of many science fiction novels and stories, also *writes* poetry, children's books, and essays. In some of *her* essays, *she* examines feminist and environmental concerns. *These essays* reflect LeGuin's political views.

Ursula K. LeGuin...writes is an example of subject-verb agreement. The pronouns *her* and *she* in the second sentence agree with their antecedent, *Ursula K. LeGuin*. In the third sentence, *essays* is modified by the demonstrative adjective *these;* both words are plural and thus in agreement.

14 a Make subjects and verbs agree.

A verb must agree with its subject in person (first, second, or third) and number (singular or plural) (see Chapter 27).

> *Seamus Heaney is* considered a fine "rural poet." [third-person singular]
>
> *I hear* echoes of the Irish countryside in his poems. [first-person singular]
>
> *We want* to hear Seamus Heaney read from his latest manuscript. [first-person plural]

Making subjects and verbs agree is rarely difficult except in the following situations.

● **1 Words and phrases between subject and verb.** Ignore words or phrases that come between the subject and verb in checking agreement. Find the subject and make the verb agree with it.

> The object of a preposition cannot be the subject of a sentence.
>
> The first two *chapters* of the book *were* exciting. [The verb agrees with the subject, *chapters*, not with the nearest noun, *book*.]
>
> The *size* of the bears *startles* the spectators.

Singular subjects followed by expressions such as *with, together with, accompanied by,* and *as well as* take singular verbs. These phrases are not part of the subject, even though they do suggest a plural meaning.

FAULTY   The *coach*, as well as the players, *were* happy about the
            unexpected victory.

REVISED   The *coach*, as well as the players, *was* happy about the
            unexpected victory.

● **2 Indefinite pronouns as subjects.** Indefinite pronouns ending in -*one*, -*body*, and -*thing* (*anyone, everybody, something*) are singular. Other singular indefinite pronouns are *another, each, either, neither,* and *one*. These pronouns always take singular verbs.

> *Everybody* in the audience *was* enthusiastic.
>
> *Another* of the pesticides *has* proved harmful to birds.
>
> *Each* of the students *needs* individual help.
>
> *Neither* of the books *is* available in the library.

The indefinite pronouns *both, few, many, others,* and *several* always take plural verbs.

> *Many use* their Super Bowl tickets, but *others scalp* them for high prices.

All, any, most, more, and *some* may take either a singular or plural verb depending on the noun to which they refer.

> *Some* of the silver *is* missing. [*Some* refers to the singular noncount noun *silver*. For a list of noncount nouns, see Section **26a**.]

Some of her ancestors *were* pioneers. [*Some* refers to the plural noun *ancestors.*]

None takes either a singular or plural verb depending on the noun to which it refers. However, *none* can also mean "not one" and so in some cases may require a singular verb even though the apparent antecedent is plural.

None of the work is finished. [*None* refers to the singular noncount noun *work.*]

None of the bees *have* swarmed although the hive is crowded. [*None* refers to the plural *bees.*]

None of these pies *is* cool enough to eat yet. [*None* means "not one" and thus requires a singular verb.]

● **3 Collective nouns as subjects.** Collective nouns are singular in form but name a group of persons or things: *audience, band, bunch, class, committee, crowd, family, herd, jury, public, team,* and the like. Use a singular verb with a collective noun when the group is considered as a unit acting together. Use a plural verb when the individual members of the group are acting separately.

The committee *is* meeting today. [The singular verb *is* emphasizes the committee acting as a unit.]

The committee *are* unable to agree on a plan. [The plural verb *are* emphasizes the individual members.]

● **4 Subjects joined by *and*.** Two or more subjects joined by *and* typically require a plural verb.

Line, proportion, and *perspective are* elements of drawing.

Lehmbruck and *Rodin were* sculptors who worked with bronze.

However, use a singular verb when the two parts of a compound subject refer to the same person or thing.

Gomez's closest *friend* and *business partner was* formerly his boss.

Ham and *eggs is* a high-cholesterol breakfast.

If *each* or *every* comes before singular subjects joined by *and*, use a singular verb.

Every *parent* and *teacher makes* rules for children to follow.

Each *boy* and *girl has* to decide whether to listen.

● **5 Subjects joined by *or* or *nor*.** When two or more subjects are joined by *or* or *nor*, make the verb agree with the subject closest to it.

Either *you* or *he has* to be here.

Either the *dean* or her *assistant was* supposed to meet with the student committee.

If one of the subjects is singular and one is plural, place the plural subject second to avoid awkwardness.

> Neither the *chairperson* nor the committee *members are* here to present their petition.

● **6 Inverted subject-verb order.** Check agreement carefully when the verb comes before the subject.

The expletive *there* is not the subject of a verb; it is a signal that the subject will follow the verb (see Section **26f**). To determine subject-verb agreement when the verb precedes the subject, change the word order so the subject comes first, as in the following examples.

> There *are* no *trees* in our yard. [The subject is *trees*: *No trees are in our yard.*]
>
> On this question, there *remains* no *doubt*. [The subject is *doubt*: *No doubt remains on this question.*]

The verb may sometimes come before the subject when a sentence begins with the adverb *here* or *there* or with an adverbial word group.

> There *goes* the *man* I was describing. [*The man I was describing goes there.*]
>
> After a big victory *come* the postgame *letdown* and *fatigue*. [*The postgame letdown and fatigue come after a big victory.*]

● **7 Who, which, and that as subjects.** When the relative pronouns *who, which,* and *that* are used as subjects of a subordinate clause, use a singular verb when the pronoun's antecedent is singular and a plural verb when the antecedent is plural.

> They are the *employees who deserve* praise. [*Who* refers to the plural *employees*; thus the verb is plural.]
>
> The *book that was* lost belonged to the library. [*That* refers to the singular noun *book; was* is singular.]

Be careful about agreement when you use the phrase *one of the* before a relative pronoun. What does the relative pronoun refer to? If it refers to the singular *one*, use a singular verb; if it refers to the plural noun in the *of* phrase, use a plural verb. Context can help you decide.

> Santini is one of the council *members* who *oppose* the plan. [*Who* refers to the plural *members*; several council members oppose the plan.]
>
> Many important people in town oppose the plan. Santini is *one* of the council members who *opposes* the plan. [*Who* refers to *one*; Santini opposes the plan and he is a council member. Note that the meaning of the sentence would not change if the phrase *of the council members* were omitted.]

● **8 Titles, business names, and words used as words.** When the subject is the title of a novel, a play, the name of a business or the like, or a word used as a word, use a singular verb even if the form of the subject is plural.

Romeo and Juliet is a Shakespearean play.

Songs and Satires is a book by Edgar Lee Masters.

Smith Brothers® *is* a brand of cough drops.

Women is the plural of *woman.*

● **9 Plural forms, singular meanings.** Nouns such as *economics, news, physics,* and *mathematics* that refer to a body of knowledge usually take singular verbs because they are singular in meaning, although plural in form. Plural-form physical ailments such as *measles* or *hives* are treated similarly.

Linguistics is the study of human speech.

The good *news has* traveled quickly.

Measles carries the threat of severe complications.

However, some plural-form nouns such as *athletics, hysterics, aerobics, politics, statistics,* and *acoustics* may be either singular or plural, depending on whether they refer to a singular idea or a plural idea. The noun *data,* however, is almost always treated as plural in formal writing.

Aerobics is an extremely strenuous form of exercise. [singular meaning]

College *athletics are* responsible for generating thousands of dollars from loyal alumni. [plural meaning: various collegiate sports]

The *data indicate* that consumers are making more credit card purchases.

● **10 Quantities as subjects.** Noun phrases indicating fixed quantities or extents (money, time, distance, or other measurements) may be either singular or plural, depending on whether they are being considered as a unit (singular) or as parts of a unit (plural).

The *majority* in the legislature *is* Republican. [unit]

The *majority* of the tourists *have* returned to the bus because of the rain. [individuals]

Three-quarters of the money *is* already spent. [unit of money]

Sixty percent of the trees *were* damaged by the hurricane. [individual trees]

Three hundred pounds is a lot for an amateur to bench-press. [unit]

Five and a half liters were needed to fill the tank. [parts of unit]

The expression *the number* takes a singular verb, but *a number* takes a plural verb.

The number of candidates for the position *was* large.

A number of candidates *were* applying for the position.

The number of people moving to the Southwest *is* increasing.

A number of business firms *have* moved from New York.

● **11 Predicate nouns.** Predicate nouns do not affect subject-verb agreement.

The best *part* of the program *is* the vocal duets.

Expensive *cars are* a necessity in his life.

Exercise 14.1

In the following sentences and paragraph, revise any errors in subject-verb agreement.

Sentence Practice

1 Every one of my friends have a more highly developed sense of smell than I, and, as a result, they have played a number of practical jokes on me that has not been funny.

2 The majority of these jokes has involved hiding pungent or rotten foods in my room or car where neither I nor my roommate have been able to find the smelly culprit for days.

3 On occasions my girlfriend, as well as my roommate, have participated in these pranks because everyone in my circle of friends delight in my utter helplessness where smells is concerned.

4 For example, this gang of conspirators schemes to trick me by putting ammonia in my cologne bottle or hiding Limburger cheese in my sock drawer.

5 Once *Sons and Lovers* were the hiding place for particularly vile-smelling wads of cloth soaked in hydrogen sulfide that was stuffed into the spine of the book.

6 Although my defective sniffer along with my helplessness as the victim greatly entertain my friends, really there is satisfaction and pleasure in knowing that I have the last laugh.

7 The number of times when I have been publicly embarrassed are many fewer than the times when either my roommate or my friends has had to suffer for days smelling the ground garlic or rotten eggs they have hidden.

8 Of course, my inability to detect most smells are an embarrassing hardship and a serious loss because I cannot share the many pleasures that the majority of my friends takes for granted.

9 For example, selecting the most fragrant bouquet of flowers and choosing the perfect perfume for my girlfriend is impossible, and my family is always having to describe the fabulous aromas of my dad's cooking during holidays.

10 The news of my defective sniffer have always made me famous at school, and even in college at least three-fourths of the people I meet has heard of my problem and the famous jokes played on me.

Paragraph Practice

One of the newest fields for researchers are the experiments on and analyses of the connection between the sense of smell and human psychology and physiology. From this quest to understand the impact of smell has come many potential applications for medicine, business, and home. The use of aromatherapy to treat everything from bad moods to learning disorders are being studied. Scientists have found that there seems to be connections between the aromas people smell and their feelings of security, relaxation, and general well-being. Thus, the commercial potential for a range of items from perfumed fabrics and furniture to fragrance-producing systems in homes and businesses are staggering to the imagination. Each of these areas hold great promise for improving the quality of life in the twenty-first century.

In Your Own Words

Write a two-paragraph discussion of the person who is the most positive influence in your life. In it write sentences which illustrate the following kinds of subject-verb agreement: (1) words and phrases coming between the subject and the verb; (2) indefinite pronoun; (3) subjects joined by *or* or *nor*; (4) inverted subject-verb order; (5) title, business name, or words used as a singular subject; and (6) singular subject with plural predicate noun.

14 b Make pronouns and antecedents agree.

A pronoun agrees in number with its antecedent, the word to which it refers.

> Bruno Bettelheim, author of *The Uses of Enchantment*, believes that fairy tales help *children* overcome *their* fears. [The plural pronoun *their* refers to the plural antecedent *children*.]

> Unlike a myth, a fairy *tale* does not have a god or goddess as *its* main character. [The singular *its* refers to the singular *tale*.]

> A *child* listening to *his or her* parent reading a fairy tale is able to identify with the human protagonist. [*His or her* is a singular pronoun referring to the singular antecedent *child*.]

● **1 Indefinite pronouns as antecedents.** In writing, use singular pronouns to refer to indefinite pronouns such as *person, one, any, each, either, neither,* and compounds ending in *-one, -body,* and *-thing,* such as *someone, anybody,* and *everything*.

Spoken English frequently uses a plural pronoun to refer to indefinite antecedents, but the singular continues to be preferred in writing.

SPOKEN	*Each* of the Cub Scouts is to bring *their* own tent to the roundup.
WRITTEN	*Each* of the Cub Scouts is to bring *his* own tent to the roundup.
SPOKEN	*None* [not one] of us mothers wants you to forget *our* children.
WRITTEN	*None* of us mothers wants you to forget *her* children.
SPOKEN	*Everyone* at the meeting should be allowed to express *their* opinions before the vote is taken.
WRITTEN	*Everyone* at the meeting should be allowed to express *his or her* opinion before the vote is taken.

● **2 Collective nouns as antecedents.** Use a singular pronoun if you are considering the group as a unit and a plural pronoun if you are considering the individual members of the group separately.

> The *band is* recording a new album. [The band is considered as a unit.]

> The *class* finished *their* lab experiments yesterday. [The class members worked individually.]

Some writers prefer not to use a plural pronoun to refer to a collective noun. If such sentences seem awkward to you, consider omitting the pronoun or replacing it with an appropriate article or other determiner.

The class finished *the* lab experiments yesterday.

● **3 Compound antecedents.** If two or more antecedents are joined by *or* or *nor*, make the pronoun agree with the antecedent that is closer to it. Or consider omitting the pronoun or replacing it with an appropriate article or other determiner.

Neither my *brother* nor my *parents* have confirmed *their* reservations.

Either *Samantha* or *Melissa* is taking *her* vacation in May.

Either *Samantha* or *Melissa* is taking *a* vacation in May.

Refer to antecedents joined by *and* with plural pronouns. In some situations, the pronoun may be omitted or replaced with an article or other determiner.

Mark and Ellen bought *their* new car yesterday.

Mark and Ellen bought *a* new car yesterday.

However, when *each* or *every* introduces a compound antecedent, use a singular pronoun.

Each state and city makes *its* own laws.

When a compound antecedent refers to a single person or thing, use a singular pronoun.

The teacher and activist has been promoting causes *she* considers vital to the welfare of the community.

Exercise 14.2

Revise the following sentences and paragraph to make every pronoun agree with its antecedent in accordance with written usage. Indicate any sentence that would be acceptable in speech. Once you have revised the pronouns, be sure to revise any verbs that no longer agree with their subjects.

Sentence Practice

1 Everyone who has begun singing an advertising jingle out of the blue can testify that they understand the power of advertising.

2 Often when we are out together, either my friend Ramon or others in our gang are likely to begin singing the latest radio or television jingle he has heard.

3 Anyone listening to us would shake their heads in disbelief at our wacky renditions of these jingles, but Ramon and his roommate are especially bold about throwing himself into the performance whether or not onlookers are staring.

4 In addition to our skill with the melodies, our group prides ourselves on never forgetting a single word of the jingles.

5 Several of us guys have trouble remembering his computer passwords and locker numbers, but nobody in the group has ever forgotten the melody or words once they began to sing.

Paragraph Practice

Several advertising techniques influence consumers to rush out and buy products that he or she has heard about in radio or television commercials. First, advertisers often use a famous athlete like Michael Jordan or celebrity like Cindy Crawford to testify that they find the product remarkable. Some ads appeal to the consumers' need for security and safety, for example, those for First Alert® smoke detectors, and others, like ads for Cadillac and other luxury cars, play on his or her need to feel successful or important. Some of the most memorable commercials rely on the clever use of language ("I heard it through the grapevine" or "It melts in your mouth, not in your hand") to make consumers feel smart and to convince him or her that buying the product shows their intelligence. Many commercials feature either the melody and words of a jingle ("Like a good neighbor, State Farm is there") or fantastic special effects like the California Raisins to mesmerize its audience into buying what it is selling.

14 **c** Eliminate sexist pronoun references.

Formal English has traditionally used masculine pronouns (*he, him, his*) to refer to indefinite antecedents and nouns that include both men and women.

> A *student* who thinks *he* is eligible for financial aid should send *his* application forms before December 1.

> *Everyone* should brush *his* teeth three times a day.

Today, many people find such usage offensive (see Section **23c** on gender stereotypes). Several alternatives are available for revising these usages.

● 1 Use plural nouns and pronouns. Changing singular nouns and pronouns to the plural eliminates the gender-specific reference.

> *Students* who think *they* are eligible for financial aid should send *their* application forms before December 1.

> *Everyone* should brush *their* teeth three times a day. [In spoken English and informal writing, the use of a plural pronoun with a singular indefinite pronoun is gaining some acceptance. In formal writing, however, this usage is not widely accepted.]

● 2 Omit the pronoun. If a personal pronoun is unnecessary to the meaning of the sentence, omit the pronoun or replace it with an appropriate article or other determiner.

A student who may be eligible for financial aid should send the application forms before December 1. [The first pronoun has been eliminated by changing *who thinks he is eligible* to *may be eligible*. *The* replaces *his* before *application forms*.]

People should brush *their* teeth three times a day. [In English, parts of the body are referred to with possessive pronouns; omitting *their* would be incorrect. Instead, the singular indefinite pronoun *everybody* has been replaced by the plural noun *people* to agree with *their*.]

● **3 Replace *he* with *he or she* and *him* with *him or her*.** Replacing *he* with *he or she* is appropriate if the phrase is not overused. A passage becomes awkward with too many repetitions of *he or she* and *him or her*.

AWKWARD   A student who thinks *he or she* is eligible for financial aid
               should send *his or her* application forms before December 1.

ACCEPTABLE   A student who thinks *he or she* is eligible for financial aid
               should send *the* application forms before December 1.

ACCEPTABLE   *Everyone* should brush *his or her* teeth three times a day.

Exercise 14.3

Using the range of available options, revise the following sentences so that pronoun references are nonsexist and reflect reality. Be prepared to discuss your choices.

Sentence Practice

1 In preparation for the crafts festival, let's call a fireman or a policeman to hear his advice about the safety precautions we have taken with the wiring for exhibition booths.
2 Each of the craftspeople will be selling some of his or her best wares at the festival; thus, we want to be sure that everything is safe.
3 We need to be sure that we can find a nurse who will be willing to donate her time to be on hand in case of a medical emergency.
4 A spokesman for the local arts council must be recruited so that he or she can handle publicity for the event.
5 An accountant can help us with the financial planning for the festival only if we give him complete information.

Paragraph Practice

In using the full range of options to revise these sentences, consider which options work together best in the paragraph as a whole.

When our social club decided to sponsor a crafts festival to raise money for a homeless shelter, we realized that we first needed to seek the advice of a lawyer about legal issues he might foresee. Then each member of the club was assigned to a committee on which his or her interests and talents might best be used. The chairman of each committee posted his progress report weekly to be sure we would be ready in time for the grand opening. One of our biggest headaches was recruiting a food server who would give up her free time to supervise plans for feeding the crowd. And one of our biggest triumphs was talking a well-known actor into putting together a talent show. All in all, each person who worked for the success of the fundraiser believed that his or her time had been well spent.

In Your Own Words

Review the rules for pronoun agreement and gender-specific pronoun references and list the four rules which give you the most problem in your writing. Then write a paragraph on your favorite recent movie, and in the paragraph use each of the four pronoun rules correctly.

14 **d** **Make demonstrative adjectives (*this, that, these, those*) and the nouns they modify agree.**

The adjective must agree in number with the noun it modifies: *this* swing …*these* swings. A demonstrative adjective in phrases with *kind of* or *sort of* modifies *kind* or *sort*. Standard usage favors agreement among the demonstrative, the noun being modified, and the object of the preposition *of*.

NONSTANDARD	Those kind of strawberries taste sweet.
STANDARD	Those kinds of strawberries taste sweet.
	That kind of strawberry tastes sweet.

NONSTANDARD	This sort of cakes is delicious.
STANDARD	These sorts of cakes are delicious.
	This sort of cake is delicious.

NONSTANDARD	These sort of things happen.
STANDARD	These sorts of things happen.
	This sort of thing happens.

Exercise 14.4

In the following sentences and paragraph, correct every error of agreement and gender-specific pronouns in accordance with written usage.

Sentence Practice

1 Anyone who wants to be a journalist should strengthen their writing skills and have a strong liberal arts background.

2 A newspaper reporter, as well as a television news reporter, have to understand such fields as history, political science, and economics, and he must know how to locate information quickly about almost any topic.

3 Even sports require the reporter to know about many other areas to do his job well.

4 Specialized areas such as arts or education also demands that the reporter know about other fields, for example, history and business, if they want to excel in reporting.

5 There is also a need for and keen interest in those newsmen who can speak more than one language now that journalism, along with business and politics, have become truly international.

Paragraph Practice

Coverage of the news in daily papers and on television news shows have changed considerably during the last few decades. The line between news and entertainment has softened so that most news coverage now include reports on such areas as health, food, and films. A newspaper reporter or the newscasters on the local TV station tries to keep his audience informed about local personalities and community interests as well as keeping them informed about accidents, crime, weather, and sports, which fills up only the most conservative news programs and newspapers today.

In its format and tone, many newspapers and news programs seem to imitate magazines, and some viewers complain that amid all of the features, he or she is finding it increasingly difficult to zero in on the real news. For many viewers, however, there is no problem and no complaints, because for him or her, sensational news about celebrities or a report detailing the latest aerobic exercises are what they want to see. Almost everyone who reads a newspaper or watches a news program are trying to keep up with important events. Now, though, keeping up with the news and understanding important issues requires readers and viewers to commit more time than ever as he or she struggles with new formats that seem to blur the news.

Writers Revising

Agreement

Grammatical agreement among subjects, verbs, and pronouns helps readers grasp the relationships among your ideas and sentences.

Muhammad's instructor asked the class to summarize the information from an informative article, documentary television show, or video. Then each student was to revise the summary and provide the instructor with an analysis of the most frequently-made error and with recommendations for avoiding that particular problem in future writing assignments. The following paragraphs come from the first draft of Muhammad's summary. Find his errors.

Draft

Before Joseph Campbell died, Bill Moyers interviewed him for many hours about his exploration and preservation of the myths of various cultures. Out of these hours of recorded interviews, a series of six videotapes were produced; the first of the series were called The Hero's Journey. As I found out, there is many myths that share the same basic structure.

Campbell says that a hero is anyone who give their lives to something other than themselves or bigger than themselves. For example, a hero might save another person or sacrifice himself for an ideal. A hero such as Telemachus go away from all they know--the place they live or the people they love--into an unknown world in which a number of things happen to them. Campbell notes the things that happens to the hero fall into two categories: trials (physical or spiritual) and revelations (seeing or hearing things that other people don't). Each really have to do with the transformation of the hero's consciousness. Neither trials nor revelations has the power to stop the hero. The hero, who often is a young adult, always succeed, and they come back from their adventures a new person.

Revision

1   Before Joseph Campbell died, Bill Moyers

interviewed him for many hours about his

exploration and preservation of the myths of

2 various cultures. Out of these hours of

recorded interviews, a series of six video-

tapes ~~were~~ [was] produced; the first of the series   14a(1)

3 ~~were~~ [was] called The Hero's Journey. As I found

out, there ~~is~~ [are] many myths that share the same   14a(6)

basic structure.

4   Campbell says that a hero is anyone who

give ~~their lives~~ [s his or her life] to something   14a(2), b(1)

other than ~~themselves~~ or bigger than ~~them-~~ [himself or herself]   14b(1), c(1)

5 ~~selves~~. For example, a hero might

save another person or sacrifice himself [or herself] for   14c

6 an ideal. A hero such as Telemachus go[es] away   14a(1)

from all ~~they~~ [he or she] know[s]--the place ~~they~~ [he or she] live[s] or   14a, b, c

the people ~~they~~ [he or she] love--into an unknown world
in which a number of things happen to ~~them.~~ [him or her]   14a, c

7 Campbell notes the things that happen~~s~~ to   14a(7)

the hero fall into two categories: trials

(physical or spiritual) and revelations

(seeing or hearing things that other people

8 don't). Each really ~~have~~ [has] to do with the   14a(2)

transformation of the hero's consciousness.

9 Neither trials nor revelations ~~has~~ [have] the power 14a(5)

10 to stop the hero. The hero, who often is a

young adult, always succeed~~s~~ and ~~they~~ [he or she] come~~s~~ 14a(1)-

back from ~~their~~ [his or her] adventures a new person.   14b, c

Analysis

Muhammad gave his instructor the following analysis and recommendations for avoiding agreement problems in future papers.

My main problem is that whenever a verb comes
right after a word that ends in s, I think the verb
should be plural. In sentences 2, 3, 6, and 10, I
made this error. Even when the word before the verb
isn't the subject, as in sentence 10 ("always"), I do
this. The other major problem in sentences 2, 6, and
10 is that several words came between the subject and
the verb, which I hadn't noticed while I was writing.

I made a lot of other agreement errors because I
didn't refer to my handbook while I was writing, but
I can't find any patterns in these errors.

To stop making subject-verb and pronoun-
antecedent errors, I need to start looking at each
sentence as a whole instead of referring to only a
few words. In the second paragraph I really got into
trouble--after I made the first error in sentence 4,
all the others followed automatically. As soon as I
wrote "give" instead of "gives" in sentence 4, "their
lives" was next because I was thinking only about
making the words sound right with "give." The same

```
thing happened in sentence 6 with "go" instead of
"goes."

    The other revision I still need to make is to
get rid of all the "himself or herself" and "he or
she" and "him or her" phrases from the beginning of
the second paragraph. I guess that after looking at
each sentence as a whole, I also need to look at big-
ger blocks of writing to see if my revisions make my
sentences sound awkward.
```

Muhammad solved this last problem in his final draft by changing all the subjects, verbs, and pronouns in the first few sentences in the second paragraph into their plural forms:

```
Campbell says that heroes are people who give
their lives to something other than or bigger than
themselves. For example, heroes save other people or
sacrifice themselves for their ideals. Heroes such as
Telemachus travel away from familiar people and
places into an unknown world, in which a number of
things can happen to them.
```

In this final revision, Muhammad also has revised his sentence structure to make his sentences more concise.

15 Pronoun Reference

A pronoun's meaning derives from an antecedent, a noun or other pronoun to which it refers. If the antecedents of the pronouns in your writing are not clear, your writing will not be clear.

15 a Revise a pronoun that refers to more than one antecedent.

Pronouns can, of course, refer to compound antecedents in such sentences as "Joan and Karen both believed they had performed well," where the pronoun *they* refers to *Joan and Karen*. However, if a pronoun can refer to either of two possible antecedents, it will be ambiguous, and readers will not know which antecedent is intended.

AMBIGUOUS   When Kathy visited her mother, she had a cold. [Who had a cold, Kathy or her mother?]

CLEAR   When she visited her mother, Kathy had a cold. Kathy had a cold when she visited her mother. Her mother had a cold when Kathy visited her. When Kathy visited her, her mother had a cold.

AMBIGUOUS   Arthur went to the airport with John, where he took a plane to Phoenix. [Who took the plane, John or Arthur?]

CLEAR   After going to the airport with John, Arthur took the plane to Phoenix.

After Arthur went to the airport with him, John took the plane to Phoenix.

Exercise 15.1

Revise the following paragraph to eliminate the ambiguous reference of pronouns.

Maureen told the other advertising agency employees that she had several designs for the client's new product and she wanted to get them together the next day. The owner of the agency told Maureen that her job required a great deal of creative ability. When the owner took Maureen to the meeting with the client the next afternoon, she introduced herself. When the client told Maureen the designs were excellent, she was pleased. Maureen told her coworker Carla that the ad agency had been given another ad campaign to plan, so she needed to get busy right away.

15 b Place each pronoun close enough to its antecedent to ensure clear reference.

The nearer a pronoun is to its antecedent, the more likely it is to be clear. The more remote the antecedent, the more difficult it will be for readers to understand the reference—particularly if other nouns come between the antecedent and the pronoun. Readers should never have to search for a pronoun's antecedent.

REMOTE   Credit cards spread throughout the United States and western Europe during the late 1960s. Card issuers make money from the fees paid by card owners and merchants and from interest charged on unpaid balances. Between 1965 and 1970, *they* increased from fewer than 5 million in use to more than 50 million. [*Credit cards* is the antecedent to which *they* refers, but readers may wonder whether *card issuers, card owners, unpaid balances,* or *merchants* is the antecedent for *they*.]

CLEAR   …Between 1965 and 1970, *credit cards* increased from fewer than 5 million…[This revision repeats the subject, *credit cards.*]
Credit cards spread throughout the United States and western Europe during the late 1960s, increasing between 1965 and 1970 from fewer than 5 million in use to more than 50 million … [The remote reference is eliminated by combining the first and third sentences.]

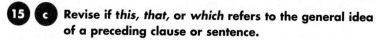

15 **c** Revise if *this, that,* or *which* refers to the general idea of a preceding clause or sentence.

The use of *this, that,* and *which* to refer to an idea stated in a preceding clause or sentence is common in informal English in such sentences as "They keep their promises, which is more than some people do." Such broad reference risks confusing readers. Ordinarily, eliminate any vague use of *this, that,* and *which,* either by recasting the sentence to eliminate the pronoun or by supplying a specific antecedent for the pronoun.

VAGUE	The disadvantages of credit cards can offset the advantages, which merits careful consideration. [What merits consideration: the advantages, the disadvantages, the offsetting of one by the other?]
CLEAR	The disadvantages of credit cards can offset the advantages, a fact which merits careful consideration. [*Fact* supplies a clear antecedent for *which.*]
CLEAR	Because the disadvantages can offset the advantages, the consequences of using credit cards should be carefully considered. [The sentence has been revised to eliminate the vague use of *which.*]
VAGUE	I announced that I was going to cut up all my credit cards. This caused a shocked silence.
CLEAR	I announced that I was going to cut up all my credit cards. This announcement caused a shocked silence. [*Announcement* clearly indicates the antecedent for *This.*]

Exercise 15.2

In the following sentences and paragraph, revise all sentences to eliminate remote or vague pronoun reference.

Sentence Practice

1 At one time the United States had over two million acres of wetlands, but because these wetlands have been drained to build cities and to create farmland, more than half of them are now gone. This is bad because wetlands provide a home for many species of birds and animals.

2 Destroying wetlands also destroys the wildlife there, which worries conservationists.

3 Wetlands such as ponds, marshes, streams, swamps, and estuaries are valuable natural resources and thus need to be preserved. Because they serve as breeding grounds for fish and birds, they are also a vital link in the chain of life.

Paragraph Practice

The duck population seems to have suffered the most as the number of America's wetlands has declined. That means that ducks have fewer wetlands in which to breed and live. For example, a mallard duck flying north in the spring may not find the same pond where it spent the previous summer. It will then have no place to make its nest. Conservationists report that the number of ducks flying south each winter has fallen in the last ten years. This has led the U.S. Fish and Wildlife Service to shorten the length of duck hunting season and to lower the number of ducks hunters can kill during the season.

15 d Revise if a pronoun refers to an implied but unexpressed antecedent.

To be clear, a pronoun must have a noun or the equivalent of a noun as its specific antecedent. Modifiers, possessives, and other words or phrases may suggest an appropriate noun but they do not provide clear and specific antecedents. Revise to provide a specific noun or noun equivalent as an antecedent for each pronoun, or otherwise revise the sentence.

FAULTY   Because we put a wire fence around the chicken yard, they can-
            not escape, [*Chicken* functions as an adjective modifying *yard.* It
            suggests but does not express the necessary antecedent *chickens.*]
REVISED   Because we put a wire fence around the chicken yard, the chick-
            ens cannot escape.

FAULTY   The guest speaker today is a banker, and that is a career I want
            to know more about. [The appropriate antecedent, *banking,* is
            implied, but it needs to be stated specifically.]
REVISED   The guest speaker today is a banker, and I want to know more
            about careers in banking.

Exercise 15.3

Revise the following paragraph to eliminate all references to unexpressed antecedents.

Mary Cassatt's paintings show the influence of the Impressionists, especially that of Edgar Degas. She was also influenced by Japanese art, emphasizing the uses of line and pattern she saw in them. Cassatt also imitated the use of figures in Japanese portraits, and that shows in such famous works as *Girl Arranging Her Hair* (1886) and *The Bath* (1891). Born in 1844 in Philadelphia, Pennsylvania, Cassatt lived much of her life in Paris, where she became a well-known American painter. This helped the French Impressionists because it influenced rich American art lovers to buy from the French painters as well as from Cassatt herself.

15 e Revise indefinite uses of *they, it,* and *you.*

The indefinite use of *they, it,* and *you* is common in speech: "In Germany, they drink beer"; "It says in the dictionary that…"; "You can never find anything where you're looking for it." In writing, these pronouns always require specific antecedents. Substitute an appropriate noun or noun equivalent, or rewrite the sentence.

| SPOKEN | Out in the country, *they* do not understand the problems of the city. |
| WRITTEN | People living out in the country do not understand the problems of the city. |

| SPOKEN | *They* said in the newspaper that Japan experienced another earthquake. |
| WRITTEN | The newspaper said that Japan experienced another earthquake. |

| INFORMAL | Many suburban towns do not permit *you* to drive more than twenty-five or thirty miles an hour. |
| FORMAL | Many suburban towns do not permit *people* (or *a person* or *one*) to drive more than twenty-five or thirty miles an hour. |

You is always correct in writing directions or in other contexts where the meaning is clearly *you, the reader.*

| CORRECT | Before turning on your air conditioner, be sure you have closed all your windows. |
| INAPPROPRIATE | In early colonial villages, you had to depend on wood for fuel. [The reader is unlikely to be living in an early colonial village.] |

| REVISED | In early colonial villages, people had to depend on wood for fuel. |
| BETTER | Early colonial villagers had to depend on wood for fuel. [This version is clearer and more concise than the first revision.] |

Exercise 15.4

Revise the following paragraph to avoid the indefinite use of *they, you,* and *it.*

In the United States, they are eating more fish, and as a result, aquaculture, which could be called fish farming, is a growing enterprise. In an article in yesterday's newspaper, it says that natural sources such as oceans and rivers aren't supplying enough fish to meet consumers' demands. To help supply those demands, they are growing fish as well as traditional crops like corn and wheat. Because of the development of aquaculture, that trout you buy for dinner may have come from a special pond on a farm instead of from a stream. In fact, on some fish farms, they let you go out and choose your own fish from the holding ponds.

15 f Use the pronoun *it* only one way in a sentence.

It is used as an expletive to postpone a subject ("It is wise to be careful"), in certain idioms ("It is cold") and colloquial expressions ("He made it to the finish line"), and as a definite pronoun referring to specific antecedents. All of these uses are acceptable, but sentences in which more than one of these uses occur are likely to be confusing.

CONFUSING	She put her car in the garage because she never leaves *it* out when *it* is bad weather. [The first *it* refers to *car*; the second is idiomatic.]
IMPROVED	She put her car in the garage because she never leaves it out when the weather is bad [or *in bad weather*].

15 **g** Match *who, which,* and *that* with appropriate antecedents.

In general, use *who* to refer to persons and *which* or *that* to refer to things.

> Many *students who* major in mathematics today find employment with computer companies.
>
> *Arkansas, which* became a state in 1836, was earlier a part of Louisiana.
>
> Among the *flowers that* [or *which*] grow most easily are petunias and marigolds.

The possessive *whose* is frequently used to refer to things when the phrase *of which* would be awkward.

> *Cinderella* is a story *whose* ending most of us know. [Compare *the ending of which.*]

The relative pronoun *that* can be used only in restrictive clauses, which limit the meaning of the word they modify and are not set off by commas. *Which* can be used in both restrictive and nonrestrictive clauses. Nonrestrictive clauses are set off by commas (see Section **32c**). Some writers prefer to introduce all restrictive clauses with *that* and to limit the use of *which* entirely to nonrestrictive clauses.

> The *Eighteenth Amendment, which* forbade the manufacture, sale, import, or export of intoxicating liquors, instituted nationwide prohibition in 1919.
>
> The *amendment that* [or *which*] repealed prohibition was ratified in 1933.

Exercise 15.5

Revise the following sentences so that pronouns are used appropriately.

1 Five types of plants who eat insects are found in the United States.
2 Because these plants live in soil that has little nitrogen in it, it is the insect organs that supply the nitrogen the plant needs to survive.
3 The venus flytrap, that is the best known of the carnivorous plants, has leaves that snap shut on insects.

Exercise 15.6

Revise the following paragraph to eliminate the faulty reference of pronouns.

> Because most people today take for granted having ice anytime you want it, it is hard to realize that ice has not always been available for chilling drinks or for filling a cooler for a picnic. In the past, it had to be hacked out of frozen

lakes and moved to icehouses, where it was kept covered in sawdust. The people that wanted ice bought it from an ice vendor which delivered blocks of it to hotels, homes, and restaurants. They had to use the ice quickly, for there was no refrigeration. It says in a book about the history of ice in the United States that in 1834 Jacob Perkins invented the first refrigeration unit. This made it possible to store ice for longer periods of time. Refrigeration and ice-making have come a long way since that: Today a person can go to your refrigerator door and fill a glass with it without ever having to open the freezer.

In Your Own Words

Review the problems of pronoun reference discussed in this chapter. List the five rules which cause you the most difficulty as a writer. Then write a two-paragraph discussion about the characteristics you look for in a friend, and in this paragraph, incorporate sentences that illustrate the correct use of those five rules.

16 Shifts

Writers keep each sentence consistent by using one subject; one tense, voice, and mood in verbs; and one person and number in pronouns, as far as grammar and meaning allow. Unnecessary shifts in any of these elements tend to obscure meaning and make reading more difficult that it has to be (see Section **6g** for a discussion of consistency within paragraphs, **29e-f** to review verbs, and **27** to review pronouns).

16 a Revise unnecessary shifts in subject or voice.

Particularly in compound and complex sentences, meaning frequently requires the writer to refer to more than one subject, as in the following sentence:

> When the *car* hit their dog, *John* ran home, and *Bill* held the dog until help arrived.

Here, meaning requires a shift of subject from one clause to another.

Less frequently, meaning may justify a shift from active to passive voice within a sentence.

> Three men *escaped* from the state prison yesterday but *were captured* before sundown.

Here, the writer could have chosen to write *but the police captured them,* changing the subject but keeping the active voice in both main clauses of a compound sentence. But by choosing to use the compound predicate, *escaped...but were captured,* the writer keeps attention focused on the important subject, *three men.*

Unlike the shifts in subject and voice in these sentences, the shifts in the following sentences are unnecessary;

FAULTY *As the boys approached* the swamp, *frogs could be heard* croaking. [Here the focus of the sentence is on *the boys*. The shifts of subject from *the boys* to *frogs* and of the voice of the verb from the active to the passive are unnecessary and distracting.]

REVISED *As the boys approached* the swamp, *they could hear* frogs croaking.

FAULTY *Ellen stayed* at a mountain resort, and most of her *time was spent* skiing. [The sentence is about Ellen. The shift of subject from *Ellen* to *time* and the resulting shift from active to passive voice blur rather than sharpen the sentence.]

REVISED *Ellen stayed* at a mountain resort *and spent* most of her time skiing.

Exercise 16.1

In the following paragraph, correct any unnecessary shifts in subject or voice.

Skyscrapers symbolize technological progress, affluence, and the excitement of urban life; for a hundred years builders have been fascinated by them and the possibilities they offer city planners. This fascination was stimulated in 1889 by the construction of the Eiffel Tower in Paris, for this marvel rose to 984 feet. Developers quickly saw that constructing tall buildings required less land in expensive urban centers, so efforts were intensified by them to encourage innovations in engineering tall structures. In 1931 the Empire State Building was completed in New York, and its 102 floors were seen as a technological wonder. Today, the 120-floor CN Tower in Toronto overshadows the Empire State Building, and the Eiffel Tower is only half the size of the CN Tower. In Japan plans are underway to build a skyscraper of 500 floors, and it will house enough stores and services that its residents will rarely need to leave the building.

Revise unnecessary shifts in person or number.

Unless meaning clearly requires such changes, keep person and number within a given sentence consistent.

In English, writers and speakers can make general statements by using either the second-person pronoun *you*, the third-person pronoun *one*, or one of various third-person general nouns such as the singular *a person* or the plural *people*. Thus any one of the following sentences is consistent:

If *you* want to play games, *you* must learn the rules.

If *a person* [or *one*] wants to play games, *he or she* must learn the rules.

If *people* want to play games, *they* must learn the rules.

Unnecessary **shifts in person** are frequently shifts from the third person (the person being talked about) to the second person (the person being talked to), as in the following:

FAULTY	When *a person* has good health *you* should feel fortunate.
REVISED	When *a person* has good health, *he or she* should feel fortunate.
	When *you* have good health, *you* should feel fortunate.
	When *people* have good health, *they* should feel fortunate.

A second kind of unnecessary shift occurs when the writer starts with the first person and shifts to the second. Such sentences are ordinarily more effective when the writer maintains the first-person point of view.

WEAK	I refuse to go to a movie theater where you can't buy popcorn.
IMPROVED	I refuse to go to a movie theater where I can't buy popcorn.

These shifts are sometimes called **shifts in point of view**. Readers count on point of view to signal their relationship to the writer and to the information being presented. Think, for example, how startling it is to be reading as a third-party "observer" and then suddenly find the language pointing remarks directly at "you."

Faulty **shifts in number** within a sentence usually involve faulty agreement between pronouns and their antecedents (see Section **14b**).

FAULTY	I like *an occasional cup* of coffee, for *they* give me an added lift. [Shift from singular to plural. The pronoun should agree with the singular antecedent *cup*.]
REVISED	I like *an occasional cup* of coffee, for *it* gives me an added lift.
	I like *occasional cups* of coffee, for *they* give me an added lift.

Exercise 16.2

In the following sentences, correct any unnecessary shifts in person or number.

1 Food lovers should never tire of eating pizza because you can order them with an almost endless variety of crusts and toppings.

2 A vegetarian and a meat lover can share a pizza if he or she carefully arranges the toppings.

3 I like the thin, crispy crusts because on it you can taste the toppings more distinctly than a person can on the medium-thick or deep-dish crusts.

4 Those people with hearty appetites often prefer the Chicago-style pizza because those have both a bottom and a top crust with a thick filling of sauce and vegetables or meat that really fills you up.

5 Pizza can even be dessert for some pizza lovers: He or she orders them with chocolate chips or fruits that you would not expect to taste good.

16 c Revise unnecessary shifts in tense or mood.

In a sentence such as "Nostalgia is a love of the way things were in our youth," meaning requires a shift of tense from the present *is* to the past *were*. Unless the meaning or the grammar of a sentence requires such changes in tense, keep the same tense throughout all the verbs in a sentence (see also Sections **29a-d**).

FAULTY	I *sat* down at the desk and *begin* to write. [The verb shifts unnecessarily from past to present tense.]
REVISED	I *sat* down at the desk and *began* to write.

FAULTY	In Chapter One she *accepts* her first job as a kitchen maid, but by Chapter Three she *was cooking* for an Austrian prince.
REVISED	In Chapter One she *accepts* her first job as a kitchen maid, but by Chapter Three she *is cooking* for an Austrian prince. [In this sentence, the revision uses the present tense in both verbs because it is customary to use the present tense in describing actions in literature. See Section **29d**.]

Shifts in mood within a single sentence or a series of related sentences are almost never justified. Such shifts often occur in writing directions. Avoid them by casting directions consistently either in the imperative or the indicative mood (see Section **29f** for an explanation of *imperative* and *indicative*).

FAULTY	*Hold* the rifle firmly against your shoulder, and then you *should take* careful aim. [Shift from imperative to indicative mood.]
REVISED	*Hold* the rifle firmly against your shoulder and then *take* careful aim. [Both verbs are in the imperative mood.]
	You *should hold* the rifle firmly against your shoulder and then [you should] *take* careful aim. [Both verbs are in the indicative. Note that here the second *you should* can be omitted since it will be understood by the reader.]

Directions are usually most economical and effective when written in the imperative mood.

Exercise 16.3

In the following paragraph, correct any needless shifts in tense or mood.

Australia offers its citizens great geographic and cultural diversity. The smallest continent, Australia featured deserts and mountains as well as tropical areas, and go to Australia to see unique plants and animals. Settled by the British in the eighteenth century, Australia was first a penal colony, but it attracts colonists increasingly during the nineteenth and early twentieth centuries. Its early attraction results from the discovery of gold and diamonds there, but in recent decades economic prosperity has drawn immigrants from many cultures. Today, Australia, the world's foremost producer of wool, manufactured significant amounts of steel, cars, textiles, appliances, and other products. In addition, visit its cities, especially Sydney, Melbourne, and Brisbane, to see the commercial, industrial, and artistic advances that make Australia a dynamic, alluring country.

16 d Revise incomplete shifts from indirect to direct discourse.

Direct discourse is the exact words of a speaker or writer. Indirect discourse reports what someone has said or written, with appropriate changes in tense, person, and the like.

DIRECT	She said, "I'm determined to win this match."
INDIRECT	She said that she was determined to win the match.

The tense in indirect discourse should ordinarily be the same as the tense of the main verb. Incomplete shifts between direct and indirect discourse often cause tense errors.

FAULTY	Lincoln asked the general *whether his army was well supplied* and *is it ready for battle.*
REVISED	Lincoln asked the general whether his army was well supplied and ready for battle. [indirect discourse]
	Lincoln asked the general, "Is your army well supplied? Is it ready for battle?" [direct discourse]
FAULTY	They wondered *if we had missed the train* and *are we trying to telephone them* to let them know.
REVISED	They wondered if we had missed the train and if we were trying to telephone them to let them know. [indirect discourse]
	They wondered, "Have they missed the train, and are they trying to telephone us to let us know?" [direct discourse]

ESL Highlight

Changing from Direct to Indirect Discourse

No change of verb tense is necessary when the verb introducing an indirect statement is in the present tense (*says, explains, mention*). When this verb is in the simple past tense (*said, remarked, stated*), do the following:

1 Change all the verbs in the reported statement, except infinitives and the main verb after a modal auxiliary (see Section **29c** on modals).

She said, "I *want* to change my major."
She said she *wanted* to change her major.
He said, "Louisa *is gaining* confidence."
He said Louisa *was gaining* confidence.
We said, "She *can* study here tonight."
We said she *could* study here tonight.

Exception: The tense does not change when the indirect statement expresses a general truth or a historical fact: "Joe said that the Mississippi River flooded in the summer of 1993."

Changes in Modal Auxiliaries

Make the following changes in modals when switching from direct to indirect discourse.

Direct discourse	Indirect discourse
can	could
may	might
must	had to
will	would

Usually, *could, would, might,* and *should* do not change.

2 Change pronouns and possessives to the second or third person unless the speaker is reporting his or her own words. Add a noun if necessary to clarify the meaning.

Sally said, "She's my favorite comedian."
Sally said that *Roseanne Barr* was *her* favorite comedian.

3 Change demonstrative pronouns (*this, that, these, those*) to *the*. Change the word *here* to indicate the location *here* refers to—for example, *in the Student Union building.*

Note that the word *that* after the introductory verb is optional in indirect discourse.

Exercise 16.4

Revise the following sentences and paragraph, correcting all needless shifts in tense, mood, voice, person, and number and any shifts from indirect to direct quotation. Be prepared to explain your revisions.

Sentence Practice

1 Although most sharks swim at speeds up to 30 miles per hour, a speed of 60 miles per hour can be attained by the mako shark.
2 The average mako shark is about 12 feet long and weighed up to 1,000 pounds.
3 If you go fishing for mako sharks, a real challenge may be in store for you.
4 A hooked mako shark may fight for hours, and they have also been known to attack boats or even leap into the boat.
5 If you want a challenge, you can fish for a mako shark, but be careful, for its teeth are long, thin, and very sharp.

Paragraph Practice

When I was swimming at a beach on the southern coast last summer, the lifeguard told me to watch out for sharks and did I know what to do if I spotted one in the water. Sharks live in all oceans, but because they are most common in warmer waters, when you swim in warm coastal waters you should be cautious, for people may encounter a shark. Fortunately, not all sharks are predators; the whale shark feeds on plankton, and they do not bother swimmers. The basking shark is another harmless shark species, and plankton is eaten by this shark. Nevertheless, one hears vivid stories of shark attacks, so you tend to become wary when you go into the water.

In Your Own Words

Assume that you are writing a letter to a friend, a letter in which you include a paragraph offering some advice to help the friend get a date. After you have written this paragraph (in the second person, singular, present and future tenses), rewrite the advice so that it reflects the advice given to a group (plural, third person) at a seminar two months earlier (past tense).

Writers Revising

Shifts and Pronoun Reference

Fran, the Placement Office intern, read a student's article for the placement newsletter. The writer was supposed to have summarized an article originally appearing in *National Business Employment Weekly*. While adapting the original for readers of the placement newsletter, the student created shifts and pronoun reference errors. See if you can correct the mismatches; then compare your revision with Fran's version, which follows the draft.

Draft

There comes a time when we must make a break and rely on ourselves as a career expert. To a large degree, you are your own expert because only you know best about your interests, challenges, and what suits you. This means your own judgment and intuition must be trusted, if you are going to take the initiative in your job search. They say we are often our own worst enemies; if you see yourself as a bungling idiot during an interview, you'll probably behave like it.

Revision

1   There comes a time when we must make a

break and rely on ourselves as ~~a~~ career

2 expert. To a large degree, ~~you~~ we are ~~your~~ our own   16b

expert because only ~~you~~ we know best about ~~your~~ our

interests, challenges, and what suits ~~you.~~ us.

> *Being our own experts means we must trust our*
> 3 ~~This means your~~ ^own judgment and intuition,   15c, 16a
>   *we*
> ~~must be trusted,~~ if ~~you~~ are going to take the
>   *our*   *We can*
> 4 initiative in ~~your~~ job search. ~~They say we~~   15e
>   *be*   *we*
> ~~are~~ often ^our own worst enemies; if ~~you~~ see
> *ourselves*   *s*
> ~~yourself~~ as ~~a~~ bungling idiot^ during an inter-
>   *we are likely to*   *idiots*
> view, ~~you'll probably~~ behave like ~~it~~.   15d

Analysis

As she considered possible revisions, Fran knew she had to choose a single point of view, addressing the audience in either first-person plural (*we*) or second person (*you*). She decided that *we* would encourage readers to identify with the article; she also wanted to avoid making readers feel bad, since some negative things were being said (for example, *bungling idiot*). Fran first revised the entire article to reflect this decision, changing all the antecedents and verbs to make them consistent with *we*.

This in sentence 3 and *They say* in sentence 4 are vague, indefinite uses of these pronouns. Fran substituted more precise language for *This* and eliminated *They say*, since it serves no useful purpose in the sentence. The *it* that ends the paragraph has no expressed antecedent that agrees with it in number and makes the end of the article seem weak; Fran simply changed it to *idiots*, which also maintains the consistent use of number with the plural pronoun *we*.

Finally, Fran reexamined *must be trusted* in sentence 3, which she thought sounded awkward. Her revision from the passive voice to the active voice the sentence much stronger.

 Misplaced Modifiers

Modern English relies heavily on word order to show relationships among words. *Dog bites man* does not mean the same thing as *Man bites dog*. If the words are reversed, so is the meaning.

Just as word order helps readers keep subject-verb-object relationships clear, it also helps them know which words are the objects of modifiers. Readers expect modifiers to be next to the words they modify, so writers must be especially careful to place phrases and clauses near the nouns they modify. Otherwise, sentences such as these can occur:

He bought a horse from a stranger with a lame hind leg.

We returned to Atlanta after a week's vacation on Monday.

At best the reader is distracted by such sentences; at worst, ludicrous literal meanings can destroy the writer's credibility. Consider, for example, the following misplaced modifier noted by a national magazine:

> "While a Legion bugler played 'To the Colors,' the first flag was hoisted on DeVane Park's 30-foot flagpole, followed by David Rinald singing the national anthem." *Lake Placid* (Fla.) *Journal*
>
> Helped him hit the high notes.

—*The New Yorker*

  Be sure limiting adverbs such as *almost, even, hardly, just, only, nearly* precede the words they modify.

Speakers commonly put *only* and similar adverbs before the verb, regardless of which words they modify. In writing, limiting adverbs must be placed before the words they modify. A limiting adverb can modify a verb, as in "Her one-year-old son couldn't *even* crawl yet," an adverb, or an adjective preceding a noun:

SPOKEN	Gina had barely just reached the parking lot when she saw the birthday balloons inside her car.
WRITTEN	Gina had just barely reached the parking lot when she saw the birthday balloons inside her car. [*Just* modifies *barely*.]
SPOKEN	I *only* ran one mile.
WRITTEN	I ran *only* one mile. [*Only* modifies *one*.]

Exercise 17.1

Revise the following paragraph so that limiting adverbs are placed before the words they modify. Then write five sentences of your own, each using a different limiting adverb (*almost, even, hardly, just, only, practically, precisely, nearly, shortly,* and so on) placed appropriately in the sentence.

> Comic strips in the newspaper practically entertain every reader because they appeal to basic human needs and desires. Even long-running strips like "Dick Tracy," "Blondie," "Dennis the Menace," and "Beetle Bailey" comfort readers because they precisely have been ever present throughout the readers' own years of trials and tribulations. Like the older strips, the newer ones reassure readers and make them believe that they almost can accomplish anything if they have only faith in themselves and the will to face problems head-on. Whether Cathy is trying another diet or another shopping spree or Charlie Brown is trying to kick just the football, a comic strip character can give readers both a laugh and a lesson about life. It hardly is a surprise that people of all ages nearly turn to the comics when they pick up the newspaper.

Move the italicized adverb to a different place in each of the following sentences so that a new meaning is created. Be prepared to explain the differences in meaning between the two sentences. Then write five sentences of your own that change the meaning with a repositioning of the adverb.

1 *Actually,* not all comic strips in newspapers are funny.
2 Every comic page offers two or three strips that are *usually* serious.
3 For example, *generally* "Mary Worth" and "Prince Valiant" reflect serious moral issues that do not elicit laughter.
4 Other serious strips that *often* make us laugh only on the surface are political cartoons like "Pogo," "B.C.," "The Wizard of Id," and "Doonesbury."
5 *Just* regularly reading those allows comic lovers to keep up with everything happening in national politics.

17 b Be sure modifying phrases refer clearly to the words they modify.

Phrases used to modify nouns must ordinarily be placed immediately after the words they are intended to modify (to review phrases, see Section **26g**). The following examples show the confusion created by misplaced modifiers.

MISPLACED   Jon borrowed a bicycle from a friend *with saddlebags.* [The writer intended the phrase *with saddlebags* to modify *bicycle,* not *friend.*]

CLEAR   Jon borrowed a bicycle *with saddlebags* from a friend.

MISPLACED   Harriet bought herself a vintage car for her birthday with all original parts.

CLEAR   Harriet bought herself a vintage car with all original parts for her birthday.

Phrases used as adverbs may usually be placed within the sentence—close to the words they modify—or at the beginning or end of the sentence. In some sentences, however, their placement requires special thought.

MISPLACED   At the bottom of the garbage can under the coffee grounds and eggshells, Katie's eyes spotted the gold bracelet. [The writer began the sentence with a phrase that modifies the last word, *bracelet.*]

CLEAR   Katie's eyes spotted the gold bracelet at the bottom of the garbage can under the coffee grounds and eggshells.

MISPLACED   A huge boulder fell as we rounded the corner *with a crash.* [*With a crash* modifies the verb *fell,* so it should be positioned immediately after *fell.*]

CLEAR   A huge boulder fell *with a crash* as we rounded the corner.

MISPLACED	Thank you for the beautiful bowl. Right now it's sitting on our buffet *full of fruit*. [That's a lot of fruit!]
CLEAR	Thank you for the beautiful bowl. Right now it's sitting *full of fruit* on our buffet.

Exercise 17.3

Revise the following paragraph so that the modifying phrases refer clearly to the words they are intended to modify.

> Although tofu is a familiar food in the Orient, the soybean product in the United States isn't well known. In the Orient for more than a thousand years tofu has been a staple of people's diets. Tofu with no cholesterol is a versatile food. To make tofu, soybeans are first soaked and then finely ground in water. Because tofu is high in protein, it is often used in dishes such as lasagna as a meat substitute.

17 **c** Be sure modifying clauses refer clearly to the words they modify.

Clauses that modify nouns usually begin with *who, which,* or *that* and follow immediately after the words they modify.

MISPLACED	The dog had a ribbon around his neck *that was tied in a bow.* [The ribbon, not his neck, was tied in a bow.]
CLEAR	Around his neck the dog had a ribbon *that was tied in a bow.*
MISPLACED	The children cautiously approached the deserted house by a winding path, *which was said to be haunted.* [The house, not the path, was said to be haunted.]
CLEAR	By a winding path, the children cautiously approached the house *that was said to be haunted.*

Adverb clauses are introduced by words such as *after, although, because, since,* and *until.* Like adverb phrases, they can usually be placed either within the sentence close to the words they modify or at the beginning or end of the sentence; they can sometimes be confusing when placed carelessly (clauses and phrases are discussed in Sections **26g** and **26h**).

MISPLACED	The police towed the stolen station wagon to the city garage *after it was abandoned.* [The clause *after it was abandoned* is intended to modify the verb *towed* but seems to modify the noun *garage.*]
CLEAR	*After the stolen station wagon was abandoned,* the police towed it to the city garage.
	The police towed the stolen station wagon, *after it was abandoned,* to the city garage.

Exercise 17.4

Revise the following paragraph to place the modifying clauses in clear relationships to the words they modify.

> A number of talk shows currently appear on television that did not exist ten years ago. These shows feature well-known hosts and usually include some debate by the audience, which may be heated. This debate generally centers on issues of concern to viewers, such as parent-child relationships, marital problems, and substance abuse, because it is a means of communicating help to a vast television audience. Guests on these shows may range from best-selling authors and film stars to homemakers and victims of crimes who are undergoing therapy as a result. Although they sometimes seem uncontrollable, every talk show host seems to have a special talent for keeping audience members from growing too insulting or too angry.

17 d Revise to eliminate squinting modifiers.

A squinting modifier is one that may modify either a preceding word or a following word. It squints at the words on its right and left and leaves the reader confused.

SQUINTING	His physician told him *frequently* to exercise.
CLEAR	His physician *frequently* told him to exercise.
	His physician told him to exercise *frequently*.
SQUINTING	He promised *on his way home* to visit us.
CLEAR	*On his way home*, he promised to visit us.
	He promised to visit us *on his way home*.

Exercise 17.5

Revise the following sentences to eliminate squinting modifiers.

1 Finding time to exercise often poses problems for many people.
2 A person may decide in the morning to exercise, but he or she may have conflicts that make exercising frequently impossible.
3 Once a person loses the momentum to exercise early in the day, he or she may not want later to exercise.
4 If the would-be exerciser plans in the evening to exercise, friends may interrupt suddenly to lure one away.
5 A person has to make a firm commitment that places exercising regularly at the top of his or her daily priorities.

17 e Revise awkwardly split infinitives.

An infinitive is split when an adverbial modifier separates the *to* from the verb. There is nothing ungrammatical about splitting an infinitive, and sometimes a split is useful to avoid awkwardness. But most split infinitives are unnecessary.

| AWKWARD | I tried not *to* carelessly *hurt* the kitten. |
| CLEAR | I tried not *to hurt* the kitten carelessly. |

AWKWARD	You should try *to*, if you can, *take* a walk every day.
CLEAR	If you can, you should try *to take* a walk every day.
	You should try *to take* a walk every day if you can.

On the other hand, note the following sentence:

The course is designed *to* better *equip* graduates to go into business.

Better squints between *designed* and *to equip*; after to *equip*, *better* modifies *graduates*; at the end of the sentence *better* is awkward and unnatural, if not entirely unclear. In this case, the split infinitive is the best choice for conveying the meaning the writer intended.

Exercise 17.6

Revise the following paragraph to eliminate awkwardly split infinitives.

People who want to improve their diets should be sure to carefully choose their breakfast cereals. Shoppers have a wide variety of cereals to, when they're at the supermarket, choose from. Therefore, consumers have to always be sure to thoroughly read the nutrition information labels on the cereal boxes, for some cereals have high fat, sugar, and salt contents. To accurately determine what's in a box of cereal, shoppers should read the "Nutrition Information" and "Carbohydrate Information" labels. Being careful about the cereals they eat is a good way for people to, if they want, start improving their diets.

17 f Use effective sentence patterns.

Readers rely on related sentence elements and known sentence patterns to help them process a sentence's meaning (see Section **26f**). Separation of a subject and its predicate, a verb and its objects, or a main verb and its auxiliary verb requires readers to hold pieces of information "in suspension" so to speak. So when you go against reader's expectations about the order of sentence patterns, you should have a good reason for doing so.

Experienced writers intentionally separate related sentence elements to achieve special effects, such as adding suspense or drama to a sentence by delaying the verb. Nevertheless, effective separation of related sentence elements can be a judgment call, and not everyone will agree on the results. Use such separations only if your subject and purpose warrant the dramatic and artificial impression that separations convey.

| EFFECTIVE | The captain, *seeing the ominous storm clouds gathering* |
| SEPARATION | *overhead,* ordered the crew to take in the sail. |

> Only when a man is safely ensconced under six feet of earth, *with several tons of enlauding granite upon his chest*, is he in a position to give advice with any certainty, and then he is silent.
>
> —Edward Newton

AWKWARD
SEPARATION

She *found*, after an hour's search, the *money* hidden under the rug.

CLEAR

After an hour's search, she *found* the *money* hidden under the rug.

AWKWARD
SEPARATION

At the convention I saw Mary Ward, whom I *had* many years ago *met* in Chicago.

CLEAR

At the convention I saw Mary Ward, whom I *had met* many years ago in Chicago.

Exercise 17.7

Revise the following paragraph to eliminate unnecessary separation of sentence parts.

> Harriet Tubman, because she worked in the Underground Railroad to lead her people to freedom, came to be called Moses. Harriet Tubman was, in 1820, born a slave, but she, in 1849, escaped and eventually became a "conductor" on the Underground Railroad. Tubman led, while risking great danger to herself, more than 300 slaves to freedom. Individuals like Harriet Tubman were crucial to the success of the Underground Railroad because the system needed, so that it could move slaves north to freedom, brave and dedicated workers.

Exercise 17.8

Revise the following sentences and paragraph to eliminate all misplaced modifiers and awkward separations. Be prepared to explain your revisions.

Sentence Practice

1 Shopping malls have become major cultural centers that many Americans decide often to visit.
2 Malls to the uninitiated only offer an almost endless string of stores, but to the seasoned mall visitor, malls offer opportunities to regularly socialize, exercise, and people-watch that are unique.
3 Some people in the mall find ice-skating rinks even, bowling alleys, and other organized entertainment, and they enjoy frequently indulging in the special food areas that have many kinds of ethnic foods, which sometimes look like sidewalk cafes.
4 Teenagers who are too young to drive soon discover that their parents will deliver them to malls, although providing a haven for teens may not have been the developers' main goal, which are safe, exciting places to routinely meet friends that have stimulating lights and sounds and smells.

5 Malls, because the many mall visitors like having them, also feature on occasion special events such as art exhibits, talent competitions, and antique shows.

Paragraph Practice

Among the most regular visitors to the mall are exercisers, whom one can encounter any time during the day or night after the mall has opened. In fact, some malls open as early as 6 A.M. to generally enable the public to, before the shopping day begins, use the facilities to keep in shape. Some mall walkers enjoy the convenience of a secure environment, warm in the winter and cool in the summer, which benefits especially the elderly exercisers or single women who do not feel safe walking in their own neighborhoods. People recovering from illness or surgery in the mall find that they have a flat surface to walk on and that there are always nearly other people who become a kind of support group. Of course, some exercisers in the mall don't wear exercise clothes or shoes or consider themselves exercisers even at all: These are the intrepid shoppers who dash from one store to the next in a mad, calorie-burning frenzy to skillfully take advantage of the sales.

In Your Own Words

In a newspaper or a magazine, find two examples of a misplaced modifier. (They are not difficult to find in print.) Write a paragraph explaining both what seems to have been the intended meaning and what meaning the writer ultimately conveyed.

18 Dangling Modifiers

A modifier must have something to modify. A **dangling modifier** has nothing to modify because the word it would logically modify is not present in its sentence: for example, "Driving through the mountains, three bears were seen." In this sentence, the modifying phrase has no logical object. The sentence says the bears are driving, but common sense tells us bears can't drive.

Dangling modifiers may be verbal or prepositional phrases (**18a-c**) or elliptical clauses (**18d**). They often come at the beginning of a sentence, but they can come at the end as well. Dangling modifiers often occur in mixed constructions when a writer begins a sentence as if he or she intends to use an active voice verb in the main clause but finishes it by shifting to a passive voice verb (see Section **20b**).

Eliminate dangling modifiers (1) by reworking the sentence so that an appropriate word is provided for the modifier to modify—in the case of a mixed construction, by using the same verb voice in both clauses—or (2) by expanding the dangler into a full subordinate clause (see Section **26h**).

The following examples—the first from a student essay, the second from a financial journal—show danglers and how to eliminate them.

DANGLING   Driving through the mountains, three bears were seen.

REVISED   While driving through the mountains, *we saw* three bears. [active voice verbs throughout; word to modify supplied]
As we were driving through the mountains, we saw three bears. [expansion to full subordinate clause]

DANGLING   When asked to explain why they borrowed money from a particular bank, previous good experience and low interest rates were most frequently mentioned as reasons.

REVISED   When asked to explain why they borrowed money from a particular bank, *people* most frequently *mentioned* previous good experience and low interest rates as reasons. [active voice verbs throughout; word to modify supplied]

Dangling modifiers can also slip into writing when an appropriate object for the modifier is present in an adjacent sentence but not in the sentence containing the dangler. Consider this paragraph from a campus newspaper:

While wearing a Halloween mask and carrying a handgun, a man entered Marsh Pharmacy and asked for all of the narcotics, said Frank Reinhart, a temporary Marsh employee. According to Reinhart, he was filling in for another pharmacist when a man came up to the desk. *Wearing a green mask and overalls*, Reinhart estimated his height at about 6 feet and his weight at about 150 pounds.

Presumably the would-be thief, rather than Reinhart, was wearing the green mask and overalls. The reporter forgot that a modifier and the word it modifies need to be located in the same sentence:

According to Reinhart, he was filling in for another pharmacist when *a man* wearing a green mask and overalls came up to the desk.

18 **a** Revise to eliminate dangling participial phrases.

A **participle** is a verb form usually ending in *-ing* or *-ed* and used as an adjective to modify a noun or pronoun. A participial phrase consists of a participle, its object, and any modifiers of the participle or object (see Section **26g**).

DANGLING   Coming home late, the house was dark. [There is nothing in the sentence that can sensibly be coming home. A revision must identify some person.]

REVISED   Coming home late, we found the house dark.
When we came home late, the house was dark.

DANGLING   Being made of glass, Rick handled the tabletop carefully.

REVISED   Because the tabletop was made of glass, Rick handled it carefully. [The participial phrase is expanded into a subordinate clause.]

Exercise 18.1

Revise the following paragraph to eliminate dangling participial phrases.

Putting together a résumé, much care must be taken in order for the résumé to be received favorably by a prospective employer. Neatly framed by a pleasingly wide margin, the job applicant should avoid strikeovers, white-out, and misspellings. In addition, the appropriate kind of organization should be used, taking great pains to give precise information about the applicant's educational background, work experience, and interests. Remembering to include volunteer jobs, offices held in clubs, and scholarships and honors awarded, the résumé also should mention skills in foreign languages and with computers. Printed on white or off-white paper of good quality, the applicant should also include a cover letter explaining why he or she is seeking an interview for the job.

18 b Revise to eliminate dangling phrases that contain gerunds.

A **gerund** is an -*ing* form of a verb used as a noun. A gerund phrase consists of a gerund, its object, and any modifiers of the gerund or object (see Section **26g**). In typical dangling phrases that contain gerunds, the gerund or gerund phrase serves as the object of a preposition.

Dangling gerunds, like the dangling infinitives discussed in Section **18c**, sometimes occur when the subject of the main clause is not the same as the implied subject of the gerund phrase. Because a shift of subject is often accompanied by a shift to passive voice, checking the main clause for passive voice verbs is a quick way to test for modifying phrases that may be dangling.

DANGLING   Before exploring the desert, our water supply was replenished. [Who replenished it?]
REVISED   Before exploring the desert, we replenished our water supply.

DANGLING   After putting a worm on my hook, the fish began to bite. [A very accommodating fish that will bait the hook for you!]
REVISED   After I put a worm on my hook, the fish began to bite.

Exercise 18.2

Revise the following paragraph to eliminate dangling gerund phrases.

After completing the résumé, the cover letter should be prepared on high quality, letter size paper that matches that of the résumé. Three main areas should be organized before writing the letter—a brief opening paragraph that identifies the job being sought, a middle section that summarizes the applicant's qualifications and refers to the résumé, and a brief closing paragraph that requests an interview. By using the cover letter to highlight one's special talents, the reader may be motivated to look carefully at the résumé. On preparing the rough draft of the cover letter and résumé, however, spelling and grammar must be double-checked so that the job application looks professional. Because of finding mechanical errors and a sloppy appearance in the cover letter and résumé, many talented applicants do not get the chance to have the job interview they badly want.

18 c **Revise to eliminate dangling infinitive phrases.**

An **infinitive** consists of the infinitive marker *to* followed by the base form of the verb. An infinitive phrase consists of an infinitive, its object, and any modifiers of the infinitive or object.

DANGLING	To take good pictures, a good camera must be used. [Who will use the camera?]
REVISED	To take good pictures, you must use a good camera.
	If you wish to take good pictures, you must use a good camera.
DANGLING	To skate well, practice is necessary.
REVISED	To skate well, you [or *one*] must practice.

Exercise 18.3

Revise the sentences in the following paragraph to eliminate dangling infinitive phrases.

To make a perfect omelet, the eggs should be very fresh. A 5- or 6-inch skillet should be used to make a two- or three-egg omelet. To make sure that the omelet won't be tough, the egg whites and the egg yolks should be mingled together, but not overbeaten. The heat under the pan should be kept at medium-high to cook the eggs without burning them. To put the finished omelet on a serving plate, the pan should be tilted toward the plate as the omelet is pushed out with a fork.

18 d **Revise to eliminate dangling elliptical clauses.**

An **elliptical clause** is one in which the subject or verb is implied or understood rather than stated. The clause dangles if its implied subject is not the same as the subject of the main clause. Eliminate a dangling elliptical clause by (1) making the dangling clause agree with the subject of the main clause or (2) supplying the omitted subject or verb.

DANGLING	*When a baby,* my grandfather gave me a silver cup.
REVISED	*When a baby,* I was given a silver cup by my grandfather.
	[The subject of the main clause agrees with the implied subject of the elliptical clause.]

REVISED   *When I was a baby,* my grandfather gave me a silver cup. [The omitted subject and verb are supplied in the elliptical clause.]

DANGLING   *While rowing on the lake,* the boat overturned.
REVISED   *While rowing on the lake,* we overturned the boat. [The subject of the main clause agrees with the implied subject of the elliptical clause.]

               While we were rowing on the lake, the boat overturned [*or* we overturned the boat]. [The elliptical clause is expanded into a subordinate clause.]

Exercise 18.4

Revise the following sentences to eliminate dangling elliptical clauses.

1 When looking for a job, several techniques may lead to quick success in the search.
2 Classified ads are not the only place to find out about jobs—or even the best place—if organized for the job search.
3 Unless using an employment agency, a school's career services office may offer the best leads about jobs.
4 Until confident of being hired, using personal contacts to network can also increase opportunities for finding a good job.
5 Even communicating with companies that have not advertised jobs can help the job searcher, unless poorly written.

Exercise 18.5

Revise the following sentences and paragraph to eliminate dangling modifiers.

Sentence Practice

1 The number of people who go to bowling alleys has not grown recently, although still the most popular indoor sport in the United States.
2 To attract more customers, computerized scoring systems, restaurants, and child-care centers have been added to bowling alleys.
3 When using the computerized scoring systems, tedious computations of strikes and spares are no longer necessary.
4 To attract young families with children, child-care centers in bowling alleys allow parents to enjoy themselves while their children play in a supervised area.
5 After an evening of bowling, a relaxing dinner can be enjoyed in the bowling alley's full-service restaurant.

Paragraph Practice

Having experienced a drop in attendance because of the popularity of home video, efforts were made to encourage customers to return to movie theaters. To make waiting before the movie more enjoyable, theater lobbies were expanded and redecorated. If hungry before or after the movie, some theaters added cafes and pizza parlors. After getting into the theater itself, comfortable seats and a temperature-controlled climate are other comforts encountered. To attract moviegoers with sophisticated sound systems at home, high-technology sound equipment is installed in most movie theaters. Today more popular than ever, people go to cineplexes to see the latest feature films.

In Your Own Words

Write a paragraph about your favorite way to spend a free afternoon. In this paragraph use two present participial phrases, one infinitive phrase, one phrase containing a gerund, and one elliptical clause. Be sure that you make these phrases clear modifiers, not dangling ones.

Writers Revising

Modifiers

Jim, a student in Freshman English, was assigned a personal experience essay. Part of the assignment was to try to achieve variety in sentence construction. When he read over his rough draft, however, Jim noticed that while varying his sentences he had created several dangling and misplaced modifiers. See if you can revise his work, keeping sentence variety but correcting faulty modification. Then compare your version with Jim's retyped revision, which appears after the draft.

Draft

Last summer I saw a hot-air balloon race. To really understand what is going on, a knowledge of hares and hounds is helpful. Taking off first, one balloon is designated the "hare" balloon, and then all the other balloons--the "hounds"--chase it.

The hare balloon after a while lands in a field some distance from the starting point. Marked with an "x," the hound balloon that is able to land on or closest to the hare balloon's spot wins the race. That balloon takes first prize and gets congratulations from all the other balloonists having "caught" the hare. Coming close to the hare balloon's landing spot is not easy particularly since hot-air balloons float with the wind and are difficult to maneuver.

Ballooning is the oldest form of aerial transportation. First flown in France, that country celebrated its 200th anniversary for ballooning in 1983.

Revision

Last summer I saw a hot-air balloon race.
To really understand what is going on, a knowl-   17e
edge of hares and hounds is helpful. Taking
off first, one balloon is designated the "hare"
balloon, and then all the other balloons--
"hounds"--chase it.

After a while the hare balloon lands in a   17f
field some distance from the starting point. The
hare balloon's landing spot is marked with an   17b
"x," and the hound balloon that is able to land
on or closest to that spot wins the race.
Having "caught" the hare, that balloonist takes   17b
first prize and gets congratulations from all
the other balloonists. Coming close to the hare
balloon is not particularly easy since hot-air   17d
balloons float with the wind and are difficult to
maneuver.

Ballooning is the oldest form of aerial
transportation. Hot-air balloons were first flown   18a
in France, where the two-hundredth anniversary
of ballooning was celebrated in 1983.

Analysis

To revise his paper, Jim first underlined the parts of sentences that
seriously obscured his meaning. For example, he saw in his draft that
the second sentence in the second paragraph (sentence 3 in the revision) suggested that the hound balloon, not the hare balloon's landing
spot, was marked with an "x." Jim completely restructured the sentence, changing the elliptical phrase *Marked with an "x"* (see Section
18d) into a part of the main clause, thus highlighting this important
information for readers. The misplaced modifier *having caught the
hare* in the third sentence of paragraph 2 made it seem as though all
the balloonists won the race; Jim placed this modifier closer to its
noun, *balloonist*, to make his meaning clear. And the last sentence of
the draft seemed to indicate that France can fly! Just as he did in sentence 3 of paragraph 2 in the revision, Jim revised the modifier to
become part of the main clause, making the origins of hot-air ballooning the main focus of the concluding sentence.

After thoroughly revising these misleading sentences, Jim read
the draft aloud to locate sentences that sounded awkward. First he

considered changing *To really understand* (part of sentence 2 in the revision) once he had identified it as a split infinitive, although he didn't find it particularly awkward. However, the only revisions he could think of were *Really to understand* and *To understand really*, neither of which was an improvement. Jim decided that his best option was to leave *To really understand* as it was.

In the second paragraph (first sentence in the revision), the phrase *after a while* caused an awkward split between subject and verb, so Jim moved it to the beginning of the sentence. He identified the word *particularly* in the last sentence of paragraph 2 as a squinting modifier which could be interpreted to mean "not particularly easy" or "not easy, particularly since hot air...." Jim had intended the first meaning and changed the placement of the modifier accordingly.

Jim located all but one of the misplaced and dangling modifiers in his draft. In the second sentence is a dangling infinitive phrase that needs an appropriate subject to perform the action of understanding. Jim could have revised this sentence to become *To really understand what is going on, one needs to know something about hares and hounds.*

19 Omissions; Incomplete and Illogical Comparisons

A sentence will be confusing if the writer omits words needed for clarity and accuracy. Sometimes, of course, writers omit words through haste or carelessness. This sort of omission can be caught with careful proofreading. Most omissions not caused by carelessness occur in three kinds of constructions: (1) constructions in which the omission of a preposition or conjunction is common in informal speech, (2) some compound constructions, and (3) comparisons.

19 a Proofread your writing for careless omissions.

The following sample sentences are confusing because they omit necessary words.

CONFUSING	Many millions people were unemployed last recession.
REVISED	Many millions *of* people were unemployed *during the* last recession.
CONFUSING	The Kentucky Derby is Louisville's best-known attraction, but far from its only one.
REVISED	The Kentucky Derby is *one of* Louisville's best-known attractions, but far from its only one.

The writer of the second example probably thought out the sentence with something like the phrase *one of* in mind and was merely careless in getting the idea down on paper.

19 **b** In writing, express relationships left implied in speech.

Some constructions such as "He left Monday" are idiomatic. In speaking we often extend this pattern to such expressions as "We became friends spring semester," or "The next few years we'll worry about prices." In writing, such relationships need to be spelled out.

SPOKEN   Space travel *the last few years* has been exciting.
WRITTEN   Space travel *during the last few years* has been exciting.

Similes or comparisons such as "I feel like a million dollars" are common in both speech and writing. The construction "feel like" also appears in idiomatic expressions such as "I feel like a cookie," but in this case no comparison is being expressed. The speaker does not actually *feel* like a cookie (he or she merely wants a cookie to eat); the spoken idiom omits the implied participle *having* or *eating*. In most written contexts, the verbal should be expressed.

SPOKEN   Do you feel like some popcorn?
                   She feels like a game of tennis.
                   I feel like a movie.
WRITTEN   Do you feel like *having* some popcorn?
                   She feels like *playing* a game of tennis.
                   I feel like *going to* a movie.

The omission of *that* can sometimes be confusing.

CONFUSING   He felt completely naked but totally private swimming
                   was indecent.
REVISED   He felt that completely naked but totally private swimming
                   was indecent.

The use of *type, make, brand,* and other similar words immediately before a noun (*this type show, this brand cereal*) is common in speech but is avoided by most writers.

SPOKEN   I have never driven this *make car* before.
WRITTEN   I have never driven this *make of car* before.

Exercise 19.1

Revise the following paragraph to correct careless omissions and to supply words that are implied but not stated.

Increasingly, men are streaming into salons to undergo facials, which until lately were the type treatment only women experienced. After consulting with specialist, the male customer, like his female counterpart, spends about two hours—and about eighty dollars—to have face and neck massaged and covered with various kinds masks. Once the masks are removed, the customer finds a vibrant face has replaced the haggard one. This treatment stimulates the circulation blood and deep-cleans the skin. The process is so relaxing that it usually makes the customer feel like a nap. Now that men more and more are competing with women for the top managerial jobs, they have discovered the beauty that is only skin deep may give them an edge in the job market.

19 **c** Include all necessary words in compound constructions.

When we connect two items of the same kind with coordinating conjunctions such as *and* or *but,* we often omit words that unnecessarily duplicate each other: "She could [go] and did go"; "He was faithful [to] and devoted to his job." But such omissions work only if the two items are in fact the same. If they are not, the resulting construction will be incomplete (see also the discussion of parallelism in Chapter 9). Such incomplete constructions usually result from omitting necessary prepositions or parts of verb phrases.

INCOMPLETE   Tanya was interested and skillful at photography.

REVISED   Tanya was interested *in* and skillful *at* photography. [*Interested* idiomatically requires the preposition *in*; if it is not present, we tend to read *interested at.*]

INCOMPLETE   My cat never has and never will eat fish.

REVISED   My cat never has *eaten* and never will *eat* fish.

INCOMPLETE   Tom's ideas were sound and adopted without discussion.

REVISED   Tom's ideas were sound and *were* adopted without discussion. [*Were* needs to be repeated here since the two verbs are not parallel; the first *were* is used as the main verb; the second is used as an auxiliary with *adopted.*]

Exercise 19.2

Revise the following paragraph to supply the omitted words.

    College students have always and continue to want to make their dormitory rooms more comfortable and homelike. Most dorm rooms are clean and functional but not really large, so students have to find ingenious ways to save space. Realizing that dorm rooms never have and never will be large enough, some roommates check with each other about what to bring before moving in; in doing so, the roommates avoid duplicating items such as stereos, refrigerators, and television sets. Students enthusiastic and interested in fitness programs often bring weights and exercise equipment with them when they arrive on campus. Those students who are not skillful and practical in arranging the mass of items they brought for their rooms may spend a year climbing over boxes, bicycles, and books.

19 **d** **Make all comparisons complete and logical.**

A comparison expresses a relationship between two things: "A is larger than B." To make a comparison complete and logical, include both items being compared and all words necessary to make the relationship clear, and be sure that the two items are in fact comparable.

● **1 Incomplete comparisons.** Sentences such as "Cleanaid is better" or "Weatherall Paint lasts longer" are popular with advertisers because they let the advertiser avoid telling us what the product is better than or lasts longer than. To be complete, a comparison must state both items being compared.

INCOMPLETE   Our new Ford gets better mileage. [better than what?]
REVISED   Our new Ford gets better mileage than our old one did.

INCOMPLETE   Louisville features more park land per person than any other in
              the nation. [any other what?]
REVISED   Louisville features more park land per person than any other
              city in the nation.

● **2 Ambiguous comparisons.** In comparisons such as "He enjoys watching football more than [he enjoys watching] baseball," we can omit "he enjoys watching" because only one meaning is reasonable. But when more than one meaning is possible, the comparison will be ambiguous.

AMBIGUOUS   I admire her more than Jane. [more than Jane admires her?
             more than you admire Jane?]
CLEAR   I admire her more than I admire Jane.
             I admire her more than Jane does.

● **3 Illogical comparisons.** A comparison will be illogical if it compares or seems to compare two things that cannot be sensibly compared.

ILLOGICAL   A lawyer's income is greater than a doctor. [The sentence com-
             pares an income to a doctor. Logic requires the comparison of
             income to income or of lawyer to doctor.]
REVISED   A lawyer's income is greater than a doctor's.
             A lawyer's income is greater than that of a doctor.
             A lawyer has a greater income than a doctor has.

● **4 Grammatically incomplete comparisons.** Comparisons using the expressions *as strong as, as good as,* and the like always require the second *as.*

INCOMPLETE   He is as strong, if not stronger than, Bob.
REVISED   He is as strong as, if not stronger than, Bob.
              He is as strong as Bob, if not stronger.

In comparisons of items in the same class of things, use *other* or *any other.* In comparisons of items in different classes, use *any.*

INCORRECT	Mount Everest is higher than *any* Asian mountain.
CORRECT	Mount Everest is higher than *any other* Asian mountain.
	Mount Everest is higher than *other* Asian mountains. [We are comparing Mount Everest, one Asian mountain, to other Asian mountains.]
	Mount Everest is higher than *any* American mountain. [We are comparing Mount Everest, an Asian mountain, with American mountains, a different class.]

Exercise 19.3

Revise the following paragraph to make all comparisons complete and logical.

> Today, technology allows weather forecasters to make better predictions about the weather. Using devices such as satellites and supercomputers, weather forecasters are able to make predictions that are more reliable than predictions in the past. Factors such as the seasons affect weather forecasting; for instance, weather in summer is less stable. Geography's role in influencing the weather is as important, if not more important than, any factor that affects the climate. Because of the unpredictability of weather patterns, short-range weather forecasters are able to make predictions that are more reliable than long-range forecasters.

Exercise 19.4

Revise these sentences and paragraph to eliminate incomplete constructions. Be prepared to explain your revisions.

Sentence Practice

1 Some fashion-conscious people find shoes make as great a fashion statement if not greater than anything they wear.

2 Ranging from platform shoes to flat-heeled or spike-heeled shoes to cowboy boots, shoes change styles as rapidly and sometimes more dramatically than clothing styles.

3 The last few decades shoe designers have used every imaginable type material for shoes, not just natural materials like cotton and leather, and they have and continue to design shoes in a wild assortment of colors for both men and women.

4 Shoe connoisseurs often are more delighted with new trends in shoes than designers, and they rush to purchase shoes in new colors and new shapes that are more exciting than last year.

5 When they feel like new shoes, some shoppers loyally stick to one brand shoe, but most buy shoes that look more fashionable and fit better.

Paragraph Practice

> The history of shoes, depicted in drawings, sculpture, paintings, and art, testifies the hardship, opulence, and whim of bygone days. Among the more

whimsical styles was the fifteenth-century English men's shoe that had a pointed toe, called a pike, which could be as long if not longer than the rest of the shoe. The next century the absurdities of shoe design were more evident in the width, shoes becoming so wide that Queen Mary limited their size. In the eighteenth century men's shoes had higher heels, and some heels, as tall as six inches, had poems written on them. Nearly as absurd if not more absurd were the development and passion for women's pointed-toed shoes and stiletto-heeled shoes in the 1950s.

In Your Own Words

Write a paragraph comparing and contrasting the characteristics of your two best friends. In the paragraph, be sure that you include the following constructions at least once: *better than, as...as, as...as if not...than,* and *any other.*

20 Mixed or Confused Sentences

Sometimes a sentence goes wrong because the predicate says something about the subject that cannot sensibly apply to that subject, or because it starts with one kind of construction and ends with a different kind of construction. The first of these is called **faulty predication**; the second, a **mixed construction**.

20 a Combine only subjects and predicates that make sense together.

Not all subjects and verbs make sense together. In each of the following sentences, inappropriate verbs create faulty predication.

> The *selection* of the committee *was chosen* by the students.

> Many *settlers*, moving into a new part of the country, *expanded* into towns.

> Any *member* who failed to do his or her job on the ship *meant* danger for the whole crew.

● 1. Subjects and complements linked illogically with *to be.*

Illogical combinations of subject and verb are particularly likely to occur when some form of the linking verb *to be* (*is, are, was, were*) is used. Linking verbs equate what comes before the verb with what comes after it—the subject with the complement: Something equals something else. Thus they cannot be used to connect things that are not equal.

FAULTY	An important step in skiing is stopping. [*Step* does not equal *stopping.*]
REVISED	An important step in skiing is learning to stop.

FAULTY   The magician's first trick was a pack of cards. [*Trick* does not equal *pack*.]

REVISED   Her first trick was one performed with a pack of cards.

FAULTY   Schools are a serious quarrel today.

In the third example, *schools* clearly is not equivalent to *quarrel*. But revision is not really possible because the subject, *schools*, is itself so vague. Perhaps the writer meant something like "*Increased taxes for schools cause serious quarrels today.*"

● **2 Illogical use of *is when* and *is where*.** Predicates that begin with *is when* and *is where* can cause faulty predication. Definitions such as "*Weightlessness is when there is no gravity*" or "*Subtraction is where you take one thing from another*" are common in speech. Written English, however, requires a noun or a word group functioning as a noun as both subject and complement in such definitions.

FAULTY   A documentary is when a movie or a television program analyzes news events or social conditions.

REVISED   A documentary is a movie or a television program that analyzes news events or social conditions.

FAULTY   A hasty generalization is when you jump to conclusions.

REVISED   A hasty generalization involves jumping to conclusions. To make a hasty generalization is to jump to conclusions.

Another acceptable revision preserves the *when* or *where* but substitutes another verb for the linking verb *is*. This revision also avoids the overreliance on *to be* verbs common in much writing.

FAULTY   Frostbite is where skin tissue has been frozen.

REVISED   Frostbite appears where the skin tissue has been frozen.

FAULTY   A safety is when a ball carrier gets tackled behind his own goal line.

REVISED   A safety occurs when a ball carrier gets tackled behind his own goal line.

● **3 *The reason is because.*** Sentences such as "The reason she didn't come was because she was sick" are common in speech, but *reason is that* is preferred at all levels of writing. *Because* means "for the reason that"; therefore, the expression "the reason is because" is redundant.

FAULTY   The reason he went to Chicago was because he wanted to visit Kareem.

REVISED   The reason he went to Chicago was that he wanted to visit Kareem. He went to Chicago because he wanted to visit Kareem.

Exercise 20.1

Revise the following paragraph to eliminate faulty predications.

> Bootlegging is where highly taxed or forbidden items are produced illegally. The term *bootlegging* is historically associated with Prohibition; Prohibition was when Congress passed a constitutional amendment in 1919 to limit liquor production and sales. The crime and violence associated with Prohibition meant a big problem for federal law enforcement authorities. One of the reasons that Prohibition was such a problem for federal authorities was because bootleggers such as Al Capone had created a huge illegal liquor industry. The repeal of Prohibition was when the Twenty-first Amendment to the Constitution was passed and ratified in 1933. Today bootlegging often means pirated computer software.

 Revise to eliminate mixed constructions.

A mixed construction is one in which a writer begins a sentence in one construction and then shifts to another. The result is a derailed sentence that must be put back on its track to be clear.

MIXED   With every effort the student made to explain his problem got him more confused.

Here the writer began with a prepositional phrase, but was thinking of *every effort* as the subject by the time he or she arrived at the verb *got.* We can untangle the sentence either by giving *got* the subject *he,* or by dropping the preposition *with* and making *every effort* the subject.

REVISED   With every effort the student made to explain his problem, he got more confused.
Every effort the student made got him more confused.

Beginnings such as *the fact that, there are,* and *it is* often cause needless complexity and lead to mixed or confusing sentences.

FAULTY   The fact that Louise was a good student she had many offers for good jobs. [*The fact that* as a beginning requires something like *results* or *leads to* as a main verb in the sentence. But the writer has forgotten that as the sentence develops.]

REVISED   The fact that Louise was a good student resulted in her having many offers for good jobs.
Because Louise was a good student, she had many offers for good jobs.

Unnecessary shifts from active-voice to passive-voice verbs can also create mixed constructions. When the implied or expressed subject of one clause becomes an implied or expressed object in another clause, readers, have a hard time sorting out meaning (see Section **16a**).

MIXED   When they were water-skiing, the tow rope was broken by my
             friends. [The subject shifts unnecessarily from *they* to *rope*.]
REVISED   When they were water-skiing, my friends broke the tow rope.

Exercise 20.2

Revise the following paragraph to eliminate mixed constructions.

With the gradual disappearance of the traditional service station has
caused many motorists to alter the way they take care of their cars. The fact
that motorists rarely find full-service facilities when they stop to buy gas they
have had to learn more about such routine maintenance as changing the oil
and checking the air pressure in the tires. By not having an attendant at the
gas station to check the transmission fluid and the brake fluid requires
motorists to find a mechanic to perform the basic services or they themselves
must learn to check the fluids. Even such a simple task as inspecting the
hoses and belts the motorists must face the responsibility of doing it—or face
a mechanic's bill for doing so. When they were all full-service, the motorists
often took for granted the customary free look under the hood at gas stations.

Exercise 20.3

Revise the following sentences and paragraph to eliminate faulty predication and mixed constructions.

Sentence Practice

1 By studying the problems of office workers it was determined that eyestrain
is the most frequent complaint among workers.
2 To prevent eyestrain is a reason health experts suggests that anyone spending
hours in front of a video display terminal should take a ten-minute break
every hour.
3 When workers take this ten-minute break, something in the distance should
be looked at to relax the eyes.
4 The reason so much eyestrain occurs is because office space is often badly
designed, and lighting is inadequate or is in the wrong place.
5 The fact that eyestrain can lead to irritability and headaches and those who
must spend all day in poorly designed or badly lighted offices can suffer.

Paragraph Practice

Another cause of eyestrain is where drivers must spend hours on the road
during long trips. Driving at high speeds means concentration for the driver,
and that intense concentration often leads to eyestrain. When they drive on
long highway trips, stops after the first 200 miles and then after every 100
miles should be made by drivers. Because the sun can cause glare on bright
days is a reason drivers should wear sunglasses to reduce that extra strain on
their eyes. By taking frequent breaks from driving and by wearing sunglasses
makes it possible to avoid eyestrain on long highway trips.

Writers Revising:

Omissions, Incomplete and Mixed Constructions

Continuing with the revision of his essay on hot-air ballooning, Jim checked for omissions, incomplete comparisons, and confused and mixed constructions. See what you can do with the passage that follows, and then compare your revision with Jim's.

Draft

```
    I learned ballooning fall semester when I attend-
ed the Albuquerque International Balloon Fiesta with
a friend. This event attracts over 700,000 enthusi-
asts interested or skilled at flying the hot-air
craft. No other ballooning event attracts more spec-
tators and participants. Several contests that are
held at the Fiesta have valuable prizes. One is where
balloonists try to snag keys hanging from the top of
a pole stuck into the ground. The keys are to the
prize, a new car.
```

Revision

```
                about      during
1    I learned ballooning  fall semester when I      19b
               ^            ^
     attended the Albuquerque International Balloon

     Fiesta with a friend. This event attracts
                                        in
2    over 700,000 enthusiasts interested or           19c
                                           ^
     skilled at flying the hot-air craft. No other

     ballooning event attracts more spectators and
     than the Albuquerque fiesta does
3    participants. Several contests that are held      19d(1)
                  ^
                                      In one contest
4    at the Fiesta have valuable prizes. One is       20a(2)

     where balloonists try to snag keys hanging

     from the top of a pole stuck into the ground.

     The keys are to the prize, a new car.
```

Analysis

Jim realized that without the preposition *about* in the first sentence, readers would assume from the first draft that he knows how to fly a balloon, but he does not. As he examined this first sentence he also added the preposition *during,* which the sentence implies but does not express in the draft. He made revision 2 because *interested* cannot be followed by the preposition *at;* this compound construction required *in* to be complete (*interested in or skilled at*). When he saw the word *more* in the third sentence (*more spectators and participants*), he knew that he needed to complete the comparison by adding *than the Albuquerque fiesta does.* Finally, Jim noticed two problems in the sentence beginning *One is where ....* First, he didn't think readers would remember what *one* refers to (*contests*) because it was back at the beginning of the previous sentence. Second, the word *where* seemed unclear, since he wasn't trying to focus his readers' attention on the place the contests are held but on the type of contest he is using as an example. By changing *One is where* to *In one contest,* Jim cleared up both these problems. His revision eliminates the ambiguities he created in his first draft.

Review Exercise

Sentence Revision

Indicate the principal error (faulty agreement, sentence fragment, run-on faulty reference, misplaced modifier, awkward separation, and so on) in the following sentences and paragraphs. Then revise to eliminate the errors.

Sentence Practice

1. Native Americans, the aboriginal peoples which lived in North, Central, and South America before the arrival of Europeans, being diverse in their languages and cultures.
2. The reason for this is because Native Americans had migrated at various times from Asia over the Bering Strait land bridge, then traveling South and Central America and all across North America are why they developed different cultures and languages.
3. The migrations began as long ago if not longer than 32,000 B.C. they were nomads who survived by hunting.
4. By 2000 B.C. some Native American societies, especially in southwestern North America, began growing corn, and they as a result settled in one place unlike other nomadic Native American societies that have relied on hunting.
5. The earliest migrants, however, like Asia where they originated, knew to kill animals, a pointed projectile must be used, and they also understood the uses of fire.
6. The type environment and culture of each society are largely responsible for the kind of housing they developed, ranging from portable teepees on the Great Plains among hunting cultures to underground rooms, wooden structures, and cave and cliff dwellings in more agricultural societies.

7 In some Native American cultures featured class structures which included the chief and other nobility, priests, commoners, and servants, and displaying wealth in the form of a surplus of food or decorative items were important customs in distinguishing class.

8 Beginning in the seventeenth century, you find the Spanish trying to make Christians of the Native Americans, which also continued at the hands of other European colonists.

9 The Proclamation of 1763 was when the land west of the Appalachian Mountains was allocated to Native Americans, but once gold was discovered in California in 1848 invalidated this settlement, and they encroached on the land more.

10 Throughout the nineteenth century there was a number of bloody wars between the white settlers and various Native American societies, however, the Native Americans were increasingly forced onto, under the terms of treaties and legislation, reservations.

Paragraph Practice

Of the numerous Native American societies, one of the most sophisticated cultures are the Pueblo. Their ancestors, called Basket-Makers around 1500 B.C., archaeologists found that the Native Americans which settled in southwestern North America developed an agricultural society in fact corn, squash, and beans were grown, and at an early date they used irrigation techniques in their cultivation. In the first century A.D., their descendants, which the Spanish later called Pueblo, became skilled architects, they built houses of stone and adobe more sophisticated than their ancestors. Their name, *Pueblo,* referred to the kind of villages they lived, which featured large, communal houses accessed from the top by a ladder. They also used for their religious rites underground rooms called kivas only entered by men, their designs related to the slab houses lined with stones and partly submerged by their ancestors. Like the pueblos, a ladder is used to enter the kiva from the roof.

Some later periods they also lived in elaborate cave and cliff dwellings, which are the forerunners of modern apartment complexes, along the walls of canyons and on the top of mesas. Discovering some of them have up to a hundred rooms, the Pueblo cliff dwellings making the society safer from enemy attack. Attacks and drought by Navaho and Apache drove the cliff-dwellers from the cliff houses and into villages.

From the Spanish the Pueblo learned to weave wool and to cultivate cattle, also they excelled at making baskets and pottery that you would find unsurpassed. Once the Spaniards began to conquer the Pueblo caused much bloodshed, but by the early seventeenth century, Spanish missionaries were building churches in Pueblo villages. The complex Pueblo religion has involved many special rites led by Pueblo priests, which exerted much influence in all areas of community life. The rich mythology, religion, and literature of the Pueblo still being celebrated practiced today. To understand more about this remarkable culture, visit both the ancient and modern dwellings of the Pueblo in Colorado, Utah, Arizona, and New Mexico.

In Your Own Words

Review your most recent two pieces of writing and list any basic sentence faults you find, such as comma splices, fragments, run-on sentences, misplaced and dangling modifiers, illogical and incomplete comparisons, and mixed constructions. Then write a two-paragraph statement about which of these errors are occurring most frequently and what you believe you can do to improve your ability to find these problems in your writing and solve them.

Part 4

Effective Words

As writers and readers we share a love for language, for how words sound, for the rhythms they can dance out, for the patterns they can be made to form; but we also share the unending responsibility for guarding language so that it remains accurate as a means by which human truths may be sought and expressed in order that we can hold together.

—Robert Pack, "On Wording"

The Dictionary

A good dictionary is more than a source for checking spelling, pronunciation, and meaning; it also records word history (*etymology*), part of speech, and, when necessary, principal parts, plurals, or other forms. Frequently it records the level of current usage. Often the dictionary offers other information as well—lists of abbreviations, rules for punctuation and spelling, condensed biographical and geographical information, the pronunciation and source of many given names, and a vocabulary of rhymes. For writers and readers a dictionary is an invaluable resource and an indispensable tool.

The various editorial staffs, contributors, consultants, and panels who work together to produce a first-rate dictionary are interested in where a word has come from, its current meaning and actual usage, and its latest important developments. As William Morris explains in his introduction to the first edition of *The American Heritage Dictionary:* "We have engaged the services of hundreds of authorities in every range of human endeavor and scholarship, from archaeology to space research, from Indo-European to computer programming… many thousands of definitions were sent to these specialists for emendation or approval." Good dictionaries record the way our language changes and provide guidance about its most effective use in our speech and writing.

21 a Become familiar with general dictionaries.

● **1 Abridged dictionaries.** Also known as desk dictionaries, abridged dictionaries usually list between 150,000 and 200,000 entries. These hardbound, one-volume works conveniently serve most people's daily reading and writing needs. These dictionaries should not be confused with paperback versions of the same title. Paperback dictionaries, while handy for carrying to class, contain many fewer words and may lack etymologies, synonymies, and full definitions as well as important front and back matter. You should have a good hardback abridged dictionary in your personal library.

Of the many dependable abridged dictionaries available, five reputable ones are described in this section. Although they differ in important ways, all contain more than 150,000 entries, provide careful etymologies (word histories) and basic grammatical information about each entry, supply usage labels, and specify distinctions among synonyms.

Merriam-Webster's Collegiate Dictionary. 10th ed. Springfield, MA:
   Merriam-Webster, 1993.
This dictionary is the successor to *Webster's New Collegiate Dictionary,*
ninth edition. It continues the Merriam-Webster tradition of being based

on *Webster's Third New International Dictionary*, unabridged. Thus, this desk dictionary is derived from a citation file of more than 14 million examples of English words and benefits from the research conducted for the preparation of the most recent edition of *Webster's Dictionary of English Usage*. The order of definitions is historical, earliest use given first: A date notes the first instance of use. The tenth edition has full etymologies, a wide range of synonymies, and full prefatory material including a two-page chart explaining how to read the entries, explanatory notes, a discussion of language systems and history, and guides to pronunciation and abbreviations. The back matter includes foreign words and phrases, biographical and geographical names, signs and symbols, and a style handbook.

Webster's New World Dictionary: College Edition. 3rd ed. Englewood Cliffs,
     NJ: Prentice Hall, 1993.
This dictionary emphasizes simplified definitions even of technical terms and includes a large number of words and phrases that are relatively informal. Usage labels are generously used. Synonymies and etymologies are full and thorough. The sequence of definitions is historical, except that common meanings are placed first before specialized ones. Identification of Americanisms and attention to the origin of American place names are special features. This dictionary is fairly liberal in allowing for variant spellings.

The American Heritage Dictionary of the English Language. 3rd ed.
     Boston: Houghton Mifflin, 1992.
The American Heritage College Dictionary. 3rd ed. Boston:
     Houghton Mifflin, 1993.
The American Heritage Dictionary and its more compact college edition are distinguished by their highly informative and entertaining notes as well as their extensive margin photographs and illustrations. In addition to etymologies, these dictionaries contain 400 word histories: one-paragraph essays on the origin and development of selected words; 500 usage notes, often including opinions of the Usage Panel (over 100 well-known writers, educators, experts, and public figures) on such matters as grammar, diction, and registers; 100 regional notes explaining variant terms used in different parts of the country. Definitions begin with what the editors judge to be the central or most common meaning, and this meaning serves as the base for the arrangement of the other senses of the word. Synonymies are generous and cross-referenced. Geographical and biographical entries appear in the main dictionary. An appendix features a lengthy discussion of Indo-European roots showing the interrelationships among many words.

The Random House Dictionary of the English Language. College ed. New York:
     Random, 1984.
This dictionary is based on the well-regarded unabridged *Random House*

Dictionary of the English Language. Definitions are ordered by frequency of use. A single alphabetical listing incorporates all biographical and geographical as well as other entries.

● **2 Unabridged dictionaries.** Unabridged dictionaries contain the most complete and scholarly description of English words. Available in most libraries, those described here are the ones most frequently used in the United States.

The Oxford English Dictionary. 2nd ed. New York: Oxford UP, 1989. 20 vols.
The Oxford English Dictionary: Additions. New York: Oxford UP, 1993. 2 vols.
Commonly referred to as the *OED*, this is the greatest dictionary of the English language. Listing a total of 616,500 word forms in its initial twenty volumes, the second edition of the *OED* amalgamates the text of the first edition, twelve volumes published in 1933 and four supplementary volumes published between 1972 and 1986. The 1933 edition was itself a reprint of the ten-volume *New English Dictionary on Historical Principles* originally published in parts between 1884 and 1928. The fact that a two-volume *Addition* has been published since the second edition was printed in 1989 attests to the continuing, rapid growth of English.

Definitions in the *OED* are ordered historically from earliest to most recent use. This dictionary is distinguished by some 2.5 million quotations dated to illustrate meaning and spelling for a given word at a particular time in its history. A single word may occupy several pages. *Set*, for example, occupies twenty-five pages, and a single one of its more than 150 definitions is illustrated by nineteen quotations from writings beginning in 1205. The pronunciation system used in the first edition has been replaced by the International Phonetic Alphabet, in which stress marks are placed before the syllable.

Webster's Third New International Dictionary of the English Language.
Springfield, MA: Merriam-Webster, 1986.
This single, large volume is the unabridged dictionary most people in the United States are likely to have used in their college or public library. The current edition has been revised regularly since its first printing in 1961. Although not as exhaustive as the *OED*, its definitions are scholarly, exact, and frequently supported by illustrative quotations. Since the 1961 edition uses style labels such as *slang* infrequently and does not use the label *colloquial*, some readers continue to prefer the second edition even though it lacks a number of new and specialized words.

Random House Unabridged Dictionary: Print & Electronic Edition.
2nd & revised ed. New York: Random, 1993. Available in print and electronic CD-ROM formats.

With nearly 320,000 entries, the one-volume *Random House Unabridged Dictionary* is considerably briefer than the *OED* and *Webster's Third*. But it is a sound and scholarly dictionary with especially up-to-date entries organized by frequency of use. It is the only entirely new unabridged dictionary to be published in recent years and, thus far, the only one also published in an electronic format. The *Random House Unabridged* contains 75,000 example phrases and sentences, twelve supplements such as "Avoiding Sexist Language," and a thirty-two-page full-color atlas.

In Your Own Words
In the library, consult the *Oxford English Dictionary* for its meanings of *nice*. Write a two-paragraph summary of the shades of meaning the word has had from its first appearance in English to the present time.

21 **b** Become familiar with specialized dictionaries.

General dictionaries bring together in a single reference all of the information you ordinarily need about a word. Special dictionaries can give more detailed, complete information because they limit their attention to a single kind of information about words or to a single category of words. Thus a dictionary of slang can devote an entire page to the word *hip*, in contrast to the general dictionary, which can afford no more than four or five lines. A medical dictionary can include thousands of specialized medical terms of which only a few hundred might be included in a general dictionary.

Specialized dictionaries abound: dictionaries for engineers, psychiatrists, scholars of music, nurses, economists, auto mechanics—just about any field that has a specialized vocabulary. You would do well to familiarize yourself with specialized dictionaries in the fields you are studying. Instructors and practitioners in these fields, as well as reference librarians, can point such dictionaries out to you. (See also the lists of reference books in Chapter 46, "Locating and Working with Sources.")

Dictionaries of usage and of synonyms can help you a great deal with your writing. When you need specialized information about words, check the most recent edition of one of the following dictionaries:

Bernstein, Theodore M. *The Careful Writer: A Modern Guide to English Usage.*
Follett, Wilson. *Modern American Usage.*
Fowler, H. W. *Dictionary of Modern English Usage.* Rev. and ed. Sir Ernest Gowers.
Harpers Dictionary of Contemporary Usage.
Lighter, J.E. *Random House Historical Dictionary of American Slang.*
Partridge, Eric. *A Dictionary of Slang and Unconventional English.* Ed. Paul Beale.
Webster's College Thesaurus.
Webster's Dictionary of English Usage.
Webster's New Dictionary of Synonyms.
Wentworth, Harold, and Stuart Berg Flexner. *Dictionary of American Slang.*

In Your Own Words

Look in a recent dictionary of slang for the meanings of two slang terms you have heard your parents or someone of their generation use. Write a paragraph explaining the history of these terms as slang.

21 **c** **Become familiar with the features of a dictionary entry.**

Because dictionaries must say a great deal in a very brief space, they use systems of abbreviations, symbols, and typefaces to condense information. Although such systems vary from dictionary to dictionary, their format is quite similar. Taking the time to read a dictionary's explanatory pages will save you some puzzlement later; and once you have become familiar with the system in one dictionary, you will find reading any dictionary's entries fairly easy.

The following sample entry, from *Webster's Third New International Dictionary*, shows most of the principal features of a dictionary entry. These are labeled and numbered to correspond with the more detailed descriptions that follow.

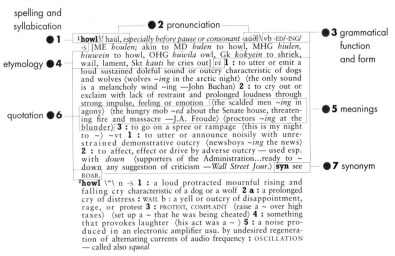

—By permission. From *Webster's Third New International Dictionary*. © 1986 by Merriam-Webster, Inc., publisher of the Merriam-Webster® dictionaries.

● **1 Spelling and syllabication.** The main entry of a word in a dictionary shows the spelling and syllabication, using centered dots between syllables to show how to separate the word properly at the ends of the lines (see Chapter 42, "The Hyphen"). The entry also gives the proper spelling of compound words, properness depending on whether the editors found them more often written as two single words (**half broth•er**), as a hyphenated compound (**quar•ter-hour**), or as one word (**drug•store**). Dictionaries also indicate foreign words that require italics (in manuscript, underlining) either by labeling them as foreign (*French, German,* etc.), printing them in boldface italics, or using a symbol such as a double dagger (‡).

Any variant spellings will also be listed in the main entry. Usually, the first listing is, in the opinion of the editors, the more common; some dictionaries indicate that two variants are equally common by joining them with *or* (**cad•die** *or* **cad•dy**) or that one is less common than the other by joining them with *also* (**wool•ly** *also* **wool•y**). In general, choose the first listed variant unless there is a special reason for choosing the second.

The main entry for *howl* shows that it is a one-syllable word, which cannot be divided at the end of a line; that it is not normally capitalized; and that it has no variant spelling.

Exercise 21.1

Referring to a dictionary, give the preferred spelling of each word.

1. judgement	4. whisky	7. turquois
2. travelled	5. surprize	8. queazy
3. manoeuvre	6. barbeque	9. catalogue

Exercise 21.2

Rewrite the following compounds, showing which should be written as they are, which hyphenated, and which written as two or more words.

1. covergirl	4. kindhearted	7. halfway
2. selfesteem	5. witchhunt	8. bullpen
3. bankcard	6. looseleaf	9. gameshow

Exercise 21.3

Copy the following foreign words, underlining those that require italics and supplying accents where needed.

1. bon appetit	4. nouvelle cuisine	7. Weltanschauung
2. quid pro quo	5. non sequitur	8. coup de grace
3. hombre	6. chutzpa	9. manana

● **2 Pronunciation.** Dictionaries indicate the pronunciation of words by respelling them with special symbols and letters. Explanation of the symbols is given either at the bottom of the page on which the entry appears or in the prefatory pages or both.

In *Webster's Third* the pronunciation appears between slant lines called reverse virgules; some other dictionaries use parentheses. Stressed syllables are indicated by accent marks (´ or '). In most dictionaries, the accent mark follows the stressed syllable. Notice, however, that *Webster's Third* (as well as *Webster's New Collegiate*, based on the *Third*) places the accent mark immediately before the stressed syllable.

Dictionaries show frequently occurring variant pronunciations as they do variant spellings. In the *Webster's Third* sample entry, for instance, you can see that an unabridged dictionary may even show variant pronunciations for such a simple word as *howl*. As with variant spellings, the first pronunciation is sometimes said to be preferred. However, unless there is a limiting label or comment attached to one or more variants, they are all equally correct. Your preference should be determined by the pronunciation you hear in conversation around you.

Exercise 21.4

Copy the dictionary pronunciation for the following words. If there is more than one acceptable pronunciation, copy all and underline the one you are most familiar with.

1. salmon	5. harass	8. perseverance
2. presentation	6. neither	9. pianist
3. Caribbean	7. envelope (as a noun)	10. route
4. pajamas		

● **3 Grammatical functions and forms.** All dictionaries indicate the part of speech to which a word belongs. If a word can serve as more than one part of speech, most dictionaries include all its functions and meanings under a single entry, grouping the meanings separately for each function. A few dictionaries list a separate entry for each part of speech—as does *Webster's Third*, which groups the intransitive *(vi)* and transitive *(vt)* verb forms in the first entry and the noun form *(n)* in the second.

Dictionaries also show a word's inflected forms, especially if they are irregular or if they might cause spelling problems (as in *travel, traveled, traveling* or *travelled, travelling*). Thus the entry for the verb *drink* lists the irregular past tense *drank* and the past participle *drunk*. The entries for the singular nouns *child* and *alumna* give the plural forms *children* and *alumnae*. Most dictionaries do not show plurals for nouns that are regular, forming their plurals with -*s*. Most dictionaries also show -*er* and -*est* for the comparative and superlative forms of adjectives and adverbs. Where this information is not supplied, you can assume the comparative and superlative forms require the addition of *more* and *most*. *Webster's Third* is one of several dictionaries that also show the regular as well as irregular forms for various parts of speech.

Other parts of speech formed from the word being defined, and related in meaning, are listed at the end of the entry. They are spelled, divided into syllables, and identified by part of speech, but not defined.

Exercise 21.5

Write the past tense and past participle of each of these verbs. Use a dictionary as necessary.

1. dream	4. burst	7. shine
2. swear	5. hang	8. wake
3. dive	6. bite	9. weave

Exercise 21.6

Write the plural (or plurals) of each of the following. Use a dictionary as necessary.

1. phenomenon	4. syllabus	7. wolf
2. crisis	5. criterion	8. medium
3. fungus	6. sister-in-law	9. radius

Exercise 21.7

Write the comparative and superlative forms of each of the following. Use a dictionary as necessary.

1. subtle	4. bad	7. terrible
2. little	5. slowly	8. alert
3. dainty	6. sly	9. beastly

● **4 Etymology.** A word's history—its origin and derivation—often helps clarify its present meaning, forms, and spelling. Because the course of history changes, restricts, or extends meanings, many original ones have been lost entirely. *Presently*, for example, formerly meant "at once, immediately"; it now usually means "shortly, in a little while."

The etymology of a word can be very useful in discriminating between synonyms so that you can select the one that comes closest to the meaning you intend. Dictionaries place etymologies after the initial grammatical label or at the very end of the entry. When they contain symbols, abbreviations, and different typefaces, you should check the key and explanation provided in the dictionary's opening pages.

The material between the brackets in the *Webster's Third* entry for *howl* shows the origin or etymology of the word: *howl* comes from a word in Middle English (ME) spelled *houlen* and is related to Middle Dutch (MD) *hūlen* and Middle High German (MHG) *hiulen* or *hiuweln*, all meaning "to howl"; to the Old High German (OHG) word *hūwila* meaning "owl"; to the Greek (Gk) *kokyein* meaning "to wail" or "lament"; and to the Sanskrit (Skt) word *kauti* meaning "he cries out."

Exercise 21.8

Explain the etymology of each of the following.

1. ghastly	4. livid	7. paradox
2. fervent	5. mawkish	8. zone
3. debris	6. sabotage	9. jacket

Exercise 21.9

From what specific names have the following derived?

1. serendipity	4. fuchsia	7. volt
2. dalmatian	5. vulcanize	8. frankfurter
3. bowdlerize	6. quixotic	9. plutonium

Exercise 21.10

From what language did each of the following words originally come?

1. chrome	6. walrus	11. marimba
2. chutney	7. kowtow	12. pigment
3. hammock	8. juggernaut	13. aardvark
4. sherbet	9. yogurt	14. yo-yo
5. tycoon	10. persimmon	15. okra

● **5 Meanings.** Strictly speaking, dictionaries do not *define* words; they record meanings that actual usage, past and present, has attached to words. When more than one meaning is recorded for a single word, *Webster's Collegiate* (and *Webster's Third*) lists them in order of historical use, earliest meaning first. Most other dictionaries list the most common or frequently used, most general, or most basic meaning first. Thus it is important to know a dictionary's system of arrangement, explained in the volume's prefatory pages, and to read *all* the meanings in an entry before choosing the one that best suits the context in which you plan to use the word.

Senses of a word within a single part of speech are shown by means of boldface numbers. Where the sense of a word can be subdivided into further shades of meaning (different but related senses), boldface, lower-case letters are used. Words in small capitals (WAIL in meaning 2 of the noun form of *howl*, for example) are both synonyms and also main entries where further related definitions can be found. Special and technical meanings are clearly indicated.

Exercise 21.11

For each of the following words, (1) indicate the total number of meanings you can find, and (2) write three sentences that illustrate three meanings.

1. deck	4. school	7. date
2. scrape	5. left	8. closet
3. troll	6. nurse	9. fortune

Exercise 21.12

Explain the changes in meaning that have taken place in each of the following words, using etymologies where helpful.

1. vaccine	6. slogan	11. mayhem
2. decimate	7. hectic	12. quarantine
3. scold	8. mundane	13. dilemma
4. frantic	9. glamour	14. libel
5. shambles	10. foible	15. dally

● **6 Quotations.** Quotations form a major part of a definition by illustrating actual usage, the context for a word. They are extremely valuable in showing differences in synonyms, distinguishing between closely related meanings, or illustrating unusual uses of a word. Those labeled by authors' names or by sources are actual quotations; those not so labeled are typical phrases created by the dictionary editors. Illustrative quotations are usually enclosed in angle brackets (< >) or set off by a colon and italicized.

Under meaning 2 of *howl* as a transitive verb, a usage note states that in this meaning *howl* is used especially with *down* in the phrase *howl down,* and an example from *The Wall Street Journal* is provided. *Webster's Third* uses a swung dash (~) in quotations to replace the word itself.

● **7 Synonyms and antonyms.** A **synonym** is a word having approximately the same general meaning as the main-entry word. An **antonym** has approximately the opposite meaning. For practical reasons, not all entries show synonyms and antonyms. Paragraph-length discussions of groups of synonyms are usually located at the end of certain entries and cross-referenced at related entries. For instance, at the end of meaning 2 in the *Webster's Third* transitive verb entry for *howl,* "**syn** see ROAR" means that the entry for *roar* contains a discussion of the synonyms for *howl.* That synonym group is reproduced here.

syn HOWL, ULULATE, BELLOW, BAWL, BLUSTER, CLAMOR, VOCIFERATE: ROAR suggests the full loud reverberating sound made by lions or the booming sea or by persons in rage or boisterous merriment (far away guns *roar* —Virginia Wolff) (the harsh north wind ... *roared* in the piazzas —Osbert Sitwell) (*roared* the blacksmith, his face black with rage —T.B. Costain) HOWL indicates a higher, less reverberant sound often suggesting the doleful or agonized or the sounds of unrestrained laughter (frequent *howling* of jackals and hyenas —James Stevenson-Hamilton) (how the wind does *howl* — J.C. Powys) (*roared* at his subject ... *howled* at ... inconsistencies —Martin Gardner) ULULATE is a literary synonym for HOWL but may suggest mournful protraction and rhythmical delivery (an *ululating* baritone mushy with pumped-up pity —E.B. White) BELLOW suggests the loud, abrupt, hollow sound made typically by bulls or any similar loud, reverberating sound (most of them were drunk. They went *bellowing* through the town —Kenneth Roberts) BAWL suggests a somewhat lighter, less reverberant, unmodulated sound made typically by calves (a woman *bawling* abuse from the door of an inn —C.E. Montague) (the old judge was in the hall *bawling* nasty orders —Sheridan Le Fanu) BLUSTER suggests the turbulent noisiness of gusts of wind; it often suggests swaggering and noisy threats or protests (expressed her opinion gently but firmly, while he *blustered* for a time and then gave in —Sherwood Anderson) (swagger and *bluster* and take the limelight —Margaret Mead) CLAMOR suggests sustained, mixed and confused outcry as from a number of agitated persons (half-starved men and women *clamoring* for food —Kenneth Roberts) (easy ... for critics ... to *clamor* for action —Winston Churchill) VOCIFERATE suggests loud vehement insistence in speaking (was not willing to break off his talk; so he continued to *vociferate* his remarks —James Boswell)

—By permission. From *Webster's Third New International Dictionary.* © 1986 by Merriam-Webster, Inc., publisher of the Merriam-Webster® dictionaries.

● **8 Labels.** Dictionaries label words or particular meanings of words to indicate that they are in some way restricted. Words and meanings not so labeled are appropriate for general use. Although the particular labels that dictionaries use vary somewhat, all labels can be divided into four general categories: geographic labels, time labels, occupational or subject labels, and usage or style labels.

Geographic labels indicate that the word or meaning is limited to a particular area. Typical labels of this sort are *British, Australian, New England, Southern U.S.,* and the like. Thus *Webster's Collegiate* labels *lift,* in the meaning of "elevator," *British,* and *outbye,* meaning "a short distance away," *Scottish. Webster's New World* labels *corn pone,* a kind of corn bread, *Southern U.S.* The label *dialectal* or *regional* usually suggests a specialized local or provincial word, often traditional. Thus *larrap,* meaning "a blow" or "to flog," is labeled *dialectal* by *Webster's Collegiate* and *regional* by *American Heritage.*

Time labels indicate that the labeled word has passed out of use entirely or no longer occurs in ordinary contexts. *Obsolete* means that a word has passed out of use entirely (for example, *absume* and *enwheel,* words that have not been used for 200 years). *Archaic* means that the labeled word or meaning is no longer generally used, although it may still be seen occasionally in older writing (for example, *belike,* meaning "probably," and *outland,* meaning "a foreign land").

Subject labels indicate that a word or a particular meaning belongs to a special field such as law, medicine, baseball, finance, mathematics, or psychology. Thus *Webster's New World* identifies *projection* as a psychiatric term (*Psychiatry*) when used to mean the process of assigning one's own undesirable impulses to others and as a photographic term (*Photog.*) when used to mean projecting an image on a screen. *American Heritage* labels as *Law* the meaning of *domain* in the sense of ownership and rights of disposal of property.

Style labels indicate that a word or meaning is restricted to a particular level of usage. Typical style labels are *slang, colloquial, informal, nonstandard, substandard, illiterate,* and *vulgar.* (See also Chapter 22 for further discussion of standard, nonstandard, and slang usage.) Variations among dictionaries are greatest in their choice of labels and in the words and meanings to which they apply them. Nonetheless, there is broad agreement on the meanings of the labels themselves.

Slang indicates that a word, though widely used, has not yet been accepted in the general vocabulary. Slang terms and meanings often are used humorously; are likely to be short-lived, limited to a particular group of people; and are used almost entirely in speech rather than writing. Typical examples are *gross out* (to fill with disgust), *dork* (a socially inept person), *shades* (sunglasses), *piece* (a handgun), and *megabuck* (a million dollars). Of the dictionaries described, *Webster's Collegiate* is by far the most sparing in its use of the label, allowing many entries labeled *slang* by others to pass without any label.

Colloquial and *informal* are almost synonymous terms. They both indicate that a word is characteristic of speech or of quite informal, rather than more formal, writing. The *American Heritage* uses the label *informal; Webster's New World* uses *colloquial. Webster's Collegiate* uses neither label and thus may be less useful for those who need to determine how appropriate a word is for a particular writing context.

Illiterate, substandard, and some other similar terms are labels indicating that a word is limited to uneducated speech, as *drownded* for the past tense of *drown.* Though dictionaries vary somewhat in the particular labels they use, their agreement in classifying a word as being limited to uneducated speech is much greater than their agreement in labeling a word *slang, colloquial,* and so on.

To use your dictionary wisely as a guide to usage, you will have to examine carefully the explanatory notes in it to determine exactly what labels are applied and how they are interpreted by the editors.

Exercise 21.13

Which of the following are standard English and which also have colloquial, informal, or slang usages, according to your dictionary? If possible, check more than one dictionary to determine if they agree.

1. jerk	4. eyeball	7. kisser	10. cream
2. rap	5. geek	8. fuzz	11. plastered
3. sponge	6. bust	9. waffle	12. badder

Exercise 21.14

In what areas of the world would you be likely to hear the following?

1. monsoon	4. chinook	7. chateau	10. sari
2. dacha	5. grandee	8. geisha	11. paella
3. bonnet	6. couscous	9. outback	12. ricksha

Exercise 21.15

Any of the desk dictionaries discussed in this chapter will help you answer the following questions. Look up the meanings of *etymology, homonym,* and *synonym,* if necessary, before answering the questions.

1. What is the etymology of the word *campaign?*
2. What are the three homonyms for the word *right?*
3. What is the syllabication of the word *extemporaneous?*
4. What are some synonyms for the adjective *authentic?*
5. Give the meanings of these abbreviations: DNB, kg, q.v., RSVP.

21 d   Increase your vocabulary to improve the effectiveness of your writing.

The English language contains well over a million words. Of these, about two-fifths belong almost exclusively to special fields (e.g., zoology, electronics, psychiatry). Of the remaining three-fifths, unabridged dictionaries list 500,000 or more, desk dictionaries between 150,000 and 200,000. Such wealth is both a blessing and a curse. On the one hand, many English words are loosely synonymous, sometimes interchangeable, as in *buy* a book or *purchase* a book. On the other hand, the distinctions between synonyms are fully as important as their similarities. For example, a family may be said to be living in *poverty*, or in *penury*, or in *want*, or in *destitution*. All these words are loosely synonymous; but each in fact indicates a slightly different degree of need, *want* describing the least severe and *destitution* describing the most severe degree. Thus only one of the words will portray the family exactly as you see it and wish your reader to see it. In short, as a writer of English you must use words carefully in order to be precise.

We all have two vocabularies: a **passive**, or **recognition, vocabulary**, which is made up of the words we recognize in the context of reading material or conversation but do not actually use ourselves; and an **active vocabulary**, which consists of "working" words—those we use daily in our own writing and speaking. A good vocabulary is the product of years of serious reading, of listening to intelligent talk, and of trying to speak and write forcefully and clearly. This does not mean other methods of vocabulary building are ineffective, but it does mean that acquiring a good vocabulary is inseparable from acquiring an education.

● **1 Prefixes and suffixes.** You can improve your recognition vocabulary by learning the meaning of common prefixes and suffixes. English includes many words derived from other languages. Consequently, it has a number of words based on common root forms to which different prefixes or suffixes have been added. The root form *spec-*, for example, from the Latin *specere* ("to look"), appears in *specter, inspection, perspective, aspect, introspection, circumspect, specimen, spectator*. Knowing the common prefixes and suffixes will help you detect the meanings of many words whose roots are familiar.

Prefixes

Prefix	Example	Meaning
ab-	absent	away from
ad-*	adverb	to *or* for
com-*	combine	with

Prefix	Example	Meaning
de-	degrade, depart, dehumanize	down, away from, *or* undoing
dis-*	disparate, disappoint	separation *or* reversal
ex-*	extend, ex-president	out of *or* former
il-*	illogical	not
im-	immobile	not
in-*	input	in *or* on
in-*	inhuman	not
ir-	irrefutable	not
mis-	misprint	wrong
non-	non-Christian, nonsense	not
ob-*	obtuse	against
pre-	prevent, precondition	before
pro-	proceed	for *or* forward
re-	repeat	back *or* again
sub-*	subcommittee	under
trans-	transcribe	across
un-	unclean	not

*The spelling of these prefixes varies, usually to make pronunciation easier. *Ad* becomes *ac* in *accuse*, *ag* in *aggregate*, *at* in *attack*. Similarly, the final consonant in the other prefixes is assimilated by the initial letter of the root word: *colleague* (*com* + *league*); *illicit* (*in* + *licit*); *offend* (*ob* + *fend*); *succeed* (*sub* + *ceed*).

Exercise 21.16

Write words denoting *negation* of the following.

EXAMPLE   movable—able to be moved
            immovable—*not* able to be moved

1. reverent	4. mature	7. judge
2. disputable	5. reputable	8. returnable
3. conscious	6. convenient	9. legible

Exercise 21.17

Write words denoting *reversal* of the following.

EXAMPLE   accelerate—to move at *in*creasing speed
            decelerate—to move at *de*creasing speed
            increase—to grow *larger*
            decrease—to grow *smaller*

1. infect	4. classify	7. generate
2. compose	5. please	8. honor
3. bend	6. cut	9. personalize

Suffixes

These fall into three groups: noun suffixes, verb suffixes, adjectival suffixes:

Noun Suffixes

Noun suffixes denoting *act of, state of, quality of* include the following:

Suffix	Example	Meaning
-dom	freedom	*state of* being free
-hood	manhood	*state of* being a man
-ness	dimness	*state of* being dim
-ice	cowardice	*quality of* being a coward
-ation	flirtation	*act of* flirting
-ion	intercession	*act of* interceding
-sion	scansion	*act of* scanning
-tion	corruption	*state of* being corrupt
-ment	argument	*act of* arguing
-ship	friendship	*state of* being friends
-ance	continuance	*act of* continuing
-ence	precedence	*act of* preceding
-ancy	flippancy	*state of* being flippant
-ency	currency	*state of* being current
-ism	baptism	*act of* baptizing
-ery	bravery	*quality of* being brave

Noun suffixes denoting *doer, one who* include the following:

Suffix	Example	Meaning
-eer (general)	auctioneer	*one who* auctions
-ist	fascist	*one who* believes in fascism
-or	debtor	*one who* is in debt
-er	worker	*one who* works

Verb Suffixes

Verb suffixes denoting *to make* or *to perform the act of* include the following:

Suffix	Example	Meaning
-ate	perpetuate	*to make* perpetual
-en	soften	*to make* soft
-fy	dignify	*to make* dignified
-ize, -ise	sterilize	*to make* sterile

Adjectival Suffixes

Adjectival suffixes include the following:

Suffix	Example	Meaning
-ful	hateful	full of
-ish	foolish	resembling
-ate	affectionate	having
-ic, -ical	angelic	resembling
-ive	prospective	having
-ous	zealous	full of
-ulent	fraudulent	full of
-less	fatherless	without
-able, -ible	peaceable	capable of
-ed	spirited	having
-ly	womanly	resembling
-like	childlike	resembling

Exercise 21.18

Make words indicating *act of, state of,* or *quality of* from the following words.

1. fraudulent
2. deceitful
3. govern
4. optimal
5. discover
6. legitimate
7. observant
8. state
9 tense

Exercise 21.19

Make nouns indicating *doer* from the following.

1. piano
2. chemistry
3. account
4. oversee
5. cartoon
6. invent
7. pamphlet
8. promote
9. nutrition

Exercise 21.20

Make verbs indicating *to make* or *to perform the act of* from the following nouns and adjectives.

1. character
2. strength
3. energy
4. signal
5. short
6. custom
7. code
8. vacant
9. glad

Exercise 21.21

Make adjectives of the following words by adding a suffix.

1. adore
2. cynic
3. score
4. glamour
5. graph
6. mass
7. fright
8. study
9. justify

● **2 Synonyms.** You can strengthen your active vocabulary by using words from your recognition vocabulary. When you acquire a new word, find opportunities to use it so that it will come to feel natural and comfortable in your speech and writing.

An excellent way to strengthen your vocabulary is to study dictionary discussions of synonyms. As you add words to your vocabulary, look them up in a dictionary to be certain of their meaning and usage, and examine their synonyms at the same time. That way you will be able to increase your vocabulary by not one but several related words at a time. Furthermore, you will have learned the distinctions in meaning that will make your use of these words accurate and effective. Synonym dictionaries and thesauruses, devoted exclusively to the grouping and differentiating of synonyms, are also good sources. Although the various editions of *Roget's Thesaurus* are valuable for long lists of closely related words, they must be used cautiously because they do not discuss distinctions in meaning and offer no guiding examples. A thesaurus should be used in conjunction with a dictionary so that you will be sure of selecting the synonym with the shade of meaning you need.

Exercise 21.22

Indicate the distinctions in meaning among the words in each of the following groups.

1 absurd, silly, preposterous, ridiculous, ludicrous
2 eccentric, anomalous, abnormal, odd, singular
3 mournful, sorrowful, sad, grievous, lugubrious
4 vacant, void, vacuous, empty, unoccupied
5 rude, uncouth, churlish, insolent, impudent

In Your Own Words
If you do not own a recent, hardback, desk dictionary, consult one in the library. Look at the information inside the front and back covers, in the pages leading up to the letter *a*, and in the appendices (everything after the letter *z*). Write a two- or three-paragraph discussion of the kinds of information you found that you didn't realize was in the dictionary.

22 Appropriateness

Several thousand years ago, the Greek philosopher Aristotle wrote that a speech is composed of three things: the speaker, the subject on which he speaks, and the audience he is addressing. Contemporary author and teacher William Zinsser states that good writing is a personal transaction between a reader and a writer. Both Aristotle and Zinsser point to the importance of choosing words that are appropriate. Your language reflects your attitude toward the subject, your attitude toward yourself, and your attitude toward your listeners or readers. If the words you choose are inappropriate, you will end up alienating your audience.

There are no words in the English language that cannot be used somewhere, sometime. Consider the range of choices involved in describing the same event to different audiences. The words you use to describe a campus party in a letter to a friend and in a paper for a psychology class will differ considerably. The writing in the letter would appropriately be informal and colloquial—easy, loose, and full of jargon and slang: "The party was radical, everybody just hanging loose and generally chilling out after too many all-nighters and heavy-duty mid-terms." In the psychology paper the writing would appropriately be more formal, edited, standard English—the "public" writing of the professions and most college courses: "Many college students release the tension and pressure resulting from concentrated study by attending parties after their exams are over." (Sections **22a-22c** discuss the differences between formal and informal English.)

Both examples are right for their situations. But the audience for the first is much more limited than the audience for the second. When you write, remember that the more diverse and general your audience, the more you need to rely on standard, formal English, which offers a huge vocabulary of widely understood words. In contrast, the vocabularies offered by slang, jargon, colloquialisms, regionalisms, and the like are narrow and specialized, limited to relatively small groups of readers, and therefore much more likely to be misunderstood. Consequently, their use should generally be limited to special contexts, audiences, and purposes.

22 a Choose the register of English appropriate to your writing task.

Edited American English, the written and spoken language of educated people, is accepted as the norm for public speech and writing: It is the language shared by a wide audience of literate people. In the following excerpt, the cultural and social importance of using standard English is discussed.

> James Baldwin once defended black English by saying it had added "vitality to the language," and even went so far as to label it a language in its own right, saying "Language [i.e., black English] is a political instrument" and a "vivid and crucial key to identity." But did Malcolm X urge blacks to take power in this country "any way y'all can"? Did Martin Luther King Jr. say to blacks, "I has been to the mountaintop, and I done seed the Promised Land"? Toni Morrison, Alice Walker and James Baldwin did not achieve their eloquence, grace and stature by using only black English in their writing. Andrew Young, Tom Bradley and Barbara Jordan did not acquire political

power by saying, "Y'all crazy if you ain't gon vote for me." They all have full command of standard English, and I don't think that knowledge takes away from their blackness or commitment to black people.

—Rachel Jones, "What's Wrong with Black English"

American English includes three general **registers,** or varieties of language used in different social contexts: formal register, informal register, and familiar register. Each register is appropriate to different writing or speaking situations. However, because *formal* and *informal* each encompass wide ranges of degree, what may seem relatively formal to one reader may strike another as fairly informal. Perceived formality or informality is highly dependent on purpose, subject matter, and audience expectations. For example, if you used the level of diction appropriate to a research report in a letter to your sister, she might consider you stuffy or even pretentious.

● **1 Formal register.** Formal register is the language of scholarly books and articles; business, scientific, and government reports; legal writing; and most literary prose. Formal register is characterized by a greater emotional distance between the writer and the audience, and between the writer and the topic, than the informal or familiar registers. Formal register is grammatically accurate and logically organized; it does not include contractions, colloquial language, or slang (see Sections **21c** and **22c**). In college writing, formal register is appropriate in research reports, examinations, and essays that call for a degree of objectivity. For example, an essay with an informative purpose (see Section **2a**) would typically be written in formal register. Compare the following paragraphs.

> Of all the riddles that have stirred the human imagination, none has provoked more lyrical speculation, more religious awe, more contentious debate. No other moment in time, aside from the Big Bang that began the universe, could be more central to the understanding of nature than the instant that life began. "Scientific" theories on the subject are as old as civilization. The ancient Egyptians believed frogs and toads arose from silt deposited by the flooding Nile. The Greek philosopher Aristotle taught that insects and worms were born of dewdrops and slime, that mice were generated by dank soil and that eels and fish sprang forth from sand, mud and putrefying algae. In the 19th century, electricity, magnetism and radiation were believed to have the ability to quicken nonliving matter.
>
> —J. Madeleine Nash, "How Did Life Begin?"

> There still remain the questions of translation and the origin of the genetic code. John Maynard-Smith offered one scenario for the emergence of these features: the use of amino acids and cofactors by ribozymes. Due to their relative size and structure, the most likely interaction was between a single amino acid and three nucleotides (hence the triplet code). As the number of amino acids used as cofactors increased, each with its own nucleic acid triplet, so the possibility of two, three, and four amino acids being brought together arose. Some

of these emerging peptides would be functional, and the nucleic acid sequence would have a selective advantage. Maynard-Smith felt that this illustrated a point that must not be overlooked in the study of evolution, namely, that adaptation of function may obscure the origin of structure: A case in point is the feather, evolved for flight from the original purpose of maintaining warmth.

—Luke O'Neill, et al., "What Are We? Where Did We Come From? Where Are We Going?"

Although the intended audiences and purposes for these examples differ considerably, both examples are in the formal register. The first, from an article in *Time*, avoids contractions, colloquialisms, and slang; it uses correct grammar and mechanics; and it does not attempt to create an intimate tone between the reader and the material. The second example, from *Science* magazine, also discusses the beginning of life forms. It does so in a much more technical way than the *Time* article, because its intended audience is a more highly specialized reader than that intended by the writer of the *Time* article. Technical language itself does not mean that this example is in a higher register than the *Time* article. Both excerpts, in fact, are in the formal register. Both have emotional distance from the reader, both employ correct grammar, and both rely on elevated language.

● **2 Informal register.** Informal register is writing that is close to general speech, similar to the casual conversations you might have with a colleague or acquaintance. Informal register suggests a fairly close relationship between the writer, audience, and topic; it would be an appropriate choice for a first-person experience essay for a college class or a short memo to a colleague at work. Informal register may include shortened forms of words such as *phone* for *telephone,* contractions, **colloquialisms** (see Section **21c**), **regionalisms** (see Section **22b**), **neologisms** (see Section **23e**), and **slang** (see Section **22c**). Consider the following passage.

Imagine your are an owl: a nice, middle-class barn owl. You raise 3.2 owlets, commute to the meadow, and have mousie-o's for breakfast.

One day, one of the farmer's kids, mistaking you for a football, grabs you off your perch, heads out to the yard, and makes a long forward pass.

You are stunned. Your beak is wide in soundless terror, and you are too shocked even to spread your wings. You plummet into the waiting hands of the receiver, who is immediately tackled by every sibling in sight, and you are on the bottom.

Welcome to the world of overnight shift. That's about what it feels like.

On the midnight shift, you are forever picking your metabolism up by the scruff of its neck, giving it a good shake and setting it down on a new track. It shudders groggily, and staggers off. Who on earth would want to do that, one wonders? Hardly anyone. But those who must include hospital care-givers, police, firefighters, utilities operators, anyone whose services are round-the-clock....

Perhaps companies should declare a shorter work-week the norm for overnight workers or concede some more vacation. Society as a whole benefits from our discomfort. Remember Three Mile Island? Happened on the midnight shift. And Chernobyl? Also on the midnight shift.

It's called burning out the midnight owl—after a while, you don't give a hoot about anything.

—Carole Treasure, "The Midnight Shift Does Murder Sleep,"
in *The Wall Street Journal*

This example of informal register uses second person, colloquialisms (such as the cliché *scruff of its neck*), and neologisms (such as *mousie-o's*). And although it uses mostly standard English, it also has some structures that would be less acceptable in the formal register—for example, the sentence fragments ("Hardly anyone" and "Also on the midnight shift"). It also plays with language in a way that the formal register does not: It uses metaphors, analogy, and even puns ("burning the midnight owl" and "don't give a hoot").

● **3 Familiar register.** Familiar register is the level of diction used with close family and intimate friends. This level of diction can be found in personal letters, journals, diaries, and in dialogue in novels and plays. Familiar register is characterized by the frequent use of the first person ("I"), colloquialisms, slang, regionalisms, and sometimes scant attention to grammatical rules. Familiar register suggests an extremely close relationship between writer and reader, and thus assumes that the reader will already understand the context of the writing. In the following excerpt from a personal letter, for example, the writer assumes that the reader (his sister) will understand that he is referring to his children's experiences on Halloween.

Superman and the Witch came home last night from a recon of the neighborhood with enough booty to feed Somalia. Superman had chocolate all over his face and a torched blood sugar level: faster than a speeding bullet. The Witch emptied the whole thing into a pile on the living room floor and ran her fingers through it like King Midas. The loot will be divided into baggies and locked in the upright freezer for parental distribution....oooh the power of being Mom and Dad.

—H. Samuel Gamble III, family letter

This description of the Halloween antics of a seven-year-old and her three-year-old brother exhibits the familiar register because it uses slang (*recon, loot, torched*, as adjectives), analogies and comic allusions (*Superman, Witch, King Midas*), and casual sentence structure and mechanics ("oooh the power of being Mom and Dad."). Familiar register is typically not an appropriate choice for writing you will do in college or on the job.

In Your Own Words

1 Write a paragraph to your roommate or a close friend explaining your career plans. Then rewrite the paragraph as if you were writing to a prospective employer. Analyze the differences in your level of language.

2 Locate two brief articles on the same topic, one in a popular magazine and the other in a more scholarly periodical. In a paragraph or two, analyze the differences in the language.

22 b Regional or nonstandard language is inappropriate in formal writing.

Regional words (sometimes called **provincialisms** or **localisms**) are words whose use is generally restricted to the speech of a particular geographical area. Examples are *tote* for *carry*, *poke* for *bag*, *spider* for *frying pan* or *skillet*. *Nonstandard* words and expressions generally occur only in the language of uneducated speakers. Examples are *ain't, could of, she done,* and double negatives such as *can't never, scarcely none,* and *don't have no.* Dictionaries label such words *nonstandard* or *illiterate.* These have no place in your writing unless you are presenting dialogue or characterizing actual speech that uses such words.

REGIONAL	She *redded up* the house for our *kinfolk.*
GENERAL	She cleaned the house for our relatives.
NONSTANDARD	They *didn't ought to have* spent the money.
STANDARD	They shouldn't have spent the money.
NONSTANDARD	I wish *I'd of drove more careful.*
STANDARD	I wish I had driven more carefully.

Exercise 22.1

If you are a native of the region in which your college is located, ask a classmate from another region to give you a list of words or expressions that strike him or her as being regionalisms in your speech. If you come from another area yourself, make up your own list of regionalisms of the college area and compare it with a classmate's.

22 c Use slang only when it suits the audience and purpose for which you are writing.

Slang consists of the rapidly changing words and phrases in popular speech that people invent to give language novelty and vigor. Slang words, in fact, are fun—unless you don't happen to know what they mean. Then they can seem like the strange tongue of a secret sect.

Slang often is created by the same process we use to create most new words: by combining two words (*ferretface, blockhead*); by shortening words (*pro, prof, vet, max*); by borrowing from other languages (*kaput, spiel*); and by generalizing a proper name (*the real McCoy*). Often slang simply extends the meaning of phrases borrowed from other activities (*lower the boom* from sailing; *tune in, tune out* from radio; *cash in your chips* from poker). A great deal of slang gives a new range of meaning to existing words (*hot button, rip off, turned on, flamed*).

Slang is—and has always been—part of the current language, adding spontaneity, directness, color, and liveliness. Over three hundred years ago, Pilgrim youngsters were inventing slang terms, turning the traditional farewell—"God be with you"—into the flippant "good-by." Thus slang often contributes directly to the growth of the language as slang terms move gradually into general use. Words like *rascal* and *sham* were originally slang terms; shortened forms such as *A-bomb, ad, gym,* and *phone* are now appropriate to most informal writing. Reports on education routinely refer to high school *dropouts.* To see soft drinks and potato chips called *junk food* in the pages of a magazine surprises no one. When slang is clear, precise, vivid, and descriptive in ways that more standard words are not, it tends to enter general usage. In informal writing, well-chosen slang terms can be very effective:

> If T. Rex hears about this, he'll roll over in his fossilized grave: paleontologists have just found his grandma. And she's a turkey.
>
> —*Newsweek*

> Nerds and geeks must stop being ashamed of who they are. It is high time to face the persecutors who haunt the bright kid with thick glasses from kindergarten to the grave. For America's sake, the anti-intellectual values that pervade our society must be fought.
>
> —Leonid Fridman

But slang has serious limitations. It is often imprecise, understandable only to a narrow social or age group, and usually changes very rapidly. You may be familiar with the latest slang, but who remembers *lollapalooza, balloon juice,* or *spooning*? The fact that *hep* became *hip* within a few years suggests how short-lived slang can be.

Enjoy slang for the life it can sometimes give to speech. But even in conversation, remember that it may not be understood and that a little goes a long way. If you rely on *stuff, cool, rad,* and *gross* to describe all objects, events, and ideas, you don't communicate much. In writing, use slang primarily when it serves some legitimate purpose, such as capturing the flavor of conversation:

> My friend Connie told me about this computer-animal in her literature class, a hyper weirdo who was zoned out in class and schizzed out before papers were due. He dissed on the class all the time, but finally this hunk asked Connie if she'd like to go grab a pizza and maybe catch a flick.

Except in carefully controlled contexts, slang and standard language usually make an inappropriate mixture:

> The very notion of venture capital is so alien in Communist China that no government official was willing to risk giving the two [young Chinese entrepreneurs] permission to set up shop. The decision was bucked up all the way to Premier Zhao Ziyang. He flashed the go-ahead last year, and the company began operation in January.
>
> —*Business Week*

While we are not likely to resist such usages as *set up shop* in a magazine aimed at a fairly broad, general business audience, the slang expressions *bucked up* and *flashed the go-ahead* here seem out of place in a news story concerning the head of the Chinese government. The best rule of thumb is to assess your audience and purpose carefully in deciding whether a slang term is appropriate.

Exercise 22.2

The following list includes both new and old slang terms. Use your dictionary or, in the case of ultra-new slang, the testimony of friends to define them and to figure out their etymology.

1. phat	5. nerd	8. ditsy
2. dis	6. zone out	9. book it
3. way cool	7. digs	10. klutz
4. hip		

In Your Own Words

For a week, list all slang terms you hear used by your friends. Look up the most interesting ten of them to see whether they are in the dictionary. If they are, note their etymology. Then choose the one that interests you most and write an extended definition of a paragraph or two (see Section **7d**).

22 d For a general audience, use jargon sparingly.

The term **jargon** has several meanings (see Section **24b**). In a famous essay, "On Jargon," Sir Arthur Quiller-Couch defined the term as vague and "woolly" speech or writing that consists of abstract words, elegant variation, and "circumlocution rather than short straight speech." Linguists often define jargon as hybrid speech or dialect formed by a mixture of languages (for example, the English-Chinese jargon known as pidgin English).

To most people, however, jargon is the technical or specialized vocabulary of a particular trade, profession, or field of interest—for example, engineering jargon, computer jargon, or horticultural jargon. Naturally, members of a specialized group use their jargon when communicating with one another. It is their language, so to speak, and its terms are often more precise, more meaningful, and more quickly comprehended than nonjargon expressions would be.

The following example shows how the author of a computer manual carefully defines terms, even though some of his readers may be very familiar with computer jargon. Because other readers may be computer novices relying on the manual for instruction, he is careful to establish meanings for Macintosh® jargon.

> The Macintosh makes a useful distinction between *applications* and *documents*, the first being used to create the second. Applications can also be

thought of, more generally, as *tools* since the Macintosh manual uses the former term somewhat restrictively. Programs, such as MacWrite and MacPaint, are what are formally referred to as applications.... The pointer is a tool, whose use will vary from place to place; the keyboard and mouse are physical tools, as is the video screen on which you see the development of your labors.... Documents, on the other hand, are the end result of the process of computing, the reason you bought a computer in the first place.

—John M. Allswang, *Macintosh: The Definitive Users Guide*

Technical jargon is inappropriate when you are writing for a general audience, unless, of course, the terms have entered everyday language and are widely understood. The mass media have broadened our understanding of many technical terms, especially those relating to newsworthy topics. *Countdown* and *liftoff* from space exploration, *carcinogenic* and *biopsy* from medicine, *printout* and *terminal* from computer technology are but a few of the words that have moved from jargon into fairly general usage. Nevertheless, you should use jargon with care, defining the terms if you think your readers might not know the meanings.

Unfortunately, jargon impresses some people simply because it sounds involved and learned. We are all reluctant to admit that we do not understand what we are reading. What, for example, can you make of the following passage?

The Turbo-Encabulator in Industry

Work has been proceeding in order to bring to perfection the crudely conceived idea of a machine that would not only supply inverse reactive current for use in unilateral phase detractors, but would also be capable of automatically synchronizing cardinal grammeters. Such a machine is the Turbo-Encabulator.... The original machine had a base plate of prefabulated amulite surmounted by a malleable logarithmic casing in such a way that the two spurving bearings were in a direct line with the pentametric fan.... The main winding was of the normal lotus-o-delta type placed in a panendermic semiboloid slot in the stator, every seventh conductor being connected by a non-reversible tremie pipe to the differential girdlespring on the "up" end of the grammeters.

—Reprinted by permission of the publishers, Arthur D. Little, Inc., Cambridge, Mass

This new mechanical marvel was a joke, the linguistic creation of a research engineer who was tired of reading jargon. The point is, you should avoid unnecessary jargon in your writing, words used merely to impress, words that clutter rather than clarify.

In Your Own Words

Make a list of ten words and/or phrases that constitute jargon in a field you know. In writing, define these terms so that a general reader could understand. Finally, explain whether you think each term is a justifiable use of jar-

gon in your field or whether a "plain English" term would work just
as well.

Exercise 22.3

From an issue of a magazine or newspaper written for a general audience,
list technical or specialized terms that have ceased to be jargon and have
entered the general usage. From what fields did these terms originally
come? How many of them are at least partially defined within the context
of the articles in which they appear?

23 Exactness

Once you have determined the type of language that is appropriate for your
subject and audience, you will want to choose words that most precisely
convey the meaning you intend. To write with precision, you need to know
both the denotation and the connotation of words. **Denotation** is the core
of a word's meaning, sometimes called the "dictionary" or literal meaning:
for example, a *tree* is "a woody perennial plant having a single stem or
trunk." **Connotation** refers to the reader's emotional response to a word
and to the associations the word carries with it. Thus, *tree* may connote
shade or coolness or shelter or stillness or strength.

If you have misunderstood the denotation of a word you are using,
you are quite likely to confuse your readers. The student who wrote "The
firefighters who risked their lives to rescue the child were praised for their
heroics" chose the wrong word. *Heroics* means "melodramatic behavior or
language," quite different from *heroism*, the word the writer surely intended.
"*Eager* to hear from you" denotes desire, but "*Anxious* to hear from you"
denotes worry.

Errors of connotation are more subtle because individual responses to
words differ and meanings can change over time. For example, *gay* commonly means "exuberant," but its secondary definition, "homosexual," has no
doubt affected the word's connotative impact. Nonetheless, many words have
quite stable connotations. *Home* generally suggests security, a sense of one's
own place. Most of us would prefer a *cozy* robe and slippers to *snug* ones.

Your words should also connotatively fit other words in the same sentence and the larger context. Consider the following:

> *Brandishing* a gun and *angrily demanding* the money, the thief *yelped threat-
> eningly* at the frightened teller, "Empty the cash drawer."

The verb *yelped* suggests animal-like anger and abruptness, perfectly appropriate to the situation being described. Yet the connotations seem to
conflict with the adverb *threateningly*. *Yelped* also connotes alarm and pain.

Since the thief appears to have the upper hand in the situation, for most of us *snarled* would suggest connotations more in keeping with the other words in the sentence.

Many words stand for abstractions: *democracy, truth, inadequacy, challenge, beauty.* Because the connotations of such words are both vague and numerous, state specifically what you mean when you use them, or make sure that the context clarifies their meaning (see Section **23g**). Otherwise, readers will think they understand your terms when they do not.

23 a Distinguish among synonyms to increase exactness.

English is rich in **synonyms**, groups of words that have nearly the same meaning: *begin, start, commence; funny, comic, laughable.* But most synonyms differ in connotation. By observing their precise shades of meaning and choosing carefully among them, you can more accurately express your ideas. Occasionally, the difference in meaning between two synonyms is so slight that it makes little difference which you choose: You can *begin a vacation* or *start a vacation*—either will do. But usually the differences will be much greater. To *commence a vacation*, for example, connotes far more formality than ordinarily goes with vacations. And it makes a much more important difference whether you describe a movie as *funny, comic,* or *laughable.*

If you increase the number of synonyms in your vocabulary (see Section **21d**) and distinguish carefully among them when you write, your use of language will be more precise and therefore a greater aid to your readers. Knowing that *fashion* and *vogue* are synonyms for *fad*, or that *renowned* and *notorious* are synonyms for *famous*, gives you the chance to make your writing more exact by selecting the synonym connoting the precise shade of meaning that best expresses your idea. On the other hand, careless use of synonyms not only makes writing inexact, but also often distorts meaning. Notice the importance of connotation in the following sentence:

> Capone was a *renowned* gangster. [*Renowned* has favorable connotations that the writer probably did not intend. *Famous* would do, but it is not very exact. *Notorious*, "known widely and regarded unfavorably," would be exact.]

Exercise 23.1

Explain the differences in meaning among the italicized words in each of the following groups.

1 an *impossible*, an *absurd*, an *unreasonable*, an *impractical* plan
2 a *stingy*, a *miserly*, a *mercenary*, a *penurious* person
3 a *precept*, an *instruction*, a *maxim*, a *prescription*
4 to *diminish*, to *dwindle*, to *decrease*, to *decline*
5 a *disrespectful*, a *supercilious*, a *contemptuous*, a *disdainful* attitude

For each of the following sentences, choose the italicized synonym that seems to connote the most appropriate and precise shade of meaning for the context.

1 The first grader's parents told him not to *tarry, dawdle, linger, lag* on the way to school.

2 The mayor had to resign after the *revelation, exposure, disclosure, divulgence* of her income tax evasion.

3 Because he was so *unskillful, incompetent, awkward, maladroit,* the juggler dropped all the plates the first time he tried to juggle them.

4 The mountain climber showed much *obstinacy, tenacity, perseverance, resolution* as he spent ten days climbing the snow-covered cliffs.

5 Wondering if they would ever get home, the dinner guests spent an hour and a half listening to the speech of the *garrulous, chatty, fluent, glib* guest of honor.

23 b Revise stereotyped references to race, ethnicity, religion, class, age, and geographical areas.

Stereotypes, biased generalizations about groups of people, are inaccurate because they ignore the uniqueness of individual members of a group. They are offensive because they often reflect or lead to discrimination and intolerance. Not all Jews are good businesspeople; not all Baptists are fundamentalists; not all Asians are good at math. Eliminating stereotypes from your writing will help you become a more critical thinker and more accurate writer.

Beyond these obvious instances, check your writing carefully for implicitly stereotypical attitudes. For example, if you write about "a well-preserved fifty-year-old woman," you are making unfair judgments about standards of female attractiveness, standards that you would be unlikely to apply to a fifty-year-old man. Similarly, don't assume that all New Yorkers are rude, people from Appalachia hillbillies, or New Englanders taciturn. In referring to various ethnic groups, find out which terms people belonging to that group prefer, and use them. For example, the term *Oriental* is considered offensive; the term *Asian* is preferred. Many American black people now prefer the term *African-American* over *Negro*; many of the indigenous people of America now wish to be called *Native Americans* rather than *American Indians*. Because such usage changes quickly over time, be guided by the usage preferred by well-respected members of the group in question or the current usage reflected in the publications of that community.

In Your Own Words

1 List ten stereotypes you have observed from ads on television or in magazines. Explain in writing what assumptions these stereotypes make and why they are inaccurate.

2 Scan the letters to the editor in a daily newspaper and find three examples of

stereotyping. Explain in writing what assumptions these stereotypes make and why they are inaccurate.

23 c Revise gender stereotypes.

Eliminating gender stereotypes from your writing helps ensure that you will not alienate any of your readers, who will typically be both women and men. (See Section **14c** for strategies to remove common-gender pronoun stereotypes from your writing.) In general, do not refer to someone's gender or marital status unless the context of the writing requires doing so. Instead of writing "Three women doctors have started a new practice in Amherst," write "Three doctors have started a new practice in Amherst." Using the phrase *women doctors* in a context in which you would not write *male [or men] doctors* is considered by many to be sexist usage. Similarly, the title *Ms.* parallels *Mr.*; neither title reveals a person's marital status. Use *Ms.* unless a woman specifically asks to be called *Miss* or *Mrs.*

● **1 Occupational stereotypes.** Professions and occupations once viewed as typically male or typically female now usually employ both sexes. Use the following chart to eliminate stereotypes about occupations from your writing.

Instead of	*Use*
anchorman, anchorwoman	anchor
businessman, businesswoman	businessperson
chairman, chairwoman	chair, chairperson
clergyman	minister, pastor, priest, rabbi
female (or woman) doctor, engineer, etc.	doctor, engineer, etc.
fireman	firefighter
freshman	first-year student
mailman	mail (or letter) carrier
male nurse	nurse
policeman, policewoman	police officer
salesman	salesperson
steward, stewardess	flight attendant
weatherman, weather girl	meteorologist, weather forecaster

● **2 Exclusionary language.** Revise any language that illogically excludes either men or women from a group of people.

Instead of	*Use*
the common man	the average person
man, mankind	humans, humanity, people, humankind, the human race
man-made	synthetic

manpower, workmen	personnel, workers, work force
mothering	parenting, nurturing, caring for
old wives' tales	superstitions

● **3 Consistency in referring to men and women.** Be sure you refer to men and women in the same way when the circumstances are similar. For example, two faculty members in the biology department should be referred to as Professor Winston and Professor Levitz, not Professor Winston and Mrs. Levitz. The two poets Richard Wilbur and Sylvia Plath should be referred to as Wilbur and Plath (once their full names have been given), not as Wilbur and Sylvia (or Miss Plath or Mrs. Hughes). Similarly, don't refer to adult males as *men* and adult women as *girls*.

Exercise 23.2

Part A

Revise the following gender stereotypes, occupational stereotypes, and exclusionary terms.

1. craftsman
2. actress
3. female priest
4. fellowship
5. housewife
6. cleaning lady
7. newsmen
8. office girls
9. councilman
10. cowgirl

Part B

Revise the following paragraph, using the context as a guide for removing gender stereotypes, occupational stereotypes, and exclusionary language.

When I visited Chicago recently, I spent several nights with my Uncle Fred, a policeman who has seen and done just about everything a man could want to do. He and his fellow officers have seen lots of violent acts and the aftermath of many more—all the stuff that television anchormen skim over on the evening news. During the visit I naturally wanted to go with him on an exciting police call, but he said that a young lady like me had no business being in on such activities. Instead, Uncle Fred took me to the Art Institute, where he said we could have a proper ladies' lunch in the restaurant and see some works by a sculptress whom I admire. Uncle Fred, who actually knows a lot about art, pointed out that each of the curators at the Institute has his own specialty. Now that Uncle Fred knows that I plan to be a painter, he has resigned himself to my fate, but he keeps muttering that I could just as easily become chairman of the board of a bank or a female doctor. Of course, I didn't want to tell him that I could also just as easily become a policeman like him.

In Your Own Words

In a paragraph or two, explain what particular terms that reinforce gender stereotyping, occupational stereotyping, or exclusion of a group have been problems for you as a writer and speaker to change to make your writing less stereotypical. Explain why you think these terms have been especially difficult for you to replace with less offensive terms.

Exercise 23.3

Put together a list of words that show how standard English is reflecting elimination of stereotyping. Be ready to discuss whether you think the preferred term is accurate and/or justified.

23 **d** **Distinguish words that have similar sound or spelling but different forms or meanings.**

Some words are **homonyms;** that is, they have the same pronunciation but different meanings and different spellings (*idol, idle, idyll; aid, aide; aisle, isle*). Other words are sufficiently similar in sound and spelling to be confusing (*marital, martial*). Treat all these words as you would any other unfamiliar term: Learn the correct spelling and meaning of each as an individual word.

Many words have two, sometimes three, adjectival forms, each having a distinct meaning (for example, a *changeable* personality, a *changing* personality, a *changed* personality). A roommate whom you *like* is not necessarily a *likeable* roommate, nor is a *matter of agreement* necessarily an *agreeable matter*. Be careful not to substitute one form for the other.

UNACCEPTABLE	The cook served our *favorable* dessert.
ACCEPTABLE	The cook served our *favorite* dessert.
UNACCEPTABLE	He is a good student; he has a *questionable* mind.
ACCEPTABLE	He is a good student; he has a *questioning* mind.

Exercise 23.4

What are the differences in meaning in each of the following pairs of words?

1. accept, except
2. affect, effect
3. elude, allude
4. credible, creditable
5. discreet, discrete
6. flaunt, flout
7. illicit, elicit
8. mitigate, militate
9. moral, morale
10. ordinance, ordnance
11. principle, principal
12. populace, populous
13. an *ingenious* person
    an *ingenuous* person
14. a *distinctive* book
    a *distinguished* book
15. an *effective* plan
    an *efficient* plan
16. an *imaginary* friend
    an *imaginative* friend
17. a *laudable* speech
    a *laudatory* speech
18. a *masterly* performance
    a *masterful* performance
19. an *ornate* table
    an *ornamental* table
20. a *valuable* painting
    a *valued* painting

23 **e** **Keep meaning clear by using established words.**

Invented words tend to confuse meaning. A **coined word** is a new and out-right creation (like *gobbledygook, blurb*). A **neologism** is either a new word or a new use of an old word or words (like computer *virus* or traffic *grid-lock*). A **nonce-word**, literally **once-word,** is a word made up to suit a spe-cial situation and generally not used more than once ("My son," he said, "suffers from an acute case of televisionitis"). Though most neologisms and nonce-words are short-lived, they are among the ways by which new words and new functions for old words are constantly working their way into a changing language. *Motel*, for example, an invented word formed from *motor* and *hotel*, is now a permanent fixture in our language.

English is relatively free in shifting words from one part of speech to another. This process, called **functional shift,** is one of the many ways in which our language grows. The noun *iron* is used as an adjective in *iron bar*, and as a verb in *iron the shirts*. The Space Age has given us *All systems are go*, using the verb *go* as a modifier. *River, paper,* and *tennis* are clearly nouns in form, but we commonly use them as modifiers in *river bank, paper bag,* and *tennis elbow*.

But the fact that such changes are common in English does not mean that there are no constraints on functional shift. In "The jury opinioned that the defendant was guilty," *opinion* is used as a verb, a grammatical function to which it is entirely unaccustomed. The meaning may be clear, but the use is not accepted. We *punish* a person. There is perhaps no good reason why we should not speak of *a punish*, but we don't: If we want a noun, we use *punishment*. Advertisers talk about *winterizing* our cars with antifreeze and snow tires, but most of us draw the line at *skiierizing* our automobiles with the addition of a ski rack.

Don't be afraid to try a new coinage if it seems to suit your purpose and audience. Do be careful, however, to avoid unintentional inventions—words that you "invent" because of spelling errors (*disallusion* for *disillusion*) or an inexact knowledge of word forms and functions (*under-standment* for *understanding*). If you have any doubt about the accepted grammatical functions of a word, consult your dictionary.

Exercise 23.5

In the following sentences, correct the words which seem needlessly invent-ed. When necessary, check your dictionary to determine whether a particu-lar word is an accepted form as used.

1 One of the fastest growing ways to shop is to order merchandise from the fantastical array of catalogs that have flooded the mailboxes of prospective consumers irregardless of the requestiveness for them.

2 From these catalogs one can order everything from athletical equipment to hot-from-designers clothing and accessorizers.

3 Some catalog companies have a specialtization such as products for book-lovers, organizers, computer whizzes, or antiquing fanatists, and catalogs provide the latest in bumperstickerness, CDs, and videos.

4 Although many people like merchandization by catalog because of the exotic items many catalog companies offer, many like catalog shopping because they can breakfast or supper as they shop or because they like to avoid the increasingly complexical giantism of malls.

5 Prices in catalogs compete with favorability when compared to those in stores, and catalog companies usually offer easy procedurization for exchanges and refunds if the customer is nonsatisfied with a product.

23 f Follow accepted usage for idioms that include prepositions.

An **idiom** is an expression that does not follow the normal pattern of the language or that has a total meaning not suggested by its separate words: *to catch fire, strike a bargain, ride it out, lose one's head, hold the bag.*[*] Such expressions are a part of the vocabulary of native speakers. In fact, we learn them in the same way we learn new words—by hearing them in the speech around us and by reading them in context. For the most part they give no more, and no less, difficulty than vocabulary itself gives us. Dictionaries usually give the common idiomatic expressions at the end of the definition of a word entry.

For many writers the most troublesome idioms in English are those that require a particular preposition after a given verb or adjective according to the meaning intended. The following list contains a number of such combinations that frequently cause trouble.

ABIDE, ABIDE BY	The counselor can't *abide* our inability to *abide by* the rules.
ABSOLVED BY, FROM	I was *absolved* by the dean *from* all blame.
ACCEDE TO	He *acceded to* his father's demands.
ACCOMPANIED BY, WITH	I was *accompanied by* several advisors. The terms were *accompanied with* a plea for immediate peace.
ACCORD WITH, ACCORDING TO	*According to* the report, his version of the event does not *accord with* mine.
ACQUITTED OF	He was *acquitted of* the crime.
ADAPTED TO, FROM	This machine can be *adapted to* farm work. The design was *adapted from* a previous invention.
ADMIT TO, OF	The clerk *admitted to* the error. The plan will *admit of* no alternative.

[*]The term *idiom* is also used to mean the characteristic expression or pattern of a dialect or language. In this sense of the word, we can speak of the *idiom* of speakers from South Boston, or we can compare English *idiom* with German or French.

AGREE TO, ON, WITH, IN	They *agreed to* [or *on*] the plan but *disagreed with* us. They *agreed* only *in* principle.
ANGRY WITH, AT	She was *angry with* me and *angry at* the treatment she had received.
CAPABLE OF	This paint is *capable of* withstanding vigorous scrubbing.
CHARGE FOR, WITH	I expected to be *charged for* my purchase, but I didn't expect to be *charged with* stealing something.
COMPARE TO, WITH	He *compared* the roundness of the baseball *to* that of the earth. [to liken to something in a different class] He *compared* the fuel economy of the Ford *with* that of the Plymouth. [to examine two things in the same class for resemblances and differences]
CONCUR WITH, IN	We *concur with* you *in* your desire to use the revised edition.
CONFIDE IN, TO	My friend *confided in* me. She *confided to* me that she was interviewing for another job.
CONFORM TO, WITH	The specification *conformed to* [or *with*] the architect's original plans.
CONFORMITY WITH	You must act in *conformity with* our rules.
CONNECT BY, WITH	The rooms are *connected by* a corridor. That doctor is officially *connected with* this hospital.
CONTEND FOR, WITH	Because she needed to *contend for* her principles, she found herself *contending with* her parents.
DIFFER ABOUT, FROM, WITH	We *differ about* our tastes in clothes. My clothes *differ from* yours. We *differ with* one another.
DIFFERENT FROM*	Our grading system is *different from* yours.
ENTER INTO, ON UPON	She *entered into* a new agreement and thereby *entered on* [or *upon*†] a new career.
FREE FROM, OF	The children were *freed from* the classroom and now are *free of* their teachers for the summer.
IDENTICAL WITH	Your reasons are *identical with* ours.
INFER FROM	I *inferred from* her expression that she was disappointed in us.
JOIN IN, WITH, TO	He *joined in* the fun *with* the others. He *joined* the wire cables *to* each other.

Different than is colloquially idiomatic when the object of the prepositional phrase is a clause:

FORMAL	This town looks *different from* what I had remembered.
COLLOQUIAL	This town looks *different than* I had remembered it.

†In many phrases, *on* and *upon* are interchangeable: *depend on* or *depend upon*; *enter on* or *enter upon*. However, *on* will be perceived as less formal and more contemporary usage than *upon*.

LIVE IN, AT, ON	The Wamplers *live at* 14 Neil Avenue and *live in* a Dutch colonial house. They *live on* Neil Avenue.
NECESSITY FOR, OF, NEED FOR, OF	There was no *necessity* [*need*] *for* you to lose your temper. There was no *necessity* [*need*] *of* your losing your temper.
OBJECT TO	I *object to* the statement in the third paragraph.
OBLIVIOUS OF	When he held her hand he was *oblivious of* the passing of time.
OVERCOME BY, WITH	I was *overcome by* the heat. I was *overcome with* grief.
PARALLEL BETWEEN, TO, WITH	There is often a *parallel between* fantasy and reality. This line is *parallel to* [or *with*] that one.
PART FROM, WITH	As I *parted from* my best friend, I knew that I had also *parted with* an important page from my past.
PREFERABLE TO	A leisurely walk is *preferable to* no exercise at all.
REASON WITH, ABOUT	Why not *reason with* them? Why not *reason about* the matter?
REWARD BY, WITH, FOR	They were *rewarded by* their employer *with* a raise *for* their work.
VARIANCE WITH	This conclusion is at *variance with* your facts.
VARY FROM, IN, WITH	The houses *vary from* one another. They *vary in* size. People's tastes *vary with* their personalities.
WAIT FOR, ON	They *waited for* someone to *wait on* them.
WORTHY OF	That candidate is *worthy of* our respect.

Exercise 23.6

Provide the idiomatic expressions needed in the following sentences and paragraph.

Sentence Practice

1 Some people are hesitant to enter _____ the spirit of adventure and try new or unusual foods.

2 In fact, many people object _____ any food that is not familiar; these people are hard to reason _____, for they're adamant that they would never try something like fried squid or goose liver.

3 These picky eaters seem oblivious _____ the possibilities of discovering new foods because they feel their old favorites like meat and potatoes are preferable _____ something exotic like goat meat stew.

4 Actually, people who never vary _____ their standard dishes are missing a lot, for if they would only agree _____ trying an unusual food like squid, they might find they like it.

5 Those diners who are capable _____ putting aside their qualms about eating unusual foods are usually rewarded _____ a tasty experience.

Paragraph Practice

When my Japanese friend invited me to have dinner at a sushi restaurant, I had to admit _____ almost total ignorance about sushi. I told my friend that I thought sushi was identical _____ raw fish; when my friend heard that, she laughed and confided _____ me that most Westerners make the same mistake. In fact, she said, in Japan raw fish is called sashimi, and sashimi is different _____ sushi in many ways. To the Japanese, sushi refers to vinegared rice. Perhaps people get sushi and sashimi confused because sashimi is normally accompanied _____ sushi when the dish is served. After my friend had made clear to me how sushi varies _____ sashimi, we joined _____ a wonderful feast of sushi and sashimi _____ several other friends.

23 g Use concrete and specific words to make abstract and general language more exact.

Abstract words name qualities, ideas, concepts: *honesty, virtue, poverty, education, wisdom, love, democracy.* **Concrete words** name things we can see, hear, feel, touch, smell. *Sweetness* is abstract; *candy, honey, molasses,* and *sugar* are concrete. To describe people as *reckless* is to describe them abstractly; to say "they ran two traffic lights in the center of town and drove eighty-five miles an hour in a restricted zone" is to make that recklessness concrete.

General words refer to all members of a class or group. **Specific words** refer to the individual members of a class. *Vegetation* is general; *grass, shrubs, trees, flowers,* and *weeds* are specific. *Animal* is general; *lions, elephants, monkeys, zebras, cats, dogs, mice,* and *rabbits* are specific.

The classes abstract and concrete, general and specific overlap with each other, and both are relative. The verb *communicate* is both abstract and general. *Speak* is concrete and specific relative to *communicate,* but it is general compared to *gasp, murmur, rant, rave, shout,* and *whisper. Music* is concrete and specific relative to *sound* but general compared to *classical music,* which in turn is general compared to *Beethoven's Fifth Symphony. Dwelling* is a general word; *apartment, cabin, barracks, house, hut, mansion, shack,* and *tent* are specific. But *dwelling* is more specific than *building,* which includes not only *dwelling* but also *church, factory, garage, school,* and *store.*

All effective writing will use both abstract and concrete words, both general and specific. There are no substitutes for such abstractions as *fairness, friendship, love,* and *loyalty.* But all abstractions need to be pinned down by details, examples, and illustrations. When they are not, they remain vague and always potentially confusing. We can all quickly agree that taxes and justice should be *fair.* But until each of us has narrowed down by detail and example what he or she means by *fairness,* we will not understand each other in any useful way.

Similarly, we cannot do without general terms. We would be hard-pressed to define *cat* if we could not begin by putting cats in the general class *animal*. But as soon as we have done so, we must then name the specific characteristics and qualities that distinguish cats from, say, armadillos or raccoons. To say "Tom enjoys reading" tells readers very little until we know whether the reading consists of *Sports Illustrated* and *People*, or of Dickens and Dostoyevsky.

Effective writing constantly weaves back and forth between abstract and concrete, between general and specific. It is the writer's use of the abstract and general that guides the reader, but it is the concrete and specific that allow the reader to see, feel, understand, and believe. "This lamp supplies insufficient light" informs us; "this fifteen-watt bulb gives no more light than a firefly in a jam jar" makes us understand what the writer means by *insufficient.*

Whenever you use abstract words, give them meaning with concrete details and examples. Whenever you use general words, tie them down with specific ones. Try constantly to express yourself and your ideas in concrete terms; search for the most specific words you can find.

GENERAL   The flowers were of different colors.
SPECIFIC   The chrysanthemums were bronze, gold, and white.

GENERAL   The cost of education has increased greatly.
SPECIFIC   Tuition at many private universities has increased as much as 1,000 percent in the past three decades.
MORE SPECIFIC Tuition at my college was $300 in 1955; forty years later it was more than $15,000.

SPECIFIC   Mateo was a stocky man, with clear eyes and a deeply tanned face. His skill as a marksman was extraordinary, even in Corsica, where everyone is a good shot. He could kill a ram at one hundred and twenty paces, and his aim was as accurate at night as in the daytime.
MORE SPECIFIC Picture a small, sturdy man, with jet-black, curly hair, a Roman nose, thin lips, large piercing eyes, and a weather-beaten complexion. His skill as a marksman was extraordinary, even in this country, where everyone is a good shot. For instance, Mateo would never fire on a wild ram with small shot, but at a hundred and twenty paces he would bring it down with a bullet in its head or shoulder, just as he fancied. He used his rifle at night as easily as in the daytime, and I was given the following illustration of his skill, which may seem incredible, perhaps, to those who have never travelled in Corsica. He placed a lighted candle behind a piece of transparent paper as big as a plate, and aimed at it from eighty paces away. He extinguished the candle, and a moment later, in utter darkness, fired and pierced the paper three times out of four.

—Prosper Mérimée, *Mateo Falcone*

Exercise 23.7

Revise the following paragraph, supporting the generalizations and abstractions with concrete and specific details so that the meaning of the paragraph is clearer and the language more exact. Before you begin to revise, list the abstract or general words you think need sharper focus.

> Going grocery shopping is an unpleasant chore, but when I have to do it, I try to find ways to make it an interesting experience. Noticing the strange types of shoppers keeps me interested so that I have done my shopping before I know it. I am always amazed at those shoppers who are well organized when they arrive and do their shopping without much trouble. It is more fun, though, to watch the disorganized shoppers who don't know where to find things and who don't really know what they want to buy. Some shoppers clearly spend a lot of time being sure that what they buy is healthful, and some seem to load up on all the junk food they can carry. Looking at the kinds of items in a shopping cart tells me a lot about what kinds of lives my companions have.

23 h Increase exactness by using apt figurative language.

Like concrete and specific words, figurative language can help readers understand your ideas. The basis of most figurative language lies in the comparison or association of two things essentially different but nonetheless alike in some underlying and surprising way. Inexperienced writers sometimes think figurative language is the monopoly of poets and novelists. In fact, it plays an important part in much prose and is one of the most effective ways of making meaning concrete. Notice how the following passage uses figurative language to illustrate a point about consumer spending:

> Any significant business recovery has to have the consumer's support, because the consumer sector accounts for two-thirds of GNP [Gross National Product]. So far there is no solid support—consumer spending is not advancing. And for good reason: Consumer incomes are growing slowly.... So consumers are not exactly dragging their feet. They are dancing as fast as can be expected.
>
> —*Business Week*

The two most common figures of speech are simile and metaphor. **Similes** make direct and explicit comparisons, usually introduced by *like, as, as if,* or *as when,* as in "Jess is as changeable as the New England weather." **Metaphors** imply comparisons, as in "Prisoned in her laboratory, she ignored the world." The figure of speech used in the preceding excerpt from *Business Week* is a metaphor that compares consumers to dancers in step with the slow growth in personal income.

Both simile and metaphor require that the two things compared be from different classes so that their likeness, when pointed out, will be fresh and surprising. The consumer-dancer metaphor accomplishes this goal because we do not usually think of consumers as dancers stepping to the tune of the economy. The image adds liveliness to the economic discussion and helps personify the generalization *consumers,* increasing our understanding of the relationship between spending and income. If similes and metaphors are extended, they must also be consistent.

> Up scrambles the car, on all its four legs, like a black beetle straddling past the schoolhouse and the store down below, up the bare rock and over the changeless boulders, with a surge and a sickening lurch to the skybrim, where stands the foolish church.
>
> —D. H. Lawrence, *Mornings in Mexico*

> Writing a story or a novel is one way of discovering *sequence* in experience.... Connections slowly emerge. Like distant landmarks you are approaching, cause and effect begin to align themselves, draw closer together. Experiences too indefinite of outline in themselves to be recognized for themselves connect and are identified as a larger shape. And suddenly a light is thrown back, as when your train makes a curve, showing that there has been a mountain of meaning rising behind you on the way you've come, is rising there still, proven now through retrospect.
>
> —Eudora Welty, *One Writer's Beginnings*

In the foregoing passage, Eudora Welty compares meaning to a mountain and writing to a journey—specifically, a train trip—a simile she uses frequently in *One Writer's Beginnings.* Extended throughout the book is the metaphor of memory, and life itself, as a journey: "The memory is a living thing—it too is in transit."

Apt figures of speech can do much to make writing concrete and vivid, and, by making one experience understandable in terms of another, they can often help clarify abstractions. But be careful when creating figures of speech; if they strain too hard, as in the first of the following examples, they will miss their mark, falling flat or seeming too contrived. When two figures are *mixed* so that they create clashing images (sometimes called *mixed metaphors*), as in the final four examples, readers will not only miss your point, they will find your writing ludicrous.

> Her smile was as warm as an electric blanket.
>
> Does your life have to be on the rocks before you will turn over a new leaf?
>
> She made her reputation as a big star early in her career, but she has been coasting on her laurels for the past ten years.
>
> He held the false belief that in a capitalist democracy we can peer deep into the veil of the future and chain the ship of state to an exacting blueprint.
>
> He [artist Thomas Hart Benton] was flat-out, lapel-grabbing vulgar, incapable of touching a pictorial sensation without pumping and tarting it up to the point where the eye wants to cry uncle.
>
> —*Time*

Exercise 23.8

Collect several examples of figurative language from newspapers and magazines. Look for some that are effective and some that are mixed metaphors. Identify what is being compared, what image is being created. Then analyze why the effective ones work and why the ridiculous ones do not. You can begin by practicing on the following paragraphs from the sports pages of a newspaper.

> A Harvard team that could do no wrong upset a Yale team that did almost everything wrong today before a crowd of 59,263 in the Yale Bowl. This victory, by a 37-20 score, deprived the Bulldogs of an outright Ivy League championship. They had to share the title with Princeton, both finishing with 6-1 records.
>
> For Harvard, there was the exquisite satisfaction of snatching a jewel away from its old rival and staining an otherwise respectable season. It was the fifth time since 1974 that a Harvard triumph in the finale took away from Yale either an outright or shared Ivy title.

Exercise 23.9

Replace the mixed or incongruous figures of speech in the following sentences and paragraph with more appropriate comparisons. Be prepared to explain why the original similes or metaphors are inappropriate.

Sentence Practice

1 My neighbor was green with envy when he saw my new red sports car.
2 The children went limp with fear at the sight of the monster and then froze in horror as it let forth a gigantic roar.
3 My brother didn't like playing second fiddle to the leader of the clarinet section, so he dropped out of the band.
4 The president tried hard to steer the ship of state through the latest diplomatic crisis, but because of bad advice from his cabinet members, he had a hard row to hoe.
5 The sales director needed information about our earnings for the year, so she asked us for a ball park figure so that she could run it up the flagpole at the next budget meeting.

Paragraph Practice

The cook had egg on his face when the chocolate souffle he had prepared for the special dinner fell flat as a pancake. As if that weren't enough, he flipped his lid when he lifted the cover of the soup pot and discovered that he'd forgotten to turn on the heat under the pan. When he realized the soup was ice cold, the cook decided this dinner wasn't going to be a bowl of cherries. He knew he had failed the acid test when he mistakenly put too much vinegar in the salad dressing. He finally threw in the towel when he realized that even though the dinner was ruined, he'd still have to spend half the night cleaning up the kitchen.

23 **i** Keep meaning exact by avoiding trite expressions.

A trite expression, sometimes called a **cliché,** or a **stereotyped** or **hackneyed phrase,** is an expression that has been worn out by constant use, as *burning the midnight oil, hopping mad, head over heels in love.* Many trite expressions are examples of figurative language that once was fresh but has lost its power because we have heard it too often. Several of the metaphors and similes in Exercise 23.9 are trite expressions: *flat as a pancake* and *threw in the towel,* for example.

Words in themselves are never trite—they are only used tritely. We cannot avoid trite expressions entirely, for they sometimes describe a situation accurately, capturing a writer's or speaker's intended meaning precisely. But such expressions can also be the crutch of a lazy thinker who chooses the worn cliché rather than searching for the exact words that will best express an idea.

> But when inflation came down … and the lingering recession and a strong dollar forced even the wealthiest business executives and foreign travelers to pinch pennies, the financial feasibility of scores of new hotel projects went down the tubes.
>
> —*Business Week*

The writer of the preceding example has chosen expressions that accurately capture the meaning. But the *pinch pennies* metaphor and the slang phrase *down the tubes* have been so overworked that they cease to be effective. Together these expressions create a mixed image (pennies down the tubes) that is likely to strike many readers as funny—probably not the effect the writer intended.

What is your estimate of the person who wrote this?

> A college education develops a *well-rounded personality* and gives the student an appreciation for *the finer things of life.* When he or she finally graduates and leaves *the ivory tower* to *play in the game of life,* the student will also have the necessary *tools of the trade.*

This writer's language suggests that her thinking is not only trite but imprecise as well. The expressions *well-rounded personality* and *finer things of life,* for example, are so abstract and vague that readers will surely wonder just what, exactly, the writer means.

Effectively used, triteness can be consciously humorous. The string of trite expressions in the following example explodes into absurdity when the writer deliberately transposes the words in the two clichés in the last clause.

> A pair of pigeons were cooing gently directly beneath my window; two squirrels plighted their troth in a branch overhead; at the corner a handsome member of New York's finest twirled his night stick and cast roguish glances

at the saucy-eyed flower vendor. The scene could have been staged only by a Lubitsch; in fact Lubitsch himself was seated on a bench across the street, smoking a cucumber and looking as cool as a cigar.

—S. J. Perelman, Keep It Crisp

Exercise 23.10

Identify all the clichés in the following passage. Then revise the passage, eliminating those expressions you think are too hackneyed to be effective and substituting fresher, more meaningful language.

> When I decided at long last to have a party and invite all my friends, I was determined to go the whole nine yards and do it up big. Because my house was a real disaster area, I worked for a week to get the place shipshape. I also slaved over a hot stove for several days so that the food would be first rate. The day before the party, I bought snacks and beverages so that my friends could eat, drink, and be merry. Finally, I asked several friends to bring their favorite tapes and CDs so that we could dance the night away. Little did I think when I was making all these preparations that the roof might fall in. First, it was raining cats and dogs the night of the party, and all the guests arrived looking like drowned rats. My friends forgot to bring their tapes and CDs, so we all sat around staring at the ceiling. The food was the only bright spot in the evening, so at least I hit a home run in that area. When the evening was over, I breathed a big sigh of relief. I've decided that you live and learn, and I've learned that giving parties may not be my cup of tea.

24 Directness

The challenge to directness comes from two fronts—wordiness and vagueness. A wordy writer uses more words than are necessary to convey meaning; a vague writer fails to convey meaning sharply and clearly. Wordiness and vagueness are found together so often as to be nearly indistinguishable, as the following example shows:

WORDY AND VAGUE	He attacks the practice of making a profitable business out of college athletics from the standpoint that it has a detrimental and harmful influence on the college student and, to a certain degree and extent, on the colleges and universities themselves.
IMPROVED	He attacks commercialization of college athletics as harmful to the students and even to the universities themselves.

Sometimes wordiness is just awkwardness; the meaning is clear, but the expression is clumsy.

AWKWARD	The notion that present-day Quakers wear flat-brimmed dark hats or black bonnets and long dresses is a very common notion.

IMPROVED   Many people think that present-day Quakers wear flat-brimmed dark hats or black bonnets and long dresses.

Wordiness and vagueness obscure meaning. Your goal as a writer should be to say things as directly and economically as possible without sacrificing clarity and completeness. Readers are always grateful for writing that is concise, that makes every word count. The following sections discuss ways to spot and eliminate wordiness and vagueness in your writing.

24 **a** Revise to eliminate the wordiness.

Wordy writing wastes readers' time and contributes nothing to meaning. Constructions that contribute to wordiness often appear in clusters. Where you find one sort, you are likely to find another. Two that frequently appear as a pair are nominals and weak verbs. Other contributors to wordiness are roundabout constructions, unnecessary phrases and clauses, redundancy, and awkward repetition.

● **1 Nominals.** Nominals are nouns created by adding suffixes to verbs: *establishment, completion, deliverance.* While there is certainly nothing wrong with these words, using unnecessary nominals in your writing tends to make it ponderous and slow-moving. The reason is that the verb, the word that conveys action in the sentence, has been transformed into a noun, an object. Learn to spot nominal suffixes such as *-ment, -tion, -ance* (also sometimes *-ity, -ize, -ness*) in your writing and to change unnecessary nominals back into verbs. Your sentences will be shorter and more vigorous.

WORDY   Strict *enforcement* of the speed limit by the police will cause
NOMINALS   a *reduction* in traffic fatalities.
REVISED   If the police strictly enforce the speed limit, traffic fatalities will be reduced.

● **2 Weak verbs.** Vague, weak verbs such as *make, give,* and *take* often occur in combination with nominals as replacements for the stronger, more energetic verbs that have been changed into nouns. Another weak verb form, the passive-voice verb, also lengthens sentences and reduces vigor because it involves subjects being *done to* rather than subjects *doing* (see Section **29e**). Consequently, a sentence using a passive-voice verb requires a prepositional phrase to identify the agent, or *doer* of the action. Your writing will be less wordy if you choose specific, concrete, active-voice verbs.

WEAK VERB   At the next meeting, the city council *will take* the firefighter's request for a raise under consideration.
REVISED   At the next meeting, the city council will consider the firefighters' request for a raise.

PASSIVE VOICE   A decision *was reached* by the council members to amend the zoning laws.

REVISED   The council members reached a decision to amend the
                zoning laws.
                The council members decided to amend the zoning laws.

● **3 Roundabout constructions.** Indirect and circuitous wording annoys
readers and wastes their time because it detracts from quick, clear understanding of your meaning. As you revise your writing, you will often be able
to strike out unnecessary words or gain directness with slight changes.
Words such as *angle, aspect, factor,* and *situation,* and phrases such as *in the
case of, in the line of, in the field of* are almost never necessary and are common obstacles to directness.

WORDY   I am majoring in the field of biology.
REVISED   I am majoring in biology.

WORDY   Another aspect of the situation that needs to be examined is the
                matter of advertising.
REVISED   We should also examine advertising.

Expletives (*there is, there are, it is, it was*) frequently add unnecessary
words and weaken the emphasis on a sentence's true subject (see Section
10c). Your sentence may be more effective if you simply begin with the
true subject. In other instances, a one-word modifier may convey meaning
more economically.

WORDY   There were fourteen people in attendance at the meeting.
REVISED   Fourteen people attended the meeting.

WORDY   It is apparent that we can't agree.
REVISED   Apparently, we can't agree.

Weak and wordy constructions such as *because of the fact that, it
was shown that,* and *with regard to* can often be reduced to a single word
or eliminated.

WORDY   Due to the fact that the plane was late, I missed my connecting
                flight to San Antonio.
REVISED   Because the plane was late, I missed my connecting flight to
                San Antonio.

WORDY   With regard to the luggage, the airline will deliver it to our hotel
                this afternoon.
REVISED   The airline will deliver the luggage to our hotel this afternoon.

● **4 Unnecessary phrases and clauses.** Wordiness often results from
using a clause when a phrase will do, or a phrase when a single word will
do. Needless constructions waste readers' time and lengthen sentences without adding meaning. Learn to spot such constructions, especially several
piled together. Where appropriate, reduce clauses to participial or appositive phrases or to single-word or compound modifiers. Reduce phrases to

single-word or compound modifiers, verbals (verb base plus -*ing*), or possessives with -*s;* or leave them out if they don't contribute to meaning.

WORDY	This shirt, *which is made of wool,* has worn well for eight years.
REVISED	This *woolen* [or wool] shirt has worn well for eight years. [The meaning of the wordy clause *which is made of wool* is conveyed as accurately, and more economically, by *woolen,* a single-word modifier.]
WORDY	The football captain, *who is an All-American player,* played his last game today.
REVISED	The football captain, *an All-American,* played his last game today. [The meaning of the clause modifying *captain* is more economically expressed as an appositive phrase.]
WORDY	The conclusions *that the committee of students* reached are summarized in the newspaper *of the college that was published today.*
REVISED	The conclusions *reached by the student committee* are summarized in *today's college newspaper.* [One-word modifiers (*student, college*), a possessive (*today's*), and a participle (*reached*) have replaced wordy clauses and phrases.]

● **5 Redundancy.** Expressions such as *I saw it with my own eyes* and *audible to our ears* are redundant; they say the same thing twice. Redundancies don't clarify or emphasize; they just sound stupid— especially ones with words that are already absolute and cannot logically be further qualified (*unique, perfect, dead,* for example). Typical examples include the following:

Redundant	Direct
advance forward	advance
continue on	continue
completely eliminate	eliminate
refer back	refer
repeat again	repeat
combine together	combine
circle around	circle
close proximity	close
few in number	few
cheaper in cost	cheaper, less costly
disappear from view	disappear
past history	history, the past
important essentials	essentials

Sometimes sentences become wordy through a writer's careless repetition of the same meaning in slightly different words.

WORDY	As a rule, I usually wake up early.
REVISED	I usually wake up early.
WORDY	In their opinion, they think they are right.
REVISED	They think they are right.
WORDY	After the close of the office at 5 P.M. this afternoon, Jones's farewell party will begin.
REVISED	After the office closes at 5 P.M., Jones's farewell party will begin.
WORDY	She is attractive in appearance, but she is a rather selfish person.
REVISED	She is attractive but rather selfish.

Similarly, some expressions are simply redundant or roundabout ways of saying things that could be stated in a single, precise word.

Wordy	Direct
call up on the telephone	telephone
this day and age	today
of an indefinite nature	indefinite
at this point in time	now, today
by means of	by
destroy by fire	burn
at all times	always
in the near future	soon

● **6 Awkward repetition.** Repetition of important words can be a useful way of gaining emphasis and coherence in your writing (see Section **6d**), but careless repetition is awkward and wordy.

AWKWARD	The investigation revealed that the *average teachers teaching* industrial arts in California have an *average* working and *teaching* experience of five years.
REVISED	The investigation revealed that industrial arts teachers in California have an average of five years' experience.
AWKWARD	The capacity of computer memory is being *improved* constantly in order to *improve* computing speed.
REVISED	The capacity of computer memory is being increased constantly to improve computing speed.

Exercise 24.1

Identify the causes of wordiness in the following sentences and paragraph, and revise them to reduce wordiness.

Sentence Practice
1 Learning to make a budget and stick to it has been the cause of much frustra-

tion for many of my friends who attend college, but most of them see that it is necessary to learn to live on a budget.

2 One factor that causes problems for most of them is that they find it hard to keep up with all the ways in which they spend the money that they do have.

3 Once they can completely account for most of their expenditures, my friends are able at that point in time to make a list of priorities for ways that they want to spend the money which they have.

4 As soon as such a list of priorities is made by them, they can keep track of the money they spend and the ways in which they spend it to see how closely it matches the list which they made of their priorities for spending.

5 Once the differences between ways they want to spend their money and ways they are actually spending it are known, then an adjustment can be made in either the habits which they have for spending or the goals which they have for spending.

Paragraph Practice

Many experts say that the habits which students form for spending and budgeting are indicative of the extent of the financial success and problems the students will have once they graduate from college in the future. No matter how little or how much money a student spends, he or she should begin at an early point to save at least 10 percent of whatever money he or she earns at a job. Experts agree that the best way for people to save money that is theirs is to pay themselves a set amount each month and put it into a savings account—before they pay any bills or obligations or plan to pay for anything else. Financial planners also advise students to be careful about using credit cards and charge accounts, which are readily available to most students, so that they can avoid having to pay high interest rates. Learning to live within one's means while one is still a student in college can lead to success down the road when the student graduates and has even more money to manage as he or she gets a full-time job in the future.

Exercise 24.2

Revise the following paragraph to eliminate wordiness and awkwardness.

Two of the well-known women in Canada who are famous writers are Alice Munro and Margaret Atwood. Atwood, a versatile writer who believes in the absolute value of literature, has written as a Canadian nationalist and a feminist. She has written many novels, short stories, poems, essays, and television and radio scripts, and her writing, which is known worldwide because it has been translated into many languages, has made her one of the most well-known contemporary writers in the world. Munro, who is most famous for her short stories, has written many stories about the failure of men and women to communicate adequately. Although in *Lives of Girls and Women* (1971) Munro attempted to write a novel and her publisher advertised it as a novel, to many critics it seems like a collection of short stories in spite of its label. Munro is a writer for whom people's experiences in separate episodes which reflect only small glimmers of truth about them and about their lives are most indicative of truth and, therefore, she find the short story a form which more accurately reflects her basic understanding about the relationships and experiences that are revealed in people's lives.

In Your Own Words

Review your two most recent pieces of writing for examples of wordiness. List all phrases and sentences that are wordy and diagnose the cause of wordiness in each case (for example, redundancy, expletive *there is,* careless repetition). Then write a brief summary of the problems you find with wordiness in your own writing.

24 b Revise to eliminate vague, pretentious diction.

Journalist Edwin Newman, well known for his writing about the English language, has noted that "direct and precise language, if people could be persuaded to try it, would...help to substitute facts for bluster...and it would promote the practice of organized thought and even of occasional silence, which would be an immeasurable blessing." Never be ashamed to express an idea in simple, direct language. Complicated, pretentious, artificial language is not a sign of superior intelligence or writing skill. If alternative forms of the same word exist, use the shorter. Choose *truth* and *virtue* over *truthfulness* and *virtuousness.* Choose *preventive* rather than *preventative.*

As many of the examples in Section **24a** illustrated, wordy language is frequently also pretentious language; diction becomes more elaborate, showy, and self-conscious than the subject requires. Vague, abstract terms and euphemisms are other characteristics of pretentious language. Instead of "we decided against it," someone writes "we have assumed a negative posture on the matter"—as if these words were better than simply saying no.

We all are familiar with this kind of diction—the pompous language of many government documents, military reports, scholarly articles, and business executives' defenses of a poor product or unprofitable year. Pretentious diction is all too frequently a means of disguising the truth rather than revealing it. Instead of admitting he wants to raise taxes, the President talks about "revenue enhancement." Rather than a press office, the Environmental Protection Agency has an "Office of Public Awareness." The military refers to a bombing raid as a "protective reaction strike," and the MX missile is named "the Peacekeeper." Instead of saying "You're fired," the boss explains that an employee is "the next candidate for staff reduction." Even when such language is meant to convey information honestly, we react negatively because we are used to associating it with bureaucratic smokescreens. It's no wonder artificial diction of this type has come to be called *businessese, bureaucratese, gobbledygook,* and *bafflegab.* In his novel *1984,* George Orwell termed such doubletalk "Newspeak"—a language designed to supplant truth with vagueness. Following Orwell's lead, since 1974 the Committee on Public Doublespeak, a group affiliated with the National

Council of Teachers of English, has presented annual Doublespeak Awards to public figures for language that is "grossly deceptive, evasive, euphemistic, confusing, or self-contradictory."

Preferring simplicity does not mean you must make *all* writing simple. Naturally, highly complex or technical subjects call at times for complex and technical language—the jargon and style appropriate to the subject and audience (see Section **22d**)—as the following passage illustrates.

> One of the simplest ways of evolving a favorable environment concurrently with the development of the individual organism is that the influence of each organism on the environment should be favorable to the *endurance* of other organisms of the same type. Further, if the organism also favors *development* of other organisms of the same type, you have then obtained a mechanism of evolution adapted to produce the observed state of large multitudes of analogous entities, with high powers of endurance. For the environment automatically develops with the species, and the species with the environment.
> —A. N. Whitehead, *Science and the Modern World* [his italics]

Within the context of its subject, purpose, and audience, this passage is neither vague, pretentious, nor artificial. It conveys its meaning directly. On the other hand, the following examples are wordy and vague.

ARTIFICIAL   Due to the fact that the outlet mechanism for the solid fuel appliance was obstructed by carbon, the edifice was consumed by fire.

DIRECT   Because the flue for the wood-burning stove was clogged with soot, the house burned down.

ARTIFICIAL   The athletic contest commenced at the stipulated time.

DIRECT   The game began on time.

ARTIFICIAL   It still looks favorable for beneficial crop moisture in central Indiana.

DIRECT   Chances for rain in central Indiana still look good. The soybeans could use a soaking.

Euphemisms, words or phrases substituted for those that are, for some reason, objectionable, have their place in effective writing. They express unpleasant things in less harsh, less direct ways: *perspire* for *sweat, elderly* for *old, deceased* for *dead.* Most common euphemisms are associated with the basic facts of existence—birth, age, death, sex, body functions— and often seem necessary for politeness or tact. We may be more comfortable describing a good friend as one who is *stout* and *disorganized* rather than as a *fat slob.* In such contexts these terms are harmless.

But using euphemisms to distract readers needlessly from the realities of work, unemployment, poverty, or war is at best misleading and at worst dishonest and dangerous. Today we take for granted terms such as *sanitation engineer* (garbage collector), *funeral director* (undertaker), and *mainte-*

nance staff (janitors). Such terms perhaps help protect the feelings of individuals and give them status; but the individuals themselves still have to pick up garbage, prepare bodies for burial, and sweep floors—in short, do work that is hard or unpleasant. And if the terms make us forget that reality, they are misleading. It is but a short step to language consciously intended to deceive. Such language give us *peace-keeping force* (military troops), *servicing the target* (killing the enemy), *strategic redeployment* (retreat), *visual surveillance* (spying), and *inoperative statements* (lies). Such phrases are downright dishonest, created for the sole purpose of distracting us from realities we need to know about. Slums and ghettos are no less slums and ghettos because a writer calls them the *inner city*. And if you're fired, you're out of a job even if you've been *terminated* or *deselected*.

Keep your own writing honest and direct. Be alert to dishonesty and pretentiousness in the writing of others. Use euphemism if tact and genuine respect for the feelings of your audience warrant it, but resist temptations to slide into artificial diction that veils, rather than conveys, meaning.

Exercise 24.3

Supply more direct words or phrases for the following euphemisms.

1. terminate
2. office assistant
3. economically disadvantaged
4. physically challenged
5. sales associate
6. preowned automobile
7. at-risk student
8. human resources department
9. substance abuse
10. information specialists
11. misspeak
12. gentrification

In Your Own Words

Find several examples of gobbledygook or pretentious, artificial diction in newspapers and magazines. Translate these into direct, natural language.

Exercise 24.4

Revise the following passage, substituting more direct, natural language for the wordy, artificial diction and unnecessary euphemisms.

At the commencement of business this morning, it was discovered that the computer system at the banking facility was in a nonoperational mode. As a result of this negative situation, the bank manager had to establish a dialogue with the supervisor of the computer department in order to determine the most advantageous method of serving the bank's customers. After the termination of this meeting, the bank manager informed the tellers that in order to effect maximum efficiency of operation, they would be required to check each customer's account before issuing payment for a check. When plans for operating had been finalized, the manager said that it was her observation that, customerwise, the bank could operate in a productive posture until repair of the computer system could be implemented.

Writers Revising

Effective Words

Ricky has become politically active recently concerning environmental issues and wants to encourage more funding for his state's Department of Environmental Quality. He has decided to write to his county representative in the legislature, asking the representative to support increased funding for DEQ. Before he mails his letter, he asks his English instructor, who is also interested in environmental issues, if she will critique it. She agrees and marks his letter with references from Chapters 22-24. Read the following excerpt from Ricky's letter and critique it. Then compare your critique with the one Ricky's instructor marked, which appears after the draft.

Draft

```
Dear Representative Maxey:

    For many, many years our state has referred to
itself as the "Sportsman's Paradise." This environ-
mental turf, which is our state, has longtime been a
haven for people who enjoy hunting and fishing to
enjoy their pastimes respectfully. But Louisiana is
presently in the wake of an enormous and tremendous
environmental crisis which poses great potential harm
for all of us citizens who live and work here and
love our state dearly. The only sure solution to this
crisis is to begin the cleaning up of our environment
and to support sufficiently those state agencies which
specialize in this area. Since the establishment of
the Department of Environmental Quality, and under
the guidelines of the Environmental Affairs Act, we
have had a proper base to commence to begin saving
our state. However, establishment is not enough.
Instead of pinching pennies, we must properly fund
the DEQ to allow for this process to proceed.
Therefore, the legislature should push for increased
general funding for the DEQ from our state.
```

Ricky's instructor asked him to go over his paper with her. When he read the paper along with her, he saw his language problems were primarily wordiness and imprecise word choice.

Revision

Dear Representative Maxey:

For ~~many, many years~~ ^{decades} our state has   24a(5)

referred to itself as the "Sportsman's

Paradise." This environmental turf, which is

our state, has longtime been a haven for ~~both~~

^{people who enjoy hunting and fishing respectively.}

~~hunters and fishermen to enjoy their pastimes~~   23c, 24a(5)

~~respectfully.~~ But Louisiana is presently in the   23d

wake of ~~an enormous and tremendous~~ ^{a great} environmen-   24a(5)

tal crisis which poses potential harm for all

~~of us~~ citizens who live and work here and ~~love~~   24a(4)

~~our state dearly.~~ The only sure solution to   23i

this crisis is to ~~begin the cleaning~~ ^{clean} up ~~of~~ our   24a(4)

environment and to support sufficiently those

state agencies which specialize in this area.

Since the establishment of the Department of

Environmental Quality, and under the guide-

lines of the Environmental Affairs Act, we

have ^{had} a proper base to ~~commence to~~ begin saving   24a(5)

our state. However, establishment is not

enough. ~~Instead of pinching pennies, we~~ ^{We} must   23i

properly fund the DEQ to allow for this

process to proceed. Therefore, the legislature

should push for increased general funding for

the DEQ. ~~from our state.~~   24a(5)

Analysis

In the first sentence, *decades* replaces the redundant *many, many years*. In the second sentence, the incorrect word *respectfully*, meaning "to show regard," is replaced by *respective*, meaning "relating to particular persons or things," to precede *pastimes*. In the third sentence, one word, *great*, can be substituted for the redundant *enormous and tremendous*. The fourth and fifth editorial changes, in Ricky's third sentence, delete the wordy *of us* and the trite expression *love our state dearly*. In the fourth sentence, a two-word verb phrase, *clean up*, replaces a cumbersome five-word weak-verb-and-nominal combination. Ricky's seventh change, in the fifth sentence, deletes *commence to*, which means the same as *begin*. The seventh sentence (editorial change eight) benefits from removing the trite expression *pinching pennies*. Ricky realized *from our state* in sentence eight (editorial change nine) was redundant because the location had been clearly established at the beginning of the letter. As a result of revising his wording, Ricky's letter moves more clearly and directly to its point and thus is more likely to hold his reader's attention.

25 Spelling

Language existed first as speech, and the alphabet is basically a visual device to represent speech. When letters of the alphabet have definite values and are used consistently, as in Polish or Spanish, the spelling of a word is an accurate index to its pronunciation, and vice versa. Not so with English. The alphabet does not represent English sounds consistently. The letter *a* may stand for the sound of the vowel in *may, can, care,* or *car; c* for the initial consonant of *carry* or *city; th* for the diphthong in *both* or in *bother*. Different combinations of letters are often sounded alike, as in *rec(ei)ve, l(ea)ve,* or *p(ee)ve*. In many words, moreover, some letters appear to perform no function at all, as in *i(s)land, de(b)t, of(t)en, recei(p)t*. Finally, the relationship between the spelling and the pronunciation of some words seems downright capricious, as in *through, enough, colonel, right*.

Much of the inconsistency of English spelling may be explained historically. English spelling has been a poor index to pronunciation ever since the Norman conquest, when French scribes gave written English a French spelling. Subsequent tampering with English spelling has made it even more complex. Early classical scholars with a flair for etymology added the unvoiced *b* to early English *det* and *dout* because they mistakenly traced these words directly from the Latin *debitum* and *dubitum* when actually both the English and the Latin had derived independently from a common Indo-European origin. Dutch printers working in England were responsible for changing English *gost* to *ghost*. More complications arose when the pronunciation of many words changed more rapidly than their spelling. The *gh* in *right* and *through*, and in similar words, was once pronounced much like the German, *ch* in *nicht*. *Colonel* was once pronounced *col-o-nel*. The final *e* in words like *wife* and *time* was long ago dropped from actual speech, but it still remains as a proper spelling form.

The complex history of the English language may help to explain why our spelling is illogical, but it does not justify misspelling. Society tends to equate bad spelling with incompetent writing. In fact, only the misspellings tend to be noticed, not the quality of the writing.

25 a Use American spellings.

Many words have a secondary spelling, generally British. Though the secondary spelling is not incorrect, you should use the spelling more widely accepted in the United States. Here is a brief list of preferred and secondary spelling forms; consult a good dictionary for others.

1 American *e*	British *ae, oe*
anemia	anaemia
anesthetic	anaesthetic
2 American *im-, in-*	British *em-, en-*
impanel	empanel
inquiry	enquiry
3 American *-ize*	British *-ise*
apologize	apologise
civilization	civilisation
4 American *-or*	British *-our*
armor	armour
color	colour
labor	labour
odor	odour
5 American *-er*	British *-re*
center	centre
theater	theatre

6 American *o*	**British *ou***
mold	mould
plow	plough
smolder	smoulder

7 American *-ction*	**British *-xion***
connection	connexion
inflection	inflexion

8 American *l*	**British *ll***
leveled	levelled
quarreled	quarrelled
traveled	travelled

9 American *e* omitted	**British *e***
acknowledgment	acknowledgement
judgment	judgement

25 b Proofread carefully to eliminate misspelling.

In writing a first draft, you form words into sentences faster than you can write them down. You concentrate not on the words you are writing, but on the words to come. A few mistakes in spelling may easily creep into early drafts. Always take five or ten minutes to proofread your final draft for spelling errors.

Lack of proofreading accounts for the fact that the words most often misspelled are not, for example, *baccalaureate* and *connoisseur*, but *too*, *its*, *lose*, *receive*, *accommodate*, and *occurred*. Most of us think we can spell a familiar word. Either we never bother to check the spelling in a dictionary, or we assume that a word pictured correctly in our mind will automatically transfer to our writing. This thinking accounts for such errors as omitting the final *o* in *too*, confusing the possessive *its* with the contraction *it's*, and spelling *loose* when *lose* is meant. You will never forget how to spell *receive*, *accommodate*, *occurred* if you will devote just a few moments to memorizing their correct spellings.

25 c Pronounce words carefully to aid correct spelling.

Many words are commonly misspelled because they are mispronounced. The following list of frequently mispronounced words will help you overcome this source of spelling error.

accident*a*lly		note the *al*
acc*u*rate		note the *u*
bus*i*ness		note the *i*
can*d*idate		note the first *d*
envir*on*ment		note the *on*
Feb*r*uary		note the *r*
gover*n*ment		note the *n*
incident*a*lly		note the *al*
lib*ra*ry		note the *r*
math*e*matics		note the *e*
prob*ab*ly		note the *ab*
quan*t*ity		note the first *t*
represen*ta*tive		note the *ta*
soph*o*more		note the second *o*
su*r*prise		note the first *r*
a*th*letics	NOT	ath*e*letics
disas*t*rous	NOT	disast*er*ous
heigh*th*	NOT	heigh*th*
gri*e*-vous	NOT	gre-*vi*-ous
ir-*rel*-e-*v*ant	NOT	ir-*rev*-e-*l*ant
mis-ch*ie*-vous	NOT	mis-che-*vi*-ous

However, pronunciation is not an infallible guide to correct spelling. Although, for example, the last syllables of *adviser,* *beggar,* and *doctor* are all pronounced as the same unstressed *ur,* they are spelled differently. Proceed cautiously when using pronunciation as a spelling aid, and check your dictionary whenever you doubt either your pronunciation or your spelling.

25 d Distinguish among the spellings of words that are similar in sound.

English abounds in **homonyms,** words whose sound is similar to that of other words but whose spelling is different (for example, *rain, rein, reign*). Some of the most troublesome homonyms are listed here.

all ready: everyone is ready
already: by this time

all together: as a group
altogether: entirely, completely

altar: a structure used in worship
alter: to change

ascent: climbing, a way sloping up
assent: agreement; to agree

breath: air taken into the lungs
breathe: to exhale and inhale

capital: chief; leading or governing city; wealth, resources
capitol: a building that houses the state or national lawmakers

cite: to use as an example, to quote
sight: the ability to see
site: location

clothes: wearing apparel
cloths: two or more pieces of cloth

complement: that which completes; to supply a lack
compliment: praise, flattering remark; to praise

corps: a military group or unit
corpse: a dead body

council: an assembly of lawmakers
counsel: advice; one who advises; to give advice

dairy: a factory or farm engaged in milk production
diary: a daily record of experiences or observations

descent: a way sloping down
dissent: disagreement; to disagree

dining: eating
dinning: making a continuing noise

discreet: reserved
discrete: individually distinct

dying: ceasing to live
dyeing: process of coloring fabrics

foreword: a preface or introductory note
forward: at, near, or belonging to the front

forth: forward in place or space, onward in time
fourth: the ordinal equivalent of the number 4

its: possessive form of *it*
it's: contraction of *it is*

loose: free from bonds
lose: to suffer a loss

personal: pertaining to a particular person; individual
personnel: body of persons employed in same work or service

principal: chief, most important; a school official; a capital sum (as distinguished from interest or profit)
principle: a belief, rule of conduct, or thought

rein: strap for controlling an animal
reign: to rule

respectfully: with respect
respectively: in order, in turn

stationery: writing paper
stationary: not moving

their: possessive form of *they*
they're: contraction of *they are*
there: adverb of place

whose: possessive form of *who*
who's: contraction of *who is*

your: possessive form of *you*
you're: contraction of *you are*

25 **e** **Learn spelling rules to aid correct spelling.**

● **1** *ie and ei.* Distinguish between *ie* and *ei.* Remember this jingle:
Write *i* before *e*
Except after *c*
Or when sounded like *a*
As in *eighty* and *sleigh.*

i before *e*	*ei* after *c*	*ei* when sounded like *a*
thief	receive	weigh
believe	deceive	freight
wield	ceiling	vein

Exceptions:
Neither sovereigns nor financiers forfeit the height of their surfeit leisure to seize the weird counterfeits of feisty foreigners.

—Christopher W. Blackwell

● **2 Final e before a suffix.** Drop the final *e* before a suffix beginning with a vowel but not before a suffix beginning with a consonant.

a Suffix beginning with a vowel, final *e* dropped:

please + sure	= *pleasure*
ride + ing	= *riding*
locate + ion	= *location*
guide + ance	= *guidance*

Exceptions: In some words the final e is retained to prevent confusion with other words.

dyeing (to distinguish it from *dying*)

The final *e* is retained to keep *c* or *g* soft before *a* or *o.*

notice + able	= *noticeable*
change + able	= *changeable*
BUT practice + able	= *practicable* (*c* has sound of *k*)

b Suffix beginning with a consonant, final *e* retained:

sure + ly	= *surely*
arrange + ment	= *arrangement*

like + ness	= *likeness*
entire + ly	= *entirely*
entire + ty	= *entirety*
hate + ful	= *hateful*

Exceptions: Some words taking the suffix *-ful* or *-ly* drop the final *e:*

awe + ful	= *awful*
due + ly	= *duly*
true + ly	= *truly*

Some words taking the suffix *-ment* drop the final *e:*

judge + ment	= *judgment*
acknowledge + ment	= *acknowledgment*

The ordinal numbers of *five*, *nine*, and *twelve*, formed with *-th*, drop the final *e*. *Five* and *twelve* change *v* to *f*.

fifth	ninth	twelfth

● **3 Final *y* before a suffix.** In general, change the final *y* to *i* before a suffix, unless the suffix begins with *i*.

defy + ance	= *defiance*
forty + eth	= *fortieth*
ninety + eth	= *ninetieth*
rectify + er	= *rectifier*
BUT cry + ing	= *crying* (suffix begins with *i*)

● **4 Doubling final consonants.** A final single consonant is doubled before a suffix beginning with a vowel when (a) a single vowel precedes the consonant, and (b) the consonant ends an accented syllable or a one-syllable word. Unless both these conditions exist, the final consonant is not doubled.

stop + ing	= *stopping* (*o* is a single vowel before consonant *p* which ends a word of one syllable)
admit + ed	= *admitted* (*i* is a single vowel before a consonant *t* which ends an accented syllable)
stoop + ing	= *stooping* (*p* ends a word of one syllable but is preceded by double vowel *oo*)
benefit + ed	= *benefited* (*t* is preceded by a single vowel *i* but does not end the accented syllable)

Exercise 25.1

Spell each of the following words correctly and explain what spelling rule applies. Note any exceptions to the rules.

1. close + ure = ?	11. thirty + eth = ?
2. sneer + ed = ?	12. fine + ness = ?

3. issue + ance = ?
4. rotate + ion = ?
5. note + able = ?
6. endure + ance = ?
7. fate + ful = ?
8. remit + ed = ?
9. measure + able = ?
10. peace + able = ?

13. entice + ment = ?
14. defeat + ed = ?
15. sure + ty = ?
16. comply + ance = ?
17. live + ly = ?
18. shop + ed = ?
19. commence + ment = ?
20. fly + er = ?

● **5 -*s* endings on nouns and verbs.** Nouns ending in a sound that can be smoothly united with -*s* usually form their plurals by adding -*s*. Verbs ending in a sound that can be smoothly united with -*s* form their third-person singular by adding -*s*.

Singular	Plural	Some Exceptions		Verbs	
picture	pictures	buffalo	buffaloes	blacken	blackens
radio	radios	tomato	tomatoes	criticize	criticizes
flower	flowers	zero	zeroes	radiate	radiates
chair	chairs				
ache	aches				
fans	fans				

● **6 -*es* endings on nouns and verbs.** Nouns ending in a sound that cannot be smoothly united with -*s* form their plurals by adding -*es*. Verbs ending in a sound that cannot be smoothly united with -*s* form their third-person singular by adding -*es*.

Singular	Plural	Verbs	
porch	porches	pass	passes
bush	bushes	tax	taxes

● **7 Nouns and verbs ending in *y*.** Nouns ending in *y* preceded by a consonant form their plurals by changing *y* to *i* and adding -*es*. Verbs ending in *y* preceded by a consonant form their third-person singular in the same way.

Singular	Plural	Verbs	
nursery	nurseries	pity	pities
mercy	mercies	carry	carries
body	bodies	hurry	hurries
beauty	beauties	worry	worries

Exceptions: The plural of proper nouns ending in *y* is formed by adding -*s* (e.g., "There are three Marys in my history class").

Nouns ending in *y* preceded by *a, e, o,* or *u* form their plurals by adding -*s* only. Verbs ending in *y* preceded by *a, e, o,* or *u* form their third-person singular in the same way.

Singular	Plural	Verbs	
day	days	buy	buys
key	keys	enjoy	enjoys
guy	guys		

● 8 **Plurals of borrowed words.** The spelling of plural nouns borrowed from French, Greek, and Latin frequently retains the plural of the original language.

Singular	Plural
alumna (*feminine*)	alumnae
alumnus (*masculine*)	alumni
analysis	analyses
basis	bases
crisis	crises
criterion	criteria
datum	data
hypothesis	hypotheses
medium	media
phenomenon	phenomena

The tendency now, however, is to give many such words an anglicized plural. The result is that many words have two plural forms, one foreign, the other anglicized. Either is correct.

Singular	Plural (foreign)	Plural (anglicized)
appendix	appendices	appendixes
chateau	chateaux	chateaus
focus	foci	focuses
index	indices	indexes
memorandum	memoranda	memorandums
radius	radii	radiuses
stadium	stadia	stadiums

Exercise 25.2

Correctly spell the plural of each of the following nouns and the third-person singular of each of the following verbs and explain what spelling rule applies. Note any exceptions to the rules.

1. reflex	8. echo	15. hasten
2. deputy	9. marry	16. podium
3. emphasis	10. destroy	17. speech
4. delay	11. jinx	18. rally
5. conspiracy	12. bless	19. coach
6. alley	13. felony	20. veto
7. annoy	14. verify	

In Your Own Words

What words do you have trouble spelling? Most people have some words which they look up in the dictionary each time they use them, because they can't remember the spelling. Think of five words that you repeatedly look up. Review the spelling rules in this chapter, and write a paragraph or two explaining which rules apply to the spelling of these troublesome words. Explain whether or not understanding the spelling rule will keep you from having to check the spelling of those words again in the dictionary.

25 **f** Spell compound words according to current usage.

Compound words usually progress by stages from being written as two words, to being hyphenated, to being written as one word (for example, *door mat, door-mat, doormat*). Since these stages often overlap, the correct spelling of a compound word may vary. For the current spelling of a compound, check a good dictionary. (For more examples and a discussion of the general use of the hyphen in compounds, see Chapter 42, "The Hyphen.")

Review Exercises

Words

Part A

Use your dictionary to help you answer the following questions.

1 What is the etymology of the word *virus*?

2 How many meanings can you find for the word *sack*?

3 What are some synonyms for the word *elegance*?

4 What are two homonyms for the word *you*?

5 What do the abbreviations EDT, i.e., and HMS mean?

Part B

Rewrite the following sentences and paragraph, eliminating poor usage of slang, inappropriate words, clichés, euphemisms, needlessly invented words, incorrect idioms, vagueness and wordiness, mixed or incongruous metaphors, and misspellings.

Sentence Practice

1 The personal director of the manufacturing company said she was looking for a person to fill a management position: The right person would have a degree in computer science, would have knowledge of government regulations, and would have experience in the business world.

2 Neither of the first two candidates she interviewed had the right stuff, so she went back to square one and ran an ad in the newspaper.

3 The next person who came to apply for the job had been involuntarily terminated from his previous position.

4 The next applicant was very eager and enthusiastic about the job; she wanted to get on the fast track to success right away, but she didn't have any managerial experience.

5 Finally, just when the personal director was ready to throw in the towel, the perfect applicant arrived: This person had worked in a management position in a government agency for five years; had received a degree in computer science; and showed poise, good judgement, and enthusiasm in the job interview.

Paragraph Practice

When I decided to take college classes at night, I knew I would have to have self-discipline since I also work full-time during the day. Nevertheless, I knew that if I wanted to climb the ladder of success, I had to dive right in and get to work on my degree. Now that I have been attending classes for a while, I'll agree to those people who told me that working full-time and going to school would effect my life. The biggest problem I have is time; when I think back to my life before I became a student, I realize I had every night to relax after work. Now I rush home, change clothes, grab a quick snack, and go to class. Sometimes, when I'm burning the midnight oil, I feel overwhelmed, but I tell myself to chill out because the attainment of a degree is worth the effort. My moral does get a little low at times also, but I always feel better when the semester is over, and I see what I have achieved.

In Your Own Words

Listen to your favorite singer's latest CD or album. List the figures of speech, slang terms, euphemisms, clichés, and stereotypical language that occur in the songs. Then write a three-paragraph analysis of the kinds of language dominant on the album. Be sure to cite many examples to support your analysis.

Part 5

Basic Grammar

Writing always presents problems, dilemmas, some of which beset all writers, even great ones; but there is no need to be baffled by all the difficulties every time you write. The effort to which you are being invited is to learn the usual pitfalls and how they are avoided, while also learning the devices—tricks of the trade—by which writing can be both improved and made easier than it seems to most people. . . . By the same effort, you may also learn to be clear and to afford pleasure to those who read what you write.

—Jacques Barzun, *Simple & Direct*

We use grammar whenever we speak or write. As a subject, grammar is a way of *describing* what happens to language when you use it. In this sense, grammar is in the same class as physics. Both are concerned with systems that operate according to principles. Physics describes how light, sound, and other kinds of energy and matter work. Grammar describes how language works. Any language is composed of individual words and grammatical devices for putting them together meaningfully. English has several devices for putting words into meaningful combinations. The three most important are word order, function words, and inflections.

In English, grammatical meaning is largely determined by **word order**. *Blue sky* and *sky blue* mean different things: In the first, *blue* describes *sky*; in the second, *sky* describes *blue*. The sentence "The thief called the lawyer a liar" is different from "The lawyer called the thief a liar" and "The liar called the lawyer a thief."

Word order can be extremely important to meaning, as the following example shows: "The shoes on the steps with the run-down heels are mine." Word order indicates that *with the run-down heels* describes *steps*, but common sense tells us that steps don't have heels. However, until our common sense overrides the meaning created by word order, we are momentarily confused.

Function words are words such as *the, and, but, in, to, because, while, ought,* and *must*. Function words express relationships among other words. Compare the following:

I am lonely *at* dark.   The cook prepared *a* rich feast.

I am lonely *in the* dark.   The cook prepared *the* rich *a* feast.

Inflections are changes in the form of words; these changes indicate differences in grammatical relationship. Inflections account for the differences in meaning in the following sentences:

The river*s* flow slowly.   Stop bother*ing* me.

The river flow*s* slowly.   Stop*s* bother me.

Readers depend on your using these grammatical devices—word order, function words, and inflections—to signal what you mean.

A distinction is sometimes made between grammar and usage. Grammar is concerned with generally applicable principles about language. **Usage**, in contrast, is concerned with choices, particularly with differences between *formal* (less conversational) and *informal* (more conversational) English and between *standard English* (well established and widely recognized as acceptable) and *nonstandard English* (generally considered unacceptable by educated speakers and writers of English) (see Chapter 22).

The differences between *tile floor* and *floor tile, he walks* and *he walked, she was biting the dog* and *the dog was biting her* are grammatical differences of word order and inflection. The differences between *I saw* and *I seen, she doesn't* and *she don't,* and *let me do it* and *leave me do it* are differences in usage. These statements may identify the persons who use them as speakers of standard or nonstandard dialects, but they do not mean different things. Because this book is concerned with writing standard English, it is concerned with both grammar and usage.

 Sentence Sense

To describe the way a language works, grammarians assign words to categories according to their functions. These grammatical function labels are called the parts of speech. The parts of speech and the functions they usually perform are as follows:

Function	Part of Speech	Example
Naming	Nouns, pronouns	*corn, summer, it*
Predicating (stating or asserting)	Verbs	*grows, was, will eat*
Modifying	Adjectives, adverbs	*tall, quickly*
Connecting	Prepositions, conjunctions	*in, and, although*

 Recognize nouns.

Nouns name or classify persons, places, things, and concepts: *women, home, dog, shoes, studio, committee, athletics, courage, wealth.* Nouns are divided into the following types.

- **Proper nouns** name particular people, places, or things: *Dorothy, Kansas, Toto.* The first letter of a proper noun is always capitalized.
- **Common nouns** name general groups, people, places, or things: *girl, state, dog.*
- **Count nouns** name people, places, and things that can be counted: one *synagogue,* three *churches,* fifteen *employees.* Count nouns have singular and plural forms: *table, tables; bus, buses; foot, feet; man, men.*
- **Noncount nouns,** also called mass nouns, name things that cannot be counted: *sugar, water, milk, coffee.* Noncount nouns do not usually have plural forms.
- **Collective nouns** name groups: *committee, family, team, class.* Collective nouns are singular in form but either singular or plural in meaning depending on the context (see Section **14a**).
- **Abstract nouns** name intangible qualities, conditions, or ideas: *justice, freedom, sympathy, peace.*
- **Concrete nouns** name things perceived by the five senses: *sky, book, teacher, cookies.*

Nouns can be distinguished from other types of words by four characteristics.

- A noun can be preceded by an article (also called a determiner): *a* team, *an* orange, *the* ball.

- Except for noncount nouns, nouns can be changed from singular to plural, usually by adding -*s* or -*es*: *dog, dogs; church, churches; child, children; woman, women; fish, fish* (for spelling of irregular plurals, see Section **25e**).
- Nouns can show ownership by the addition of an apostrophe and -*s*: *child, child's.*
- Certain endings, italicized in the following words, also are characteristic of nouns: relev*ance*; excell*ence*; real*ism*; activ*ity*.

ESL Highlight

Articles and Nouns

Use *a* or *an* with a singular count noun when your reader or you do not know its specific identity, unless another noun marker precedes the noun: *a friend,* but *her friend.*

Common Noun Markers

ARTICLES	*a* computer, *an* orange, *the* house
NUMBERS	*fifteen* credits, *16,000* years old
POSSESSIVE PRONOUNS	*my, your, his, her, its, our, their*
POSSESSIVE NOUNS	*President Clinton's* health care plan
OTHER PRONOUNS	*all, any, each, every, either, neither, few, many, more, most, much, this, that, these, those, several, some, whose*

Do not use *a* or *an* with plural nouns or noncount nouns.

Common Noncount Nouns

ABSTRACT NOUNS	advice, beauty, confidence, courage, employment, fun, happiness, health, honesty, information, intelligence, knowledge, love, luck, satisfaction, truth, violence, wealth
GROUPED ITEMS	clothing, equipment, food, furniture, homework, jewelry, money, success, traffic, vocabulary
FOOD AND DRINK	beef, beer, bread, butter, candy, cereal, cheese, coffee, flour, fruit, ice, milk, pasta, salt, sugar, tea, water
NATURAL ELEMENTS	air, blood, coal, dew, darkness, dirt, fire, fog, gold, heat, ice, iron, light, rain, scenery, silver, smoke, snow, sunshine, water, weather, wind, wood

Use *the* with a noun when your reader knows its specific identity, unless the noun is a plural or noncount noun meaning "in general" or "all" or a proper noun:

"the tower in the center of town," but "Towers are tall buildings."

"the street," but "First Street"

 **Recognize pronouns.**

Pronouns are words that can replace or refer to nouns:

Birds sing at dawn.   Anne likes apples.
They sing at dawn.   *She* likes *them.*

The noun that a pronoun replaces or refers to is called its **antecedent**.
In the sentence "Jesse Jackson is the man who founded Operation PUSH,"
the pronoun *who* refers to its antecedent, *man.* Some pronouns also serve
as adjectives modifying nouns: *"These* books are overdue."

English has eight types of pronouns: personal, indefinite, relative,
interrogative, intensive, reflexive, and reciprocal.

Personal pronouns refer to specific persons or things. Personal pronouns have different forms depending on their function in the sentence:
"She was amazed by *her* own good luck" (see Chapter 27).

SINGULAR   I, me, you, she, her, he, him, it
PLURAL   we, us, you, they, them

Indefinite pronouns do not refer to specific persons or things; thus, they
do not require antecedents: *"Anyone* who loves dogs will enjoy this event."

Common Indefinite Pronouns			
all	both	many	one
another	each	most	some
any	everyone	none	someone
anyone	everybody	no one	somebody
anybody	everything	nobody	something
anything	few	nothing	

Relative pronouns introduce subordinate clauses and refer to a noun or
pronoun that the clause modifies: "My friends found an owl *that* was hurt."
That introduces the clause *that was hurt* and refers to the noun *owl* (see
Section **26h**).

that, who, whom, whose, which

Interrogative pronouns introduce questions: *"Who* ate my cookie?"
"Whose coat is lying on the floor?"

what, who, whom, whose, which

Demonstrative pronouns (also called demonstrative adjectives when they
precede nouns) point to or identify particular people or things: *"This* is
Toni Morrison's new novel." *"Those* trees are evergreens."

SINGULAR   this, that
PLURAL   these, those

Intensive and reflexive pronouns have the same forms but perform different functions. Intensive pronouns emphasize their antecedents: "The musician *himself* realized the audience was losing interest." Reflexive pronouns refer to a receiver of an action who is the same as the doer of the action: "My daughter dressed *herself*."

SINGULAR	myself, yourself, himself, herself, itself
PLURAL	ourselves, yourselves, themselves

Reciprocal pronouns refer to the separate parts of a plural antecedent: "As a family we have to take care of *one another*."

      each other, one another

26 **c** Recognize verbs.

A verb makes an assertion about the subject: The clock *ticks*, A deer *runs*. Verbs indicate actions (*ask, eat, give*), occurrences, (*become, happen*), or states of being (*seem, appear, live, be*).

ACTION	The children *played*.
OCCURRENCE	The thunder *became* louder.
STATE OF BEING	This answer *seems* wrong.

Verbs change form to show the time of the action or occurrence, the person and number of the subject, and the voice and mood of the verb (see Chapter 29).

TIME	We *jump*, we *jumped*
PERSON	I *run*, she *runs*
NUMBER	one person *arrives*, two people *arrive*
VOICE	they *call*, they are *called*
MOOD	Curtis *knows*, if Curtis *knew*

Main verbs may combine with auxiliary verbs to create verb phrases. Auxiliary verbs (also called helping verbs) include forms of *be, have,* and *do* and the modal auxiliaries, which do not change form: *can, could; will, would; shall, should; may, might, must.* In sentences with verb phrases, the main verb always follows any auxiliary verbs (see Section **29c**).

    Verbs sometimes can be identified by their suffixes, or word endings. Some common verb suffixes are italicized in the following verbs:

implic*ate*	oper*ate*	wid*en*	hast*en*
lique*fy*	simpli*fy*	recog*nize*	modern*ize*

26 **d** Recognize adjectives and adverbs.

Modifiers are words or word groups that identify, limit, or qualify the words or word groups to which they refer. The principal one-word modifiers are adjectives and adverbs.

● **1 Adjectives.** Adjectives modify, or limit the meaning of nouns or pronouns: *brown* dog, *Victorian* house, *yellow* one, *good* pass. Adjectives answer questions such as *which one?, what kind of?,* or *how many?* about the nouns or pronouns they modify. Adjectives change form in the positive, comparative, and superlative: *happy, happier, happiest; beautiful, more beautiful, most beautiful; good, better, best.*

● **2 Adverbs.** Adverbs modify verbs, adjectives, adverbs, or whole sentences: "stayed *outside*"; "horribly *angry*"; "very *slowly*"; "*fortunately,* the accident was not serious." Adverbs often answer one of the following questions: *how? when? where? why? to what extent? to what degree?*

Some adverbs may be identified by their *-ly* ending (*slowly, carefully*), but not all adverbs end in *-ly* (*not, always, never*) and not all words ending in *-ly* are adverbs. For example, *lovely* and *homely* are both adjectives.

Like adjectives, many adverbs change form to indicate the comparative and superlative degree: *carefully, more carefully, most carefully.*

See Chapter 28 for more information about adjectives and adverbs.

ESL Highlight

Modifiers Preceding a Noun
When more than one modifier precedes a noun, the following order is usual:

Determiner: *the, my, all*
General characteristic: *beautiful, soft, ugly*
Size: *big, little, large, long, short*
Age: *old, new*
Color: *red, black*
Material: *wood, metal, plastic*
Noun being modified: *chair, house, dog*

The ugly old metal desk is my favorite piece of furniture.

This new green pencil belongs to my friend Camille.

In general, use no more than two or three modifiers between the determiner and the noun being modified.

26 e Recognize prepositions and conjunctions.

Connecting words allow writers to combine words and word groups to express the relationships between ideas more concisely and clearly. For example, we don't need to say "We talked. We played cards. We went home." Rather, we can say "After we talked and played cards, we went home" or "After talking and playing cards, we went home." Prepositions and conjunctions enable us to make these connections among related ideas.

● **1 Prepositions.** A preposition shows the relationship between a noun or a pronoun (called its **object**) and some other word in the sentence. The preposition, together with its object, almost always modifies the other word to which it is linked.

> Skaters glide *over* the ice. [*Over* links *ice* to the verb *glide; over the ice* modifies *glide.*]

Although a preposition usually comes before its object, in questions it sometimes follows its object.

> In what town do you live?
>
> What town do you live in?
>
> To whom do I send the check?
>
> Whom do I send the check to?

Common Prepositions

about	below	into	through
above	beside	near	to
across	by	next	toward
after	down	of	under
among	during	off	until
around	except	on	up
as	for	out	upon
at	from	over	with
before	in	past	within
behind	inside	since	without

Many single-word prepositions combine with other words to form phrasal prepositions, such as *down from, in addition to, such as, at the point of.*

Some words, such as *below, down, in, out,* and *up,* occur both as prepositions and as adverbs. Used as adverbs, they never have objects. Compare "He went below" with "He went below the deck."

Other words function as both prepositions and subordinating conjunctions. Examples are *after, as before, since,* and *until.*

● **2 Conjunctions.** A conjunction shows the relationship between the words, phrases, or clauses it connects. **Coordinating conjunctions**—*and, but, or, nor, for, so, yet*—join words, phrases, or clauses of equal grammatical rank (see Sections **26g** and **26h**).

WORDS JOINED   We ate ham *and* eggs.

PHRASES JOINED   Look in the closet *or* under the bed.

CLAUSES JOINED   We wanted to go, *but* we were too busy.

See Section **32a** for a discussion of punctuating clauses joined with coordinating conjunctions.

Correlative conjunctions are coordinating words that work in pairs to join words, phrases, clauses, or whole sentences. The most common correlative pairs are *both . . . and, either . . . or, neither . . . nor, not . . . but,* and *not only . . . but also.*

> *both* courageous *and* loyal
>
> *either* before you go *or* after you return
>
> *not only* as a child *but also* as an adult

Subordinating conjunctions join clauses that are not equal in rank. A clause introduced by a subordinating conjunction is called a *dependent* or *subordinate* clause (see Section **26h**) and cannot stand by itself as a sentence; it must be joined to a main, or independent, clause.

> We left the party early *because we were tired.*
>
> *If the roads are icy,* we will have to drive carefully.

Common Subordinating Conjunctions

after	even if	so that	when
although	even though	than	whenever
as	if	that	where
as if	in order that	though	wherever
as though	rather than	unless	whether
because	since	until	while
before			

See Sections **32b-32d** on punctuating clauses joined with subordinating conjunctions.

Conjunctive adverbs connect only independent clauses. Unlike other kinds of conjunctions, they can occupy different positions within a clause. A semicolon separates two clauses joined by a conjunctive adverb, and the conjunctive adverb is set off from the rest of the sentence with commas.

> Scientists have discovered a new receptor site for the HIV virus; *however,* it may be several years before an effective vaccine is developed.
>
> Scientists have discovered a new receptor site for the HIV virus; it may be several years, *however,* before an effective vaccine is developed.
>
> Scientists have discovered a new receptor site for the HIV virus; it may be several years before an effective vaccine is developed, *however.*

Common Conjunctive Adverbs

accordingly	however	namely	specifically
also	incidentally	nevertheless	still
anyway	indeed	next	subsequently
besides	instead	nonetheless	then
certainly	likewise	now	therefore
consequently	meanwhile	otherwise	thus
finally	moreover	similarly	undoubtedly
furthermore			

See Section **33b** on punctuation with conjunctive adverbs.

Exercise 26.1

In the following sentences and paragraph, identify the adjectives (ADJ), adverbs (ADV), prepositions (P), coordinating conjunctions (CC), correlative conjunctions (CorC), subordinating conjunctions (SC), and conjunctive adverbs (CA). Then use each sentence as a model for writing a sentence of your own that uses adjectives, adverbs, prepositions, and conjunctions as they are used in the model. For a topic, you might write about events in your own life.

Sentence Practice

1 One of the earliest and most important writers to call attention to women's issues was Mary Wollstonecraft, who wrote *A Vindication of the Rights of Woman* in 1792.
2 When her attempts to support herself as a governess and school administrator failed, she worked diligently as a writer and translator of several languages.
3 With her small child she bravely traveled to remote areas of Scandinavia, writing about the plight of women she observed there.
4 Early in her life she suffered at the hands of an abusive father, and later she was repeatedly betrayed by her lover, Gilbert Imlay.
5 She labored tirelessly to achieve both legal rights and a useful, challenging education for women.
6 Eventually she married the philosopher William Godwin, who earlier had argued against the institution of marriage; however, at age thirty-eight she died just after giving birth to their daughter, Mary Godwin.

Paragraph Practice

    Like her famous mother, Mary Godwin wrote both fiction and nonfiction. After she married the poet Percy Bysshe Shelley, Mary Godwin Shelley penned her most famous work, *Frankenstein; or The Modern Prometheus*, written in 1816 when she was only nineteen years old. Following the drowning of her husband in 1822, she supported herself and her son by editing Shelley's poems and prose. Among her works are five additional novels, many short stories, and numerous biographical and critical works about Shelley's life and work. Although some of her late works were popular, Mary Shelley's fame as a writer was secured by the publication of the celebrated *Frankenstein*.

Exercise 26.2

Expand each of the following sentences, using adjectives, adverbs, prepositions, and conjunctions to add information. After expanding the sentences, go back and label the adjectives, adverbs, prepositions, and conjunctions.

1 Philippe wanted a pizza for lunch.
2 He went to a pizzeria.
3 He could not decide on the toppings for the pizza.
4 His friend, Marguerite, made a suggestion.
5 He shared the pizza with her.

In Your Own Words

Write a paragraph about an embarassing moment you experienced. Include adjectives, adverbs, prepositions, and conjunctions, and label them.

26 f Recognize sentence parts and patterns.

A **sentence** is a grammatically independent group of words that expresses a complete thought. The term *grammatically independent* means that a sentence does not depend on any other word group to complete its meaning. For example, "Marcos is listening to music" and "Is Marcos listening to music?" are sentences. But "although Marcos is listening to music" is not a sentence because the connecting word *although* makes the whole word group dependent on something else for completion, as in "Although Marcos is listening to music, he will hear the baby if she cries." Every sentence has two main parts, a subject and a predicate.

● **1 Subjects.** The subject of a sentence is a noun or pronoun and any modifiers of the noun or pronoun. The subject names the person, thing, or concept that the sentence is about.

> *Joan Didion* has written essays, novels, and plays.
>
> Has *anyone in the class* read her work?
>
> *Didion's voice* is considered unsentimental.

The subject of a statement can be located by asking "who?" or "what?" about the verb: Who has written essays, novels, and plays? *Joan Didion.* To identify the subject of a question, change the question to statement form and apply the question "Who or what?" about the verb: Anyone in the class has read her work. Who has read her work? *Anyone in the class.*

● **2 Predicates.** The predicate consists of a verb or verb phrase and all its

modifiers, objects, and complements. The verb itself may be a single word (*teaches*) or a main verb preceded by auxiliary verbs (*are attending, will have started*). Note that other words may come between the parts of a verb phrase: in the sentence "He is not thinking clearly," the verb phrase is *is thinking*. The predicate, which always includes a main verb, makes a statement or asks a question about the subject or tells the subject what to do.

> Newborn babies *sleep an average of sixteen hours a day.*

> The average amount of time that people sleep *declines with increasing age.*

> *Do* you *get enough sleep?*

● **3 Basic sentence patterns.** All English sentences are built on five basic patterns. Differences among the patterns lie in the predicate—the verb and what follows it. (ESL students see also Section **29e**.)

Sentence Pattern 1	
Subject +	*Verb (+ any modifiers of the verb)*
The snow	fell.
The powdery snow	fell silently to the ground.

In a sentence using Pattern 1, the verb is **intransitive**—that is, its meaning does not need to be completed by an object or a complement. However, intransitive verbs are often modified by adverbs (*silently*) and prepositional phrases (*to the ground*).

Sentence Pattern 2		
Subject +	*Transitive Verb +*	*Direct Object*
Dogs	eat	bones.
The carpenter	will repair	the roof.

Transitive verbs transfer their action to a **direct object.** The direct object is always a noun, a pronoun, or a group of words serving as a noun. A direct object completes the sentence by answering the question "what?" or "whom?" about the verb: What do dogs eat? *Bones.*

Sentence Pattern 3			
Subject +	*Transitive Verb +*	*Direct Object +*	*Object Complement*
The press	calls	him	a star.
We	are making	the clerk	angry.

An **object complement** is a noun or adjective that renames or describes the direct object. Only a few verbs, such as *appoint, believe, call, consider, find, judge, make,* and *name,* allow this pattern.

Sentence Pattern 4

Subject +	Transitive Verb +	Indirect Object +	Direct Object
My friend	lent	me	her car.
Gandhi	brought	India	independence.

After such transitive verbs as *ask, give, send, tell,* and *teach,* the direct object may be preceded by an **indirect object** that tells to whom or for whom the action of the verb is intended: My friend lent her car to whom? *Me.*

Sentence Pattern 5

Subject +	Linking Verb +	Subject Complement Predicate Noun (or) Predicate Adjective
Einstein	was	a genius.
Cool water	tastes	good.

The fifth pattern occurs only with **linking verbs.** Linking verbs connect the subject with either a **predicate noun,** a noun that renames the subject, or a **predicate adjective,** an adjective that describes the subject. The most common linking verbs are forms of the verb *be* (for example, *am, is, are, was, were, has been, might be*). Other linking verbs are *appear, become, seem,* and in some contexts *feel, grow, act, look, smell, sound,* and *taste.* A linking verb acts as an equal sign between the subject and the complement: *Einstein = a genius.*

● **4 Changes in basic patterns.** Variations in the five basic sentence patterns occur in questions, commands, sentences in the passive voice, and sentences beginning with expletives.

Questions

Auxiliary Verb +	Subject +	Main Verb	
Will	they	run	in the first race?

Function Word +	Subject +	Verb	
Do	they	run	in the first race?

Commands
Omission of Subject

(You) Open the door.
(You) Stay calm.

In **passive sentences,** the subject is not the performer of the action; instead, the subject receives the action of the verb. The original active subject may be omitted or placed in a phrase beginning with *by.* The verb in passive sentences consists of a form of *be* and the past participle (see Section **29e**).

Passive

Subject +	Passive Verb +	(Original Subject)
My recovery	was called a miracle	(by the doctor).
Independence	was brought to India	(by Gandhi).
He	was killed in action.	(actor unknown)

When an **expletive** (*there* or *it*) begins a sentence, the subject is delayed until after the verb (see Section **14a**).

Expletive +	Verb +	Complement	Subject
It	is	certain	that they will arrive.
There	was		no reply.
It	will be	hot	early next week.

ESL Highlight

Verbs Beginning Sentences
English usage does not permit a sentence to begin with a verb except in questions. In statements, an expletive (*it* or *there*) must precede the verb: not *Is a dark room* but *It is a dark room* or *Is it a dark room?*

Exercise 26.3

In the following sentences and paragraph, identify the subjects (S), verbs (V), direct objects (DO), indirect objects (IO), and complements—that is, object complement (OC), predicate noun (PN), predicate adjective (PA). Remember that some sentences, such as those using passive voice or the expletive construction, vary from the five basic sentence patterns; indicate the patterns you find in the following sentences. Then use each sentence as a model for writing a sentence of your own, using subjects, verbs, direct objects, indirect objects, and complements as in the model.

Sentence Practice

1 There are many causes of temporary insomnia.
2 Anxiety over upcoming tests or projects, for example, is often disturbing at bedtime.
3 Even such delights as chicken curry or an extra spicy pizza can give some normal sleepers a bad case of insomnia.
4 More serious conditions such as depression, sleep apnea, or narcolepsy make would-be sleepers insomniacs.

5 Some extreme sleep disorders like apnea can be cured only by surgery.

6 Prolonged sleep deprivation, regardless of the reason, is a serious health problem.

Paragraph Practice

Fortunately, there are many ways to cure the less serious forms of insomnia. Tryptophan-rich foods like milk and turkey can make sleep-deprived people drowsy. In addition, going to bed at the same time each night gives many sleepers the biological rhythm necessary for sleep. Sound sleep is also aided by regular exercise early in the day. The substitution of decaffeinated coffees and teas for caffeine-laced morning beverages also can relieve some kinds of temporary insomnia.

In Your Own Words

Write a paragraph about your favorite musical group. In it, include at least one example of each of the five sentence patterns, an example using the passive voice, and an example using an expletive construction.

26 g Recognize phrases.

A **phrase** is a word group that has no subject or predicate and is used as a single part of speech. Phrases cannot express complete thoughts by themselves. *I fell on the sidewalk* is a complete thought; *on the sidewalk* is not.

Phrases can be prepositional, verbal, or absolute.

● **1 Prepositional phrases.** Prepositional phrases consist of a preposition (see Section **26e**), its object, and modifiers of the object (*under the ground, without thinking, in the blue Honda*). Prepositional phrases function as adjectives or adverbs and occasionally as nouns.

> He is a man *of action.* [adjective modifying *man*]
>
> The plane arrived *on time.* [adverb modifying *arrived*]
>
> She came early *in the morning.* [adverb modifying *early*]
>
> *Before breakfast* is too early. [noun, subject of *is*]

● **2 Verbal phrases.** A verbal is a word derived from a verb: *to see, seeing* (see Section **29a** on verb forms). Unlike verbs, verbals cannot function by themselves as predicates. Like verbs, however, they can take objects and complements and be modified by adverbs. A verbal with its objects, complements, and modifiers is called a **verbal phrase.**

> I prefer *to believe him.* [*Him* is the object of the verbal *to believe.*]
>
> *Screaming loudly,* I jumped out of bed. [The adverb *loudly* modifies the verbal *screaming.*]
>
> *Swimming in the Atlantic* is refreshing. [The prepositional phrase *in the Atlantic* functions as an adverb modifying the verbal *swimming.*]

Verbal phrases function as nouns, adjectives, or adverbs, depending on whether they are classified as infinitives, participials, or gerunds.

Infinitive phrases consist of an infinitive (*to* + base form: *to see, to earn*), its modifiers, and/or its object (*to see the world, to earn money quickly*). Infinitive phrases function as nouns, adjectives, or adverbs.

> *To learn calculus quickly* is my first objective. [noun, subject of verb]
>
> I wanted *to buy the house*. [noun, object of verb]
>
> It is time *to go to bed*. [adjective modifying *time*]
>
> We were impatient *to start the game*. [adverb modifying *impatient*]

Participial phrases consist of a present participle (*screaming, eating, running*) or a past participle (*screamed, eaten, run*), its modifiers, and/or its object: *lying on the beach, found in the street*. Participial phrases always function as adjectives describing nouns or pronouns.

> The dog *running in the yard* belongs to my mother.
>
> The man *walking his dog* is my father.
>
> *Covered with ice*, the road was dangerous.
>
> *Beaten into stiff peaks*, the egg whites were prepared for meringue.

See Section **29b** for a list of irregular past participles.

Gerund phrases consist of a present participle (*telling, acting*), its modifiers, and/or its object: *telling the truth, acting bravely*. Gerund phrases always function as nouns, either as subjects or objects.

> *Running in the yard* keeps the dog fit. [subject]
>
> She earned extra money *by working overtime*. [object of preposition]
>
> He hated *living alone*. [object of verb]
>
> *Walking his dog* is my father's only exercise. [subject]

ESL Highlight

Infinitives and Gerunds as Direct Objects of Verbs

Certain verbs may be followed by a gerund or an infinitive as the object with no change in meaning.

Either infinitive or gerund: advise, allow, attempt, begin, continue, dislike, dread, forbid, hate, intend, like, love, need, neglect, permit, prefer, start

After *need*, a passive infinitive must be used: "This computer monitor needs *to be fixed*." After a few verbs (*advise, allow, forbid, permit*), a noun or pronoun object is used before the infinitive: "I forbid *you* to leave."

NO CHANGE IN MEANING   John likes *to play* tennis.
                                            John likes *playing* tennis.

After some other verbs, only a gerund or only an infinitive may be used.

INFINITIVE ONLY   John wants *to cook.*
GERUND ONLY   Elena enjoys *eating.*

The following is a list of verbs that must be followed by either an infinitive only or a gerund only.

Infinitive only: afford, agree, appear, ask, care, claim, choose, decide, demand, deserve, expect, fail, happen, have, hope, learn, manage, need, offer, plan, prepare, pretend, promise, refuse, seem, wait, want, wish
Gerund only: admit, appreciate, avoid, consider, deny, discuss, enjoy, escape, finish, imagine, mention, mind, miss, practice, quit, recall, resent, resist, risk, suggest, tolerate

A few other verbs may be followed by either a gerund or an infinitive; however, the meaning of the sentence changes depending on which is used.

Meaning changes: forget, mean, propose, regret, remember, stop, try, used to

I remembered *to lock* the door before I left. [completed an action after calling it to mind]

I remembered *locking* the door before I left. [reflection on a past action]

Ask your instructor for assistance if you are unsure of the meaning of a gerund or infinitive used as the object of one of these verbs.

● **3 Absolute phrases.** Absolute phrases consist of a noun or pronoun and a participle. Unlike other kinds of phrases, absolute phrases do not modify particular words in the sentence to which they are attached. Rather, they modify the whole sentence.

The whole family sat silently, *their eyes glued to the TV screen.*

Mortgage rates having risen, Isabel gave up searching for a new house.

The old man lay sprawled on the sofa, *eyes closed, arms folded across his chest, his loud snores almost rousing the dog sleeping near him.*

In absolute phrases with the participle *being* followed by an adjective, *being* is often omitted so that the phrase consists only of a noun followed by an adjective and any other modifiers.

Final examinations over, Linda returned to work.

The ski lodge was thoroughly inviting, *the lights low, the long sofa and over-stuffed chairs luxuriously comfortable, the logs burning brightly in the fireplace.*

Exercise 26.4

In the following sentences and paragraph, underline the verbal phrases once and put the prepositional phrases in parentheses. Note that a prepositional phrase may sometimes be part of a verbal phrase or vice versa, as in the verbal phrase *lying on the beach,* or the prepositional phrase *after going to bed.* After marking the sentences, write five sentences of your own, using these sentences as models for the use of verbal and prepositional phrases.

Sentence Practice

1 The beverage known as coffee comes from the berries of the coffee tree.
2 Standing about six feet high, coffee trees have shiny evergreen leaves covering slender, vertical branches.
3 Before A.D. 1000, Ethiopians ate the fruit of the coffee tree and used it to make wine.
4 Drinking coffee had become a pastime for Europeans by the mid-seventeenth century.
5 To grow well, coffee plants need to have a hot, moist climate and rich soil.

Paragraph Practice

Caffeine, a stimulant contained in coffee, can create problems for you. After drinking lots of coffee, you may find yourself getting restless or irritable. Going to sleep may be difficult, for caffeine also contributes to insomnia. Other beverages containing caffeine include tea and cola, so you should be careful to avoid these drinks before going to bed. You may find that drinking hot cocoa before bedtime keeps you awake also, for in drinking cocoa, you are also ingesting caffeine.

In Your Own Words

Write a paragraph about your first job. In it use two gerunds, two present participles, two past participles, and two infinitives, and an absolute phrase. Also include four prepositional phrases.

26 h Recognize clauses.

A **clause** is a group of words containing a subject and a predicate. The relation of a clause to the rest of the sentence is shown by the position of the clause or by a conjunction. There are two kinds of clauses: (1) main, or independent, clauses and (2) subordinate, or dependent, clauses.

● **1 Main clauses.** A main clause has both subject and verb, and it is not introduced by a subordinating word. A main clause makes an independent statement; by itself, it can stand as a simple sentence. It is not used as a noun or as a modifier.

Eagles are beautiful.

Will you please come forward?

● **2 Subordinate clauses.** Subordinate clauses are usually introduced by a subordinating conjunction (*as, since, because,* etc.) or by a relative pronoun (*who, which, that*). A **relative pronoun** is a connecting word that refers to a noun or pronoun in the main clause. Subordinate clauses function as adjectives, adverbs, or nouns. They cannot stand alone but must be attached to a main clause. They express ideas that are subordinate to or dependent on the idea expressed in the main clause. The exact relationship between the two ideas is indicated by which subordinating conjunction or relative pronoun joins the subordinate and the main clause.

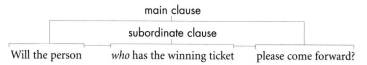

main clause | subordinate clause

Eagles are beautiful *when* they soar high above the cliffs.

main clause

subordinate clause

Will the person *who* has the winning ticket please come forward?

An **adjective clause** modifies a noun or pronoun. It usually begins with a relative pronoun that serves as the clause's subject or object.

> This is the jet *that broke the speed record.* [The subordinate clause modifies the noun *jet.*]

> Anyone *who is tired* may leave. [The subordinate clause modifies the pronoun *anyone.*]

> Basketball is the sport *he plays best.* [The subordinate clause modifies the noun *sport,* with the relative pronoun *that* understood.]

An **adverb clause** modifies a verb, adjective, another adverb, or a whole main clause. It explains when, where, why, how, or with what result.

> The child cried *when the dentist appeared.* [The subordinate clause modifies the verb *cried.*]

> My head feels sore *where I bumped it.* [The subordinate clause modifies the predicate adjective *sore.*]

> She thinks more quickly *than you do.* [The subordinate clause modifies the adverb *quickly.*]

> We can leave for home *unless you are too tired to drive.* [The subordinate clause modifies the entire main clause.]

A **noun clause** functions as a noun. It may serve as subject, predicate noun, object of a verb, or object of a preposition.

> *What you need* is a vacation. [The subordinate clause is the subject of the verb *is.*]

This is *where we came in.* [The subordinate clause is a predicate noun.]

Please tell them *I will be late.* [The subordinate clause is the object of the verb *tell*, with the relative pronoun *that* understood.]

I have no interest in *what I am reading.* [The subordinate clause is the object of the preposition *in.*]

ESL Highlight

Omission of Subject or Verb
Unlike some other languages, English requires both a subject and a main verb in every clause, with two exceptions. A subject may be omitted in commands such as "Look at me" because the subject, *you,* is understood. A verb may be omitted in elliptical constructions: "She was a beauty; he, a beast" (see Section **18d**).

Exercise 26.5

Underline the main clauses once and subordinate clauses twice in the following sentences, and identify each subordinate clause as an adjective, adverb, or noun clause. Then use each sentence as a model for writing a sentence of your own, using adjective, adverb, and noun clauses in similar ways.

1 Two early leaders in the women's rights movement and the antislavery movement were the sisters Angelina and Sarah Grimké who were born into a slave-holding family in Charleston, South Carolina.

2 Once they concluded that slavery should not be tolerated, the Grimké sisters moved to the Northeast, freed their own slaves, and began working as abolitionists.

3 Living in New York in the 1830s, the sisters made impassioned antislavery speeches to large gatherings, and they wrote pamphlets and letters that promoted their cause.

4 Authorities in South Carolina, where the works of the Grimké sisters were burned, said that the sisters would be imprisoned if they returned to the state.

5 Although their antislavery stand initially drew the Grimké sisters into public debate, their work also propelled them to the forefront of the women's movement because they were forced to defend their right as women to be heard in what had largely been the political sphere of only men.

Exercise 26.6

In the following sentences and paragraph, underline each main clause once and each subordinate clause twice. Indicate the function of each subordinate clause as adjective, adverb, or noun. Then use each sentence as a model for writing a sentence of your own, with similar structure.

Sentence Practice

1 Santa Fe, which is the capital of New Mexico, was founded in 1609 by the Spanish, who saw that the site was well located to be a center of trade with the southwestern Indians.

2 Although Santa Fe was officially founded in 1609, the Pueblo Indians had already used the site as a living place where they stayed for part of the year.

3 What makes Santa Fe the oldest capital city in the country, even though the city didn't become part of the United States until 1846, is that it has served as a center of government since its founding.

4 Whenever tourists visit modern Santa Fe, they often go first to the Plaza, a tree-shaded area that has been the heart of the city since 1610.

5 If they walk a block east of the Plaza, visitors can see the St. Francis Cathedral, which was begun in 1869 by Jean Baptiste Lamy, who was Santa Fe's first archbishop.

Paragraph Practice

The American painter Georgia O'Keeffe, who spent much of her life in New Mexico, often used elements of southwestern landscape in her works. Although she spent most of the later part of her life in the Southwest, O'Keeffe was born in Sun Prairie, Wisconsin, in 1887; in 1924 she married photographer Alfred Steiglitz. Steiglitz owned the gallery where O'Keeffe's work was first exhibited. Many of Georgia O'Keeffe's paintings are of abstract forms, but what sets them apart from other abstract works is their vivid coloring. Whenever people think of O'Keeffe's work, they often recall her flower paintings, which have become well known after the works were exhibited throughout the United States.

● **3 Sentence classification.** The number and types of clauses in a sentence determine its classification: simple, compound, complex, or compound-complex.

A **simple sentence** has a single main clause.

The wind blew.

A sentence remains a simple sentence even when the subject, the verb, or both are compounded and modifying words and phrases are added.

The cat and the dog fought. [compound subject]

The dog barked and growled. [compound predicate]

With its back arched, the cat jumped to the top of the bookcase and hissed nastily at the dog. [compound predicate]

A **compound sentence** has two or more main clauses.

The wind blew, and the leaves fell.

A **complex sentence** has one main clause and one or more subordinate clauses.

When the wind blew, the leaves fell.

A **compound-complex sentence** contains two or more main clauses and one or more subordinate clauses.

When the sky darkened, the wind blew, and the leaves fell.

See Chapter 8 for a discussion of creating compound, complex, and compound-complex sentences. See Chapter 11 for a discussion of how sentence structure and length can be varied to create emphasis and accentuate meaning.

Exercise 26.7

In the following sentences and paragraph, underline each main clause once and each subordinate clause twice. Then indicate whether the sentence is simple, compound, complex, or compound-complex. Revise the simple sentences and the compound sentences, adding the necessary subordinate clauses to make them complex or compound-complex.

Sentence Practice

1 One of the early twentieth century's major African-American writers was Zora Neale Hurston, whose works have been recently rediscovered and applauded by general readers and academics alike.

2 Best known for her novel *Their Eyes Were Watching God,* which was published in 1937, Hurston wrote several other novels and numerous short stories.

3 Hurston, who graduated from Howard University in 1928 with a degree in English, studied anthropology at Barnard College, and this interest in anthropology is reflected in her nonfiction books and articles about African-American folklore.

4 Born in Eatonville, Florida, then an all-black community, Hurston moved to New York City in the 1920s and participated in the Harlem Renaissance, a cultural revival among black writers.

5 Hurston was the most productive African-American writer of her day, but when she died in 1960, she was so poor that her grave was left unmarked until 1973, when African-American novelist Alice Walker had a tombstone erected as a tribute to Hurston.

Paragraph Practice

Alice Walker, who as a writer was inspired by the works of Zora Neale Hurston, has written extensively about Hurston. Walker's research and critical writing about Hurston helped rekindle critical interest in Hurston's work, and Walker's work helped create the demand to republish Hurston's. Like Hurston, Walker has written about African-American heritage and creativity as well as the racial and sexual abuse of black women. The first of Walker's works to be published, a collection of poetry in 1968, had as one of its themes the civil rights movement. She wrote the widely acclaimed novel *The Color Purple,* which won the Pulitzer Prize in 1982, and she has written several other novels, many short stories, and numerous essays, lectures, and poems.

Exercise 26.8

Sentence Practice

Using coordinating and subordinating conjunctions, combine the following
sets of simple sentences in two ways. First combine each set into a single
compound sentence. Second, combine each set into a single complex or
compound-complex sentence, changing wording and compounding and
subordinating sentence parts as necessary.

1 Fast-food restaurants are convenient. They provide popular foods at reasonable prices.

2 Fast-food restaurants used to serve mostly hamburgers. Now they offer sal-
ads, yogurt, and even cooked vegetables. Some fast-food restaurants specialize
in ethnic foods.

3 For children, food is perhaps not the main attraction of fast-food restaurants.
Children like the colorful playgrounds at fast-food restaurants. They also like
having their birthday parties at fast-food restaurants. They like the toys in
kids' meals. They like the promotional materials and mascots found at some
fast-food restaurants.

Paragraph Practice

In the following paragraph, use coordinating and subordinating conjunctions to combine most of the simple sentences into either compound,
complex, or compound-complex sentences.

> Fast-food restaurants may not be beneficial in the long run. Some fast-
> food meals contain high levels of sodium, sugar, and fat. Eating too many
> fast-food meals can cause poor nutrition and health problems. Some fast
> food costs more than home-cooked equivalents. In a sense, fast food is
> expensive. Some families rely on fast food for most meals. Family members
> may go for days without eating together at home. Having birthday parties
> and other celebrations at fast-food restaurants may make home seem less
> important than in the past. The sameness of fast-food restaurants may even
> encourage passivity and boredom.

In Your Own Words

Write a paragraph describing your personality. In it include at least one
simple sentence, one compound sentence, one complex sentence, and one
compound-complex sentence. Label them.

27 Case of Nouns and Pronouns

Case shows the function of nouns and pronouns in a sentence. Case indicates whether a noun or pronoun is being used as a subject (**subjective
case**), an object (**objective case**), or as a possessive (**possessive case**).

subjective   objective   possessive
  | | |
He gave   *me* a   *week's* vacation.

Nouns have only two case forms: the possessive form and the common form, which serves all other functions.

Nouns

	Common	Possessive
SINGULAR	student	student's
PLURAL	students	students'

Pronouns typically have three case forms: the subjective, objective, and possessive. These forms are shown here.

Personal Pronouns

Singular	*Subjective*	*Objective*	*Possessive*
FIRST PERSON	I	me	my, mine
SECOND PERSON	you	you	you, yours
THIRD PERSON	he, she, it	him, her, it	his, her, hers, it
Plural			
FIRST PERSON	we	us	our, ours
SECOND PERSON	you	you	you, yours
THIRD PERSON	they	them	their, theirs

Relative or Interrogative Pronouns

	Subjective	*Objective*	*Possessive*
SINGULAR	who	whom	whose
PLURAL	who	whom	whose

27 **a** Use the subjective case to show subjective functions.

We use the subjective form for all pronoun subjects and for all pronouns after forms of the verb be (such as *is, are, were,* or *have been*). "They won the game, but in terms of sportsmanship the real victors were *we*." Native speakers of English are unlikely to say or write "Us are happy" or "Him is going away." But compound subjects and some constructions in which the subject is not easily recognized may cause problems.

● 1 **In all parts of a compound subject.**

He and *I* went shopping for a doll for my mother.

My father and *she* collect dolls, so my brother and *I* wanted to buy one for her birthday.

If you are unsure about the pronoun form in a compound subject, you can test for the correct case by saying each pronoun against the verb separately. For example, "My father collect(s) dolls / she collects dolls," so "my brother wanted to buy one/I wanted to buy one" for her birthday.

● 2 **After *than* and *as*, if the pronoun is the subject of an understood verb.**

My brother is better at choosing collectible dolls than *I*. [*I* is the subject of *am at choosing them*, which is understood by the reader.]

I am not as expert at judging value as *he* [is].

● 3 **In an appositive renaming a subject or a subject complement.** An **appositive** is a word or phrase set beside a noun or pronoun that identifies or explains it by renaming it. When an appositive renames a subject or subject complement, it is grammatically equivalent to the subject or complement and thus takes the same case.

We two, *Sam and I*, went to an antique shop. [*Sam and I* is an appositive renaming the subject *We two*.]

We children had seen a doll there that our mother might like. [Not *Us children*. *Children* is an appositive defining the pronoun *We*.]

● 4 ***Who* and *whoever* as subjects of a clause.**

The person <u>*who* thinks dolls are inexpensive</u> should price antique dolls. [*Who* is the subject of the verb *thinks* in the clause *who thinks dolls are inexpensive*.]

<u>*Whoever* is familiar with antiques</u> knows they can be costly. [*Whoever* is the subject of the verb *is* in the underlined clause.]

The form of the pronoun is always determined by its function in its own clause. If it serves as the subject of its own clause, use the subjective form even though the whole clause may be the object of a verb or preposition.

Antique dealers can tell <u>*who* is educated about price and value</u>. [*Who* is the subject of the verb *is educated* in the subordinate clause, which is the object of the main clause's verb *can tell*.]

They will usually negotiate a fair price for <u>*whoever* knows an object's true worth.</u> [The *whoever* clause is the object of the preposition *for*. *Whoever* is the subject of the clause.]

Note that the form of the pronoun does not change when such expressions as *I think* and *he says* come between the subject and its verb.

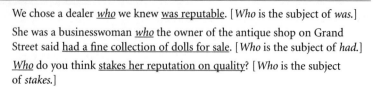

We chose a dealer _who_ we knew <u>was reputable</u>. [_Who_ is the subject of _was._]

She was a businesswoman _who_ the owner of the antique shop on Grand Street said <u>had a fine collection of dolls for sale</u>. [_Who_ is the subject of _had._]

Who do you think <u>stakes her reputation on quality</u>? [_Who_ is the subject of _stakes._]

If you are not sure which form to use in sentences such as these, temporarily omit the interrupting words.

She was a businesswoman (who, whom) had a fine collection of dolls for sale.

(Who, Whom) stakes her reputation on quality?

The test will help you determine in each case whether the pronoun _who_ is the subject of the verb in the subordinate clause.

● **5 After forms of the verb _be_, except when writing dialogue.**
In spoken English, using objective pronouns after forms of _be_, including _to be_, is common. In writing, however, choose the subjective case for these pronouns: "This is she." "It is I."

It was _he_, my brother, who first noticed the antique Japanese doll, not _I._

When you are writing dialogue, make the choice between the subjective or objective case based on the formality of the speaker and the situation.

● **6 For a pronoun following the infinitive _to be_ when the infinitive has no expressed subject.** Spoken English commonly uses the objective case of the pronoun in this construction. Written English uses the subjective case. (See Section **27b(5)** for the case of the pronoun after the infinitive when the subject is expressed.)

WRITTEN   I would like to be _she_ when she opens the package.
               [The infinitive _to be_ has no expressed subject.]
SPOKEN   I would like to be _her_ when she opens the package.

Exercise 27.1

In the following sentence and paragraph, correct any errors in the use of subjective and objective case after the verb _to be_. Assume that you are writing formal English. Explain which errors would be acceptable in dialogue and informal speech or writing.

Sentence Practice

1 Every family has a true eccentric or two, and in my family I am pleased to say that it is me and my cousin Estaban who are them.

2 It was him who realized that in temperament and energy it is us who delight in oddities and differences.

3 Of course, I had never thought much about our eccentricities until later when our Aunt Marguerite introduced us to her friends by saying, "These two misfits are them, my niece and nephew, Rita and Estaban, the weird duo whom I described to you as the ones who aim to shock the rest of the family."

4 From that moment on, Estaban and I found that it is them, the rest of the family, who wait to see what we will wear, eat, and argue about, and we have accepted that the trendsetters of our family, the standard-bearers of the *avant-garde* are us.

5 Now the family would be disappointed if the two of us showed up in normal clothes and argued moderate views, and we have determined that the burden of moving the family's identity into the next century means much work for us; but the effort is worth all the work every time we hear the family say, "It is Estaban and her who keep the rest of us young!"

Paragraph Practice

My friend Gail has an uncle, Aubrey, who is one of the oddest people I have ever met, and it is him to whom I owe most of my success as a *bona fide* eccentric. Known for wearing wild kaftans and elaborate jewelry, Aubrey shared his secrets with us: "These ideas are they, the beliefs that people really do not want to conform, that they love to be shocked, that oddity prolongs life." "But," he confessed, "it is you who must realize that in becoming eccentrics, you are not really them but are conformists instead." It was me who saw in a second what he meant, but it was them, Gail and Anita, who briefly acknowledged that true eccentricity is not easy to find. Nevertheless, it was him who showed me what fun it is to try to be strange.

Exercise 27.2

In the following sentences and paragraph, correct any errors of case in accordance with formal written usage. Be ready to explain your reasons.

Sentence Practice

1 We two, my roommate Chong and me, have just equipped the kitchen in our new apartment.

2 First, we bought four pots and a skillet from a sales assistant whom I thought did not know how to use a stove as well as us students.

3 Next, Chong, who is a better cook than me, insisted that we buy expensive utensils no one except he knows how to use.

4 Also, it was him who recommended that we stock up on dishtowels, potholders, and trivets, but fortunately, my sister, who Chong has a crush on, gave us her extras.

5 Finally, much to my relief, it was easy for Chong and she to agree that we should buy a microwave so that cooking could be done by whoever wants to dish up the next meal.

Paragraph Practice

At my first cooking lesson when I asked the chef to identify whisks amid the tools on the counter, he picked up two large wire beater-like implements and disdainfully said, "These are they." I suspected that my classmates were learning much more than me, but this feeling was confirmed by the behavior of one student, a man my age who, I thought, was being pretentious to ask

about the advantages of a convection oven. The other students who I observed also seemed more skillful than me, but it was them who helped me relax when they teased me a bit. At that first lesson everyone except the pretentious man and I managed to prepare a delicious dish to share with whomever wanted to sample it. The pretentious classmate, who said he was a better cook than us eight beginners, burned a hole in his pot. With due modesty, I must say that it was me who contributed most to the success of the first class: I washed the dishes.

 27 b Use the objective case to show objective functions.

Objective pronoun forms are used for the objects of all verbs, verbals, and prepositions.

OBJECT OF VERB	Did you see *him* yesterday?
	Our friends visited *us*.
OBJECT OF VERBAL	Visiting *them* was pleasant. [object of gerund *visiting*]
	I wanted to invite *her* to lunch. [object of infinitive *to invite*]
OBJECT OF PREPOSITION	Give the check to *me*.
	We will split the total between *us*.

Problems with objective pronoun forms usually occur in the same kinds of constructions that cause problems with subjective pronoun forms (see Section **27a**).

● 1 In all parts of a compound object.

We discovered the cat and *him* under the bed. [Not *the cat and he*; *him* is a part of the compound object of the verb *discovered*.]

They were afraid of you and *me*. [Not *of you and I*; *me* is a part of the compound object of the preposition *of*.]

To decide whether a singular pronoun form is in the correct case, say the sentence aloud, changing the pronoun to the plural. It may be easier for you to hear the correct form in "They were afraid of *us*." *Us*, the objective form, is equivalent to *me*, the corresponding singular pronoun form.

● 2 After *than* and *as*, if the pronoun is the object of an understood verb.

He fears the Great Dane more than [he fears] *me*.
The cat dislikes the Great Dane as much as [it dislikes] *us*.

In these examples, an error in pronoun case would change the meaning of the sentences. The subjective pronoun, used instead of the objective pronoun, would indicate a different understood verb and, hence, a different meaning.

He fears the Great Dane more than *I*. [fear the Great Dane.]
The cat dislikes the Great Dane as much as *we*. [dislike the Great Dane.]

● 3 In an appositive renaming the object of a verb or the object of a preposition.

> The two of them stared at us—*me* and the dog—and refused to come out from under the bed. [*Me and the dog* is an appositive renaming *us.*]

● 4 *Whom* and *whomever* as objects.

WRITTEN   *Whom* do you fear?
SPOKEN   *Who* do you fear?

WRITTEN   Of whom are you afraid?
SPOKEN   *Who* are you afraid of?

In subordinate clauses, use *whom* and *whomever* for all objects. Remember that the case of the relative pronoun in a subordinate clause depends on its function in its own clause and not on the function of the whole clause.

> The visitors <u>whom we had expected</u> did not come. [*Whom* is the object of the verb *had expected.* The underlined clause modifies *visitors.*]

> <u>Whomever you like best</u> is the person you should invite. [*Whomever* is the object of the verb *like* in the subordinate clause. The entire clause is the subject of the sentence.]

A helpful test is to put the words in the clause in subject-verb-object order (*you like whomever best*). That way you will be able to tell more easily which case form of the pronoun is appropriate.

ESL Highlight

Omission of Relative Pronouns

A relative pronoun introducing a subordinate clause can be omitted from a sentence if it functions as the direct object of the verb or as the object of a preposition.

Direct object. The relative pronoun may be omitted if a subject and verb immediately follow the relative pronoun.

The visitors [whom] we expected did not come. [direct object of *expected*]

Object of preposition. When the preposition comes at the end of the clause, the pronoun may be omitted.

Here is the flower [that] I was telling you about. [object of the preposition *about*]

If the preposition is not at the end of the clause, the relative pronoun must be included.

My brother is one person with whom I feel comfortable. [object of the preposition *with*]

● **5 For the object of a verb that also functions as the subject of an infinitive.**

> We wanted *him* to take the part. [*Him* is the object of the verb *wanted* and the subject of the infinitive *to take.*]
>
> Tim believed *her* to be me. [*Her* is the object of the verb *believed* and the subject of the infinitive *to be.*]
>
> The voters selected *them* to be the state senators.

27 **c** **Use the possessive case to show ownership functions.**

● **1 Indefinite pronouns and nouns naming living beings.** The possessive case of such words usually is formed by adding an apostrophe (') and the letter *s* (see Section **41a**). With nouns naming inanimate things, the *of*-phrase (*the point of the pen*) is sometimes preferred, but the *s*-form occurs very often.

INDEFINITE PRONOUNS	anyone's guess; everybody's understanding
ANIMATE NOUNS	Jane's hair; the cat's meow; a friend's car
INANIMATE NOUNS	the point of the joke, the wing of the airplane; the words of the title; the city's newsstands; the article's tone

The *s*-possessive is commonly used in expressions that indicate time (*moment's notice, year's labor*) and in many familiar phrases (*life's blood, fool's gold*). Choice of possessive form may also depend on sound or rhythm: The *s*-possessive is more terse than the longer, more sonorous *of*-phrase (the President's signature, the signature of the President). *The title's words,* however, seems more awkward than *the words of the title.*

Note that the possessive form of personal and interrogative or relative pronouns (*its, whose*) is *not* formed with *'s* (see Section **41b**).

● **2 A noun or pronoun preceding a gerund.** In informal English the objective case (pronoun) or common form (noun) before a gerund is typical. A **gerund** is a verb with the suffix *-ing* (*skiing, reading, driving*) that functions as a noun. Formal English, however, requires the possessive case.

FORMAL	What was the reason for *my* studying Japanese?
INFORMAL	What was the reason for *me* studying Japanese?
FORMAL	You know about *Japan's* dominating the world marketplace.
INFORMAL	You know about *Japan* dominating the world marketplace.

Even in formal English the common form is frequently used with plural nouns.

> I understand *people* wanting to learn about another culture.

Your choice of case may sometimes depend on the meaning you want
to convey.

> Imagine *my* traveling to Japan. [The act of traveling is emphasized.]
>
> Imagine *me* traveling to Japan. [The emphasis is on *me*. *Traveling* is used here
> as a participle modifying *me*.]

● 3 ***Whose* with impersonal antecedents to avoid awkwardness.**

> We bought two tickets for a flight *whose* destination was Tokyo. [Compare *We
> bought two tickets for a flight the destination of which was Tokyo.*]
>
> Japanese companies *whose* products sell well internationally have captured a
> large market share. [Compare *Japanese companies the products of which sell
> well internationally have captured a large market share.*]

Exercise 27.3

In the following sentences and paragraph, revise the errors of case in accordance with formal written usage. Be prepared to explain your answers.

Sentence Practice

1 Our art instructor gave my friend and I tickets to a modern photography
  exhibit at the local art museum.
2 Many of we viewers at the exhibit were particularly interested in documentary photography of the Great Depression and World War II.
3 During these periods, documentary photographers such as Margaret Bourke-
  White and Dorothea Lange contributed photographs to popular picture
  magazines like *Life*; when I saw their work, I admired them having the skill
  to get such images on film.
4 In some of the photographs taken during the Great Depression, the people
  who the photographer captured on film seem to have a look of despair on
  their faces.
5 Looking at these photographic images of the Great Depression was an unset-
  tling experience for us—my friend and I—because we had not realized the
  kinds of hardships the people who we were gazing at had faced.

Paragraph Practice

> My friend liked the contemporary photograph section of the exhibit more
> than me. In that section of photographs, we saw lots of innovative photo-
> graphic techniques such as collage and multiple images; when I saw the work
> of these photographers. I thought they to be very skillful at their art. I won-
> dered, however, who do you think would want to pose for a photograph of a
> face broken into thousands of tiny images? My friend likes the work of these
> artists and believes that them trying out new techniques will lead to even
> more unusual uses of photography.

Exercise 27.4

In the following paragraph, revise the errors in case forms in accordance
with formal written usage. Be prepared to explain your answers.

Finding good part-time jobs that fit our class schedules posed real problems for my cousin Susan and I. Susan and me share an apartment, and it was her who came up with the idea of working the same hours so that we could share a car. Our friends who we asked about job leads had no useful suggestions, and the counselor in the campus job placement office could not place we two together. Whoever we called in response to classified ads had just hired someone. Us pounding the pavement did little good either. One shop owner who I thought wanted to hire me obviously did not want to hire Susan. Two sisters who run a floral shop offered us a job for ten hours a week each, but it required us being there by 5:30 A.M.! It was them, however, who suggested our best lead—the local bookstore. The manager offered Susan and I flexible hours and decent pay, but she insisted on paying Susan more than I because Susan has more work experience than me. Our parents cannot quite picture us—Susan and I—buying books at a discount and actually reading for fun, but these have been the perks of the job.

In Your Own Words

Review the rules governing pronoun case. Which rules cause problems for you as a writer? Write a paragraph discussing the two most troublesome rules, explaining why you believe these confuse you and ways you might be able to overcome your confusion.

28   Adjectives and Adverbs

Adjectives and adverbs modify—that is, limit or qualify—the meaning of other words. **Adjectives** modify nouns and pronouns; they are usually placed either immediately before or after the word they modify. Adjectives qualify meaning by indicating *what kind of, how many,* or *which one* about the words they modify.

> Our *local* doctor told me I probably needed *new* glasses; *blurred* vision was giving me headaches too *severe* to treat with aspirin *alone*.

Adverbs normally modify verbs, adjectives, and other adverbs, although they may sometimes modify whole sentences. When they modify adjectives or other adverbs, they are adjacent to the words they modify. When they modify verbs, they are frequently, but not always, adjacent to the verbs.

Adverbs qualify the meaning of the words they modify by indicating such things as *when, where, how, why, in what order,* or *how often.*

> The office closed *yesterday*. [*Yesterday* indicates when.]

> Deliver all mail *here*. [*Here* indicates where.]

> She replied *quickly* and *angrily*. [*Quickly* and *angrily* describe how she replied.]

> *Consequently*, I left. [*Consequently* describes why.]

He *seldom* did any work. [*Seldom* indicates how often.]

Most adverbs are distinguished from their corresponding adjectives by the ending -*ly*: *strong—strongly, happy—happily, doubtful—doubtfully, hasty—hastily, wonderful—wonderfully*. But the -*ly* ending is not always a dependable adverbial indicator, since some adverbs have two forms (*quick, quickly; slow, slowly*); others have the same form as adjectives (*fast, much, late, well*); and some adjectives also end in -*ly* (*lovely, lonely*). (See Section **21d**, for a discussion of the ways adjectives are formed from nouns.) Nevertheless, where there is a choice between a form with -*ly* and a form without it, formal English prefers the -*ly* form for the adverb—*runs quickly* rather than *runs quick, eats slowly* rather than *eats slow*—even though the shorter forms are widely used in informal English, particularly in such commands as *Drive slow*.

28 a Use an adverb to modify a verb.

INCORRECT   He writes *careless*. [*Careless* is an adjective.]
CORRECT   He writes *carelessly*. [The adverb *carelessly* is needed to modify the verb *writes*.]

Note that *badly* always functions as an adverb; *bad* always functions as an adjective. Use *badly* to modify a verb. Similarly, *good* always functions as an adjective. Choose the adverb *well* to modify a verb.

INCORRECT   The chorus sang *bad* from the first song to the last.
CORRECT   The chorus sang *badly* from the first song to the last. [*Badly* modifies the verb *sang*, telling *how* they sang.]

INCORRECT   He plays that saxophone *good*, doesn't he?
CORRECT   He plays that saxophone *well*, doesn't he? [*Well* modifies the verb *plays*, telling *how* he plays.]

Remember, *good* and *bad* as adverbs are nonstandard, as in "She talks good but writes bad." Standard English requires the use of the adverbs *well* and *badly*: "She talks well but writes badly."

28 b Use adverbs to modify adjectives and other adverbs.

INCORRECT   I am *terrible* nearsighted.
CORRECT   I am *terribly* nearsighted. [The adverb *terribly* is needed to modify the adjective *nearsighted*.]

INCORRECT   Contact lenses cost *considerable* less than they used to.
CORRECT   Contact lenses cost *considerably* less than they used to. [The adverb *considerably* is needed to modify the other adverb *less*.]

Using adjectives in place of adverbs is more common in conversation than in writing. The use of the adjective *real* as a substitute for *really* or as an emphatic *very* to modify adjectives and adverbs is heard at all levels of speech. Similarly, the adverb form *surely* should replace *sure* in formal speech and writing.

| FORMAL | My flight was *really* late. |
| COLLOQUIAL* | My flight was *real* late. |

| FORMAL | I will *surely* be glad to get home. |
| INFORMAL | I will *sure* be glad to get home. |

28 **c** After a linking verb, use an adjective to modify the subject.

The common linking verbs are be, *become, appear, seem,* and the verbs pertaining to the senses: *look, smell, taste, sound, feel.* Predicate adjectives after such verbs modify the subject and should be in adjective form. The verb simply links the two.

> You look *tired* tonight. [*Tired* modifies *you.*]
>
> The milk smells *sour.* [*Sour* modifies *milk.*]

One of the most frequent errors in this construction is *I feel badly* in place of the correct subject-linking-verb-predicate adjective form *I feel bad.* Though *badly* is common even in educated speech, *bad,* an adjective, correctly modifies the subject *I.*

FORMAL	He feels bad [ill].
COLLOQUIAL	He feels *badly.*
FORMAL	He felt *bad* about it.
COLLOQUIAL	He felt *badly* about it.

Some verbs, such as *look* and *sound,* can function as either action or linking verbs, depending on the intended meaning.

| LINKING VERB | The cat looked *sly* to the canary. [The adjective *sly* modifies the subject *cat.*] |
| ACTION VERB | The cat looked *slyly* at the canary. [The adverb *slyly* modifies the action verb *looked.*] |

Exercise 28.1

In the following sentences, identify all adverbs. For each adverb which can also be used as an adjective, write a sentence showing its use as an adjective.

Sentence Practice

1 One of the less familiar threats to ecology is the steadily increasing destruction of coral reefs nearly everywhere in the world's oceans.

2 Daily, the fragile reefs are undergoing damage and exploitation that are fast

---

Colloquial means characteristic of or appropriate to conversation but not to formal writing.

depleting the reefs' many benefits.

3 Only relatively remote reefs have escaped the rather rapid destruction caused by fishing, diving, tourism, construction, and mining.

4 Almost too late, scientists have discovered just how promising the reefs are in their search today for new medicines.

5 Now scientists question whether or not we ever will be able to use the almost incredible richness of the reefs without ultimately destroying them.

Paragraph Practice

In the following paragraph, revise any errors in the use of adjectives and adverbs in accordance with formal written usage.

> Coral reefs, which nurture approximate one-fourth of all organisms in the sea, are a good example of a perfect balanced, mutual beneficial relationship. Corals support the algae that, in turn, efficient produce food and oxygen for the coral through photosynthesis. Dead corals steady build up a limestone base that supports the living corals, but if they all die, the reef dies gradual. The death of the reef displaces both fish who feed normal on the algae growing there and the predatory fish that eat them. Inhabitants of the more than one hundred countries bordered by reefs must sure strive to reverse the rapid escalating destruction of the reefs, which significant protect the land from being eroded by the sea.

28 d Use comparative and superlative forms correctly.

The positive, comparative, and superlative forms of adjectives and adverbs show degrees of quality or quantity.

Positive	Comparative	Superlative
rich	richer	richest
joyous	more joyous	most joyous
delicious	more delicious	most delicious
carefully	more carefully	most carefully

● **1 Use of comparatives and superlatives.** Use the comparative form to compare two persons or things and the superlative form to compare three or more persons or things.

COMPARATIVE   This car is *cheaper* than that one.

SUPERLATIVE   This car is the *cheapest* compact car on the market.

COMPARATIVE   Ruth runs *more quickly* but *less gracefully* than her teammate Elaine.

SUPERLATIVE   Ruth runs the *most quickly* but *least gracefully* of the three sprinters.

● **2 Form of comparatives and superlatives.** Most one-syllable adjectives and a few one-syllable adverbs form the comparative and superlative with *-er* and *-est*. Adjectives of two syllables often have two possible forms (*fancier, more fancy; laziest, most lazy*). When there is a choice, use the form that is better suited to the rhythm of the sentence. Adjectives and adverbs of three or more syllables always take *more* and *most* (or *less* and *least*): *more beautiful, most regrettably, less interesting, least happily.*

Irregular Adjectives and Adverbs

	Positive	Comparative	Superlative
Adjectives	good	better	best
	well	better	best
	bad	worse	worst
	little	less	least
	many	more	most
	much	more	most
Adverbs	badly	worse	worst
	well	better	best

Consult a dictionary when in doubt about the appropriate form.

● **3 Illogical comparisons.** Some adjectives and adverbs cannot logically be compared: A person is either *dead* or *alive*, a room is either *empty* or *not empty*, a jewel is *unique* or not. Although common in informal usage, such illogical comparisons should be avoided in formal writing.

INFORMAL   His diving form is *more perfect* than mine.
FORMAL   His diving form is *more nearly perfect* than mine.

● **4 Double comparatives or superlatives.** Check your writing for double comparatives and superlatives such as *more luckier* and *most craziest*. When an *-er* or *-est* ending is added to an adjective or adverb, *more* and *most* are redundant.

Exercise 28.2

In the following sentences and paragraph, revise in accordance with formal written usage any errors in the use of the comparative and superlative forms of adjectives and adverbs. Then use each revised adjective and adverb in a sentence of your own.

Sentence Practice

1 Being on time is one of the most tricky challenges of modern life, causing numerous problems for everyone from the punctualest to the casualest person.
2 One of the most clear reasons is that people general have trouble synchronizing their watches and clocks.
3 Thus, even the carefulest appointment-keeper may arrive two minutes more early or more late than his or her appointment at the dentist, for a job interview, or for a date.
4 A more subtler problem occurs when cultural expectations of time differ as, for example, when Americans, who are ruled by precise hours and minutes, do business with Arabs, who divide time into much less preciser segments.
5 But perhaps the most odd realization is that the most perfect measurement of time is inaccurate, though less so than the better quartz-crystal watches and clocks that are considered to keep time especially good.

Paragraph Practice

From about 1650 until the 1920s, the precisest timekeepers were pendulum clocks. The exactest of these counteracted temperature changes with materials that lost heat at different rates. Even more finer timekeeping appeared in the 1920s with, first, modifications to the pendulum and then the development of the quartz-crystal oscillator, which was off only 0.1 millisecond per day. The recentest refinements are atomic clocks, which compensate for the motion of the earth and thus achieve the most high standards, required for use in laboratories, space exploration, and satellite technology. Of the three modern kinds of clocks, the atomic clock is the more accurate and has given its name to IAT, international atomic time, considered the standard international time by the International Bureau of Weights and Measures.

28 e Choose adjectives over noun modifiers.

The use of nouns to modify other nouns in expressions such as *rock garden, steel mill, silver mine,* and *telephone booth* is both common and correct. But when nouns are used to replace appropriate adjectives or when the series of nouns modifying other nouns is long, such expressions are awkward or even confusing.

● 1 Adjectives and noun modifiers.

| AWKWARD | corporation report | Canada Rockies |
| IMPROVED | corporate report | Canadian Rockies |

● 2 Long series of noun modifiers.

CONFUSING	office management personnel report [A report about the management of office personnel? A report by personnel who are managing an office? Something else?]
CLEAR	a report about the management personnel in this office
CONFUSING	teacher education program analysis [An analysis of a program for educating teachers? An analysis by teachers of an educational program? Something else?]
CLEAR	teachers' analysis of an educational program

Exercise 28.3

In the following sentences and paragraph, revise in accordance with formal written usage any errors in the use of adjectives and adverbs. Then use the revised forms in sentences of your own.

Sentence Practice

1 Modern zoo planners are doing away with cages and bars in order to provide a naturaler environment for the animals.

2 Although traditional zoo practices still exist, these practices are rapid disappearing as zoo designers construct habitats that realistic re-create the animals' natural environment.

3 To create these natural environments, zoo designers often have to duplicate exotic landscapes such as a Brazil rain forest or an Alaska ice field.

4 Visitors observing these environments frequent have to watch patient, for the animals often hide in the underbrush or in the foliage of the trees.

5 Fortunate, the wait is worthwhile, since visitors to these zoos feel that they have entered a faraway world where they see the animals behaving natural in conditions much like their native environment.

Paragraph Practice

Many zoos in the United States exemplify changes that have recent taken place in zoo planning and design. For example, the Bronx Zoo, the country's larger urban zoo, has an area called Himalayan Highlands where visitors can see rare Tibetan snow leopards chasing each other playful in a mountain setting. The Brookfield Zoo, west of downtown Chicago, was one of the first zoos in the country to have no bars enclosing its animals; today this zoo has a glass-covered jungle habitat that accurate depicts Asia, Africa, and South America rain forests. Another real popular exhibit at the Brookfield Zoo is the Seven Sea Panorama, an expanded marine habitat including an outdoor Pacific Coast seascape and an indoor dolphin pool that is sure a hit with children. In Tucson, Arizona, the Arizona-Sonora Desert Museum is a very unique combination of natural history museum, botanical garden, and regional zoo; the desert display is spectacular colored in March and April when the desert plants bloom.

In Your Own Words

Write a paragraph describing your favorite place to be alone. In it use at

least four adjectives and four adverbs, including at least one comparative adjective form and one superlative adjective form and at least one comparative adverb form and one superlative adverb form.

29 Verbs

The form of a verb or verb phrase indicates three things about the action or state of being it names. It tells what time the action occurs (tense); whether the subject is performing the action or receiving it (voice); and what the attitude of the writer or speaker is (mood). Verbs agree in person and number with their subjects (see Section **14a**).

29 a Recognize verb forms.

All verbs except *be* have five forms.

Verb Forms

Base Form	Past Tense	Past Participle	Present Participle	-s Form
live	lived	lived	living	lives
play	played	played	playing	plays
eat*	ate	ate	eating	eats
break*	broke	broken	breaking	breaks

*Irregular verb. See Section **29b**.

The base form, past tense, and past participle form are known as the three **principal parts** of verbs.

● **1 Base form.** Dictionaries list verbs according to their base forms. In the present tense, the base form of a verb is used with subjects that are plural nouns and pronouns ("People *work* to live; they don't *live* to work") the pronouns *I* and *you* ("I *play* all day").

The base form is used after all auxiliary verbs except *be* and *have* to indicate various shades of meaning: "Lisette may *enjoy* the movie, but Pierre will *find* it offensive."

● **2 Past tense and past participle.** The past tense and the past participle share the same form in regular verbs: base form + -ed or -d. The past tense indicates completed action that occurred entirely in the past. The past participle preceded by *has, have,* or *had* forms the perfect tenses (see Section **29d**). Combined with forms of *be,* the past participle forms the passive voice (see Section **29e**). Used alone, the past participle functions as an adjective.

Fatima *has developed* an earache. [perfect tense]

The car *was being driven* across the country. [passive voice]

The *signed* contract clearly indicates our agreement. [adjective]

● **3 The present participle: base form + -ing.** Combined with *am, is, are, was, were,* or *will be,* the present participle forms the progressive tenses (see Section **29d**).

Gardeners *are chuckling* over their harvest now, but they *will be drowning* in zucchini by mid-August.

The present participle alone cannot be used as the main verb of a sentence.

● **4 Base form + -s.** The *-s* form is used only in the present tense with the following kinds of subjects: singular nouns and third-person singular pronouns (*Michael Jordan, he; Wendy Wasserstein, she; cat, it*) and most indefinite pronouns (such as *each, anybody, someone*). The verbs *be* and *have* are irregular in this form: *is, has.*

Wendy Wasserstein *writes* plays about modern women.

Star Wars is the modern equivalent of the ancient Greek *Odyssey.*

● **5 The verb be.** The verb *be* has eight forms:

Base form: be

Past participle: been

Present participle: being

Present-tense forms: I *am*; he / she / it *is*; you / we / they *are*

Past-tense forms: I / he / she / it *was*; you / we / they *were*

● **6 Omission of -s and -ed endings.** The *-s* and *-ed* endings on verbs are sometimes incorrectly omitted in writing because they are not pronounced clearly in speech. With the following types of subjects, verbs in the present tense must end in *-s*: (1) *he, she,* or *it*, (2) singular nouns, (3) indefinite pronouns such as *someone* or *anybody*.

She *attends* school board meetings each month.

My cat *catches* mice and *brings* them home to us.

Everyone *wants* to be respected.

All regular verbs in the past-tense or past-participle forms should end with *-ed* or *-d* (for irregular verbs, see Section **29b**).

Professor Sanchez *asked* us to write seven essays this semester.

Each paper *required* extensive drafting and revising.

Exercise 29.1

In the blanks in the following sentences and paragraph, supply the correct present-tense form of the verbs given in parentheses. Then use each of the sentences as a model to construct a similar sentence of your own.

Sentence Practice

1 My roommate always (disagree) _____ with me about what movies we should see; she (like) _____ horror films, but I hate scary movies.

2 Each week she (search) _____ the movie listings and then (ask) _____ me to go with her to see the latest gruesome film.

3 If someone (mention) _____ to my roommate that Stephen King has written a new novel, she then (wait) _____ eagerly for the novel to be made into a movie.

4 Whenever anyone (ask) _____ me to go to a horror movie, I try to say no, but my roommate always (insist) _____ on dragging me to see the latest movie.

5 As a result, I (go) _____ with her, but I (sit) _____ next to her and (keep) _____ my eyes closed while she (sit) _____ there and (enjoy) _____ every horrible minute.

Paragraph Practice

My sister often (go) _____ with me to the movies, but she always (sit) _____ several rows in front of me. She (say) _____ that I distract her by munching popcorn too loudly, but, in truth, she (be) _____ the problem. She can't settle down and watch the movie, and she constantly (ask) _____ questions about the plot and characters. No matter how much candy she (buy) _____ before we go in, she (get) _____ hungry before the movie is over and (rush) _____ to the concession stand several times. Now that she (know) _____ that we can't sit together, we're much happier on those numerous occasions when she (invite) _____ herself to tag along to the movies with me.

29 b Recognize regular and irregular verbs.

● **1 Regular verbs.** A verb is regular if both the past tense and past participle are created by adding *-ed* or *-d* to the base form: *combed, completed.* (The final consonant sometimes must be doubled when adding *-ed* or *-d*: *planned, tripped.* See Section **25e**.)

● **2 Irregular verbs.** Irregular verbs form the past and past participle in some other way, usually by changing an internal vowel. Some irregular verbs have the same forms for the past tense and past participle: *spin, spun, spun.* Others change in all three principal parts (*give, gave, given*) or stay the same in all three parts (*cut, cut, cut*).

The dictionary lists only the base form if a verb is regular. If the dictionary lists the base form and one other (*bend, bent*), the second form is used for both the past tense and past participle. If an irregular verb changes form in all three parts, the dictionary will list all three (*begin, began, begun*).

The principal parts of commonly used irregular verbs are listed here. When two forms are listed, both are acceptable, although the first form listed is preferred according to most dictionaries. Keep a list of irregular verbs you find troublesome.

Principal Parts of Irregular Verbs

Base Form	Past Tense	Past Participle
arise	arose	arisen
awake	awaked *or* awoke	awaked *or* awoken
be	was/were	been
bear	bore	borne *or* born
beat	beat	beaten
become	became	become
begin	began	begun
bend	bent	bent
bind	bound	bound
bite	bit	bitten
blow	blew	blown
break	broke	broken
bring	brought	brought
build	built	built
burn	burned *or* burnt	burned *or* burnt
burst	burst	burst
buy	bought	bought
catch	caught	caught
choose	chose	chosen
cling	clung	clung
come	came	come
cost	cost	cost
cut	cut	cut
dig	dug	dug
dive	dived *or* dove	dived
drink	drank	drunk
drive	drove	driven
eat	ate	eaten
fall	fell	fallen
feed	fed	fed
feel	felt	felt
fight	fought	fought
find	found	found
fly	flew	flown
forbid	forbade *or* forbad	forbidden
forget	forgot	forgotten *or* forgot
freeze	froze	frozen
get	got	got *or* gotten
give	gave	given
go	went	gone
grow	grew	grown
hang (suspend)	hung	hung
hang (execute)*	hanged	hanged
have	had	had

Base Form	Past Tense	Past Participle
hear	heard	heard
hide	hid	hidden
hit	hit	hit
keep	kept	kept
know	knew	known
lay	laid	laid
lead	led	led
leave	left	left
lend	lent	lent
lie	lay	lain
let	let	let
lose	lost	lost
make	made	made
mean	meant	meant
pay	paid	paid
prove	proved	proved *or* proven
read	read	read
ride	rode	ridden
ring	rang	rung
rise	rose	risen
run	ran	run
say	said	said
see	saw	seen
send	sent	sent
set	set	set
shake	shook	shaken
shine (glow)	shone	shone
shine (polish)*	shined	shined
shrink	shrank	shrunk
sing	sang	sung
sink	sank *or* sunk	sunk
sit	sat	sat
sleep	slept	slept
speak	spoke	spoken
spend	spent	spent
spin	spun	spun
spring	sprang *or* sprung	sprung
stand	stood	stood
steal	stole	stolen
stink	stank	stunk
strike	struck	struck
strive	strove	striven
swear	swore	sworn
swim	swam	swum
swing	swung	swung
take	took	taken
teach	taught	taught

Base Form	Past Tense	Past Participle
tear	tore	torn
tell	told	told
think	thought	thought
throw	threw	thrown
wake	woke *or* waked	woken *or* waked
wear	wore	worn
wind	wound	wound
write	wrote	written

*A regular verb with this meaning.

Exercise 29.2

In the blanks in the following sentences, supply the correct forms of the verbs given in parentheses.

Sentence Practice

1 Yesterday at sunrise my friends and I (swim) _____ in a cold stream just as the sun (shine) _____ over the top of the mountains.
2 One at a time we (swing) _____ out over the stream on a heavy rope and (hang) _____ suspended over the sparking water until the time was just right to drop into it.
3 Then we (catch) _____ the limbs of a tree and (ride) _____ out over the rapids.
4 As the limbs (shake) _____ from our weight, we (spring) _____ into a deep pool and (dive) _____ to the bottom.
5 We (know) _____ this dive was dangerous, but we swimmers (feel) _____ brave and happy as we (drink) _____ in the sounds and smells of the morning.

Paragraph Practice

Revise the errors in verb form in this paragraph. Use each corrected verb form in a sentence of your own.

Our family has grew to love this mountain retreat, and in the last few years, we have stole whatever time we could from school and work and took in the beauty of this soothing place. Once the sun has rose each morning, this magic place holds something special for each of us. The last time we went, for example, my mother choose fly-fishing, and my sisters begin cleaning a site for the future picnic area. Dad, who had just broke in his new hiking boots, talked my two friends into a six-mile walk. I drawed straws with my brother to see which of us got the hammock on the porch. When he win, I lead my dog into the woods, and we take a nap for several hours until I was awoke as I was being bit by mosquitoes.

● 3 *Lie* and *lay*, *sit* and *set*. These pairs of irregular verbs are often confusing. The intransitive verbs *lie* and *sit* cannot pass action to objects or occur in the passive voice. *Lay* and *set*, which are transitive verbs, must either have objects or be in the passive voice. In written English, the distinction is important to communicating meaning precisely. *Lie* means "to recline"; *lay* means "to place." *Sit* means "to occupy a seat"; *set* means "to place."

> The dog *lay* under the table while Jo *set* it for dinner.
>
> Roberto *laid* the book on the table before *sitting* down.

The following chart shows the parts of these irregular verbs.

Base Form	Past Tense	Past Participle	Present Participle
lie	lay	lain	lying
lay	laid	laid	laying
sit	sat	sat	sitting
set	set	set	setting

See Section **26f(3)** for more information on intransitive and transitive verbs.

Exercise 29.3

Sentence Practice

Supply the correct form of *lay, lie, sit,* or *set* in the blanks. For which blanks are two answers possible? Then in a sentence of your own, use each verb form that you insert in a blank.

1 After an exhausting day of moving into my new apartment, I decided to _____ down for a nap before unpacking, so I just left all of the clutter _____ everywhere.
2 I had just _____ down on my unmade bed when I remembered that I had _____ my keys on the windowsill outside the door.
3 Fortunately they were still _____ where I had _____ them as I was unloading the truck.
4 As I _____ down again and drifted off to sleep, I heard an odd noise and _____ up in bed.
5 Across the room a large mouse was _____ next to the table where I had _____ my keys.
6 _____ there, frozen in fear, I screamed for Beza, my Siamese cat, who was _____ in a patch of sunshine by the dining room window.

Paragraph Practice

Revise this paragraph, correcting the errors in the forms of *lay, lie, set,* and *sit*.

> The state of my dorm room is beyond my control, because my two room-mates leave everything laying just where it doesn't belong. For example, Carlos lays his dirty clothes on top of the bookcase, and Steve sits his empty soda cans on the dresser. Setting on my desk for a month, two pizza boxes grew mold before I finally lay them on Steve's desk. Of course, it was hard to see them lay-

ing there amid the collection of dirty dishes and take-out cartons. If I set down at my desk to study, the mess in the room distracts me. I had just laid down to go to sleep last night, however, when I realized that the chaos is a small price to pay for two great friends. Now I've decided to set my own dirty clothes and left-over food in the few available nooks and crannies where nothing has been lain.

In Your Own Words

Review the list of irregular verbs in Section **29b**. List ten which have principal parts that surprise you. Write a paragraph using the past tense or past participle of at least five of these troublesome verbs. Also include at least one use of *to lie* or *to lay* (in any tense) and at least one use of *to sit* or *to set* (in any tense).

Exercise 29.4

In the blanks in the following sentences and paragraph, supply the correct form of the verb or verbs given in parentheses. Then use each of the sentences to construct a similar sentence of your own.

Sentence Practice

1 Christopher Columbus (become) _____ the first European to (sit or set) _____ foot on Cuba when he visited the island in 1492.
2 During the 1600s and 1700s, the number of people on the island (rise) _____ when immigrants from Spain (come) _____ to the island.
3 Cuba, which (lie or lay) _____ 90 miles south of Florida, (consist) _____ of the large island of Cuba as well as many small nearby islands.
4 Sugarcane, which (be) _____ Cuba's major crop today, has been (grow) _____ on the island for hundreds of years.
5 Today, Cuba's population (consist) _____ of people of Spanish, African, and Spanish-African descent, most of whom (speak) _____ Spanish.

Paragraph Practice

In the harbor of Havana, Cuba's capital, (lie or lay) _____ the U.S. battleship *Maine;* the ship (explode) _____ and (sink) _____ on February 15, 1898. Although experts never (determine) _____ the cause of the explosion, some American journalists (write) _____ stories blaming the Spanish. After the sinking of the *Maine,* the U.S. (ask) _____ the Spanish to withdraw from Cuba, but on April 24 Spain (declare) _____ war on the U.S. During the Spanish-American War, Theodore Roosevelt and his Rough Riders (win) _____ fame when they (ride) _____ up San Juan Hill. American troops captured the city of Santiago de Cuba on July 17, an event which (lead) _____ to the end of the war a month later.

29 c Recognize main and auxiliary verbs.

The **main verb** of a sentence creates its principal meaning. **Auxiliary verbs** (also called helping verbs) that precede the main verb indicate changes in time or attitude. The main verb, which is always the last verb in the verb phrase, can be the base form (*walk, drive*), the present participle (*walking, driving*), or the past participle (*walked, driven*).

Auxiliary Verbs

Forms of *be: be, am, is, are, was, were, being, been*
Forms of *have: have, has, had*
Forms of *do: do, does, did*
Modal auxiliaries: *can, could, may, might, must, shall, should, will, would*

● **1 Be.** The forms of *be* used with the present participles of main verbs form the progressive tenses (see Section **29d**). The forms of be used with the past participles of main verbs form the passive voice (see Section **29e**).

> Silvio *was questioning* some of Ralph Waldo Emerson's ideas.
>
> He *was given* a collection of Emerson's works as a gift.

● **2 Have.** The forms of *have* used with the past participles of main verbs form the perfect tenses (see the chart in Section **29d**).

> Silvio *has read* and *reread* Emerson's *Self Reliance*. He isn't completely sure what Emerson meant when he wrote, "I hope in these days we *have heard* the last of conformity and consistency."

● **3 Do.** Forms of *do* create questions, express negative statements when used with the adverbs *never* or *not*, or emphasize the meaning of the main verb.

> *Do* you *know* what he meant? The part about consistency *does* not *seem* clear to me. Silvio *did say* he needs to read Emerson several times to grasp his ideas.

● **4 Modal auxiliaries.** Unlike *be, have,* and *do,* the modal auxiliaries do not change form. Modals combine with main verbs to indicate possibility, obligation, necessity, ability, permission, and the like.

> He *would* probably feel happier if you *would* visit his mother now and again.
>
> It *must have been* difficult for Alice to raise five children by herself—she *might* seem demanding but surely you *could* understand her point of view if you tried.

ESL Highlight

Modal Auxiliaries

Following are some of the choices in using modal auxiliaries.

To ask for permission to do something now or in the future, you can use *can, could,* or *may. May* is the most formal; *could* is more polite than *can.* Although

can is used to ask permission in informal conversation, *may* is preferred; *can* is reserved for expressing ability. "*May* I please see my course schedule?" "*Could* I use your VCR Friday night?" "*Can* I have a donut, please?" (conversation) "*May* I have a donut, please?" (writing)

To indicate a strong possibility of something happening now or in the future, as the result of another action, choose *can* or *could*: "If you don't start studying more, you *could* fail biology."

To indicate a weak possibility of something happening now or in the future, use *may* or *might*. *May* expresses a somewhat more likely possibility than *might*: "You *may* confuse your students if you don't prepare for class." "She *might* go with us to the zoo if we tell her that the animals are no longer in cages."

To indicate ability in the present tense, choose *can* if the ability is not dependent on specified conditions: "Jonas *can* recite the entire Declaration of Independence." Choose *could* if the ability is dependent on certain conditions: "If she had the money, she *could* come with us to France." (But she doesn't have the money.) In the past tense, use *could* to express ability: "Before I started smoking, I *could* run five miles at a time."

To indicate obligation or responsibility, use *should*: "We parents *should* think about the consequences of our anger." (We may or may not always do so, however.)

To indicate necessity, use *must*: "I *must* get my driver's license before I look for a job." Alternatively, use *need to*: "I *need to* get my license so I can drive to interviews."

29 d Recognize verb tenses.

Tense is the time of the action expressed by the verb. The **simple tenses** indicate the general time of an action or state of being: past, present, and future. The **perfect tenses** indicate completed actions. The **progressive tenses** indicate continuing actions. The **perfect progressive tenses** indicate actions that continue up to some point in time. The following chart summarizes the tenses for the regular verb *play* and the irregular verb *eat*. (ESL students see Chapter 30 for more information on verbs.)

	Present	*Past*	*Future*
SIMPLE	play	played	will play
	eat	ate	shall eat
PERFECT	has played	had played	will have played
	have eaten	had eaten	will have eaten
PROGRESSIVE	is playing	was playing	will be playing
	are eating	were eating	will be eating
PERFECT	has been playing	had been playing	will have been playing
PROGRESSIVE	have been eating	had been eating	will have been eating

---

ESL Highlight

Be, Have, and *Do*

In all tenses except the simple present and the simple past tense, the auxiliaries *be* and *have* carry the tense *and* create questions, negative statements, and added emphasis. In the simple present and simple past tenses, however, a question, negative statement, or special emphasis is indicated by a form of the auxiliary *do* (see Section **29c(3)**).

Has he *received* my letter? [present perfect tense]
Did he *receive* my letter? [simple past tense]

● **1 The present tense.** The present tense expresses general truths and accepted facts: "The earth *rotates* around the sun." In addition, the present tense expresses habitual actions: "The class *practices* yoga each morning at six o'clock."

The present tense is typically used in academic writing to refer to information from a report, article, book, or other written source:

SOCIOLOGY   Gerontologist Ken Dychtwald *points* out that during most of human history only one person in ten lived to the age of 65.

LITERATURE   In Dickens's novel, David Copperfield's harsh stepfather *sends* him to London, where David *works* in a warehouse pasting labels on bottles.

The present tense is often used to indicate future action:

Our tour *begins* tomorrow.

Classes *start* in two weeks.

● **2 Tense sequence with infinitives and participles.** Infinitives and participles express only a time that is relative to the time indicated by the main verb of the sentence. The infinitive and participle forms of the regular verb *want* and the irregular verb *begin* are as follows.

	Infinitives	*Participles*
PRESENT TENSE	to want	wanting
	to begin	beginning
PAST TENSE	—	wanted
	—	begun
PERFECT TENSE	to have wanted	having wanted
	to have begun	having begun

A present infinitive or present participle expresses an action occurring at the same time or later than the time of the main verb. A perfect infinitive, past participle, or perfect participle expresses a time earlier than the time of the main verb.

> She *wants* [*wanted, had wanted, will want*] *to study* law. [The present infinitive *to study* indicates the same time or time later than that of the main verb *want*.]

> She *would have* preferred *to study* [not *to have studied*] law. [The present infinitive *to study* indicates that studying law would occur at the same time or a later time than the expression of her preference.]

> She *was* [*is, will be*] glad *to have studied* law. She would like *to have studied* law. [The perfect infinitive *to have studied* indicates that the study occurred earlier than the time indicated by the main verbs *was, is, will be,* or *would like*.]

> *Wanting* to study law, she *works* [*worked, had worked, will work*] hard. [The present participle *wanting* indicates the same time or a time later than that of the main verb.]

> *Having passed* the entrance exam, she is *celebrating* [*has celebrated, will celebrate*]. [The perfect participle *having passed* indicates passing the exam occurs before the celebrating.]

> *Defeated* in the election, the candidate *retired* [*has retired, had retired, will retire*] from politics. [The past participle *defeated* indicates that the defeat occurred before the time indicated by the main verb *retire*.]

Exercise 29.5

In the following sentences and paragraph, choose the infinitive or participle form that is in appropriate sequence. Be prepared to explain your choices. Do any of the sentences have more than one possible answer?

Sentence Practice

1 (Thirsting, Having thirsted) for violence and gore, at an early age I began (to love, to have loved) reading murder mysteries by such writers as Agatha Christie, John Dickson Carr, and Ngaio Marsh.

2 (Having convinced, Convincing) myself that I did not have time to study French or to do my math problems, I hastened (to read, to have read) about gruesome murders and brilliant detection.

3 (Reading, Having read) about a third of a detective novel, I could easily begin (to figure out, to have figured out) the killer's identity.

4 (Reaching, Having reached) the end of the book, however, I usually was shocked (to learn, to have learned) that I had been duped by the author.

5 Once again my attempts (to match, to have matched) wits with the detective convinced me that by graduation I will be wise (to prepare, to have prepared) myself for something other than a career as a detective.

Paragraph Practice

(Reading, Having read) most of the best classic British detective novels, I have recently begun (to appreciate, to have appreciated) several modern mystery writers, especially the Americans Sue Grafton and Sarah Paretsky. Their novels feature female detectives who are brave enough (to take on, to have taken on) the toughest cases and bright enough (to solve, to have solved) them in less time than the male police officers with whom they match wits. (Having agreed, Agreeing) to solve a case, these female detectives—Grafton's Kinsey Milhone and Paretsky's V. I. Warshawski—never fail (to catch, to have caught) the criminals. They are rarely able (to succeed, to have succeeded) without experiencing danger and romance, (being, having been) both beautiful and brave. Both Kinsey Milhone and V. I. Warshawski, (solving, having solved) the case, usually debate whether or not (to give, to have given) up both detecting and romance, but, fortunately for those who love (to read, to have read) these authors, the detectives never give up either.

Exercise 29.6

In the following sentences and paragraph, choose the verb form in parentheses that is in appropriate tense sequence. Be prepared to explain your choices. Do any of the sentences have more than one possible answer?

Sentence Practice

1 Tropical rain forests (affect, affected) our lives in many ways.
2 Tropical rain forests (contain, contained) 40 to 50 percent of all species of life on earth, even though these rain forests (cover, covered) only 6 to 7 percent of the earth's surface.
3 The author of a recent article about ecology (states, stated) that if we (act, acted) now, we can preserve these valuable rain forests.
4 When I went to the drugstore to have a prescription filled, my pharmacist (tells, told) me that tropical rain forests (supply, supplied) the sources for many medicines.
5 Tropical rain forests (play, played) a part in climate control, and they (are, were) also sources of food and timber.

Paragraph Practice

My community (has, has had) a trash recycling program for nearly a decade; consequently, I always (separate, separated) my trash into recyclable categories. Because glass and metal do not decompose rapidly, recycling these materials (reduces, reduced) the amount of solid waste at our trash dumps. Recently, when I took a walk around my neighborhood, I (realize, realized) that every week people (throw, threw) away trash that could easily be recycled. However, I've also learned that some people (think, thought) that recycling trash (is, was) too much work. For instance, when I talked to my neighbor, she (tells, told) me that sorting her trash (is, was) too much trouble.

In Your Own Words

Write a paragraph giving directions for a simple activity, such as grooming a pet or making a pizza. Use the second person (you) present tense. Then, rewrite the paragraph in the third person singular (he or she) in the present tense, as if you were observing what someone is doing. Finally, rewrite it in the third person singular past tense (using other tenses as needed for tense sequence). as if you are telling about an action that happened some time ago.

● **3 Tense sequence in complex sentences.** When the verb in the main clause of a complex sentence is in any tense except the past or past perfect, the verb in the subordinate clause will be in whatever tense the meaning requires.

> The weather service *predicts* that it *will be* hot again tomorrow. [The prediction occurs in the present but refers to the future.]

> Our friends *will* not *know* that we *were* here unless we *leave* them a note. [future, past, present]

If the verb in the main clause is in the past tense or past perfect tense, the verb in a subordinate clause following it will typically be in the past or past perfect tense, unless the subordinate clause states a general truth.

> You *said* that you *wanted* [not *want*] to live in an apartment.

> I *thought* that I *had left* my coat in the car.

> The owners *discovered* later that the fire *had destroyed* their house. [The destruction of the house occurred at a time before the owner's discovery of it.]

> BUT The child *discovered* painfully that fire *burns*. [Here *fire burns* states a general truth. Thus the verb is in the present even though the child's discovery occurred in the past.]

29 **e** Recognize voice.

Voice shows whether the subject performs or receives the action of the verb. When the subject performs the action, the verb is in the **active voice.** When the subject receives the action, the verb is in the **passive voice.**

ACTIVE The elephant *dragged* its trainer.
PASSIVE The trainer *was dragged* by the elephant.

The passive voice is formed by using a form of *be* (*am, is, was, were, been, being*) with the past participle of the main verb: *was driven, will have been driven, is being driven.* Even when the passive verb phrase includes other auxiliary verbs, a form of *be* must come immediately before the main verb.

ESL Highlight

Intransitive Verbs
Only transitive verbs (i.e., verbs that can take an object) can show both active and passive voices: "The student wrote the paper" (active) or "The paper was written by the student" (passive). Intransitive verbs express actions that are complete in themselves; thus, they cannot

take the passive voice: "He slept" (active) but not "He was slept" (see Section **26f (3-4)**).

● **1 The active voice.** The active voice is almost always more direct, economical, and forceful than the passive (see Sections **10f** and **24a**).

PASSIVE   The lead role *was played* by Tom Cruise.
ACTIVE   Tom Cruise *played* the lead role.

● **2 The passive voice: when the actor is unknown.**

The play was first performed in 1591.

The cash was taken.

● **3 The passive voice: when the receiver of the action is more important than the actor.**

The new bridge was completed by the contractor.

The results of the experiment have been duplicated by other scientists.

When named in the sentence, the actor appears in a prepositional phrase beginning with *by* or *with*.

See Section **16a** for a discussion of ineffective shifts from one voice to another and Section **24a** on the unnecessary use of the passive.

Exercise 29.7

In the following sentences and paragraph, identify the verb as active or passive. Then revise each sentence, making active verbs passive and passive verbs active. Add whatever information you need to change the voice. Then compare the original and your revision and decide whether the active or passive voice seems better. Be prepared to explain your choices.

Sentence Practice

1 For a part-time job in a computer store near campus, I was interviewed by the owners, Mrs. Wexler and Mr. Alberti.
2 Of course, I was asked about my academic background, but I was surprised by their questions about my interest in sports and Chinese cooking.
3 Most of their questions, in fact, did not address my knowledge of computers, and so I began to anticipate being turned down for the job.
4 I was depressed by this possibility because I needed this job to help with school expenses.
5 My feelings of dejection were quickly swept away when the owners asked me if I could start work the next day.

Paragraph Practice

Job interviews make most people nervous, but the stress can be reduced considerably if the job seeker takes the proper steps to prepare for the interview. First, the applicant must double-check the time and place of the interview to reduce the chance of being late or becoming lost. Also the applicant can be relieved of stress by reading about the company to prepare questions that might be asked by the interviewer. Such preparation shows the interviewer that the applicant has been motivated to find out about the company. Questions that might be asked by the interviewer should also be anticipated and the answers practiced out loud before the interview. Finally, every effort should be made to look professional and to act courteously.

In Your Own Words
Using the active voice, write five sentences about your best birthday ever. Then, rewrite them in the passive voice. Remember that linking verbs like *to be* and *to seem* as well as intransitive verbs like *stumble* and *arrive* cannot be active and passive voice: only transitive verbs are active and passive voice.

29 f Recognize mood.

The mood of a verb indicates whether the writer or speaker regards the action as a fact, as a command, or as a wish, request, or condition contrary to fact. The **indicative** mood is used for ordinary statements and questions ("She is quiet," "Is she happy?"); the **imperative** mood, for commands ("Be quiet"); and the **subjunctive** mood, for conditions contrary to fact and in clauses following certain verbs such as *demand, insist, recommend, request, suggest,* and *urge.*

English speakers typically have problems only with the subjunctive form, which uses the base form of the verb (without the *-s*), *have* instead of *has*, and *were* or *be* instead of *am, is, are, was,* or *were.*

● 1 The subjunctive in *if* clauses expressing conditions contrary to fact.

> If the rose bush *were* healthy, it would have more buds. [The bush is not healthy.]
>
> Last year, the bush looked as though it *were* going to die. [But it didn't die.]

However, not all clauses beginning with *if* necessarily express a condition contrary to fact: "If my experiment is successful, I will have proven my point." (Here the clause states a condition that has not yet occurred; the experiment may or may not be successful.)

ESL Highlight

Tense in Conditional Sentences
In conditional sentences expressing contrary-to-fact situations, shift the tense of the *if* clause backward in time. For example, if the true

situation takes place in the present, the verb in the *if* clause is in the past tense:

I would buy the car today, if I *had* the money.

Notice that the form of the verb in the independent clause is modal + base form *(would + buy)*.

If the true situation takes place in the past, the verb in the *if* clause is in the past-perfect tense:

If I *had had* the money yesterday, I would have bought a car.

The form of the verb in the independent clause is modal + perfect infinitive *(have* + past participle).

Wish and **Hope.** Although the verbs *wish* and *hope* are often used interchangeably, the verb *wish* requires the same backward shift of tenses, but the verb *hope* does not. *Hope* uses "real" time.

I wish you *were* here now. [present]

I wish you *had been* here yesterday. [past perfect]

● **2 The subjunctive in *that* clauses after verbs expressing wishes, commands, requests, or recommendations.**

The law requires that there *be* a prompt trial.
I move that this meeting *be* adjourned.

The reporter asked that Senator Schroeder *repeat* her last reply.

I wish I *were* in Rome. [*That* is unexpressed.]

● **3 The subjunctive in a few surviving idioms.**

Peace *be* with you.

Long *live* the Queen!

Heaven *help* us!

Be that as it may.

Exercise 29.8

In the sentences in the following paragraph, choose the appropriate verb form. Be prepared to explain your choices.

     Instead of sitting here listening to an economics lecture, I wish I (was, were) lying on the beach. While lying there on the beach, I would request of my friends that I (am, be) left alone to read and relax. If I (was, were) on my ideal stretch of beach, I'd also have palm trees to shade me from the sun and soft breezes to cool me. While I was sitting there daydreaming about my beach, my instructor called my name and recommended that I (pay, paid) more attention in class. I guess I'd better forget about my beach for a while, since my instructor also requested that I (am, be) the person who explains the concept of laissez-faire in class tomorrow. Far (is, be) it from me to let a glorious dream of the beach stand in the way of intellectual progress in economics!

In Your Own Words
Write two sentences illustrating each of these uses of the subjunctive mood: (1) condition contrary to fact; (2) expressions of wishes, commands, requests, or recommendations; and (3) idiomatic expressions. Write all sentences in the present tense.

Exercise 29.9

Sentence Practice
In each of the following sentences, choose the correct form of the verbs, infinitives, or participles from each of the pairs given in parentheses. Do any of the sentences have more than one possible answer? Use each verb form you choose in a sentence of your own.

1 (Having been dragged, Being dragged) into my first game of Frisbee®, I (was surprised, have been surprised) at how quickly I (learned, have learned) to play.

2 I never (have been, had been) good at any sports, so I was reluctant (to play, to have played) the first time.

3 (Having thrown, throwing) the Frisbee a couple of times, I quickly got the hang of it, (realizing, having realized) that catching it (is, was) harder than throwing it.

4 My friend pointed out that the spin and force of the throw (keep, kept) the Frisbee flying and that my grip on the Frisbee (affects, affected) its spin and force.

5 I also (discovered, have discovered) that Frisbee is a relatively safe sport: A few bruises from (bumping, having bumped) into people and some sore muscles are (expected, to be expected), but more serious injuries happen only when players (do, did) not look where they (step, were stepping).

Paragraph Practice
Correct any errors you find in the use of verbs and verbals in this paragraph.

> The Frisbee has its origin in the bakery business. Students who used to have bought pies and cookies from the bakery owned by the Frisbee family in Connecticut begun tossing the pie tins and lids from cookie tins in informal games. In 1947 a Frisbee was marketed for children, and the name Frisbee had been bought in 1957. The development of plastics made it possible for more efficient Frisbees to have been made, and people's excitement over a miniature flying saucer helped make Frisbees bestsellers. By the 1970s, the International Frisbee Association was formed. Today many kinds of competitions and organized games with the Frisbee have taken place worldwide—even contests for dogs, who have been natural Frisbee players.

Writers Revising

Verbs

For his introductory psychology class, Keith was writing a research report on nightmares and anxiety. Following is a section of Keith's second draft. To create this second draft, Keith revised the content and organization of his earlier work; his next step was to make sure that all the verbs were in the appropriate forms. Revise any problems with verbs that you find in this draft. Then compare your revision to the changes Keith made in his final version, which follows the draft.

Draft

Nightmares are not an uncommon occurrence. They do not necessarily occur nightly, but, nonetheless, many individuals experienced them. Are these "bad dreams" generally preceded by an elevated level of anxiety, or vice versa? Wood and Bootzin (1990) perform a study to test the assumptions that (a) frequent nightmares were uncommon among normal adults, and (b) nightmares reflect generally elevated levels of anxiety.

The study by Wood and Bootzin use daily sleep logs to record ongoing observations about nightmares. This was a first in published nightmare studies to date. The logs were used in comparison with reports which were used previously. The study also reexamined the relationship between nightmares and anxiety.

The 220 subjects in the study come from a pool of undergraduate introductory psychology students. To begin, retrospective self-reports were taken on three estimates. Subjects were first asked how many nightmares they had had over the past year; if they had had a nightmare over the previous year, how many; and how many nightmares they had experience over the previous month. Next, the subjects written in response to a series of questionnaires that ask about anxiety, creativity, and sleep disorders. Finally, the subjects were gave 14-page dream logs which they filled out each morning for two weeks. In the logs, subjects were suppose to comment on whether they had had a nightmare the previous night, and if so, how many. To prevent false or exaggerated reports, the subjects were tole that the researchers were interested in non-nightmare

as well as nightmare subjects, and that credit would
be give regardless. Also, subjects required to hand in
nightly reports within four days.

Revision

Nightmares are not an uncommon occurrence.

They do not necessarily occur nightly, but,

1 nonetheless, many individuals experienced   29d(1)

them. Are these "bad dreams" generally pre-

ceded by an elevated level of anxiety, or

2 vice versa? Wood and Bootzin (1990) perform^ed   29a(6)

a study to test the assumptions that (a)

3 frequent nightmares ~~were~~ *are* uncommon among nor-   29d(3)

mal adults, and (b) nightmares reflect gener-

ally elevated levels of anxiety.

4   The study by Wood and Bootzin use^d daily   29a(6)

sleep logs to record ongoing observations

about nightmares. This was a first in pub-

lished nightmare studies to date. The logs

were used in comparison with reports which

5 ~~were~~ *had been* used previously. The study also reexam-   29d

ined the relationship between nightmares and

anxiety.

6   The 220 subjects in the study ~~come~~ *came* from a   29b(2)

pool of undergraduate introductory psycholo-

gy students. To begin, retrospective self-

reports were taken on three estimates.

Subjects were first asked how many nightmares

they had had over the past year; if they had

had a nightmare over the previous year, how

many; and how many nightmares they had expe-

7 rience^d over the previous month. Next, the   29a(6)

8 subjects ~~written~~ *wrote* in response to a series of   29b(6)

9 questionnaires that ask^*ed* about anxiety, cre-   29a(2)

ativity, and sleep disorders. Finally, the

10 subjects were ~~gave~~ *given* 14-page dream logs which   29b (2), 29e

they filled out each morning for two weeks.

11 In the logs, subjects were suppose^d to com-   29a(6)

ment on whether they had had a nightmare the

previous night, and if so, how many. To pre-

vent false or exaggerated reports, the sub-

12 jects were ~~tole~~ *told* that the researchers were   29b(2)

interested in non-nightmare as well as

nightmare subjects, and that credit would be

13,14 give^n regardless. Also, subjects ^*were* required to   29b(2), 29e

hand in nightly reports within four days.

Analysis

To correct the verb errors in his second draft, Keith first checked for the kinds of mistakes he typically makes, which he had become aware of by keeping an error log in his English class. Keith knew that he often omitted the endings *-ed* and *-d* from past-tense verbs and that he sometimes made errors in using irregular verbs. Searching for omitted endings, Keith added the appropriate endings to the verbs *perform* (error 2 in the revision), *use* (error 4), *asked* (error 9), and *suppose* (error 11). As he consulted his handbook, he briefly wondered whether he ought to change the first sentence of the second paragraph to the present-tense form *uses* (see Section **29d(1)** on academic writing); however, he decided to keep to the past tense throughout the entire paper because the research study about which he was reporting was not ongoing but had been completed.

On this first pass, Keith also found two mistakes in the forms of irregular verbs (errors 6, 8).

Keith knew from class discussion and from reading his research sources that social scientists use the passive voice more frequently than researchers in the humanities (see also Chapter 50), so he concentrated on checking the forms of these verbs instead of worrying about overusing the passive voice. When he examined his sentences, he found three errors in the use of irregular past participles (errors 10, 12, 13). Keith also noticed that he had neglected to use a form of *be* before the past participle *required* (error 14) in the last sentence, so he added *were* to make the passive voice verb *were required*.

Keith decided to take a break from revising and then read the draft again with fresh eyes. When he did so the next day, he found several errors in verb tense. In the first paragraph, Keith had begun by using the present tense because he was discussing general ideas and questions that Wood and Bootzin's study was designed to test. However, at the end of the first sentence (error 1) he shifted to the past tense: *many individuals experienced them.* Keith remembered reading in his handbook that the present tense is used to express habitual actions; he realized that nightmares qualify as habitual actions, so he changed *experienced* to *experience.* In looking carefully at the sentence beginning "Wood and Bootzin (1990) performed a study," Keith noticed that he had used a past-tense verb (*were*) in part (a) but a present-tense verb (*reflect*) in part (b). Keith decided to change *were* to *are* (error 3) and leave *reflect* in the present tense to emphasize that these two statements refer to general truths, or at least beliefs that are so widely accepted that researchers found them worthy of study.

In the second paragraph, Keith questioned his second use of *were used* (error 5) because he was discussing studies done before Wood and Bootzin's. He checked Section **29d** and then revised the sentence to better distinguish the respective times of the studies: "The logs were used in comparison with reports which had been used previously." Since it had become obvious to Keith that he had failed to identify tense errors in his first two passes, he carefully examined the tenses of all the verbs in the third paragraph. Keith found one more error (error 7): He had neglected to put the *-d* on *experience* to form the past perfect tense: *had experienced.*

Look again at the sentence in which error 7 occurs. Can you think of a way to rewrite the sentence to make it more succinct?

Verbs: Special Concerns for ESL Writers

Non-native speakers of English may have trouble deciding which verb form most accurately states their intended meaning. For example, the meanings of some verbs change depending on which tense is used, and other verbs indicate fixed relationships between subject and object. The following section details some of the rules governing verb usage in English (see also Chapter 29, "Verbs").

30 a Examine progressive forms for time relationships.

The **progressive** forms of verbs indicate continuing action or emphasize the duration of an action. Usually, the progressive forms also convey a sense of incompleteness. The progressive forms of some verbs indicate repeated actions, and in a few special cases, the progressive expresses completed actions. (See Section **30b** for verbs whose meanings do not usually permit them to be used in the progressive forms.)

● **1 Formation of the progressive forms.** Following is a summary of the auxiliary verbs used to create the progressive tenses. The main verb in the progressive tenses is always the present participle (base + *-ing* form): *waiting, learning.*

Formation of the Progressive Forms

The auxiliary verbs listed here are followed by the present participle of the main verb, for example, *eating.*

	Auxiliary Verb
PRESENT PROGRESSIVE	present form of *be* [*am, is, are*]
PRESENT PERFECT PROGRESSIVE	present form of *have* + *been*
PAST PROGRESSIVE	past form of *be* [*was, were*]
PAST PERFECT PROGRESSIVE	*had been*
FUTURE PROGRESSIVE	*will be* or *going to be*
FUTURE PERFECT PROGRESSIVE	*will have been*

● **2 The present progressive.** The present progressive is used to indicate an action occurring as you write or speak: "I am sitting at my computer." "My daughter is playing in her bedroom." This form can indicate an action occurring over a given period of time, not necessarily at this moment: "This year, I am making Christmas gifts for each member of my family." When used with a word referring to a future time or in a context clearly indicating the future, the present progressive indicates an action that will occur in the future: "My mother's train is arriving at 10:30 tomorrow morning. I am taking her out to lunch at Chez Louis."

● **3 The present perfect progressive.** The present perfect progressive emphasizes the duration of an action begun in the past and continuing at this moment: "She has been sitting there for hours." (She is still sitting there.)

Do not use the present perfect progressive to express an action that is not continuous. Use the present perfect tense (present tense form of *have* + past participle of the main verb) instead.

INCORRECT   Ana has been leaving the party.
REVISED   Ana has left the party.

Do not use the present perfect progressive with words that state the number of times something has been done or the number of things that have been done. Instead, use the present perfect tense.

INCORRECT   They have been going to Colorado to ski six times.
REVISED   They have gone to Colorado to ski six times.

To indicate a single action, use the present perfect progressive form if the action is continuing; use the present perfect tense if the action is completed.

CONTINUING ACTION   Bill has been singing folk songs all evening. [Bill is still singing.]
COMPLETED ACTION   Bill has sung folk songs. [But he isn't singing now.]

● **4 The past progressive.** Used with a word expressing an exact time or a given period of time, the past progressive form indicates an action whose exact beginning and ending are unknown.

EXACT TIME   I didn't call to tell you the news because I knew you were taking your exam at 3:30. [Taking the exam began before 3:30 and probably continued after 3:30.]
PERIOD OF TIME   What was I doing last evening? I was listening to all my old Patsy Cline albums.

Used with words indicating duration, the past progressive expresses the beginning and ending of an action: "From November to March, I was working at a resort in Miami."

The past progressive indicates that two actions were occurring at the same time in the past: "While Susan was cleaning the living room, her husband was cooking dinner."

To indicate an action that began before another past action and probably continued after it, use the past progressive for the continuing action and the simple past for the other action: "They were eating dinner when the telephone rang."

The meaning you wish to convey often will determine whether the past progressive or the simple past form is the appropriate choice:

SIMPLE PAST   When Margaret finished her shower, I got ready to run.
                      [Margaret was finished before I started to get ready.]
PAST PROGRESSIVE   When Margaret finished her shower, I was getting ready
                      to run. [I started getting ready before she was finished.]

Do not use the past progressive to indicate that a single past action occurred. Use the simple past tense instead.

INCORRECT   He was leaving Indianapolis last year.
REVISED   He left Indianapolis last year.

Do not use the past progressive to indicate an action that continued for a period of time in the past and then ended at a later time in the past. Use the past perfect tense instead.

INCORRECT   I had been saving every cent I earned for two years.
REVISED   I had saved every cent I earned for two years.

● **5 The past perfect progressive.** Use the past perfect progressive to emphasize the continuous nature of a past action taking place before a more recent past action: "They had been waiting for the store manager for half an hour when they walked out in disgust."

Like the present perfect progressive, the past perfect progressive is not used when the number of times something has been done is mentioned. Use the past perfect tense (past tense form of *had* + past participle of the main verb) instead.

INCORRECT   We had been visiting Nepal twice already, so this year we decid-
                      ed to go to Tibet.
REVISED   We had visited Nepal twice already, so this year we decided to
                      go to Tibet.

● **6 The future progressive.** Use the future progressive form to indicate an action that will be in progress at a given time in the future: "At 8:00, we will be leaving for New York." The future progressive can indicate an action that will continue to happen at different times in the future: "I am going to be giving your cat three leukemia shots at six-month intervals." Use the future progressive to indicate an action that will occur at some unknown future time: "You'll be hearing from our collection agency if you don't pay this bill immediately."

Do not use the future progressive to indicate an action that will be completed at a future time. Use the future perfect tense (*will have* + past participle of the main verb) instead.

INCORRECT   By October 30, I will be moving into my new apartment.
REVISED   By October 30, I will have moved into my new apartment.

● **7 The future perfect progressive.** The future perfect progressive is used in the same situations as the future perfect tense, but the future perfect progressive can only be used with verbs that indicate continuing action.

INCORRECT She will have been completing her studies in January.
REVISED She will have completed her studies in January.
CORRECT On September 19, she will have been teaching for exactly twenty years.

● **8 Repeated actions.** Used with verbs that express momentary actions, such as *beat, blink, hit, knock, rap, shake, spit, hit, wink,* the progressive forms indicate repeated actions: "Marlene is kicking the candy machine because it won't refund her money."

Exercise 30.1

In the following sentences and paragraph, revise the inappropriately used progressive forms of the verbs. Be prepared to explain why they are not appropriate.

Sentence Practice

1 The field of international communications is rapidly becoming critical to the global market that is developing.
2 When businesspeople are misunderstanding one another, business is being lost and often feelings are being hurt as well.
3 What has been being seen as rudeness is also being perceived as a reason not to be doing further business with an individual or company.
4 For example, when an American businessperson is trying to negotiate a contract with Latin Americans, he or she perhaps is pressing the Latin American company to make a quick decision; and the Latin Americans likely are perceiving this rush as rude behavior, because lengthy, slow decision making is being practiced in their culture as an important element of business.
5 Other considerations which are playing important roles in international business are concepts of space, time, status, and values.

Paragraph Practice

Two of my college friends have been going into international business, and both have been losing two important deals because they have not been understanding and respecting cultural differences. Last year my friend Greta was being sent on a one-week trip to Saudi Arabia to negotiate the sale of electrical supplies to a hotel chain. When she was attending a dinner in her honor and was being invited to sit in a separate room with the wives of Arab businessmen, she was responding in anger and was leaving the party early. This behavior was hurting her status there, and she finally was losing the contract—to another businesswoman who was knowing how to interpret Arab culture. My friend Keith was having a similar experience last year in Japan. He was failing to understand that a decision there is typically being made by a team, not by one individual. When he was continuing to pay attention to only one person and when he was pushing for that person to decide, the Japanese team was being offended and was ending the negotiations abruptly.

In Your Own Words

Review the discussion of rules for using the progressive forms of verbs. Then write three sentences (each in a different tense) illustrating the use of the progressive forms. Then write a paragraph explaining which uses are most confusing to you and why.

30 **b** **Check state-of-being verbs in the progressive form.**

State-of-being verbs express a sense of being or existing that does not have a definite beginning or ending. These verbs have an inherent sense of time-lessness or duration and are usually not used in the progressive form.

INCORRECT   I am knowing her very well.
CORRECT   I know her very well.

● **1 Perception.** State-of-being verbs express sensory perception (e.g., *hear, see, seem, smell, taste, look, appear, feel*).

> The soup tastes good.
> That fruit tree appears healthy.

● **2 Mental conditions.** State-of-being verbs express mental or intellectual conditions (e.g., *believe, know, remember, imagine, mean, think, understand, wonder, recognize*).

> I understand what you mean.
> Tom remembered to buy gasoline.

● **3 Emotional conditions.** State-of-being verbs express emotional conditions (e.g., *hate, like, want, prefer, love, dislike, need, hope, appreciate*).

> I want to go to the movies.
> I dislike having to wait for people.

● **4 Ownership.** State-of-being verbs express ownership or a relationship (e.g., *own, have, possess, belong to, involve, require*).

> Your classmates require your help.
> This plan involves you.

● **5 Measurement.** State-of-being verbs express conditions of measurement (e.g., *weigh, measure, contain*).

> This room measures twelve feet by six feet.

● **6 Exceptions.** The progressive form may be used to express an activity rather than a state of being:

HAVE   I have a car. [possession; state of being]
                She is having a party. [activity]

TASTE   The coffee tastes good. [perception]
             The chef is tasting the soup. [activity]
CONSIDER   I consider you [to be] my friend. [mental condition]
             I am considering taking a job with a more progressive company.
             [activity]

The progressive form may be used to express politeness:

> We are hoping to see you next week.

The verb *be* is used in the progressive when it is followed by an adjective or noun expressing a certain behavior or particular role the subject is assuming.

> Leonard is being silly.
> He is being a clown.

Exercise 30.2

In the following sentences and paragraph, determine which sentences use the progressive forms correctly with state-of-being verbs. Revise inappropriate uses. Be prepared to explain your choices.

Sentence Practice

1 I am feeling confused about what to major in.

2 I am loving my English courses, but I am wondering what I can do with an English major.

3 Since I am having a hard time with economics and accounting, I am thinking that a business major is not being for me.

4 Career counseling has been helping a little, but I am being overwhelmed by my inability to decide on a major and stick to it.

5 Since my freshman year, I have been having four different majors, nearly a different one each term.

Paragraph Practice

Friends who are wanting to help me have been making some good suggestions. Della is believing that an internship would help me make up my mind. Austin, who is knowing how much I am hating business, says that I ought to make appointments with people in different kinds of careers and visit them at their jobs to see what these jobs are requiring in terms of training. My professors tell me that my confusion is being typical. Finding the right career path is involving more work and distress than I was believing it would. Of course, I am seeing that no major will be containing all of the answers for my happiness with a career.

In Your Own Words

Write one sentence each to illustrate the use of the progressive form of state-of-being verbs to express the following: (1) perception, (2) mental conditions, (3) emotional conditions, (4) ownership, (5) measurement, and (6) exceptions.

Identify verbs as transfer or reaction verbs.

In most sentences, the subject and verb phrase together express an action. If the verb is **transitive**, an object completes the action. **Intransitive** verbs are complete without an object.

TRANSITIVE	The dog licked Jon's hand.
	Samantha wrote a letter.
INTRANSITIVE	The train arrived.
	Lani ran around the block.

(See transitive and intransitive verbs in Section **26f**.)

However, some verbs do not direct action to an object; instead, they transfer sensation to an object or receiver or express reactions to sensations or experiences.

Snakes scare Tom.

Snakes, the subject of this sentence, is the source of the sensation. *Tom*, the object of the verb, receives the sensation. The verb *scare* is a transfer verb.

Tom fears snakes.

In this sentence, the source of the sensation is still *snakes*, but now *snakes* is the object of the verb. *Tom* is still the receiver of the sensation, but now *Tom* is the subject. The verb *fears* is a reaction verb. In sentences using reaction verbs, the flow of action is from the object to the subject.

Note that the two example sentences convey the same meaning.

● **1 Transfer verbs.** In a sentence that follows subject-verb-object order, the subject of a transfer verb (often inanimate or nonhuman) is the *source* of the sensation conveyed by the verb.

Science fiction movies bore Chika.

The President's illness worries most citizens.

Verbs That Express Transfer		
amuse	excite	please
annoy	fascinate	satisfy
bore	frighten	scare
challenge	impress	surprise
confuse	insult	terrify
damage	offend	worry

● **2 Reaction verbs.** In a sentence that follows subject-verb-object order, the subject of a reaction verb (usually animate or human) is the *receiver* of the sensation conveyed by the verb.

Morgan dislikes homework.
Christine understands his concern.

Reaction verbs describe a condition or state of being and usually cannot be used in the progressive tenses (see **30b**).

INCORRECT   Bob is loving weightlifting.
REVISED   Bob loves weightlifting.

Verbs That Express Reaction

admire	enjoy	hate	miss	trust
dislike	fear	love	respect	understand

● **3 Subject and objects.** In sentences that follow subject-verb-object order, the subjects and objects of transfer and reaction verbs cannot be interchanged.

INCORRECT   Social situations fear me. [reaction verb]
REVISED   I fear social situations.

INCORRECT   I interest his remarks. [transfer verb]
REVISED   His remarks interest me.

30 d Examine the present participles (*amusing, missing*) and past participles (*amused, missed*) of transfer and reaction verbs for subject-object relationships.

Both transfer and reaction verbs can be expressed in the active and passive voices (see Section **29e** on voice).

TRANSFER VERB   The boss's opinion surprised me. [active voice]
                I was surprised by the boss's opinion. [passive voice]
REACTION VERB   The psychologist respects her ideas. [active voice]
                Her ideas are respected by the psychologist. [passive voice]

● **1 Transfer verbs: voice.** The animate receiver of a sensation can be the subject of a transfer verb only in the passive voice.

INCORRECT   The crowd excites by the ballgame.
              The crowd excites the ballgame.
REVISED   The ballgame excites the crowd. [active voice; *The crowd* is the object of the verb.]
              The crowd is excited by the ballgame. [passive voice; *The crowd* is the subject.]

INCORRECT   My niece bored by my story.
              My niece bored my story.
REVISED   My story bored my niece. [active voice]
              My niece was bored by my story. [passive voice]

Note that when transfer verbs occur in the passive voice, a preposition (usually *by*) normally introduces the source of the sensation: "She was impressed by the doctor's caring attitude." An exception occurs when the source of the sensation appears in a noun clause beginning with *that*.

NOUN PHRASE   The manager was annoyed *by his late arrival.*
NOUN CLAUSE   The manager was annoyed *that he was late.*

● **2 Transfer verbs: the present participle.** The present participle (base + *ing*) of transfer verbs can modify only the source of the sensation, not the receiver.

INCORRECT   The crowd is exciting by the ballgame.
REVISED   The ballgame is exciting to the crowd.
             The crowd is excited by the ballgame.
             [past participle substituted for present participle]

Note that one can say *The crowd is exciting [to people].* In this sentence, *the crowd* is the source of the sensation; *people* are the receivers of the sensation.

Exercise 30.3

The following sentences contain transfer and reaction verbs. Revise the sentences that are incorrect. Be prepared to explain your corrections.

Sentence Practice

1 Many parents are overwhelmed the great variety of toys available today.
2 Children delight toys, especially toys that are stimulating their imaginations.
3 Children are quickly bored battery-powered toys.
4 Children are challenging toys that are unstructured.
5 Unstructured toys enjoy children because these toys force children to pretend and create.

Paragraph Practice

In the following paragraph, choose the correct verb form from those in parentheses.

A recent trip to the toy store (was amazing, amazed) me, because for a few minutes I (was believing, believing, believed) that I (had been going, was going, had gone) to another planet. I (was fascinated, was fascinating, was being fascinated, fascinated) by all of the noises, controls, colors, and lights that (are, were, are being, were being) typical of modern toys. I (was confusing, was being confused, was confused) by my inability to locate a simple ball or doll. Many of the toys I (was seeing, seeing, was seen, saw) imitated figures from television programs or (had, were having, having) names of companies on them. For example, I saw miniatures of fast-food restaurants and equipment that (were delighting, delighting, delighted) children gathered around them.

In Your Own Words

Review the discussion of progressive forms, state-of-being verbs in the progressive form, and transfer and reaction verbs. Which areas are confusing you? Write a paragraph explaining as precisely as possible the problems you are having understanding these uses of verbs.

Writers Revising

Troublesome Verbs

State-of-being verbs, the progressive tenses, and transfer and reaction verbs are often troublesome for ESL writers. The author of the following essay, Yingfan, first revised his writing for overall organization and transitional expressions. Because he knew that he often had difficulty deciding on appropriate verb forms, he examined each verb as a second step in revising.

Examine the following paragraphs from Yingfan's draft and correct any errors in verb usage. Then compare your corrections to those in his revised essay to see if you were able to identify and explain all the problems with verbs.

Draft

It was in the late summer when I began my travel in China with my grandma. Our first stop was Changso, a small city near Suchang. I was knowing a lot about Changso because my grandma had told me a lot about that place. That was the city where my mom was born and lived until she entered college. That was the city where my grandma and grandpa were having a small business for many years. My grandma was spending half her life there. She was very exciting by our arrival at the railway station. My curiosity about the city grew bigger and bigger. It was no doubt a beautiful place in a thirteen-year-old child's mind.

However, my first sight of the city was a dirty, overcrowded station. The station walls were grey and stained with smoke, and piles of rubbish and boxes made islands in the large room. I surprised by such things. There were many people, but the place seemed dead. Most of the people sit on the dirty ground, smoking, speak less, some even slept there. Like every other station in this colorful world, you could find different people there, workers, farmers, and teachers; however, they were not colorful. This world was

only belonging to the grey and blue; this world
belonged to that particular time in China. I could
read the tired expressions of their faces, but I was
too young to recognize that they were not satisfied
with their lives.

Revision

It was in the late summer when I began my

travel in China with my grandma. Our first stop

was Changso, a small city near Suchang. I ~~was~~

1 ~~knowing~~ **knew** a lot about Changso because my grandma   30b(2)

had told me a lot about that place. That was

the city where my mom was born and lived

until she entered college. That was the city

2 where my grandma and grandpa ~~were having~~ **had** a   30b(4)

small business for many years. My grandma ~~was~~

3 ~~spending~~ **had spent** half her life there. She was very   30a(4)

4 ~~exciting~~ **excited** by our arrival at the railway sta-   30d(1)

tion. My curiosity about the city grew bigger

and bigger. It was no doubt a beautiful place

in a thirteen-year-old child's mind.

However, my first sight of the city was a

dirty, overcrowded station. The station walls

were grey and stained with smoke, and piles

of rubbish and boxes made islands in the

5 large room. I ^**was** surprised by such things. There   30d(1)

were many people, but the place seemed dead.

6 Most of the people ~~sit~~ **were sitting** on the dirty ground,   30a(4)

7,8 smoking, ^**not speaking and** ~~speak less~~, some ^**were** even ~~slept~~ **sleeping** there.   30a(4)

Like every other station in this colorful

world, you could find different people there,

workers, farmers, and teachers; however, they

were not colorful. This world ~~was~~ only

belonged
9 ~~belonging~~ to the grey and blue; this world   30b(4)

belonged to that particular time in China. I

could read the tired expressions of their

faces, but I was too young to recognize that

they were not satisfied with their lives.

Analysis

First, Yingfan checked the verbs in his sentences to see if they were state-of-being, transfer, or reaction verbs. Then he examined these sentences to see if he had overused the past progressive. To do this, he checked his sentences to determine if the actions being described were completed actions or if they indicated duration. Based on this preliminary examination, he corrected his essay.

Yingfan recognized *know* (error 1 in the revision) and *have* (error 2) as state-of-being verbs which cannot be used in the progressive. He changed the verbs to the simple past: *I knew* and *my grandma and grandpa had*.

When he examined *was spending* (error 3), he realized that he was discussing an event that was completed. His grandma no longer lived in Changso. Therefore, it was appropriate to use the past perfect tense to indicate an action that took place before another past action (the trip being described). He changed the sentence to read *My grandma had spent half her life there*. Yingfan recognized that *exciting* (error 4) is the participle of a transfer verb and cannot be used to modify the receiver of the sensation. He knew that to have his grandma as the subject of the sentence, he had to use the passive voice.

When Yingfan looked at *surprised* (error 5), he realized that it, too, is a transfer verb and that to have the receiver of the sensation, himself, be the subject, he had to use passive voice. He rewrote the sentence to read, *I was surprised by such things*. The sentence about the people in the railway station presented several problems. He had intended to describe what the people were doing as he walked through the station. The verbs could be either simple past or progressive. To emphasize the duration of the actions, he decided to use the past progressive. *Sit* (error 6) was incorrect in the present tense; he changed it to *were sitting. Speak less* (error 7) sounded awkward. He decided to use a direct negative, *not*, with the participle: *not speaking*. The final part of the sentence, *some even slept* (error 8), was not parallel to the other verbs because it had a subject: *some*. He decided to correct this problem by making it a second clause separated by a *comma* and *and*. The sentence now read, *Most of the people were sitting on the dirty ground, smoking, not speaking, and some were even sleeping there.* Yingfan recognized the verb *belong* (error 9) as another state-of-being verb which cannot be used in the progressive. He changed the verb to the simple past tense.

Review Exercise

Basic Grammar

Part A

In the following sentences, first identify the basic sentence pattern used (see Section **26f**); then for each sentence identify the adjectives, adverbs, prepositions, coordinating conjunctions, and subordinating conjunctions.

1 I recently took a ride in a hot-air balloon.
2 Passengers in hot-air balloons drift quietly over fields and rivers.
3 Ballooning is a relaxing way of traveling.
4 The balloon pilot told me the history of hot-air ballooning.
5 The hot-air balloon was invented by two Frenchmen.

Part B

In the following sentences, identify all phrases—prepositional, infinitive, gerund, or participial; then underline each main clause once and each subordinate clause twice; finally, identify each sentence as simple, compound, complex, or compound-complex.

1 Hot-air balloon flights take place in early morning or late afternoon when winds are light.
2 First, a fan fills the balloon with cold air; next a burner, fueled by propane gas, heats the air in the balloon.
3 As the air in the balloon becomes hotter, the balloon becomes buoyant and begins to rise.
4 The balloon pilot can control the altitude of the balloon by heating or cooling the air in the balloon.
5 Even though balloon pilots can control altitude, they cannot control direction, so balloon passengers go where the winds take them.

Part C

In the following sentences and paragraph, correct in accordance with formal written usage any errors in the use of pronouns, adjectives, adverbs, or verbs.

Sentence Practice

1 George Washington Ferris, whom was an engineer from Pittsburgh, invent the Ferris wheel in 1893.

2 Ferris designs the wheel for the 1893 World's Columbian Exposition in Chicago, and the wheel was the colossolest structure many people had ever saw.

3 The hub of the original Ferris wheel weighed more than seventy tons, making it the larger single piece of steel that had been forged up to that time.

4 Whomever rode on the original Ferris wheel gotten a twenty-minute ride and a view of Lake Michigan.

5 The Chicago Exposition closing, it took workers twelve weeks to have dismantled the giant Ferris wheel.

Paragraph Practice

I asked my little brother if him and his friends would like to go to the amusement park with my friend and I. My brother said yes quick because he love to ride on roller coasters. My little brother like roller coasters more good than me, for I get scared easy, and I sure don't like being upside down when I'm riding. However, people like my brother seem to love screaming loud as they go up steep inclines and then rapid drop down again. If I was them, I'd get sick because some roller coasters race along the dips and curves at seventy miles an hour. If that doesn't make me feel badly enough, amusement park owners keep building even frighteninger roller coasters; it seems like every week someone advertises the most longest and fastest roller coaster in the world. Anybody whom thinks I'm going to get on one of them roller coasters is crazy. While my brother and his friends spent the afternoon on the roller coaster, I'm going to ride the merry-go-round. I'll sure be the safer of the people at the amusement park.

Part 6

Punctuation

Punctuation [is a] code that serves to signal structural, semantic, and rhetorical meanings that would otherwise be missed by the reader ... and from the reader's point of view, punctuation provides a map for one who must otherwise drive blindly past the by-ways, intersections, and detours of a writer's thought.

–Mina Shaughnessy, *Errors and Expectations*

When we speak, we use pauses and gestures to emphasize meaning, and we vary the tempo, stress, and pitch of our voices to mark the beginning and end of units of thought. In other words, we "punctuate" our speech. We punctuate writing for the same purposes, drawing on a whole set of conventional devices developed to help readers identify chunks of information and to give them clues to what we are trying to communicate.

The first of these devices is **spacing:** that is, closing up or enlarging the space between letters or words. For example, we do not runwordstogetherthisway. Instead, we identify a word as a word by setting it off from its neighbors. Spacing is the most basic of all punctuating devices. We use spacing also to separate sentences, to set off paragraphs, to list items as in an outline, to mark lines of poetry, and the like.

But spacing, of course, is not the only punctuation we need. What, for example, can you understand from the following string of words?

> the smaller size costs much more than it should on the average the product performs poorly in test markets the labels do not appeal to younger shoppers that seems to be what were up against and what we must resolve bellowed the vice president of marketing before we can think of redoing our advertising campaign

To make this passage intelligible, we need to add two other kinds of punctuation: (1) changes in the size and design of letters, namely, **capitals** and **italics**; and (2) marks or points, namely, **periods, commas, quotation marks, apostrophes**, and other special signs.

> "The smaller size costs much more than it should, on the average the product performs poorly in test markets, the labels do not appeal to younger shoppers—that seems to be what we're up against and what we must resolve," bellowed the vice president of marketing, "before we can think of redoing our advertising campaign."

The example shows four functions of punctuation:

1 **End punctuation.** Capitals, periods, question marks, and exclamation points indicate sentence beginnings and endings.

2 **Internal punctuation.** Commas, semicolons, colons, dashes, and parentheses within sentences show the relationship of each word or group of words to the rest of the sentence.

3 **Direct-quotation punctuation.** Quotation marks indicate speakers and changes of speaker. Brackets and ellipses indicate that words have been added to or omitted from the original text.

4 **Word punctuation.** Capitals, italics, quotation marks, apostrophes, and hyphens indicate words that have a special character or use.

In questions of punctuation there is often no absolute standard, no authoritative convention to which you can turn for a "correct" answer. But two general rules serve as reliable guides:

1 Punctuation is a part of meaning, not a substitute for clear and orderly sentence structure. Before you can punctuate a sentence properly, you must construct it properly.

2 Observe conventional practice in punctuation. Though many of the rules are not hard and fast, still there is a community of agreement about punctuating sentences. Learning and applying the punctuation rules that follow will help you observe these conventions.

31 End Punctuation

Periods, question marks, and exclamation points signal the end of a sentence. Use a **period** after statements or commands; use a **question mark** after questions; use an **exclamation point** after strongly emotional expressions.

Ordinarily, the character of the sentence dictates the proper end punctuation; for instance, a clearly interrogative sentence calls for a question mark. Occasionally, however, your readers will not be able to tell from content or structure alone what you intend the meaning of a sentence to be. In such cases, end punctuation is vital to meaning. For example, notice the different intentions of the three following sentences and how the end punctuation contributes to meaning:

> He struck out with the bases loaded.
>
> He struck out with the bases loaded?
>
> He struck out with the bases loaded!

The Period

31 a Use a period to signal the end of a statement, a mild command, or an indirect question.

STATEMENT	She swam the mile with easy strokes.
COMMAND	Swim with easy strokes.
INDIRECT QUESTION	I asked her where she learned to swim with such easy strokes.

31 b Use periods with initials of names and abbreviations ending with lower-case letters.

Robert A. Heinlein	Mr.	Ms.	Sen.
Dr. J. I. Kalwani	Mrs.	etc.	St.

The trend is to omit periods in abbreviations made up of capital letters. Always omit periods in abbreviations that serve as names of organizations, corporations, and government agencies.

RN	PhD	NY	NFL
CPA	BS	CA	UNICEF
PTA	MBA	CARE	CIA

If you are unsure whether to use periods in an abbreviation, consult a good dictionary or the style manuals of professional organizations in your field.

The Question Mark

31 c **Use a question mark after a direct question.**

Direct questions often begin with an interrogative pronoun or adverb (*who, when, what,* etc.) and usually have an inverted word order, with the verb before the subject.

> When did you study chemistry?
>
> Do you ever wonder what your future will be?
>
> You want to make a good impression, don't you?

31 d **Use a question mark inside parentheses (?) to indicate doubt or uncertainty about the correctness of a statement.**

This device shows that, even after research, you could not establish the accuracy of a statement. However, using it does not serve as a substitute for checking facts.

> John Pomfret, an English poet, was born in 1667 (?) and died in 1702.

Rather than using (?), you may simply use *about*:

> John Pomfret, an English poet, was born about 1667 and died in 1702.

Do not use a question mark as a form of sarcasm:

> It was an amusing (?) play.

31 e **Do not use a question mark after an indirect question.**

An **indirect question** is a statement implying a question but not actually asking one. Though the idea expressed is interrogative, the actual structure is not: The subject and verb are not inverted.

> They asked me whether I had studied chemistry in high school.
>
> He asked me whether I wished to make a good impression.
>
> I wonder what my future will be.

A polite request phrased as a direct question may sometimes be followed by a period rather than a question mark, especially when the intent is more like that of a mild command than an actual question.

> Here is my draft of the committee's report. *When you have finished adding your comments, would you please return it to me.*

However, if you do not use a question mark, you run some risk of your reader's failing to realize that a request has been made. The safest practice is to use the question mark with such requests, particularly if you want a direct response on the reader's part.

The Exclamation Point

31 **f** Use an exclamation point after an interjection or after a statement that is genuinely emphatic or exclamatory.

Fire! Help! Oh, no!

Mom! Dad! Guess what! I've been accepted to law school!

The rocket's engines have ignited, and we have liftoff!

31 **g** Do not overuse the exclamation point.

Used sparingly, the exclamation point gives real emphasis to individual statements. Overused, it either deadens the emphasis or introduces an almost hysterical tone in your writing.

> War is hell! Think of what it does to young people to have their futures interrupted and sometimes cut off completely! Think of what it does to their families! Think of what it does to the nation!

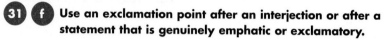

Exercise 31.1

Supply the appropriate punctuation marks in the following sentences and paragraph. If you feel that a choice of marks is possible, state why you chose the one you did. After completing the sentences, go back and revise the indirect questions to make them direct questions, and punctuate accordingly.

Sentence Practice

1 My roommate asked me last night if I knew what the term *Cinco de Mayo* means

2 According to my history professor, Muriel B. Harrison, *Cinco de Mayo* is a Mexican holiday that celebrates the anniversary of the Battle of Puebla on May 5, 1862

3 Who was involved in the Battle of Puebla

4 Dr Harrison, who has a PhD in Latin American history, told us that the Mexican troops, who were outnumbered three to one, defeated the French troops of Napoleon III

5 Wow Defeating an army when you're outnumbered three to one is quite a feat.

Paragraph Practice

Diego Rivera is one of Mexico's most famous modern painters, but did you realize that you can also see his work at the Detroit Institute of Arts If you ever go to Detroit, be sure to see Rivera's murals in which he painted scenes of industry in America When I was there last spring, a museum guide

asked if I had ever seen any of Diego Rivera's paintings in Mexico In fact, I
did see his huge murals of Mexican life when I visited the Palace of Fine Arts
in Mexico City several years ago The murals were fantastic

In Your Own Words

Write a paragraph about a suspenseful situation you found yourself in.
Include at least one sentence ending with a question mark and one sentence
ending with an exclamation mark.

Internal Punctuation

End punctuation indicates whether a whole sentence should be read as
a question, a statement, or an expression of emotion. Internal punctuation
indicates the relationships and relative importance of elements within
the sentence. Five punctuation marks are used for this purpose: **commas,
semicolons, colons, dashes,** and **parentheses**.

In studying the rules discussed in the following chapters, notice
not only how each mark is used but also how it contributes to the total
meaning of the sentence.

32 The Comma

Commas separate the parts of a sentence from one another. When commas
are used in certain conventional ways, they can help readers understand your
intended meaning and guide them through complex sentence structures.

 **Use a comma to separate main clauses joined by
a coordinating conjunction.**

● 1 **The coordinating conjunctions are** *and, but, or, nor, for, so,*
and *yet.* When any one of these conjunctions is used to connect main
clauses, it is always preceded by a comma. The comma acts as a signal that
one independent clause has ended and the next is about to begin.

> Half a million colonists remained loyal to the British Crown during the
> American Revolution, *and* for their loyalty many of them lost their homes,
> property, and livelihoods.

> History books used to portray Loyalists as conniving aristocrats with British
> connections, *but* research has revealed that most were ordinary hard-working
> farmers and tradespeople.

> Rebel patriots physically abused some Loyalists, *or* more often they verbally
> abused those who would not shift their allegiance.

There are, however, two exceptions, noted next.

● **2 Some writers omit the comma before the coordinating conjunction when one or both of the main clauses are very short.**

> The spirit is willing but the flesh is weak.
>
> Get your coat and let's go.

The use of a comma in such sentences is not wrong, and since the comma is sometimes necessary for clarity, it's a good idea simply to establish the habit of using a comma regularly.

● **3 When one or both of the main clauses joined by a coordinating conjunction are long or internally punctuated, use a semicolon before the coordinating conjunction.**

> The Canadian Mounted Police were established in the 1870s to assure peaceful settlement of the northwest wilderness; and they became symbols of political and social order.
>
> The Mounties, dressed in red tunics and riding well-trained horses, were a familiar sight on the Canadian frontier; but few people in the United States saw Mounties except in the movies.

Exercise 32.1

Sentence Practice

Combine the following sentences by using a coordinating conjunction and a comma. If one or both of the main clauses are long or internally punctuated, use a semicolon before the coordinating conjunction. If you have a choice of conjunctions, be prepared to explain your selection.

1　In Amsterdam, the tall and narrow seventeenth-century house where Anne Frank and her family spent two years hiding during World War II is now a museum. Over 500,000 visitors come to the house each year.

2　When they tour the museum, visitors can see permanent displays of photographs of the Frank family, various documents, and World War II materials. The museum also presents changing exhibitions, many of which deal with events of the war and the Holocaust.

3　The German-Jewish Frank family had to go into hiding in rooms in the upper part of the house. The Nazis would have sent them off to the death camps.

4　Anne Frank and her family were discovered on August 4, 1944. Anne and her sister were first sent to Westerbrook, a Jewish transit camp, then to Auschwitz, and finally to Bergen-Belsen, the concentration camp where they died.

5　Anne Frank was only sixteen when she died. She left a diary which is an insightful account of the horrors of war and repression as well as an account of the goodness of people such as those who risked their own lives to hide the Frank family.

6 *The Diary of Anne Frank* was published in 1947 and remains popular today. Editions of the book have been printed in over thirty countries.

Paragraph Practice

Using coordinating conjunctions preceded by commas, combine at least eight of the sentences in the following paragraph. Use a semicolon before the coordinating conjunction if main clauses are long or internally punctuated.

> Amsterdam is the capital of the Netherlands. The city is also one of Europe's great commercial and artistic cities. Visitors to Amsterdam should not miss seeing the Rembrandt collection in the Rijks Museum. They should also not leave the city without seeing the Van Gogh collection at the Municipal Museum. Amsterdam is also an important European port. The city is built on two rivers, the Ij and the Amstel. Canals running through the city link it to the North Sea and the Rhine River, one of Europe's most important waterways. Visitors can stroll across some of the bridges that cross Amsterdam's canals. They can wander through the narrow streets and admire the seventeenth-century architecture.

In Your Own Words

Write a paragraph describing your room. In it use five of the coordinating conjunctions (*and, or, for, nor, but, so,* and *yet*). Use at least two of them between main clauses.

32 **b** Use a comma to separate introductory phrases and clauses from a main clause.

Introductory phrases and clauses may be adverbial, modifying the verb in the main clause or the whole main clause; or they may serve as adjectives, modifying the subject of the main clause. Whatever their function, they should always be separated from the main clause by a comma unless they are very short and there is no possibility of misreading.

INTRODUCTORY   *According to legend,* Hercules had enormous strength. [adverbial]
PREPOSITIONAL   *Like any man of sense and good feeling,* I abominate work.
PHRASES   [adjectival]

—Aldous Huxley

INTRODUCTORY   *To succeed as a long-distance runner,* a person must have strong
VERBAL   legs. [adverbial]
PHRASES   *Announcing a recess,* the judge retired to his chambers. [adjectival]
                Exhausted by her effort, the swimmer fell back into the pool.
                [adverbial]
                To be quite honest about it, that dog has been known to climb
                trees. [adverbial]

INTRODUCTORY   *As soon as she had finished studying,* she left the library. [adverbial]
CLAUSES   *If your job is to write every day,* you learn to do it like every
                other job. [adverbial]

—William Zinsser

> *Whenever I hear anyone arguing for slavery,* I feel a strong
> impulse to see it tried on him personally. [adverbial]
> —Abraham Lincoln

● **1 Verbal modifiers and verbals used as subjects.** Introductory
verbal modifiers are set off from the rest of the sentence by a comma;
verbals used as subjects are not.

VERBAL MODIFER	*Having been an arbitrator between labor and management for a decade,* he felt confident in tackling one more labor dispute.
VERBAL AS SUBJECT	*Having been an arbitrator between labor and management for a decade* made him feel confident in tackling one more labor dispute.

● **2 Very short clauses and phrases.** The comma is frequently omitted
after very short introductory clauses or phrases. However, even when the
introductory clause or phrase is very short, a comma is necessary if its
omission can cause misreading.

CLEAR	When they arrived she was taking the cat out of the piano. After my defeat I retired from public life.
CONFUSING	When he returned home was not what it used to be.
CLEAR	When he returned, home was not what it used to be.

Exercise 32.2

In the following sentences and paragraph, insert commas wherever they are
needed after introductory elements. Then write five sentences of your own
containing correctly punctuated introductory elements.

Sentence Practice
1 In spite of many differences between them Elvis Presley shares some interesting similarities with the nineteenth-century British poet Lord Byron.
2 Just as Byron caused crowds of female admirers to shriek and swoon in his
presence Presley also was mobbed by screaming fans who adored him.
3 Criticized widely for their immorality Byron and Presley traveled widely in
search of acceptance and inner peace and turned to drugs to combat their
loneliness and artistic frustrations.
4 To revolutionize their art was not the aim of either Byron or Presley though
Byron did expand the forms and uses of poetry just as Presley transformed
popular music in the United States.
5 Dying suddenly at age forty-two in 1977 in Memphis Presley today is still
being mourned by adoring fans, and Byron also was widely mourned when
he died at age thirty-six.
6 To see the tremendous similarity in Presley and Byron one need look no further than the fame and cultural impact each had.

Paragraph Practice

Among the many differences in Presley and Byron was their social class. Inheriting the title of baron at age ten Byron attended exclusive schools; Presley, on the other hand, was born into a poor family and attended public schools. Although both men suffered bouts of depression Byron responded to his suffering with a kind of cynicism and bitterness not as evident in Presley. Being drafted into the U.S. Army in 1958 Presley served two years, but Byron, who died after one year's fighting in Greece, joined the Greek rebels because he believed in their cause. Even though Byron and Presley differed from each other in many ways the significant cultural impact of each is strikingly similar.

In Your Own Words

Write a paragraph about an outdoor event you attended. In it use examples of at least one introductory clause and several short introductory words and phrases.

  **Use commas to set off nonrestrictive elements.
Do not use commas with restrictive elements.**

A **restrictive** element defines, limits, or identifies the meaning of the noun or pronoun it modifies. A restrictive element is essential to the meaning of the sentence; if it is removed, the meaning changes significantly. Restrictive words, phrases, clauses, and appositives *are not* set off with commas. (To review phrases, see Section **26g**; for clauses, see Section **26h**; for appositives, see Sections **8c** and **27a**.)

RESTRICTIVE A person *who is honest* will succeed.
MODIFIER REMOVED A person will succeed.

The second version of the sentence omits the most essential piece of information in the sentence: Only the *honest* person will succeed. Thus, *who is honest* is restrictive and should not be set off with commas.

A **nonrestrictive** element does not carry the basic meaning; thus, commas separate it from the rest of the sentence. Removing nonrestrictive elements omits some information but does not change the essential meaning of the sentence. Commas *are* used to set off nonrestrictive modifiers.

NONRESTRICTIVE Jacob North, *who is honest,* will succeed.
MODIFIER REMOVED Jacob North will succeed.

In the second version, the essential meaning of the sentence is preserved. *Jacob North* will succeed; his honesty may contribute to his success but is not a requirement for his achieving it. Commas set off the nonessential information.

● **1 Nonrestrictive elements: Use commas.** Words, phrases, clauses, and appositives are nonrestrictive if they refer to only one possible person, place, or thing. Elements that immediately follow proper nouns are usually nonrestrictive.

NONRESTRICTIVE CLAUSE	Oprah Winfrey, whose talk show I regularly watch, features controversial topics. [The proper noun is *Oprah Winfrey*.]
RESTRICTIVE CLAUSE	The talk show that I regularly watch features controversial topics. [The clause *that I regularly watch* is essential to the meaning of the sentence.]
NONRESTRICTIVE PHRASE	Oprah Winfrey, with her interest in social problems, educates her audience about ways to improve their situations. [The prepositional phrase is *with her interest in social problems*.]
RESTRICTIVE PHRASE	A talk show with an interest in social problems may educate its audience about ways to improve their situations.
NONRESTRICTIVE APPOSITIVE	Oprah Winfrey, one of the most popular talk show hosts, stimulates her audience to think about social issues.
RESTRICTIVE APPOSITIVE	The popular talk show host Oprah Winfrey stimulates her audience to think about social problems. [Notice that the proper noun comes after *The popular talk show host*. Removing *Oprah Winfrey* would omit the most essential piece of information.]

● **2** *Two* **commas set off a nonrestrictive element.** Unless the nonrestrictive element begins or ends the sentence, the "opening" comma must have a "closing"comma to balance it.

NOT	The gate, unlocked and wide open swung on its hinges.
BUT	The gate, unlocked and wide open, swung on its hinges.
	Unlocked and wide open, the gate swung on its hinges.

● **3 Restrictive elements: No commas.** Words, phrases, clauses and appositives that are needed to identify precisely "who" or "which one" are restrictive. Words, phrases, clauses, and appositives modifying indefinite pronouns (such as *anyone, somebody,* etc.) are usually restrictive. Adjective clauses beginning with *that* or having an unexpressed introductory word are restrictive (see Section **26h**).

RESTRICTIVE CLAUSE	The bank that I use recently increased its service charge. [adjective clause beginning with *that*]
NONRESTRICTIVE CLAUSE	First National Bank, which has been my bank for five years, recently increased its service charge.
RESTRICTIVE CLAUSE	The service charge I already pay is high. [*That* is unexpressed in the clause *that I already pay*.]

NONRESTRICTIVE CLAUSE	The current service charge, which I pay monthly, is already high.
RESTRICTIVE PHRASE	Everyone who has an account at this bank must be angry about the increase. [indefinite pronoun]
NONRESTRICTIVE PHRASE	My parents, who also have an account at First National, are angry about the increase.
RESTRICTIVE APPOSITIVE	My friends Alex and Judith have already changed banks as a result of the new fees. [identifies which friends]
NONRESTRICTIVE APPOSITIVE	The new service charge, a 50 percent increase, will probably cost the bank some other customers.

● **4 Ambiguous meaning.** In some sentences, setting or not setting off the modifier with commas is the only way to make your meaning clear to readers. Decide which meaning you intend and use commas appropriately.

RESTRICTIVE	The onions simmering in beef broth taste sweet.
NONRESTRICTIVE	The onions, simmering in beef broth, taste sweet.

The first sentence implies that there are other onions not being simmered in beef broth that don't taste sweet. The second sentence indicates that there is a single batch of onions, all of which are being cooked in broth.

RESTRICTIVE	The student recognized for the discovery will be eligible for a large scholarship.
NONRESTRICTIVE	The student, recognized for the discovery, will be eligible for a large scholarship.

The nonrestrictive sentence has as its subject a particular student who will be eligible for a scholarship, and the fact that the student has been recognized for the discovery is additional detail about the student. The restrictive sentence makes recognition for the discovery a condition for receiving the scholarship; that is, *only* the student who has made the discovery will be eligible for the scholarship.

Exercise 32.3

In the following sentences and paragraph, insert commas to set off nonrestrictive elements. Indicate which sentences are correct as written. Then write five sentences of your own—correctly punctuated—by creating three sentences with nonrestrictive elements and two sentences with restrictive elements.

Sentence Practice

1 Bread which seems to be a universal food appears in a variety of shapes throughout the world.
2 Anyone who has been to France has seen rows and rows of crisp baguettes in the bakeries.

3 Challah the traditional Jewish braided loaf is a symbol of the ceremonial bread that the priest in the ancient Temple of Jerusalem placed on the table.

4 Pita bread with its handy "pocket" for holding fillings is a traditional Middle Eastern bread.

5 People who think of bread only in terms of plastic-wrapped white loaves don't know what they're missing by not sampling some of these satisfying breads.

Paragraph Practice

Some of the most delicious breads in the world come from India where most breads are unleavened. In India the term *roti* means bread, and many of these unleavened breads resemble the tortilla which is a well-known Mexican bread in shape. *Pooris* which puff up like balloons are flattened disks of dough fried in hot oil. The *chapati* a bread made out of finely ground whole-wheat flour is a basic bread that is eaten throughout most of northern India. *Naan* bread one type of leavened bread made in India is baked in a *tandoor* a large clay oven.

In Your Own Words

Write a paragraph about your favorite food. In it include at least two examples of a nonrestrictive modifier and at least two examples of a restrictive modifier.

 Use a comma to set off adverbial phrases and clauses that follow the main clause and explain, amplify, or contrast it. Do not set off such elements if they are closely related to the main clause.

Adverbial phrases and clauses often *restrict* the meaning of main clauses that follow and are therefore essential to the meaning of the main clause. When they follow the main clause, restrictive adverbial clauses should not be set off by a comma. When adverbial clauses merely introduce additional *nonrestrictive* information, however, a comma is used to indicate that they are not essential to the meaning.

Consider the logic and meaning of the sentence when deciding whether to set off adverbial clauses and phrases. Note the following:

> We won't miss the beginning of the movie if we hurry.

> We haven't missed the beginning of the movie, even though we're late.

The first of the examples sets up *if we hurry* as the necessary condition for not missing the beginning of the movie. In the second, the main clause makes an unqualified statement of fact; the *even though* clause adds some information but does not change the meaning of the clause.

> Mrs. Jones must have decided not to go outdoors today because the snow hasn't been shoveled from the walk.

Mrs. Jones must have decided not to go outdoors today, because the snow hasn't been shoveled from the walk.

The first example states that the unshoveled walk is the reason Mrs. Jones has not gone outdoors. The unshoveled walk is an essential condition for keeping her indoors, as indicated by the lack of a comma before the *because* clause. In the second example, the comma before *because* tells us that the writer intends the clause to be nonrestrictive and the information to be understood as nonessential to the basic meaning of the sentence. The *because* clause merely provides evidence for the fact that Mrs. Jones has not gone outside.

Exercise 32.4

Insert commas in the following paragraph wherever they are needed to set off adverbial clauses or phrases. Indicate which sentences are correct as written. Then write five sentences of your own containing correctly punctuated adverbial clauses or phrases.

The ingredients and cooking methods involved in making chili often arouse heated debate because everyone seems to have a different opinion about what constitutes a perfect pot of chili. Some Texans claim that chili isn't authentic unless it's made with tiny cubes of chopped beef. Others believe that only pure chili powder should be used although many chili cooks use chili seasoning made of a blend of several spices. Some people think chili should contain only beef, tomato, and chili peppers even though many people add onions and beans. Finally there's also a hardy group of chili eaters who think that the concoction is truly authentic only if it's so spicy it burns the mouth.

32 e Use commas to set off all absolute phrases.

Absolute phrases consist of a noun or a pronoun followed by a present or past participle: *the sun shining brightly.* These economical but information-rich phrases modify the entire main clause in which they stand rather than any particular word or words in that clause. Always nonrestrictive, they supply explanatory detail rather than essential information. Thus they should always be set off by commas.

He was stretched out on his reclining chair in the full sun, *his eyes covered, his head thrown back, his arms spread wide.*

Other things being equal, short familiar words are better than long unfamiliar words.

They were waiting for us, *their figures defined by the light from the half-open door.*

Exercise 32.5

Insert commas in the following sentences to set off absolute phrases. Then write five sentences of your own that contain absolute phrases.

1 Their mats and steps placed before them the new students eagerly awaited the instructor's first directions in the step-aerobics class.

2 The students their fidgety bodies clad in the latest exercise fashions peered at each other and mentally critiqued each other's weight and shape.

3 The music blaring from gigantic speakers in the corner of the gym the class came to life under the instructor's increasingly difficult commands.

4 Several of the students lasted only ten minutes before they stumbled to the water fountain their lack of conditioning revealed in flushed and grimacing faces.

5 After forty-five minutes of torture, the class their bodies glistening with perspiration began to smile as they enjoyed the relaxing cool down and thought about their achievement.

32 **f** Use commas to set off parenthetical elements.

Words, phrases, and clauses that slightly interrupt the structure of a sentence are often called **parenthetical elements.** Although such elements may add to the meaning of the sentence or relate the sentence to a preceding sentence or idea, they are not essential to grammatical structure. Such elements include words of direct address, mild interjections, the words *yes* and *no*, transitional words and expressions, and phrases expressing contrast.

DIRECT ADDRESS	Can you show me, *Kathy,* how to punctuate this sentence? Will you speak a little louder, *George?*
MILD INTERJECTIONS	*Well,* Caridad said she was sorry. *Oh,* I hate stewed prunes.
TRANSITIONAL WORDS AND PHRASES	Sales taxes, *moreover,* hurt poor people severely. *On the other hand,* Quakers are opposed to military service.
CONTRASTED ELEMENTS	He had intended to write 1868, *not 1968.* Tractors, *unlike horses,* require gasoline. Insecticides and garden sprays now available are effective, *yet safe.*

Note that other elements of a sentence will interrupt its structure and require commas when they are inserted out of their normal grammatical order. Compare the following:

My grandmother always told me that work never killed anyone.
Work, *my grandmother always told me,* never killed anyone.

The exhausted and thirsty construction workers welcomed the cold beer.
The construction workers, *exhausted and thirsty,* welcomed the cold beer.

Always use two commas to set off a parenthetical element unless it begins or ends a sentence.

NOT   She noticed, however that tact worked wonders.
NOT   She noticed however, that tact worked wonders.
BUT   She noticed, however, that tact worked wonders.
       She noticed that tact worked wonders, however.

Exercise 32.6

In the following sentences and paragraph, insert commas to set off parenthetical elements. Then write five sentences of your own that contain parenthetical elements requiring commas.

Sentence Practice

1 Martina I am enjoying the works of some interesting Latin American writers for example Gabriel García Márquez and Jorge Luis Borges.
2 Latin American writers in fact have written some of the most innovative modern short stories and novels.
3 García Márquez like Borges and many other Latin American writers emphasizes political and intellectual issues.
4 Yes I do remember my dear friend that you did not like the beginning of *One Hundred Years of Solitude,* but you should try again I think because García Márquez won the Nobel Prize for it and other work.
5 A better beginning point with his work on the other hand perhaps would be his short stories for instance "A Very Old Man with Enormous Wings" and "The Handsomest Drowned Man in the World."

Paragraph Practice

    I can tell you in addition that Latin American writers developed a technique called *magical realism.* This technique makes the novels and stories seem real and believable, but on the other hand it allows the writer to introduce absurd characters and elements and treat them as if they were utterly believable. In Isabel Allende's novel *House of the Spirits* for instance one of the main characters is Clara the Clairvoyant, a woman with green hair who can foretell the future. In García Márquez's story "A Very Old Man with Enormous Wings," to cite a second example the reader is supposed to believe matter-of-factly that a poor man and his wife could pen up a scruffy fallen angel in their yard and charge money for the public to view him. Jorge Borges's story "The Garden of Forking Paths" seems to be a stimulating puzzle about the nature of time not simply a straightforward espionage story. Magical realism therefore helps the reader identify with seemingly real places and events while in contrast it makes the reader imagine reality in a new way through the introduction of nonreal elements.

32 g   Use commas to separate the items in a series.

A series consists of three or more words, phrases, or clauses of equal grammatical rank. The items of such a series are said to be *coordinate:* They have approximately equal importance. Typical series take the form *a, b,* and *c,* or the form *a, b,* or *c.*

St. Theresa was *humble, sincere,* and *devout.* [three adjectives]

Only a generation ago, the Navaho were *horsemen, nomads, keepers of flocks, painters in sand, weavers of wool, artists in silver,* and *singers of the yei-bie-chai.* [seven nouns, some modified by prepositional phrases]

—Edward Abbey

Her sails ripped, her engines dead, and *her rudder broken,* the vessel drifted helplessly. [three absolute phrases]

After the accident, the driver of the car had no idea of *who he was, where he came from,* or *how the accident happened.* [three dependent clauses]

And that's the news from Lake Wobegon, *where all the women are strong, all the men are good-looking, and all the children are above average.* [three dependent clauses introduced by a single conjunction]

—Garrison Keillor

Some writers treat three or more short, closely related independent clauses not joined by coordinate conjunctions as a series, separating them by commas rather than semicolons.

Some of the people said the elephant had gone in one direction, some said he had gone in another, some professed not even to have heard of any elephant.

—George Orwell

Use semicolons in such a series if you are not sure commas are appropriate.

Some writers omit the comma before *and* in simple *a, b,* and *c* series: violins, flutes and cellos; men, women and children. But since the comma is sometimes vital for clarity, it is preferable to establish the habit of always including it.

I am interested in a modern, furnished apartment with two bedrooms, kitchenette, living room, bathroom with shower, and garage.

Without the comma after *shower,* the writer seems to be asking for an apartment with a garage in the bathroom.

32 **h** Use commas to separate coordinate adjectives in a series. Do not use commas to separate cumulative adjectives.

Adjectives in a series are *coordinate* if each adjective modifies the noun separately. They are *cumulative,* not coordinate, if any adjective in the series modifies the total concept that follows it.

COORDINATE   The British colony of Hong Kong grew up around a *beautiful, sheltered, accessible* port.

CUMULATIVE   Hong Kong is the *third-largest international financial* center in the world.

In the first example, each adjective is independent of the other two; the three adjectives could be rearranged without seriously affecting the meaning of the sentence: *accessible, beautiful, sheltered* port; *sheltered, accessible, beautiful* port. Moreover, the conjunction *and* could be inserted in place of the commas and the basic meaning would remain—*beautiful* and *sheltered* and *accessible* port.

But in the second sentence the adjectives are cumulative and interdependent. *And* cannot be inserted between the adjectives, nor their order changed, without making nonsense of the original meaning: *third-largest* and *international* and *financial center; financial third-largest international center.* The adjectives in the second sentence constitute, in effect, a *restrictive* phrase, as distinct from the *nonrestrictive* quality of the adjectives in the first sentence, and therefore are not separated from one another by commas.

The same principles apply when only two modifiers precede the word being modified.

> *Huge, lumbering* freighters share Hong Kong's *busy deepwater* port with *ancient Chinese* junks.

In actual usage, punctuation of coordinate adjectives varies a great deal. Consider the following sentences:

CUMULATIVE   The *powerful new water-cooled* engine is very fuel-efficient.
COORDINATE   The *powerful, new, water-cooled* engine is very fuel-efficient.

Both sentences may be punctuated correctly: The lack of commas, or their inclusion, signals the writer's intentions and tells the reader how a series of adjectives is to be understood.

Exercise 32.7

In the following sentences and paragraph, supply commas where they are needed to separate sentence elements in a series. Then write five sentences of your own containing correctly punctuated elements in a series.

Sentence Practice

1 T-shirts and sweat shirts offer an amazingly varied colorful display of political slogans memorable places marketable products and art works.

2 T-shirts may come in shocking or sedate colors they may be long-sleeved or short-sleeved and they may have designs on the front or back or both.

3 The lowly utilitarian beginning of the T-shirt as underwear has nearly been forgotten in an age when people wear T-shirts to concerts restaurants and offices.

4 Similarly, sweat shirts no longer serve their original purpose as humble exercise clothing but advertise everything from environmental campaigns to athletic teams orchestras and universities.

5 Collectors of flamboyant unusual T-shirts and sweat shirts don't always have

to buy them because these kinds of shirts are often available free at such events as political rallies and fundraising events they are often included in convention packages and they are often gifts from friends and family who travel to exciting exotic places.

Paragraph Practice

Wearing sweat shirts and T-shirts has become so popular that I have collected a whole closet full: For parties I have glitzy sequined sweat shirts with ribbons for such public activities as shopping and movies I have several sedate looking ones for impressing my friends I have shirts with university logos and witty slogans and for cleaning and exercising I have some well-worn raggedy shirts. My friends and I wear these shirts to shock our more conservative friends to advocate our position on political concerns and to express our sense of belonging to certain groups. Detracting attention from our imperfect physiques protecting us from chills stretching with our every move, sweat shirts provide all sorts of comfort. In a pinch a sweat shirt can also serve as a rain jacket as a night shirt or as a pillow. When they are too faded and torn for even me to wear, sweat shirts and T-shirts make great dust rags serve excellently as packing material for breakable fragile objects and work well as bedding for pets.

In Your Own Words

Write a paragraph about an interesting place you have visited. In it, include at least one example of coordinate adjectives, one example of words in a series, one example of phrases in a series, and one example of clauses in a series (dependent or independent).

32 **i** Follow conventions for the use of commas in dates, addresses, geographical names, titles, and large numbers.

● **1 Dates.** If a date is written as month-date-year, use a comma between the date and the year. If such a date is in a sentence, use a comma after the year as well.

> The German surrender ended World War II in Europe on May 7, 1945.

> World War II began on September 1, 1939, when Germany invaded Poland.

If only the month and year are given, do not use commas.

> The Vietnam Women's Memorial was unveiled November 11, 1993, in Washington, D.C.

> The Vietnam Women's Memorial was unveiled in November 1993 in Washington, D.C.

If a date is written as day-month-year, use no commas.

> 11 November 1993   20 July 1946

● **2 Addresses.** Standard comma punctuation of addresses is as follows:

205 Hayes Street, San Francisco, California 94102

39 West 12th Street, Olean, NY 71402

When a geographical name or address appears within a sentence, use a comma after each part, including the state if no zip code is given. Do not use a comma between the state and the zip code.

ADDRESSES   She gave 39 West 12th Street, Olean, New York 71402, as her forwarding address.

GEOGRAPHICAL   He spent a month at Bremen, Germany, and the rest of his time
NAMES   in Tunbridge Wells, Kent, a small village in England.

● **3 Titles.** Use commas to separate names from titles when the title follows the name. If the name followed by a title occurs within a sentence, use a comma after the title as well as between the name and the title.

Katherine Dugald, M.D.

William Harrington, Sr.

The university recently announced the appointment of Katherine Dugald, M.D., to the faculty of the medical school.

● **4 Large numbers.** Use commas in large numbers to indicate thousands. Do not use commas in social security numbers, telephone numbers, zip codes, and the like.

1,249	Social Security number 391-07-4855
89,129	Telephone number (515)555-7669
1,722,843	Jamaica Plain, MA 02130

Use a comma to prevent misreading.

Sometimes in a sentence two words fall together so that they may be read two ways. In such instances, a comma may be necessary to prevent misreading even though no standard punctuation rule applies.

Long before, she had left everything to her brother.

Inside the house, cats are sometimes a nuisance.

People who can, take vacations in the summer.

Without a comma after *before*, the first sentence would momentarily confuse a reader, who would read *Long before she had left* as a single chunk of information. The comma in the second sentence prevents one from reading *house cats* as an adjective and noun, and in the third sentence from reading *can take* as a verb phrase. Often it is best to rewrite such sentences to avoid confusion.

For the misuse of the comma, see Section **36**. For the use of commas in quoted material, see Sections **37d–37f**.

Exercise 32.8

In the following sentences and paragraph, insert commas where conventional usage requires them or where they are needed to prevent misreading.

Sentence Practice

1 Sir Arthur Conan Doyle MD created Sherlock Holmes, the fictional detective who is as popular today as he was when he first appeared in the late 1800s.

2 Doyle's first story about Sherlock Holmes appeared in 1887, and since then over 1000 books have been written about the fifty-six stories and four novels that feature the brilliant detective.

3 Today Holmes's fans try to find the detective's fictional dwelling place at 221-B Baker Street London England.

4 In addition to Sherlock Holmes, Doyle also created John Watson MD Holmes's companion and foil.

5 To Watson Holmes often seems to be a genius as he explains to his friend that the deductions he has reached about a complex case are merely elementary.

Paragraph Practice

Edgar Allan Poe, who was born on January 19 1809 in Boston Massachusetts is often called the father of the modern detective story. Poe spent a year at the University of Virginia in Charlottesville Virginia and then entered West Point in July 1830. Poe stayed at West Point less than a year and then went to Baltimore Maryland to live with a relative and work as a journalist. "The Murders in the Rue Morgue," Poe's first detective story, appeared in *Graham's Magazine* in April 1841. Soon after C. August Dupin, the detective Poe had created for the story, became well known among readers for his courage and his deductive powers.

Writers Revising

Commas

Brad's English 101 assignment was to narrate a significant event so that readers would understand why and how it seemed significant to the writer. The following paragraphs are from one block of his paper on his six-week trip to Europe. Add commas wherever you think they are necessary, remove any you think are unnecessary, and then compare your editing choices with Brad's. His revision follows the draft.

Draft

```
     In Austria, I spent an unforgettable week with
the Staudlbauer family. As I look back now I realize
that the entire week I was learning about their cul-
ture. At the time however I didn't think of the
significance of this particular homestay. One evening
my homestay mother cooked a typical Austrian meal
```

that included Rindsbraten (pork roast) sauerkraut
knudel (dumplings) and a salad. After dinner my homestay father Peter and brother Patrick and I took a
leisurely bike ride on some of the beautiful winding
country roads. My father said he didn't speak English
but ironically the whole conversation was in English.
He followed my thoughts the best he could his eyes
speaking clearly what he could not say in words.

If you can go abroad and meet new friends. I've
never had so much fun learning before. I hope to
visit the Staudlbauers in 1997, after I get my
degree. Learning German, before I go back will help
me understand my homestay family and their culture
even better.

Revision

1 In Austria, I spent an unforgettable week   32b(2)
   with the Staudlbauer family. As I look back
2 now, I realize that the entire week I was   32b
3 learning about their culture. At the time, how-   32f
   ever, I didn't think of the significance of this   32f
   particular homestay. One evening my homestay
   mother cooked a typical Austrian meal that
4 included Rindsbraten (pork roast), sauerkraut,   32g
   knudel (dumplings), and a salad. After dinner
5 my homestay father, Peter, and brother, Patrick,   32c(1),
   and I took a leisurely bike ride on some of   32g
6 the nearby winding country roads. My father   32h
7 said he didn't speak English, but ironically   32a
   the whole conversation was in English. He fol-
8 lowed my thoughts the best he could, his eyes   32e
   speaking clearly what he could not say in
   words.
9 If you can go abroad and meet new friends.   32j
   I've never had so much fun learning before. I
10 hope to visit the Staudlbauers in 1997, after   32d
11 I get my degree. Learning German, before I go   32b(1)
   back will help me understand my homestay family and their culture even better.

Analysis

Brad's instructor had her students exchange papers and describe to their peer reviewers how they identified errors to correct during revision. Here is part of Brad's conversation with his peer reviewer, Knok.

"When I'm writing I don't pay much attention to things like commas. The last time I turned in a writing assignment, though, Ms. Rosen told me that I need to pay more attention to them. So when I was ready to edit this paper, I did two things: First, I put in the commas I was sure I needed. The ones I knew I needed were the commas in the series (error 4 in the revision) and the comma before *but* (error 7). This comma was easy for me to figure out because there were two different sets of subjects and verbs in the sentence, *father said* and *conversation was.*

"Second, I reviewed the chapter on commas in the handbook. It was just like learning a new game, which I love to do. I looked at a rule and then at my paper to see if the rule applied. I skipped the rules I already knew, so I started with Section 32b on introductory phrases and clauses. My very first sentence has an introductory phrase, but after reading the whole section I knew that *In Austria* was a very short one that didn't need a comma (error 1). The second sentence had an introductory clause, and when I compared my sentence to the examples in the book, I thought it was long enough to need a comma after it (error 2). The last sentence started with a verbal, *Learning German,* so I had to decide whether it was a verbal modifier or a verbal used as a subject. I figured out that if I couldn't find another subject in the sentence, the verbal must be the subject. I couldn't find another subject, so I didn't put a comma after the verbal (error 11).

"I thought Section 32c was hard to understand, and it took me a while to look at all my sentences for restrictive and nonrestrictive elements. But luckily, the book had an example in Section 32c1 that was just like my sentence about my father and Peter (error 5). So I ended up putting commas before and after the nonrestrictive appositives *Peter* and *Patrick.* Comparing Section 32d with my sentence about wanting to visit my homestay family again (error 10), I decided that because I definitely want to get my degree before I go back, the clause *after I get my degree* was a necessary condition—so I didn't need to put a comma before it."

Brad discussed with Knok his method for finding seven of the eleven comma questions he found. Look at errors 3, 6, 8, and 9 in Brad's revision to find the remaining comma questions, and use the

Chapter 32 to explain to yourself why he decided to make the other changes he did. The appropriate sections are listed on the right side of the revision.

Finally, ask yourself this question: Did Brad adequately fulfill the original assignment? From these paragraphs, is it obvious to you why this homestay was significant to Brad? Why or why not? Refer to Chapters 2, 3, and 6 if you are not sure.

Review Exercises

Comma Usage

Part A

Insert commas where they are needed in the following sentences and paragraph.

Sentence Practice

1 *Martial arts* a phrase that refers to various forms of self-defense have become popular today as a method of learning how to protect oneself without a weapon.
2 Although many people think that martial arts refers only to karate a technique using blows with the side of the hand this group of self-defense methods also includes judo and kendo.
3 Created in the 1880s in Japan judo is based upon the principle of *jujitsu* a term referring to the basic techniques of martial arts.
4 Technically jujitsu skills should enable a smaller weaker person to overcome a larger stronger opponent.
5 Kendo is unusual in the array of martial arts forms leather-covered bamboo sticks being used as weapons by opponents.

Paragraph Practice

When modern marathon runners cross the finish line in famous races such as the New York Marathon the Boston Marathon or the Berlin Marathon they are participating in a run that has its roots in ancient Greece. According to tradition the first marathon runner an ancient Greek named Pheidippedes left the city of Marathon Greece to carry to Athens the news of a Greek victory over the Persians. When Pheidippedes made his run in 490 B.C. he covered a distance of 22 miles but today the modern marathon distance has been set at 26 miles and 385 yards. Modern marathons unlike that first run with its single runner include a field of thousands of runners who have an astonishing range of ages, abilities, and nationalities. In a recent New York City Marathon in fact three participants were 90 years old.

Part B

In the following paragraphs, insert any necessary commas.

American novelist Willa Cather who was born in the east and grew up in Nebraska wrote of the immigrants who settled the western prairies. Cather was born in Back Creek Valley Virginia but when she was ten years old her family moved to Nebraska. The Cather family settled on the Divide a high area of grassy windblown plains near the Kansas border. In this area which was often affected by blizzards droughts and invasions of insects Willa Cather came to know the various groups of immigrants who had also settled there. The Cathers' neighbors included French Swedish Czech German and Scotch-Irish settlers and several of her early short stories and novels such as *My Antonia* and *O Pioneers!* deal with the prairies and the people who started a new life in this harsh environment.

In 1884 the Cather family moved from the prairie to Red Cloud Nebraska and in 1890 Willa Cather went to the University of Nebraska at Lincoln. Planning to study science Cather however turned to writing. After leaving the university and the plains Cather went first to Pittsburgh and then to New York.

In 1912 Cather visited the southwestern part of the United States an area that continued to draw her back and to influence her later novels. For example Cather's novel *The Professor's House* draws upon experiences she had when she visited Mesa Verde a southwestern national park that could be reached only by wagon when Cather visited in 1915. In addition to *The Professor's House* Cather also set her novel *Death Comes to the Archbishop* in the southwest. In that 1927 novel set in New Mexico Cather writes of Jean Baptiste Lamy who was the first Archbishop of New Mexico. Although she had spent much of her life in the west Willa Cather spent her last years on Grand Manon Island which is located off Canada's east coast and she is buried in Jaffrey New Hampshire.

In Your Own Words

As you review the comma rules discussed in this chapter, list those that cause you problems in your writing. Write a paragraph analyzing why you think these particular comma problems are still occurring in your writing.

 # **The Semicolon**

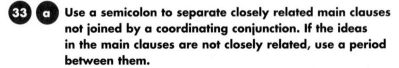 **Use a semicolon to separate closely related main clauses not joined by a coordinating conjunction. If the ideas in the main clauses are not closely related, use a period between them.**

Coordinating conjunctions (*and, but, or, nor, for, so,* and *yet*) add meaning to sentences, establishing explicit relationships of equality, addition, simultaneity, choice, contrast, and so forth between independent clauses: "Columbus 'discovered' America in 1492, *but* the Vikings got here before that. Norsemen writing to the Vatican reported voyages from Greenland to

Canada, *and* some people believe Columbus was aware of this information." At times, however, you may wish only to suggest relatedness between thoughts, rather than to add meaning. In those instances, a semicolon can be a very effective tool. Compare the following sentences.

> Columbus "discovered" America in 1492. The Vikings got here before that. Norsemen writing to the Vatican reported voyages from Greenland to Canada. Some people believe Columbus was aware of this information.

> Columbus "discovered" America in 1492; the Vikings got here before that. Norsemen writing to the Vatican reported voyages from Greenland to Canada; some people believe Columbus was aware of this information.

A period is a full stop, marking a complete break between sentences; in contrast, a semicolon separates and stops but does not fully break the flow of thought between grammatically independent statements. Be aware that a semicolon may be used only between word groups of equal grammatical rank (see Section **36i**).

> We organize time and myth with music; we mark our lives by it. Music is the way that our memories sing to us across time.
>
> —Lance Morrow

> At high tide the whole Atlantic rushed in, tossing the seaweeds in his mane; at low tide he rushed out, growling and gnashing his granite teeth.
>
> —Mary Antin

> Children begin by loving their parents; as they grow older they judge them; sometimes they forgive them.
>
> —Oscar Wilde

A comma is sometimes used to separate very short main clauses not joined by coordinating conjunctions, particularly if the clauses are parallel, as in "She is not a person, she is a legend" or "Some allow it, some don't." But the semicolon is always correct in such sentences—and safer for the inexperienced writer.

33 b   Use a semicolon to separate main clauses joined by a conjunctive adverb.

Conjunctive adverbs are words like *however, moreover, therefore, consequently, indeed,* and *then* that carry a thought from one main clause to the next. (See Section **26e** for a more extensive list; see Section **13b** for a discussion of semicolons and comma splices.)

> I ordered the concert tickets by mail; *therefore,* I didn't have to stand in line.

> Our muscles were tired and sore; *nevertheless,* we kept on jogging.

> On February 2 the groundhog saw its shadow; *consequently,* according to folk wisdom, we can expect six more weeks of winter weather.

You can distinguish conjunctive adverbs from other kinds of connecting words if you remember that they are the only ones that can be moved from the beginning of a clause to another position in that clause without changing the clause's meaning.

The band struck up a familiar tune; *indeed,* they were playing our song.

The band struck up a familiar tune; they were, *indeed,* playing our song.

When a conjunctive adverb comes within the second main clause instead of at the beginning, the clauses still must be separated by a semicolon and the conjunctive adverb set off by a pair of commas. Note that a conjunctive adverb that begins a main clause is followed by a single comma.

33 c Use a semicolon to separate main clauses joined by a coordinating conjunction if the clauses are long or internally punctuated.

The meeting last night, the most argumentative and confusing thus far, lasted until midnight; and unless something unexpected happens in the meantime, the next meeting may last even longer.

When New England was first settled, lobsters were plentiful all along the coast; and since the settlers depended heavily on the sea for their food, especially in the early years, they certainly must have eaten lobster frequently.

In some instances, even when relatively short main clauses are joined by a coordinating conjunction, a semicolon instead of a comma may be used for emphasis.

He could hear the excitement of their talk from the next room; but he could not distinguish what they were saying.

33 d Use a semicolon to separate the items of a series if the items themselves contain commas.

Compare the following sentences:

At courtside were Mr. Jones, the owner and the general manager, a referee, the coach, a former star player, and the current trainer of the team.

At courtside were Mr. Jones, the owner and the general manager; a referee; the coach, a former star player; and the current trainer of the team.

The number of people at courtside varies considerably, depending on the punctuation. Without semicolons, readers may have difficulty separating items into subsets.

In other cases, semicolons help to group items with accompanying lengthy modifying phrases or explanations.

The march had been an extraordinary conglomeration of different types of people: students; young middle-class families with children; punks with stiff green Mohawks; a band of bikers with fifties-style pompadours and big Moto Guzzi motorcycles.

—*The New Yorker*

Snobbery has traditionally been founded on birth; knowledge or pseudo knowledge, or merely self-assured ignorance, all of them amounting to the same thing in snob terms; access to power, status, celebrity; circumstances, such as the place one lives or even the things one does not do, such as watch television.

—Lance Morrow

Occasionally, semicolons add an effective emphatic touch as well as provide separation where commas exist.

The bureaucracy consists of functionaries; the aristocracy, of idols; the democracy, of idolators.

—G. B. Shaw

Note that in all the preceding examples semicolons are used to separate items of equal rank—coordinate elements.

Exercise 33.1

Part A

In the following sentence, insert semicolons or substitute them for commas wherever needed.

The itinerary for my trip this summer includes two days in Atlanta, Georgia, where I plan to visit my cousin at Morehouse College, three days in Orlando, Florida, where I want to spend some time at Disney World, a stop at Cape Canaveral, where I hope to get a glimpse of the launch site for the space shuttle, and finally, five days in Key West, where I plan to lie by the pool, do some skin diving, and eat some conch chowder.

Part B

In the following sentences, insert semicolons or substitute them for commas wherever needed.

1 Soccer is the world's most popular sport, this simple kicking game involves millions of players and probably billions of fans around the world.

2 The game of soccer most likely had its origins in a kicking game played in China 2,000 years ago, what we think of today as modern soccer originated in England in the 1850s.

3 Soccer is known as "football" in England, the sport goes by the name of football in many other countries as well.

4 Although it used to be played in the United States mainly at colleges and East Coast prep schools, soccer has become a popular sport for children because it requires little special equipment, furthermore, the activity suits children's physical development, and girls and boys can play on the same team.

5 Soccer's championship series, the World Cup, attracts a tremendous number of fans, although millions of American sports fans tune into the Super Bowl and the World Series, billions of television viewers around the world will watch the World Cup Tournament.

Part C

Combine at least eighteen of the twenty-two sentences in the following paragraphs by using a semicolon and conjunctive adverb that expresses the correct relationship between the clauses (see Section **26e** for a list of conjunctive adverbs). You may need to delete or rearrange some words to achieve smooth sentences.

Earthquakes have always been among nature's most frightening and devastating phenomena. The term *earthquake* describes a trembling or shaking movement of the earth. This trembling or shaking motion occurs because of the movement of opposing plates of rock along fault lines in the earth's crust. Most people have heard of the San Andreas Fault. It is part of a series of faults extending along an area of more than 600 miles in California. When the sections of a fault rub against each other, vibrations move through the earth. An earthquake occurs. These vibrations can also cause a *tsunami,* or tidal wave. These waves attain tremendous speed and force and can devastate coastal areas. *Tsunami* are often set off by earthquakes. Volcanic eruptions can also set off these giant ocean waves.

Earthquakes terrified and mystified people in the past. Sophisticated systems now allow modern scientists to measure the movements of the earth. These scientists, who are called seismologists, can sometimes predict that an earthquake may occur. Earthquakes themselves are measured on the Richter scale. The Richter scale indicates the amount of energy released at the earthquake's origin deep within the earth.

Not all parts of the earth are subject to frequent or severe earthquakes. Some areas are considered earthquake belts because they are near known fault lines. In the twentieth century, advances in science and technology have enabled city planners in earthquake belts to construct new buildings that are better able to withstand the shock of an earthquake. Today, buildings are less likely to suffer severe damage in an earthquake than they were in the past. Nothing is totally earthquake proof. These frightening movements of the earth can still cause much damage and destroy life, as the San Francisco and Los Angeles earthquakes of the 1990s proved.

In Your Own Words

Write a paragraph about shopping for a recent purchase. In the paragraph include at least one example of a semicolon used to join main clauses and one example of a semicolon separating items in a list when some of the items contain commas.

 The Colon

Whereas the semicolon always indicates a full stop, the colon indicates that what follows will explain, clarify, or illustrate the information in the preceding clause.

Use a colon to separate a main clause and another sentence element when the second explains, illustrates, or amplifies the first.

It is safe to predict what prices will do in the next decade: They will go up.

If you're considering a hat, remember this cardinal rule: Never try to wear a hat that has more character than you do.

Charm, in the abstract, has something of the quality of music: radiance, balance, and harmony.

—Laurie Lee

There are two times in a man's life when he should not speculate: when he can't afford it and when he can.

—Mark Twain

34 b **Use a colon to set off a list or series, including those introduced by *the following* or *as follows*.**

Anything is possible on a train: a great meal, a binge, a visit from card players, an intrigue, a good night's sleep, and strangers' monologues framed like Russian short stories.

—Paul Theroux

If you are interested in reading further about usage, we recommend the following books: Evans, *A Dictionary of Contemporary American Usage;* Follet, *Modern American Usage;* and Bernstein, *The Careful Writer.*

The recommended treatment for a cold is as follows: plenty of fluids, bed rest, and aspirin for fever.

Make sure that a *complete* sentence precedes the colon. *Do not use a colon after a partial statement,* even when that partial statement uses words like *including* or *such* as that indicate a list will follow.

NOT   We rented several classic Bogart movies, including: *Casablanca, Key Largo,* and *The Maltese Falcon.*

BUT   We rented several classic Bogart movies, including *Casablanca, Key Largo,* and *The Maltese Falcon.*

NOT   Tours to Australia feature stops such as: Melbourne, Sydney, and Canberra.

BUT   Tours to Australia feature stops such as Melbourne, Sydney, and Canberra.

OR   Tours to Australia feature such stops as the following: Melbourne, Sydney, and Canberra.

NOT   My favorite foods are: strawberries, chocolate cake, shrimp, and asparagus with hollandaise sauce.

BUT   My favorite foods are strawberries, chocolate cake, shrimp, and asparagus with hollandaise sauce.

See Section **36k** for more discussion of inappropriate use of colons in lists.

34 **c** Use a colon to introduce a formal quotation.

The Sixteenth Amendment set up the income tax: "The Congress shall have power to lay and collect taxes on incomes, from whatever source derived, without apportionment among the several states, and without regard to any census or enumeration."

In *Counseling Psychology,* Charles J. Gelso and Bruce R. Fretz offer a definition of cross-cultural counseling that is gaining acceptance among counselors and psychologists: "We share the emerging current view that cross-cultural counseling should refer to *all* counseling that deals with clients whose values and perceptions of reality are different from the counselor's. From this perspective, men counseling women or women counseling men are engaging in cross-cultural counseling. An Asian-American counseling a Hispanic, an atheist counseling a fundamentalist, and a black 25-year-old counseling a black 85-year-old are all engaged in cross-cultural counseling."

34 **d** Use a colon to separate items in biblical citations, titles and subtitles, and divisions of time.

BIBLICAL CITATION   Isaiah 40:28-31
SUBTITLE   *The Panda's Thumb: More Reflections in Natural History*
DIVISION OF TIME   9:20 A.M.   10:10 P.M.

Exercise 34.1

In the following sentences and paragraph, insert colons wherever they are needed. Then write five sentences of your own that use colons in various ways.

Sentence Practice

1 Travel teaches us valuable lessons tolerance for ideas different from our own, knowledge of others' customs and cultural history, and the importance of self-reliance and independence.

2 Whether it's a quick weekend at a favorite campsite or a leisurely trip to China, a trip transforms most travelers in one major way it makes them more flexible.

3 When travelers overcome their prejudices and rigid expectations, everything becomes a welcome adventure the new foods they try, the challenges they meet in an unfamiliar train or bus system, they challenges they may confront in scheduling meals and sleep.

4 My Aunt Victoria, who has traveled to more than thirty countries, recently expressed to me the secret of her happiness as a traveler "Always assume that you will be spending the rest of your life in whatever place you visit and that you must, therefore, learn as much as you can about everything and make friends with as many people as you can so that you can be a member of the community all the quicker."

5 Thus, if my plane lands in Minneapolis or Denver at 320 P.M., by 4 P.M., I am trying to follow my Aunt Victoria's advice I am trying to converse with other passengers on the local bus, I buy and scan the local newspaper, and I make plans to take in one or two of the nontourist places and events the locals enjoy.

Paragraph Practice

On a recent trip to Ireland with my university's choral group, I was overwhelmed by the beauty of the country the haunting starkness of the stoney Burren contrast strikingly with the lush greenness of the countryside. Having only three days in Dublin frustrated us because the city offers a wide array of sights Phoenix Park, Dublin Castle, Trinity College, St. Patrick's Cathedral, and the Abbey Theatre, to name only a few of the famous sights. My favorite place in all of Ireland, however, is the most remote spot we visited the Aran Islands, which are about thirty miles out in the Atlantic from Galway. As much as I loved the pony cart ride to an old Roman fort and a long hike, the blowing cold rain made me happy, nevertheless, to see our ferry arrive at 530 P.M. After this splendid trip to Ireland, I have reached one conclusion the luck of the Irish is that they get to live in beautiful Ireland!

In Your Own Words

Write a paragraph about a personal goal and some steps you are taking to achieve it. In the paragraph include at least one sentence which uses the colon to separate a main clause and another sentence element (either another main clause, a dependent clause, a phrase, or a single word).

 ## **The Dash and Parentheses**

Both dashes and parentheses set off interrupting comments, explanations, examples, and other parenthetical elements from the main thought of the sentence. Commas are ordinarily used when parenthetical elements are closely related in the main thought of the sentence. Dashes and parentheses are used when the interruption is abrupt and the element set off is only loosely related to the main thought of the sentence.

Dashes emphasize the element being set off and give it greater importance than parentheses do. Parentheses are used when the element enclosed is an incidental explanatory comment, an aside, or a nonessential bit of information.

A single dash is used following an introductory element or preceding a final sentence element. A pair of dashes is used to enclose an element within a sentence. Parentheses are always used in pairs around the enclosed element. In handwriting, distinguish the dash from the hyphen by making the dash longer. In typewritten copy and computer printouts, use two hyphens, with no spacing between them or on either side, to indicate the dash.

The Dash

35 a Use the dash or a pair of dashes to mark an abrupt shift in sentence structure or thought.

Could she—should she even try to—borrow money from her aunt?

The Queen of England never carries money—too unseemly—but travels with ladies in waiting who pay from the royal purse for whatever Her Majesty fancies.

That puppy is going to grow up to be enormous—check out the size of his paws—and will eat us out of house and home.

35 b Use the dash to emphasize nonrestrictive appositives and other parenthetical elements.

See Sections **32c** and **32f** for a discussion of appositives and parenthetical elements.

Resorts seeking to expand to other base facilities, such as Winter Park, are also considering the use of funiculars—railroad cars pulled along a track—which can carry up to 5,000 [people] hourly.

—Skiing

I think extraterrestrial intelligence—even beings substantially further evolved than we—will be interested in us, in what we know, how we think, what our brains are like, the course of our evolution, the prospects for our future.

—Carl Sagan

An American reader of translated Chinese poems may be taken aback—even put off—by the frequency, as well as the sentimentality of the lament for home.

—Yi-Fu-Tuan

Each person is born to one possession which overvalues all his others—his last breath.

—Mark Twain

35 c Use the dash to set off internally punctuated appositives or other parenthetical elements.

To prevent confusion, use dashes rather than commas to set off appositives containing punctuated items in a series. In the following sentence the word *object* appears to be one item in a series.

Putting a spin on an object, a top, a bullet, a satellite, gives it balance and stability.

But when the commas are replaced by dashes, the meaning is clear.

Putting a spin on an object—a top, a bullet, a satellite—gives it balance and stability.

Here is another example:

> Because I have so little regard for most of O'Neill's plays, and especially for those hallowed late plays of his—*A Moon for the Misbegotten, The Iceman Cometh,* and *A Touch of the Poet*—I am relieved to have a chance to repeat my opinion that *Long Day's Journey Into Night* is the finest play written in English in my lifetime.
>
> —Brendan Gill

35 d Use the dash to set off introductory lists or summary statements.

Gather data, tabulate, annotate, classify—the process seemed endless to the research assistant.

Black flies, horseflies, little triangular flies, ordinary house flies, unidentified kinds of flies—those are what I mean when I say I'm sick of flies.

35 e Use the dash to show interruption or hesitation in speech.

"Why don't you—" He stopped abruptly and looked away.

"Well, I—uh—we—some of us really want to drop your plan."

Parentheses

35 f Use parentheses to set off information, explanation, or comment that is incidental or nonessential to the main thought.

But according to Hall, in many Mediterranean Arab cultures there are only three sets of time: no time at all, now (which is of varying duration) and forever (too long).

> —Robert Levine and Ellen Wolff

More than 1,000 years ago, the Hopis (the word means "the peaceful ones") settled in the mesa-dotted farmland of northern Arizona.

> —Time

Among the narratives in the text, Maya Angelou's (pp. 58-68) is my favorite.

35 g Use parentheses to enclose numbers or letters labeling items listed within sentences.

To check out a book from our library, proceed as follows: (1) check the catalog number carefully; (2) enter the catalog number in the upper left-hand corner of the call slip; (3) fill out the remainder of the call slip information; and (4) hand in the call slip at the main desk.

Exercise 35.1

In the following sentences and paragraph, insert dashes or parentheses wherever they are needed.

Sentence Practice

1 Crossword puzzles are a great pastime some would say a complete waste of time for many people who love language or who love puzzles.

2 Special phrases, puns, odd definitions those are the elements that make crosswords especially intriguing to many people.

3 Crossword lovers usually do the puzzles for one of several reasons to pass the time pleasantly, to improve their vocabulary, or to sharpen their memory.

4 Some people buy leading daily newspapers the *New York Times,* the *Boston Globe,* or *The Los Angeles Times,* for example not for the news but for the crossword puzzles.

5 My friend Claude I should say my fellow crossword addict Claude does not consider reading the headlines of the daily newspaper until he has worked the crossword with an ink pen, no less!

Paragraph Practice

One day I decided to educate Claude never a simple task about the history of the crossword, offering to treat him to a pizza if he could tell me when and where the crossword originated. Thoughtful for a couple of minutes, Claude seemed stumped, but then he said falteringly: "Crosswords well let me see they were uh, now I recall they were introduced in England in the last century as a pastime for children." He was right he nearly always is and I ended up buying the pizza and hearing more detailed history of the crossword. Claude intrigued me with the following: 1 the first crossword published in the United States appeared December 21, 1913, in the New York *World*; 2 within ten years crosswords were in high demand in most daily newspapers; and 3 from the United States the popularity of crosswords traveled back to England, where they became a craze among adults. Claude, who has been doing crosswords since he was eight he is now twenty-nine says that no matter what reason they give for doing the puzzles, people do them for only one reason completing or nearly completing a crossword makes them feel intelligent.

In Your Own Words

Write a paragraph about a couple of habits you have that other people often find annoying. In this paragraph include at least one sentence which uses parentheses and at least one sentence that uses dashes.

 # Superfluous Internal Punctuation

Careful punctuation helps readers separate words and ideas and group related words together. Inadequate punctuation can force a reader to go over a passage several times to get its meaning. But too many marks of punctuation confuse a reader as much as too few marks.

The following sentence, for example, is jarring because of unnecessary and confusing punctuation.

> The people of this company, have, always, been aware, of the need, for products of better quality, and lower prices.

None of the commas in this sentence is necessary. Many of them are probably the result of pauses in the writer's thinking. Remember that correct punctuation does not derive from such pauses—but from the meaning the writer intended.

Use all the punctuation marks that will make the reader's work easier or that are required by convention. But do not insert unnecessary marks. Especially avoid the misuses of the comma, the semicolon, and the colon.

36 a Do not separate a subject from its verb unless intervening words require punctuation.

NOT The feminist movement, has rekindled interest in the Nancy Drew mysteries.

BUT The feminist movement has rekindled interest in the Nancy Drew mysteries.

Any intervening words requiring punctuation use **balanced** punctuation: a pair of commas, dashes, and so forth.

36 b Do not separate a verb from its object unless intervening words require punctuation.

NOT Caroline Keene wrote, the Nancy Drew series.

BUT Caroline Keene wrote the Nancy Drew series.

36 c Do not separate a preposition from its object.

NOT Caroline Keene was the pen name for, Edward L. Stratemeyer and also for, his daughter Harriet.

BUT Caroline Keene was the pen name for Edward L. Stratemeyer and also for his daughter Harriet.

36 d Do not separate a single or a final adjective from its noun.

NOT Stratemeyer's daughter took over writing the best-selling, highly entertaining, series.

BUT Stratemeyer's daughter took over writing the best-selling, highly entertaining series.

36 e Do not set off a restrictive modifier.

See Section **32c**.

NOT The plots, which she invented, were based on incidents from her own childhood and early adulthood.

BUT The plots which she invented were based on incidents from her own childhood and early adulthood.

NOT Many of her stories, about Africa, South America, and the Orient, reflect her travels to those places as a researcher and photographer.

BUT Many of her stories about Africa, South America, and the Orient reflect her travels to those places as a researcher and photographer.

Often, adverbial phrases and clauses that interrupt or follow a main clause *restrict* the meaning of the word or clause to which they are attached. They are therefore essential to the meaning and should *not* be separated by commas from what they modify (see also Section **32d**).

NOT Several Nancy Drew films, in 1939, added to the growing popularity of the series.

BUT Several Nancy Drew films in 1939 added to the growing popularity of the series. [The phrase *in 1939* restricts the meaning of the verb *added to*, telling when, and is thus essential to the meaning.]

NOT A whole generation of baby boomers grew up admiring Nancy Drew, for her courage and spirit of adventure.

BUT A whole generation of baby boomers grew up admiring Nancy Drew for her courage and spirit of adventure. [The phrase *for her courage and spirit of adventure* restricts the meaning of the participle *admiring*, telling why, and is thus essential to the meaning.]

36 f Do not separate two words or phrases joined by a coordinating conjunction.

NOT Harriet Stratemeyer wrote more than a hundred books, and created outlines for many others.

BUT Harriet Stratemeyer wrote more than a hundred books and created outlines for many others.

NOT Other pen names she used include Laura Lee Hope, and Franklin W. Dixon.

BUT Other pen names she used included Laura Lee Hope and Franklin W. Dixon.

36 g Do not separate an introductory word, brief phrase, or short clause from the rest of the sentence unless clarity or emphasis requires it.

NOT As Franklin Dixon, she wrote several books in the Hardy Boys series.

BUT As Franklin Dixon she wrote several books in the Hardy Boys series.

36 h Do not separate quotations that are part of a sentence's structure from the rest of the sentence.

NOT Harriet Stratemeyer said, she was lucky to have the creative influence of her gifted father.

BUT Harriet Stratemeyer said she was lucky to have the creative influence of her gifted father.

NOT My professor said that the Nancy Drew and Hardy Boys series have been, "substantially underrated" in terms of their influence on at least two generations of young readers.

BUT My professor said that the Nancy Drew and Hardy Boys series have been "substantially underrated" in terms of their influence on at least two generations of young readers.

36 i Do not use a semicolon to separate a main clause from a subordinate clause, a phrase from a clause, or other parts of unequal grammatical rank.

NOT Contemporary author Judy Blume writes novels that girls find appealing; because the books deal with problems they face.

BUT Contemporary author Judy Blume writes novels that girls find appealing because the books deal with problems they face.

NOT One of her books, *Are You There God? It's Me, Margaret.*, portrays a twelve-year-old; coping with uncertainty about religion.

BUT One of her books, *Are You There God? It's Me, Margaret.*, portrays a twelve-year-old coping with uncertainty about religion.

36 i Do not use a semicolon before a direct quotation or before a list.

NOT One reviewer said of Blume's *It's Not the End of the World*; "She believably delineates the bewilderment and anxiety afflicting the children of about-to-be-divorced parents."

BUT One reviewer said of Blume's *It's Not the End of the World*, "She believably delineates the bewilderment and anxiety afflicting the children of about-to-be-divorced parents."

NOT Blume realistically and sensitively addresses many things that worry young people; a new baby in the family, emerging sexuality, fitting in with new friends.

BUT Blume realistically and sensitively addresses many things that worry young people: a new baby in the family, emerging sexuality, fitting in with new friends.

36 k Do not use a colon between a verb and its object or complement or between and preposition and its object.

Even though the words that comprise the object or complement may be in series, as in a list, a colon is not needed to precede them. A colon precedes a list only when the words before it form a complete statement (see Section **34b**).

NOT Over more than twenty years, Blume has written: *Freckle Juice, Superfudge, Iggie's House,* and *Here's To You, Rachel Robinson!*, to name a few of her books.

BUT Over more than twenty years, Blume has written *Freckle Juice, Superfudge, Iggie's House,* and *Here's To You, Rachel Robinson!*, to name a few of her books.

NOT *Tiger Eyes* explores the feelings of a fifteen-year-old confused by: grief over her father's death, anger about her mother's dating, and dismay at a school friend's drinking problem.

BUT *Tiger Eyes* explores the feelings of a fifteen-year-old confused by grief over her father's death, anger about her mother's dating, and dismay at a school friend's drinking problem.

NOT Blume's books belong to the genre called "problem novels," and although the books have sad moments, they are not: depressing, bitter, or hopeless.

BUT Blume's books belong to the genre called "problem novels," and although the books have sad moments, they are not depressing, bitter, or hopeless.

Exercise 36.1

In the following sentences and paragraph, eliminate any superfluous commas, semicolons, or colons, substituting other punctuation as necessary.

Sentence Practice

1 Most people know that butterflies are among the many species of animals and insects that migrate; although most people do not realize the great distances these migrations cover, and the huge numbers of butterflies involved.

2 Scientists have tracked some migrations of: up to 2,400 butterflies, and they have been amazed to find that some butterflies can travel, up to 600 miles over water.

3 Even when migrating butterflies cannot see one another, amazingly they all follow, the same direction; not deviating from the route even when they encounter obstacles.

4 A recent article on migrating butterflies states that, a single migration in one area of the world can involve: as many as one and a half billion butterflies.

5 In the fall, one of the well-known, long-distance, migrants, the monarch butterfly, travels from Canada, and the northeastern United States to Mexico, a distance of, nearly 2,500 miles.

Paragraph Practice

Although scientists know that butterflies migrate long distances; they still do not know how the butterflies find their destination. Several of the possible methods that have been suggested are: that the butterflies follow the angle of the sun, that they use visual landmarks as guides, and that they are aided, by the earth's magnetic field. Not surprisingly, most butterflies travel, to escape unfavorable, drastic, changes in climate; moving from wet to dry areas or cold to warm ones. Some butterflies, that do not hibernate or become dormant, are constantly moving; never settling in one place. Most areas of the world, even deserts, have butterflies, and in most parts of the world some butterflies participate in long-distance migrations; while others are part of undramatic, hardly noticeable, migrations.

In Your Own Words

Review the discussion of superfluous internal punctuation. Then look over the last two pieces of writing you did. If you find that you have used unnecessary punctuation within sentences, write a paragraph explaining what you believe led you to do so. If any rules for internal punctuation are confusing, explain which ones seem to be giving you trouble.

Review Exercises

Internal Punctuation

The following sentences and paragraph require various kinds of internal punctuation. Supply the needed punctuation marks, and be prepared to explain your choices.

Sentence Practice

1 Because scuba diving equipment has become lighter safer and easier to use more people are trying out diving for recreation.

2 Before setting off for a diving vacation in a place like Key West Florida however amateur divers should take a scuba diving course.

3 These diving schools which usually offer classroom sessions as well as open water instruction are often run by diving shops therefore divers can rent or buy their equipment at the same time they sign up for classes.

4 To make sure a diving school is reputable prospective students should ask if the school is certified and they should also visit a class to see how diving training is conducted.

5 Once people learn to dive they often fall into one of two categories the kind of dedicated diver some might use the word *crazy* who puts on a wet suit to dive in December and the recreational diver who prefers to take off for the warm waters of the southern coast.

6 Some divers do what is called skin diving this popular fairly inexpensive form of diving involves using a face mask and a snorkel to dive just below the surface of the water.

7 If divers wish to go to greater depths they need to use a SCUBA an acronym that stands for Self-Contained Underwater Breathing Apparatus.

8 More serious underwater exploration requires a diving suit these suits were first invented in the seventeenth century but high-tech versions of them are still used by divers today.

9 Once divers learn the technique and feel comfortable underwater they often say they feel as though they have entered another world a world where the human being is the intruder.

10 Divers can participate in various types of group dives for example some diving shops organize tours to Florida or the Caribbean others set up dives to explore shipwrecks and some lead shark dives that allow divers to view sharks from the safety of underwater cages.

Paragraph Practice

The Cayman Islands three small islands located in the middle of the Caribbean Sea are a diver's paradise for the islands' beaches are protected by barrier reefs. The Cayman Islands the largest of which is Grand Cayman today have a population of over 17000. The islands are a British dependency their capital George Town is located on Grand Cayman. The islands' attractions white beaches clear and silt-free water and a tropical climate bring in many tourists each year but the area is still fairly unspoiled by overdevelopment. Short diving courses snorkeling trips and week-long advanced courses the islands' diving operators offer programs for both the inexperienced and the experienced diver.

 Quotation Marks

Direct quotations—that is, direct discourse and material quoted word for word from other written sources—must always be set off distinctly from a writer's own words. Quotation marks usually indicate the distinction, although when quotations from written sources are long, the distinction may be shown instead by indentation. Chapter 37 describes the conventional uses of quotation marks and indentation to set off quoted material; the use and punctuation of explanatory words such as *he said*; the conventions controlling the placement of other marks of punctuation with quotation marks; and the special uses of quotation marks in certain titles and with words used as words.

An explanatory comment inserted in a quotation or the omission of some part of the original quotation calls for the use of brackets or the ellipsis mark. These are discussed in Chapter 38.

 Use double quotation marks to enclose a direct quotation from speech or writing.

"Don't dive from that rock," she warned me.

James Baldwin wrote, "It is a terrible, an inexorable, law that one cannot deny the humanity of another without diminishing one's own."

In dialogue, each change of speaker is indicated by a new paragraph.

> "And after dinner, as your personal Mephistopheles, I shall take you up a high hill and show you the second-best place in the world. You agree? A mystery tour?"
>
> "I want the best," she said, drinking her Scotch.
>
> "And I never award first prizes," he replied placidly.
>
> —John Le Carre

Remember not to set off indirect quotations with quotation marks.

She warned me not to dive from that rock.

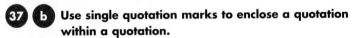
Wasn't it Baldwin who wrote that when we deny another person's humanity we diminish our own?

37 b Use single quotation marks to enclose a quotation within a quotation.

E. B. White wrote, "As an elderly practitioner once remarked, 'Writing is an act of faith, not a trick of grammar.' "

Notice that the end punctuation of the sentence within single quotation marks serves also as the end punctuation for the entire sentence of which it is a part. For the rules governing end punctuation used with quotation marks, see Section **37g**.

37 c Indent prose quotations of more than four lines and poetry quotations of more than three lines.

● **1 Long prose quotations.** Each line of a prose quotation of more than four lines should be indented from the left-hand margin. In typewritten papers, indent the quotation ten spaces from the left, and double-space it. Do not enclose an indented quotation in quotation marks. If quotation marks occur *within* such material, use them exactly as they are in the original.

```
William Zinsser's comment in his book Writing to Learn is
worth quoting:

          If you think you can dash something off and have it come
          out right, the people you're trying to reach are almost
          surely in trouble. H. L. Mencken said that "0.8 percent
          of the human race is capable of writing something that
          is instantly understandable." He may have been a little
          high. Beware of dashing. "Effortless" articles that look
          as if they were dashed off are the result of strenuous
          effort. A piece of writing must be viewed as a constant-
          ly evolving organism.

Zinsser knows what he's talking about.
```

● **2 Quoted poetry.** Single lines of poetry are ordinarily run into the text and enclosed in quotation marks unless the writer wishes to give them particular emphasis by setting them off.

```
In the line "A spotted shaft is seen," the hissing s sounds echo
Emily Dickinson's subject: a snake.
```

Two or three lines of poetry may be either enclosed in quotation marks and run into the text or indented ten spaces from the left. If they are enclosed in quotation marks and run into the text, divisions between lines are indicated by a slash mark (/).

```
     Published anonymously in Punch on December 6, 1915, John
McCrae's extremely popular poem "In Flanders Fields" is one reason
poppies have come to symbolize World War I and, in fact, all
British and American war dead: "In Flanders fields the poppies
blow / Between the crosses, row on row, / That mark our place."
```

```
     Published anonymously in Punch on December 6, 1915, John
MaCrae's extremely popular poem "In Flanders Fields" is one reason
poppies have come to symbolize World War I and, in fact, all
British and American war dead:
                    In Flanders fields the poppies blow
                  Between the crosses, row on row.
                    That mark our place.
```

Poetry quotations of more than three lines should be double-spaced and indented ten spaces from the left. Any special spacing or indention appearing in the original should be preserved.

```
McCrae uses the voice-from-the-grave device to focus on the
ironic contrast between lovers' beds and the soldiers' graves
where "we now lie":
                    We are the Dead. Short days ago
                  We lived, felt dawn, saw sunset glow,
                      Loved and were loved, and now we lie
                      In Flanders fields.
```

Exercise 37.1

In the following sentences, insert double or single quotation marks or slash marks wherever needed.

1 My younger brother is reading *Hamlet* in his high school literature class, and last night he asked me Do you know what the line To be or not to be—that is the question means?

2 I told him I thought that the line might indicate that Hamlet is thinking of suicide.

3 I recall that when I read *Hamlet* in my English literature class, the professor announced: This play has probably created more critical controversy than any other play ever written.

4 After reading *Hamlet*, I also read Shakespeare's sonnets; my favorite sonnet begins with the lines Let me not to the marriage of true minds Admit impediments.

5 After his class had discussed *Hamlet*, my brother said, I enjoyed that play a lot, even though I had to work hard to understand it, and I think I'd like to see a performance of *Hamlet* on the stage.

37 **d** **In punctuating words introducing a quotation, be guided by the length and formality of the quotation.**

Commas typically separate words such as *she said* from a quotation which follows. However, when the quotation that follows is grammatically closely related, explanatory words may not be followed by any punctuation. When quotations are relatively long and formal, they may be followed by a colon.

NO PUNCTUATION   I yelled "Stop!" and grabbed the wheel.

Auden's poem "In Memory of W. B. Yeats" begins with the line "He disappeared in dead of winter."

F. Scott Fitzgerald wrote that "genius is the ability to put into effect what is in your mind."

PUNCTUATION WITH   The old rancher said very quietly, "Under no circum-
COMMA   stances will I tell you where the money is hidden."

The chairman asked him, "Have I stated your motion correctly?"

PUNCTUATION WITH   The speaker rose and began to rant: "The party in power
COLON   has betrayed us. It has not only failed to keep its election promises but has sold out to special-interest groups." [See also examples in Section **37c**.]

 Use a comma to separate an opening quotation from the rest of the sentence unless the quotation ends with a question mark or an exclamation point.

"The man is dead," he said with finality.

"Is the man dead?" he asked.

"Oh, no!" he screamed hysterically. "My brother can't be dead."

  When quoted dialogue is interrupted by words such as *they said,* use a comma after the first part of the quotation. To decide which punctuation mark to place after the interrupting words, apply the rules for punctuating clauses and phrases.

"I am not aware," she said, "of any dangers from jogging." [phrase]
"I have always worked hard," he declared. "I was peddling newspapers when I was eight years old." [independent clause]
"Jean has great capacities," the supervisor said; "she has energy, brains, and personality." [independent clause]

Exercise 37.2

In the following sentences, insert appropriate punctuation marks where necessary to separate quotations from the rest of the sentence.

1   "Do you ever have trouble using your VCR" asked Kevin.
2   Kevin said that the instructions for his VCR state "Operating this machine is simple after reading these instructions."

3 "One thing I have discovered" said Kevin "is that the term *simple* doesn't mean the same thing to everyone."

4 "Some newer models are voice activated" I replied "or have on-screen directions that simplify programming. That's *so* much easier than the older videocassette recorders" I exclaimed.

5 Maybe Kevin should do what my neighbor did, for he recently told me "Whenever I want to record anything on my VCR, I get my twelve-year-old daughter to do it for me, and she has no trouble."

37 **g** **Follow American conventions in placing other punctuation with quotation marks.**

● **1 Place commas and periods inside quotation marks.** Commas are generally used to separate direct quotations from unquoted material.

> "There comes a time," said the politician, "to put principle aside and do what's right."

Note that this rule applies regardless of the reason for using quotation marks.

> According to Shakespeare, the poet writes in a "fine frenzy."

> The words "lily-livered coward" derive from an earlier expression, "white-livered," which meant "cowardly."

The only exception to this rule is punctuation of in-text citations using *MLA* style (see Section **48c**).

● **2 Place semicolons and colons outside quotation marks.**

> According to Shakespeare, the poet writes in a "fine frenzy"; by "fine frenzy" he meant a combination of energy, enthusiasm, imagination, and a certain madness.

● **3 Place a dash, question mark, or exclamation point inside the quotation marks when it applies only to the quotation; place it outside the quotation marks when it applies to the whole sentence.**

> She said, "Will I see you tomorrow?"
> Didn't she say, "I'll see you tomorrow"?

> "You may have the car tonight"—then he caught himself abruptly and said, "No, you can't have it—I need it myself."

When a mark applies to both quotation and sentence, use it only once— putting it inside the quotation marks.

> Have you ever asked, "May I come in?"

Exercise 37.3

In the following sentences, insert whatever punctuation marks are appropriate for use with quotation marks.

1 When my roommate took a course in Romantic literature. I asked her, "What have you learned about Wordworth's sister, Dorothy, and her influences on his work"

2 "Quite a bit" she replied. "The professor said that Dorothy Wordworth was, to quote my professor, 'the spirit inspiring Wordworth's poems' "

3 "Did she really say 'the spirit inspiring Wordworth's poems' " I asked. "I have always thought of Dorothy as being just a housekeeper for Wordsworth"

4 "What a crazy thing to think" snapped my roommate. "Dorothy did keep house for her brother, but keeping house for him hardly means that she was not also an intelligent woman capable of helping Wordsworth with his poetry. And what do you mean by saying 'just a housekeeper' "

5 "Hold on" I interrupted "and let me explain that I was not being derogatory when I said 'just a housekeeper' but neutral"

6 My roommate had obviously overreacted to my phrase "just a housekeeper" I would have to work hard to get back in her good graces.

7 Clearly her reaction meant that I was in for a bad time because I had said "just a housekeeper" first she would yell a lot about the role of women, and then she would haul out several feminist writers for me to read in order to overcome my biases.

8 Exasperated, I finally inquired. "Have you ever asked yourself, dear roomie, 'Why do I yell at my friends so much' "

In Your Own Words

Locate two books that were published in another country. Consider the choice of single or double quotation marks and the placement of quotation marks with commas and periods. Write a paragraph explaining the differences in usage in those books and in American usage.

  Use quotation marks to set off titles of poems, songs, articles, short stories, and other titles that are parts of a longer work.

For the use of italics for the titles of longer works, see Sections **39a** and **39b**.

> Theodore Roethke's poem "My Papa's Waltz" appeared in his book *The Lost Son and Other Poems.*

> "The Talk of the Town" has for many years been the opening column of *The New Yorker.*

> The song "I Left My Heart in San Francisco" has become an anthem for that city.

> "Beowulf to Batman: The Epic Hero in Modern Culture," an article by Roger B. Rollin, originally appeared in the journal *College English.*

  Use quotation marks to set off words used in a special sense.

When a new book comes into the library, it is first of all "accessioned."

Is this what is known as "functional" architecture?

37 (i) **Do not use quotation marks in certain situations.**

Do not use quotation marks around common nicknames. Do not use them for emphasis. And do not use them apologetically to enclose slang, colloquialisms, trite expressions, or for imprecise words or phrases when you cannot find the right word. Replace inappropriate words with precise language. If, however, you wish your reader to recognize a slang term, colloquialism, or specialized term as such (to prevent misunderstanding the usage), then you may need to use quotation marks to indicate that the word is being used in a special sense: "In Britain a car's trunk is the 'boot.'"

> NOT   A neighbor kid, "Butch" Jackson, taught me to whistle.
>
> BUT   A neighbor kid, Butch Jackson, taught me to whistle.
>
> NOT   Bennazir brought an "awesome" souvenir back from her two-week hike—a baby black snake.
>
> BUT   Bennazir brought a squeal-inspiring, squiggly souvenir back from her two-week hike—a baby black snake.

Exercise 37.4

In the following paragraph, insert quotation marks wherever they are needed.

> Because they believed that the South needed to turn from an industrial to an agricultural economy, a group of prominent southern writers of the 1930s are often referred to as the agrarians. This group included the poets Allen Tate, Robert Penn Warren, and John Crowe Ransom, who wrote the poem Bells for John Whiteside's Daughter. Ransom was also one of the seven founders of *The Fugitive*, a magazine that became a focus for what might be called a southern literary renaissance. Allen Tate's best-known poem is Ode to the Confederate Dead, which was published in 1937 in a volume entitled *Selected Poems.* Robert Penn Warren, who wrote poetry, fiction, and criticism, was a Rhodes Scholar at Oxford; there he wrote the short story Prime Leaf, a story he later developed into the novel *Night Rider.*

Brackets and the Ellipsis Mark

Brackets and ellipsis marks signal that a writer has made changes in material being quoted directly. Brackets are used to indicate that a writer has inserted into the quotation some information, comment, or explanation not in the original. The ellipsis mark is used to indicate that something has been deliberately omitted from the material being quoted.

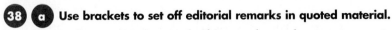

38 **a** Use brackets to set off editorial remarks in quoted material.

You will sometimes want to insert a clarifying word or explanatory comment in a statement you are quoting. Enclosing such information in brackets lets the reader know at once that you are speaking rather than the original author.

> My professor said, "Alice Munro's novel [*Lives of Girls and Women*] is one of the most profound modern initiation stories—and one of the few about women."

> The favorite phrase of their [English] law is "a custom whereof the memory of man runneth not back to the contrary."
>
> —Ralph Waldo Emerson

In bibliographical notations, use brackets to enclose the name of a writer reputed to be the author of the work in question.

> [Ned Ward], *A Trip to New England* (1699)

38 **b** Use the word *sic* ("thus it is") in brackets to indicate that a mistake or peculiarity in the spelling or the grammar of a foregoing word appears in the original work.

> The high school paper reported, "The students spoke most respectively [sic] of Mrs. Hogginbottom."

38 **c** Use an ellipsis mark (...) to indicate an intentional omission from quoted material.

When you want to quote from an author but omit some words within a sentence or omit one or more sentences, in fairness to the original author and to your readers you must indicate that you have omitted material from the original. Such omissions are indicated by inserting an ellipsis mark at the point of omission.

For an omission within a sentence, use three spaced periods, leaving a space before and after each period. When the omission comes at the end of a sentence, use four periods; the first is the usual sentence period, and the last three are the ellipsis mark. If the quotation continues, leave one space between the last of the periods and the first letter of the next word. If a parenthetical reference, such as a page number or the like, follows the ellipsis mark at the end of a sentence, use three spaced periods and put the sentence period immediately after the final parenthesis.

ORIGINAL   Mickey's is a child's world, safe (though occasionally scary), nonviolent, nonideological, where all the stories have happy endings. Characterization is strong and simple—Mickey is bright and friendly, Minnie eternally feminine, Goofy happily stupid, Donald of the terrible temper a raffish, likeable rascal. No Disney strip ever gave a child bad dreams or an adult anything to ponder.

                                              —Russel Nye, *The Unembarrassed Muse*

QUOTED WITH
OMISSION

Mickey's is a child's world, safe . . . nonviolent, nonideological, where all the stories have happy endings. Characterization is strong and simple—Mickey is bright and friendly, Minnie eternally feminine. . . . No Disney strip ever gave a child bad dreams . . . (157).

If you must omit an entire line or more of poetry or an entire paragraph or more of prose, use a full line of ellipsis marks to indicate the omission. The following example is from Edgar Allan Poe's poem "The Raven."

Once upon a midnight dreary, while I pondered, weak and weary,
Over many a quaint and curious volume of forgotten lore—
While I nodded, nearly napping, suddenly there came a tapping.
. . . .
" 'Tis some visitor," I muttered, "tapping at my chamber door—
Only this and nothing more."

Review Exercises

Punctuation of Quoted Material

In the following sentences and paragraph, supply the appropriate punctuation.

Sentence Practice

1 In his book *Hillerman Country,* mystery writer Tony Hillerman includes a chapter entitled The Dineh and the Turquoise Mountain in which he describes Tsoodzil, one of four mountains sacred to the Dineh, in English called Navajos.

2 Hillerman explains how he viewed the mountain daily for twenty-five years from the off-ramp of I-40 as he drove home from the University of New Mexico Tsoodzil Turquoise Mountain never seems to look quite the same, but it always turns my mind away from the city to thoughts of fir-spruce forests, and a spirit called Blue Flint Girl who lives there, as Navajo ritual poetry tells us, in a house made of morning mist, a house made of dawn.

3 Aren't his mystery novels set on the Navajo reservations in Arizona and New Mexico queried my friend Claudia in an e-mail conversation Is Hillerman a Native American?

4 Yes, his detectives are Navajo police officers, I wrote back to her, but Hillerman is not a Native American. His knowledge comes from observing and studying Navajo and other southwestern Indian cultures extensively and respectfully.

5 In fact, I continued in my e-mail message to Claudia, Gloria Duus, an administrator for the U.S. Bureau of Indian Affairs and a Navajo herself, said that many of her people regard Hillerman as a valued spokesperson to the outside world for Navajo customs, rituals, and beliefs; He presents a positive image, portraying us the Navajo as a people who never separate ourselves from nature, for whom nature, religion, and culture are all one she said at a lecture I attended last week on mystery writers.

Paragraph Practice

Would you like to go see a production of Lorraine Hansberry's play
A Raisin in the Sun at the university theatre this Friday night my sister asked
me when I saw her at lunch today. I would I said because I've read the play
but I've never seen it performed. I wish I knew where Hansberry got her title
for that play my sister said for the title intrigues me. I told her that the title
comes from a poem entitled A Dream Deferred by Langston Hughes. In fact,
the phrase a raisin in the sun appears in the third line of Hughes's poem.

In Your Own Words

Review your writing with regard to the way in which you use quotation
marks, the ellipsis, and brackets. Which rules cause problems for you?
In a paragraph explain the problems with quoting that you still need to
work on.

Word Punctuation

Italics, capitals, apostrophes, and hyphens identify words that have a special
use or a particular grammatical function in a sentence.

> Our two-week reading program, assigned in Wednesday's class, focuses on
> Shakespeare's *King Lear*.

Here the italics set off the words *King Lear* as a single title. The capitals
identify *Wednesday's, Shakespeare's, King,* and *Lear* as proper names. The
apostrophes indicate that *Shakespeare's* and *Wednesday's* are singular possessives and not plurals. The hyphen between *two* and *week* makes the two
words function as a single adjective.

Italics

Italics are printing typefaces that slope toward the right. In typed or handwritten manuscript, italics are indicated by underlining.

> On the printed page: *italics*
> In typewritten copy: `italics`
> In handwritten copy: <u>italics</u>

39 a Italicize the titles of books, newspapers, magazines, works of art, music, movies, television and radio programs, record albums, cassettes, CDs, and all publications issued separately.

"Issued separately" means published as a single work and not as an article
or story in a magazine, nor as a chapter or section of a book. (For the proper punctuation of such titles, see Section **37h**.)

The New York Times	*The Thinker*
People	*Death of a Salesman*
Northern Exposure	*Webster's New Collegiate Dictionary*
the *Star-Spangled Banner*	*The Lord of the Rings*
Brandenburg Concerto No.1	

Be careful not to add the word *The* to titles unless it belongs there and not to omit it if it does belong.

NOT   *The Reader's Digest*
BUT   the *Reader's Digest*

NOT   the *Red Badge of Courage*
BUT   *The Red Badge of Courage*

Note that the titles of some very well-known works and documents are not italicized nor placed in quotation marks.

the Bible	Psalms
the Koran	the Constitution of the United States
the Magna Carta	Matthew
the Declaration of Independence	the Bill of Rights

39 b **Italicize the names of ships, spacecraft, and aircraft.**

Titanic	the *Concorde*
Spirit of St. Louis	*Challenger*
U.S.S. *Saratoga*	

Note that for ships and the like, the prefix U.S.S. (or H.M.S.) is not italicized: U.S.S. *Nimitz*; H.M.S. *Pinafore*.

39 c **Italicize letters, numbers, and words used as words.**

Your *r*'s look very much like your *n*'s, and I can't decide if this is a *7* or a *1*.

The early settlers borrowed Indian words like *moccasin*, *powwow*, and *wigwam*.

Quotation marks are also sometimes used to set off words as words (see Section **37i**). However, if a subject you are discussing in a typewritten or handwritten paper requires you to set off many words as words, underlining (italics) will make your manuscript look less cluttered.

39 d **Italicize foreign words and phrases that have not yet been accepted into the English language. Italicize the Latin scientific names for plants, animals, and so forth.**

She graduated *magna cum laude*.

Many of the works of the *fin de siècle* judged so sensational when they were written now seem utterly innocent.

In the fall, the ginkgo tree (*Ginkgo biloba*) produces a yellow fruit that smells indescribably foul.

You may sometimes feel that a foreign word or phrase expresses your meaning more aptly or concisely than an English one. If you are sure that your readers will understand the expression, use it. But overuse of such words is pedantry. Many foreign words have been accepted into the English language and need no longer be italicized. The following words, for example, do not require italics:

bourgeois   milieu   denouement   liqueur

To determine whether a foreign word should be italicized, consult a good dictionary (see Section **21a** for a list).

39 **e** Use italics to give a word or phrase special emphasis.

Always turn off the electricity before attempting to work on the wiring.

We have government *of* the people, *by* the people, and *for* the people; dictatorships have government *over* the people.

39 **f** Avoid the overuse of italics.

Distinguish carefully between a real need for italicizing and the use of italics as a mechanical device to achieve emphasis. The best way to achieve emphasis is to write effective, well-constructed sentences. The overuse of italics will make your writing seem immature and amateurish, as in the following:

Any good education must be *liberal.*

America is a *true* democracy, in every sense of the word.

This book has what I call *real* depth of meaning.

Exercise 39.1

Italicize words as necessary in the following sentences and paragraph.

Sentence Practice

1 A pioneer in the fight for women's rights, Jane Grey Swisshelm (pronounced Swiz-em) was one of the first female journalists in the United States, founding the Pittsburgh Saturday Visiter, which she edited from 1847 to 1857.

2 The term feminist hardly does justice to her impassioned fight for women's rights, a fight which in 1850 forced the press gallery in Washington, D.C., to open its doors to women reporters.

3 Jane Grey Swisshelm (nee Cannon) left her husband of twenty-one years, moving to St. Cloud, Minnesota, where she founded another newspaper, the Visiter, which she later renamed the St. Cloud Democrat.

4 Democrat is not a word readily applied to Swisshelm, however, because she worked hard to maintain her independence from all political groups, though her views were undoubtedly Republican.

5 Her autobiography, Half a Century (1880), reveals her passionate campaign against slavery, which was, in her view, the sine qua non of human rights and a much more important issue than women's fight to vote.

Paragraph Practice

My friend Bert, who is in one of my journalism classes, says that he first heard about Jane Grey Swisshelm on a television series, Pioneering Journalists. Bert said he believes everyone would be impressed with Swisshelm's career, especially her antislavery campaign, but he said that another early woman journalist featured in the television series impressed him almost as much: Sara Payson Willis (1811-1872). Using the pen name Fanny Fern, she wrote a weekly column for twenty-one years in the New York Ledger, and she used this column to attack snobbery, the ill treatment of the poor, and the oppression of women. Her columns were collected into books such as Fern Leaves from Fanny's Portfolio (1853) and Fresh Leaves (1857), and she also wrote three novels, including the widely read Ruth Hall, which argued that women should use their talents to write. Bert said, "I really admire Fanny Fern for the tough way in which she set forth the ABC's of women's issues: the right of women to vote, to receive pay equal to men's, and to win recognition as the intellectual equal of men."

In Your Own Words

Review the discussion of italics, and write a one-paragraph discussion of the rules which were new to you or those which have been problems in your writing.

40 Capitals

Modern writers capitalize less frequently than did earlier writers, and informal writing permits less capitalization than formal writing. Some three hundred years ago, a famous author wrote,

> Being ruined by the Inconstancy and Unkindness of a Lover, I hope a true and plain Relation of my Misfortune may be of Use and Warning to Credulous Maids, never to put much Trust in deceitful Men.
> —Jonathan Swift, "The Story of the Injured Lady"

A contemporary writer would capitalize no letters but the initial *B* and the pronoun *I*.

40 a Capitalize the first word of grammatically independent structures.

Capitalize the first word of a sentence, a direct quotation that is not structurally part of another sentence, a complete sentence enclosed in parentheses or brackets, or—in some cases—a complete sentence following a colon.

● 1 A sentence.

Education is concerned not with knowledge but with the meaning of knowledge.

● 2 A direct quotation.

She thought, "Where shall we spend our vacation—at the shore or in the mountains?"

Notice that the preceding example shows a quotation that is grammatically independent. Before the quotation are words that introduce and attribute it to a speaker, but the quotation itself could stand alone and is, in fact, an independent thought. The capital letter signals this independence.

When a quotation is grammatically incorporated into the sentence in which it appears, the first word of the quotation is not capitalized unless it is a proper noun.

She knew that "the woods are lovely, dark, and deep," but sun, sand, and sea appealed to her, too.

The newspaper's motto was "all the news that's fit to print," which made me wonder how bad the news had to be before it became unfit.

● 3 A complete sentence enclosed in parentheses or brackets.

The survey shows that cigarette smoking has declined nationally in the last ten years but that smoking among women and teenagers has increased. (See Table 3 for numerical data.)

"The Black Death killed anywhere between one-third to one-half of the entire population of Europe. [Exact numbers are impossible to derive, given the state of recordkeeping in medieval Europe.] Those who survived were often too few to bury the dead."

When a parenthetical or bracketed statement appears within another sentence, the first word is ordinarily not capitalized and the ending period is omitted.

The survey shows that cigarette smoking has declined nationally in the last ten years but that smoking among women and teenagers has increased (see Table 3 for numerical data).

● 4 A complete sentence following a colon. Typically, an independent statement following a colon is not capitalized, particularly when it is closely related to the preceding sentence. However, if the writer wishes to emphasize the independence of the statement, a capital letter may be used.

There were fifteen or twenty women in the room: None of them was his mother.

40 b   Capitalize the first word of a line of poetry.

True ease in writing comes from art, not chance,
As those move easiest who have learned to dance.

         —Alexander Pope, *Essay on Criticism*

Some poets ignore the convention of capitalizing each line of poetry. When quoting poetry, follow the capitalization of the original exactly.

a man who had fallen among thieves
lay by the roadside on his back
dressed in fifteenthrate ideas
wearing a round jeer for a hat

        —e. e. cummings, "a man who had fallen among thieves"

40 c   Capitalize the pronoun *I* and the interjection *O*.

How long must I wait, O Lord?

Do not capitalize the interjection *oh* unless it is the first word of a sentence.

Oh what a mess we made in the cabin.

Chong felt oh so glad to settle back into a comfortable routine.

40 d   Capitalize proper nouns, their derivatives and abbreviations, and common nouns used as proper nouns.

● 1 Specific persons, races, nationalities, languages.

Willa	Bob	Rita Mae Brown	Semitic
Asian	American	Mongolian	Cuban
Canadian	English	Swahili	Zulu

Usage varies for the term *black (blacks)* as an ethnic designation. Although it is often not capitalized, and is never capitalized in the phrase "blacks and whites," many authors regularly capitalize other uses in current writing.

● 2 Specific places.

Atlanta	Buenos Aires	California	Lake Erie
Newfoundland	India	Jerusalem	Snake River

● 3 Specific organizations, historical events and periods, and documents.

African National Congress	the French Revolution
the Locarno Pact	the Renaissance
Declaration of Independence	the Battle of Hastings

● 4 Days of the week, months, holidays, and holy days.

Thursday	Good Friday	the Fourth of July
Easter	Christmas	Ramadan
November	Hanukkah	Yom Kippur

● **5 Religious terms, deities, and sacred texts.**

the Virgin Allah Holy Ghost Jehovah the Torah

● **6 Titles of books, plays, magazines, newspapers, journals, articles, poems, computer software, and copyrighted or trademarked names or products.** Capitalize the first word and all others except articles (*a/an, the*) and conjunctions and prepositions of fewer than five letters (see also Sections **37h** and **39a**).

> *Dust Tracks on a Road: An Autobiography* *Business Week*
> *Paradise Lost*   *Leisure Studies*
> *War and Peace*   *Microsoft Word*
> *Ebony*   *Oreo cookies*
> *Much Ado About Nothing*

● **7 Titles, and their abbreviations, when they precede a proper noun.** Such titles are an essential part of the name and are regularly capitalized. Abbreviations for academic degrees and professional certificates are also capitalized when they follow a proper name.

> Professor Berger   John Leland, PhD
> Mr. Rothstein   Thomas Hass, MD
> Vice Chairman Diaz   Valarie Petroski, CPA
> Dr. Carolyn Woo   Editor-in-Chief Weil
> Justice Sandra Day O'Connor Secretary-General Boutros-Ghali
> President Clinton   Associate Dean G. P. Bass

When a title follows a name, capitalize it only if it indicates high distinction:

> Bill Clinton, President of the United States
> William Renquist, Chief Justice of the Supreme Court
> BUT Sally S. Fleming, director of corporate communications
> J. R. Derby, professor of biology

Often the "in-house" conventions of a particular organization include capitalizing titles after names. For example, in an annual report or employee newsletter you would probably see the following:

> Sally S. Fleming, Director of Corporate Communications

This use of capitals suggests that the concept of high distinction is strongly related to audience and context. Although a title following a name may not warrant the distinctive treatment of capitalization for a general audience (the readers of your paper about corporate research and development), that same title may well be capitalized for a specialized audience (Fleming's coworkers).

● **8 Common nouns used as an essential part of a proper noun.** These are generic names such as *street, river, avenue, lake, county, ocean, college, church, award.*

Vine Street	Fifth Avenue	Pacific Ocean
Lake Sammamish	General Motors Corporation	Penn Central Railroad
Hamilton College	Pulitzer Prize	Mississippi River

When the generic term is used in the plural, it is not usually capitalized.

Vine and Mulberry streets
the Atlantic and Pacific oceans
Hamilton and Lake counties
the Catholic and Protestant churches in town

40 **e** **Avoid unnecessary capitalization.**

A good general rule is not to capitalize unless a specific convention warrants it.

● **1 Capitalize *north, east, south, west* only when they come at the beginning of a sentence or refer to specific geographical locations, not when they merely indicate direction.**

Birds fly south in the winter, some stopping north of South America.

If the United States looks east and west, it sees economic competitors in the Far East and Western Europe.

● **2 The names of seasons need not be capitalized.**

fall   autumn   winter   midwinter   spring   summer

● **3 Capitalize nouns indicating family relationships only when they are used as names or titles or in combination with proper names. Do not capitalize such nouns when they are preceded by possessive adjectives.**

I telephoned my mother.
BUT   I telephoned Mother.

My uncle has four children.
BUT   My Uncle Ben has four children.

● **4 Ordinarily, do not capitalize common nouns and adjectives used in place of proper nouns and adjectives.**

I went to high school in Cleveland.
BUT   I went to John Adams High School in Cleveland.

I am a university graduate.
BUT   I am a Stanford University graduate.

I took a psychology course in my senior year.
BUT   I took Psychology 653 in my senior year.

She received a bachelor's degree in computer science.
BUT   She received a Bachelor of Science degree from the Computer Science Department.

Exercise 40.1

In the following sentences and paragraph, capitalize words as necessary. Remove unnecessary capitals.

Sentence Practice

1 sojourner truth, whose original name was isabel baumfree, was born in 1797 in hurley, new york.

2 although sojourner truth was born a slave, She was freed by the new york state emancipation act of 1827.

3 Sojourner Truth was one of the first Black women to speak out against Slavery, and later in her life she became a Crusader for Women's rights.

4 After the civil war, truth spoke out for equal treatment for african americans, especially for Equality in Education.

5 even though sojourner truth was Illiterate, she was a powerful speaker; for example, in 1852 she attended the national women's suffrage convention in akron, ohio, and gave the speech that made her famous, a speech entitled "ain't i a woman."

Paragraph Practice

women's suffrage, or the right of Women to vote, was first proposed in the united states in 1848. women such as elizabeth cady stanton, susan b. anthony, and lucretia mott led the Fight to win for women the Right to Vote. stanton was a journalist who became President of the national woman suffrage association. Mott was a quaker who had helped slaves come North during the civil war. Anthony, who had organized the daughters of temperance, the first women's temperance association, helped to write the first three Volumes of a work called *the history of woman suffrage*, the Dedication of women such as these three paid off, for in 1920 the constitution of the united states was amended to give women the right to vote.

In Your Own Words

Write a paragraph identifying the problems with capitalization that you have had in recent papers. Which particular rules confuse you or are difficult to remember?

41 The Apostrophe

41 a Use an apostrophe to show the possessive case of nouns and indefinite pronouns.

● **1 Add an apostrophe and *s* to form the possessive of singular nouns, indefinite pronouns, and plural nouns that do not end in *s*.**

the woman's decision	the women's decision
the child's toy	the children's toys
the man's feet	the men's feet

someone's sandwich   the people's sandwiches
the duchess's ring
James's gym shoes
Keats's famous poem

● **2 Add only an apostrophe to form the possessive of plural nouns ending in *s*.**

the boys' blue jeans
the Smiths' house [referring to at least two persons named Smith]
The miners' strike lasted three months.
the duchesses' rings

● **3 In compounds, make only the last word possessive.**

nobody else's fault
I can't find my brother-in-law's pen. [singular possessive]
Their mothers-in-law's birthdays are a day apart. [plural possessive]

● **4 In nouns of joint possession, make only the last noun possessive; in nouns of individual possession, make both nouns possessive.**

Margo and Paul's office is down the hall. [joint possession]
Margo's and Paul's offices are down the hall. [individual possession]

41 **b**   **Do not use an apostrophe with the possessive form of personal pronouns. Be particularly careful not to confuse *its* with the contraction *it's* (it is).**

The personal pronouns *his, hers, its, ours, yours, theirs,* and the pronoun *whose* are possessives as they stand and do not require an apostrophe.

    his CD player   an idea of *hers*   a friend of *theirs*

The possessive form of *it* is *its.* Do not use an apostrophe to form the possessive. The word *it's* (with an apostrophe) is a contraction for *it is* and is not possessive.

    Although we couldn't find *its* nest, we saw the bird. We know *it's* a robin.

41 **c**   **Use an apostrophe to indicate the omission of a letter or number.**

can't	cannot	o'clock	of the clock
doesn't	does not	blizzard of '89	blizzard of 1989
it's	it is	will-o'-the-wisp	will of the wisp

In reproducing speech, writers frequently use an apostrophe to show that a word is given a colloquial or dialectical pronunciation.

    "An' one o' the boys is goin' t' be sick," he said.

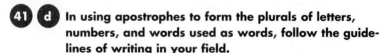

41   d   In using apostrophes to form the plurals of letters, numbers, and words used as words, follow the guidelines of writing in your field.

The style manual of the Modern Language Association recommends using an apostrophe to form the plurals of letters but not the plurals of numbers, abbreviations, or words used as words.

> CPAs in the 1990s will have to mind their *p*'s and *q*'s while leading their clients through the *A, B, C's*—the *ifs, ands*, and *buts*—of the income tax code.

Other style manuals differ. In fact, many no longer require apostrophes with the plurals of letters.

Exercise 41.1

In the following sentences and paragraph, insert apostrophes or apostrophes plus *s* as necessary. Then write five sentences of your own that use apostrophes in various ways.

Sentence Practice

1 Because more and more people are taking tours to Antarctica, scientists are becoming concerned about the impact of the increased number of visitors on the regions fragile environment.

2 Scientists concerns involve protecting Antarcticas mosses, grasses, and lichens.

3 Penguins, seals, and seabirds inhabit the Antarctic continents ice shelves and peninsulas, and scientists are also worried that increased tourism will affect these animals habitats.

4 The 1980s were a time of growing interest in travel to Antarctica, and more and more people journeyed to the worlds coldest continent.

5 As a result, its vital that the visitors be aware of the importance of preserving Antarcticas unique environment.

Paragraph Practice

Roald Amundsens journey to the South Pole in 1911 made him the first human being to reach the earths southernmost point. Amundsens trek to the South Pole was followed by that of British explorer Robert Scott. Scott didnt achieve the distinction of being the first to reach the South Pole, because Scotts group of five, who had pulled sledges through Antarcticas subfreezing conditions, arrived at the Pole just a month after Amundsen. This second groups return from the South Pole was tragic: Scott and his men suffered from hunger, became ill, and encountered blizzard conditions that resulted in the mens deaths on the return trip. Amundsens and Scotts expeditions to the South Pole opened the way to further explorations of the earths fifth largest continent, although its tragic that the British explorers lives were lost in the effort.

In Your Own Words

In your neighborhood find signs that do not use the apostrophe to indicate possession even though they should. Scan newspaper ads for examples of mistakes in spelling possessives. Write a paragraph sharing your examples.

42 The Hyphen

In handwriting, distinguish the hyphen from the dash by making the hyphen shorter. In typewriting and word processing, the hyphen is typed immediately next to the letter it follows, with no space in between.

The hyphen has two distinct uses: (1) to form compound words, and (2) to indicate that a word is continued from one line to the next.

Convention in the latter use of the hyphen, called *syllabication* or *word division*, is arbitrarily fixed (see Chapter 45). However, convention in the use of hyphens with compounds not only shifts rapidly but is unpredictable. As a noun, *short circuit* is spelled as two words; but the verb *short-circuit* is hyphenated. *Shorthand* and *shortstop* are spelled as single words, but *short order* is spelled as two words. *Short-term* in *short-term loan* is hyphenated, but in *the loan is short term* it is spelled as two words.

In such a rapidly changing and unpredictable matter, your only safe recourse is to consult a good, up-to-date dictionary (see Chapter 21). The following uses of the hyphen in forming compound words are widely accepted.

42 a Use a hyphen to form compound words that are not yet accepted as single words.

The spelling of compound words that express a single idea passes through successive stages. Originally spelled as two separate words, then as a hyphenated word, a compound word finally emerges as a single word.

> *base ball* became *base-ball* became *baseball*
> *post mark* became *post-mark* became *postmark*

Similar words pass through these stages at different rates—and some perhaps not at all. Compare the following words, selected from a recently published dictionary.

bull's-eye	bullhorn
fire-eater	flame thrower
speed-reading	speedboating

African-American or African American

There is no certain way of determining the proper spelling of a compound at any given moment. Your dictionary is your most authoritative reference.

42 b Use a hyphen to join two or more words serving as a single adjective before a noun.

Do not hyphenate such an adjective if it follows the verb as a predicate adjective.

> a well-known speaker
> BUT The speaker was well known.
>
> a grayish-green coat
> BUT The coat was grayish green.
>
> nineteenth-century American fiction
> BUT American fiction of the nineteenth century

Omit the hyphen when the first word is an adverb ending in *-ly*.

> a slow-curving ball
> BUT a slowly curving ball
>
> a quick-moving runner
> BUT a quickly moving runner

42 c Use a hyphen to avoid an ambiguous or awkward union of letters.

> re-create [for "create again"]
> NOT recreate
>
> bell-like
> NOT belllike

There are many common exceptions, however.

> coeducational   coordinate   cooperate   readdress
> NOT co-educational   co-ordinate   co-operate   re-address

42 d Use a hyphen to form compound numbers from twenty-one through ninety-nine and to separate the numerator from the denominator in written fractions.

twenty-nine   fifty-five   two-thirds   four-fifths

42 e Use a hyphen with the prefixes *self-, all-, ex-,* and the suffix *-elect.*

self-important   all-conference   ex-mayor   governor-elect

Do not capitalize the prefix *ex-* or the suffix *-elect*, even when used in titles that are essential parts of a name.

ex-Mayor Sanchez   Governor-elect Jones   ex-President Bush

Exercise 42.1

Insert hyphens as needed in the following passage. Then write five sentences containing compound adjectives, some of which precede nouns and some of which follow verbs as predicate adjectives.

Frederick Douglass, an abolitionist who was an ex slave, is an important figure in nineteenth century American history. Douglass was born in Maryland in 1817 and died in 1895; thus his life spanned almost three fourths of the nineteenth century. His autobiography, *Narrative of the Life of Frederick Douglass, an American Slave,* was published in the mid nineteenth century and is one of the best known accounts of the experiences of pre Civil War slaves. The book quickly became a best seller in its own time. In addition to being a deeply moving account of the young Douglass's life as a slave, the autobiography is also a record of his self discovery of his role as a spokesman for his people.

Review Exercises

Word Punctuation

Supply the necessary italics, capitals, apostrophes, and hyphens in the following sentences and paragraph.

Sentence Practice

1 Although the adventure packed histories of pirates have always appealed to the publics imagination, few people know that some of the most ruthless, blood thirsty pirates were women, for example, grace o'malley, mary read, anne bonny, and ching shih.

2 Using piracy to advance irelands fight against england, o'malley, a sixteenth century irish pirate, eventually renounced piracy in 1586 and was pardoned by queen elizabeth I.

3 The englishwoman mary read, who disguised herself as a soldier in flanders, became a pirate after the death of her husband when she ran away from the army and signed on to a ship going to the west indies; she was forced to join in the pirates deeds when the ship on which she was sailing was captured by marauders.

4 Turning down an offer of amnesty in 1717, mary met the irish born anne bonny, and these two female pirates raided spanish treasure ships in the caribbean until they were caught in 1720, marys and annes pregnancies saved them from execution.

5 Managing nearly 2,000 ships and a pirate network of 70,000 to 80,000 men and women, the nineteenth century chinese pirate ching shih was widely admired as a businesswoman, according to alexander darymples book, memoir concerning the pirates on the coast of china (1806).

Paragraph Practice

Pirate lore has been transformed into famous works of art which havent lost their appeal in the 1990s when piracy has more to do with hijacking and

computer fraud than with the sea. One of the most villainous and best loved fictional pirates is Captain Hook, who made his stage debut in j. m. barries play peter pan in 1904. In 1926 the silent film the black pirate starred douglas fairbanks as its dagger wielding pirate, and in 1935 the film captain blood featured a talking errol flynn as its hero. Robert louis stevenson wrote the well known treasure island in 1883. treasure islands famous one legged pirate, long john silver, and his cohorts nearly succeeded in taking the schooner hispaniola from its captain. The world of music has also paid homage to pirates: for example, the corsair (1814), a long poem by lord byron, inspired an opera by verdi and a famous ballet. The word pirate simply means "robber on the sea," but its a word that suggests a world of romance and adventure.

In Your Own Words

Write a paragraph about a recent film you have seen or a book you have read. In the paragraph, include at least one example of italicizing a title, italicizing a word spoken of as a word, a singular possessive noun, a plural possessive noun, and a hyphenated word. Double-check the paragraph to be sure that all capitalization is correct.

Review Exercises

Punctuation

Part A

In the following sentences and paragraph, make all necessary corrections in internal punctuation and in the use of quotation marks, capitals, italics, apostrophes, and hyphens.

Sentence Practice

1 The american poet langston hughes was born in joplin missouri in 1902 in addition to poetry Hughes who died in 1967 also wrote drama fiction television scripts songs and childrens books.

2 Hughes was one of the prominent figures in the Harlem Renaissance a period in the 1920s marked by a surge of writing and music by black artists many of whom were associated with the harlem section of new york city.

3 Many of Hughes poems deal with Harlem and in his volume of poems entitled Montage of a Dream Deferred Hughes depicts the life of urban black americans.

4 Other writers associated with the Harlem Renaissance include Countee Cullen a poet who used traditional verse forms to express black themes James Weldon Johnson a lawyer who wrote both novels and poetry and Zora Neale Hurston an anthropologist and writer who studied african american folktales.

5 Because of the work of these artists harlem became a literary and artistic center but the period known as the Harlem Renaissance ended with the beginning of the Great Depression in the 1930s.

Paragraph Practice

Because i had grown up in a small town in nebraska i was excited by the diversity and overwhelmed by the size of new york city when I made my first

but certainly not my last visit there. To get oriented to the huge metropolis
I took a guided tour of the city. The two day tour took us to several famous
sites the empire state building the world trade center and the statue of liberty.
On the first day of the tour our guide said to us I want you to remember
that this city which is the largest in the U.S. was established as a dutch settlement in 1624. The tour guide also told us that even before the dutch came to
the area the english explorer henry hudson had been there moreover it is
believed that Giovanni da Verrazanno 1480-1527 an italian explorer may have
been the first european to arrive in the area. Verrazanos name stays in New
Yorkers minds today as part of the Verrazano-Narrows bridge. The bridge has
a main span of 4260 feet making it the countrys longest suspension bridge
used by vehicles. When I saw that bridge at the entrance of new york harbor
one word came to mind awesome.

Part B

In the following paragraphs, insert any needed internal punctuation, as well
as capitals, italics, apostrophes, hyphens, and quotation marks.

When people think of fairy tales the first name to come to mind is probably Grimm the family name of two german brothers who collected and edited over 200 tales and legends, jacob grimm the older of the two brothers was
born in 1785 and his brother wilhelm was born in 1786. The brothers studied
law but they also became interested in gathering folktales and legends particularly those passed on through the oral tradition. Their first collection of
tales was called Kinder-und Hausmärchen a german title that is more familiar
to english speakers as Grimm's Fairy Tales. The collections contain such well
known stories as Hansel and Gretel Rapunzel Snow White and the Seven
Dwarfs and The Frog Prince. Although the Grimms book had been published
as a serious scholarly collection of tales it also gained popularity with general
readers. Eventually seven editions of Kinder-und Hausmärchen appeared
during the brothers lifetime. Today the fairy tales have been translated into
seventy languages and characters such as Rumpelstiltskin and the Bremen
Town-Musicians as well as many others are favorites of children and adults
everywhere.

The grimm brothers became most famous for their work with fairy
tales yet they also studied the german language and began work on an
etymological dictionary a dictionary which would trace the history of words
in the german language. The brothers began work on the dictionary in 1852
however Wilhelm died in 1859 jacob died in 1863 and the dictionary was
not completed for over a hundred years.

Part C

In the following sentences and paragraph, determine which punctuation
marks are used correctly, correct any marks used incorrectly, and add any
needed punctuation.

Sentence Practice

1 The Vietnam Memorial an angle of polished black granite situated near
   the Lincoln Memorial, and the Washington Monument on the Mall in

Washington, D.C., has become one of the most frequently visited sites in the nations capital.

2 The Memorial was designed by Maya Lin who was an undergraduate, architectural student at Yale when she submitted the winning design, for the Memorial in 1981.

3 After considerable controversy over the unusual design construction finally began in March, 1982; the 3000 cubic feet of granite for the panels came from Barre Vermont.

4 Etched into the granite of the Vietnam Memorial, are nearly 60000 names of individuals, who were killed in Vietnam, or are listed as missing in action.

5 Visitors, to the Vietnam Memorial touch the names of those they knew and some leave medals photographs letters and other personal mementos.

Paragraph Practice

Although nearly sixty years have passed, since Amelia Earharts disappearance in the South Pacific in July 1937 the mystery of what happened on the world famous aviators last flight remains unsolved today. After the disappearance of the plane, and in the years since then many searches have been conducted their participants hoping to find the remains of Earharts plane. Earhart who had been the first woman to fly across the Atlantic in 1928 and later the first woman to fly across the Atlantic alone had set out in 1937 to fly around the world. On what turned out to be her last flight Earhart was accompanied by her navigator Fred Noonan. Earhart, and Noonan, were headed for Howland Island a tiny bit of land in the Pacific however their plane disappeared somewhere between New Guinea and Howland Island. The whereabouts of Earhart Noonan and the plane remain a mystery.

Part 7

Mechanics

Of all forms of symbolism, language is the most highly developed, most subtle, and most complicated. It has been pointed out that human beings, by agreement, can make anything stand for anything.

—S. I. Hayakawa, *Language in Thought and Action*

Many practices of written English are merely conventions. Logic does not justify them; they simply represent standard ways of doing things—codes of meaning that people recognize and accept. The mechanics of using numbers, abbreviations, and word division (syllabication) are such conventions.

43 Numbers

Conventions governing the choice between spelling out numbers (*twenty-two*) and using figures (*22*) vary with the kind of writing. Writing in general publications uses spelled-out numbers more frequently than does scientific or technical writing. Consider the following examples:

> There remained to the seventy-five-year-old King only one great-grandson, a pink-cheeked child of two, the last surviving infant in the direct line. . . . This new little Dauphin remained miraculously alive and lived to rule France for fifty-nine years as Louis XV. On his deathbed, Louis XIV called for his great-grandson and heir who then was five. Face to face, these two Bourbons who between them ruled France for 131 years regarded each other.
>
> —Robert K. Massie, *Peter the Great: His Life and World*

> In alphanumeric mode, the video circuit displays characters in 80 or 40 columns by 25 rows. Sixteen foreground and background colors are available, except with character blinking, which reduces available background colors to eight.
>
> In graphics mode, low resolution provides 16 colors and 160 by 200 pixels, medium resolution provides 4 colors and 320 by 200 pixels, and high resolution offers 2 colors and 640 by 200 pixels.
>
> —"The Tandy 1000," *Byte: The Small Systems Journal*

> What is America's biggest regional repertory company, employing as many as 63 actors to mount a dozen productions for a total of 676 performances a year? What company features three spaces ranging from a stripped-down, experimental "black box" . . . to a 1,173-seat outdoor Elizabethan playhouse? . . . What company annually attracts more than 300,000 playgoers, 90% of them from more than 150 miles away? . . . The answer in each case is the Oregon Shakespearean festival. . . .
>
> —"Only 2,500 Miles from Broadway," *Time*

As different as these passages appear to be in their use of numbers versus figures, each follows a coherent set of guidelines used by writers of general nonfiction (the first example), technical description (the second example), and journalism (the third example).

Your own use of numbers and figures should be governed by the conventions of the field for which you are writing. Those conventions can be discovered by examining style manuals published by the professional organizations in the field. See Chapters 49-52 for discussion of writing in various disciplines.

43 a Use words and figures for numbers.

Generally, use words for numbers nine and less. Use figures for numbers ten and over. If a discussion contains few numbers, one- or two-word numbers may be spelled out, and other numbers may be written as figures. Related numbers should all be expressed in the same style.

> The larvae of swallow-tail moths feed only on one plant. The leaves, located 15 to 20 meters up into a forest canopy, are difficult to see.
>
> —*Chemistry*

> Tired volunteers rescued 17 whales beached or stranded Thursday along Cape Cod. . . . Up to 70 scientists and volunteers had worked two days, sometimes in 50-degree water, to aid the giant mammals.
>
> —*USA Today*

> I wouldn't give you fifty cents for that car, not even if I lived to be one hundred years old. No, not even if I lived to be 199!

> The ornithologist reported that two of the 50 bald eagles known to be living in Ohio had recently been sighted in Belmont County. The sightings were at 5-, 12-, and 27-day intervals during the three summer months of June, July, and August.

Remember that the words for compound numbers twenty-one to ninety-nine are hyphenated (see Section **42d**).

43 b Use figures for dates and addresses.

Dates	*Addresses*
May 4, 1914	13 Milford Avenue
23 April 1978	57 East 121st Street
1862-1924	Route 1 P.O. Box 739
17 B.C. to A.D. 21	Apt. 2B
21 B.C.E.-15 C.E.	Grinnell, Iowa 50112

Ordinal numbers (numbers that indicate order: *first, third, twenty-ninth*) or the forms 1st, 3rd, 9th, may be used in dates if the year is not given: *March 1, March first, March 1st.*

   In formal invitations, dates are usually written out: *Tuesday, September first, nineteen hundred and eighty-seven.* (See Section **32i** for the punctuation of dates and addresses.)

Use figures to express precise measurements.

DECIMALS	8.72 13.098
PERCENTAGES	72% or 72 percent
MIXED NUMBERS AND FRACTIONS	27½ 19⅔ (but *one-half* pound of coffee)
SCORES AND STATISTICS, NUMBERS BEING COMPARED	score of 35-10 vote of 86-53 it was 5-10 degrees warmer
IDENTIFICATION NUMBERS	Channel 5 Interstate 70
VOLUME, CHAPTER, AND PAGE NUMBERS	Volume V, Chapter 7, page 518
ACT, SCENE, AND LINE NUMBERS	*King Lear*, 2.1.18-47
NUMBERS FOLLOWED BY SYMBOLS OR ABBREVIATIONS	5 cu. ft. 93°F. 31°C. 55 mph 60 Hz 1200 baud
EXACT AMOUNTS OF MONEY	$24.98 56¢
TIMES	4:30 P.M. 11:55 P.M. (but *half past two, quarter of six, seven o'clock*)

Sums of money that can be expressed in two or three words or in round numbers are sometimes written out: *twenty million dollars in losses, fifty cents on the dollar.*

When writing a compound-number adjective, spell out the first of the two numbers or the shorter of the two to avoid confusing the reader: *sixteen 10-foot poles, 500 one-liter bottles.*

 Except where clarity requires it in legal or business writing, do not repeat in parentheses a number that has been spelled out.

BUSINESS	The original order was for eight (8) pumps.
STANDARD	Katie lost all six credit cards yesterday.

 Spell out numbers that occur at the beginning of a sentence.

Although you may frequently see figures at the beginning of newspaper headlines, such usage is a journalistic space-saving convention.

> 17 Whales Saved; 11 Killed
> —*USA Today*

If you use a number to begin a sentence, spell it out or revise the sentence so it begins with a word instead of a figure.

FAULTY	217 bales of hay were lost in the fire.
REVISED	Two hundred and seventeen bales of hay were lost in the fire.
FAULTY	1994 was the year the Dallas Cowboys won the Super Bowl.
REVISED	In 1994 the Dallas Cowboys won the Super Bowl.

Exercise 43.1

In the following sentences and paragraph, make any necessary corrections in the use of numbers. Assume a general audience.

Sentence Practice

1 Consumers can find up to twelve types of milk and cream on their supermarket shelves, but often shoppers aren't sure just what makes each type of milk different from the others; basically, the main difference in these types of milk is the amount of fat in each.

2 For instance, whole milk has at least three and a quarter percent fat, while lowfat milk, which has had some fat removed, usually contains one or two percent of fat.

3 Skim milk, sometimes called nonfat milk, has less than one percent fat; at the other end of the scale, heavy cream has thirty-six percent fat.

4 The various types of milk and cream on the supermarket shelves have all been pasteurized to destroy bacteria; pasteurizing involves heating the milk or cream at one hundred and forty-five°F. for 30 minutes or at one hundred and sixty-five°F. for 15 seconds.

5 Often, cream is ultrapasteurized, a process in which the liquid is heated at two hundred and eighty°F. for a minimum of 2 seconds.

Paragraph Practice

Although the Food and Drug Administration has required that labels on 1,000s of foods be more informative than ever before, some consumers still feel overwhelmed and confused by the nutritional information on packages. For example, the package for one brand of cheeze crackers says that a serving is 1 ounce, or about 8 crackers, and that this serving provides about 2% of the daily recommended amount of iron. That much is clear, but is the serving generous or deficient in its 180 milligrams of potassium? The label says that the serving contains four percent of the recommended daily protein, or 3 grams. Does that mean that the consumer should multiply 25 times 3 to get the full required protein for a day—or, figured another way, 200 crackers? 140 calories per serving, however, means that to get the full protein requirement by eating cheeze crackers, a person would end up consuming thirty-five hundred calories and 200 grams of fat! These numbers hardly add up to good health today when many consumers' 1st priority is eating healthy food. Given the twenty fifty-foot food aisles in some grocery stores, it's no wonder that some consumers give up in frustration rather than read nutritional information that requires the math skills of a nuclear physicist.

In Your Own Words

Use the library to locate both a technical or scientific article and a humanities article which contain numbers. List the ways in which the two types of articles differ in spelling out or using figures for numbers. Write a paragraph analyzing what rules the editors of each periodical seem to have for using numbers.

44 Abbreviations

Abbreviations are common in writing for specialized audiences. These readers are usually familiar with the abbreviations common to their field and find them a convenient shorthand. When writing for a general audience, however, you will typically want to avoid abbreviations—with some standard exceptions.

44 a Use appropriate abbreviations in formal and informal writing.

● **1 Titles before proper names.** Use such abbreviations as *Mr., Mrs., Ms., Dr.* only when the surname is given: *Dr. Hart* or *Dr. F. D. Hart.*

FAULTY He has gone to consult the Dr.
REVISED He has gone to consult Dr. Hart [*or* the doctor].

Use abbreviations such as *Hon., Rev., Prof., Sen.* only when both the surname and given name or initials are given: *The Hon. O. P. Jones,* but not *Hon. Jones.* In more formal usage, spell out these titles and use *The* before *Honorable* and *Reverend.*

INFORMAL Rev. W. C. Case delivered the sermon.
FORMAL The Reverend W. C. Case delivered the sermon.

Use *St.* (Saint) with a Christian name that refers to a person or place: *St. Theresa, St. Louis.*

● **2 Titles after proper names.** Use the following abbreviations only when a name precedes them: *Jr., Sr., Esq.* Abbreviations of academic degrees and professional certifications (*MS, PhD, LLD, MD, JD, CPA*) can be used after a name, or they can stand by themselves. "Robert Reese, Jr., has an MA in philosophy." Do not, however, use equivalent titles and/or abbreviations both before and after a name.

NOT Dr. Carolyn Haas, *MD,* is a pediatrician.
BUT Carolyn Haas, *MD,* is a pediatrician.

● **3 Abbreviations of dates, times, and units of measurement.** These terms should be abbreviated only when they appear with figures specifying exact numbers: *34 B.C., A.D. 1066, 6:54 a.m.* (or *A.M.*), *7:15 p.m.* (or *P.M.*), *$87.59, no. 6* (or *No. 6*), *55 mph.*

B.C., which means "before Christ," is always abbreviated and capitalized and always follows the year. *A.D.,* which means "in the year of our Lord" (*anno Domini*), is always abbreviated, capitalized, and always precedes the year. Similarly, *a.m.* (*ante meridiem,* "before noon") and *p.m.* (*post meridiem,* "after noon") are always abbreviated.

The use of abbreviations without numbers should be avoided.

> NOT   We met in the p.m. to check the no. of ft. the river had risen.
>
> BUT   We met in the evening to check the number of feet the river had risen.

See Section **44g** for further discussion of scientific and technical abbreviations.

● **4 Latin abbreviations.** Although Latin abbreviations such as *i.e.* (that is), *e.g.* (for example), *etc.* (and so forth) have been common in writing, in formal writing the English equivalent is increasingly used. Do not use *etc.* as a catch-all. It is meaningless unless the extension of ideas it implies is unmistakably clear. Do not write *and etc.*; the *and* is redundant.

> CLEAR   The citrus fruits—oranges, lemons, etc.—are rich in vitamin C. [The reader has no difficulty in mentally listing the other citrus fruits.]
>
> INEFFECTIVE   We swam, fished, etc. [The reader has no clues to the implied ideas.]
>
> REVISED   We swam, fished, rode horses, and danced.

● **5 The names of agencies, organizations, and corporations.** These abbreviations fall into two groups: **acronyms,** formed from the initial letters of words and pronounced as a single word, and **initialisms,** also formed from initial letters but pronounced separately.

> AGENCY   OSHA   Occupational Safety and Health Administration [acronym]
>
> ORGANIZATION   MADD   Mothers Against Drunk Driving [acronym]
>
> CORPORATION   IBM   International Business Machines [initialism]

If you frequently use a name that may be unfamiliar to readers, spell it out on first mention and give the abbreviation in parentheses: *Zimbabwe African National Union (ZANU).* Use only the abbreviation in subsequent references.

Dictionaries of abbreviations and acronyms are available in library reference rooms.

44 **b** **Spell out the names of people; countries and states; days, months, and holidays; and academic courses.**

> FAULTY   Eliz., a student from Eng. who joined our bio class last Wed., expects to go home for Xmas.
>
> REVISED   Elizabeth, a student from England who joined our biology class last Wednesday, expects to go home for Christmas.

The District of Columbia is spelled out when it is used alone but abbreviated as DC when it follows the city name, Washington. The United States can be abbreviated as the USA (or U.S.A.) or the US.

44 c Spell out place names and the words *street, avenue, route,* and the like, except in addresses.

FAULTY   The office is near the Michigan St. exit of I-70.
REVISED   The office is near the Michigan Street exit of Interstate 70.

44 d Spell out references to books and parts of books.

Except in footnotes and bibliographies, references to volume, chapter, page, or line should be spelled out:

FAULTY   Rumi is discussed in Ch. 7, pp. 130-154 in *The Sufis.*
REVISED   Rumi is discussed in Chapter 7, pages 130-154 in *The Sufis.*

44 e Spell out the names of companies.

Use abbreviations such as *Bros., Ltd.* (for *Limited*), *Co., Corp.,* and the ampersand (*&* for *and*) only if the firms themselves use them: *Barnes & Noble, Inc.* but *Western Union Telegraph Company.*

44 f Avoid clipped forms in formal writing.

Words such as *dorm* (dormitory) and *lab* (laboratory) are clipped forms. Clipped forms are fairly common in the jargon of particular fields, as in *lab tech* in medicine. In informal writing meant for a general audience, clipped forms give writing a conversational tone. Technically not abbreviations, clipped forms are not followed by periods.

44 g When writing for a general audience, spell out most scientific and technical words.

The number of technical and scientific abbreviations in general use—in everyday speech, newspapers, and magazines—increases constantly. Thus we are more likely to recognize the abbreviation DNA than we are its long form, deoxyribonucleic acid.

If you are unsure whether to abbreviate a technical word, follow your common sense and prevailing general usage. If your readers may be unfamiliar with an abbreviation, first use the full name followed by a brief explanation or the abbreviation in parentheses. Thereafter, use the abbreviation alone.

> Thanks to computer-aided design and computer-aided manufacturing (CAD-CAM), automobile companies are able to test new models on the drawing board. CAD-CAM saves thousands of dollars and hundreds of hours in engineering time.

Whether to use abbreviations for units of measurement in writing for a nontechnical audience can be a judgment call. For instance, most of us probably accept the use of "45 rpm" in the example that follows:

> Record industry analysts say the 45 rpm single is a thing of the past; revolutions per minute don't mean much when your compact disc player holds just one size.

But many readers resist such usage in general writing:

> The canoe was 8 ft long and 3 ft wide. Empty, it weighed 100 lb.

44 h Punctuate abbreviations according to the conventions of the field for which you are writing.

In technical writing, the periods are omitted from abbreviations unless they could be confused with words of the same spelling: "The cable is 23 ft 8 in. long." In general writing, omit the periods or not, as you choose, as long as the abbreviations are not confusing and are used consistently throughout the document.

The *MLA Handbook*, the style manual for writing about literature, English, and other modern languages, notes the trend to use neither periods nor spaces between letters of an abbreviation, particularly when the abbreviation is composed of capital letters: *MBA, BC, AD, NY, CPA, USA*. An exception is initials of given names, which require both periods and spacing: *E. F. Hutton, J. Ross Brown*. Periods are recommended for abbreviations ending in lower-case letters: *a.m., i.e., e.g., Dept. of Defense*.

Conventions regarding abbreviations vary widely between fields and sometimes even within fields. Familiarize yourself with the conventions of the group for which you are writing by examining style manuals and periodicals in the field; then apply those conventions with consistency and common sense.

Exercise 44.1

Correct any misuse of abbreviations in the following sentences and paragraph.

Sentence Practice

1 The site for the White House, which is located on Penn. Ave. in Wash., DC, was chosen by George Washington.

2 Although Washington chose the location for the White House, John Adams was the first pres. who actually lived in the Exec. Mansion.

3 The White House, which was built of stone from Virg., was not originally white, but after being burned by the Brit. in 1814, it was restored and painted white.

4 Although the building had been referred to earlier as the White House, that name finally became official during the time Theo. Roosevelt was in office.

5 Like the White House, the official residence of the Brit. Prime Minister is also a tourist attraction; the house, located at 10 Downing St. in London, can be viewed from several yds. away, but Downing St. itself cannot be entered.

Paragraph Practice

My Am. hist. prof., Dr. Mary Samuels, Ph.D., asked me to come by her office in the a.m. to discuss my research paper. I need to have this paper finished by the end of Nov., so I have to get my idea approved by this Fri. I plan to do a paper on the work of Dr. Eliz. Blackwell, M.D., the first woman in the USA to receive a med. degree. Dr. Blackwell graduated from medical col. in 1849 and in 1857 helped to start the N. York Infirmary for Women and Children. The Dr. also helped to found the Women's Med. Col. at the Infirmary.

In Your Own Words

Scan newspapers and magazines for abbreviations you are not familiar with. Look them up in a recent dictionary. List five clipped forms you have found in the newspaper or magazines. Write a paragraph explaining whether or not the abbreviations and clipped forms were appropriate for the intended audience of the newspapers or magazines from which they came.

45 Word Division

When only part of a word will fit at the end of a line, divide the word between syllables and use a hyphen to indicate the break. Always place the hyphen at the end of the line after the first part of a divided word, not at the beginning of the next line on which you complete the word.

When you are in doubt about the syllabication of a word, consult a good dictionary. Desk dictionaries normally use dots to divide words between syllables: *bank-rupt, col-lec-tive, ma-lig-nant, punc-ture.* Note that not every syllable marks an appropriate point at which to divide a word at the end of a line (see Sections **45b** and **45c**). If a word cannot be correctly divided between syllables, move the entire word to the beginning of the next line.

 **Do not divide words pronounced as one syllable.**

WRONG	thr-ee	cl-own	yearn-ed	scream-ed
REVISED	three	clown	yearned	screamed

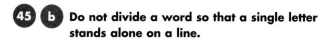

45 b Do not divide a word so that a single letter stands alone on a line.

WRONG	wear-y	e-rupt	a-way	o-val
REVISED	weary	erupt	away	oval

45 c When dividing a compound word that already contains a hyphen, make the break only where the hyphen occurs.

AWKWARD	pre-Dar-winian	well-in-formed	Pan-Amer-ican
REVISED	pre-Darwinian	well-informed	Pan-American

45 d Divide compound words only between the parts.

When possible, divide words with suffixes or prefixes between the parts.

COMPOUND WORDS	snowmobiles (snow-mobiles)	headache (head-ache)
PREFIXES	misinterpret (mis-interpret)	disengage (dis-engage)
SUFFIXES	resentment (resent-ment)	joblessness (jobless-ness)

45 e Do not divide figures, abbreviations, or contractions.

WRONG	36,-000	YW-CA	NA-TO	were-n't	did-n't
REVISED	36,000	YWCA	NATO	weren't	didn't

Exercise 45.1

Which of the following words may be divided at the end of a line? Indicate appropriate divisions with a hyphen. Refer to your dictionary if necessary.

event	premature	roommate
ill-mannered	slouched	completely
asleep	improvement	NAACP
unmistakable	couldn't	oversight
cowardice	habit-forming	NOW

Review Exercise

Mechanics

Correct any errors in the following sentences and paragraph. Remember to check for faulty hyphenation. Assume a general audience.

Sentence Practice

1 Among the most famous universities in the world are 2 in England, Oxford University and Cambridge University, each conveniently accessible from London in just under an hr. by train.

2   35 separate colleges comprise Oxford University, and 31
colleges make up Cambridge University today, each univ. having
1000s of undergraduate and grad. students as well as 100s of
profs, call-
ed dons.

3   Each univ. has a large no. of specialized libraries,
including, for ex., the Bodleian Librar-
y and Radcliffe Camera in Oxford and Pepys Lib., Wren Library,
and University Library at Cambridge.

4   Both universities date from the MA: Oxford, slightly older,
was founded early in the 13 century, and by 1,230 a.d. Cambridge
also was thriving as a center of learning.

5   Fem. students were not allowed at Oxford and Cambridge until
late in the 19th century, and they weren'-
t given degrees until the mid 20th century.

Paragraph Practice

In Oxford, only 59 mi. from the metropolis of London,
visitors may feel that they have suddenly walk-
ed back seven hundred yrs. as they view the many buildings from
the med. period, such as Merton Chapel, etc. Visitors need 2 or
3 days to see the colleges and related pts. of interest such as
the Ashmolean Mus. In Cambridge 1 of the most famous sights is
Kings College Chapel, which features elaborate fan-vaulting that
is extraordinary for its time, a-
round 1,512-1,515. For the equivalent of a dollar and fifty cents, a visitor to Cambridge may tour a college like St. John's College, where the Bridge of Sighs over the River
Cam connects the older bldgs. of the col. with the newer ones.
From the bridge, one can watch students and townspeople using 10 ft. poles to propel flat-bottom-
ed boats slowly along, in an activity called punting.

In Your Own Words

Review the last two pieces of writing you have done and list the problems
you had with numbers, abbreviations, and word division. In a paragraph
explain why you believe you made these errors.

Part 8

Research Writing

Research is … the attempt to take external events and data and, by passing them through the sensibilities of the writer, to produce a text that reflects both the outer and the writer's inner worlds of meaning.

—James V. Catano, "Navigating the Fluid Text"

Knowledge is of two kinds. We know a subject ourselves, or we know where we can find information upon it.

—Samuel Johnson, Boswell's *Life of Johnson*

46 Locating and Working with Sources

47 Drafting and Revising the Research Paper

48 Documenting the Research Paper

46 Locating and Working with Sources

Conducting research is a basic human activity. Broadly speaking, everyone engaged in acquiring knowledge is engaged in research. The research you will do in college may include observing events, interviewing people, performing laboratory experiments, or systematically reading the ideas of researchers and thinkers in your field of study. However, research is more than just gathering data; it also requires the critical thinking skills of selecting, organizing, analyzing, interpreting, and evaluating that data so that valid statements can be made about some aspect of reality.

Whether they are college students or rocket scientists, researchers frequently present the results of their work in writing so that others can share and evaluate their ideas. These results may appear as an article in a scholarly journal or magazine, a business presentation, a patent application for a new drug, or a term paper for a college political science course. Whatever form the research publication takes, the fundamental research process is similar across disciplines. (For more on writing in the humanities, social sciences, other sciences, and business, see Part 9, "Writing in Different Disciplines.")

Chapters 46, 47, and 48 chart the process of producing writing from your research. These chapters follow Bonnie Lin, a student writer, as she collects material and writes a research paper for her English 102 course. Although many variations are possible in the research process, you will see one effective method of investigating sources and writing up your results: planning a search strategy; locating and working with sources; sorting, evaluating, and organizing material; and writing, documenting, and revising the paper.

46 **a** Plan a search strategy.

● **1 Develop a research question.** An effective search strategy begins with a research question. Sometimes you will be intrigued by an idea from a lecture or class discussion that you wish to research; sometimes your general reading of newspapers, magazines, or books will lead to an interesting topic of inquiry. Other times, you will need to think carefully about a topic to find an aspect of it that you would like to know more about. However you arrive at your research question, check to be sure that it is neither too broad nor too narrow for the length of the paper you will eventually write. The best way to ensure that you have chosen a suitably narrowed research question is to discuss your idea with your instructor.

Bonnie Lin remembered hearing that McDonald's Corporation was phasing out its styrofoam clamshell packaging and replacing it with recyclable material. She wondered what had prompted the company to recycle.

How had McDonald's made this decision? Did the company feel a responsibility to protect the environment? When Bonnie discussed her questions with her instructor, Professor Sorrenson recommended that Bonnie broaden her question to include other companies' recycling efforts because she doubted Bonnie would find enough sources of information about McDonald's for a fifteen-page paper. Bonnie broadened the scope of her research question accordingly.

Once you have identified an appropriate research question, you can begin to develop a working bibliography, a list of articles, books, and other sources you plan to consult to research your subject. Before you go to the library, however, consult with people who are knowledgeable about your topic.

● **2 Talk to knowledgeable people.** The college itself is your best source of people who are knowledgeable on a wide range of topics. You can explore potential sources of information with professors, graduate students, or other researchers at your school before you ever open a book, saving yourself much time and frustration. Professors can frequently provide information about prevailing schools of thought on a subject and tell you about the most authoritative scholars and sources. In fact, your professors may be authoritative sources themselves.

Bonnie's instructor suggested that she talk to a business professor about her research question before she started compiling a working bibliography. Doing so, she found that there was heated controversy among business leaders about what responsibility corporations had to protect the environment. Since the whole topic was relatively new, the professor recommended that she get an overview of her subject by reading recent magazine and newspaper articles (see Section **46b**). Further, Bonnie learned that she had access in her college library to a business-oriented segment of PRO-QUEST (an on-line CD-ROM database) called ABI/Inform which she could use to find the relevant articles. To put her research question into context, the professor suggested a newly published business textbook (*Corporations in the Moral Community*) as background reading. In about half an hour, Bonnie gained a basic understanding of her research topic and knew what her next steps should be.

● **3 Start keeping a research log.** Recording the results of your research at each step of the process will help you keep track of the sources you have consulted so that you don't duplicate your efforts. The log can also help you if you need to refer to sources you located earlier once you have focused your thesis (see Sections **47a-47b**). As you check the various kinds of indexes referred to in Section **46d**, note which search terms you have tried, as Bonnie did in the following section of her research log.

Research Log

<u>Monday Afternoon</u>

1. Spoke with the reference librarian about how to search on PROQUEST, our library's on-line system--it follows the Library of Congress subject headings.
2. Found the <u>Library of Congress Subject Headings</u> (the large red volumes). Wanted to check out headings related to my topic, business and the environment.

<u>Monday Evening</u>

3. Searched PROQUEST's ABI/Inform first, since it lists business-oriented articles. Had to keep trying different search terms to find some narrow enough to look at.

--Tried the search term "environment"--4,104 "hits"
--Tried the search term "environment and marketing"--601 "hits"
--Tried the search term "environmental protection"--445 "hits"
--Tried the search term "environment and McDonald's"--24 "hits"
--Tried the search term "business ethics"--665 "hits"
--Tried the search term "business ethics and the environment"--44 "hits"

Found several promising leads under the search term "business ethics and the environment." Skimmed some articles and photocopied a couple of them.
4. Next searched the "Periodicals Index (1991-93)." Found some new sources under the same term I used to search ABI/Inform. Photocopied some articles.
5. In "Newspaper Abstracts (1991-93)" found several good articles on the McDonald's recycling program with the Environmental Defense Fund. Made copies of useful articles from microfilm and microfiche.

--Tried the search term "corporate responsibility"--535 "hits"
--Tried the search term "corporate responsibility and the environment"--37 "hits"

<u>Tuesday Afternoon</u>

6. Checked library's list of college-held serials and periodicals against the PROQUEST printout. Some of the promising magazines and journals we didn't have, like the <u>Columbia Journal of World Business.</u> Filled out interlibrary loan request forms for copies of articles and turned them in at the reference desk. Should take a week to get copies.
7. Needed background in business theory. Checked books in our system but many aren't recent enough. Found several good leads in the recent <u>Books in Print.</u> Filled out more interlibrary loan slips. This time I can't get what I want for at least 2 weeks!

<u>Tuesday Evening</u>

8. Checked the <u>Readers' Guide to Periodical Literature</u> volumes
from 1991-93. Used search term "business, environmental
aspects." What I found doesn't add anything new. Feel satisfied
with what I have so far.

9. Remember seeing an ad for Sun Oil in one of the magazines I
read which listed the company's environmental principles.
Decided to write and find out more about their program. Asked
the reference librarian where I could find Sun's corporate
address. Located it in <u>Hoover's Handbook of American Business.</u>

10. Began draft of letter to Sun Oil. Hope they answer soon!

Notes for letter:

What are the Sun Principles?
Why did Sun decide to endorse the CERES Principles?
What does Sun think about their environmental responsibility?

46 b Draw on your library's resources.

Libraries offer a variety of important research resources. The primary ones
are reference librarians; the general collection of books; collections of periodicals (in some libraries these holdings are called *serials*) that include newspapers, magazines, journals, bulletins, and pamphlets (including microfilm
and microfiche); collections of reference works; and electronic media such as
audio and video tapes. The following chart shows how to access each of
these resources as well as the types of material typically available.

Major Types of Library Resources

Resources	Where to access	What is listed	How to obtain
Reference Librarians	library's reference desk	how to begin search; locating information	in person or by telephone (some libraries)
General Collection: Books	catalog of holdings: computerized or card file	general and specialized books	can be checked out
Periodicals, Bulletins, etc.	indexes: printed computerized, or microfiche	general and specialized magazines, journals, newspapers	must be used in library

Resources	Where to access	What is listed	How to obtain
Reference Collection: Books	catalog of holdings: computerized or card file	general and specialized encyclopedias, dictionaries, handbooks, atlases, etc.	must be used in library
Electronic Media	catalog of holdings: computerized or or card file	audio and video tapes; films	sometimes can be checked out

● 1 **Consult the reference librarian.** The reference librarian is your most important resource. This knowledgeable specialist can tell you how to begin your search or help you at any point when you are unsure where to look next. Reference librarians know about dozens of indexes and reference works, alternative key words to try if you can't find material under the search term you are using, and resources that may be available in other libraries. Some libraries have telephone references services you can call to check a statistic or a fact.

● 2 **Get an overview of your topic from reference books.** If you are focusing and narrowing your research subject, or if you need basic knowledge, your next stop should be general reference works such as encyclopedias, dictionaries, handbooks, and other sources that provide overviews and definitions for the topic or field you are investigating. You may want to move from a general reference work to a more specialized one (such as a specialized encyclopedia) for a more detailed view of the subject area. A list of general and specialized references books appears later in this chapter.

● 3 **For current topics, search periodical indexes (newspapers, magazines, journals).** Because books take several years to write and produce, recent information about many topics is best found in newspapers, magazines, and scholarly journals that cover the subject. Your library has indexes organized alphabetically by key-word headings. Under each heading you will find a list of articles pertaining to the key word. Your library's indexes may be in two formats: (1) printed volumes with supplements shelved in the reference section and (2) computerized indexes, accessible on-line by means of a modem and telephone line or accessible from disks on CD-ROM. Many computerized indexes provide an abstract (brief summary) of an article as well as its author, title, and publication information. Libraries can subscribe to a number of periodical indexing services which supply the computerized indexes. These may be general, or they may be specialized such as indexes of business or scientific and technological information or even information restricted to ethnic topics.

Even when they offer computerized indexes, libraries usually also continue to subscribe to the leading printed indexes as well. Don't ignore the print indexes just because the computerized listings are fast and easy to use. Be aware that the computerized listings may not include exactly the same periodicals as the printed indexes. For instance, some may index newspapers and some may not. Also, be sure to check the dates covered by the computerized listings. You may need to consult printed indexes for older references or for listings in additional periodicals. Think of computerized and printed indexes as companion research tools rather than relying exclusively on one or the other. A listing and discussion of useful indexes follows in this chapter.

Your library may not subscribe to all the periodicals referenced in various indexes. The ones your library carries will be listed either in the general library catalog along with books or in a separate serials catalog, either as a computer printout or on microfiche.

● **4 Rely on books for more extended analyses and interpretations of your topic.** Researching recent periodicals will give you the most current factual information. Then you can consult books for additional information, background, and analysis. The length afforded by a book allows authors to discuss issues in depth, dig deep into background, analyze information to determine its meaning, debate points of view, and elaborate causes and effects.

As you research your subject, you will need to evaluate your sources carefully, choosing a good mixture of primary and secondary sources—examining many and selecting the best. Section **46f** explains how to evaluate sources.

Recognizing Primary and Secondary Sources

Primary sources: First-hand reports or other original material
- surveys, investigations, research studies, and interviews reported by the original investigators and recorders
- original accounts of events by first recorders in newspapers, magazines, on television, radio, or film
- autobiographies, notes, letters, diaries, or other original documents or tapes, novels, short stories, poems, plays, films, music, or original works of art

Advantages: Most accurate with least amount of filtering and distortion. You can evaluate the information and draw your own conclusions.

Disadvantages: Technical or specialized information may be difficult to understand or interpret. Even primary investigators and eye-witness reporters may distort or filter information.

Secondary sources: Reports on the work or words of others, second-hand information
- essays, articles, and books that report or interpret the work of others
- histories (by other than eye-witnesses), biographies, television, radio, or film documentaries (other than parts contributed by eye-witnesses)
- encyclopedias or other reference works

Advantages: Summaries, interpretations, and evaluations may prove helpful. Difficult or technical material may be explained. Gaps or biases in original information may be noted.
Disadvantages: Secondary source may be guilty of substantial omissions, distortion, filtering, or bias. Secondary source may lack qualifications to understand or report adequately on subject.

46 **c** Check standard reference sources.

To familiarize yourself quickly with a topic or area of research, check sources such as encyclopedias, handbooks, dictionaries, biographical dictionaries and indexes, almanacs, and other standard references. The reference librarian can tell you which ones are likely to be relevant for your research subject. Some of the most helpful types of reference works are described next.

- **Abstracts.** Brief summaries of journal, magazine, and newspaper articles appearing with the citation information for each article.
- **Almanacs, fact books, year books.** Lists of facts and data updated annually. Good for demographics and statistics, newsworthy events of the year in politics, economics, sports, the arts, notable births and deaths. May be national or international in scope.
- **Atlases and gazetteers.** Books of maps and geographical data. Often include population data.
- **Biographical references.** Include various *Who's Who* publications, biographical indexes, and dictionaries. Give information about or tell where to find information about important people, living or dead. May be general (*International Who's Who*) or specialized (*American Men and Women of Science*).
- **Bibliographic indexes.** Listings of articles and books on subjects arranged alphabetically.
- **Book review indexes and digests.** Listings of books reviews, where they have been published, and sometimes a quoted passage from the review.
- **Citation indexes.** Listings of references to works after they have been published. Useful for tracing reactions to authors, works, and ideas.
- **Dictionaries.** Definitions of terms. Specialized dictionaries exist for many fields. Good to consult throughout your research if your subject is technical, specialized, or unfamiliar to you.
- **Encyclopedias.** Broad overview of a subject, including historical background. Besides general encyclopedias, there are many specialized ones such as the

Encyclopedia of Computer Science and Technology. Entries often include a brief bibliography.

- **Guides to the literature.** Compilations of references sources in various disciplines. Works include such things as guides to statistical sources, government publications, British literature, Islamic art. A very broad and flexible category of reference works.
- **Handbooks.** Facts and information about such particular fields as chemistry, music, psychology, grammar, auto repair, economics, and photography. Sometimes arranged alphabetically, like a dictionary, with a focus on "how to" or "what is."
- **Periodical indexes.** Alphabetized listings of magazines, journals, and newspapers under key-word headings. Some indexes may be general, listing numerous subjects in periodicals of all sorts, including wide-circulation magazines and newspapers. Others may be specialized by type of subject matter (business, literature, law, medicine) or by type of publication indexed (only *The New York Times,* only mass circulation magazines, only scholarly journals in the social sciences).

The following is a representative list of reference books available in most libraries. Some reference books are revised or updated periodically, appear in new editions, or have supplements. Unless you want to locate historical information, you will usually want to look for the most recently published version.

Guides to Reference Sources

Brownstone, David, and Gorton Carruth. *Where to Find Business Information.* Directory to over 5,000 sources including databases, information services, government publications, books, and periodicals.

Galin, Saul, and Peter Spielberg. *Reference Books: How to Select and Use Them.*

Gates, Jean Key. *Guide to the Use of Books and Libraries.*

Sheehy, Eugene P. *Guide to Reference Books.* Supplement.

Shove, Raymond H. et al. *The Use of Books and Libraries.*

Statistical Sources. A subject guide to locating statistics sources.

Catalogs

Books in Print. Author and title indexes for *Publishers' Trade List Annual Subject Guide to Books in Print.*

Cumulative Book Index. Monthly listing of published books in English. Cumulated annually.

Monthly Catalog of U.S. Government Publications. 1895 to date.

National Union Catalog. Subject and author listings of Library of Congress holdings as well as titles from other libraries, motion pictures, recordings, and film strips.

Union List of Serials in Libraries of the United States and Canada. Lists of periodicals and newspapers. Supplemented monthly by *New Serial Titles.*

Vertical File Index. 1935—. Supplements to date (formerly called *Vertical File Service Catalog.* 1935-1954). Monthly, with annual cumulations. Subject and title index to selected pamphlet material.

General Encyclopedias

Collier's Encyclopedia. Multivolume.
Encyclopedia Americana. Multivolume.
Encyclopedia Britannica. Multivolume.
Encyclopedia International. Multivolume.
New Columbia Encyclopedia. 1 vol.
Random House Encyclopedia. 1 vol.

Dictionaries, Word Books

Abbreviations Dictionary. International in scope.
Acronyms, Initialisms and Abbreviations.
American Heritage Dictionary. Good notes on usage.
Dictionary of American English on Historical Principles. 4 vols. 1938-1944.
Dictionary of American Regional English.
Evans, Bergen, and Cornelia Evans. *A Dictionary of Contemporary American Usage.*
Fowler, Henry W. *Dictionary of Modern English Usage.* 2nd ed. Rev. by Sir Ernest Gowers.
Funk & Wagnalls New Comprehensive Dictionary. Unabridged.
Oxford Dictionary of English Etymology.
Oxford English Dictionary. 2nd ed. 20 vols. Also known as *New English Dictionary.* Unabridged.
Partridge, Eric. *A Dictionary of Slang and Unconventional English.*
Random House Dictionary of the English Language. Unabridged.
Roget's International Thesaurus. Several editions available.
Webster's Dictionary of Proper Names.
Webster's New Dictionary of Synonyms.
Webster's Third New International Dictionary. Unabridged.
Wentworth, Harold, and Stuart B. Flexner. *Dictionary of American Slang.*

Almanacs, Fact Books, Yearbooks

Americana Annual. 1924—.
Britannica Book of the Year. 1938—.
Congressional Quarterly Almanac.
Congressional Record. 1873—. Issued daily while Congress is in session: revised and issued in bound form at end of the session.
Facts on File. A weekly digest of world events. 1940—.
Historical Statistics of the United States: Colonial Times to 1970. 2 vols. 1975. Supplement to *Statistical Abstract.* Both published by U.S. Bureau of the Census.
Information Please Almanac.
Negro Almanac. 1967—.
New International Year Book. 1907—.
Official Associated Press Almanac. 1969—. An almanac with longer articles, strong emphasis on statistical data and biographical information.
Statistical Abstract of the United States. 1878—.
United Nations Statistical Yearbook. 1945-1968. Monthly supplements.
World Almanac and Book of Facts. 1868—.

Atlases and Gazetteers
Columbia-Lippincott Gazetteer of the World.
Commercial and Library Atlas of the World. Frequently revised.
Encyclopedia Britannica World Atlas. Frequently revised.
National Atlas of the United States.
National Geographic Atlas of the World.
New Cosmopolitan World Atlas. Issued annually.
The Times Atlas of the World.
Webster's New Geographical Dictionary.

General Biography
American Men and Women of Science.
Biographical Dictionaries Master Index. A guide to over 725,000 listings of
    biographies appearing in current dictionaries and collective biographical
    sources.
Biography Almanac.
Biography Index. 1946—. Quarterly. Cumulated annually, with permanent
    volumes every three years.
Current Biography: Who's News and Why. 1940—. Published monthly with
    semiannual and annual cumulations.
Dictionary of American Biography. 17 vols., supplements.
International Who's Who 1936—.
McGraw-Hill Encyclopedia of World Biography.
Webster's Biographical Dictionary.
Who's Who. (British) 1849—.
Who's Who in America. 1899—.
Who's Who of American Women. 1958—.
Who Was Who. 1897-1960.
Who Was Who in America. Historical Volume. 1607-1896.

Books of Quotations
Bartlett, John. *Familiar Quotations.*
Evans, Bergen. *Dictionary of Quotations.*
The Macmillan Book of Proverbs, Maxims, and Famous Phrases.
Oxford Dictionary of Quotations.

Mythology and Folklore
Brewer's Dictionary of Phrase and Fable.
Bullfinch, Thomas. *Bullfinch's Mythology.*
Funk & Wagnalls Standard Dictionary of Folklore, Mythology, and Legend.
    2 vols.
Hammond, N. G., and H. H. Scullord. *The Oxford Classical Dictionary.*
Larousse World Mythology.

Literature, Drama, Film, and Television
Aaronson, C. S., ed. *International Television Almanac.* 1956—.
Adelman, Irving, and R. Dworkin. *Modern Drama: A Checklist of Critical
    Literature on Twentieth Century Plays.*
Baugh, Albert C., ed. *A Literary History of England.*

Benét, William Rose. *The Reader's Encyclopedia.*
Bukalski, Peter J. *Film Research: A Critical Bibliography.*
Cassell's *Encyclopedia of World Literature.*
Cawkwell, Tim, and John Milton Smith, eds. *World Encyclopedia of the Film.*
Columbia Dictionary of Modern European Literature.
Contemporary Authors: A Bio-bibliographical Guide to Current Authors and Their Works. 1962—.
Dictionary of World Literary Terms.
Hart, J. D. *Oxford Companion to American Literature.*
Hartnoll, Phyllis. *The Oxford Companion to the Theatre.*
Harvey, Sir Paul, and J. E. Heseltine. *Oxford Companion to Classical Literature.*
———. *Oxford Companion to English Literature.*
Holman, C. Hugh. *A Handbook to Literature.*
International Encyclopedia of the Film.
Literary History of England. 4 vols.
Literary History of the United States. 2 vols.
MLA International Bibliography of Books and Articles on the Modern Languages and Literatures. Published annually since 1922.
New York Times Film Reviews, 1913-70.
Spiller, Robert E. et al., eds. *Literary History of the United States.*
Whitlow, Roger. *Black American Literature.*
Woodress, James, ed. *American Fiction 1900-1950: A Guide to Information Sources.*

History, Political Science
Almanac of American Politics.
Asian American Studies: An Annotated Bibliography & Research Guide.
Cambridge Ancient History. 5 vols. Plates.
Cambridge Medieval History. 1967—.
Dictionary of American History. 8 vols.
Durant, Will, and Ariel Durant. *The Story of Civilization.* 11 vols.
Encyclopedia of American History.
Harvard Guide to American History. 2 vols.
Historical Abstracts.
International Political Science Abstracts.
Johnson, Thomas H. *Oxford Companion to American History.*
Langer, William L. *An Encyclopedia of World History.*
Latinos in the United States: A Historical Bibliography.
The Native American: An Illustrated History.
New Cambridge Modern History. 14 vols.
Political Handbook and Atlas of the World. Published annually.
Political Science: A Bibliographical Guide to the Literature.
Schlesinger, Arthur M., and D. R. Fox, eds. *A History of American Life.* 13 vols. 1927-1948.

The Arts
Apel, Willi. *Harvard Dictionary of Music.*
Bryan, Michael. *Bryan's Dictionary of Painters and Engravers.* 5 vols.

Canaday, John C. *The Lives of the Painters.* 4 vols.
Chujoy, Anatole, and P. W. Manchester. *The Dance Encyclopedia.*
Encyclopedia of American Art.
Encyclopedia of Painting.
Encyclopedia of World Art. 15 vols.
Feather, Leonard. *Encyclopedia of Jazz.*
Fletcher, Sir Banister F. *A History of Architecture.*
Focal Encyclopedia of Photography. 2 vols.
Myers, Bernard S. *McGraw-Hill Dictionary of Art.* 5 vols.
New Grove Dictionary of Music and Musicians.
Osborne, Harold. *Oxford Companion to Art.*
Popular Music: An Annotated List of American Popular Songs. 6 vols.
Roach, Hillred. *Black American Music: Past and Present.*
Scholes, Percy A. *Oxford Companion to Music.*
Stambler, Eric. *Encyclopedia of Pop, Rock, and Soul.*
Thompson, Oscar, and N. Slonimsky. *International Cyclopedia of Music and Musicians.*

Philosophy, Religion

Adams, Charles, ed. *A Reader's Guide to the Great Religions.*
The Concise Encyclopedia of Western Philosophy and Philosophers.
Encyclopedia Judaica. 16 vols.
Encyclopedia of Philosophy. 4 vols.
Ferm, Vergilius. *Encyclopedia of Religion.*
Grant, Frederick C., and H. H. Rowley. *Dictionary of the Bible.*
New Catholic Encyclopedia. 17 vols.
New Schaff-Herzog Encyclopedia of Religious Knowledge 12 vols. and index.
Universal Jewish Encyclopedia. 10 vols.

Science, Technology

Chamber's Technical Dictionary. Revised with supplement.
Chemical Abstracts.
Dictionary of Physics.
Encyclopedia of Chemistry.
Encyclopedia of Biological Sciences.
Encyclopedia of Physics.
Gray, Peter, ed. *The Encyclopedia of the Biological Sciences.*
Handbook of Chemistry and Physics. 1914—.
McGraw-Hill Encyclopedia of Science and Technology. 15 vols.
Universal Encyclopedia of Mathematics. 1964.
Van Nostrand's Scientific Encyclopedia.

Social Sciences, Business, and Economics

Davis, John P., ed. *The American Negro Reference Book.*
Deidler, Lee J., and Douglas R. Carmichael. *Accountant's Handbook.*
A Dictionary of Psychology.
Dow Jones Irwin Business Almanac.
Encyclopedia of Computer Science and Technology.

Encyclopedia of Educational Research.
Encyclopedia of Human Behavior: Psychology, Psychiatry, and Mental Health.
Encyclopedia of Psychology.
Encyclopedia of Social Work. (formerly *Social Work Yearbook*, 1929-1960)
Good, Carter V. *Dictionary of Education.*
Greenwald, Douglas. *The McGraw-Hill Dictionary of Modern Economics.*
Heyel, Carl. *The Encyclopedia of Management.*
International Encyclopedia of the Social Sciences. 17 vols. Supplement.
Klein, Barry T., ed. *Reference Encyclopedia of the American Indians.*
Mitchell, Geoffrey, D. *A Dictionary of Sociology.*
Munn, G. G. *Encyclopedia of Banking and Finance.*
Standard & Poor's Register of Corporations, Directors and Executives. 3 vols.
  Updated annually.
Thomas Register of American Manufacturers. 1910—. Multivolume. Updated
  annually. Includes alphabetical listings of company profiles, also brand
  names and trademarks.
White, Carl M. et al. *Sources of Information on the Social Sciences.*

46 d Search the periodical indexes.

You will find the most current information in newspaper, magazine, and journal articles. These are accessed by means of general and special indexes listing articles under subject headings. General indexes list articles on many different topics. Special indexes limit themselves to articles in specific areas. Choose a general index when you want an overview of a subject. Articles listed in general indexes are more likely to be secondary sources, reports written by journalists about the work of others. Look in special indexes when you want to locate articles written by the experts themselves. For example, a general index such as the *Readers' Guide to Periodical Literature* will lead you to articles written for the general public about AIDS. However, if you want to read articles about AIDS research written by the scientists conducting the research, consult *Index Medicus*, which lists articles in medical journals. For college-level research writing, you should draw on the most authoritative and most primary sources available that you can understand. Certainly you should begin to read specialized and scholarly periodicals in your major field of study.

● **1 General indexes.** The following five indexes are particularly helpful for conducting general research.

Readers' Guide to Periodical Literature. 1900 to date. Published semimonthly;
  cumulated every three months and annually. Gives entries under author,
  title, and subject for articles appearing in about 160 popular periodicals.
International Index. 1907-1965. Became *Social Sciences and Humanities Index.*
  1965-1973. Divided into *Social Sciences Index*, 1974—, and *Humanities
  Index*, 1974—.

Poole's Index to Periodical Literature. 1802-1881. Supplements through January 1, 1907. This is a subject index to American and English periodicals.

Popular Periodicals Index. 1973——. An author and subject guide to popular articles appearing in about twenty-five periodicals not indexed by major indexing services.

Vertical File Index. 1932/1935——. Lists pamphlets on all subjects.

Reading a *Readers' Guide* Entry

The *Readers' Guide to Periodical Literature* is the most widely known and used of the general indexes. Because many periodical indexes use systems similar to that of the *Readers' Guide*, it is worth examining the following sample entries.

1 DIVALL, LINDA
        about
  And on the right ... A. Siegel. por *Working Woman* 17:69 F '92
2 DIVAS *See* Opera singers
3 DIVER, CHUCK
  Mixture madness. il *Flying* 119:114-15 Jl '92
4 DIVERS *See* Diving
5 DIVERSIFICATION IN AGRICULTURE
  Unusual ... and proud of it [ADAPT3 conference] B. Freese. il
    Successful Farming 90:20-1 mid-F '92
6 DIVERSIFICATION IN INDUSTRY
  The corporation. See issues of Business Week
  Un-diversifying [PacifiCorp] il *Forbes* 150:16+ S 14 '92
                 Japan
  If at first you don't succeed ... [Nippon Steel] G. Eisenstodt. il
    Forbes 149:68 Ja 20 '92
7 DIVERSITY (BIOLOGY)
    See also
  Conservation biology
  Convention on Biological Diversity
  Instituto Nacional de Biodiversidad de Costa Rica
  All creatures great & small [Endangered Species Act; cover
    story] C. Oliver. il *Reason* 23:22-7 Ap '92
  Are the tropics a cradle of diversity or only a museum? [work of
  David Jablonski] R. A. Kerr. *Science* 257:486 Jl 24 '92
     ·
       —From *Readers' Guide to Periodical Literature 1992.*

The headings for entries 2, 4, 5, 6, and 7 are **subject entries**. Entries 1 and 3 are **author entries**. Entry 6, a subject entry, indicates that an article on the subject of diversification in industry was published in the September 14, 1992 (volume 150) issue of *Forbes* magazine, starting on page 16. (The + sign indicates that the article continues on a page or pages after 16.) Titled "Un-diversifying," it was illustrated (*il*) and unsigned. (All abbreviations and symbols used are explained in the first pages of any issue of the *Readers' Guide.*)

Under entry 7 is a **see also** listing which gives other subject headings on the subject of diversity in biology to which the reader could

turn for further listings. Next it cites the cover story of the April 1992 issue of *Reason* titled "All Creatures Great and Small," by C. Oliver, and notes that the illustrated story appears on pages 22-27. In the brackets after the title it also notes that the article contains a discussion of the Endangered Species Act.

Entries 2 and 4 are **cross-references** to the places in the guide at which the reader can find the subject listed.

● **2 Special indexes.** These indexes list articles published in periodicals devoted to special concerns or fields.

> *The Bibliographic Index.* 1938—. Indexes current bibliographies by subject; includes both bibliographies published *as* books and pamphlets and those that appear *in* books, periodical articles, and pamphlets.
>
> *Book Review Digest.* 1905—. Monthly, cumulated annually. Lists books by author and quotes from several reviews for each. Covers seventy-five journals and newspapers.
>
> *Book Review Index.* 1965—. Covers 230 journals and lists books that have one or more reviews.
>
> *Current Book Review Citations.* 1976—. Indexes over 1,000 periodicals and includes fiction, nonfiction, and children's books.
>
> *Editorials on File.* 1970—.
>
> *Essay and General Literature Index.* 1934—. Indexes collections of essays, articles, and speeches.
>
> *Facts on File.* 1941—.
>
> *Newspaper Index.* Lists articles from the *Chicago Tribune, New Orleans Times-Picayune, Los Angeles Times*, and *Washington Post.*
>
> *New York Times Index.* 1913-. Semimonthly, with annual cumulation. Since this index provides dates on which important events, speeches, and the like occurred, it serves indirectly as an index to records of the same events in the other newspapers.
>
> *Ulrich's International Periodicals Directory.* 2 vols. Lists 65,000 periodicals under the subjects they contain, with detailed cross-references and index, thus indicating what periodicals are in a particular field. Also indicates in what other guide or index each periodical is indexed, thus serving indirectly as a master index.

The titles of most of the following special indexes are self-explanatory.

> *Accountants' Index.* 1944—.
>
> *Agricultural Index.* 1916 to date. A subject index, appearing nine times a year and cumulated annually.
>
> *Applied Science and Technology Index.* 1958 to date. (formerly *Industrial Arts Index*)
>
> *The Arts Index.* 1929 to date. An author and subject index.
>
> *Articles on American Literature.* 1900-1950. 1950-1967. 1968-1975.
>
> *Business Periodicals Index.* 1958 to date. Monthly. (formerly *Industrial Arts Index*)

Dramatic Index. 1909-1949. Continued in *Bulletin of Bibliography*, 1950 to date. Annual index to drama and theater.

The Education Index. 1929 to date. An author and subject index.

Engineering Index. 1884 to date. An author and subject index.

General Science Index. 1978—. Supplements monthly except June and December.

Granger's Index to Poetry.

Index Medicus. Lists medical articles.

Index to Legal Periodicals. 1908 to date. A quarterly author and subject index.

Industrial Arts Index. 1913-1957. An author and subject index, monthly, with annual cumulations. (In 1958 this index was split into *Applied Science and Technology Index* and *Business Periodicals Index.*)

International Nursing Index.

Monthly Catalog of United States Government Publications. 1905—.

Physical Education Index. 1978—. Covers not only physical education but sports in general. Published quarterly.

Play Index. 1978.

Public Affairs Information Service Bulletin. 1915 to date. Weekly, with bimonthly and annual cumulations. An index to materials on economics, politics, and sociology.

Quarterly Cumulative Index Medicus. 1927 to date. A continuation of the *Index Medicus,* 1899-1926. Indexes books as well as periodicals.

Short Story Index. 1953—. Supplements.

Social Sciences Index. 1974—.

Song Index. 1926. Supplement.

United Nations Documents Index. 1950—.

● **3 Electronic indexes and databases.** Many libraries offer electronic access to periodical indexes as well as the printed volumes listed previously in this chapter. Electronic indexes may be general or specialized, on-line (terminal connected to database by modem and telephone line) or CD-ROM. You may be able to access an index such as Periodical Abstracts–Research I (over 1,000 popular magazines, business periodicals, and academic publications) or *Cumulative Index to Nursing and Allied Health Literature* (articles from 300 journals, pamphlets, and dissertations) from a CD-ROM terminal or dial up DIALOG Information Retrieval Service on-line from your library—or even your computer at home. Check with your library to see what electronic databases, indexes, or on-line catalogs are available and how to use them.

Typically, electronic searches enable you to scan entries, select the ones you want to see in full detail, and then display a selected entry in "full-record" form, as shown in the following screen samples. Most computer search systems provide for printing screens so you do not have to copy down the information by hand. Many electronic indexing systems also feature abstracts and sometimes full texts of the indexed articles.

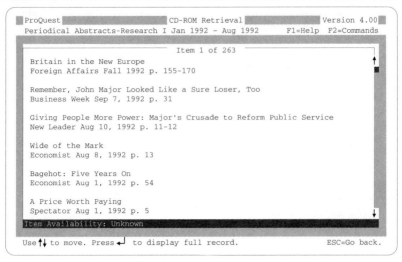

Electronic Index Title Screen

Electronic Index Full Record Screen

In Bonnie Lin's search for information about corporate responsibility for the environment, she used PROQUEST's "Newspaper Abstracts." Before copying any articles (which her library stores on microfilm and microfiche), she read the abstracts (summaries) onscreen to make sure they directly related to her research question. Two of the abstracts she read are printed next.

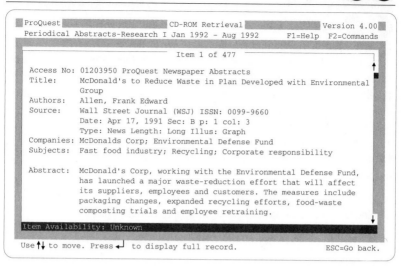

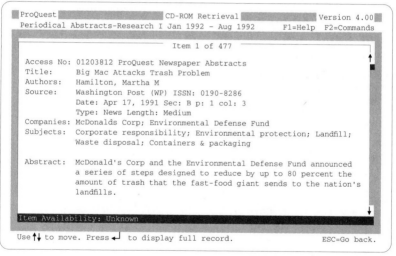

Onscreen Newspaper Abstracts

Although Bonnie read both of these articles, she found that the Hamilton article was more detailed than the Allen article, and she ended up citing only the former in her research paper, which appears in Section **48e**.

 **Continue your search at the union catalog.**

Once you have gained an overview of your subject, tentatively decided on a direction, and begun compiling a preliminary bibliography, you will be able to use the library's union catalog more effectively. This catalog unifies all the library's holdings, listing alphabetically all the books, periodicals, films, and other media the library contains. Its entries tell you the call number you need to locate books on the shelves. Your library may list periodicals in a separate serials catalog, either on cards, microfiche, or computer printout. In fact, some libraries store their entire catalog listing on microform or in computer files.

● **1 Classification systems.** The classification system on which a library catalog is based is a kind of map of library holdings. Library holdings are divided into categories with numbers or letters assigned to each. Consequently, if you know the numbers or letters for the general category you need, you occasionally might want to bypass the catalog, go directly to the appropriate shelves, and browse through the books.

The chief purpose of a classification system is to permit easy retrieval of stored materials. To further that objective, every item in the library is given a call number. Be sure to copy the call number fully and exactly as it appears in the catalog entry.

American libraries use either the **Dewey decimal system** or the **Library of Congress system** to classify books.

The Dewey system divides books into ten numbered classes:

000-099	General works	500-599	Pure science
100-199	Philosophy	600-699	Useful arts
200-299	Religion	700-799	Fine arts
300-399	Social sciences	800-899	Literature
400-499	Philology	900-999	History

Each of these divisions is further divided into ten parts, as

800	General literature	850	Italian literature
810	American literature	860	Spanish literature
820	English literature	870	Latin literature
830	German literature	880	Greek literature
840	French literature	890	Other literatures

Each of these divisions is further divided as

821	English poetry	826	English letters
822	English drama	827	English satire
823	English fiction	828	English miscellany
824	English essays	829	Anglo-Saxon
825	English oratory		

Further subdivisions are indicated by decimals. *The Romantic Rebels,* a book about Keats, Byron, and Shelley, is numbered 821.09, indicating a subdivision of the 821 English poetry category.

The Library of Congress classification system, used by large libraries, divides books into lettered classes:

A	General works	M	Music
B	Philosophy, Religion	N	Fine arts
C	History, Auxiliary sciences	P	Language and literature
D	Foreign history and topography	Q	Science
E-F	American history	R	Medicine
G	Geography, Anthropology	S	Agriculture
H	Social sciences	T	Technology
J	Political science	U	Military science
K	Law	V	Naval science
L	Education	Z	Bibliography, Library science

Each of these sections is further divided by letters and numbers that show the specific call number of a book. *English Composition in Theory and Practice* by Henry Seidel Canby and others is classified in this system as PE 1408.E5. (In the Dewey decimal system this same volume is numbered 808 C214.)

● **2 Search headings.** If your library uses the Library of Congress classification system, you will find near the catalog several volumes entitled *Library of Congress Subject Headings.* By looking up key words (descriptor terms, subject headings) related to your topic in these volumes, you will learn which headings to check in the subject section of the catalog.

If your library uses the Dewey decimal system, you will have to compare your list of key words directly with the catalog's subject entries to discover which ones are used as subject headings relevant to your topic. A reference book entitled *Sears List of Subject Headings* lists headings applicable to either the Dewey system or the Library of Congress system. Bonnie chose the most likely looking headings with which to begin her key word search at the library's on-line electronic catalog. The headings would serve equally well for searching a card catalog.

Besides **subject entries**, library catalogs also contain **author entries** and **title entries** (no title entry is used when the title begins with words as common as "A History of ..."). Following are author, title, and subject cards for a book found by looking under the subject heading "Environmental Policy" in a library's card catalog. Following the cards is an explanation of some of the information they contain.

Subject
Card

1 ENVIRONMENTAL POLICY--UNITED STATES.

2 HC
110   **3** Environmental policy in the 1990s :
E5   toward a new agenda / edited by
E49876   **4** Norman J. Vig, Michael E. Kraft.--
1994   **5** 2nd ed.--Washington D.C. : CQ
             Press, c1994.
         6 xviii, 422 p. ; 24 cm.
         7 Includes bibliographical references
         and index.

         8 1. Environmental policy--United
         States. 2. Environmental policy. I.
         Vig, Norman J. II. Kraft, Michael E.

9   17 DEC 93   28222232 AUMMsc   93-2116r93

Title
Card

HC
110   Environmental policy in the 1990s :
E5   toward a new agenda / edited by
E49876   Norman J. Vig, Michael E. Kraft. --
1994   2nd ed.--Washington D.C. : CQ
             Press, c1994.
             xviii, 422 p. ; 24 cm.
             Includes bibliographical references
             and index.

             1. Environmental policy--United
         States. 2. Environmental policy. I.
         Vig, Norman J. II. Kraft, Michael E.

     17 DEC 93   28222232 AUMMat   93-2116r93

Author
Card

Vig, Norman J.

HC
110   Environmental policy in the 1990s :
E5   toward a new agenda / edited by
E49876   Norman J. Vig, Michael E. Kraft. --
1994   2nd ed. -- Washington D.C. : CQ
             Press, c1994.
             xviii, 422 p. ; 24 cm.
             Includes bibliographical references
             and index.

             1. Environmental policy--United
         States. 2. Environmental policy. I.
         Vig, Norman J. II. Kraft, Michael E.

     17 DEC 93   28222232 AUMMat   93-2116r93

1 "ENVIRONMENTAL POLICY—UNITED STATES" is the **heading** under which the card is filed in the subject section of the catalog.

2 HC
110   gives the **call number**
E5   for the book in the Library
E49876   of Congress classification system.
1994

Except for the difference in call number, catalog cards using the Library of Congress system or the Dewey system contain identical information.

3 "Environmental policy in the 1990s: toward a new agenda" is the **full title** (including the subtitle) of the book. Note that the library practice of capitalization differs from standard practice.

4 "Norman J. Vig" and "Michael E. Kraft" are the editors of the book. Their names appear separately, in last-name-first order, as headings on author cards.

5 "2nd ed." means that this book is the second edition. Place of publication, publisher, and year of publication (copyright date) follow.

6 "xviii, 442 p.; 24 cm." indicates that the book contains 18 introductory pages numbered in Roman numerals and 422 pages numbered in Arabic numerals. There are no portraits or illustrations in the book; if there were, they would be listed next as "ports" and "ils." The book is 24 centimeters high (an inch equals 2.54 centimeters).

7 This **contents note** tells readers whether a book contains a bibliography or index. Make a habit of checking the contents note because a book with bibliography listings may lead you to other useful research sources.

8 "1. Environmental policy …" are **tracings** showing that the book is listed in the catalog under two subject headings (indicated by Arabic numerals) and two author headings (indicated by Roman numerals). When doing research, pay attention to subject tracings because they can lead you to other books related to your topic.

9 The line at the bottom of the card contains acquisition and cataloging information that is useful to library staff.

● **3 Electronic catalog searches.** If your library's catalog of holdings is electronic and accessible by computer, you will perform your searches in much the same way as if you were using a traditional card catalog. You will be able to search by author, title, or subject. If you conduct a subject search, you will need to use key-word headings such as those from the *Library of Congress Subject Headings*. Often it helps to narrow your search by combining key words or phrases with *and*—for instance, *smoking and cancer* rather than just *smoking* or *cancer*. The instructions posted at the catalog computer terminals will explain how to conduct an efficient search.

The information that appears on the computer screen may or may not look like the catalog cards shown previously. Different systems have different features. However, the standard bibliographic and location information will be there, and you will usually be able to print out the entry for future reference. The following example shows one such on-line catalog printout for a video recording.

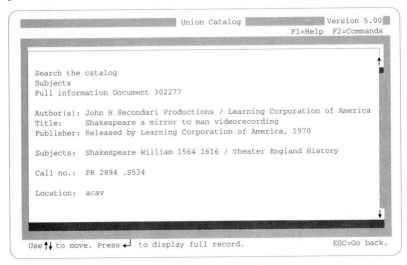

```
┌──────────────────────────────────────────────────────────────────────────┐
│              ████████ Union Catalog ████████  ██████ Version 5.00█        │
│                                         F1=Help  F2=Commands              │
│  ┌───────────────────────────────────────────────────────────────────┐↑  │
│  │                                                                   │██  │
│  │ Search the catalog                                                │    │
│  │ Subjects                                                          │    │
│  │ Full information Document 302277                                  │    │
│  │                                                                   │    │
│  │ Author(s): John H Secondari Productions / Learning Corporation of America │
│  │ Title:     Shakespeare a mirror to man videorecording            │    │
│  │ Publisher: Released by Learning Corporation of America, 1970      │    │
│  │                                                                   │    │
│  │ Subjects:  Shakespeare William 1564 1616 / Theater England History │   │
│  │                                                                   │    │
│  │ Call no.:  PR 2894 .S534                                          │    │
│  │                                                                   │    │
│  │ Location:  acav                                                   │    │
│  │                                                                   │    │
│  │                                                                   │↓   │
│  └───────────────────────────────────────────────────────────────────┘   │
│                                                                           │
│  Use ↑↓ to move. Press ↵ to display full record.        ESC=Go back.      │
└──────────────────────────────────────────────────────────────────────────┘
```

On-line Catalog Screen; Subject—Shakespeare

46 f Evaluate your selections.

Not everything you locate will be useful research material. Before you check a stack of books out of the library or photocopy dozens of pages from periodicals, spend a few minutes evaluating these sources. In addition to skimming the pages, examine the following:

In Books

Table of contents. It indicates what chapters might be useful.

Preface. It usually explains the book's purpose and the author's method. The preface may indicate that certain material has been omitted or included and why.

Introduction. It often gives a critical overview of the subject, establishing the focus and summarizing the approach taken.

Glossary. If included, it lists and defines terminology.

Index. It lists specific names, subjects, events, terms, and concepts covered in the book. Look to see if what you are looking for is listed.

Bibliography, footnotes, endnotes. These may list additional important books and articles.

About Books

Book Review Digest. Located in the library's reference collection, the *Digest* lists where book reviews have been published. Checking a review may tell you if the book is worthwhile.

About Magazines and Journals

Abstracts. Before searching for an article in a journal or magazine, see if the reference collection has an abstract volume for the field or subject area. See if an abstract of the article is available.

Classified List of Periodicals for the College Library. By Evan I. Farber. Provides publication information, types of subject matter, authors, and readers usually associated with scholarly and professional journals in the liberal arts and sciences by field. Does not cover technology or engineering. Helpful in evaluating a particular periodical's biases, authority, and credibility.

Magazines for Libraries. By Bill and Linda S. Katz. Describes most popular and many scholarly periodicals. Helpful in evaluating a periodical's biases, authority, and credibility.

Some preliminary evaluation of sources before you spend time reading them fully helps you make the best use of your research time. You'll want to narrow your sources to those that are the most relevant, reliable, and authoritative on your topic (see Sections **4b**, **6e**, and Chapter 7). You should continue your evaluation with all sources that you do read in part or in full so that the materials you ultimately use will result in a well-researched, well-balanced paper.

Exercise 46.1

Draw a diagram of the reference room of your library, indicating on it the position of the following reference books and indexes.

1 *Encyclopaedia Britannica*
2 *Encyclopedia of Religion and Ethics*
3 *Jewish Encyclopedia*
4 *Dictionary of American History* (DAH)
5 *Dictionary of American Biography* (DAB)
6 *American Authors, 1600-1900*
7 *Who's Who*
8 *Facts on File*
9 *World Almanac*
10 *New English Dictionary* (NED), often referred to as *Oxford English Dictionary* (OED)
11 union card or electronic catalog (if not in a separate room)
12 *Readers' Guide to Periodical Literature*
13 *The New York Times Index*
14 *The Art Index*
15 *Business Periodicals Index*

Exercise 46.2

Answer each of the following questions by consulting one of the standard reference guides listed in Exercise 46.1.

1   Where can you find articles published on AIDS in 1994?
2   Where can you find information on Alaska, its government, and the events leading to its statehood?
3   Among which tribe of American Indians is the highest development of shamanism found?
4   What was the first invention of Peter Cooper, American inventor, manufacturer, and philanthropist (d. 1883)?
5   What did the word *gossip* mean in twelfth-century England?

Exercise 46.3

To find a magazine article in *Readers' Guide* (or any periodical index), you must first know how to convert its information into conventional English. Demonstrate your familiarity with the *Readers' Guide* by examining the following excerpt and filling in the blanks.

> JOB APPLICATIONS
> *See also*
> Employment interviewing
> Employment references
> Applying yourself [applying for job as pastry chef to support painting and writing] N. Ring. il *The New York Times Magazine* p14+ N 15 '92
> Careers & opportunities 1992. B. W. O'Connor. il *Black Enterprise* 22:61-2+ F '92
> Get the job you want [address, May 11, 1991] H. Mackay. il *Reader's Digest* 140:83-6 My '92
> How to plan a super job search. A. M. White, il *Career World* 21:28-30 S '92
> If family members ask for a job. D. Bork. il *Nation's Business* 80:50+ Ap '92
> Job-hunting strategies for recent college grads. D. M. Baskerville. il *Black Enterprise* 23:155-6+ O '92

Articles on employment resumés are collected in the periodical index under the subject heading _____. These articles are arranged alphabetically by the _____ of the article. "How to Plan a Super Job Search" is the title of an article written by _____. "il" means the article includes _____. The title of the periodical in which this article appeared is _____. The article is in _____21, on _____ 83 to 86. "S '92" stands for the _____ and _____ the article was published.

Exercise 46.4

Select a specific research subject of interest to you. Then use your library's resources to answer the following questions.

1   What are the titles of general or special encyclopedias (or handbooks or other general works such as textbooks) that have articles providing information on your subject?
2   If any of these articles contain relevant bibliographies, write down the full bibliographic information for a few of the most useful items.

3 What three subject headings found in the *Library of Congress Subject Headings* or *Sears List of Subject Headings* volumes are most closely related to your subject?

4 Examine the tracings on at least two relevant subject entries in the union catalog. Which tracings fit your subject best?

5 Names of people and organizations appear in the subject section of the union catalog. What names related to your subject are listed?

6 Using the subject headings in the catalog, look for the subject division "—Bibliography." If you find any book-length bibliographies, cite a few of those that look most useful.

7 Use the catalog subject headings and list two books that have bibliographies in them. Give the page numbers for the bibliography sections if they are listed in the catalog entry.

8 In a book review index, locate reviews for one of the books relevant to your subject. Which book review index did you use? Where and when did the review originally appear?

9 List four periodical indexes (including one newspaper index and one collection of abstracts) showing useful articles on your subject. Write out the title, author (if any), and publication information for three articles. Using Katz's *Magazines for Libraries* and/or Farber's *Classified List of Periodicals for the College Library*, summarize their comments about the periodicals in which the articles are published.

10 Using the *Essay and General Literature Index*, give the following information pertaining to your research subject: (a) subject heading(s) used; (b) author of relevant essay; (c) title of that essay; (d) title of the book in which the essay appears; (e) call number of the book, if the library owns it.

In Your Own Words

Write a two-paragraph update to a friend or to your teacher about the progress of your research project. Mention particularly useful sources you have found, and mention the kind of information you are still seeking and ways in which you plan to search for it.

47 Drafting and Revising the Research Paper

47 a Understand the purposes of research papers.

The paper that reports "all about" a subject is not research. The aim of a true research paper is not just to summarize information or to show that you can use the library and know correct documentation form. Although these skills contribute to a research paper's success, your task as a writer is also to analyze and interpret information, to explore ideas and demonstrate their application, to think critically about the available evidence and draw valid conclusions from it.

Research projects usually start with a need for knowledge, or with an observation about what is known, and then systematically explore the subject with the aim of furthering the reader's understanding or breaking new ground. Consequently, research papers frequently test a theory, follow up on previous research, or explore a problem posed by other research or by events.

The opening section of a research paper typically introduces the broad subject and narrows it to the specific aspect the author intends to discuss. The opening often notes previous research, provides a context for the paper, or alerts the reader to points of view that will be explored later. First-year student Bonnie Lin's paper, reprinted at the end of Chapter 48, begins with a two-paragraph introduction that does all of these things. The author's research method or approach may also be mentioned in the introduction. And finally, the author indicates his or her point of view regarding the subject—the thesis or conclusions that the paper will demonstrate. Although these points may appear in a different order and with varying amounts of detail, they are usually all present in successful research papers.

47 **b** Determine your purpose and approach.

Instead of taking notes with the nearly impossible aim of "learning everything," you should direct your reading. Once you have an overview of your subject, you may decide you want to apply an accepted theory to a particular aspect of the subject. Or you may want to disagree with or modify someone else's conclusions, adding to and reinterpreting the evidence. Or perhaps your subject requires careful observation and field or lab work, the recording of data, and then hypothesis formulation and testing, as do the research subjects in Chapters 50 and 51. In any case, part of your research strategy should be deciding where you can make a contribution to the body of knowledge about your subject and then reading your sources with that goal in mind.

Bonnie Lin thought carefully about the purpose and audience for her research paper. As she read articles reporting opposing viewpoints of corporations' responsibility to protect or clean up the environment, she was surprised by the number of corporate managers who believe their only role is to generate profits for their stockholders. However, part of her assignment was to report on her findings as objectively as possible, so she knew she should not simply take the side of pro-environmentalists. Instead, she needed to draw on a variety of sources to give a fair presentation of all the perspectives of the business community.

As discussed in Chapter 46, Bonnie had broadened her original research question from "Why did McDonald's decide to start recycling?" to "Why do any companies decide to participate in recycling or other environmental measures?" After reading her preliminary sources, Bonnie changed the focus of her question to "What can companies who want to be environmentally responsible do to ensure that environmental protection becomes a reality?" She thought that by attempting to answer this question in her paper, she could discuss both the importance of corporate responsibility and the problems a company faces in making protection of the environment one of its priorities.

Bonnie's instructor had specified that the research paper should be written to an audience of her classmates and instructor. Since the course was English 102, Bonnie knew she had to assume that her audience would not have specialized knowledge of her subject matter. However, classmates would have a general knowledge of recent environmental problems from watching TV news and reading news magazines or newspapers. In her introduction she decided to cite some facts on environmental disasters that would make it obvious why some companies think that environmental protection should be a corporate goal.

Her research goal and approach decided, Bonnie drew up a rough outline of questions based on her preliminary reading, incorporating a few notes to herself to remember what her focus in each section would be. Bonnie then used this outline as a plan for further reading on her topic.

I. What widely publicized environmental disasters of recent years could I use to show why some companies think environmental protection needs to be part of their corporate goals? (check newspapers)
II. What kind of evidence could I use to show that environmentalism is becoming increasingly important to consumers? (and having an effect on companies that depend on consumers)
III. What are the different viewpoints of what business's role in protecting the environment should be?
   A. What companies have good plans for environmental protection? (McDonald's, Sun, need others)
   B. Which companies don't? (need more here)
   C. From an overall business point of view, what are the arguments either way? (profits and ethics)
IV. Exactly what have companies done to promote environmental concerns?
V. What are some of the problems companies face as they try to become environmentally responsible?

This working outline differs from the final one Bonnie submitted with her research paper, of course. It would undergo several revisions as her research developed, but at this stage it served her purpose well: to help her organize her thinking and plan her note-taking.

Record exact bibliographic information for each source.

You will need exact bibliographic information for the "Works Cited" pages at the end of your research paper. Therefore, throughout your preliminary search, carefully record publication information about each source that you

think you might use. Many researchers write an individual bibliography card for each source to make compiling the final bibliography list easier. Others prefer to make a computer file of these entries, and some programs will alphabetize the final list of entries for you. Another method is to record all bibliographic information in your research notebook or log. If you use this last method, writing on one side of the page only will help you arrange your citations more easily. Whichever method you choose, use it consistently. Failing to get all the necessary bibliographic information when you are consulting a book, article, or reference source such as an index or the library catalog usually delays and inconveniences you later. Omitting a particularly useful piece of information may necessitate looking through several books, periodicals, or bibliographies to relocate exact information for a bibliographic citation.

If you use the bibliography card method, you may want to use the 3" x 5" size for your entries. Record the information for a single source on each card so that later all you will have to do is to sort out the cards for the works you actually used in your final draft and then arrange them in alphabetical order for typing as "Works Cited" (in the MLA system of citation).

After you have checked with your instructor to find out which documentation (bibliographic) style you should use, write out the bibliographic information in the exact format required by that style. Doing so will ensure that you record all the information you will need for your "Works Cited" or other bibliography list.

Recording Complete Publication Information

To compile your bibliography, list:

- Author and/or editor or translator, if there is one
- Full title and subtitle of book or article
- Publisher's name and place of publication
- Year of publication for a book; volume number and date for an article
- Page numbers on which an article appears

Consult the style manual for the documentation style you will use for the kinds of information to record for nonprint sources. See the chart in Section **49c** for the names of style manuals and the sample citation entries of MLA style in Chapter 48, APA style in Chapter 50, CBE style in Chapter 51, and CMS style in Chapter 52.

To find your source again if you need more information, list:

- The call number or other information on location in the library
- The name of the index in which you found the source listed
- Printouts of database searches

Take careful notes: summary, paraphrase, and direct quotation.

Taking notes on 4" x 6" or 5" x 8" index cards is usually more efficient than writing them on full sheets of paper; cards are easier to carry and easier to rearrange when you are deciding on the organization for your paper. Limiting each note card to a single subject or even a single subtopic facilitates such rearrangements.

Some students write all their research notes as direct quotations from their sources. However, this method is tedious, time-consuming, and unnecessary. Furthermore, the act of transcribing prevents you from assimilating and evaluating the material as you read it. Take most of your notes in summary or paraphrase form, reserving direct quotations for material that is especially well stated or for points that might require the clout of a respected authority's exact words. No matter what form your notes take, all notecards should include the following information.

Notecard Information

- Shortened publication information such as author's last name for cross-referencing to complete publication information on bibliographic cards or notes
- Page numbers of the source. If the note includes information from several pages, show which information is from which page.
- Topic heading for easy sorting while drafting the paper
- Brackets around your own ideas and notes to separate them clearly from the source material

● **1 Summary notes.** A **summary** is a brief note that captures information quickly without regard for style or careful expression. Your purpose is simply to record the facts or important points, to give a rough sketch of the material. Whenever you include a summary in your research paper, be sure to cite the source appropriately.

Summary

deceptive companies

"Environmental Group"
WP, 28 Aug. 1991, sec. F 3

Friends of the Earth, an environmental interest group,
cited DuPont's dismal environmental record based
on comparative studies and EPA data. Striking contrast
to company's self-image as environmentally friendly.
[Compare Swasy on P & G.]

● **2 Paraphrase notes.** A **paraphrase** is a restatement of the source material in your own words, syntax, and style but preserving the tone of the original (humor, doubt, etc.) and of approximately the same length. A paraphrase uses the original author's idea and presents it in your own language. Since in paraphrasing you are borrowing someone's thoughts, you must cite the source when you use the paraphrase in your paper.

Paraphrase

> Kodak and environmental responsibility
> and corporate structure
>
> Poduska, 287
>
> Kodak has a environmental management program that reveals how the company makes environmental responsibility part of its structure. Corporate and group teams are key. Headed by the CEO and made up of group presidents and senior staff vice presidents, the Committee on Environmental Responsibility is concerned with the company's environmental policies worldwide. Next the Health, Safety and Environment Coordinating Committee advises and counsels. Finally, the largest staff (400) makes up the Corporate Health, Safety and Environment Organization, which acts as a resource for the other committees.

● **3 Direct quotation notes.** A **direct quotation** records exactly the words of the original source (as well as the exact punctuation and even any spelling errors; see Section **38b** for the use of *sic* in such instances). Like summaries and paraphrases, direct quotations require citations in your paper crediting the source from which you copied them. Always put quotation marks around all the material you take word for word from any source. In general, use direct quotations only for particularly telling phrases or for information that must be rendered exactly as you found it.

Direct Quotation

> N. Craig Smith, 59
>
> Henry Ford's definition of a socially responsible company (environmental responsibility is good business)
>
> "There is no longer anything to reconcile...between the social conscience and the profit motive.... Improving the quality of society...is nothing more than another step in the evolutionary process of taking a more far-sighted view of return on investment."

Bonnie used ellipsis marks to indicate omissions from the source (see Section **38c**). She wanted to include only those ideas that directly related to the focus of her paper.

47 e Be careful not to plagiarize the work of others, either by accident or by design.

Plagiarism consists of passing off the ideas, opinions, conclusions, facts, words—in short, the intellectual work—of another as your own. **Plagiarism is dishonest and carries penalties** not only in academic environments but in all professions, as well as in copyright law.

The most obvious kind of plagiarism occurs when you appropriate whole paragraphs or longer passages from another writer for your own paper. Long word-for-word quotations are rarely appropriate to a paper, but when they are, you must indicate clearly that they *are* quotations and indicate their exact source. No less dishonest is the use of all or most of a single sentence or an apt figure of speech appropriated without acknowledgment from another source.

Suppose, for example, that you are working on a paper about families and have read a book by Jane Howard entitled *Families*. You have a note card on which you have written the partial sentence "Good families have a switchboard operator—someone who cannot help but keep track of what all the others are up to...." Your notes indicate that this is a quotation. But when you turn to writing your paper, this and other phrases from the same source seem so apt to your purposes in a slightly different context that you yield to temptation and write, as if in your own words, "All families need at least two things: someone around whom others cluster and someone who cannot help but keep track of what all the others are up to—a kind of switchboard operator." You have plagiarized just as badly as the writer who has appropriated a whole paragraph. The words are not yours, they are Jane Howard's, and honesty requires that you give her credit for them.

You are unlikely to copy directly from another writer without being consciously dishonest as you do so. But even though you acknowledge the source in a citation, you are also plagiarizing when you incorporate in your paper faultily paraphrased or summarized passages from another author in which you follow almost exactly the original's sentence patterns and phrasing. Paraphrasing and summarizing require that you fully digest an author's ideas and interpretations and restate them in your own words—and you must reference the source. It is not enough simply to modify the original author's sentences slightly, to change a word here and there. Consider the following original together with the sample paraphrases and summary:

Original

The craft of hurricane forecasting advanced rapidly in the Sixties and early Seventies, thanks to fast computers and new atmospheric modeling techniques. Now there is a lull in the progress, strangely parallel to the lull in the storm cycle. The Center shoots for a 24-hour warning period, with 12 daylight hours for evacuation. At that remove, it can usually predict landfall within 100 miles either way. Longer lead times mean much larger landfall error and that is counterproductive. He who misses his predictions cries wolf.

—William H. Macleish, "Our Barrier Islands," *Smithsonian* Sept. 1980: 54.

Faulty Paraphrase

Hurricane forecasting made rapid progress in the sixties and seventies due to fast computers and new atmospheric techniques, but there is now a lull in the progress. The Warning Center tries for a 24-hour warning period, including 12 hours of daylight. That close to a storm, it can usually predict landfall within 100 miles either way. If lead times are longer, there will be a much larger error, which will be counterproductive (Macleish 54).

Even though the writer acknowledges the author (as indicated by the citation at the end of the paragraph), this is a clear example of plagiarism. The author has combined the first two sentences of the original and changed a few words here and there but in no way indicated that most of the paragraph's structure and phrasing is almost exactly that of the original.

Improved Paraphrase

New techniques, together with computers, have significantly increased the accuracy of hurricane forecasting. Now it is possible to predict where a hurricane will hit land with an error of not more than 100 miles if a warning of 24 hours is allowed. If more than 24 hours is required, the error will be proportionately greater (Macleish 54).

This paraphrase successfully puts the information in the words of the researcher. Both the sentence structure and the phrasing are clearly the researcher's, not the original author's. But such a full paraphrase of a relatively simple passage is probably much more complete than someone researching hurricane warning problems and developments in a variety of sources would need. In many contexts, a simple, brief summary statement like the following might well be sufficient:

Summary

With computers and new techniques, forecasters can now provide a 24-hour hurricane warning and predict within 100 miles either way where a storm will hit (Macleish 54).

In Your Own Words

For each of the following passages, write a summary note and a paraphrase note. If you think a passage contains subtopics that would best be handled as separate notes, prepare a summary and paraphrase for each subtopic. Be sure that you have avoided plagiarism: restate the original ideas in your own words. If you think that in a few spots there is no adequate substitute for the original language, put those words in quotation marks.

1 "But rock music has one appeal only, a barbaric appeal, to sexual desire—not love, not eros, but sexual desire undeveloped and untutored. It acknowledges the first emanations of children's emerging sensuality and addresses them seriously, eliciting them and legitimating them, not as little sprouts that must be carefully tended in order to grow into gorgeous flowers, but as the real thing. Rock gives children, on a silver platter, with all the public authority of the entertainment industry, everything their parents always used to tell them they had to wait for until they grew up and would understand later."
—Allan Bloom, from *The Closing of the American Mind*

2 "Any education that matters is *liberal*. All the saving truths and healing graces that distinguish a good education from a bad one or a full education from a half-empty one are contained in that word. Whatever ups and downs the term 'liberal' suffers in the political vocabulary, it soars above all controversy in the educational world. In the blackest pits of pedagogy the squirming victim has only to ask, 'What's liberal about this?' to shame his persecutors. In times past a liberal education set off a free man from a slave or a gentleman from laborers and artisans. It now distinguishes whatever nourishes the mind and spirit from the training which is merely practical or professional or from the trivialities which are no training at all. Such an education involves a combination of knowledge, skills, and standards."
—Alan Simpson, from *The Marks of an Educated Man*

3 "In almost every college or university, the library is acknowledged by faculty, students, and administrators as the 'heart of the campus.' Yet on many college campuses the potential of the library goes unrealized. The library becomes an underutilized, expensive storehouse. Librarians are seen as, or what is worse, perform as keepers of the books, or, in the words of a Cambridge University faculty member, 'warehouse managers.' Consequently, library materials purchased to support the curriculum lie unused on the shelves. Students who frequent the library often use it as a study hall or as a convenient location for a social gathering. In addition when students have a course assignment or research paper that requires the use of library materials, they often perform poorly and spend more time than necessary. The reason for such poor performance is that most students do not have the necessary skills to effectively identify and use appropriate library materials."
—Carla J. Stoffle, "The Library's Role in Facilitating Quality Teaching"

47 **f** **Learn when and how to use quotations.**

A research paper loaded with quotations or consisting of long quotations stitched loosely together with brief comments will almost always be an unsatisfactory paper. The point of research is to present in your own words the interpretations and judgments you have come to as a result of your investigation, making clear and accurate references to the sources you have consulted.

The almost irresistible temptation for inexperienced writers is to justify every major point they make in their research paper with a quotation from an authority. First, you are entitled to draw conclusions about your research subject; not everything you say requires backing up with a source. Second, use paraphrases and summaries instead of quotations in most cases where sources are cited. Frequently, the point can be made better in your own words, with proper citation, than in the words of the original.

Learning to use quotations wisely when you have good reason and learning how to fit them easily, naturally, and logically into your paper are signs of effective composition. Your *use* of a quotation, not the quotation itself, is part of your research contribution. When readers come upon a quotation, they should never feel that it has been "chopped" from the original source and "dropped" on them suddenly. One of your tasks as a researcher and writer is to provide appropriate contexts for the quotations you are using. Consequently, it is often a good idea to mention the source or the importance of a quotation in the text of your paper. By providing an introductory phrase such as "according to a leading authority," or "a recent government study shows that…," you not only supply a frame of reference for the quotation but you also establish its authority and credibility in your reader's mind. Thus the quotation becomes an intrinsic part of the whole weave of your paper.

Many contexts can support the use of brief and—less frequently—long quotations. But the contexts in which they are most likely to be preferable to paraphrase or summary are those in which the original phrasing is striking, memorable, or lends concreteness or authenticity; the force of the statement is important and would be lost in paraphrase; the quotation is an example of what is being discussed; or, in writing about a writer or a literary work, the quotations exemplify the writer's style or typify a character, theme, or the like.

In her paper (see Section **48e**), Bonnie Lin uses four quotations long enough to be indented (see Section **37c**). The first, on pages 4 and 5 of her paper, lists the ten CERES Principles. Bonnie listed these principles instead of including them in a series of phrases within a single sentence because she wanted to focus her readers' attention on their broad application to any kind of business. To make sure that she did not misinterpret Exxon's reasons for refusing to sign a set of environmental principles, Bonnie quoted Exxon officials' exact statement on page 5. She used the long quotation from a McDonald's executive on page 6 to emphasize the questionable nature of McDonald's refusal to support the CERES principles, which are so broadly stated that they hardly "have little or no application in the hamburger business." Finally, Bonnie quotes Henry Ford toward the very end of her paper as a way to remind readers that paying attention to social issues (such as environmentalism) is compatible with the profit motive that drives companies' activities. She uses the quotation as a backboard off which to bounce her own concluding sentences.

Bonnie provides suitable introductions for the long quotations, making clear the purpose they serve and establishing the context in which they are to be understood. She also has been selective, using ellipses in the last quotation to indicate omitted material extraneous to her purpose. Such omissions are desirable as long as they do not change the meaning of the original.

Like long quotations, short ones need to be fitted naturally into the flow of your paper. Short quotations should be worked smoothly into the syntax of your sentences; furthermore, they should be introduced in a way that establishes the connection between the source and the point you are making. Notice how the following examples by student writers achieve these goals with phrases such as *John Frederick Nims remarks, reports that, in McCarthy's words,* or *preaching that…those who tell us that.* The numbers in parentheses are in-text page citations.

> Not all Victorian women were the shy, timid, modest beings they are sometimes imagined to be. Elizabeth Barrett Browning once submitted a poem about women as sex objects which her editor rejected "for indecency." As John Frederick Nims remarks, "Who would have expected such a poem from a Victorian lady with three names?" (187).

> Any study of the music of Bela Bartok can well begin by taking note of the commanding presence of the man himself. Yehudi Menuhin, describing his first meeting with the composer, reports that he "felt at once that I was facing someone pared down to the essential core" (16).

> The book which is most informative about Mary McCarthy as a person is perhaps her *Memories of a Catholic Girlhood,* which reflects, in part, her early life with her great-aunt, who, in McCarthy's words, "had a gift for turning everything sour and ugly" (49).

> There is nothing like a time of inflation, declining productivity, burgeoning government expenditures, and increasing taxes to unleash a flood of conflicting economic theory. Our own period is fertile ground for such debate, and we find ourselves choosing sides between those who believe that only a return to the virtues of old-line capitalism can save us, preaching that we must untax the rich so that they may invest, since "the creation of wealth is the only salvation of the poor," (Abelson 21) and those who tell us that only a "fundamental restructuring of American society" (Fitzpatrick 383) will keep us from going down.

Whenever you use direct quotations in your writing, be sure to transcribe them accurately. Make it a rule to check and recheck each quotation, including its punctuation. Make sure that you understand the mechanical conventions of quoting material. Indicate omissions from a quotation by using ellipses (see Section **38c**), and make sure that what you retain is grammatically coherent. If you insert words of your own in the original, indicate your insertion by placing brackets around it (see Section **38a**). If the quotation contains a mistake or peculiarity of spelling or grammar, retain it in your quotation but indicate that it appears in the original by using *sic* ("thus it is") in brackets immediately following it (see Section **38b**).

In Your Own Words

Choose one of the passages from the previous "In Your Own Words" exercise and write a paragraph or two about the topic the passage discusses. Incorporate at least two direct quotations from the passage into your paragraph. Work them smoothly and naturally into your writing, avoiding "chop-and-drop" quotations. Be sure to use punctuation correctly, including any ellipses and brackets.

47 g Revise the research paper.

Writing a successful research paper requires uniting many parts into a coherent whole. Because of its length and scope, the argumentative nature of its thesis, and the complexity and variety of evidence gathered to support that thesis, a research paper presents a very challenging task for the writer. Sometimes writers discover that their paper does not prove the point they set forth in the beginning and does not succeed as a coherent whole, even though they have worked very hard at the research and drafting. Major revisions may be necessary. Several steps will help you manage your research paper and revise it as necessary.

● **1 Allow yourself enough time to research the subject and write the paper.** A paper begun Friday night when it is due Monday morning will be an extremely superficial paper, if not a total failure. You will suffer from short-term memory overload, be unable to see crucial connections between ideas, and use only whatever research materials you can quickly lay hands on—rather than those materials that will best aid your work. It is not too soon to start your paper a month before it is due. Some research projects will require even longer, possibly a whole term. Professional researchers may spend years on their projects.

● **2 Give the paper a cooling-off period—at least two or three days—after you have completed the first draft.** You will need the objectivity several days can provide if you want to be able to reread your paper critically and revise it effectively.

● **3 Check each paragraph before you revise to be sure it has clear and explicit connections to the thesis and adds something new and important to the proof.** Check your paper to be sure all the parts relate to the thesis. Compare the paper and its final outline against the rough outline or idea tree you worked from when you began your research. Has your paper wandered from its focus? Or does your draft improve upon your original scheme? Second, when you have worked hard to research and compile evidence, it is very tempting to include too much material in the first draft. Make sure that everything in your paper is necessary. Ruthlessly cut the portions that are repetitious or off the main line of your argument.

● **4 Be sure you have provided adequate transitions between ideas and sections.** What seems obvious to you because you have been thinking about the subject so intensely may not be obvious to your readers. Provide your audience with clear road signs: Spell out the logic of your argument wherever it might not be clear.

● **5 Look at every quotation.** Is each one necessary, or would a paraphrase or summary be better? Does the paper provide sufficient and correct documentation (see Chapter 48)? Are the quotations integrated into the paper (no "chop-and-drop")? Does the paper supply appropriate contexts for the words or ideas of others?

● **6 Have you written a paper that shows you have thought critically about your subject and the work of others on that subject?** Your research paper should be more than a conglomeration of other people's words and ideas. It should show your critical analysis of those ideas, persuasively present your informed conclusions, and express your contribution to an on-going dialogue on the subject.

Research Writing

Revision Checklist

Meaning Changes
- **Subject.** Is the subject clear? Are the ideas in the paper all related to the subject? (Chapters 2-4)
- **Focus.** In addition to the subject, does the paper have a clear, controlling idea? Are all the paragraphs in the paper related to the controlling idea? (Chapter 3)
- **Thesis.** Is there a thesis statement that expresses the controlling idea? Because of their length and complexity, research papers need a clear statement of thesis. (Chapter 3)
- **Development.** Are the ideas and points of view in the paper adequately explained? Will connections between ideas, between threads of the argument, and between sections of the paper be obvious to readers or should they be explained? (Chapters 4, 6)
- **Organization.** Do the ideas and paragraphs in the paper progress in an organized fashion? Have clear transitions been provided? Will readers be able to

follow the progression of ideas and explanations of points of view easily? (Chapter 6)

- **Logic.** Are the assertions adequately supported with evidence? Are ideas presented fairly, without bias? Have fallacies in reasoning been avoided? Is the presentation of point of view balanced? Have the pros and cons of various points of view been weighed honestly? (Chapter 7)

- **Use of sources.** Are the sources used in the paper credible, reliable, and authoritative? Is the information the most recent obtainable? Are quotations exact? Have summaries and paraphrases been written without plagiarizing language from the original? (Chapter 47)

- **Documentation of sources.** Has all the information used in the paper— facts, summaries, paraphrases, and quotations from research sources—been acknowledged accurately and appropriately with in-text references, documented citations, and bibliography entries? (Chapter 48)

- **Audience.** Has the paper taken audience into account? Has sufficient background information been provided? Has the audience's level of expertise, interest, and point of view regarding the subject been considered? Are definitions of technical or unfamiliar terms supplied where necessary? (Chapter 2)

- **Opening and closing.** Does the paper have an effective beginning and a strong conclusion that ties the threads of the paper's argument together? (Chapter 4)

- **Purpose.** Does the paper have a clear aim? Has it fulfilled that aim? (Chapter 2)

- **Title.** Does the paper have a title that captures the reader's interest and clearly indicates what the paper is about? (Chapter 4)

Surface Changes

- **Documentation of sources.** Have all in-text citations and bibliography entries been carefully checked for complete and accurate information and correct documentation format? (Chapter 48)

- **Grammar, punctuation, spelling.** Has proofreading for these errors been thorough? Have mistakes been corrected? (Chapters 12-20, 26-29, 31-42, 25)

- **Mechanics.** Have the conventions of capitalization, use of abbreviations, numbers, and so forth that are appropriate for the subject and audience been observed? (Chapters 40, 43-45)

- **Level of language.** Is word choice precise and appropriate for the subject and audience? (Chapters 22-23)

- **Wordiness.** Have words been used economically and effectively, avoiding wordiness, unnecessary jargon, and vagueness? (Chapter 24)

- **Sentence structure.** Are sentences logical, well constructed, and effective in their use of subordination, variety, parallelism, and emphasis? (Chapters 8-11)

 # Documenting the Research Paper

One of the purposes of keeping accurate bibliography cards and notes that carefully distinguish between direct quotation and summary or paraphrase is to provide the information you will need for documenting the source material you have used in your research paper. You must acknowledge all the facts, ideas, interpretations, opinions, and conclusions of others that you incorporate into your own paper by documenting the sources—whether they be books, periodicals, interviews, speeches, or lab or field studies.

48 a Decide what to document and what not to document.

● **1 What to acknowledge.** Always acknowledge all direct quotations, statistics, charts, diagrams, tables, and the like that you reproduce entirely or partially in your paper. Always acknowledge your paraphrases and summaries of the interpretations, opinions, and conclusions presented in your sources. Keep in mind that the interpretations and conclusions reached by researchers and scholars are in many ways more important contributions than the bald facts they may have gathered and are therefore even more deserving of acknowledgment.

● **2 What not to acknowledge.** You do not have to provide documentation for facts that are considered common knowledge. "Common knowledge" consists of standard historical and literary information available in many different reference books—the fact that John F. Kennedy died in 1963, the fact that Charles Dickens created such characters as Uriah Heep and Mr. Micawber, or that Darwin's theory of evolution was the subject of great intellectual debate in the nineteenth century. Such information is considered common knowledge as far as documentation is concerned, even though you may have learned it for the first time when you began your research.

In contrast, common sense will tell you that highly specialized facts— the cost of a six-room house in the 1830s, the number of Polaroid cameras sold between 1980 and 1990, the estimated population of Mongolia in 1960, the highest recorded tide in San Francisco Bay, or the number of earthquakes in Peru during the twentieth century—are unlikely to be common knowledge, and so the sources of information should be documented.

In addition to information that is widely available and undisputed, facts agreed on by nearly all authorities discussing a particular subject are considered common knowledge. As soon as you explore any subject to some depth, you will quickly come to see that certain material is taken as established fact while other material is disputed or has been established by some special investigation. A student writing on the poet Wordsworth for the first time, for instance, may not have known initially that the *Preface to the Lyrical Ballads* was first published in 1800, but it will not take long to discover that everyone writing on the subject accepts this as an established fact. Such information will not need to be acknowledged. In contrast, the exact date of a particular poem may be a matter of dispute or may have been established by a scholar's diligent research. This kind of information must be acknowledged.

48 **b** **Use appropriate documentation form.**

Documentation is the means by which you acknowledge material you have used from outside sources. In professional scholarship, documentation forms are complex and varied. Most forms have evolved from the demands of professional scholarship, itself a precise and exacting business. Furthermore, the preferred form for citations and bibliographic entries varies considerably among disciplines. Each of the natural sciences, the American Medical Association, the American Bar Association, such fields as linguistics, and many other disciplines have their own preferred styles, each of which is described in the particular group's style manual (see Chapters 49-51). For any discipline in which you write, *always check the professional publications and relevant style manuals to determine the appropriate documentation form.* When you write for a specific assignment, ask your instructor which documentation style he or she prefers.

48 **c** **Use the MLA name and page system in most humanities courses.**

The **name and page system** described by the Modern Language Association in its *MLA Handbook for Writers of Research Papers* (1988) is the documentation form used by some eighty professional journals in the languages, humanities, and some social sciences. This system uses **in-text citations** (rather than footnotes or endnotes) to acknowledge the words or ideas of outside sources where they are used in a paper. The only exceptions are **content and bibliographical endnotes** (see Section **48c3**).

● **1 MLA in-text citations.** In-text citations provide the documentation for outside sources in parentheses that appear as close as possible to the documented material without disrupting the grammar or sense of the material. Usually this location is at the end of the sentence.

MLA Standard Parenthetical In-Text Citation Format

- author's last name (or shortened title of work, if there is no author)
- one space (no punctuation)
- page number (Number only: Do not use "p." or "pp." or "pgs.")

Work by one author.

```
     In fact, EPA estimates by the year 2000, nearly 3 percent of
the nation's Gross National Product (GNP)--$160 billion--will be
spent on protecting the environment (Thomas 21).
```

Notice that in the parenthetical reference, the name of the author of the source (Thomas) and the page number (21) have no punctuation between them, nor does any abbreviation for "page" (such as "p.") precede the page number.

All references cited in the text are listed alphabetically in a section called *Works Cited* at the end of the paper. As illustrated on pages 12 and 13 of Bonnie Lin's paper (Section **48e**), the "Works Cited" list functions as a bibliography, usually listing references by author's last name, if known, or by title if the author is not known. Sometimes a work will be listed by an editor's, translator's, or other person's name. Thus, the "Works Cited" entry for the aforementioned Thomas material would be listed as follows:

```
Thomas, Lee M.   "The Business Community and the Environment: An
     Important Partnership."   Business Horizons 35 (1992): 21+.
```

In the Thomas in-text citation, the author's name is not mentioned in the text of the sentence; thus it must be given in the citation so that readers can find the appropriate "Works Cited" entry. However, the citation usually includes only the page number if the author's name has been stated in the sentence itself:

```
     According to Peter A. French, author of Corporations in the
Moral Community, "Environmental quality is the issue which will be
the single most important issue facing corporations...in the twen-
ty-first century" (117).
```

What you cite in the text has a direct bearing on what you place in parentheses: that is, when information appears in a text sentence, it is not repeated in parentheses.

For the sake of readability, look for ways to integrate citations smoothly into your sentences. Your goal should be to keep parenthetical references concise. If you can do so in a convenient and readable fashion, integrate reference information into the text:

```
     Hamlet's well-known "To be, or not to be" lines (56-89) in
Act II, scene 1 are probably the most famous of Shakespeare's
soliloquies and also probably one of the most misinterpreted.
```

rather than

```
     The well-known "To be, or not to be" lines are probably the
most famous of Shakespeare's soliloquies and also probably one of
the most misinterpreted (Hamlet, 2.1.56-89).
```

Besides at the end of a sentence, references may sometimes be placed conveniently at the ends of phrases or clauses, after statistics, and so forth.

For example,

> Norton and Monroe's survey found that 57 percent of America's drivers do not use their seat-belts (73), but we suspect the percentage is much higher.

The name-page system enables readers to find a source in your bibliography and also the place in the source where the cited material appears. Giving the author's last name and the page number usually fulfills this purpose, but some cases require additional in-text information. For example,

Two or three authors; more than three authors.

> The question then becomes whether "work produced by the institutional computer is looked upon as the work of the organization" (Pendergast, Slade, and Winkless 130); in contrast, the personal computer is identified with the individual (Elbring et al. 54).

Work by an author of two or more works cited; anonymous author.

> Vonnegut believes large families, whether biological or artificial, help sustain sanity (Sunday 66), and they nurture idealism. As the protagonist in Jailbird says, "I still believe that peace and plenty and happiness can be worked out some way. I am a fool" (57-58). This idealism endears Vonnegut to his readers ("Forty-Six" 79).

When a "Works Cited" section lists more than one work by the same author, in-text citations should contain the title (or a shortened version, such as *Sunday* for *Palm Sunday*) so readers will know which of the author's works you are referring to. For references to unsigned (anonymous) works, cite the title (or shortened form) and page number. The preceding example refers to an unsigned book review entitled "Forty-Six and Trusted."

Literary works.

> P. D. James uses lines from a play by John Webster as clues in her detective novel The Skull Beneath the Skin--for instance in the note left at the murder scene (145; bk. 3, ch. 4): "Other sins only speak; murder shrieks out" (Duchess of Malfi, 4.2.261).

Novels or plays that appear in several editions are best cited not only by page number (given first in the entry) but also by such information as chapter (ch.), part (pt.), or book (bk.) number, so that readers can follow your citations in editions other than the one you refer to. References to verse plays or poems customarily omit page numbers, instead listing more helpful information such as division numbers (act, scene, canto, etc.) followed by line numbers. The numbers 56-89 and 261 in the citations of *Hamlet* and *The Duchess of Malfi* are line numbers.

Multivolume work; several works in one citation.

> The last half-dozen years of Queen Elizabeth's reign began

```
with Shakespeare's Love's Labour's Lost and ended with her death
at age 70 (Harrison, vol. 2).  As Harrison puts it, on March 24,
1603, the queen died "having reigned 44 years 5 months and odd
days" (2: 383).  Historians regard her as a master of statecraft
(Johnson 2; Elton 46; Bindoff 377).
```

When citing an entire volume as you would a general reference to an entire work, give the author and the volume number preceded by the abbreviation *vol.* When citing specific material in a multivolume work, give first the volume number and then the page number, but omit abbreviations, as in the second reference to Harrison in the preceding example. Here, *2* stands for Volume 2 and *383* is the page number. Note the use of a colon and a space to separate volume number from page number. When documenting several works in a single parenthetical reference, cite each as you normally would, separating the citations with semicolons. If multiwork references get too bulky, place them in a bibliographical endnote (see Section **48c3**).

Indirect sources.

```
      The failure of his play Guy Domville seems to have had
positive benefits for Henry James's later novels in that he spoke
of transferring to his fiction the lessons he had learned from
the theater, using those "scenic conditions which are as near an
approach to the dramatic as the novel may permit itself" (qtd.
in Edel 434; pt. 6, ch. 1).
```

It is always best to cite original sources in your work, but sometimes a secondary source may be all that is available. In that case, indicate the secondary nature of the source by using *qtd. in* (quoted in) followed by pertinent reference information. In the preceding reference, the source is indicated by author's name, page (434), and, since the book is divided formally into parts and chapters, by part and chapter numbers (pt. 6, ch. 1). Note that a semicolon and a space separate the main reference information (author and page) from the rest of the identifying information (part and chapter numbers).

You will find examples of these and other types of in-text citations in the sample research paper at the end of this chapter. Study them to familiarize yourself with the form and to see how information may be introduced smoothly into the text.

● **2 The "Works Cited" page.** As we discussed in Chapter 47, sources are acknowledged both within the paper and in an alphabetized list of works cited at the end of the research paper. The bibliographic entries are alphabetized by the author's last name or by the first word in the title (excluding *A, An,* and *The*) if there is no author.

Just as there are specific guidelines for citing sources within the paper, there are also guidelines for preparing entries for the "Works Cited" page. The following bibliographic entries show the types of information and the form required for bibliographies using the conventions established by the MLA.

Notice that different types of entries require different types of infor-mation. For example, if your source is a translation or an edited book, you will need the name of the translator or editor as well as that of the author. If your source is an article in a periodical, you will need to record the inclu-sive page numbers of the article. Writing the library call number on the bibliography card is also helpful for locating sources on the shelves later. You will also notice that the bibliography entries use shortened forms for publishers, such as Prentice for Prentice Hall or UP for University Press. They also use common abbreviations for months (Apr., Oct.) and for such things as "no date" (n.d.) and "translator" (trans.). A list of common scholarly abbreviations appears in Section **48d**.

"Works Cited" Formats

Books

MLA Standard "Works Cited" Reference: Book

- author's last name
- comma
- one space
- author's first name (followed by middle name or initial, if there is one)
- period
- two spaces
- title (including subtitle, if any). Underline or italicize the entire title. Capitalize all important words.
- period
- two spaces
- city of publication
- colon
- one space
- publisher
- comma
- one space
- year of publication
- period

Book with one author.

Eban, Abba. Personal Witness: Israel Through My Eyes.
        New York: Putnam, 1992.

The major parts of an entry—author, title, and publication information (place of publication, publisher, date of publication)—are each separated by a period, followed by two spaces. Give the author's name in its fullest or most usual form, last name first. Obtain the information for bibliographical entries from the title page of the work cited, not from library catalog entries, other bibliographies, or indexes. These other sources may omit capital letters or use different punctuation that is specific to the style conventions of those sources only. You *must* use the information as it is presented on the work itself. If the copyright date is not located on the title page, it usually appears on the copyright page—the back of the title page—with other publication information. In books published outside the United States, publication information may be located in the colophon (publisher's inscription) at the back of the book.

Notice that only the city is given for the place of publication. If the city is outside the United States, also provide an abbreviation of the country name (or Canadian province) if the city name is ambiguous or likely to be unfamiliar to your readers. For example, you would probably need to include the country abbreviation for Bern (Bern, Switz.: Bohner, 1992) or for Cambridge (Cambridge, Eng.: Cambridge UP, 1995), because it might be confused with Cambridge, Massachusetts, but not for London, England (London: Longman, 1989). If the publisher lists more than one city on the title page or copyright page, list only the first in your citation. If an entry requires more than one line of type, indent the second and any subsequent lines five spaces from the left margin.

Book with two or three authors.
```
Guth, Hans P., and Gabriele L. Rico.  Discovering Literature:
     Fiction, Poetry, and Drama.  Englewood Cliffs: Prentice, 1993.
```

Notice that in citations involving multiple authors only the first author's name is inverted. Other authors' names appear in normal order.

Book with more than three authors.
```
Whiteford, Andrew Hunter, et al.  I Am Here: Two Thousand Years of
     Southwest Indian Arts and Culture.  Santa Fe: Museum of New
     Mexico P, 1989.
```

Et al. ("and others") is an abbreviation indicating that the work has more than three authors. Note that in the entry *et al.* should not be capitalized. If there are no more than three authors, list them as you would for a work with two authors.

Book in edition other than the first.
```
McQuade, Donald, and Robert Atwan.  Popular Writing in America:
     The Interaction of Style and Audience. 5th ed.  New York:
     Oxford UP, 1993.
```

When citing editions other than the first, it is correct to use *2nd, 4th, 17th,* etc. rather than *second, fourth, seventeenth,* and the like. *Edition* is abbreviated *ed.* If a work has a subtitle, as in the preceding example, be sure to use a colon between the main title and subtitle (even though some indexes and bibliographies may show the punctuation as a comma).

Book in a series.

```
Ryf, Robert S.   Henry Green.   Columbia Essays on Modern Writers 29.
     Ed. William York Tindall.   New York: Columbia UP, 1967.
```

Work in two or more volumes.

```
Morrison, S. E., and H. S. Commager.   The Growth of the American
     Republic.   3rd ed.  2 vols.  New York: Oxford UP, 1942.
```

Translation.

```
Kundera, Milan.   The Unbearable Lightness of Being.   Trans.
     Michael Henry Heim.   New York: Harper, 1984.
```

See also the entries and discussion under the heading "Book with Author and Editor."

Republished book (reprint).

```
Heilbrun, Carolyn G.   Writing a Woman's Life.   1988.   New York:
     Ballantine, 1989.
```

The publication date of the original hard cover printing is *1988. New York: Ballantine, 1989* is the publication information for the paperback reprint. Such information is important because although the reader needs to know exactly which edition was used in the research, it is also important to know when a work was initially published.

Edited book.

```
Stone, Robert, ed.   The Best American Short Stories 1992.   Boston:
     Houghton, 1992.
```

Book with author and editor.

```
Melville, Herman.   Billy Budd: Sailor.   Eds. Harrison Hayford and
     Merton M. Sealts, Jr.   Chicago: U of Chicago P, 1962.
Hayford, Harrison, and Merton M. Sealts, Jr., eds.   Billy Budd:
     Sailor.   By Herman Melville.   Chicago: U of Chicago P, 1962.
```

Compare the two entries for *Billy Budd*. These are entries for exactly the same book. The first one is appropriate for a paper about *Billy Budd* and/or Herman Melville. The second one is appropriate for a paper that discusses Hayford's and Sealts's work as editors. When an editor's name is the first (alphabetizing) information unit in an entry, *ed.* (editor) comes after the name and is not capitalized; otherwise, it precedes the name and is capitalized. (If there is more than one editor, make the abbreviation plural by adding an *s*.) The same distinctions apply to translations and *trans.* (translator) and other such works and contributors.

Selection in anthology or collection.

```
Chang, Curtis.   "Streets of Gold: The Myth of the Model Minority."
     Student Writers at Work and in the Company of Other Writers.
     3rd ed.   Ed. Nancy Sommers and Donald McQuade.   New York:
     St. Martin's, 1989.   90-99.
```

The title of the selection appears first after the author's name and is enclosed in quotation marks. The title of the work in which the selection appears is listed next and is underlined or italicized. A period separates the two titles. The inclusive page numbers of the selection appear at the end of the entry.

Article reprinted in a casebook, anthology, or collection.

Spenser, Theodore. "Hamlet and the Nature of Reality." <u>Journal of English Literary History</u> 5 (1938): 255-71. Rpt. in Cyrus Hoy, ed. <u>Hamlet</u>. By William Shakespeare. New York: Norton, 1963. 142-57.

Summers, Joseph P. "The Poem as Hieroglyph." <u>George Herbert, His Religion and Art</u>. London: Chatto, 1954. 123-46. Rpt. in <u>Seventeenth Century English Poetry</u>. Ed. William R. Keast. New York: Galaxy-Oxford UP, 1962, 215-37.

The two preceding entries are for essays reprinted, first in a casebook and second in a collection. Notice that the first essay originally appeared in a scholarly journal (as indicated by the manner of the journal's citation). Also notice that in the citation of the reprint casebook the editor's name (Cyrus Hoy) is listed first and Shakespeare, the author of the play for which the casebook is entitled, is listed later. This manner of listing, with the emphasis on the editor, indicates the casebook format of the text—that it features a major literary work accompanied by essays of literary criticism compiled by the editor and pertaining to the literary work. The manner of the second entry indicates that the article originally appeared as part of a book authored by Summers and has been reprinted in a collection of essays.

Notice also that the second entry cites a publisher's special imprint (Galaxy). When you cite a book that is a publisher's special imprint, list the imprint first, followed by a hyphen and then the publisher.

Anonymous book.

<u>Norwegian Folk Tales</u>. Trans. Pat Shaw Iversen and Carl Norman. Oslo: Dreyers Forlag, 1961.

Works without an author, editor, or other acknowledged "authorlike" person are alphabetized in "Works Cited" by the first important word in their title. They are not listed as *anonymous* or *anon.*

Pamphlet.

Latin, Giorgio Lilli. <u>Art in Italy</u>. Rome: Italian State Tourist Dept., 1978.

Unpublished dissertation.

Gorlier, Juan Carlos. "Processes of Social Democratization during Periods of Political Transition." Diss. U of Mass., 1991.

Published conference proceedings.

<u>Quaker Education As Ministry</u>.   Proc. of 4th Annual Conference.
      Haverford: Friends Assn. for Higher Education, 1983.

Proc. is the abbreviation for *Proceedings.*

Articles in Reference Books

Signed article.

Upjohn, Everard M.   "Cathedrals and Churches."   <u>Encyclopedia</u>
      <u>Americana</u>. 1992 ed.

Unsigned article.

"Antimonide."   <u>Encyclopaedia Britannica: Micropaedia</u>. 1992 ed.

Familiar reference books, especially those that are reprinted frequently in
new editions, are cited by edition-year only. When the abbreviation *ed.*
appears with a year, it stands for *edition* rather than *editor.* Full publication
information is not necessary. However, less familiar reference works, or
those that have been printed in only one edition, should be accompanied
by full publication information, as in the entry that follows.

Unsigned article in first edition.

"28 July 1868 Reconstruction."   <u>The Almanac of American History</u>.
      Ed. Arthur M. Schlesinger, Jr.   New York: Putnam, 1983.

Periodicals

MLA Standard "Works Cited" Reference: Periodical

- author's last name
- comma
- one space
- author's first name (followed by middle name or initial, if there is one)
- period
- two spaces
- title of article in quotation marks. Capitalize all important words.
- period (inside the closing quotation marks)
- two spaces
- title of periodical. Underline or italicize the entire title. Capitalize all
  important words.
- one space
- volume number. (Number only: Do not use *Vol.* or any other word
  or abbreviation.)
- one space
- month (or season), if given, and year of publication in parentheses
- colon
- one space

- page number, or inclusive page numbers if the article is multipaged
- period

Article from journal with continuous pagination throughout volume.

```
Jay, Gregory S.  "Knowledge, Power, and the Struggle for
     Representation."  College English 56 (1994): 9-29.
```

The title of the journal is followed by the volume number, the year of publication in parentheses, a colon, and the pages on which the article appears. Some documentation styles may use *Vol.* for *volume* and roman instead of Arabic numerals. MLA style uses no abbreviation and Arabic numerals only. Notice that the colon is the only separating punctuation used after the journal title and that abbreviations such as *p.* or *pp.* (*page* or *pages*) are not used.

Article from journal with each issue paginated independently.

```
Mendelson, Michael.  "Business Prose and the Nature of the Plain
     Style."  Journal of Business Communication 24.2 (1987): 3-11.
```

Because pagination begins over again with each issue of the journal rather than with each volume, it is necessary to give the issue number. Here the order is journal title, volume number, separating period, issue number, year of publication in parentheses, colon, and page numbers.

Article from weekly or biweekly periodical.

```
Pennisi, E.  "Immune Therapy Stems Diabetes' Progress."  Science
     News 15 Jan. 1994: 37.
```

Notice that the date of the periodical's publication is inverted and presented in "military" or "continental" style as well as abbreviated: 15 *Jan.* 1994. As in other periodical citations, the abbreviations *p.* or *pp.* are not used. Instead, the meaning of the numbers is indicated by their placement in the entry.

Article from monthly or bimonthly periodical.

```
Rebeck, George.  "Truly Public Schools."  Utne Reader Jul./Aug.
     1993: 36-38.
```

Article from daily newspaper.

```
Morris, Betsy.  "Thwack! Smack! Sounds Thrill Makers of Hunt's
     Ketchup."  Wall Street Journal 27 Apr. 1984, midwestern ed.,
     sec. 1:1+.
```

This newspaper article carried a by-line, so the author's name is known. If the article were unsigned, it would be alphabetized in "Works Cited" by its title rather than by its author. For newspaper articles, give the date of publication, the edition if the paper is printed in more than one edition (either location or time of day, whichever is relevant), and the section number as well as the page number if the newspaper is divided into sections that are paginated separately. The citation given here refers to pages 1 and following of the midwestern edition of the *Wall Street Journal* for April 27, 1984.

Signed book review.

```
Morris, Jan. "Visions in the Wilderness."  Rev. of Sands River, by
     Peter Matthiessen.  Saturday Review Apr. 1981: 68-69.
```

Unsigned article or review.

```
"Form and Function in a Post and Beam House."  Early American Life
     Oct. 1980: 41-43.
```

Government and Legal Documents; Corporate Authorship

Government publication.

```
United States.  Dept. of Health, Education, and Welfare.  National
     Center for Educational Statistics.  Digest of Educational
     Statistics.  Washington: GPO, 1968.
```

This entry shows an example of "corporate authorship." That is, an institution is considered the author, although clearly one or several people wrote the document. Corporate authorship is not uncommon for works from governmental and educational institutions, foundations, agencies, or business firms.

Constitution.

```
U.S. Const.  Art. 2, sec. 4.
```

Court cases.

```
Bundy v. Jackson.  24 FEP Cases 1155 (1981).
Seto v. Muller.  395 F. Supp. 811 (D. Mass. 1975).
```

Methods for citing court cases and legal documents vary: The ones shown here are representative, however. The name of the case is given first, followed by identification numbers, references to courts and relevant jurisdictions (for example, "FEP Cases" means "Federal Employment Practices Cases"; "F. Supp." means "Federal Superior Court"), and the year in which the case was decided. The best guide for legal references is the most recent edition of *A Uniform System of Citation* (Cambridge: Harvard Law Rev. Assn.). It should be available in your college or university library.

Letters and Interviews

Published letter.

```
Mills, Ralph J. Jr., ed.  Selected Letters of Theodore Roethke.
     Seattle: U of Washington P, 1968.
```

Unpublished letter.

```
McCracken, Virginia.  Letter to Colonel Thomas McCracken.
     1 July 1862.
```

Interviews.

Silber, John R.   Personal interview.   5 June 1979.
Kennedy, Senator Edward.   Telephone interview.   3 May 1994.

Information Services, Computer Software

Information service.

Beam, Paul.   <u>COMIT English Module</u>.   ERIC ED 167 189.
Labe, P.   "Personal Computer Industry."   Drexel Burnham Lambert,
       Inc.   23 Apr. 1987: n. pag.   Dow Jones News/Retrieval
       Investext file 12, item 32.

Material from information services and databases is cited the same way as
any other printed material, with the addition of a reference to the source—
in this case ERIC (Educational Resources Information Center) and Dow
Jones News/Retrieval. Notice that the Dow Jones entry is unpaginated (n.
pag., meaning "no page"). Be aware that information services, data banks,
microform services, and other suppliers sometimes indicate how they
should be cited in references. Follow their suggestions but, if necessary,
adapt them to the particular documentation style you are using.

Software.

Micro Grade.   <u>Computer software</u>.   Chariot Software Group, 1993.
       Macintosh version 3.0, disk.

For an entry documenting computer software, supply the following information: the author of the software (if known), the title of the program
(treated like the title of any work and underlined or italicized), a descriptive
label (Computer software), the name of the distributor, and the year of
publication. Other information can be included at the end if it will be
important to the reader. For example, this entry lists the type of computer
on which the program can be used (Macintosh) and its form (disk).

Films, Television, Radio, Recordings, Works of Art

Film.

<u>Children of a Lesser God</u>.   Dir. Randa Haines.   Paramount, 1986.

Films, television programs, movies, works of art, recordings, and the like
are treated similarly to printed works except that the type of medium logically dictates the type of information to be included. The title of the work is
always given. If the performer, composer, director, producer, or artist is of
primary importance, then the name of that person will head the entry,
appearing in the author position. If the work is more important than its
creator or performer, then the title will occupy the lead position in the
entry—as in the case of the audio tape *Footloose*, listed below. Provide
whatever information the reader will need to identify or locate the work,

such as dates of performances, broadcasts, or recordings; networks; recording companies; catalog numbers; etc. The following examples are representative.

Television and radio.
<u>Casey Stengel</u>. Writ. Sidney and David Carroll. Perf. Charles
    Durning. PBS, Boston. 6 May 1981.
Keillor, Garrison. "The News from Lake Wobegon." <u>A Prairie Home
    Companion</u>. Minnesota Public Radio. WBAA, West Lafayette.
    11 June 1994.

Record.
Moussorgsky, Modeste. <u>Pictures at an Exhibition</u>. Leonard
    Pennario, piano. Capitol, P-8323, n.d.

Audio tape; compact disc; video tape.
<u>Footloose</u>. Audio tape. Perf. Kenny Loggins et al. Columbia, JST
    39242, 1984.
Beethoven, Ludwig van. <u>The Five Piano Concertos</u>. Perf. Rudolf
    Serkin. Cond. Seiji Ozawa. Compact disc. Boston Symphony
    Orchestra. Telarc, CD 80061-5, 1984.
Allen, Woody, dir. <u>Hannah and Her Sisters</u>. Video cassette.
    HBO Video, 1985, 1 hr., 43 min.

Work of art (painting).
Picasso, Pablo. <u>A Woman in White</u>. The Metropolitan Museum of
    Art, New York.

Exercise 48.1

Revise the following to make a "Works Cited" page in the MLA format. Remember to alphabetize the list.

1 "The Stories That Cry to Be Read," <u>The Washington Post</u>, July 2, 1992, volume 115, p. C1, 40 inches, by Jacqueline Trescott.

2 Director, Matteo Bellinelli, <u>A Conversation with Alice Walker</u>. 1992 production of RTSI-Swiss Television.

3 Alvin P. Sanoff, <u>U.S. News & World Report</u>, June 3, 1991, "The Craft of Survival," p. 51, vol. 110, num. 21.

4 <u>Alice Walker</u>, by Donna Haisty Winchell, New York, Twayne Publishers, 1992.

5 Editor, Henry Louis Gates, Jr., <u>Reading Black, Reading Feminist: A Critical Anthology</u>, "The Highs and Lows of Black Feminist Criticism," by Barbara Christian. New York, Meredian Press, 1990, pages 44-51.

6 Felipe Smith, <u>Alice Walker's Redemptive Art, in African American Review</u>, Fall 1992, vol. 26, n3, pages 437-452.

● **3 Content and bibliographic notes.** Two types of notes may be used along with MLA in-text citations: content and bibliographic notes. Both kinds of notes are placed at the end of the research paper (endnotes) before the "Works Cited" page or at the bottoms of pages (footnotes). In the text of the paper, notes are indicated by raised (superscript) numbers.

Content notes provide a place to put explanatory information that is relevant to the content of the paper but too digressive or complex to put in the text itself. However, some editors discourage the use of content notes, believing that if the information is important it should be included in the text. Check with your instructor before you use content notes.

The following example comes from a sociology paper on the future social roles of the elderly. The author wanted to note a disagreement among experts without spending time discussing the varying definitions they use in the text of the paper itself. Note that the author cites two sources in her content note. These citations correspond to information listed on the "Works Cited" page.

Superscript Number in Text

Why, then, lump the "young old" (those between 60 and 74) together with the "oldest old" (those 85 and above)?[2]

Content Note

   [2]The term "oldest old" was coined by the National Institute on Aging.   There is some disagreement about exactly which ages are included in each category, but the most frequently cited age groups are as follows: young-old, 60-74; old or old-old, 75-84; oldest-old, 85+ (Fowles 45).   One authority defines young-old as 55-75 (Foner 4).

Bibliographic notes are used to offer information about a source or to cite several sources for one point when such citations would become awkward if put in the text itself.

Superscript Number in Text

One of the constant themes in gerontological research is the heterogeneity of the elderly.[1]

Bibliographic Note

   [1]See, for example, Naugarten and Maddox, who discuss the heterogeneity of the elderly. See also Morton, 217-25; Sand 92; Oscar 109-12.

48 d Common scholarly abbreviations.

The following list contains many of the scholarly abbreviations you are likely to need in writing a bibliography or that you are likely to see while conducting research.

anon.	anonymous
art., arts.	article(s)

c., ca.	*circa* (about); used with approximate dates
cf.	*confer* (compare)
ch., chs., chap., chaps.	chapter(s)
col., cols.	column(s)
dir.	director, directed by
diss.	dissertation
ed., edn.	edition
ed., eds.	editor(s)
e.g.	*exempli gratia* (for example)
et al.	*et alii* (and others)
ERIC	Educational Resources Information Service
f., ff.	and the following page(s)
GPO	Government Printing Office
ibid.	*ibidem* (in the same place)
i.e.	*id est* (that is)
illus.	illustrator, illustrated by, illustration
introd.	introduction
l., ll.	line(s)
loc. cit.	*loca citato* (in the place cited)
ms, mss	manuscript(s)
n.b.	*nota bene* (take notice)
n.d.	no date (of publication) given
n.p.	no place (of publication) given
n. pag.	no pagination
no., nos.	number, numbers
NTIS	National Technical Information Service
numb.	numbered
op. cit.	*opere citato* (in the work cited)
p., pp.	page(s)
passim	throughout the work, here and there
perf.	performed by, performer
proc.	proceedings
prod.	produced by, producer
q.v.	*quod vide* (which see)
qtd.	quoted in
rev.	review, revised
rpt.	reprint, reprinted
sec.	section
sic	thus it is
trans., tr.	translator, translated
univ., U, UP	university, university press
v. (vs.)	versus (against)
vol., vols.	volume(s)

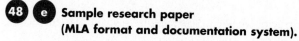 **Sample research paper (MLA format and documentation system).**

Bonnie Lin's research paper, presented in this section, is a successful student paper. For this assignment she had to choose a subject, narrow its scope to a manageable focus, gather authoritative information from a number of sources, analyze the information, and then organize it clearly in a paper of approximately ten–fifteen pages, excluding bibliography.

The paragraphs of the paper are numbered. On adjoining pages you will find commentary on the contents, argumentative structure, mechanics, and format of Bonnie's paper as well as comments about her research and writing process.

Title page

Always ask your instructor whether a separate title page is expected.
Bonnie's professor instructed students to attach a separate title page to
their research papers. Many instructors prefer the use of a title page
because it provides a cover sheet on which they can write summary
comments and the grade. MLA research paper format, however, does not
call for a title page but instead includes all identifying information on
the first page of the paper. If Bonnie's instructor had requested MLA
format exclusively (and not asked for an outline), the paper's first page
would have appeared as follows:

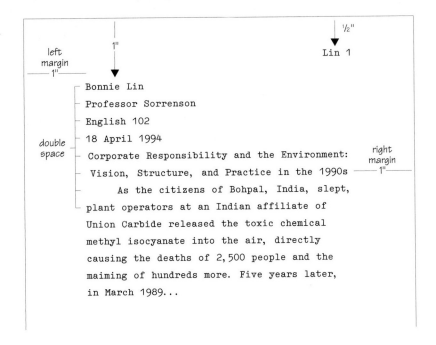

Corporate Responsibility and the Environment:
Vision, Structure, and Practice in the 1990s

by
Bonnie G. Lin

Professor Ingrid Sorrenson
English 102
18 April 1994

Outline

Bonnie submitted a formal, sentence outline with her research paper. It is headed with a statement of the thesis, which appears near the end of the paper's second paragraph. Notice that the pages of the outline are numbered with lower-case Roman numerals; the first page of the text of the paper begins with the Arabic numeral 1. For a full discussion of outlining, see Section **5c1**.

Lin i

Outline

<u>Thesis statement</u>: The best way for a company to ensure
success in meeting health and safety priorities is to
incorporate environmental concern into its corporate
vision, its structure, and its practice.

I.   In the 1990s, the public is concerned about the
     state of the environment.
     A.   Damaging environmental incidents in the 1980s
          were costly in lives, natural resources, and
          property.
     B.   People depend on the Environmental Protection
          Agency to enforce federal regulations protect-
          ing the environment.
     C.   Corporate cooperation in maintaining a safe
          and healthy environment is essential.
II. Companies have a responsibility to protect their
     stakeholders as well as their shareholders.
III. Companies can form alliances with environmental
     interest groups.
     A.   McDonald's cooperated with the Environmental
          Defense Fund in a repackaging campaign.
     B.   The Coalition of Environmentally Responsible
          Economies (CERES) encourages corporate
          environmentalism.
IV. Companies can agree to sign a set of environmen-
     tal principles.
     A.   The CERES Principles, a ten-point environmen-
          tal checklist, has had some supporters.
     B.   Some companies are wary of voluntary
          compliance.
          1.   Exxon thought signing the Principles was
               not cost-effective.

      2.   Union Carbide considered CERES an extremist group.

      3.   McDonald's believed the Principles irrelevant to the fast food business.

  C.   Sun Company accepted and modified the CERES Principles.

V.   One company, Kodak, has incorporated environmental concern into its vision, structure, and practice.

  A.   Health, safety, and environmental issues are top priorities.

  B.   A tri-level environmental management structure features "interlocking teams" with a variety of functions.

  C.   Recycling and corporate funding of environmental education programs are ongoing.

VI.   Some companies have trouble being environmentally responsible.

  A.   Some have been deceptively "green," angering consumers.

  B.   Some place blame on misleading and confusing federal and state regulations.

VII.   Corporate environmental committment will continue to be a public concern in the twenty-first century.

  A.   Companies can continue to reassess their commitment to a sound environment.

  B.   Environmental responsibility is compatible with corporate success.

Paragraphs 1 and 2

Bonnie uses her first paragraph to arouse interest and provide background. She cites environmental crises of the 1980s that her audience might recall and includes startling statistics to highlight the devastation. In the second paragraph she introduces the idea of environmental responsibility, presenting the thesis for the paper in the last sentences. The remainder of the paper discusses how some companies have worked to become more environmentally responsible by using their corporate vision, structure, and practices to address environmental concerns.

Paragraph 2 includes a quotation that contains ellipses, three spaced periods indicating that words from the source have been omitted.

Paragraphs 3 and 4

In contrast to the well-known information about toxic waste sites and nuclear power safety, the information about fish populations at the end of paragraph 3 is not common knowledge and so requires an in-text citation of the source. Because the source has no listed author, the citation gives the shortened title and page number for reference.

In paragraph 4, Bonnie notes how the federal government's role in maintaining a safe and healthy environment is an outgrowth of the public's concern. Her last sentence refers to the thesis by stating the need for corporate cooperation in this task. Notice in this paragraph how Bonnie handles abbreviations correctly. Before using an abbreviation that may be unfamiliar to her readers, she supplies the words for which the abbreviation stands and then provides the abbreviation itself in parentheses (EPA and GNP). Regarding the citing of authorities (part of her argumentative strategy), Bonnie is careful to let readers know why a particular source is a worthy authority. She does so by giving credentials, in this case that Bradley Smith is director of the EPA's Office of Environmental Education and thus an able spokesman on environmental issues.

Lin 1

Corporate Responsibility and the Environment:
Vision, Structure, and Practice in the 1990s

As the citizens of Bhopal, India, slept, plant   **1**
operators at an Indian affiliate of Union Carbide
released the toxic chemical methyl isocyanate into the
air, directly causing the deaths of 2,500 people and the
maiming of hundreds more. Five years later, in March
1989, the tanker Exxon Valdez ran aground in Alaska's
Prince William Sound, spilling 11 million gallons of
crude oil, fouling the waterway and killing fish and
wildlife by the score.

These environmental catastrophes pointed up the   **2**
need for companies to be more environmentally responsible. An editorial in the Washington Post proclaimed that
"there is growing awareness . . . that industrial activity has been part of the environmental problem and that
companies must be part of the solution" (Smart A 19).
If a company truly wants to become environmentally
responsible, it must make the health and safety of the
public a corporate priority. The best way for a company
to ensure success in meeting this priority is to incorporate environmental concern into its corporate vision, its
structure, and its practice. Some companies have tried
to adhere to these with varying degrees of success.

Environmentalism is clearly a major issue of the   **3**
1990s. Besides being dismayed by the Bhopal and Prince
William Sound incidents, the American public is concerned
about the cleanup of toxic waste sites. The safety of
nuclear power plants continues to be an issue fourteen
years after the accident at Three Mile Island. Four
years after the Exxon Valdez incident, fishermen in Prince
William Sound reported that pink salmon and herring runs
are weaker than before the spill ("Alaska Fishermen" A8).

When it created the Environmental Protection Agency   **4**
(EPA) two decades ago, the federal government was
responding to citizens' concern about protecting people

Paragraphs 5 and 6

In these paragraphs Bonnie focuses on the role she believes companies ought to play in protecting the environment. Paragraph 5 sets up the issue and provides transition. Paragraph 6 gives important definitions of shareholders and stockholders which Bonnie will use to build the case that companies are obligated to others besides their financial investors.

Paragraph 7

Bonnie introduces the idea of how a company's organizational structure can reflect and influence its environmental commitments. Compare the quotation attributed to Ralph Cavanagh in this paragraph to the unattributed quotation in paragraph 6. Bonnie decided that a parenthetical citation was sufficient in paragraph 6 because Professors Sothi and Bok were presenting a generally accepted definition of stakeholders. Cavanagh, on the other hand, needed to be named because of his position with an environmental organization and his point of view. Without the attribution to Cavanagh, the quotation would lack argumentative credibility.

and communities from both the ravages of pollution and
corporate irresponsibility about the environment.
Legislators added new laws and regulations to support and
expand the EPA's mission.   In fact, the EPA estimates
that by the year 2000 nearly 3 percent of the nation's
Gross National Product (GNP)--$160 billion--will be spent
on protecting the environment (Thomas 21).   However, corporate support and compliance are essential to make such
a tremendous outlay financially worthwhile.   Dr. Bradley
Smith, the EPA's director of the Office of Environmental
Education, stated that increasing corporate stewardship
of the environment is one of the agency's goals in the
1990s.   According to the agency, corporations need to
assume a larger role in protecting the environment,
instead of leaving the task to the federal government
(Smith).

But before addressing corporate compliance with   **5**
environmental principles as an issue, we must ask certain
fundamental questions about corporate roles.   What should
business's role be in the protection of the environment?
Where is the line between profits and responsibility?

One view holds that corporations have a responsibility not just to the shareholders who own stock in the   **6**
company but to all the company's stakeholders.
Stakeholders are "groups of individuals other than the
shareholders of a corporation to whom corporate managers
are directly responsible" (Sethi and Bok 144).
Stakeholders include citizens who live near a plant location, communities in which a corporation's workforce
resides, and even the customers who buy a company's
products. According to this way of thinking, the public
good thus becomes as important as profits in setting a
company's goals.   The public good in the 1990s includes
the protection and maintenance of a safe and healthy
environment.

To achieve these goals, companies can institute an   **7**
environmental program within the corporate structure.

Paragraphs 8, 9, and 10

Here Bonnie introduces a key piece of evidence to support her claim that corporations can develop environmentally sound business practices: They can form alliances with environmental interest groups. She provides an in-depth discussion of the partnership between McDonald's and the Environmental Defense Fund in the fast-food company's repackaging campaign to show how a cooperative rather than adversarial relationship is possible—to mutual benefit. Anticipating skeptical readers' questions, she points out in paragraph 10 that the alliance was not necessarily cost-effective for the company and that the real environmental impact may be unknown for some time.

Here and elsewhere in the paper, Bonnie had to rely on second-hand quotations, statements quoted by one source from another (for example, the words of Joel Makower). Notice that her in-text reference indicates this situation with the citation "qtd. in Fierman 92," meaning that she has recorded Makower's statement as "quoted in" the Fierman article.

Lin 3

However, such a program may be doomed to failure unless
the company shows management commitment through leadership from the top (Wybrew 82). One way for a company to
show leadership and commitment is naming an environmen-
tal-policy officer as part of the management team. This
individual should "be able to change the direction of the
company from the top" and "be someone who has the ear of
the CEO," states Ralph Cavanagh, energy program director
for the Natural Resources Defense Council (Lublin B1).
When a company's structure reflects its commitment to the
environment by including a high-level individual to plan
and implement programs, environmentally sound action
rather than lip service is much more likely to occur.

    Another method of making sure that environmental   **8**
concern remains in the forefront is for companies to
forge an alliance with an environmental interest group.
One successful partnership involved McDonald's
Corporation and the Environmental Defense Fund (EDF).
In an interview on National Public Radio, Terry
Capatasto, director of communications for McDonald's,
explained that "neither McDonald's nor the Environmental
Defense Fund had ever heard of a collaboration this
close" between a big corporation and an environmental
group (Glass 31). In creating this partnership,
McDonald's seemed to be taking a bold move toward being
more environmentally responsible.

    In April 1991, McDonald's and the EDF announced a   **9**
program for reducing the company's trash output by 80
percent. Officials of both organizations expressed the
wish that their partnership be an earnest attempt to
"weave waste management into the corporate fabric"
(Hamilton B1). In fact, in taking this stance,
McDonald's was reinforcing the move it made in November
1990 to discontinue using its polystyrene clamshell containers. In the new program, the company promised to
recycle its corrugated containers, insist its suppliers
use recycled products, investigate composting its in-

Paragraphs 11 and 12

This paragraph introduces Joan Bavaria's group, CERES. Bonnie quickly outlines how Bavaria founded the group and created the CERES Principles. In earlier drafts of the paper, this section was much longer. It took several revisions and a conference with her instructor for Bonnie to see that readers need some, but not too much, detail to understand the development of the Principles. The focus must be the stockholders' and environmentalists' alliance to pressure corporations and on the Principles themselves, not on Bavaria. So that readers will focus on the Principles, Bonnie displays them vertically in a list rather than writing them as a series of phrases in a paragraph.

Lin 4

house generated waste, and provide its customers with
reusable instead of disposable containers (Hamilton B1).
It later dropped the fourth and final element of the
program as largely impractical.

Working with EDF, McDonald's hoped to create good- 10
will as well as maintain its healthy profit margin in the
fast-food business. However, some critics saw that the
environmental program's actual cost-effectiveness was
questionable. The company was taking a risk. In fact,
both the company and EDF admitted the program would be
neither more nor less cost-effective in the long run
(Hamilton B1). Also, Joel Makower, author of <u>The Green
Consumer Supermarket Guide</u>, stated that whether the company's "one giant leap for environmentalists" would be
"even a small step for the planet" will be unknown for
years (qtd. in Fierman 92). Only future evaluation will
reveal how much the McDonald's/EDF partnership actually
benefitted the environment.

Another way for companies to be most environmental- 11
ly responsible is to commit to a set of working environmental principles. One of the more prominent sets of
principles developed out of the <u>Exxon Valdez</u> disaster.
The Valdez Principles (currently known as the CERES
Principles) were the brainchild of Joan Bavaria, director
of Franklin Research and Development Corporation, a
Boston-based company which manages its clients' "green"
portfolios of environmentally sound investments (Hinden
44). Bavaria spearheaded the formation of the Coalition
for Environmentally Responsible Economies, or CERES, a
loose federation of investors and environmentalists which
works with coporations to make them more environmentally
responsible (Hinden 44). Some members include the Social
Investment Forum, a New York State local of the American
Federation of State, County, and Municipal Employees, as
well as the National Audubon Society and the National

Paragraphs 13, 14, and 15

These paragraphs explore the reasons that some companies such as
McDonald's and Exxon refused to sign on to the CERES Principles.
To show both sides of the sign-or-not-to-sign controversy, Bonnie gives a
CERES member's response in paragraph 14. Bonnie believed that Exxon's
refusal to sign the Principles needed to be quoted exactly, rather than para-
phrased, so that there could be no misinterpretation on her part. Notice

Lin 5

Wildlife Federation (Bavaria 28).   The set of ten CERES
Principles pledges companies to
- protect the biosphere
- work for sustainable use of natural
  resources
- reduce and dispose of waste
- use energy wisely
- reduce environmental risk
- market safe products and services
- compensate for damages
- freely disclose risk or potential harm
- employ environmental directors and managers
- annually assess and audit progress
  on fulfilling the principles. (Bavaria 30)
Signing such a set of principles indicates a company's
firm commitment to environmentally sound policies and
practices.

In encouraging companies to sign on to the CERES   **12**
Principles, stockholders have played an important role in
making companies aware of their broader social responsibilities.   In 1992, U.S. shareholders filed 44 Valdez
[CERES] resolutions and 11 others asked for management
input regarding the Principles (Cogan 53).   Statistics
from the four-year history of the CERES Principles reveal
some progress in company response to stockholders'
interest. As of mid-1992, 37 private companies and three
small publically traded firms had signed the Principles
(Cogan 54).

Unfortunately, the Principles' overall reach has   **13**
been limited.   Exxon, the company whose environmental
incident spurred the creation of the CERES Principles,
has refused to sign them.   The company said it
         do[es] not recognize the need to balance envi-
         ronmental protection with the importance of
         adequate energy resouces and a stable, healthy

how she blends this lengthy quotation (correctly presented as a ten-space indented, doubled-spaced block) into her paragraph and uses brackets to indicate a change she made in the verb form (do[es]) in the first line so that the grammar between her words and those of the quotation will be correct. Bonnie presents McDonald's position similarly in paragraph 15: a blocked quotation with her own explanatory insertions in brackets.

economy. The Principles stress environmental
values to the virtual exclusion of all other
consideratations, such as relative cost as
well as benefit. (Cogan 54)
It appears the company has a negative view toward
voluntary compliance with this set of environmental
principles.

And other companies have failed to respond to   **14**
stockholders' pressure to sign the Principles. Although
5 percent of Union Carbide's investor resolutions supported signing the Principles, Robert D. Kennedy, its
chairman and chief executive officer (CEO), did not agree
that the company should make such a move. At its 1992
annual meeting, he called CERES a "self-appointed vigilante group" (Cogan 54). CERES countered by stressing
the voluntary nature of the Principles. Ariane van Buren
of the Interfaith Center on Corporate Responsibility, who
led a stockholders campaign for the Principles on behalf
of her group, stated that CERES would not "in any way
infringe upon the board of directors' authority or
responsibility for sound environmental management" (Cogan
55). Even though CERES stressed the voluntary nature of
the Principles, some CEOs perceived the group as threatening company authority.

Furthermore, McDonald's, which showed its willing-   **15**
ness to work with EDF, also refused to support the CERES
Principles. The company asked shareholders to defeat an
endorsement proposal by stating that

McDonald's was committed to sound environmental practices long before the Valdez [tanker]
oil spill [in Alaska in 1989], and solutions
designed for that problem may have little or
no application in the hamburger business.
("McDonald's Is Opposing" B6)
Instead of endorsing them, the company said it was ready-
ing its own waste-reduction plan ("McDonald's Is

Paragraphs 16 and 17
Bonnie explains Sun Company's unique response to the CERES Principles, which was to endorse them and create its own environmental guidelines, the Sun Principles. The quotations from Sun's chief executive officer not only support Bonnie's claim that environmental responsibility is good business but also support another of her claims, that environmental policy must be actively supported by top management. One of her sources for this section of the paper is a press release she obtained from corporate headquarters. In a news magazine, she had seen a company advertisement championing the Sun Principles. She wrote to Sun requesting further information and was rewarded with a personal letter from the director of media and public relations. He answered her questions as well as providing the press release and other printed information. These primary sources proved more valuable than secondary sources in presenting Sun's environmental position.

Paragraph 18
Balancing her optimism about the soundness of the Sun Principles, Bonnie cautions that Sun will have to prove its environmental commitment over time.

Lin 7

Opposing" B6). And, by the 1992 shareholders' meeting, McDonald's investors had withdrawn all resolutions asking endorsement of the CERES Principles. Even though the Principles are so broadly stated that they do seem generally applicable to any industry, resistance and misperceptions have slowed the pace of their general acceptance by companies.

Although it is true that the CERES Principles are **16** not agreeable to all corporations, one company has compromised by tailoring them to its vision and practice. In February 1993, Sun Oil endorsed the CERES Principles, the first Fortune 500 company to do so. In a press release announcing the move, Sun also stated that it had, in addition to championing the CERES Principles, drafted its own set of ten environmental guidelines which it called the Sun Principles (News Release 1). Joan Bavaria lauded Sun's move: "Sun's endorsement demonstrates its leadership and vision in this critical area of corporate social responsibility" (News Release 1).

What reasons did Sun give for agreeing to endorse **17** the CERES Principles in the first place? According to Sun CEO Robert H. Campbell, "Our business is energy and chemicals. But our business is really [the] environment" (Roberts 1). Campbell went on to explain the importance of Sun's decision from a purely business standpoint. The way Campbell sees it, Sun's decision to be environmentally responsible is more than just a case of acting morally. In his view, if a company decides to do the right thing from the beginning, it is working to avoid costly damage in the future (Roberts 26).

However, just because Sun took this giant step, it **18** is still not off the environmental hook. Many others will be watching to see if the company makes good on its promises. Jack Doyle, an analyst with Friends of the Earth, an environmental interest group, said that "community groups and environmentalists are going to be looking very carefully to see they measure up to this" (Roberts

Paragraphs 19, 20, and 21

Bonnie introduces Kodak as a company whose environmental commitment embodies her thesis in paragraph 19: Kodak exhibits environmental responsibility in its corporate vision, structure, and practice. She notes her use of a journal article written by three Kodak environmental officers as her main source for this section. Paragraph 19 explains the relationship between the environment and Kodak's corporate vision. Paragraph 20 details the way environmental awareness has been built into the company's organizational structure. Paragraph 21 highlights Kodak's recycling and environmental education programs as examples of how corporate vision and organizational structure translate into company practice.

Notice that most of the information in these paragraphs is presented in summary form. Unless the exact words of the source are important to understanding or credibility, summary and paraphrase should be used more frequently in a research paper than direct quotation. Nevertheless, whenever you use information you have obtained from sources other than yourself, you must cite the sources of that information in the text of the paper—as Bonnie has done. Failing to cite the sources of your information is plagiarism.

26).   As time goes on, Sun will have to prove the validity of its environmental commitment.

One company, Kodak, has made environmental respon-   **19**
sibility a key element of its structure, policies, and
practices.   In an article for the <u>Columbia Journal of
World Business</u>, three Kodak environmental officers laid
out Kodak's corporate commitment to environmental responsibility.   They spoke of a "corporate vision" which
involves attention to health, safety, and environmental
issues (Poduska, Forbes, and Bober 287).   And the company
design for making this vision a reality involves more
than rhetoric.

Kodak has created a formal program managers can use   **20**
to make environmental responsibility part of the company's operations.   Keys to the program are corporate and
group teams.   At the top, the Management Committee on
Environmental Responsibility (MCER), is headed by the
company's CEO, group vice presidents, and senior staff
vice presidents.   The MCER oversees the company's environmental policies and practices worldwide. As a source
of new ideas, the company's Health, Safety, and
Environmental Coordinating Committee (HSECC) works under
the MCER.   Finally, the 400 staff members of the
Corporate Health, Safety, and Environment Organization
(HSE) aid the MCER and HSECC in keeping company operations environmentally responsible (Poduska, Forbes, and
Bober 287).

In addition to having an overall plan and corporate   **21**
officers charged with environmental responsibility, Kodak
puts these into practice.   Like McDonald's, Kodak champi-
ons and practices recycling.   And although the company
did not negotiate a direct relationship with an environmental interest group similar to McDonald's partnership
with EDF, Kodak has made good on a related commitment:
environmental literacy.   According to the company
spokespersons, in 1992 Kodak contributed over $2 million

Paragraph 22

Here Bonnie introduces the issue of companies who only pretend to be "green." An important part of her argument's point/counterpoint, the following four paragraphs supply a contrast between companies such as Sun and Kodak, whose actions seem to support their words, and companies whose actions undercut their "environmentally correct" proclamations.

Paragraphs 23-26

First, Bonnie details consumer disfavor with Procter & Gamble's inconsistent environmental campaign: redesigning its laundry softener packaging to benefit the environment while at the same time working to defeat a tax on its disposable diapers which pollute the environment. Next, she calls DuPont to task for being a major polluter, according to EPA data, while running a self-congratulatory image advertising campaign that portrayed the company as a friend of the environment.

Lin 9

to the World Wildlife Fund to develop the "Windows on
the Wild" program, an environmental education package
aimed at children (Poduska, Forbes, and Bober 288). Kodak
seems to have combined McDonald's and Sun's approaches to
being more environmentally responsible.

It seems clear that some companies in the 1990s are **22**
working to become more environmentally responsible.
However, vigilant consumers and interest groups have
begun to question whether some companies are just pretending to be "green." Backsliding companies may anger
consumers and activists alike, thus running the risk of a
drop in profits. Richard Lawrence, president of the consulting firm Marketing Intelligence Service, Ltd., noted
that companies have a difficult time attending to the
financial interests of stockholders, protecting the environment, and pleasing consumers (qtd. in Swasy B1).
Companies are feeling the pressure from a public concerned about corporate responsibility for the quality of
the environment.

Procter and Gamble (P&G) provides a case in which a **23**
company's public image of environmental responsibility
and its actual behavior turned out to be inconsistent.
In January 1991, <u>Advertising Age</u> published the results of
a Gallup Organization poll, which listed P&G as the most
"environmentally conscious" U.S. corporation (Swasy B1).
However, consumer advocates found that the company's
image did not match its practices.

On one hand, the company was promoting the recy- **24**
cling of its plastic containers and concentrating its
Downy liquid fabric softener so it could be packaged in
less bulky bottles. At the same time, the company
fought efforts to curb the sale of its difficult-to-recy-
cle disposable diapers, Pampers and Luvs. It actively
fought attempts to levy a special sales tax on the diapers in Kentucky, where interest groups claimed the product fouled the landscape. It also successfully lobbied

against similar efforts in Wisconsin, Illinois, and
Connecticut. P&G charged such moves unnecessarily singled
out its product and only penalized low-income consumers
who would be more severely affected by a tax increase
than higher income groups (Swasy B6). The company seemed
unwilling to see these contradictory policies as inconsistent with what it considered to be its self-image as
an environmental champion.

Environmentalists refused to be lured by a company
suggestion that consumers compost the offending diapers
minus their plastic backsheets. Joan Mulhern, legisla-
tive director of Vermont's Public Service Research Group,
commented that "you can grind up a bus and put it in
with manure and call it compost. . . . But it's a back-
wards approach to the problem" (Swasy B6). Richard
Denison, senior scientist at EDF, noted that consumers
find disposable diapers appealing because they don't have
to give much thought to where the products end up
(Fierman 101). So, when P&G stalled a New York State
Consumer Protection Board brochure discussing the pros
and cons of using disposable diapers, environmentalists
were outraged (Swasy B6). They, as well as ordinary
consumers, questioned the quality of the company's commitment to the environment.

DuPont Company has also come under attack for not
practicing what it preaches environmentally. A report
issued by Friends of the Earth, an environmental interest
group, claimed that despite DuPont's insistence in television ads that it cares about the environment, the company is the "single largest corporate polluter in the
United States" ("Environmental Group" F3). In addition,
the report cites DuPont's record of excessive environmental infractions. In compensation for these abuses, the
company paid out a whopping $1 million monthly between
1989 and June 1991 in EPA and state fines ("Environmental
Group" F3).

25

26

Paragraph 27

This paragraph serves two argumentative purposes. First, it concedes that companies have a difficult time meeting all the federal and state environmental regulations, many of which work at cross purposes. Then it reaffirms one of the paper's major claims that to become more environmentally responsible companies need to be open to new ideas and should constantly reassess their self-image, policies, and procedures. The quotation from Bruce Smart, a former chief executive officer of a Fortune 500 company, drives home Bonnie's point that companies and environmental advocates need to find common ground to guarantee a viable environment for all.

Paragraph 28

Bonnie's conclusion is cautiously optimistic: Companies have made progress in becoming more environmentally committed since the environmental disasters of the late 1980s. But she restates her belief that more can and should be done as we approach the twenty-first century. A block quotation from Henry Ford echoes the paper's thesis that a company's success should always be compatible with its responsibility to the larger society.

Lin 11

On the other hand, companies defend themselves by
pointing to the monumental environmental task they face.
First, in order to avoid huge penalties, they must adhere
to a staggering number of federal and state environmental
regulations. Sometimes these guidelines seem confusing
or misleading. In an effort to clarify regulations, the
EPA has been working to define more precisely the meanings of words like "recyclable" and "recycled content"
(Fierman 92). Still, companies themselves need to reex-
amine their assumptions. For instance, they can view a
set of voluntary guidelines, like the CERES Principles,
as a weapon used by environmental extremists, or they can
view endorsing environmental principles as a sound business decision. As a spokesperson for reevaluation, Bruce
Smart, former CEO of the Continental Can Company, in a
1990 editorial in the <u>Washington Post</u> commemorating Earth
Week, pleaded for "cooperation, moderation, and construc-
tive dialogue" on the part of business and those advocat-
ing strong industry responsibility toward the environment
(A19). He urged everyone involved to stand back and
develop a broader perspective. "Successful policies," he
said, "will be reached by compromise and consensus, not
by insistence on absolutes" (Smart A19). Alone and in
partnerships, companies can restate their vision,
redesign their structure, and change their practices to
become more environmentally responsible.

It seems clear that business has been making steady
progress in becoming more environmentally responsible
since the dark days of the Bhopal and the <u>Exxon Valdez</u>
disasters. But more needs to be done. In fact, according to the authors of <u>Corporations in the Moral
Community</u>, "Environmental quality . . . will be the single most important issue facing corporations in the twenty-first century" (French et al. 117). Through practices
like endorsing a set of guidelines like the CERES
Principles and forming alliances with environmental

27

28

Lin 12

interest groups, some companies are making environmental
responsibility more than just a politically correct
phrase.   Perhaps Henry Ford, one of the architects of
American business, said it best.   At the turn of the
century he wrote:

> There is no longer anything to reconcile
> between the social conscience and the profit
> motive. . . Improving the quality of society
> . . . is no more than another step in the
> evolutionary process of taking a more far-
> sighted view of return on investment. (qtd. in
> Smith 59)

Companies need to understand and act upon the idea that
environmental responsibility is everyone's business, that
it is not incompatible with success.   Through the 1990s
and into the twenty-first century, environmentally
responsible companies will continue to note how their
wise decisions meant good business.

Works Cited

Bonnie has followed MLA style in preparing this paper for her English Composition class. Thus, the list of sources she has used in her paper is headed "Words Cited" rather than "Bibliography" or "References." For examples of documentation styles in disciplines other than English, refer to Chapters 49-52.

Because Bonnie's topic is a current one, she found relevant research materials largely in periodicals rather than books. Of the twenty-two sources listed in the "Works Cited," only four of them are books. The rest are magazines, journals, newspapers, and electronic media. Note the difference in citation style between magazines (publication month and year cited) and journals (volume number and year cited). Also note the citation formats for the references to a press release, a printed transcript of a radio interview (Glass), and a telephone interview (Smith). Be mindful that although style manuals and handbooks try to cover citation formats for as many types of sources as possible, they cannot be exhaustive. If you cannot find a format example for a particular type of reference source, find an example of a similar type of source and use it as a guide in preparing your citation. Remember that your responsibility is to provide sufficient information so that readers can locate the source themselves if they wish to do so.

Works Cited

"Alaska Fishermen Blockade Tankers." New York Times 23
    Aug. 1993, sec. A: 8.

Bavaria, Joan. "An Environmental Code for Corporations."
    Issues in Science and Technology 6 (1990): 28-31.

Cogan, Douglas G. "Shareholders Press Environmental
    Issues." Directors & Boards 16 (1992): 53-57.

Corcoran, Elizabeth. "Thinking Green: Can
    Environmentalism Be a Strategic Advantage?"
    Scientific American Dec. 1992: 22-23.

"Environmental Group Calls DuPont's Ads Deceptive."
    Washington Post 28 Aug. 1991, sec. F: 3.

Fierman, Jaclyn. "The Big Muddle in Green Marketing."
    Fortune 3 Jun. 1991: 91-101.

French, Peter A., et al. Corporations in the Moral
    Community. New York: Harcourt, 1992.

Glass, Ira. Interview. Printed transcript. "Weekend
    Edition." National Public Radio. 21 Apr. 1991:
    30-32.

Hamilton, Martha M. "Big Mac Attacks Trash Problem."
    Washington Post 17 Apr. 1991, sec. B: 1+.

Hinden, Stan. "Joan Bavaria Changing the Bottom Line."
    National Wildlife Oct./Nov. 1991: 44.

Lublin, Joann S. "'Green' Executives Find Their Mission
    Isn't a Natural Part of Corporate Culture." Wall
    Street Journal 5 Mar. 1991, sec. B: 1+.

"McDonald's Is Opposing Broad Environmental Plan." Wall
    Street Journal 18 Apr. 1991, sec. B: 6.

News Release. Issued jointly by Sun Company, Inc. and
    CERES, 10 Feb. 1993: 1-3.

Poduska, Richard, Richard Forbes, and Maria Bober. "The
    Challenge of Sustainable Development: Kodak's
    Response." Columbia Journal of World Business 27
    (1992): 286-91.

Roberts, William L.   "Sun's Bold Strategy for
        Environment."   <u>Philadelphia Business Journal</u> 12
        (1993): 1+.

Sethi, S. Prakash, and R. H. Bok.   "Stakeholders and
        Shareholders."   <u>Corporate Responsibility and
        Legitimacy: An Interdisciplinary Analysis</u>.   Ed.
        James J. Brummer.   Westport, CT: Greenwood P, 1991.
        140-49.

Smart, Bruce.   "Quit Bludgeoning Business."   <u>Washington
        Post</u> 10 Jul. 1990, sec. A: 19.

Smith, Bradley.   Telephone interview.   3 April 1994.

Smith, N. Craig.   <u>Morality and the Market: Consumer
        Pressure for Corporate Accountability</u>.   New York:
        Routledge, 1990.

Swasy, Alecia.   "P&G Gets Mixed Marks as It Promotes
        Green Image But Tries To Shield Brands."   <u>Wall
        Street Journal</u> 26 Aug. 1991, sec. B: 1+.

Thomas, Lee M.   "The Business Community and the
        Environment: An Important Partnership."   <u>Business
        Horizons</u> 35 (1992), 21+.

Wybrew, John.   "Corporate Responsibility."   <u>The Greening
        of Business</u>.   Ed. David A. Rhys.   Brookfield, VT:
        Gower, 1991.   78-82.

Part 9

Writing in Different Disciplines

Writing...can't be taught or learned in a vacuum. We must say to students in every area of knowledge: "This is how other people have written about this subject. Read it; study it; think about it. You can do it too." In many subjects, students don't even know that a literature exists—that mathematics, for instance consists of more than right and wrong answers, that physics consists of more than right or wrong lab reports.

—William Zinsser, *Writing to Learn*

The term *discipline* comes from a Latin word meaning "instruction" or "knowledge." When we talk about disciplines in colleges and universities, we mean branches or fields of knowledge. Different fields of study are loosely grouped under four major headings:

- **The humanities**—history, philosophy, religion, literature, and the fine arts (music, art, and drama)
- **The social sciences**—anthropology, sociology, psychology, geography, education, political science, economics
- **The natural and applied sciences**—biology, chemistry, physics, geology, biochemistry, engineering, computer science, mathematics
- **The professions**—business, law, medicine

Overlapping occurs, of course. For example, economics can be viewed as a subcategory of business; medicine is obviously related to the natural sciences.

According to its broadest definition, *discipline* means training designed to produce a specified character or pattern of behavior. When you choose a college major within a particular discipline, that is exactly what happens: From the courses and instructors in your major you begin learning not only new information but also the patters of behavior and habits of mind that characterize the discipline.

Disciplines differ in their ways of viewing the world.

One of the most important things about a college education is that it introduces you to new ways of looking at information and ideas. Your introductory courses in the humanities, social sciences, natural sciences, and professional fields such as business are windows not just on new information but also on new ways of thinking about it. As you take more courses in these disciplines, you will notice that the people who teach and work in them share certain vocabularies, research procedures, approaches to problems in their field, professional interests, and even ways of looking at things. Later, as you strive to become a member of your chosen field, one of your chief goals will be to progress from novice to expert. You will learn to "walk the walk and talk the talk" of those in biology, accounting, acting, photography, engineering, teaching, computer programming, radiology, or whatever your field happens to be.

When you are new to a field—encountering its vocabularies, assumptions, concepts, and procedures for the first time—the experience is very much like learning the norms, values, rites, and rituals of a foreign culture. Even basic things like how to approach a problem or how to write a research paper may seem bound by bewildering conventions that everyone but you appears to know. When you ask why your chemistry professor wants a different documentation format for a research report than your English professor wants for a term paper, the answer "Because that's how it's done in chemistry" does not seem particularly helpful, or even rational. However, unstated in that reply and behind the apparently nit-picking differences lie the historical and intellectual evolution of the fields. While all serious researchers and practitioners in all fields universally value careful, honest, rigorous, and accurate work, they think about and write about things differently.

Consider an example. A major earthquake hits southern California, leaving several dozen people dead, hundreds injured, and billions of dollars in damage to homes, businesses, hospitals, schools, and highways. Thousands of people need disaster relief of all kinds. Some months later a personal computer user "netsurfing" on Internet might come across drafts of four research papers posted for comments in four different usenet groups. The titles are "Using Aftershock Data to Map Thrust Faults in Southern California"; "Drawing as Therapy for Post-Earthquake Trauma: A Case Study of a Second Grade Class"; "An Economic Model of Job Loss and Job Creation Following Natural Disasters"; and "Paradise Lost: California as a Setting in 20th-Century American Fiction."

The earthquake, the source or inspiration for all of these papers, receives quite different treatment from the four authors—a geologist, an educational psychologist, a PhD student in economics, and a literature professor. The technical jargon in the titles provides clues that identify the authors' disciplines. The scientist writes about "data" and "thrust faults." The social scientist presents a "case study" of "trauma" and "therapy." The business school doctoral student has used a statistical "model" to analyze the "economic" impact of the earthquake. The humanities professor refers ironically to Milton's epic poem *Paradise Lost* to make a point about literary "setting." Whatever their personal feelings regarding the earthquake, the writers of these papers have brought the tools of their field to bear on events. Each has conducted a different sort of research with different, valuable results.

Disciplines have similar standards for research and writing.

Whatever discipline you choose to study in college, whatever field you select for your professional life, you will find important similarities in the research and writing you encounter.

- All research draws on primary and secondary sources, although the types and balance of sources will vary among disciplines. For example, a research report in organic chemistry is likely to cite fewer secondary sources than a research paper in English literature. The reason is that chemistry research is concerned with creating new compounds by means of scientific experiments, whereas literary research is concerned with interpreting previously written texts.
- All sources are cited accurately and given credit for their contributions to the research. Plagiarism is not tolerated and will result in the ruin of a researcher's career.
- All research is based on careful observation and accurate recording of infor-

mation, whether the information is data from an experiment or survey or quotations from a speech or a poem.

- All writing pays close attention to purpose, audience, thesis, sufficient and logically presented support for the thesis, coherent organization of the material, and careful documentation of sources.

Be mindful of a discipline's practices.

The next four chapters examine the thinking and writing that characterize four of the major disciplines in the college curriculum: the humanities, the social sciences, the sciences, and business. These chapters are not intended to make you proficient in these fields but to provide an overview of the conventions and some examples of the kinds of writing assignments you might encounter while taking courses in these disciplines.

Be aware that even within a single discipline, thinking and writing practices will vary from field to field. This is most obvious in superficial things like documentation format. For example, researchers in literature follow the style of the Modern Language Association (MLA) for bibliographical citations. Researchers in linguistics follow the style of the American Psychological Association (APA). Researchers in philosophy may follow *The Chicago Manual of Style* (CMS) format. This kind of variation occurs in other disciplines as well. In *How To Write & Publish a Scientific Paper*, Robert Day reports that one person looked in fifty-two scientific journals and found thirty-three different styles for listing references. The point is you must check with your professors to learn what documentation style is usual in a particular field or consult the field's major research periodicals to see what style is used. One of the important rites and rituals of becoming a member of a field is following its research, writing, and documentation practices.

49   Writing for the Humanities

49 a   Purposes and methods of inquiry in the humanities.

Students and researchers in the humanities explore questions about the meaning of human existence: What makes a person a human being? What is our relationship to the past? How can the past prepare us for the future? What are our responsibilities to others? Is there life after death? What is the meaning of a painting or a poem? These are big questions without definite answers, questions that humans have asked through the ages about themselves, the universe, and their place and role in it. A person, a society, or an era may claim to have a definitive answer, but the questions resurface and renewed debate ensues.

Because these issues about who we are and how we should live are debatable, argumentation is the typical form of discourse in the humanities. The principal method of inquiry is to contemplate a text (written or spoken word, works or art, music, dance, drama) and then respond to it by analyzing, interpreting, evaluating, or critiquing it. Researchers and students in the humanities develop and test their ideas through inductive or deductive reasoning. They present their conclusions as an argumentative thesis and then support and defend these conclusions with evidence drawn from the text and other relevant sources. Chapter 7 explores argumentation in detail.

Inductive and Deductive Reasoning

Induction. This form of reasoning is based on observations of particular instances from which a generalization about a whole class is formulated. The step from observed or experienced particular instances to a generalization about a whole class is called an *inductive leap*.

Hazards of induction. A generalization based on particular cases is only as good as the quantity and quality of the particular instances observed. The greater the number of samples and the greater the consistency (similarity) of samples, the more likely the generalization is true. Nevertheless, induction can result only in *probability*, not in certainty.

Deduction. This form of reasoning concerns itself with logically sound relationships among statements. This logical soundness is called *validity*. Deduction is almost mathematical in precision, expressing these relationships as a *syllogism*—a series of three propositions:

MAJOR PREMISE a generalization about a large group or class, arrived at inductively from observing particular cases
MINOR PREMISE a statement about a member of the large group or class
CONCLUSION a statement that links the first two premises, declaring something to be true about the person or thing cited in the minor premise

Example

MAJOR PREMISE Only rodents have long front teeth adapted for gnawing.
MINOR PREMISE Squirrels have long front teeth adapted for gnawing.
CONCLUSION Therefore, squirrels are rodents.

Hazards of deduction. Validity and truth are not the same thing. If one or more of the premises are not true, the conclusion will be false even if the logical relationship is consistent. This is obvious from the syllogism "All dogs have four legs. Bowser has four legs. Therefore, Bowser is a dog." Bowser, of course, might be a cat. In this case, the fallacy is one of cross-classification: Two things that share an attribute are not necessarily of the same class.

49 b Common types of documents in the humanities.

For a course in the humanities you might be asked to write an analysis, a review, or a research paper.

● **1 Analysis.** This document is based on close reading of (viewing of or listening to) a "text" to understand how the parts work together to form the whole and create a particular impression. Such an analysis requires an understanding of the components of the work. For example, in analyzing a Shakespearean play, you would need to be able to discuss plot, character, and scene. An analysis may require comparison or contrast between a particular work and others of its type (for example, two paintings in Van Gogh's "Starry Night" series, the blues styles of Muddy Waters and Doc Watson, or the theological differences between Islam and Christianity). An analysis assignment may require that you develop your own theory about how the parts of the work operate together, or the assignment may require you to apply someone else's theory—for instance, a Freudian analysis of Eugene O'Neill's play *Desire Under the Elms* or an analysis of Picasso's painting *Guernica* as a political statement about the Spanish Civil War.

● **2 Review.** Book reviews are common in all disciplines, but in the humanities reviews are also written about works of art, performances (music, theater, film, television, dance), and events such as speeches, exhibitions, and conferences. The review's task is to evaluate, to help readers decide if they wish to see, hear, or participate in the event or work under discussion. The parts of a review are as follows:

- An announcement of the subject
- A description or summary of the subject
- A discussion of the subject's method and technical qualities
- A discussion of its merit, as compared to others in its class
- Information about where to obtain, hear, or view the work or event (some of this information may appear earlier)

Book reviews differ from the books reports you may have written in high school. A typical school book report usually devotes the majority of its space to plot or information summary and ends with the student's brief personal response. A book review, in contrast, provides only enough summary information for the reader to understand the evaluation of the work, which is the reviewer's principal focus.

● **3 Research paper.** The most common type of research paper in the humanities is an extended analysis that uses both primary and secondary sources to place individual works or events in larger contexts to better interpret their meaning, causes, effects, or influences. Many books have started out as research papers and grew longer and more complex.

Research papers in the humanities often incorporate substantial material from secondary sources. The writer is responsible for "knowing the literature" on the subject. That means he or she must read what others have written, analyze it, and present the relevant points as part of his or her own discussion, acknowledging these secondary sources wherever their words and ideas appear in the paper. Thus research writing in the humanities requires the ability to synthesize, drawing together information and ideas from many sources and using the synthesis to construct the argument on behalf of one's own interpretation. The expression "we stand on the shoulders of giants" (the thinkers who have preceded us) is especially relevant in the humanities, in which debates about meaning are the principal subject matter.

Although there are differences among fields, the following organization is typical of research papers in the humanities:

Introduction
    Purpose of study: question or issues to be explored
    Literature review
    Thesis statement
Body
    Analysis and interpretation of text or work of art
    Supporting evidence from primary and secondary sources
Conclusion
    Summary of key points
    Restatement of thesis
Works Cited or Bibliography (begin on a new page)
    Bibliography of works cited in the paper

49 c Documentation styles and guides in the humanities.

Depending on the field, research writers in the humanities use a variant of the name and page system, the name and year system, or the endnote/footnote system. The major style manuals and supporting organizations are listed next. The MLA name and page system is illustrated by the research paper at the end of Chapter 48. The APA name and year system is illustrated by the research paper at the end of Chapter 50, "Writing for the Social Sciences." The endnote/footnote system is illustrated by the research paper at the end of Chapter 52, "Writing for the Professions: Business."

Name and page system

MLA (Modern Language Association)

Achert, Walter S., and Joseph Gibaldi. *The MLA Style Manual.* New York: The Modern Language Association of America, 1985.

Principal characteristics

In-text citations of sources quoted, summarized, or paraphrased.
In-text citations give author's last name and page number of source.
"Works Cited" give full publication information, alphabetized by
    author, at end of document.

Name and year system

APA (American Psychological Association)

Publication Manual of the American Psychological Association. 4th ed.
    Washington, DC: The American Psychological Association, 1994.

Principal characteristics

In-text citations of sources quoted, summarized, or paraphrased.
In-text citations give author's last name and publication year of source.
"References" give full publication information, alphabetized by author,
    at end of document.

Endnote/footnote system

CMS (Chicago Manual of Style: University of Chicago Press)

The Chicago Manual of Style. 14th ed. Chicago: University of Chicago Press,
    1993.
Turabian, Kate L. *A Manual for Writers of Term Papers, Theses, and
    Dissertations.* 5th ed. Chicago: University of Chicago Press, 1987.

Principal characteristics

Superscript number given at end of quotation, summary, or paraphrase
    from source.
List of sources, identified by corresponding superscript number, given
    at bottom of page, end of chapter, or end of document in same order
    as they appear in the text. Citation gives author's last name and page
    number of source.
"Bibliography" gives full publication information, alphabetized by author,
    at end of document.

Sample papers from the humanities: Literary analysis and history research (MLA documentation style).

This section presents papers written for an introductory literature course
and an introductory history course. Both use the MLA name and page documentation system. Since the literary analysis cites only the primary source,
James Joyce's short story "Araby" as it appeared in the student's textbook,
there is no bibliography. In-text citations give page references to the textbook. To help you see how the author structured her analysis, the thesis
statement and supporting evidence from the short story have been marked.

The history paper includes a bibliography along with in-text citations. The thesis, supporting claims, and evidence have been marked to show how the author structures the evidence from his sources. In this paper the writings of Pericles, Aristotle, and Sophocles are primary sources.

Literary Analysis (MLA style)

Scott 1

Julie Scott

Dr. Tarvers

English 210

March 3, 1994

                        The End of the Innocent

        Perhaps nothing is certain but death and taxes, but
in James Joyce's story "Araby" another distressing
predicament is examined--the loss of a child's innocence.
In a harrowing manner, Joyce relates the dawning of
awareness in a young boy who has a crush on the sister
of one of his playmates. Through his descriptive imagery
concerning the boy's environment, his infatuation with
Mangan's sister, and his subsequent awakening, Joyce   thesis
makes the theme of "Araby" painfully realistic to his
readers.

        The boy lives in an extremely dreary setting, one
which forces him to seek some form of escape. The set-
ting is established largely through images of darkness,   supporting
decay, and imprisonment. The boy lives on a "blind"   statement
street, and plays near "sombre houses," "dark muddy
lanes," "dark dripping gardens," and "dark odorous sta-
bles" (348). His house is cluttered with outdated newspapers and faded books, and has a shabby garden with "a
few straggling bushes" (348). The air in the house is
"musty from having been long enclosed" (348), and his
only escape, the school, is described as a prison. These
negative characteristics have symbolic as well as literal
meanings; his world is morally, spiritually, and
intellectually blind, and unable to encourage growth of
any sort.

Scott 2

supporting statement

The boy's escape from this world comes when he discovers Mangan's sister. Here, Joyce uses descriptive imagery to show the boy's idealistic point of view. The boy perceives Mangan's sister as a beautiful angel who piously forgoes a visit to the exciting Araby bazaar to attend a religious retreat at her convent school. Like a saint, she becomes the object of his "strange prayers and praises" (349). He idealistically imagines himself a knight of the Holy Grail, out to serve this perfect lady, with his love "a chalice . . . [he bears] through a throng of foes" (349). He determines to find an offering worthy of this angel/saint at the exotic Araby bazaar. The religious images Joyce employs show us how innocent and idealistic the boy is, and thereby set him up for the harrowing disillusionment the bazaar will provide.

supporting statement

The trip to Araby--the one the boy hoped would be the most gratifying of his life--ends his innocence. The darkness, emptiness, and triviality of the bazaar represent the cold realities of the life the boy cannot escape. The greater portion of the hall where the bazaar is held is in a darkness, and "a silence like that which pervades a church after a service" (350) engulfs it. Most of the booths are closed; only a handful of people attend those which are still open. The only noticeable activity is that of two men counting money. As the boy examines the few "treasures" Araby still contains, he overhears a flirtatious conversation:

> "O, I never said such a thing!"
> "O, but you did!"
> "O, but I didn't!"
> "Didn't she say that?"
> "Yes, I heard her."
> "O, there's a . . . fib!" (350)

And in a flash--what Joyce later called an epiphany--the boy realizes that his notions of life, love, and escape, are false. Life is not an exotic, faraway bazaar or a

Scott 3

holy church, but a dark, deserted hall containing only
moneychangers. Love is not a chivalrous, holy experience,
but trivial, lustful infatuation--a fib. As he stands in
complete darkness, the boy sees himself as a "creature
driven and derided by vanity; and [his] eyes [burn] with
anguish and anger" (351). And there is no escape; he
cannot pretend that he "never said such a thing" or felt
such dreams. The innocent is innocent no more.

On a superficial level, "Araby" is a very subdued
story; the initiation of the boy into manhood employs
little action and few characters--most of them nameless.
But Joyce more than compensates for this lack of action
with abundant descriptive imagery, which readers must   closing
consider carefully if they are to comprehend the full   reference
story. Without such consideration, the story appears as   to thesis
insignificant as the conversation the boy overhears at
the bazaar.

Approaches to Writing About Literature

For an analysis of a literary text (short story, novel, poem, or play),
consider one or more of the following elements.

Speaker and point of view. Through whose eyes is the work of literature
presented? Is it a first-person *I*? An all-knowing third person? What role does
the speaker have in the work: active or detached observer? What effects does
the author achieve by having that particular voice recount events? How
would the work be different if another voice told it?

Character. Who are the main characters? What roles do they play? What are
their attributes, and how do you know? Do their actions indicate their
natures? Do they sound and act like real people or like stereotypes? Are the
characters meant to stand for anything, function as symbols?

Plot. What happens? Are any actions or events more important than others?
Why? Does anything besides time bind the action together? Do any
significant patterns or repetitions of action emerge? Are any actions or events
symbolic, representing something other than just themselves?

Pace and structure. What kind of rhythm or pace does the work have? When do actions speed up or slow down? Are there discernible parts to the work? What parts get the author's most and least attention? Why?

Setting. Where and when does the work take place? What is important about the setting? Do the time and location have an effect on the people and actions in the work?

Language. Do rhythm or rhyme, metaphor, simile, or other figurative language and word choice create a particular image or impression? Can the author's style be described and analyzed in terms of its effect on the reader? Does the language especially reveal or reinforce character or theme?

Genre. What genre (form) is the work written in—poetry, fiction, or drama? Does the choice of genre give the writer particular advantages or handicaps that another genre would not? Is this work typical of its genre, or does it challenge the conventions you associate with the genre?

Theme. Do the character, setting, plot, and so forth work together to develop a theme—a central or dominating idea? What issues or questions about human existence does the work raise? Does it suggest any insights or answers concerning these questions and issues?

For a research paper about a literary text, the following list gives an idea of the range of approaches you can take.

- Relate the work to other works by the same author.
- Compare the work to those of other authors. (Be sure you have an adequate basis for comparison: for example, treatment of the same theme in works by different authors; treatment of the same historical event, such as the Great Depression or World War I, in the works of several authors.)
- Investigate how the author wrote the work, using letters, diaries, journals, and drafts as sources of evidence about the author's writing process.
- Relate the work to its time—the political, social, and artistic developments of an era.
- Relate the work to a literary theory or movement.
- Relate the work to the author's life.
- Fit the work into a literary tradition—other works of its kind that preceded and followed it.
- Investigate the textual history of the work—significant changes made by the author or others after the work was first published.
- Investigate the critical and/or popular reaction to the work (when it was first published or over a period of time) and the effect on the author's reputation.

History Research Paper (MLA style)

Brett Nachman

Professor Newell

History 101

12 September 1993

Realism and Idealism in Athens

The image of classical Athens is that of a society at the pinnacle of democracy, justice, peace, and harmony. The mention of Athens conjures up visions of Western civilization during a golden age. The prevailing imagery, put forth by contemporary as well as future writers and historians, was of a land where all were equal and peace was the predominant condition. While these idealized images of our Western predecessors surely had an effect on what civilizations to come would strive toward, the reality surrounding life in Athens was far less perfect. Everyone in Athens was not equal, justice was not always the rule, and peace was not as prevalent as the ideologies of classical Athens would have one believe.

qualification

thesis claims

Western society, especially the United States, looks to ancient Greece as the basis for the democracy it prizes today. Indeed classical Athens does deserve a nod for its idealistic beliefs regarding democracy and equality. In practice, however, the brand of democracy practiced by Athenians applied only to a relative few. The people for whom democracy was a reality were the free male citizens. Pericles in his funeral speech refers to equal justice for all and advancement irrespective of class or wealth (Wiesner 25). These espousals seem less magnificent when one realizes that they apply only to adult male citizens. When a policy is deemed to be for the good of "the people," it must be understood that "the people" is not all people.

claim 1

evidence 1

Women in classical Athens were viewed as much lower in status than men, as were children, and slaves were regarded as little more than tools.

evidence 1

Aristotle reflects this view when speaking about the deliberative faculty of these three groups: He states that it "is not present at all in a slave, in a female it is inoperative, in a child undeveloped" (Wiesner 31). It must also be understood, however, that this hierarchical view was a common characteristic of the time and thus an Athenian would not see it as going against the ideals of democracy and equality.

claim 2

As recently as the 1930s historians such as Edith Hamilton viewed the Athenian ideals of peace and equality as truth rather than just ideologies. It is now known that the Athenians were anything but peaceful. Athens was a warring state that sought to exercise control over all that surrounded it. The Peloponnesian War lasted 27 years, during which Athens conquered many peoples, occasionally slaughtering the males and selling the women and children into slavery (Wiesner 30).

evidence 2

Athenians saw these conquests as logical extensions of their ideologies. It made sense that their more advanced ideals be extended to, or imposed on, neighboring city-states. In this way the values which they espoused, and which they believed to be the most ideal, would be propagated.

claim 3

It is also now well understood that the ideal of equality was reserved strictly for males. The lack of equality in Athenian society is perhaps best shown in Sophocles' Antigone. Creon, although a fictitious character, exhibits a very realistic Athenian attitude toward

evidence 3

women and children. As king, he has decreed that of Antigone's two brothers (who have killed one another in combat), only the "loyal" one may be buried. Antigone eloquently argues that no such distinction should be made and that both must be buried. Had Antigone been

male, her fate might possibly have been different. As
it is, however, Creon orders her buried alive, and she
subsequently hangs herself at the tomb.

Creon's vehement rejection of Antigone and her
argument illustrates the Athenian view of women as infe-
riors: "I am not the man, not now: she is the man/if
this victory goes to her and she goes free" (Flagles
83). Later he affirms his position, saying that no woman
will rule over him (86). The father as the most important member of the household was a belief shared by the
Athenians and reflected in the writings of Aristotle and
Sophocles. Creon embodies this belief as both king and
father, and it is apparent in the scene between himself
and his son, Haemon. Creon becomes very upset because
Haemon dares to contradict his father and side with his
fiancée, Antigone. Haemon's action is expressly against
the Athenian hierarchical family order. These scenes,
however fictional, help detail the inequalities which
dominated classical Athens.

It is perhaps wrong to judge the values and practices of another time according to our own. It is
equally wrong, however, to idealize another society
which was, in fact, as full of problems as any society
seen since. More than any culture prior to it, Athens
strove toward ideals which it believed to be pure and,
in the truest sense, human. It is obvious that reality
did not live up to those ideals of democracy, peace,
and equality as we define them today. Athens was replete
with problems from war to sexism to slavery. The fact
that Athens was unable to live up to these ideals does
not set aside the fact that Athenians did have these
ideals. Perhaps it is the introduction and emphasis on
ideals such as peace, equality, and democracy which
should be Athens's most important legacy.

Margin annotations:

evidence 3

qualification

restatement
of
thesis claims

qualification

Nachman 4

Works Cited

Flagles, Robert, ed. "Antigone." Sophocles: The Three
     Theban Plays. New York: Penguin, 1982.

Wiesner, Merry E., Julius R. Ruff, and William Bruce
     Wheeler. Discovering the Western Past: A Look at
     the Evidence. Boston: Houghton, 1993.

In Your Own Words

Compare the sample history research paper "Realism and Idealism in Athens" to the humanities research paper structure given in Section **49b**. Write a two-paragraph explanation of the ways in which the sample paper follows the structure and the ways in which it differs. Identify any missing parts and offer reasons.

50 Writing for the Social Sciences

50 a Purposes and methods of inquiry in the social sciences.

Researchers in the social sciences study social issues. Their goal is to understand the behavior of individuals and groups. As the name of the discipline implies, social science often employs controlled investigation and a scientific method of inquiry to collect information, analyze it, and draw conclusions about human behavior. (For a description of scientific method, see Chapter 51, "Writing for the Natural and Applied Sciences.") Social scientists do two types of research: **quantitative research**, which relies numerical data, and **qualitative research**, which relies on field observations. Besides field observations, research in the social sciences may take the form of surveys, interviews, focus groups, and laboratory experiments.

The sample social science lab report that appears in this chapter explores the question "Is there a relationship between nightmares and anxiety?" To answer the question, the researchers conducted a quantitative study. They collected and analyzed numerical evidence captured by sleep logs that research subjects filled out each morning for two weeks. They chose this method of data collection rather than using anecdotal evidence (what people tried to remember later about the frequency of their bad dreams). In this way, the researchers hoped to separate fact from subjective recollection.

Quantitative and Qualitative Research

Quantitative research
- Numerical data used to establish the truth about human behavior.
- Data collected during laboratory experiments or other controlled conditions, or through surveys, questionnaires, and the like.
- Data measured and analyzed to discover nonrandom relationships among variables.
  > For example
  > Is there a connection between positive reinforcement and learning?
  > Is there a cause-and-effect relationship between increases in welfare benefits and frequency of childbirths to welfare mothers?
- Researcher is careful not to interfere in ways that might bias results (nonparticipative).

Sample experiment: Researchers record number of times first-grade teachers call on male students and number of times they call on female students to identify potential patterns of sexual discrimination in elementary school classrooms.

Qualitative research
- Personal observations of behavior recorded in the field, in the research subject's natural environment or social context.
- Researcher analyzes and interprets recorded observations, inferring their significance to answer research questions about human behavior.
- Researcher may interact with research subjects during field observations (participative).

Sample experiment: Researchers observe employment interviews and then interview the employment recruiters to study how recruiters choose among job applicants with similar skills.

---

50 b Common types of documents in the social sciences.

For a course in the social sciences, you might be asked to write a field report, a case study, a literature review, a research paper, or a laboratory report.

● 1 Field report. Field reports are based on the observations the researcher has recorded in the field. The usefulness of these observations depends upon careful, detailed, unbiased description. For any type of writing in the social sciences, develop the habit of taking full and accurate notes. Field reports typically contain the following sections:

> Introduction: statement of the research question or issue being investigated, the reason the question or issue is worth studying, and a brief review of other relevant research to date.
> Identification of the research population being observed in this field study.
> Relevant history or other background about the research population.
> Research method and materials being used in the study.

Observation of the research population's behavior. Opinion and analysis are not appropriate here.

Analysis (significance) of observed behavior.

Conclusions drawn from the analysis regarding research question or issue; recommendations, if any.

● **2 Case study.** This type of research document focuses on a particular case, one individual or group observed over a specific period of time. The components of a case study are generally the same as for a field report, although they may be structured somewhat differently depending on the goals of the study. Be aware that the findings or conclusions in one case study should not be generalized to populations outside the study, although a series of case studies may be compared or contrasted to help identify trends, patterns of behavior, and so forth.

● **3 Literature review.** Literature reviews may appear independently or as parts of other documents in both the social sciences and the natural and applied sciences. They pull together the published research on a topic or question to provide an overview of the current knowledge on the subject. The purpose of a literature review may be purely informative, or its purpose may be to supply the background for a new interpretation of existing information. When the review is part of a larger document, its purpose is to provide a context in which to view the original research presented later in the document. Literature reviews usually concern themselves with the most recent research on an issue, the most important research, or the most relevant research. Their aim is not necessarily to review everything that has been written but to winnow what has been published and present what is most useful to other researchers.

Writing a literature review requires good summarizing and paraphrasing skills. Be sure to give complete and accurate bibliographic information so that readers can find the cited research articles if they desire. An example of a research review appears in Chapter 51.

● **4 Research paper.** A research paper in the social sciences has much in common with a literature review, since it consists mostly of secondary-source information and reports on other people's primary research. Papers of this type help students become familiar with important questions, issues, and research in the field. The organization will be similar to that of a research paper in the humanities, with a focused thesis statement supported by evidence from a variety of relevant sources. Sources are credited by means of name-and-date in-text citations and a list of references at the end of the paper.

● **5 Laboratory report.** Laboratory reports record and analyze the data obtained from laboratory experiments. A sample social sciences laboratory report appears at the end of this chapter. Organized like lab reports in the natural sciences, a typical social sciences report would include the following sections:

Abstract (on a separate page; may be omitted or incorporated in Introduction if report is short)
  Summary of key points of paper
Introduction (begin on a new page)
  Purpose of study and necessary background
  Literature review (may appear as separate major section)
  Research question being investigated
Methods and Materials
  How research was conducted
    Subjects
    Research design and procedures
    Research setting, measurements, apparatus if any
Results
  Description of data collected or of observed behavior of research subjects
Discussion
  Analysis and interpretation of data or observed behavior
  Significance of results in answering research questions (may appear as separate Conclusion section)
  Recommendations, if any, and suggestions for future investigations
References (begin on a new page)
  Alphabetized bibliography of works cited in the report

50 **c** **Documentation style and guide for the social sciences.**

Much research writing in the social sciences follows the American Psychological Association **name and year documentation system** known as APA style. A fully illustrated discussion of this style appears in *Publication Manual of the American Psychological Association*, 4th edition (Washington, DC: The American Psychological Association, 1994). This documentation system uses parenthetical in-text citations for information from outside sources, giving the author's last name and publication year of the source, and a list of references at the end of the document, giving full publication information alphabetized by author.

APA In-Text Citation Format

- **Quotations of fewer than forty words.** Place the citation information in parentheses at the end of the quotation, followed by the quotation's end punctuation. The sample laboratory report at the end of this chapter contains an example. Other examples appear later in this chapter.
- **Quotations of forty words or more.** Block the quotation by starting it on a new line and indenting all lines of the quotation five spaces from the left margin. Place the citation information in parentheses at the end of the quotation, one space after the quotation's closing punctuation mark. Do not put quotation marks around a blocked quotation.

- **All quotations.** Always give page numbers, using *p.* for one page or *pp.* for more than one page. If a quotation ends before the completion of the sentence, insert the parenthetical citation one space immediately after the end of the quotation, no matter where the quotation stops in the sentence. For summaries or paraphrases of information, page numbers are unnecessary unless you think the reader will need to consult the specific pages (or unless your instructor requests that you supply them).
- **Writing in the social sciences uses fewer quotations** than writing in the humanities. In-text citations are still plentiful, because writers refer frequently to findings or research conducted by others in the field.

APA Standard Parenthetical In-Text Citation Format

- author's last name
- comma
- one space
- year of publication
- comma, if page number follows
- one space
- *p.* or *pp.*, if citation refers to immediately preceding quoted material
- one space
- page number, if citation refers to quoted material

EXAMPLE   According to recent studies, "the finding that someone has been having frequent nightmares would not necessarily be indicative of an anxiety disorder" (Wood & Bootzin, 1990, p. 67) nor even that the subject was under any particular stress (Calvados, 1991).

A work by one author. Use the citation format shown in the preceding example.

A work by two or more authors. Use the citation format shown in the preceding example. Note that APA style substitutes an ampersand—&—for the word *and* in parenthetical citations but not when authors are listed in the text.

EXAMPLE   Wood and Bootzin (1990) concluded that there is no significant correlation between nightmares and anxiety.

If a work has fewer than six authors, list them all in the first citation; in second and subsequent citations use the first author's last name and the abbreviation *et al.* ("and others"). For six or more authors, use only the first author's last name and *et al.* in all parenthetical citations. In APA style, *et al.* is not underlined or italicized.

EXAMPLE   Past studies (Bixler, Kales, Soldatos, Kales, & Healy, 1979) have focused on nightmares and their possible

```
relationships to general mental and physical health.
Also, they have tended to focus on specific types of
anxiety (Bixler et al.).
```

Author's name given in the text of the sentence. Do not repeat the name in the parenthetical citation. Place the year of publication in parentheses immediately after the author's name (see the example under "A work by two or more authors"). If the publication year is also mentioned in the text, the parenthetical citation of publication year should also be omitted.

EXAMPLE   In their 1969 study, Gottschalk and Gleser examined
            death anxiety.

A work cited more than once in a paragraph that cannot be confused with other studies. Second and subsequent citations may include only the author's last name and page (for quotations), omitting the year. However, *when more than one work by the same author(s) is cited in a paragraph,* citations must include the publication year so readers will know which work is being referred to. *When several works by the same author are mentioned together,* group them in the citation in order of publication starting with the earliest one. *If two of more works published in the same year by the same author are cited in a paper,* assign them lower-case letters (*a, b, c,* etc.), sequenced according to their alphabetical order by title in the References list.

EXAMPLE   Because of its size, Ramstein's pioneering study (1972)
            provided the benchmark for research in this area.
            Therapists were encouraged to change patients' treatment
            as a result of findings that showed a high degree of
            correlation between anxiety and nightmares (Ramstein).
            However, subsequent studies (1975a, 1975b, 1979) suggest
            that these conclusions may have been premature.

Different authors with the same last name cited in the paper. To avoid confusion, include their first and middle initials (with a space following the periods) in all citations even if the publication years differ.

EXAMPLE   S. A. Brown (1989) identified the therapeutic uses, and
            later research confirmed the results (C. B. Brown,
            1991).

A reference to two or more authors' works. List them alphabetically in the parenthetical citation, separated by a semicolon and a space.

EXAMPLE   Several later studies (C. B. Brown, 1991; Ramstein,
            1993) confirmed the results.

Corporate authorship. For an agency, association, or corporation, give the complete name of the group in the first citation. If the group's name has a well-recognized abbreviation, follow the name with its abbreviation in brackets. You may then use the abbreviation in subsequent citations.

A reference to a work with no author. Give the title or first few words of the title along with the year of publication in the citation. Indicate chapter or article titles with quotation marks and book or periodical titles with underlining or italics. All important words in all titles are capitalized in in-text citations. Note that capitalization in the References list differs (see Section **50d**). *When a work's author is designated as anonymous,* the in-text citation should reflect that designation.

EXAMPLE   The village records (Anonymous, 1634) mention nine inci-
           dents of "possession by evil spirits," which can proba-
           bly be explained as "waking" dreams or nightmares.

APA Reference List Format

Indention. *The Publication Manual of the American Psychological Association,* 4th ed., differentiates between the "final" manuscript that student writers produce to submit to their professors for grading and the "copy" manuscript of an article that an author submits to a scholarly or professional journal for typesetting and publication. In final published form, the entries in a journal article's reference list will feature "hanging" indents: the first line of the entry is flush with the left margin, and the second and subsequent lines are all indented five spaces. The APA *Style Manual* also notes that many professors may prefer their students to use the hanging indent format in their research papers, because these papers are final copy.

HANGING INDENT   Perry, B. D. (1991). Inclusion and the deaf
(final manuscript   student. <u>Educational Research, 33,</u>
or journal)   56- 63.

Clearly, when a reader wishes to find a reference quickly, hanging indents make the source's name easier to see. However, for reasons having to do with electronic typesetting, the APA *Style Manual* requests that authors preparing copy manuscripts for publication format the reference list entries of the copy manuscript with regular indention: the first line of the entry is indented five spaces, and the second and subsequent lines are all flush with the left margin.

REGULAR INDENT   Perry, B. D. (1991). Inclusion and
(copy manuscript)   the deaf student. <u>Educational Research, 33,</u>
                      56- 63.

The following reference list examples in this chapter of the *Prentice Hall Handbook* are formatted with hanging indents, because most *Handbook* users are preparing final manuscripts rather than copy manuscripts. The reference examples in the *Handbook* and the examples in APA *Style Manual* are formatted alike in all other respects. You should always check with the person to whom you are submitting your paper to determine whether the reference list format should be final manuscript-hanging indent or copy manuscript-regular indent. If you are instructed to use copy manuscript format, all you need to do is reverse the indention. And, of course, you should consult the *Style Manual* itself for detailed information.

Alphabetization. Arrange entries by the last name of the first author in an entry. If there is no author, alphabetize the entry by the first word of the title, excluding *A, An,* and *The.* If the references include listings with the same first author but different second or third authors, arrange entries according to the alphabetization of subsequent authors.

EXAMPLE   Burford, A. M., & Arnold, V. (1992).
                Burford, A. M., Smyth, W. K., & Arnold, V.(1983).

References to different works by the same author(s). Arrange by year of publication, earliest first.

EXAMPLE   Burford, A. M., & Terrel, J. B. (1987).
                Burford, A. M., & Terrel, J. B. (1989).

References to works published in the same year by the same author(s). Arrange the entries alphabetically by title, excluding *A, An,* and *The.* In the in-text citations and the list of references, designate them by lower-case letters *a, b, c,* and so forth following the publication year (see example in "APA In-Text Citation Format").

EXAMPLE   Perry, B. D. (1991a). Inclusion and the deaf student.
                Educational Research, 33, 56-63.
                Perry B. D. (1991b, April 23). My turn: The deaf can
                speak for themselves. Newsweek, p. 61.

Works designated as Anonymous. Alphabetize as if Anonymous were the author's name. This designation applies *only* if the work is signed "Anonymous." Otherwise alphabetize the work by title.

Punctuation, spacing. Use one space after the periods that separate the major parts of a reference citation. Use one space after the period that follows the initials in personal names. Use no space after internal periods in abbreviations. Use one space after commas, semicolons, and colons.

Spacing of bibliographic entries. Start the first line at the left margin. Second and subsequent lines in an entry are indented five spaces from the left margin. Double space between lines in an entry and between entries in the reference list. For examples, see the sample laboratory report at the end of this chapter.

APA Standard Format for a Reference: Book

- author's last name
- comma
- one space
- author's initials (full name is *not* used), with one space between them

- one space
- year of publication, in parentheses
- period
- one space
- title of work. Capitalize *only* the first word of the title, the first word of the subtitle (if any), and proper nouns. Underline the entire title including final punctuation, if any.
- period
- one space
- city of publication (if the city is not well known or could be confused with another publishing location, follow it with a comma, a space, and the postal abbreviation for state)
- colon
- one space
- publisher
- period

EXAMPLE   Webb, S. L. (1991). <u>Step forward: Sexual harass-</u>
                      <u>ment in the workplace.</u> New York: MasterMedia.

A work by one author. Use the format shown in the preceding example.
A work by two or more authors. Invert the names of all the authors, giving last name and then initials. List all the authors, regardless of the number. Use commas to separate an author's name from initials and to separate one author from another. Use an ampersand (&) before the last author's name. *For an edited book,* place the editors' names in the author position and add the abbreviation *Ed.* or *Eds.* in parentheses.

EXAMPLE   Frost, P. J., Moore, L. F., Louis, M. R., Lundeberg,
                  C. C., & Martin, J. (Eds.). (1985). <u>Organizational</u>
                  <u>culture.</u> Newbury Park, CA: Sage.

An article or chapter within an edited book. The title of the article or chapter appears without underlining or italics or surrounding quotation marks. Capitalize only the first word and proper names. When the editor's name is not in the author position, do not invert it. List all editors, regardless of the number. Use an ampersand before the last editor's name, but if there are only two editors do not use a comma before the ampersand. Give inclusive page numbers for the chapter or article in parentheses after the book's title.

EXAMPLE   Jones, M. O. (1985). Is ethics the issue? In P. J.
                  Frost, L. F. Moore, M. R. Louis, C. C. Lundeberg,
                  & J. Martin (Eds.), <u>Organizational culture</u> (pp.
                  235-252). Newbury Park, CA: Sage.

An entry in a reference book. If the entry is signed, begin with the author's name and follow the style given here. If it is unsigned, begin with the title of the entry, as shown.

EXAMPLE   Behaviorism. (1978). In <u>Concise encyclopedia of the</u>
<u>sciences</u> (p. 66). New York: Facts on File.

Editions other than the first. Give the edition information in parentheses
after the title. Use the abbreviation *rev. ed.* for "revised edition."

EXAMPLE   Kramer, M. G., Leggett, G., & Mead, C. D. (1995).
<u>Prentice Hall handbook for writers</u> (12th ed.).
Englewood Cliffs, NJ: Prentice Hall.

Corporate author, government publication. Use the complete name of
the government agency or corporate author if individuals are not listed as
authors. If the corporate author is also the publisher, put Author in the
publisher's position.

EXAMPLE   U.S. Economic Cooperation Administration. (1950). <u>A</u>
<u>report on recovery progress and United States aid.</u>
Washington, DC: Government Printing Office.

         U.S. Dept. of Labor. (1992). <u>Workforce 2000.</u> Washington,
DC: Author.

APA Standard Format for a Reference: Periodical

- author's last name
- comma
- one space
- author's initials (full name is *not* used), with one space between them
- one space
- publication year, in parentheses. For magazines and newspapers,
  follow the year with a comma, one space, the month, one space, and day
  (if given).
- period
- one space
- title of article. Capitalize *only* the first word of the title, the first word of
  the subtitle (if any), and proper nouns. Do *not* underline, italicize, use
  quotation marks, or otherwise set off the title.
- period
- one space
- title of periodical. Capitalize *all* important words in the title. Underline or
  italicize the title.
- comma (underlined)
- one space
- volume number, in Arabic numbers. Underline the volume number.
  Follow the volume number with the issue number in parentheses *only* if
  each issue begins with page 1.
- comma (underlined)
- one space
- inclusive page numbers. Use *p.* or *pp.* only for newspapers, not for journal

or magazine articles. Use all digits for page numbers: 344-349, not 344-49.
• period

EXAMPLE   Higgins, F., Flower, L., & Petraglia, J. (1992).
Planning text together: The role of critical
reflection in student collaboration. <u>Written
Communication, 9</u>, 48-84.

Journal article. See the preceding example.

Journal article from periodical paginated by issue. Because every
issue begins with page 1, readers need the issue number as well as the
volume number to locate the article. Place the issue number in parentheses
after the volume number.

EXAMPLE   Pomerenke, P. J. (1993). Surveying the writing assigned
in functional areas. <u>The Bulletin of the Association for Business Communication, 56</u>(4), 28-31.

Monthly magazine article. Give the year and the month of publication in
parentheses. Do not abbreviate the month. Give volume number but not
issue number. Do not use *p.* or *pp.* with page numbers. If an article appears
on discontinuous pages, list all pages numbers, separated by a comma and
one space.

EXAMPLE   Barbier, S. M. (1993, August). How to win allies and
influence snakes. <u>Working Woman, 28</u>, 34-37, 39.

Weekly magazine, weekly or daily newspaper. Give the year, month,
and day of publication in parentheses. Do not abbreviate the month. Give
volume number but not issue number. Use section numbers for newspapers
when sections are numbered separately, each beginning with page 1. For
newspapers, indicate pages with *p.* or *pp.* List all discontinuous pages. If the
article has no author, alphabetize the entry by the first important word in
the title and place the date in parentheses after the article title.

EXAMPLES   Deutsch, J. S. (1994, February 9). Black History Month
comes to classrooms. <u>Gaithersburg Gazette,</u> p. A-22.
Searching for the missing pieces. (1994, January 17).
<u>Time, 143,</u> 20-23.

Sources Requiring Special Identifying Information
Some sources need more identification than standard book and periodical
entries supply. For these sources, additional information is included in
brackets or parentheses. Use brackets to identify the form or content of the
source, such as interview, print review, film, or computer software. Use
parentheses to identify the print sources in which the referenced work
appeared. The following examples are representative.

Review, letter to the editor, editorial. Place identifying information in brackets after the article title.

EXAMPLE   Watkins, T. H. (1990, August 19). Loren Eiseley: The nature of a naturalist. [Review of Fox at the wood's edge: A biography of Loren Eiseley]. The Washington Post, p. H4.

Recorded interview, television or radio program, video cassette, or film. Give the function of the originator, performer, etc. in parentheses following his or her name. Provide the year; supply month and day of the broadcast if relevant. Indicate the form or medium in brackets.

EXAMPLE   Lord, B. B. (Speaker). (1993, April 21). Homelessness. [Interview]. All things considered [Radio program]. Washington, DC: National Public Radio. WETA.

Computer program.

EXAMPLE   Seidel, J. V., Kjolseth, R., & Seymour, E. (1988). The ethnograph [Computer program]. Littleton, CO: Qualis Research Associates.

Abstract or full text of article on CD-ROM. Give the form of the medium in brackets. So that a reader can retrieve the item using the same medium, provide location information such as file and item or access number. When citing an entire article on CD-ROM, substitute the words "Full text from" for "Abstract from."

EXAMPLE   Simms, M. (1994). Defining privacy in employee health screening cases: Ethical ramifications concerning the employee/employer relationship [CD-ROM]. Journal of Business Ethics, 13, 315-325. Abstract from: ProQuest File: ABI/INFORM (R) Select: Item: 00831923.

On-line database, article, or other information. After author, date, and title information, which is displayed according to the usual format, indicate the form or medium in brackets and supply availability information, as shown in the following example. Because electronic media and on-line information are still developing technologies, exact reference formats for these sources are still developing as well. You should include whatever "path" information will help reader retrieve the reference—for example, protocol, directory, and file name for items retrieved via computer networks. For more information on reference citations, see Li and Crane's *Electronic Style: A Guide to Citing Electronic Information* (Westport, CT: Meckler, 1993).

EXAMPLE   Richardson, G. M. (1992, July). Applicants and employees with mental disabilities [2 pages]. HR Focus [On-line], 69, (7). Available: CARL Systems Network: Business Index & ASAP.

Technical and research reports. After the author and title information, in parentheses supply any number that has been assigned to the report for identification purposes. Follow that with the publication information (location and publisher), giving the publishing agency, department, or institution exactly as it appears on the report. When a publishing department is not well known, precede it with the name of its institution, as shown in the following example. If the report is obtainable from a document deposit service such as ERIC, place the document number in parentheses at the end of the entry (see the example that follows at "Information service").

EXAMPLE   Consortium on Automated Analytical Laboratory Systems
(CAALS). (1994). <u>Communications protocol specifi-</u>
<u>cation</u> (CAALS Communication Rep. No. 1).
Gaithersburg, MD: National Institute of Standards
and Technology, CAALS.

Information service. Include information about the service in parentheses at the end of the entry.

EXAMPLE   Miller, E. P., & RiCharde, R. S. (1991). <u>The relation-</u>
<u>ship between the portfolio method of teaching</u>
<u>writing and measures of personality and motiv-</u>
<u>ation.</u> (ERIC Document Reproduction Service No.
332-184)

Dissertations, theses. For doctoral dissertations abstracted in *Dissertation Abstracts International*, follow the first example. For dissertations and master's theses that have not been abstracted or published, follow the second example.

EXAMPLE   Peterson, N. R. (1991). Effectiveness of semantic
mapping as an instructional technique in English
for mainstreamed learning disabled ninth graders.
<u>Dissertation Abstracts International, 52,</u> 05A.
(University Microfilms No. 91-92, 138)
Sherman, J. E. (1985). <u>Passive-aggressive behavior in</u>
<u>terminally ill patients.</u> Unpublished master's
thesis, Purdue University, West Lafayette, IN.

50 d Sample papers from the social sciences: Laboratory report and case study (APA documentation syle).

This section presents papers written for an introductory psychology course and an introductory geography course. Using the APA name and date documentation system, the psychology paper is a second-hand report of an experiment conducted by two researchers rather than a first-hand report of quantitative research conducted by the writer. However, its general organization follows that of a laboratory report, and so it provides a good example of this type of social sciences paper. The first paragraph serves as the report's introduction, identifying the research questions to be investigated. The results and discussion are combined in this paper; they might appear as separate sections in many social science reports. As one of the author's tasks in this report was to assess the researchers' methods, he placed this evaluation in a concluding section. Because of its brevity, the paper has no abstract. A full laboratory report appears in Chapter 51.

The geography paper takes the form of a case study. Focusing on a single group, the population of Prince George's Country, Maryland, it is an analysis of the local landscape from colonial times to 1980. As part of a larger field study of the current population, this paper provides an historical overview of the county's geographical evolution. Because the information for the case study is historical data supplied by the professor in lectures and class handouts, there is no list of references. Presented here are portions of the study's four major sections.

Notice that the headings for this paper differ from those of the psychology lab report. Each geography heading informs readers of the topic content that follows, whereas the lab report headings describe the category of information. As you familiarize yourself with various types of writing in different fields, pay attention to whether headings are used and how they are written.

Psychology Laboratory Report (APA style)

Nightmares and Anxiety

Keith Bennis

Psychology 101

Section 006

April 28, 1994

Nightmares   2

Nightmares are not an uncommon occurrence. They do not necessarily occur nightly, but nonetheless many individuals experience them. Are these "bad dreams" generally preceded by an elevated level of anxiety, or vice versa? Wood and Bootzin (1990) performed a study to test the assumptions that (a) frequent nightmares are uncommon among normal adults, and (b) nightmares reflect generally elevated anxiety in those who have them.

introduction

research question

Method

To further the research on the occurrence of nightmares, the study used daily sleep logs to record on-going observations. This method was a first in published nightmare studies to date. The logs were used in comparison with standard retrospective reports, the data collection method that had been used previously.

The 220 subjects were selected from a pool of undergraduate introductory psychology students. To begin, retrospective self-reports were taken on three estimates. Subjects were first asked how many nightmares they had had over the past year and how many nightmares they had experienced over the previous month. Next, the subjects were given a series of questionnaires dealing with anxiety, creativity, and sleep disorders. Finally, the subjects were given 14-page dream logs which they were to fill out each morning for two weeks. In the logs, the subjects were asked to comment on whether they had had a nightmare the previous night and, if so, how many. To deter false or exaggerated reports, the subjects were told that the researchers were interested in non-nightmare as well as nightmare subjects, and that credit was given regardless. Also, subjects were required to hand in nightly reports within four days.

methods and materials

Results and Discussion

results
discussion

Upon compiling the retrospective self-reports, the researchers found that the mean number of nightmares over the past year was very close to those in previous studies at 9.29. Since the first two estimates were so similar to existing figures, the authors chose not to elaborate on those numbers. However, when asked about the number of nightmares in the previous month, the subjects' mean nightmares per month was 1.03. This calculates to an approximate 12.37 annual mean nightmare frequency, which is 25% higher than the retrospective mean for the whole year. This suggests that nightmare frequency is slightly higher than had been documented in previous studies.

results
discussion

Analysis of the daily logs showed that over 46% of the subjects had at least one nightmare over the two-week period. In fact, one subject had 10 nightmares over the course of the study. The mean, however, was .909. This suggests an estimated annual mean frequency of 23.6. This is 150% higher than the estimated mean from the 12-month retrospective self-reports. The frequency of nightmares appears again to be much higher than indicated by retrospective self-reports. The results of this portion of the study are enough to provoke interest. However, more study using dream logs is needed to augment these findings, especially since the dream logs are a new method of nightmare study.

Past studies have focused on nightmares, as well as other sleep disorders, and their possible relationship to general mental and physical health (Bixler, Kales, Soldatos, Kales, & Healy, 1979). These studies were somewhat broad and all-encompassing. Also, the sample populations were not always as high (53 for nightmares) as Wood and Bootzin's study (1990). The current study focuses more on general anxiety than on death, guilt, or shame anxiety, to name a few from other sleep-anxiety studies (Gottschalk & Gleser, 1969).

The current study first found that a genuine, though very low, association may exist between anxiety and nightmare frequency when retrospective self-reports are used (Wood & Bootzin). However, when subjects used daily logs to measure frequency, the findings suggested that anxiety does not necessarily result in more nightmares, but that an anxious individual might be more likely to recall and report nightmares. | discussion |

The researchers used a stimulus-response example to suggest that although previous research implies anxiety is a stimulus and the nightmare is the response, actually nightmares may precede and cause anxiety. The study presented nightmares as common among college students and unassociated with anxiety level. The authors went on to say, "The finding that someone has been having frequent nightmares would not necessarily be indicative of an anxiety disorder" (Wood & Bootzin, 1990, p. 67).

In one last aspect of the study, the researchers assessed the relation of nightmare frequency and distress. Distress was divided into two levels, those with a current nightmare problem and those without. Using product-moment correlations, nightmare distress was found to correlate .39 using two-week logs, and .60 | results |

using 12-month retrospective self-reports. Also, nightmare distress correlated .03 with the Taylor Manifest Anxiety Scale (one of the questionnaires initially given to the subjects). This correlation, or lack thereof, suggests no relation between expressed nightmare distress and anxiety. Correlations displayed a | discussion |

stronger possible relation between nightmare distress and frequency in retrospective self-reports.

Conclusions

Overall, the study was effective. First the population was of adequate size. At 220, it was larger than many of the groups cross-referenced. The representation could have been better. The subjects were college students at a mean age of 19 years. Bower (1990) notes that nightmare frequency and dream recall decrease during adulthood and stabilize around age 40. Thus, this group of college students may be more prone to nightmares and remember them more frequently than a group of college graduates studied at a 20-year reunion.

evaluation
of study's
methods
and results

Measurements of anxiety among college students are likely to be high, with or without nightmares. Given the daily worries of exams, money, and relationships, it may be difficult to say for sure that a nightmare causes anxiety or vice versa. That is, it would be difficult to pinpoint the source of anxiety in a subject-group of this type.

The methods used in conducting this study appeared to be appropriate. Most intriguing were the sleep logs and the results associated with them. However, due to the pioneering nature of this method, it needs to be researched further. This particular pilot portion of the study provided enough difference to warrant further study. After all, using the dream diaries produced nightmare frequency numbers 2.5 times greater than previous studies had shown.

Finally, the study seemed to achieve its desired impact. It was thorough and statistically complete. As previously stated, the population sample could have been more diverse according to age, or several groups could have been compared. The results appeared logical and were compared to past studies in a reasonable manner. Overall, the results appeared convincing.

References

Bixler, E. C., Kales, A. M., Soldatos, C. J., Kales, J. R., & Healy, S. W. (1979). Prevalence of sleep disorders in the Los Angeles metropolitan area. American Journal of Psychiatry, 136, 1257-1262.

Bower, B. R. (1990). Nightmare numbers surprisingly high. Science News, 137, 132.

Gottschalk, L. A., & Gleser, G. C. (1969). Anxiety scale. In C. B. Winget & M. H. Kramer (Eds.), Dimensions of dreams (pp. 46-50). Gainesville: University Presses of Florida.

Wood, J. P., & Bootzin, R. M. (1990). The prevalence of nightmares and their independence from anxiety. Journal of Abnormal Psychology, 99, 64-68.

Geography Case Study (APA style)

The Evolution of a Cultural Landscape
in Prince George's County, Maryland
Matthew Wallas
Professor Silverman
Geo. 100
Oct. 4, 1993

Cultural Landscapes   2

Geographers explain the evolution of a cultural
landscape by describing the spatial components of a
given area as they change over time. The three basic
spatial concepts are lines, nodes, and areas. Lines
are the routes people travel, such as roads and waterways (Interstate 495, the Potomac River). Nodes are
points where lines intersect and development occurs,
such as towns and cities (Bladensburg, Lanham). Areas
are groups of nodes and lines with specific boundaries
defining the largest unit under discussion (Prince   introduction
George's County, the state of Maryland, the District of
Columbia).

The various processess that effect landscape evolution can be categorized as geographic, political, psychological, and economic. Geographic changes involve
spatial diffusion, regional interdependencies, spatial
mobility, resource evaluation, and technological innova-
tion (transportation).

The present-day landscape of Prince George's   research
County is one of mostly suburban areas. Some small   population
areas of the county remain rural, however. How did
this change from rural communities to suburban areas   research
come about? By examining the geography and history of   question
Prince George's county, as well as how the four main
landscape evolution processes affected its growth, this
question can be answered.

Relative Location of Prince George's County
Physical Aspects of Location

Most of Prince George's County is located in the
Atlantic Coastal Plain and Tidewater areas with parts
located in the Appalachia area. The point where these
two areas meet is called the fall zone. At this point   relevant
water transportation becomes blocked by rapids (the   history
Great Falls on the Potomac River, for example). In
addition, the landscape changes from a lower to a higher
elevation. Because of these changes in area, the early
eighteenth-century settlers did not go past this point,

which became known as the Tidewater Frontier. However,
certain factors caused landscape modification in the

relevant history

county. These were great and middling planters, commercialization, industrialization, and the advent of
super highways and mass transit.

Situational Factors and Landscape Modification

The early settlers followed an agrarian lifestyle.
Of the two main classes of farmers, the "great
planters" owned large plots of land that were next to
navigable water where they developed wharves for loading
and unloading boats and rafts. "Middling planters"
developed smaller estates some distance from the river
and built primitive dirt roads to transport their goods
to the wharves, and thus to the ports of trade. Around
these wharves and ports populations grew to serve them.
Navigable rivers were the colonial "highways." The
important Prince George's County colonial ports of
Bladensburg on the Anacostia River, Piscataway on
Piscataway Creek, and Nottingham, Upper Marlboro, and
Queen Anne on the Patuxent River allowed county
planters to ship their commercial agricultural products,

relevant history

such as tobacco, directly to England.

The commercialization and industrialization of the
landscape brought about the end of the Tidewater
Frontier. George Washington, who owned land west of the
Appalachians, believed the country could develop only if
a way were found to open up the potential of the west.
Technological innovations such as the steamboat and the
railroad eventually made that possible and further
changed Prince George's County. The steamboat allowed
goods to be transported more quickly and created a
trade route on the Patuxent River between Baltimore and
Washington, giving the county a link with the
Chesapeake Bay. As a result, towns sprang up along the
Patuxent between the two cities.

Cultural Landscapes   4

The railroad's advent in the nineteenth century resulted in further development of the county. The Baltimore & Ohio line from Washington to Baltimore caused towns to be located along the route. The construction of the Baltimore & Potomac Railroad, which ran close to the route of present-day Rt. 301, with a spur to Huntington, opened up the southern part of the county. As towns flourished along the railway lines, the center of attention shifted from riverine wharves and primitive roads to the railroad.

relevant history

Trolley car lines and interurbans were introduced at the beginning of the twentieth century. The trolley line from downtown Washington, DC, through Mount Rainier to Laurel was opened in 1910. These trollies brought about the development of the original "street car suburbs" such as Mount Rainier and Brentwood. Middle class and working class families were able to move out of the city and but could still commute back downtown to work. . . .

Relative Population Change and Landscape Evolution

The Relative Population Change map (Figure 1) shows the changes in population in 21 areas of Prince George's County between 1930-1950 and 1960-1980. Between 1930 and 1950, the areas furthest from the District of Columbia experienced a loss in population while those closest to the nation's capital experienced a gain in population. Between 1960 and 1980, there were relative losses in those areas closest to the District of Columbia and in the southern end of Prince George's County. The other areas further from the District had a relative population gain. . . .

observation of population's behavior

Analysis of Population Change

The areas of population growth during the 1930-1950 period are close to Washington and mainly along trolley and interurban lines (e.g., area 2). The federal government's growth during the New Deal in the 1930s

analysis of observed behavior

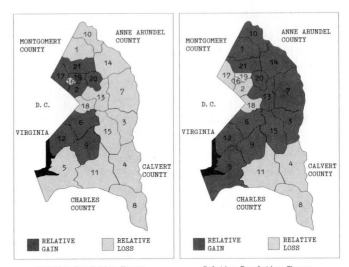

Relative Population Change   Relative Population Change
Prince George's County 1930-1950   Prince George's County 1960-1980

Figure 1. Relative population changes 1930-1980.

and World War II created an in-migration of people from
other parts of the United States. The Cold War after
World War II led to the maintenance and growth of
defense installations in the southern and western sections of the county, (e.g., areas 6, 9, and 12). The GI
Bill, enabling returning servicemen to receive a college
education, contributed to the growth of the University
of Maryland at College Park (area 21).

analysis
of
observed
behavior

  Government workers sought affordable, convenient
housing. Many families did not own a car and relied on
public transportation. In addition, there was an out-
migration from the District as families sought more space
and a higher standard of living in the suburbs. . . .

  The areas showing a relative decline in population
were mainly in the eastern and southern rural areas of
the county. This decline was due to increased mecha-
nization of farms and the cessation of farming in many
areas. During this period many landowners reassessed

their land use; in many cases agricultural acreage lay idle for many years--no longer under cultivation but not yet developed. . . .

    The areas that showed a relative gain in the 1960-1980 period are largely those that showed a relative loss in the 1930-1950 period. This population shift is caused by a number of factors. . . . The building of interstate highways I-95 and I-495, Rt. 50, and Rt. 301 and the potential improvement in total travel time from point to point encouraged greater personal car use and opened up rural areas to residential development. . . .

analysis of observed behavior

    The Federal Fair Housing Act of 1966, and the riots in downtown Washington following the 1968 assassination of Dr. Martin Luther King, brought about an out-migration of affluent black families. (These migrants were quite possibly the children of those who migrated into DC in the 1930-1950 period.) . . .

Conclusion:
The Processes That Changed Prince George's
Cultural Landscape

    The change processes primarily responsible for landscape evolution in Prince George's County are naturally interconnected. However, they can be usefully categorized as follows:

    <u>Transportation development (geographic/technological)</u>: The development of larger ships unable to navigate Prince George's silted-up waterways (the result of soil depletion and erosion from tobacco cultivation) rendered the ports obsolete. The development of rapid transportation methods--first steam railways and steamboats, then railways and trollies, followed by interstate highways and personal car ownership--has opened all parts of the county to development.

conclusion drawn form analysis

    <u>The growth of the federal government (economic)</u>: In-migration to the nation's capital began in the 1930s, but it has accelerated since World War II as people

move to the area to take advantage of government and
defense jobs. Transportation developments enabled the
growing population to spread into Prince George's County
from the District.

conclusion
drawn from
analysis

> The passage of civil rights legislation (politi-
cal): From the 1864 Constitutional Amendment abolishing
slavery in Maryland to the 1966 Federal Fair Housing
Act, strong black communities have developed in the
county. Today Prince George's County has the largest
middle-class black population in the nation.

The landscape of Prince George's County today is
very different from the landscape of its past. It has
changed from one of mostly rural areas supporting agricultural interests with navigable waterways to one of
suburban areas supporting residential and commercial
interests dependent largely on personal automobiles and
super highways. While a few areas remain rural, in the
near future these areas will be overcome by the change
processes that have affected the rest of Prince
George's County.

In Your Own Words

Read the two sample social science reports carefully. Write a two-paragraph
comparison of the use of the tone, the headings, the overall structure, and
the documentation in them.

51 Writing for the Natural and Applied Sciences

51 a Purposes and methods of inquiry in the sciences.

Students and researchers in the natural sciences are interested in answering questions concerning natural phenomena. To do this, they seek to discover new knowledge that may lead them to answers. The applied sciences, as the name suggests, apply new knowledge to the development of practical solutions to problems. For example, engineering applies physics and other natural sciences to design, construction, and manufacturing problems.

Researchers in the sciences seek irrefutable facts through laboratory and field observation. They use these facts to test hypotheses, which are proposed explanations of scientific phenomena. For a fact to be irrefutable (or at least have a high probability of being irrefutable), it must be repeatedly observed or repeatedly reproducible. Consequently, scientific experiments or data collection must be repeatable and yield identical or comparable results so that others can verify their existence, the truth of the conclusions, and so forth. Scientists use a process called the scientific method of inquiry to help ensure the accuracy of their results and the truth of their hypotheses. When writing for science courses, you will need good describing, synthesizing, analyzing, and evaluating skills to compare hypotheses and collected information.

Scientific Method of Inquiry

- Propose a hypothesis—an explanation of a scientific phenomenon.
- Review previously published research bearing on the hypothesis.
- Plan a method of investigation to test the hypothesis.
- Perform the investigation, using scrupulous, exacting standards and care in following procedures.
- Take detailed notes, recording all observations and results accurately.
- Analyze the results to decide if the data prove the truth of the hypothesis.
- If the hypothesis is unproved, rethink the experiment's design, adjust it, and repeat.
- Write up the results as a research report. Suggest other experiments or related hypotheses for future research, if warranted.

51 b Common types of documents in the sciences.

Reviews and research reports are the most common types of papers written in the sciences. Another term for a research report is laboratory report.

● **1 Review.** A research review pulls together the published information on a topic, issue, or research question. Usually the writer's task is to survey, summarize, and sometimes evaluate the current research. Occasionally a review takes a broader approach, providing a complete historical overview. Reviews are especially valuable because researchers can be brought up to date quickly without having to perform a bibliographic search and read all the material themselves. An example of a review written for a sophomore organic chemistry course appears at the end of this chapter.

● **2 Research or laboratory report.** These papers report on field observations or laboratory experiments. The following organization, known by the acronym IMRAD (for introduction, methods, results, discussion), is typical of research reports in the sciences.

    Abstract (on a separate page)
        Summary of key points of paper
    Introduction (begin on a new page)
        Purpose of research
        Hypothesis
        Background
        Literature review
    Methods and Materials
        Research design and procedures
        Research setting, measurements, apparatus
    Results
        Description of data collected, presented in the past tense
    Discussion
        Analysis and interpretation of data: conclusions that can
            be drawn from the data along with a brief summary of the
            evidence that supports each conclusion
        Discussion of whether results and interpretation support the hypothesis
        Discussion of whether results and interpretation agree with
            previously published research; if not, why not
    Conclusion (may be included as last subsection of Discussion)
        Significance of results in answering research questions
        Theoretical implications of the research
        Suggestions for future research
    References (begin on a new page)
        Works cited in the report

Verbs in Scientific Writing

Verb Tense

When a scientist publishes his or her research, it becomes *established fact* in the scientific community, indeed in the world at large. For this reason, there are writing conventions governing when to use present- and past-tense verbs. The following guidelines will help you know how to handle verb tense when writing scientific papers.

- **To quote or discuss previously published work,** use the present tense. Such work is established knowledge.

EXAMPLE   This behavior appears to be induced by some other stimulus (either chemical or physical).

- **To refer to your own work,** use the past tense. Your work is not established knowledge until it has been published (or reported in a paper written for your instructor).

EXAMPLE   This behavior appeared to be induced by some other stimulus (either chemical or physical).

- **Tenses will shift throughout the paper** as you move back and forth between reporting on your own work and that of others. Tense usage for various parts of the paper would typically be as follows:

    Abstract: past tense, when reporting your own research results of the present.
    Introduction: present tense, when reporting knowledge already established.
    Materials and Methods: past tense, when describing what you used and what you did.
    Results: past tense, when describing what you found.
    Discussion: present tense, when discussing knowledge already established; past tense, when discussing your findings in comparison with established knowledge.

Exceptions to the preceding guidelines:

Attribution of work usually requires both past (the work that was done) and present tense (the research results that are now established fact).

EXAMPLE   Hamilton reported that *Callinectes* pluck *Littorina* off of *Spartina.*

Calculations and statistical analyses should be in present tense, even when the statistics refer to data collected in the past.

EXAMPLE   The 8.3% difference in mortality rates does not match the anticipated results. Treatment 2 had the highest mortality rate, but we had not expected Treatment 1 or Treatment 3 mortality rates to be as high as they were.

General statements or known truths should be in present tense.

EXAMPLE   The snail secretes a band of mucus at the anterior lip of the shell which allows the animal to climb and remain attached to the *Spartina* above the high water mark during high tide.

Passive Voice Versus Active Voice

Scientific writing abounds with passive-voice verbs. When asked, users of the passive voice defend their choice on grounds that it is more impartial and hence more "scientific" because the agent of the action (the subject in an active-voice sentence) often remains unidentified. In other words, passive-voice sentences emphasize the materials, the methods, and the results. Up to a point this is true. But the downside of the passive voice is long, windy sentences stuffed with nominal constructions, flabby verbs (see Chapter 24), and expressions that result from bad habits rather than sound writing choices. The best science writers vote overwhelmingly for less passive voice in research writing. Robert A. Day, one of the best writers about science writing, says this about active versus passive voice:

> Let us now talk about *voice.* In any type of writing, the active voice is usually more precise and less wordy than the passive voice.... Why, then, do scientists insist on using the passive voice? Perhaps this bad habit is the result of the erroneous idea that it is somehow impolite to use first-person pronouns. As a result, the scientist typically uses such verbose (and imprecise) statements as "It was found that" in preference to the short, unambiguous "I found."
>
> I herewith ask all young scientists to renounce the false modesty of previous generations of scientists. Do not be afraid to name the agent of the action in a sentence, even when it is "I" or "we." Once you get into the habit of saying "I found," you will also find that you have a tendency to write "*S. aureus* produced lactate" rather than "Lactate was produced by *S. aureus*" (Note that the "active" statement is in three words; the passive requires five.)
>
> You can avoid the passive voice by saying "The authors found" instead of "it was found." Compared with the simple "we," however, "the authors" is pretentious, verbose, and imprecise (which authors?).
>
> —Robert A. Day, *How to Write and Publish a Scientific Paper*

51 c Documentation styles and guides for the sciences.

Various disciplines within the natural and applied sciences have developed their own documentation styles, often standardized by the scholarly association representing a particular discipline—for example, the American Chemical Society (ACS) for chemists, the American Institute of Physics (AIP) for physicists, or the Council of Biology Editors (CBE) for biologists. Some of the most widely used style guides are as follows:

American Institute of Physics. *Style Manual.* New York: American Institute of Physics, 1990.

American Medical Association, Publications Division. *Style Book: Editorial Manual.* Acton, MA: Publishing Sciences Group, 1976.

American National Standards Institute, Inc. *American National Standard for the Preparation of Scientific Papers for Written or Oral Presentation.* ANSI Z39.16-1979. New York: American National Standards Institute, 1979.

American Society for Microbiology. *ASM Style Manual for Journals and Books.* Washington, DC: American Society for Microbiology, 1985.

CBE Style Manual Committee. *CBE Style Manual: Guide for Authors, Editors, and Publishers in the Biological Sciences.* 5th ed. Bethesda, MD: Council of Biology Editors, 1983.

Dodd, Janet S. *The ACS Style Guide: A Manual for Authors and Editors.* Washington, DC: American Chemical Society, 1986.

Huth, E. J. *Medical Style & Format: An International Manual for Authors, Editors, and Publishers.* Philadelphia: ISI Press, 1987.

Michaelson, Herbert B. *How to Write & Publish Engineering Papers and Reports.* 3rd ed. Phoenix: Oryx Press, 1990.

Documentation systems in the sciences vary widely but can be grouped into three principal categories: the **name and year system** (also known as the Harvard system), the **number from alphabetical list system,** and the **number in order of citation system.** Most specialties within the natural and applied sciences use a variation of one of these systems in their research writing. The formats below follow the Council of Biological Editors (CBE) *Style Manual.*

CBE Name and Year System

- **Author's last name and year of publication** appear in parentheses in the text sentence. This in-text citation format is virtually the same as the APA format shown in Section **50c**, with the exceptions as follows.

- **No comma between author's name and publication date.**

EXAMPLE   This behavior appears to be induced by some other stimulus (Wells 1980).

- **A work by two or more authors.** The final author is joined by *and.* An ampersand—*&*—is not used.

EXAMPLE   These snails are often found in estuaries from New York to Texas (Clench and Turner 1956) and are very common in the estuaries of Charleston.

- **A work by three or more authors.** List the first author and substitute *et al., and others,* or *and coworkers* for the other authors. These substitutions are not underlined or italicized in CBE style.

EXAMPLE   The results have been inconclusive (Ryan et al. 1993). Morrisey and others (1989) repeated the original experiment (Baker and coworkers 1986), but their data did not agree with Baker's.

- **Page numbers.** Do not list page numbers in the in-text citations unless your instructor requests you do to so or unless the journal for which you are writing requires it. If you include page numbers, follow the example shown here. Use *p.* in the in-text citation, rather than *pp.*, even when multiple pages are being cited.

EXAMPLE   The procedures of the initial study were replicated (Jones 1986, p. 342-351).

CBE Number from Alphabetical List System

- **Reference numbers.** Alphabetize the list of references by author, and assign each entry a number beginning with the first entry in the list.

- **Placement.** Where a source citation is necessary in the text, insert only the number of the corresponding reference in parentheses. As shown by the following example, the numbered citations in the text will not necessarily be sequential. Some journals and professors require superscript reference numbers (either with or without parentheses) rather than on-line numbers. Be sure to determine which style you are to follow.

EXAMPLE   In the Charleston area, the main predator is *Callinectes sapidus*, the ubiquitous blue crab (5). Hamilton (3) has witnessed *Callinectes* plucking *Littorina* off of *Spartina* stalks as much as 7 cm above the water. The snails' climbing behavior would seem to be a successful mechanism for allowing *Littorina* to avoid predation (6, 7).

CBE Number in Order of Citation System

- **Reference numbers.** Assign a number to each entry in the list of references—in *order of mention in the text* rather than alphabetical order.

- **Placement.** Place only the number assigned to the reference in parentheses in the text where a source citation is necessary. Citation numbers in the text will be sequential. The list of references at the end of the paper will follow the in-text citation order, not alphabetical order. Some journals and professors require superscript reference numbers (either with or without parentheses) rather than on-line numbers. Be sure to determine which style you are to follow.

EXAMPLE   In the Charleston area, the main predator is *Callinectes sapidus*, the ubiquitous blue crab (1). Hamilton (2) has witnessed *Callinectes* plucking *Littorina* off of *Spartina* stalks as much as 7 cm above the water. The snails' climbing behavior would seem to be a successful mechanism for allowing *Littorina* to avoid predation (3, 4).

CBE Reference List Format

- **Arrangement.** Arrange references according to the citation system being used: alphabetically (then chronologically by earliest publication date when authors of two or more entries are the same) or by order of first mention in the text.

CBE Standard Format for a Reference: Book

- author's last name
- comma
- one space
- author's initials (full name is not used unless two authors by the same last name have the same initials), with one space between them
- two spaces
- title of work. Capitalize only the first word and any proper names. Do not underline or italicize the title.
- period
- two spaces
- city of publication (if the city is not well known or could be confused with another publishing location, follow it with a comma, a space, and postal abbreviation for state)
- colon
- one space
- publisher (abbreviations such as Univ. and Co. may be used)
- semicolon
- one space
- year of publication
- period

EXAMPLE
    Wilkins, A. S.   Tidewater plants and animals.
    Charlottesville, VA: Univ. of Virginia Press; 1991.

A work by one author. Use the format shown in the preceding example. Treat a *corporate author* the same as any other author. If the author and publisher are the same, repeat the author's name in the publisher position.

EXAMPLE
    American National Standards Institute, Inc.
    American national standard for bibliographic refer-
    ences, Z39.29-1979.   New York: American National
    Standards Institute; 1977.

A work by two or more authors. Invert the names of all authors, giving last name followed by initials. List all authors, regardless of number. Use a semicolon to separate one author from another. Do not use *and* or *&* before the final author. *For an edited book,* place the editors' names in the author position, followed by the word *editors*, unabbreviated.

EXAMPLE
    Wilkins, A. S.; Foreman, J. T., editors.   The
    effects of ozone depletion on amphibians.
    Charlottesville, VA: Univ. of Virginia Press; 1994.

Multiple works by the same author(s). Arrange the entries in order of publication year, starting with the earliest, regardless of the titles' alphabetization.

EXAMPLE
    Foreman, J. T.   Frogs and the biosphere.   New
    York: Wiley & Sons; 1985.

```
Foreman, J. T.   Amphibian habitats.   Woods Hole,
MA: Pond Press; 1988.
```

Selective pages or chapter within a book. For a section or selective pages, add a colon and inclusive page numbers at the end of the entry. If the selection is separately titled or by persons other than the authors or editors of the whole work, follow the format in the second of the following examples. The title of the section or chapter should appear without underlines, italics, or quotation marks.

EXAMPLES
```
Wilkins, A. S.; Foreman, J. T., editors.   The
effects of ozone depletion on amphibians.
Charlottesville, VA: Univ. of Virginia Press;
1994: 45-102.

Lee, G. W.   An investigation of the disappearance
of amphibians in Oregon.   In: Wilkins, A. S.;
Foreman, J. T., eds.   The effects of ozone deple-
tion on amphibians.   Charlottesville, VA: Univ. of
Virginia Press; 1994: 103-121.
```

Selection in a reference work. If the entry is signed, list the signer as author. If the entry is not signed, begin the entry with the title. Include volume number (use the abbreviation *vol.*) or page numbers at the end if these will help readers locate the reference.

EXAMPLE
```
Respiration.   In: Yule, J. D., ed.   Concise
encyclopedia of the sciences.   New York: Facts on
File; 1978: 481.
```

CBE Standard Format for a Reference: Journal

- author's last name
- comma
- one space
- author's initials (full name is not used unless two authors by the same last name have the same initials), with one space between them
- two spaces
- title of article. Capitalize only the first word and any proper names. Do not underline or italicize a word in the title unless it is a genus, subgenus, species, or subspecies of plant or animal being used as a scientific term. Do not put quotation marks around the article title.
- period
- two spaces
- title of periodical. Abbreviate the journal title according to the guidelines that follow under "Abbreviations of periodical titles." Capitalize all words in the title. Do not underline, italicize, or put quotation marks around the journal title.
- period

- two spaces
- volume number. Use arabic numerals, even if the original numbers on the journal are roman numerals.
- issue number, in parentheses. Include it only if the pages of the journal are numbered by issue rather than by volume.
- colon
- one space
- page numbers, inclusive. Do not use the abbreviations *p.* or *pp.*
- semicolon
- one space
- year of publication
- period

EXAMPLE   McKillup, S. C. The selective advantage of
             avoidance of the predatory whelk *Lepsiella vinosa*
             (Lamark) by *Littorina unifasciata* (Philippi). J.
             Exp. Mar. Biol. Ecol. 63: 59-66; 1982.

Abbreviations of periodical titles. In the preceding example, *J. Exp. Mar. Biol. Ecol.* stands for *Journal of Experimental Marine Biology and Ecology.* Journal titles in the natural and applied sciences have standard abbreviations, usually those recommended in the *American National Standard for Abbreviations of Titles of Periodicals.* A list may be obtained from the American National Standards Institute, 1430 Broadway, New York, NY 10018. Listings are also available in *Chemical Abstracts Service Source Index (CASSI), BIOSIS List of Serials,* and *Publications Indexed for Engineering* (located in your college library). Other science periodical indexes also list these standard abbreviations in the front, and some journals list them in their instructions to authors (usually published in the first or last issue of a volume or year). A list for a particular field can often be found in that field's style manual, such as the *ACS Style Guide* for chemistry. Of course, the journal itself will display its standard abbreviation. One-word titles, such as *Johnsonia* or *Science,* are not abbreviated. If you cannot find an abbreviation for a word in a journal title, spell it out. Do not abbreviate newspaper and magazine titles.

Works by multiple authors. Treat multiple authors of journal articles the same as multiple authors of books.

Multiple works by the same author(s). In an alphabetical system (name and date; number from alphabetical list), if two or more works have the same author, or authors with the same names in the same order, they should be arranged chronologically with the earliest publication first. If works by the same author(s) have the same publication year, order them alphabetically by title and designate them for reference purposes with lower-case letters after the dates. In the first of the following examples, note the **treatment of discontinuous pages** in an article.

EXAMPLES

Gamble, H. S. Hurricane Andrew and the John Pennekamp Coral Reef State Park. Aquarium 48: 174, 176, 179; 1993a.

Gamble, H. S. Red algae nutrients. FAMA 14(2): 86; 1993b.

Article from a journal paginated by issue. After the volume number, place the issue number in parentheses, as in the second of the preceding examples. Follow the issue number with a colon, the page number(s), a semicolon, space, publication year, and a period.

Sources Requiring Special Identifying Information

Research writing in the natural and applied sciences relies heavily on references to journal articles because scholarly journals are the principal means for communicating scientists' work. References to technical reports and conference proceedings are also fairly frequent, with references to magazines, newspapers, and electronic media being less frequent. As in APA documentation style, brackets are used to identify the form or medium of a source. Information about availability or sponsorship may also be supplied in an entry. The following examples are representative.

Technical report. In addition to the usual bibliographic information, supply any cataloging or ordering identification numbers that may help readers identify or obtain the report, along with relevant addresses.

EXAMPLE

Consortium on Automated Analytical Laboratory Systems. CAALS Modularity and Control Communications Working Group. Communications protocol specification. CAALS communication report no. 1; 1994; 165p. Available from: CAALS, National Institute of Standards and Technology, Gaithersburg, MD 20899.

Proceedings of a conference. Proceedings are the printed version of scholarly papers or speeches presented at a conference. The newest and most cutting-edge research is often reported at conferences before it is published in journals; sometimes it may be work in progress rather than completed research. In addition to the usual bibliographic information, give the full official title of the conference or meeting, the date (in year, month, day order), and the location of the conference. Provide the location and name of the publisher, date of publication, and inclusive pages. If you are referring to specific pages in a proceedings publication, cite those pages in parentheses.

EXAMPLE
    Weber, D. J.; Hess, W. M. Diverse spores of
    fungi. Gerhardt, P.; Costilow, R. N.; Sadoff, H.
    L., eds. Spores VI: selected papers from the
    sixth international spore conference; 1974 October
    10-13; Michigan State University, East Lansing,
    MI. Washington, DC: American Society for
    Microbiology; 1975; 97-111 (p. 102-103).

Magazine article. Follow the same general format as for a journal article.

EXAMPLE
    Reinhardt, A. Building the data highway. BYTE
    19(3): 46-74; 1994.

Newspaper article. If the article is unsigned, alphabetize the entry by its first word (excluding *A* and *The*). Note that in the publication information the year precedes month and day. Give section and column numbers if possible, as shown here.

EXAMPLE
    McDonald K. A. Who killed the SSC? The Chronicle
    of Higher Education. 1994 March 19; Sect. A:10
    (col.1).

Electronic media, computer program. Indicate the form of the medium in brackets and provide whatever publication information will help in identifying or locating the resource.

EXAMPLE
    Internet [video cassette]. Columbia, MD: New
    Technologies; 1993. VHS; 90 min.

51 d Sample papers from the natural sciences: Literature review (ACS documentation style) and research report (CBE documentation style).

The two sample papers that follow illustrate (1), the name and date documentation system used by the American Chemical Society, and (2), the number in order of citation system, one of the formats described by the Council of Biology Editors. You will see that there are several differences between these two documentation systems for the sciences—as major as how the reference page is organized, as minor as what appears in boldface or italics.

    For the literature review, sophomores in organic chemistry were asked to conduct a library search on a chemistry-related topic of current interest to both the scientific community and the general public. The students' professor also instructed them to use at least one non-scientific publication. His purpose was to get students to think about the difficulties of explaining complex chemistry topics to the general public. Thus the literature review cites not only scientific periodicals such as *JAMA* (*Journal of the American Medical Association*) but also general publications such as *The New York Times*.

Because general publications are rarely cited in scholarly scientific writing, the chemistry student could find no guidelines or examples in *The ACS Style Guide*. If you face a similar situation when preparing the references list in a particular discipline, use another well-known style as your "default" format, advises Janet Dodd, editor of *The ACS Style Guide*. For instance, American Chemical Society editors adopt the format shown in the current edition of *The Chicago Manual of Style* when a particular type of reference is not covered by their own style manual.

The biology paper reports a field experiment conducted in a tidewater area near Charleston, South Carolina. Including an abstract, it follows the organization of a traditional laboratory report: introduction, methods and materials, results, discussion, and references. In the interest of saving space, the figures and appendix referred to in the report have been omitted. From this report you can see that scientific studies do not always corroborate their hypotheses. Frequently, cause-and-effect relationships remain hidden, and new hypotheses must be formulated, new experiments planned, or additional data collected before the reasons behind a scientific phenomenon become clear.

Chemistry Literature Review (ACS style)

1

Searching for an Answer:

Gene Therapy and Cystic Fibrosis

Emily Boone

Chemistry 13

October 21, 1993

Professor Hansen

2

Cystic fibrosis (CF), a hereditary disorder affecting children and young adults, is characterized by respiratory infections caused by a thick mucus buildup in the lungs. The gastrointestinal system, reproductive system, sweat glands, salivary glands, pancreas, and liver can also be affected, causing this disorder to be fatal before most patients reach the age of 30. Currently, the only treatment available consists of "chest percussion" to clear the lungs, antibiotics to treat infection, replacement of enzymes in the pancreas, and nutritional monitoring (Collins 1992). Scientists are working, however, on finding more permanent medicines or cures for cystic fibrosis. The most promising solution for the future seems to be gene therapy. In general, gene therapy involves adding a healthy gene as a supplement to the defective gene already in the cell (Beardsley 1990). Many different methods of gene therapy are being studied, so it is important for researchers to know as much as possible about what is causing the disorder before trying to fix it.

Cystic fibrosis is believed to be caused by a mutation in the cystic fibrosis transmembrane conductance regulator protein (CFTR), whose gene is located near the center of the long arm of chromosome seven. In 85% of CF patients, the disease appears to be caused by a 3-nucleotide deletion in the gene, resulting in the absence of phenylalanine at the 508 amino acid position in the 1480 amino acid long protein. It is thought that the absence of phenylalanine in CFTR makes the protein incapable of transporting chloride ions across the cell membrane (Merz 1989). This closed channel traps chloride in the cell and causes a reduction in extracellular water, resulting in a buildup of thick mucus in the lungs (Roberts 1990). Researchers are not sure, however, what causes the other 15% of cases (Merz 1989).

It is known that CFTR can be found in the membranes of the cells lining the airways of the lungs, so most of the research has been directed to that area (Beardsley 1990). Unfortunately, the lung is too complex an organ from which to remove cells in the lab, so researchers such as Dr. Ronald Crystal of the National Heart, Lung and Blood Institute had to develop a way of getting the gene to the cell. His team discovered that a virus, specifically a form of cold virus, an adenovirus, could be used (AP 1991). A portion of DNA is removed from the normal virus and replaced with the missing gene before infecting an individual's cells (Andrews 1993). Ideally, then, the CFTR gene starts producing the CFTR protein once it enters the cell, and the problem is corrected.

On paper, the solution seems fairly simple. In reality, though, it is very complex. Genetic testing in labs has shown that the CFTR gene can be introduced into a cell culture, causing the cells to regain the ability to regulate chloride ions (Beardsley 1990). Crystal administered a similar test using living cotton rats and an adenovirus that had been modified so that it could not reproduce itself. The virus was administered direct- ly to the rats' lungs with the results that the human CF gene was active for at least six weeks in their lung cells (Marx 1992).

Although Crystal's experiment was successful, it also raised some important concerns that need to be addressed before humans can be involved in research testing. For the moment, gene therapy seems to be only a temporary solution that would have to be repeatedly administered since the adenoviral DNA that contains the CF gene does not become permanently incorporated at the cellular level (Marx 1992). Wilson also recognized the possibility that although the adenovirus has been altered by gene deletion, if a natural adenovirus were to infect the lungs, it would provide the missing genes to activate the virus (Marx 1992).

One has to consider as well the fact that scien-

4

tists are not fully positive that chloride regulation is the sole defect of cystic fibrosis. As Richard Boucher, a researcher at the University of North Carolina, points out, CF appears to be more than just a failure to clear mucus, since CF patients contract other infections not seen in patients with other lung diseases (Beardsley 1990). Part of the problem is that so little is actually known about the CFTR protein which seems to act as both an ion channel and a regulator of ion channels (Angier 1991).

While gene transfer as a cure for cystic fibrosis is still a long way off, scientists are making definite progress. Other gene therapy techniques involving liposomes and alpha antitrypsin are already being investigated (Beardsley 1990). For a gene that was only discovered in 1989, CFTR has been fairly well researched (Collins 1992). The outlook for the future seems promising.

5

Literature Cited

Andrews, E. "Patents; Increasing Production of a Virus"; *The New York Times*, 11 January, **1993**; p. 2.

Angier, N. "Flawed 2-in-1 Protein Causes Cystic Fibrosis"; *The New York Times*, 26 February **1993**; p. 3.

The Associated Press. "Gain Seen in Quest for Genetic Treatment of Cystic Fibrosis"; *The New York Times*, 23 April **1991**; p. 3.

Beardsley, T. "Clearing the Airways: Cystic Fibrosis May Be Treated with Gene Therapy"; *Sci. Am.* **1990**, *263*: 28-33.

Collins, F. "Cystic Fibrosis: Molecular Biology and Therapeutic Implications"; *Science* **1992**, *256:* 774.

Marx, J. "Gene Therapy for CF Advances"; *Science* **1992**, *255*: 289.

Merz, B. "Capture of Elusive Cystic Fibrosis Gene Prompts New Approaches to Treatment"; *JAMA* **1989**, *262*: 1567-73.

Roberts, L. "Cystic Fibrosis Corrected in Lab"; *Science* **1990**, *249*: 1503.

Biology Research Report (CBE style)

Observations on the Mortality of
Littorina irrorata
Within the Estuaries of Charleston,
South Carolina

Leigh Truett and Maria Carter
BIOL 341
December 1, 1995

Abstract

Littorina irrorata, the marsh periwinkle, is often found on stalks of cord grass (*Spartina alternifora*) in the estuaries near Charleston, South Carolina. These snails exhibit circatidal vertical migration along the *Spartina*. This behavior is believed to be a mechanism which evolved to allow avoidance of predation. *Callinectes sapidus*, the blue crab, is the primary predator on the marsh periwinkle in the area chosen for this study. We hypothesized that snails which were made vulnerable to predation in experimental transects would exhibit higher mortality rates that those which were protected from blue crab predation by tethering or caging mechanisms. The fact that this study was per- formed during only one season may have yielded artifi- cial estimates of mortality, since blue crabs are believed to migrate offshore in early to mid-autumn to wintering grounds. Snails that were made vulnerable to predation did exhibit high mortality rates (26.6%). However, protected snails (both caged and tethered above substratum) exhibited higher mortality rates than antic- ipated (18.3% and 13.5%, respectively). This leads us to believe that perhaps other deleterious effects may induce mortality and that snails may migrate vertically to avoid these effects as well.

3

Introduction

Littorina irrorata is often found on stalks of
Spartina alterniflora in estuaries from New York to Texas
(1) and is very common in the estuaries of Charleston.
The snail exhibits circatidal behavior patterns. A band
of mucus is secreted at the anterior lip of the shell,
which allows the animal to climb and remain attached to
the Spartina above the high water mark during high tide.
At low tide they move down onto the substratum to feed.
This cycle is repeated with every tide (2, 3).

This behavior appears to be an avoidance behavior
in that it allows Littorina to obtain refuge from predators before they actually arrive. This climbing appears
to be induced by some other stimulus (either chemical or
physical), which may be why the behavior evolved in the
first place (4).

The climbing behavior does not seem to allow
Littorina to escape predators. In the Charleston area,
the main predator is Callinectes sapidus, the ubiquitous
blue crab (5). Callinectes is not just a substratum
feeder. They can and do swim up in the water column to
obtain food. Hamilton (3) has witnessed Callinectes
plucking Littorina off of Spartina stalks as much as 7
cm above the water. They will then chip away at the
shell until they are able to extract the animal.
Evidence of their predation would be empty shells or
fragments, broken shells, or living snails which bear
scars. When selecting snails to be included in this
study, we encountered many that did bear the scars.
These, however, were excluded from study.

The climbing behavior would seem to be a successful mechanism for allowing Littorina to avoid predation
(6, 7). Our study involved testing to determine whether
climbing actually reduces mortality of Littorina.
Transects were established in which snails (a) were
allowed to climb above the high water mark and (b) were

4

restricted to the area near the substratum with tethers
similar to those used by Warren (8).

We would have liked to carry out this study over
four seasons. Estuaries are places of high seasonal
activity. Fall (our study time) is a season in which
many adult blue crabs winter in deeper water offshore
(9). Perhaps studying *Littorina* over four seasons would
be the only true way to gauge mortality, but that was
beyond the scope of this project.

Materials and Methods

An area was selected behind Folly Beach where the
Spartina was relatively dense. . . . Two sites were
established using wooden stakes and utility rope. These
sites were separated from one another by a small, sandy
knoll. In Site 1, the area closest to the open water,
the *Spartina* was much taller (average height was 33 cm)
and more dense than in the back area. In Site 2, the
area further inshore, *Spartina* height averaged 26 cm.

The site consisted of four plots, 55 cm x 55 cm,
each receiving a different treatment. One transect
served as the control group. This area was neither tethered nor caged; the *Littorina* were allowed to behave in
a normal, unobstructed way. Treatments 1, 2, and 3
required the tethering of *Littorina* to the *Spartina*.
Tethering materials consisted of monofilament line and
superglue. . . .

Data collection occurred on alternating days
between October 22 and November 9. The sites were examined at low tide and evaluated in one of four ways: (a)
number of *Littorina* still alive within the designated
area; (b) number of damaged shells or dead snails; (c)
number of snails missing from the site; (d) number of
Littorina which migrated out of the site, including the
number found free from the tethers within Treatments 1,
2, and 3. Unmarked *Littorina* that migrated into the site
were not excluded from the site. Thus, the number

of deaths would be underestimated rather than overesti-
mated. The snails that migrated from the transect were
removed from the surrounding area, so as not to be
counted more than once.

Results

    The experiment ran for 19 days, from October 22
until November 9. A longer sampling period would have
been desirable but was not logistically feasible.
Snails were counted every other day at low tide. The raw
data tables in the appendix of this paper present an
accounting of the snails continued in each site. Because
one site was much closer to the water, we expected to
observe differing mortality rates between the two chosen
sites, but this was not the case (see appendix). Since
the rates were not significantly different, a mean of
dead/damaged, migrated, living, or missing snails was
obtained between the two areas. These means were then
used in any calculations of mortality.

    Rates of injury/mortality to the snails seemed to
occur steadily over the course of the study (see Figure
1), with the exception of the control sites. These sites
had lost most snails due to migration within the first
week (see Figures 1 and 2). Treatment 2 snails (tethered
at substratum) experienced the highest mortality in week
2 of the experiment (see Figure 1). Treatment 2 snails,
which were the most vulnerable, were expected to
decrease drastically within the first week.

    Treatment 1 snails (tethered above substratum) had
a higher mortality rate than expected. Four out of 30
snails (13.5%) were injured or killed (see Figures 2 and
3A). These snails, which were allowed to remain well
above the mean high water mark, should have been free of
predators. Obviously, some other factor was making them
vulnerable. . . .

6

Discussion

The mortality rates observed were not as predicted. We had expected to see differing mortality rates
between the three treatments, with Treatment 2 (tethered
at substratum) exhibiting the highest mortality rates.
We had not expected Treatment 1 (tethered above substratum) or Treatment 3 (caged) mortality rates to be as
high as they were. Reasons for these high mortality
rates could be the subject of further investigation.

The caged area was predicted to have the lowest
mortality rate. The *Littorina* within this transect were
protected against their most common predator,
Callinectes sapidus. The *Littorina* in Treatment 2, tethered at the substratum, were expected to experience the
highest mortality. These snails were vulnerable to predation due to hindered circatidal movement. Therefore,
Treatment 1 should have experienced intermediate mortality. The animals were able to exhibit normal circatidal
movement, accessing the top of the *Spartina* grass during
high tide. Thus they would be less susceptible than the
snails in Treatment 2.

Treatment 1 was placed higher than the caged
region for several reasons. It is known that blue crabs
often pluck *Littorina* from above the water column. The
marsh grass was markedly higher than the high water
mark; however, this area was inaccessible at high tide,
and an accurate measurement was unobtainable. Other
predators such as birds could also influence the mortality in this transect. The most probable reason would be
stalk selection. Selection of a stalk appears to be random; a snail could select any given stalk, not necessarily one above the high water mark. Therefore, the snail
might become stranded below the high water mark.

The mortality data do not match these predicted
results. Treatment 2 was indeed found to have the highest mortality (26.6%). However, the caged area experienced a slightly higher mortality (18.3%) than did

7

Treatment 1 (13.5%). Any of several factors could have
been the cause. The mesh net could have hindered water
flow-through in the area in some fashion or have provided a substrate for increased sedimentation; but these
results are unlikely since the net has provided successful enclosure of particulate feeders such as *Mercenaria
mercenaria*. There may be other predators at work. . . .

The high rates of migration were not expected
either. The control group had an especially high rate of
migration. . . .

Since Site 1 was located closer to the open water,
it was predicted to have higher mortality than the back
site, Site 2. However, this result was not observed; the
differences between the two sites were negligible (see
appendix for raw data). The back site should have experienced less inundation because it is closer inshore and
was located on slightly higher ground. The topography
could have been offset by the height of the *Spartina*,
since it was shorter in this area. Also, the front area
closest to the water may be subject to greater currents
and, therefore, less suitable for habitation. . . .

Although the results did indicate higher mortality
in the experimental group attached near the substratum,
the number of deaths differed from our prediction. The
major governing factor was the time of year. Because
adult blue crabs move offshore for the fall and winter,
predation levels should have dropped throughout the
experiment. However, this does not appear to be the
case. Juvenile blue crabs, on the other hand, remain in
the estuary during fall and winter. Clam pens belonging
to Atlantic Littleneck Clamfarm experience blue crab
predation throughout the year. Therefore, these juveniles
must play some role in predation. Since mortality rates
would increase with increased predator population, conducting this experiment during all four seasons would

8

show the importance of adult and juvenile *Callinectes* predation.

    Callinectes sapidus, a known predator of *Littorina*, is voracious, crushing the shell of its prey. The blue crab showed distinct predation within the experimental area, evidenced by the amount of scarred shells discovered. More accurate results would probably be obtained during the spring and summer months when the blue crab population is at its greatest. Perhaps, aside from predator avoidance, the *Littorina* climb to avoid some other deleterious effect. We suggest another, longer study to explore additional causes of *Littorina* climbing behavior.

9

References

1.   Clench, W. J.; Turner, R. D. The family
       Melongenidae in the western Atlantic. Johnsonia 3:
       161-183; 1956.

2.   Bingham, F. O. The influence of environmental
       stimuli on the direction of movement of the
       supralittorial gastropod, *Littorina irrorata*.
       Bull. Mar. Sci. 22: 309-335; 1972.

3.   Hamilton, R. V. Predation on *Littorina irrorata*
       (Mollusca: Gastropoda) by *Callinectes sapidus*
       (Crustacea: Portunidae). Bull. Mar. Sci. 26: 403-
       409; 1976.

4.   Wells, R. A. Activity pattern as a mechanism of
       predator avoidance in two species of acmaeid
       limpets. J. Exp. Mar. Biol. Ecol. 48: 151-168;
       1980.

5.   Wilbur, T. P.; Hernkind, W. F. Rate of new shell
       acquisition in a salt marsh habitat. J. Crust.
       Biol. 2: 588-592; 1982.

6.   Hadlock, R. P. Alarm response of the intertidal
       snail *Littorina irrorata* to predation by the crab
       Carcinus meanas. Biol. Bull. 159: 269-279; 1980.

7.   McKillup, S. C. The selective advantage of avoid-
       ance of the predatory whelk *Lepsiella vinosa*
       (Lamark) by *Littorina unifasciata* (Philippi). J.
       Exp. Mar. Biol. Ecol. 63: 59-66; 1982.

8.   Warren, J. H. Climbing as an avoidance behavior in
       the salt marsh periwinkle *Littorina irrorata* (Say).
       J. Exp. Mar. Biol. Ecol. 89: 11-28; 1985.

9.   Nishimota, R. T. Orientation, movement patterns,
       and behavior of *Callinectes sapidus* Rathburn
       (Crustacea: portunidae) in the intertidal.
       Tallahassee: Florida State Univ.; 1980. 222 p.
       Dissertation.

Exercise 51.1

Applying the guidelines for verb tense and passive voice in a scientific
paper, make any editorial changes you think would improve the biology
research report. Be ready to justify your changes.

52 Writing for the Professions: Business

In business, writing is a tool used to get things done. Because its fundamental goal is to help people do business, good business writing has efficiency as its hallmark. Writers should assume that their readers are busy individuals who have little time to spend extracting information from a document. Thus, an efficient business document makes its point quickly, often telling the reader what he or she needs to know in the opening paragraph. Extensive background information and detailed explanations are typically saved for later sections of the document.

52 a Purposes and methods of inquiry in business.

Business professionals collect and analyze information to use in the efficient, productive, and profitable operation of the business. For instance, marketing analysts gather sales data so that they can assess how well a product is selling and project future sales. A prediction of future sales is necessary so that the production department can anticipate how many items to make, how much raw material to purchase, and how many employees to assign to a production run.

Business people gather information from a variety of sources including internal reporting systems (weekly, monthly, or quarterly reports prepared by employees), surveys, focus groups, interviews, direct observation, and secondary-source research. They use the data to determine findings, draw conclusions about those findings, and make recommendations for action.

Findings, Conclusions, and Recommendations

Findings. What has happened or is happening. (description, synthesis)
What are the sales this month?
How much did we sell during the last quarter?
Are our profits up or down?

Conclusions. What the information means in the present; predictions about what it will mean in the future. (analysis)
Sales are higher this month compared to last month, so our profit margin will improve.

Recommendations. What should be done, based on the conclusions drawn about the findings. (interpretation, evaluation)
Because our profits have improved, we can afford to invest in a new computer system.

52 b Common types of business documents.

Whether you are studying business or working in business, you may be asked to write a variety of types of documents. Some of the most common ones are memoranda, letters, employment documents such as job-application letters and résumés, and reports.

● **1 Memos.** The principal difference between a memorandum (memo) and a letter is the audience. A memo is **internal** correspondence written to fellow employees, whereas a letter is **external** correspondence written to someone outside your company or organization. A memo reflects this difference in its format. The sender-receiver **routing information** in the upper left of a memo's first page replaces the return and inside addresses, salutation, complimentary close, and signature found on a business letter. In most other respects, memos differ little from letters. Both are single-spaced with double-spacing between paragraphs and sections.

```
TO:        Robin Kaufman, Sales Representative
FROM:      Jo Carter, District Manager     J.C.
DATE:      March 13, 199-
SUBJECT:   April Sales Meeting Agenda

           As we agreed on the phone yesterday, the April
           sales meeting should be used to develop new
           strategies for improving the sales of our summer
           sportswear line. Historically, the most
           unprofitable territory has been New England, even
           though
```

● **2 Letters.** Business letters are used for external correspondence. The standard business letter has six parts:

Heading, which includes the writer's return address and the date
Inside address, giving the recipient's name, title (if any), company or
    organization, street address, city, state, zip code
Salutation
Body
Complimentary close
Signature block, which includes a handwritten signature with the
    typed signature beneath it

Sample letter 1 in Section **52d** illustrates a widely used format—*full block style*—with the six parts labeled. Another common format—*modified block style*—places the heading, date, complimentary close, and signature block on the right side of the page (instead of flush left, as in the block style). The modified block format may use either indented or flush-left (not indented) paragraphs. *Simplified style*, a more unusual format, replaces the salutation with a subject line and eliminates the complimentary close. Simplified format uses a full block style, with all parts flush at the left margin. This format is easy to type because no tab stops are needed. Furthermore, the subject is immediately clear, and the lack of salutation solves problems when the name of the recipient is not known. Simplified format is useful for routine requests or when personalization is unimportant. **Sample letter 2** in Section **52d** shows this format.

Request letters. Letters asking someone to do something, to provide information, to send something, or to correct a mistake should be direct, businesslike, and courteous, even when you are registering a complaint. Request letters can be grouped into two categories: those with reader benefit—fulfilling the writer's request benefits the reader in some way—and those without reader benefit—the reader has little or nothing to gain from fulfilling the request. **Sample letter 2** in Section **52d,** although registering a complaint, falls into the reader-benefit category because the company clearly gains when its customers are satisfied and loses when they are unhappy. When there is no apparent reader benefit, you must rely on the reader's goodwill. Take up as little of his or her time as possible, make your request reasonable, and—if you can—encourage the reader's goodwill by paying an honest compliment or establishing some common ground. Requests for information can frequently be handled in this way.

- **Opening:** Directly state what you want the reader to do, and briefly state why. Refer to any common ground that may exist.
- **Explanation:** Give the exact information your reader needs to meet your request. Provide the reasons and explanations to support your request.
- **Action ending:** Conclude by telling the reader what results you expect. Provide sufficient information for the reader to get in touch with you.

Transmittal letters. This type of letter has two main purposes: to say "here is the item (or information) you requested" and to generate goodwill.

- **Opening:** Tell the reader what is being transmitted and why.
- **Explanation:** Supply any necessary information about whatever is being transmitted. If the transmitted item is a lengthy document such as a report, a brief summary of the most important information in the accompanying document may be appropriate.
- **Goodwill ending:** Express pleasure at being able to provide the reader with what is being transmitted, offer to be of further assistance (if appropriate), and include courteous remarks that will encourage the reader to view you and your organization in a positive light.

Employment letters. Letters of application for employment fall into two categories: solicited applications (applications are being solicited for an existing employment opening) and unsolicited or prospecting applications (you have no direct knowledge that an opening currently exists, but you want to be considered if a job is available). **Sample letter 1** in Section **52d** is a solicited application. Usually accompanied by a résumé, a job-application letter contains the following parts.

- **Opening:** At the beginning of a solicited application letter, be sure to mention your source of information about the job (newspaper advertisement, placement office posting, referral, etc.) in addition to specifying the position for which you are applying. At the beginning of an unsolicited application letter, identify the type of position you desire (for instance, bookkeeper, computer programmer, library aide) and briefly explain why you are interested in working for the company you are addressing.

- **Education and experience.** In the body paragraphs of the letter, describe those parts of your education and experience that prepare you for the job you want. Relevant extracurricular activities and volunteer work are also appropriate. Don't just list education and experience: explain how it qualifies you for the job. Talk about what you can bring to the company, rather than what you want the company to do for you. Your tone should be confident and courteous. Be brief, direct, and factual, but also persuasive. In this section of the letter you should refer directly to your accompanying résumé.

- **Action ending.** Close by asking the reader to let you know when it would be convenient for you to come for an interview. A stronger, but permissible, ending is to say courteously that you will call to arrange an interview—as does the author of sample letter 1. Always tell the reader when, where, and how you can be reached if you are not available at your return address during the reader's business hours. Include a telephone number if possible.

● **3 Employment résumés.** The résumé that follows sample letter 1 in Section **52d** illustrates a widely used, traditional format. This format works well when you want to emphasize your education and experience. Another format organizes information according to skills, placing education and a list of employers near the end of the résumé. This format can be effective if you want to emphasize capabilities and may be advantageous for people whose work experience is varied or not continuous, or whose education or employment history is not obviously applicable to the job they are seeking.

Whatever format you choose, apply the following guidelines.

- Be sure your name, address, and telephone number are easy to read and located at the head of your résumé.

- List items in order of importance, section by section and within each section. It is not necessary to list work experience in chronological order if when it occurred is not the most important factor.

- Remember that work experience applies not only to jobs for which you were paid but also to volunteer work, community service, and leadership roles in campus organizations. The only requirement is that the experience be relevant to the job for which you are applying. Similarly, education need not be limited to completed college degrees. Training courses, evening classes, and seminars at work may be mentioned if they are relevant to the job.

- Use action verbs to describe your experience. Write *organized, developed, managed, sold, built, assisted, completed,* instead of *duties included* or *responsibilities were.* Indicate any measurable results: *increased sales by $2,000, saved the sorority $700 on heating bills, increased the student newspaper's circulation by 20%.*

- Do not include information not pertinent to the job. Employers do not want your life story. Personal information such as height or weight are not likely to be relevant. Laws forbid job discrimination based on marital status, age, sex, race, or religion. Prospective employers should not ask you questions about these matters, although you may volunteer such information if you think it will be to your advantage. The best policy is to provide only information that pertains to bona fide job qualifications. For example, you might list willingness to travel or relocate if the job involves transfers or significant time on the road; but you need not indicate whether you are male or female, single or married.

- Offer to provide references. Since the résumé's purpose is to secure an interview, standard practice is to offer to furnish references upon request rather than to include them on the résumé—unless the job notice specifically says to send references with the application letter. If the interviewer thinks you are a good candidate, he or she will ask for references. So remember to take your reference list with you to the job interview. Be sure you have contacted prospective references beforehand and received their permission to be listed. These should be people who know your work firsthand: former employers or instructors with whom who have taken relevant courses. Your reference list should include their names, business titles, addresses, and business telephone numbers.

● **4 Reports.** Business reports are typically of two types: *informational* and *analytical* or *problem solving*. Some reports combine the two, supplying information that is analyzed to provide the basis for recommending solutions to a problem that has been identified. Reports may be as short as a one- or two-page memo or long enough to require a table of contents, subdivisions, a list of references, and perhaps an appendix. A **sample research report** written for business appears in Section **52d** at the end of this chapter. Long business reports typically include the following sections:

Abstract or executive summary
    summary of main findings, conclusions, and recommendations
    (may appear as part of the introductory section in some reports)
Introduction
    authorization (who approved the report assignment)
    purpose of report, identification of problem
    scope
    background
    sources, methods, limitations
    definitions (if necessary)
    report organization (topics covered, in what order)
Body
    data obtained from research
    explanations of data
Conclusions
    summary of key findings resulting from data presented in body of report

analysis and interpretation of findings (answers to questions or solutions to problems identified in the introduction)

Recommendations

courses of action to resolve questions or solve the problem

recommendation of optimum course of action

Notes (if appropriate to documentation style used)

References (begin on a new page)

bibliography of works cited in report

52 **c** Documentation style and guides for business.

Research articles and reports written for business may use one of several documentation styles, depending on which academic discipline they are most closely allied with. For instance, papers on human resources or organizational behavior topics may use American Psychological Association (APA) style because these fields are most closely allied with the social sciences. Writers in production or manufacturing, on the other hand, might choose a style from engineering publications, whereas research and development writers might use a documentation format from the sciences, such as American Chemical Society (ACS) style. General business writers may use a format based on the endnote system illustrated in *The Chicago Manual of Style* [CMS], 14th ed., Chicago: University of Chicago Press, 1993. A less expensive, more concise style guide that illustrates CMS is Kate L. Turabian's *A Manual for Writers of Term Papers, Theses, and Dissertations*, 5th ed., Chicago: University of Chicago Press, 1987.

CMS Reference Note (Endnote) Format

- **Placement of reference note numbers.** Place a superscript (raised slightly above the line) Arabic numeral where the reference occurs: at the end of a quotation, summary, paraphrase, or other reference to a source. The number follows any punctuation marks, unless the punctuation mark is a dash, in which case the number precedes it.
- **Sequence of reference note numbers.** Numbering should be sequential, in the order that the references are made in the text, beginning with 1. Reference note numbers are not repeated, even if the reference is to a work previously cited in the text. The only exception is some scientific documentation systems which repeat the number initially assigned to a work whenever it is cited (see Chapter 51).
- **Placement and spacing of reference notes.** Reference notes should appear at the end of the document, beginning on a separate page headed "Notes" or "Reference Notes." If there is a bibliography or other separate list of references, the notes should precede this list. The first line of each note is indented consistently, six to eight spaces, from the left margin. All subsequent lines in the note are flush with the left margin. Reference notes are single-spaced with double-spacing between them.
- **Quotations of two sentences and four or more lines of text.** Block the quotation by starting it on a new line and indenting all lines of the quotation

four spaces from the left margin. Single-space the quotation block. Do not use quotation marks at the beginning or end of a block quotation.

CMS Reference Note Format

- superscript note number (beginning with 1 and following sequential order)
- author's name in normal order: first name, middle name or initials (if any), last name
- comma
- one space
- title of work (underlined or italicized)
- one space
- publication information (in parentheses)
- comma
- one space
- page(s) (Do not use *p.* or *pp.;* use numerals only.)
- period

EXAMPLE   [1]Sonja A. Sackman, <u>Cultural Knowledge in Organizations</u> (Newbury Park, Calif.: Sage, 1991), 166.

Parts of a note are separated from one another with a **comma** followed by a space, as shown in the preceding example. Reference notes end with a period.

CMS Reference List (Bibliography) Format

- **Sequence of reference list entries.** Entries in the reference list or bibliography are alphabetized by authors' last names.
- **Placement and spacing of reference list or bibliography.** The reference list should appear at the end of the document, beginning on a separate page after the notes. The list should be headed "References," "Reference List," or "Bibliography." The first line of each entry in the reference list should be flush with the left margin; subsequent lines should be indented six to eight spaces from the left margin. References are single-spaced within the entries and double-spaced between them.

CMS Reference List (Bibliography) Format

- author's name in inverted order: last name, first name, middle name or initials (if any)
- period
- space
- title of work (underlined or italicized)
- period
- space

- publication information (no parentheses)
- period, if a book. If a periodical, use a colon followed by a space
- page(s), if a periodical (Do not use *p.* or *pp.*; use numerals only.)
- period

EXAMPLE Sackman, Sonja A., <u>Cultural Knowledge in</u>
<u>Organizations</u>. Newbury Park, Calif.: Sage, 1991.

Parts of a bibliography entry are separated from one another with a **period** followed by a space, as shown in the preceding example. Bibliography entries end with a period.

Reference notes and bibliography entries contain the same information with slightly different punctuation and indentation. Compare the following examples for similarities and differences in form.

A work by one author.

NOTE   [1]Edward R. Tufte, <u>The Visual Display of</u>
<u>Quantitative Information</u> (Cheshire, Conn.: Graphics Press, 1983), 71.

BIBLIOGRAPHY   Tufte, Edward R. <u>The Visual Display of</u>
<u>Quantitative Information</u>. Cheshire, Conn.: Graphics Press, 1983.

A work by two or three authors.
In the note, present the names of all authors in normal order. In the bibliography entry, present the first author's name in inverted order and all other authors' names in normal order.

NOTE   [2]Drusilla Campbell and Marilyn Graham, <u>Drugs</u>
<u>and Alcohol in the Workplace</u> (New York: Facts on File Publications, 1988), 45.

BIBLIOGRAPHY   Campbell, Drusilla, and Marilyn Graham. <u>Drugs and</u>
<u>Alcohol in the Workplace</u>. New York: Facts on File Publications, 1988.

A work by four or more authors.
In the note, cite the first author by name and all other authors collectively as "et al." or its English equivalent, "and others." In the bibliography, all authors must be cited by their full names.

NOTE   [3]Richard W. Brislin et al., <u>Intercultural</u>
<u>Interactions: A Practical Guide</u> (Beverly Hills, Calif.: Sage Publications, 1986), 63.

BIBLIOGRAPHY   Brislin, Richard W., Kenneth Cushner, Craig Cherrie, and Mahealani Yong. <u>Intercultural</u>
<u>Interactions: A Practical Guide</u>. Beverly Hills, Calif.: Sage Publications, 1986.

No author given. Begin both the note and the bibliography entry with the title of the work. Do not use "Anonymous" unless "anonymous" is listed on the title page in place of an author's name.

Corporate or institutional authorship.

NOTE
[4]Association of Professional Writing Consultants, <u>Policy Manual of the Association of Professional Writing Consultants</u> (Tulsa, Okla.: Association of Professional Writing Consultants, 1993), 10.

BIBLIOGRAPHY
Association of Professional Writing Consultants. <u>Policy Manual of the Association of Professional Writing Consultants</u>. Tulsa, Okla.: Association of Professional Writing Consultants, 1993.

Reprint edition. If a work is identified as a reprint of another edition by another publisher, provide publication information about the earlier edition if possible. This form of citation may be particularly appropriate for some paperback editions.

NOTE
[5]Thomas J. Peters and Robert H. Waterman, Jr., <u>In Search of Excellence</u> (New York: Harper & Row, 1982; Warner Books, 1984), 123.

BIBLIOGRAPHY
Peters, Thomas J., and Robert H. Waterman, Jr. <u>In Search of Excellence</u>. New York: Harper & Row, 1982; Warner Books, 1984.

Article or chapter by one author in a work by another. The included selection should be indicated with quotation marks. The title of the complete work is indicated by underlining or italics. In the bibliography entry, inclusive pages should be given. Note that the page numbers in the bibliography entry follow the editors'/authors' names rather than coming at the end of the entry.

NOTE
[6]Meryl Reis Louis, "An Investigator's Guide to Workplace Culture," in <u>Organizational Culture</u>, ed. Peter J. Frost et al. (Newbury Park, Calif.: Sage Publications, 1985), 74.

BIBLIOGRAPHY
Louis, Meryl Reis. "An Investigator's Guide to Workplace Culture." In <u>Organizational Culture</u>, ed. Peter J. Frost, Larry F. Moore, Meryl Reis Louis, Craig C. Lundberg, and Joanne Martin, 73-93. Newbury Park, Calif.: Sage Publications, 1985.

Journal article.

NOTE   [7]Kenneth M. Coughlin, "Expanding Employee
                        Assistance Programs Is Paying Dividends," Business
                        & Health 10 (August 1992): 45.

BIBLIOGRAPHY   Coughlin, Kenneth M. "Expanding Employee
                        Assistance Programs Is Paying Dividends."
                        Business & Health 10 (August 1992): 45-53.

Magazine article. Note that the punctuation preceding the page number in
the citation for a magazine article (comma) differs from the punctuation
for page numbers in citations for journal articles (colon).

NOTE   [8]William C. Symonds, "How to Confront--And
                        Help--An Alcoholic Employee," Business Week, 25
                        March 1991, 9.

BIBLIOGRAPHY   Symonds, William C. "How to Confront--And Help--An
                        Alcoholic Employee." Business Week, 25 March
                        1991, 25 March 1991, 9.

Newspaper article. Include section and column numbers, if helpful in
locating the article.

NOTE   [9]Kimberly Murphy, "Employee Assistance Plans
                        Help Companies as Well," The Washington Post, 28
                        June 1992, sec. H2, col. 2.

BIBLIOGRAPHY   Murphy, Kimberly. "Employee Assistance Plans Help
                        Companies as Well," The Washington Post, 28
                        June 1992, sec. H2, col. 2.

Unpublished interview.

NOTE   [10]Victor Marino, president, Financial &
                        Estate Planners, Inc., personal interview, 7 April
                        1994, Towson, Md.

BIBLIOGRAPHY   Marino, Victor, president of Financial & Estate
                        Planners, Inc. Personal interview, 7 April
                        1994, Towson, Md.

Material from electronic information service.

NOTE   [11]Melinda G. Kramer, Suddenly, I Was One of
                        Them! Why Writing Consultants Must Learn the
                        Lessons of the Organization, paper presented at
                        Conference on College Composition and
                        Communication, San Diego, Calif., 1 April 1993,
                        Dialog, ERIC, ED 357 381.

BIBLIOGRAPHY   Kramer, Melinda G. Suddenly, I Was One of Them!
                        Why Writing Consultants Must Learn the
                        Lessons of the Organization. Paper presented
                        at Conference on College Composition and

Communication, San Diego, Calif., 1 April
1993. Dialog, ERIC, ED 357 381.

Audio or video cassette. If a particular artist or performer is featured, that person may be listed in the author position. Otherwise begin with the title of the work.

NOTE   [12]Your Total Robotic Solution, 13 min.,
Aquila Film & Video, Inc., 1994, videocassette.

BIBLIOGRAPHY   Your Total Robotic Solution. 13 min. Aquila Film &
Video, Inc., 1994. Videocassette.

Multiple references in a single note. When a citation refers to information from several sources, they may be listed in a single note, using semicolons between works and listing them in their order of citation. The references should be listed alphabetically in the normal way in the bibliography.

NOTE   [13]See Susan Ince, "Getting In-House Help,"
Working Woman, December 1992, 86; and Beverly A.
Potter and Sebastian Orfali, Drug Testing at Work
(Berkeley, Calif.: Ronin Publishing, 1990), 130.

Previously cited sources. When referring to a source that has been previously cited in the paper, give the author (or short title, if there is no author) and page only. If the reference is to the same page of a source cited in the immediately preceding note, use the abbreviation "Ibid." (for the Latin word that means "in the same place"). Do not underline or italicize it. Ibid. and a page number may be used if the second citation is to a different page.

NOTES   [14]Kenneth M. Coughlin, "Expanding Employee
Assistance Programs Is Paying Dividends," Business
& Health 10 (August 1992), 45.
[15]Susan Ince, "Getting In-House Help,"
Working Woman, December 1992, 86.
[16]Ibid.
[17]Coughlin, 46.

52 **d**   **Sample business documents: Letters, résumé, and research report (CMS endnote documentation style).**

Following are the letters and résumé referred to earlier in this chapter, along with a business report. The report omits a separate abstract or executive summary and instead combines these with the introduction. The conclusions and recommendations are also presented in a single section, not uncommon in shorter business reports. This research report follows the organization, visual format, and stylistics of a business report, and it uses Chicago Manual of Style endnote format for its reference citations. Portions of the report have been omitted; these are indicated by ellipses.

Sample Letter 1: Block Style
Single-space text; double-space between paragraphs and sections.

848 Plains Street
Fort Pierre, South Dakota 57067   heading
April 4, 199-

Judith Stafford
Curator
W. H. Over Western Museum   inside
University of South Dakota   address
Vermillion, South Dakota 57069

Dear Ms. Stafford: salutation

I believe I can offer practical ideas, backed by experience in several museum settings, that will help the W.
H. Over Western Museum attract funding, increase community interest, and improve quality--constant goals even in
well-managed facilities such as yours. I would like the
opportunity to put my ideas to work for your museum.

As the enclosed résumé shows, my experience includes the
following museum operations:

* collecting and cataloging specimens   body
* researching and mounting exhibits
* designing special children's programs
* working with academics, students, funding agencies,
  the media, and the general public
* writing successful grant proposals

One of the most rewarding aspects of this experience has
been seeing community participation broaden and financial
resources increase as a result of my efforts. I have a
talent for explaining things, as illustrated by the college teaching award I received and the children's natural
history program I developed. This skill will be an asset
for the educational activities that are an important part
of museum work.

My college and summer museum experiences have been a
very good introduction to my chosen career. I would like
to talk with you about employment possibilities at the
W. H. Over Western Museum and will call your office next
week to see about scheduling an interview. I look forward to meeting you.

Sincerely,   complimen-
                                        tary close

John Lewkowski   signature

John Lewkowski   typed
                                        signature

Résumé

Single-space text; double-space between sections.

John Lewkowski
848 Plains Street
Fort Pierre, South Dakota 57067
605-555-9745

Employment Objective

A museum staff position leading eventually to a curator-
ship.

Education

B.A., Earlham College, Richmond, Indiana, 1995.
Major: history   Minor: biology   GPA: 3.85/4.00=A
State University of New York, course in researching,
cataloging, and mounting exhibits, summer 1993.

Experience

Museum volunteer, Joseph Moore Museum, Earlham College,
1993-95. Assisted director of small natural history
museum. Developed traveling museum program for four
local elementary schools. Identified and cataloged specimens, maintained exhibits.

Summer intern, Tippecanoe County Historical Museum,
Lafayette, Indiana, 1994. Wrote grant proposal resulting
in $10,000 award for archeological dig at 18th-century
French and Indian trading settlement. Worked with state
and federal agencies, university faculty, museum staff.

Laboratory assistant, Earlham College, spring term,
1995. Supervised freshman biology lab, prepared lab
materials and specimens, answered students' questions,
and graded lab reports. Was selected Outstanding
Teaching Assistant in the Natural Sciences.

Honors and Activities

Earlham Alumni Scholarship, 1992-95
Outstanding Teaching Assistant, 1995
Earlham College tennis team, 1993-95

Personal Data

Speak and write French. Interests: travel and photography.

References Furnished Upon Request

Sample Letter 2: Simplified Style

Single-space text; double-space between sections.

444 West Wilson Street
Madison, Wisconsin 53715
July 9, 199-

Cambridge Camera Exchange, Inc.
7th Avenue and 13th Street
New York, N.Y. 10011

INCOMPLETE SHIPMENT

The Minolta SRT 201 camera outfit I ordered from you on
June 21 arrived today and appears to be in good working
order. However, your advertisement in The New York
Times for Sunday, June 16, listed six items as being
supplied with this outfit, including a film holder and
a sun shade. Neither of these items was included in the
package I have just received, nor do I find any notice
that they will be sent at a later date.

I am sure that this omission is unintentional and that
you will correct it. Will you please let me know when
I may expect to receive the film holder and sun shade,
as advertised. If there is a dealer in the immediate
area, I would be happy to get them from him or her if
you will authorize me to do so at your expense.

Marilyn S. Conway

Marilyn S. Conway

Research Report (CMS style)

EMPLOYEE ASSISTANCE PROGRAMS

Prepared for
Dr. Courtney Paige
President
CP & Associates

Prepared by
C. A. Frechette and R. K. Mills

April 1, 1994

CONTENTS

omitted
from the
report

EMPLOYEE ASSISTANCE AT CP & ASSOCIATES

identification
of problem
Supervisors and managers suspect that employee problems such as substance abuse, family dysfunction, and job stress are harming productivity and morale at CP & Associates. Accordingly, on February 3 we were assigned to investigate appropriate ways that these problems might be addressed in the workplace, since ultimately they affect the workplace.

authorization

summary of
findings
Following is the report resulting from our research. We have found that an increasing number of mid- and small-sized firms have followed the lead of many larger U.S. companies by adopting employee assistance programs (EAPs). After surveying the available literature (books, newspaper and magazine articles, and research printed in business journals) and interviewing managers at several local companies that have implemented EAPs, we have concluded that such a program is not only within the means of CP & Associates but would be a wise investment for the firm.

method

summary of
conclusions
and recom-
mendations
Thus we recommend that top management consider the development of a broadbrush, off-site employee assistance program. Definitions of terms, information supporting our recommendation, and detailed explanations of program alternatives are contained in subsequent sections of this report.

introduction

WHAT IS AN EMPLOYEE ASSISTANCE PROGRAM?

body
An employee assistance program (EAP) is a tool that may be used by an employer to assist employees whose job performance has been negatively affected by personal problems. In the early 1970s, business, industry, and government agencies became aware of the loss of productivity from workers impaired by drug and alcohol abuse. Tardiness, absenteeism, and accidents added to the loss of earnings in the private sector and increased the cost to government. Cost analyses showed that it was less cost effective to hire and train new employees than to rehabilitate often longtime, highly skilled workers and professionals. From the modest early EAPs, employers have learned that assisting and, if need be, rehabilitating impaired employees results in cost savings. It keeps employees productive and off unemployment and welfare rolls, and it reduces health care costs. Today, EAPs are set up to help employees deal with family problems, financial crises, relationship difficulties at the workplace and at home, depression, stress, and various addictions. Some EAPs even offer workshops and seminars on such health-related issues as obesity, stress, and smoking cessation. [1]

The major difference between an EAP and a community-based social service agency is that the EAP is concerned with the personal well being of employees and their productivity in the workplace, while the community-based social service agency is concerned with the health and well being of its clients and their role in the community.

LOOKING AT DIFFERENCES IN EAPs

After making the decision to start an EAP, the employer must weigh several options. The first option to be considered is whether the EAP will be a single-issue program or a broadbrush program. The second option is whether the EAP is to consist of an in-house contract or an off-site contact. These options will be presented and discussed in this section of the report.

Single-Issue Programs

body

Single-issue EAPs address only drug and alcohol problems within the company. This type of program is set up to offer help to employees whose job performance is affected by substance abuse. They may be referred to the EAP by their supervisors because of behavior, loss of productivity, or results of drug testing. In businesses using a single-issue EAP, the position of the employer on the use of drugs and alcohol is quite clear. If identified as a substance abuser, an employee is offered treatment and a chance at rehabilitation or is terminated.[2] Because the single-issue EAP addresses only substance abuse, and because counseling and rehabilitation are usually supplied by the health insurance provider, cost to the employer is kept to a minimum.

A disadvantage of this type of EAP is that an employee may have misgivings about seeking help for fear of being labeled a drunk or an addict. Furthermore, since the single-issue program addresses only alcohol and drug abuse, supervisors tend to look for such obvious signs as intoxication and slurred words. They may overlook the more subtle signs of tardiness, absenteeism, and poor job performance. By the time such affected employees are identified, they may be well into their addiction. Help becomes much more difficult, and relapse by alcoholics and drug abusers in the later stages of addiction is quite frequent. As the director of a single-issue EAP at a women's wear company in New Mexico explained:

> Our utilization was low and our relapse rate was high because everybody who came through the program was in the late stage of alcoholism where the

relapse risk is the greatest . . . you practically
had to be falling down drunk to get the supervisors
to refer you. Meanwhile, there's absenteeism and
accidents and all the rest of it going on all over
the plant. . . . Supervisors were too busy smelling
breath and checking to see if the forklift operator
had fresh marks on his arm. [3]

This example may seem extreme, but unfortunately it
is quite typical of a single-issue EAP. Single-issue
programs seem to lack preventive power.

Broadbrush Programs

Broadbrush EAPs address all types of problems that
could hinder the job performance of an employee. Besides
drug and alcohol addiction, these programs could include
treatment for depression, illness, loss of a loved one
by death or separation, financial hardships, marital
problems, family concerns (spouses, children, siblings,
aging parents), relationships with co-workers or supervisors, and job stress. All of these problems can and do   body
impact negatively on the performance of employees.

With a broadbrush EAP, many more employees can be
helped than with a single-issue EAP. One advantage of
the broadbrush program is that employees are less hesitant to self-refer, and they are more willing to take
advantage of the services offered. . . .

The major disadvantage of a broadbrush EAP is its
higher cost, since it deals with more issues. However,
employees receive help with personal problems that
affect their job performance. Many human resource specialists believe the savings of retaining these employees and returning them to full productivity more than
make up for the cost. [4] General Motors estimates that
"for every dollar spent on its EAP and outside treatment, two dollars are returned in regained productivity." [5]

Once a company has selected the type of EAP it
will use--single-issue or broadbrush--the next determi-
nation is whether to provide an in-house or off-site
program.

In-House EAPs

An in-house EAP will need at least one coordinator.
The coordinator will be the person with whom the employee whose work is suffering will make the first contact.
The coordinator will evaluate the employee and recommend
appropriate treatment. Usually, continuing therapy,
counseling, or rehabilitation would not be in-house, but
conducted by outside professionals. [6] A disadvantage of

an in-house EAP is that employees may not feel comfortable going to an in-house coordinator who would be a
fellow employee, even though the coordinator would be
required to use great discretion and assure confidentiality. . . .

Off-Site EAPs

An employer's other choice is to contract an
employee assistance service at an off-site location.
Employees needing help may contact such an EAP directly.
An off-site program can be more effective than in-house
assistance because it gives employees a greater sense of
confidentiality and provides an environment in which
they feel more at ease. Most employees dealing with personal issues that may affect their job performance do
not want these problems known to others within their
company. Also, employees seem more willing to go to off-
site centers than to in-house centers. . . .

IMPLEMENTING AN EMPLOYEE ASSISTANCE PROGRAM

After considering the advantages and disadvantages
of a single-issue versus a broadbrush EAP, on-site or
body off-site location, and the cost factor, the employer
must decide on the type of program to be provided. For
an EAP to be successful, the review and decision-making
process should involve not only management but also
supervisors and employees. A policy statement and proce-
dural statement must then be prepared to set forth the
organization's guidelines. Supervisors and employees
should also provide input during the preparation of
these statements. . . .

Employee Awareness

It is very important that employees understand what
the employer is offering through the EAP and be encouraged to use it. Management should publicize the program
using such methods as office meetings, special handouts
in pay envelopes, and posters.[7] . . .

CARRYING OUT THE PROGRAM

Once adopted, EAP policies and procedures must be
adhered to. Supervisors must be consistent in their
approach to employees suspected of having a problem and
in making referrals. Consistency will ensure fairness
and prevent a potential problem with an employee who
claims preferential treatment of others or who claims
discrimination. Also, managers and supervisors need to
conduct timely performance reviews of staff members and

5

employees and maintain reliable records to document job
performance and possible problems. [8]

Besides an analysis of the number of employees
referred and treated, supervisors and employees should
be asked to evaluate the EAP periodically. Simple survey
forms can provide answers to such questions as awareness
of the program, why employees do or do not use it, how
it can be improved, or what its shortcomings and benefits are. [9] Such ongoing input can make the difference
between the success and failure of an EAP.

Following these procedures allows employers to
realize the goals of employee assistance programs: to
identify troubled employees, to encourage them to seek
and accept help, to provide the most cost-effective
help, to retain employees in the work force, and to
return them to full productivity.

CONCLUSIONS AND RECOMMENDATIONS FOR CP & ASSOCIATES

Since the early 1970s, EAPs have grown from dealing
with employees with drug and alcohol abuse problems to
assisting employees with a wide range of personal,
interpersonal, and mental health problems. The Christian
Science Monitor reported in 1990 that 80 percent of
large American firms offer EAPs. With the increasing
cost of health care and expansion of EAPs into the mental health care field, more and more employers are likely to offer such assistance to their employees. At a
time when many benefits have been cut, the number of
EAPs continues to grow. [10] The main reason for this
growth is that employers realize a financial benefit by
providing this service to their employees.

With this growth in the field of employee assistance, we must be careful in our selection of an EAP and
be sure to staff it with well-trained, dedicated professionals. As health-care consultant Dr. Gary VandenBos
points out, a well-managed EAP can be the best thing to
happen to a company's employees, whereas "the worst ones
are utter disasters and nothing but a waste of money." [11]

Our research has shown that employee assistance
programs have become an important fixture of corporate
America. We believe our company would benefit greatly
from the implementation of such a program. We recommend
that serious consideration be given to the implementation of a broadbrush, off-site EAP. This type of program
is the one that the evidence suggests would be of the
greatest benefit to CP & Associates.

If you have questions or would like to discuss any
of the issues raised in this report, we would be glad to
meet with you at your convenience.

Margin labels: body · conclusions · recommendation

6

NOTES

[1]Kenneth M. Coughlin, "Expanding Employee Assistance Programs Is Paying Dividends," Business and Health, 10 (August 1992), 45.

[2]William C. Symonds, "How to Confront--And Help-- An Alcoholic Employee," Business Week, 25 March 1991, 9.

[3]Drusilla Campbell and Marilyn Graham, Drugs and Alcohol in the Workplace (New York: Facts on File Publications, 1988), 182.

[4]Catherine Foster, "More Firms Aid Drug-Using Workers," The Christian Science Monitor, 30 January 1990, 9.

[5]Beverly A. Potter and Sebastian Orfali, Drug Testing at Work (Berkeley: Ronin Publishing, 1990), 130.

[6]Susan Ince, "Getting In-House Help," Working Woman, December 1992, 86.

[7]Campbell and Graham, 207.

[8]Ibid., 324.

[9]Coughlin, 47.

[10]Foster, 9.

[11]Gary VandenBos, managing partner, McLean & Sterling, telephone interview, 24 March 1994, Portland, Oregon.

7

REFERENCES

Campbell, Drusilla, and Marilyn Graham. <u>Drugs and Alcohol in the Workplace</u>. New York: Facts on File Publications, 1988.

Coughlin, Kenneth M. "Expanding Employee Assistance Programs Is Paying Dividends." <u>Business & Health</u>, 10 (August 1992), 45-53.

Foster, Catherine. "More Firms Aid Drug-Using Workers." <u>The Christian Science Monitor</u>, 30 January 1990, 9.

Ince, Susan. "Getting In-House Help." <u>Working Woman</u>, December 1992, 86.

Murphy, Kimberly. "Employee Assistance Plans Help Companies as Well." <u>The Washington Post</u>, 28 June 1992, sec. H2, col. 2.

Potter, Beverly A., and J. Sebastian Orfali. <u>Drug Testing at Work</u>. Berkeley, Calif.: Ronin Publishing, 1990.

Symonds, William C. "How to Confront--And Help--An Alcoholic Employee." <u>Business Week</u>, 25 March 1991, 9.

VandenBos, Gary, managing partner, McLean & Sterling. Telephone interview, 24 March 1994, Portland, Oregon.

Writers Revising

The university debate team has asked Dennis to write a letter which will be sent to all heads of high school speech departments in the county advertising a debate workshop to be held on campus. The team is especially eager to have good attendance to boost a closer relationship with the high schools from which the speech department will be recruiting students and to raise the level of competition at this year's high school debate rally to be held on campus. Read Dennis's first draft and suggest ways for him to improve his letter using the material in this section and that in Chapters 1 through 5 on the writing process. Then compare your suggestions with Dennis's revision.

Draft

> 4262 July St.
> Baton Rouge, LA
> 70812
> February 14, 1995

Mrs. Susie Tanner
Speech Coordinator
Valley High School
243 Yellow St.
Baton Rouge, LA 70809

Dear Mrs. Tanner,

A special debate workshop will be offered for you and your debate team to orient you with this year's topic, Resolved: that the American judicial system has overemphasized the freedom of the press.

The six-hour workshop will familiarize your debaters with the major court cases regarding freedom of the press, major sources of evidence, including the books of Ben Bagdikian and the major theories that will enable your teams to prepare for this year's rally.

The workshop will be held on Saturday, March 16, 1995, at Coates Hall (Speech Lab) on the State University campus. We have enclosed a map for your convenience. We will begin at 9:00 a.m. and work until 12:00 p.m. You will have a one hour break for lunch. You might consider eating at the many fast-food establishments just a block away. The workshop will resume at 1:00 p.m. and go through 4:00 p.m. During this time Judge Roy Hebert of the State Supreme Court will answer any questions related to the judicial system. A formal schedule with more details is enclosed.

Please call the Speech Department anytime between 8:00 a.m. and 4:30 p.m. and tell them if you plan to attend. We need to know this information to prepare the proper amount of packets for the seminar. A nominal amount of $5.00 per debater is also needed when you arrive at the workshop. This money will be used to provide theory packets, notebook, glue sticks, and miscellaneous materials for each participant.

Please seriously consider attending the seminar. It could benefit your teams immensely. It will give them the edge in the race for this year's championship. We look forward to seeing you at 9:00 a.m. on Saturday, March 16.

Sincerely,

Dennis Jones

Dennis Jones

Revision

4262 July St.
Baton Rouge, LA 70812
February 14, 1995

Mrs. Susan Tanner
Speech Coordinator
Valley High School
234 Yellow St.
Baton Rouge, LA 70809

Dear Mrs. Tanner:

The State University debate team is offering you and your debate team a special six-hour debate workshop on Saturday, March 16, from 9:00 a.m. to 4:00 p.m., in

Coates Hall, Room 210. The workshop program will focus on this year's topic for the high school debate rally-- Resolved: that the American judicial system has overemphasized the freedom of the press.

The workshop will familiarize your debaters with the major court cases regarding freedom of the press, major sources of evidence, including the books of Ben Bagdikian, and the major theories that will enable your teams to prepare for this year's rally. Our main speaker will be Judge Roy Hebert of the State Supreme Court, who will also answer any questions your debaters might have on this year's topic.

The morning session will begin at 9:00 and go until 12:00. After a lunch break, we will resume at 1:00 and end at 4:00. Several fast-food restaurants are nearby and will be able to accommodate students during the lunch break. A map and a detailed program of the day's activities are enclosed for your convenience.

Please call the Speech Department at 766-3833 any time between 8:00 a.m. and 4:30 p.m. from Monday to Friday to make your reservations. Your call will enable us to make packets for all your students. A nominal fee of $5.00 per debater, to cover the cost of theory packets, notebooks, glue sticks, and miscellaneous materials, is due upon arrival.

We here at State hope you will bring your debaters to the workshop. It could benefit your teams immensely, giving them the edge in the race for this year's championship. We look forward to seeing you at 9:00 on Saturday, March 16.

Sincerely,

Dennis Jones

Dennis Jones
State Debate Team

Enclosures

Analysis

The revision gets to the point of the letter quickly in the first paragraph. Next, it follows with crucial information about the program content and the featured speaker to nail down the importance of the workshop for Mrs. Tanner's students. Then comes the schedule to answer questions about lunch, and then a note about enclosures. A firm request for reservations and an announcement about the cost of the workshop and what the cost will cover precedes a friendly, positive appeal for action in the concluding paragraph. Finally, the format and spelling are corrected, and an enclosure line is added.

53 Writing Essay Exams in the Disciplines

What you have learned from this handbook about effective writing also applies to writing essays for exams. You will be expected to write standard English, to organize material intelligently, and to provide evidence and detail to support generalizations. When you have several days to write a paper or a take-home exam, you spend a good part of the time on planning—thinking about the subject, gathering material, making notes, organizing your ideas, outlining. You also have time to revise your first draft, correcting errors and clarifying your meaning. However, you cannot expect to do all this in the limited time you have for an in-class exam. You are writing under pressure. Therefore, it saves time to go into essay exams knowing how to proceed.

Prepare for exams.

Most of your planning must be done before you go to the exam. How can you do that when you don't know what questions will be asked? You won't have free choice of subject; it will be chosen for you—or, at best, you will be allowed to choose from among two or three. You do know the *general subject* of the exam, however; it is the subject matter of the course or one part of the course. Your goal, then, is *to go to the exam having in mind a rough outline of the course segments and the contents of each.*

This process of outlining should begin with the first lecture or reading assignment and continue uninterrupted to the day of the exam. Take notes during lectures, underline key passages and make marginal notations in the margins of your textbooks, summarize your reading, look over your gathered material from time to time, evaluate it, and structure it. As you study, write a more formal outline based on an overview of the course

material and any guidelines suggested by your instructor. Writing such an outline and studying it can help to fix the general subject in your mind.

Also think about your audience (see Section **2b**). What expectations will your instructor have concerning the subject matter and its treatment? What is the focus of the exam? To answer these questions, think about the emphasis your instructor has placed on various topics during the term. As a general rule, the more time spent on a topic, the more important or complex the instructor judges it to be. Although you should review all relevant course material, you may be able to anticipate some exam questions if you think about topics and issues that have been stressed during the term. On the other hand, don't forget about readings that may have been assigned but not discussed. The exam may contain questions on this material, too. If you are not sure, by all means ask your instructor just how much material an exam will cover.

Plan your answer.

As soon as you see the specific questions in an exam, your subject is limited for you. Say, for example, your general subject is the history of Europe from 1815 to 1848—the segment of the course on which you are being examined. Now you are given fifty minutes to answer four questions, the first of which is, "What were the four major political and social developments in Europe during the period of 1815-1848?" Or, your general subject is three stories by Nathaniel Hawthorne and two by Herman Melville—the stories you discussed in class. Now you are given fifty minutes to answer two questions, the first of which is this: "Hawthorne has been called a 'moralist-psychologist.' Define the term and evaluate Hawthorne's effectiveness as moralist-psychologist by making specific reference to two of his tales."

● **1 Read the question carefully.** Never start writing without thinking critically about the task you are being asked to do. One of the most common errors students make during examinations is to read too hastily, and they consequently misunderstand the question. Underlining key words in the exam question can be helpful. For example, if the question says "compare and contrast," you are being asked to discuss both similarities *and* differences, not just one or the other. As you read an exam question, identify the task you are being asked to perform (see Section **2a**). Are you being asked to summarize or to analyze? Are you being asked to comment on a given statement, possibly to disagree with it, or to prove it by providing supporting evidence? Instructors think carefully about their exam questions; the wording will frequently provide you with a structure for your answer. The Hawthorne question, for instance, assigns two distinct tasks: defining and evaluating. If a student's response provides a thorough and well-supported evaluation but does not define "moralist-psychologist" adequately, his or her exam score will suffer despite the sound evaluation.

The following chart shows key words that frequently appear in essay examination questions.

Key Words Appearing on Exams

Analyze. Divide the topic into its parts or elements and discuss each part: *Analyze the therapeutic relationship in family counseling.*

Classify. Organize according to categories: *Classify four kinds of sampling and give an example of each.*

Compare and contrast. Show the similarities and differences: *Compare and contrast the economic and social roles of American women before and after World War II.*

Describe. Explain the features of the event, process, object, or procedure in enough detail to make the topic clear: *Describe the food chain in the ecosystem of the mature Northeastern forest.*

Evaluate. Give your well-supported opinion about the significance of the topic: *Evaluate Heisenberg's impact on the field of subatomic physics.*

Explain. Give reasons (and examples if necessary) for something: *Explain the fact that solar energy is not widely used to heat homes and businesses.*

Illustrate. Give examples of the topic: *Illustrate the effects of the Zebra mollusk on the Great Lakes region.*

Summarize. State the major points of the topic: *Summarize the events leading to the invasion of Afghanistan by the Soviet Union.*

Support, defend, or reject; agree or disagree. Give arguments in favor of or against a statement: *Support or reject the position that controlling the world population should involve more than distributing birth control devices to areas where they are not presently available.*

The European history question directs you to summarize information (what *are* the four major developments?). You have only about ten minutes to answer the question, so you will not be able to go into great detail. Don't try to fill up half a blue book with everything you know about the subject. In the second question, you are asked to define and evaluate; you must make a critical judgment on the basis of specific evidence in Hawthorne's stories. You have approximately twenty-five minutes to organize and write the essay. Make it a rule to take a minute or two to think about the question, and answering it will be easier.

● **2 Prepare a rough outline of the limited topic.** Typical notes for the history question could include the following:

1815—Congress of Vienna
1848—Revolutions

Nationalism—C. of V. denied rights to Poles, Belgians, Greeks, etc.
Conservative-Liberal Conflict—Cons. anti-reform. Lib. underground
Industrial Expansion—Intro. of machines. Transportation—railroads, steam
transport, etc.
Class conflict—Lower class vs. middle class

An answer to the question on Hawthorne could develop from the
following notes:

How human beings behave (psych.) and how they ought/ought not
to (moral)
"Ambitious Guest"—psychological study of human ambitions—
moralistic application
"Wakefield"—integration of psych. and moral—people tied to systems

After briefly studying such notes, you have only to number them in the
order you wish to present them—and you have an outline.

As in all outlining and other such planning, you should not feel rigidly bound to the material and its structure. As you write, other ideas may
come to you and a better structure may suggest itself. The student who
answered the Hawthorne question, for example, decided to write on
"Egotism" rather than "The Ambitious Guest." With time looking over your
shoulder, though, you probably cannot afford to change your plans more
than once.

  Compose a cover statement.

On the basis of your notes, you should now be able to begin your examination essay by writing a sentence or two that will serve as a thesis statement.
The students who answered the aforementioned questions began as follows:

Although there were no major conflicts among the European powers
between the Congress of Vienna (1814-1815) and the Revolutions of 1848,
important developments were taking place that would affect the future
history of Europe. Four of these developments were the rise of nationalism,
the conflict between the conservatives and the liberals, the conflict between
the lower and middle classes, and the expansion of industry.

Hawthorne is a moralist-psychologist who is concerned not only with
how people behave but also with how they *ought* or *ought not* to behave. He is
most successful when he integrates the two approaches, as in "Wakefield," and
least successful when his moralizing gets away from him, as in "Egotism; or,
The Bosom Serpent."

Often, of course, the pressure of the exam keeps you from composing
such a thorough cover statement. If coming up with a good cover statement
is delaying you, limit your opening to what is specifically required by the
question (e.g., Define "moralist-psychologist").

53 d Write your answer.

Provide supporting evidence, reasoning, detail, or example for each general-ization you make. Nothing weakens a paper so much as vague, unsupported generalizations, and wordiness. Don't talk about "how beautiful Hawthorne's images are and what a pleasure it was to read such great sto-ries," etc., etc. If necessary, go back to your jotted notes to add supporting material. If you have written a cover statement, look at it again and then jot down some hard evidence in the space at the top of the page.

Say you have been asked to discuss the proper use of the I.Q. score by a teacher. Your notes read, "Intelligence—capacity for learning. Must inter-pret carefully. Also child's personality. Score not permanent. Measures ver-bal ability." You have formulated this cover statement: "*Intelligence* is a vague term used to describe an individual's capacity for learning. The teacher must remember that I.Q. scores tell only part of the story and that they are subject to change." Now you must provide the evidence. Think about specific I.Q. tests, specific studies that support your generalizations. Notes such as the following will help you develop your essay:

> 10% of children significant change after 6 to 8 years
> High motivation often more important than high I.Q.
> Stanford-Binet—aptitude rather than intelligence
> Verbal ability—children from non-English-speaking families—culturally
>   divergent—low verbal score
> N.Y. study—remedial courses, etc.—40% improvement in scores

You now have some raw material to work with, material you can organize and clearly relate to your cover statement. Even if you do not fully succeed in integrating your data into a perfectly coherent and unified essay, you will have demonstrated that you read the material and have some understanding of it. Padding, wordiness, and irrelevancies prove only that you can fill up pages.

Does this mean that you can never toss in a few interesting tidbits not specifically called for by the question? There is nothing wrong with begin-ning a discussion of the significance of the Jefferson-Adams correspon-dence with, "In their 'sunset' correspondence of more than 150 letters, Jefferson and Adams exchanged their ideas on world issues, religion, and the nature and future of American democratic society, almost until the day they both died—July 4, 1826." Although only the middle third of this sen-tence is a direct response to the question, the other information is both rel-evant and interesting. Such details cannot *substitute* for your answer, but they can enhance it, just as they would an out-of-class essay.

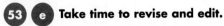 **Take time to revise and edit.**

Try to leave time at the end of the exam to read and revise what you've written. Check to see if you have left out words or phrases. See if you can add an additional bit of detail or evidence; you can make insertions in the margins. Correct misspellings and awkward sentences. See if your cover statement can be improved. You are not expected to write a perfectly polished essay in an exam, but make your essay as readable as you can in the time you have left.

Exercise 53.1

With a classmate, think of a question that might appear on an essay exam in one of your classes. Create the question as if you were the instructor preparing the test. Separately, outline an answer to the question, supplying the specific information, evaluation, organization, and presentation the question requires. Then compare your outlines and jointly determine where they can be improved with more facts, better analysis, clearer relationships between ideas, and sharper focus on the tasks the question specifies.

Writers Revising

When Melissa got her mid-term literature test back, her instructor pointed out that although Melissa had some good detail in one of her answers, she had not provided a cover statement tying her answer together. Read the test question and Melissa's answer; then try your hand at providing a cover statement and compare it with Melissa's revision.

Question: Although Ivan Ilych is clearly the main character of "The Death of Ivan Ilych," the minor characters play important roles. Briefly discuss the roles of Peter Ivanovich, Ivan's colleague, and Gerasim, Ivan's servant.

Draft

Peter Ivanovich is a colleague of Ivan's. They've known each other since they were young boys at school and have remained friends. Peter is like Ivan in many ways; in fact, his name "Ivanovich," means "son of Ivan." He is arrogant and proud and enjoys having a good time. He has a wife but doesn't seem to be a family man. He doesn't want to go to the funeral because it will cut into his time for playing bridge. He thinks of the promotions and transfers that will occur after Ivan dies, something Ivan himself would have done at Peter's funeral. Understanding Peter helps to understand Ivan. Gerasim was a servant of Ivan Ilych's home. After Ivan became ill it was Gerasim who took care of him. Ivan liked Gerasim. He was a happy, cheerful young man and did not mind caring for Ivan. The main thing Ivan liked about Gerasim was that he knew Ivan was dying and didn't pretend that he wasn't. He was sympathetic and understanding when no one else was. He helped make Ivan's miserable illness a little easier. Gerasim contrasts both Peter and Ivan. He also ties in with the theme of the story—that love and self-sacrifice make life more rewarding than riches and station in life.

Revision
Two minor characters—Peter Ivanovich and Gerasim—play major roles in revealing character and theme in "The Death of Ivan Ilych."

Analysis
The cover statement is created by referring to the question itself for the base of the cover statement—two minor characters play minor roles—and to the analysis itself for the function of the minor characters—to reveal character and theme.

In Your Own Words
Write a two-paragraph analysis of your biggest fears and weaknesses in taking essay exams. Also explain which of the suggestions in the text you believe will help you overcome some of these problems.

Glossaries

What grammarians say should be has perhaps less influence on what shall be than even the more modest of them realize; usage evolves itself little disturbed by their likes and dislikes. And yet the temptation to show how better use might have been made of the material to hand is sometimes irresistible.

—H. W. Fowler, *Modern English Usage*

54 Glossary of Grammatical Terms

This glossary provides brief definitions of the grammatical terms used in this text. Cross-references refer you to pertinent sections of the text. For further text references to terms defined, as well as for references to terms not included in the glossary, consult the index.

absolute phrase Absolute constructions modify the sentence in which they stand. They differ from other modifying word groups in that (1) they lack any connective joining them to the rest of the sentence and (2) they do not modify any individual word or word group in the sentence. Compare *Seeing the bears, we stopped the car,* in which the participial phrase modifies *we,* with *The rain having stopped, we saw the bears,* in which the construction *the rain having stopped* is an absolute modifying the rest of the sentence. The basic pattern of the absolute phrase is a noun or pronoun and a participle. (*She having arrived,* we all went to the movies. We left about ten o'clock, *the movie being over.*) Such phrases are sometimes called **nominative absolutes,** since pronouns in them require the nominative case.

Absolute phrases may also be prepositional phrases (*In fact,* we had expected rain) or verbal phrases. (It often rains in April, *to tell the truth. Generally speaking,* July is hot.) For the punctuation of absolute phrases see **32e.**

abstract noun See *noun.*

acronym An abbreviation formed from the initial letters of words, pronounced as a single word. (*MADD* means *Mothers Against Drunk Driving.*) See **44a.**

active voice See *voice.*

adjectival Any word or word group used as an adjective to modify a noun. Some modern grammars limit the meaning of **adjective** strictly to words that can be compared by adding *-er* and *-est* (*new, newer, newest; high, higher, highest*). Such grammars apply the term **adjectival** to other words that ordinarily modify nouns, and to any other word or word group when it is used as an adjective. In such grammars the italicized words below may be called **adjectivals.**

LIMITING ADJECTIVES (ALSO CALLED NOUN MARKERS)	*my* suit, *a* picture, *one* day
NOUNS MODIFYING NOUNS	*school* building, *home* plate, *government* policy
PHRASES MODIFYING NOUNS	man *of the hour; Swinging wildly,* I struck out.
CLAUSES MODIFYING NOUNS	girl *whom I know,* the flavor *that she likes*

adjective A word used to describe or limit the meaning of a noun or its equivalent. According to their position, adjectives may be (1) **attributive,** i.e., placed next to their nouns (*vivid* example; *a* boy, *strong* and *vigorous*), or (2) **predicative,** i.e., placed in the predicate after a linking verb (She was *vigorous*).

According to their meaning, adjectives may be (1) **descriptive,** naming some quality (*white* house, *small* child, *leaking* faucet); (2) **proper,** derived from proper nouns (*Roman* fountain, *French* custom); or (3) **limiting.** Limiting adjectives may indicate possession (*my, his*), may point out (*this, former*), may number (*three, second*) or may be articles (*a, the*). See **26d** and Chapter 28.

adjectival clause A subordinate, or dependent, clause used as an adjective.

> The man *who lives here* is a biologist. [The adjective clause modifies the noun *man.*]
>
> Dogs *that chase cars* seldom grow old. [The adjective clause modifies the noun *dogs.*]

See also **26h.**

adjectival phrase See *phrase.*

adverb A word used to describe or limit the meaning of a verb, an adjective, another adverb, or a whole sentence.

According to function, adverbs may (1) modify single words (went *quickly, quite* shy, *nearly* all men); (2) modify whole sentences (*Maybe* he will go); (3) ask questions (*When* did he go? *Where* is the book?); or (4) connect clauses and modify their meaning (see *conjunctive adverb*).

According to meaning, adverbs may indicate (1) manner (*secretly* envious); (2) time (*never* healthy); (3) place (*outside* the house); or (4) degree (*quite* easily angered). See **26d** and Chapter 28.

adverbial A term used to describe any word or word group used as an adverb. Common adverbials are nouns in certain constructions (She went *home*), phrases (She went *in a great hurry*), or clauses (She went *when she wanted to go*). Compare *adjectival.*

adverbial clause A subordinate, or dependent, clause used as an adverb.

> *When you leave,* please close the door. [The adverbial clause, indicating time, modifies the verb *close.*]
>
> The sheep grazed *where the grass was greenest.* [The adverbial clause, indicating place, modifies the verb *grazed.*]

Adverbial clauses also indicate manner, purpose, cause, result, condition, concession, and comparison. See **26h.**

adverbial conjunction See *conjunctive adverb.*

adverbial objective Sometimes applied to nouns used as adverbials. (They slept *mornings.* He ran a *mile.*)

adverbial phrase See *phrase.*

agreement A correspondence or matching in the form of one word and that of another. Verbs agree with their subjects in number and person (in *She runs,* both *she* and *runs* are singular and third person). Pronouns agree with their antecedents in person, number, and gender (in *He wanted his way, he* and *his* are both third-person singular, and masculine). Demonstrative adjectives match the nouns they modify in number (*this kind, these kinds*). See Chapter 14.

antecedent A word or group of words to which a pronoun refers.

> She is a *woman who* seldom writes letters. [*Woman* is the antecedent of the pronoun *who.*]
> *Uncle Henry* came for a brief visit, but *he* stayed all winter. [*Uncle Henry* is the antecedent of the pronoun *he.*]

appositive A word or phrase set beside a noun, a pronoun, or a group of words used as a noun, that identifies or explains it by renaming it.

> John, my *brother*
> Albany, that is, *New York's state capital*
> his hobby, *playing handball*
> modifiers, *words that describe or limit*

The appositives in the preceding examples are **nonrestrictive:** They explain the nouns they follow but are not necessary to identify them. When appositives restrict the meaning of the nouns they follow to a specific individual or object, they are **restrictive:** *my sister Sue* (that is *Sue,* not *Carol* or *Lisa*); *Huxley the novelist* (not *Huxley the scientist*). See **32c.**

article The words *a, an,* and *the* are articles. *A* and *an* are **indefinite** articles; *the* is a **definite** article. Articles are traditionally classed as limiting adjectives, but since they always signal that a noun will follow, some modern grammars call them **determiners.**

auxiliary A verb form used with a main verb to form a verb phrase; sometimes called a **helping verb.** Auxiliaries are commonly divided into two groups. The first group is used to indicate tense and voice. This group includes *shall, will,* and the forms of *be, have,* and *do* (*shall* give, *will* give, *has* given, *had* given, *does* give, *is* giving, *was* given).

The second group, called **modal auxiliaries,** includes *can, could, may, might, must, ought, should,* and *would.* These are used to indicate ability, obligation, permission, possibility, etc., and they do not take inflectional endings such as *-s, -ed,* and *-ing.* See **29c.**

cardinal numbers Numbers such as *one, three, twenty,* used in counting. Compare *ordinal numbers.*

case The inflectional form of pronouns or the possessive form of nouns to indicate their function in a group of words. Pronouns have three cases: (1) **nominative or subjective** (*we, she, they*), used for the subject of a verb, or a subjective complement; (2) the **possessive,** used as an adjective (*their dog, anybody's guess*); and (3) the **objective** (*us, her, them*), used for objects of verbs, verbals, and prepositions. Possessive pronouns may also stand alone (The car is *his*). Nouns have only two cases: (1) a **common** case (*woman, leopard*) and (2) a **possessive** case (*woman's, leopard's*). See Chapter 27.

clause A group of words containing a subject and a predicate. Clauses are of two kinds: main, or independent; and subordinate, or dependent. **Main clauses** make independent assertions and can stand alone as sentences. **Subordinate clauses** depend on some other element within a sentence; they function as nouns, adjectives, or adverbs, and cannot stand alone.

MAIN   *The moon shone*, and *the dog barked*. [two main clauses, either of which could be a sentence]

SUBORDINATE   *When the moon shone*, the dog barked. [adverb clause]
    That he would survive is doubtful. [noun clause]

See **26h.**

collective noun A noun naming a collection or aggregate of individuals by a singular form (*assembly, army, jury*). Collective nouns are followed by a singular verb when the group is thought of as a unit and a plural verb when the component individuals are being referred to (the majority *decides*; the majority *were* college graduates). See **14a** and **14b.**

comma splice A sentence error in which two independent clauses are joined only by a comma without a coordinating conjunction. See Chapter 13.

common noun See *noun.*

comparison Change in the form of adjectives and adverbs to show degree. English has three degrees: (1) **positive,** the form listed in dictionaries (*loud, bad, slowly*); (2) **comparative** (*louder, worse, more slowly*); and (3) **superlative** (*loudest, worst, most slowly*). See **28d.**

complement In its broadest sense, a term for any word, excluding modifiers, that completes the meaning of a verb (direct and indirect objects), a subject (subject complements), or an object (object complements).

VERB COMPLEMENTS   Give *me* the *money*. [*Money* and *me* are direct and indirect objects, respectively.]

SUBJECT COMPLEMENTS   Helen is a *singer*. She is *excellent*. [The noun *singer* and the adjective *excellent* refer to the subject.]

OBJECT COMPLEMENTS   We elected Jane *secretary*. That made Bill *angry*. [*Secretary* and *angry* refer to the direct objects *Jane* and *Bill*.]

complete predicate See *predicate.*

complete subject See *subject.*

complex sentence See *sentence.*

compound Made up of more than one word but used as a unit, as in compound noun (*redhead, football*), compound adjective (*downcast, matter-of-fact*), or compound subject (Both *patience* and *practice* are necessary). See also *sentence.*

compound-complex See *sentence.*

compound sentence See *sentence.*

compound subject See *subject.*

concrete noun See *noun.*

conjugation A list of inflected forms for a verb, displaying the forms for first-, second-, and third-person singular and plural for each tense, voice, and mood. A synopsis of the third-person singular (*he, she, it,* and singular nouns) forms for a regular and an irregular verb is shown in the list that follows.

Active Voice	*Simple Form*	*Progressive Form*
PRESENT	*he/she* asks/drives	*he/she* is asking/driving
PAST	*he/she* asked/drove	*he/she* was asking/driving
FUTURE	*he/she will* ask/drive	*he/she* will be asking/driving
PRESENT PERFECT	*he/she* has asked/driven	*he/she* has been asking/driving
PAST PERFECT	*he/she* had asked/driven	*he/she* had been asking/driving
FUTURE PERFECT	*he/she* will have asked/ driven	*he/she* will have been asking/ driving
Passive Voice		
PRESENT	*he/she* is asked/driven	*he/she* is being asked/driven
PAST	*he/she* was asked/driven	*he/she* was being asked/driven
FUTURE	*he/she* will be asked/driven	*he/she* will be being asked/driven
PRESENT PERFECT	*he/she* has been asked/ driven	*he/she* has been being asked/ driven
PAST PERFECT	*he/she* had been asked/ driven	*he/she* had been being asked/ driven
FUTURE PERFECT	*he/she* will have been asked/driven	*he/she* will have been being asked/driven

Forms for first- and second-person singular and all plural forms may be described briefly as follows:

The present-tense forms for other persons are *I/you/we/they* ask/drive.

The past- and future-tense forms for all persons are the same as those shown for the third person.

All perfect-tense and passive-voice forms that use *has* as an auxiliary in the third person use *have* in all other persons.

All perfect-tense and passive-voice forms that use *is/was* in the third person use *am/was* for the first person *(I)* and *were* in all other persons.

conjunction A part of speech used to join and relate words, phrases, and clauses. Conjunctions may be either coordinating or subordinating.

Coordinating conjunctions connect words, phrases, and clauses of equal grammatical rank: *and, but, or, nor, for.*

Subordinating conjunctions join dependent clauses to main clauses: *after, although, as if, because, since, when.*

See **26e**.

conjunctive adverb An adverb used to relate and connect main clauses in a sentence. Common conjunctive adverbs are *also, consequently, furthermore, hence, however, indeed, instead, likewise, moreover, nevertheless, otherwise, still, then, therefore, thus.* Conjunctive adverbs, unlike coordinating and subordinating conjunctions, are movable and can thus occupy different positions within the main clause in which they stand. See **33b** for punctuation of conjunctive adverbs.

connective A general term for any word or phrase that links words, phrases, clauses, or sentences. Connectives thus include conjunctions, prepositions, and conjunctive adverbs. See **26e**.

construction A general term describing any related groups of words such as a phrase, a clause, or a sentence.

coordinate Having equal rank, as two main clauses in a compound sentence. See **8a**.

coordinating conjunction See *conjunction.*

correlatives Coordinating conjunctions used in pairs to join sentence elements of equal rank. Common correlatives are *either...or; neither...nor; not only...but also; whether...or; both...and.* See **26e**.

count noun Count nouns name things that can be counted individually. They have plural forms. (Where are the garden *tools?*) See *noun* and **26a**.

dangling modifier A modifying word or phrase that has no grammatically logical word to modify in a sentence. (*While on vacation,* the neighbors fed our cat.) See Chapter 18.

declension See *inflection* and *case.*

degree See *comparison.*

demonstrative pronoun *This, that, these,* and *those* are called **demonstrative pronouns** or **demonstratives** when used as pointing words. (*That* is my favorite painting.) When they precede nouns they are called *demonstrative adjectives.* (Someone must have turned off *that* percolator, because *this* coffee is cold.)

dependent clause See *clause.*

derivational suffix See *suffix.*

determiner A word such as *a, an, the, his, our, your,* that indicates that one of the words following it is a noun.

direct address A noun or pronoun used parenthetically to point out the person addressed, sometimes called **nominative of address** or **vocative.** (*George,* where are you going? I suppose, *gentlemen,* that you enjoyed the lecture.)

direct and indirect discourse Direct discourse is an exact reporting of a speaker's or writer's words. In indirect discourse the speaker's or writer's thought is reported without direct quotation. See **16d.**

DIRECT   She said, "I must leave on the eight o'clock shuttle."
INDIRECT   She said that she had to leave on the eight o'clock shuttle.

direct object See *object* and *complement.*

double negative The use of two negative words within the same construction. In certain forms, two negatives are used in the same statement in English to give a particular emphasis to a positive idea. (He was *not* entirely *un*prejudiced.) In most instances, the double negative is nonstandard. (He *didn't* do *no* work. We *didn't* see *no*body.) See **22b.**

elliptical construction An omission of words necessary to the grammatical completeness of an expression but assumed in the context. The omitted words in elliptical expressions are understood. (*She is older than I* [am]. *Our house is small, his* [house is] *large.*)

expletive The word *it* or *there* used to introduce a sentence in which the subject follows the verb. See **26f, 10c, 24a.**

>   *It* is doubtful that he will arrive today. [The clause *that he will arrive today* is the subject of the verb *is.*]
>   *There* are two ways of solving the problem. [The noun *ways* is the subject of *are.*]

faulty predication A grammatical fault that results when a subject and its verb or a subject and its complement in a subject/linking verb/complement construction are mismatched in meaning. See **20a**.

finite verb A verb form that makes an assertion about its subject. Verbals (infinitives, participles, gerunds) are not finite forms. All finite verbs can add *-s* in the third-person singular of the present tense to show agreement with their subject. Nonfinite verb forms cannot make this inflectional change. See Chapters 29-30.

function word A term used to describe the words, such as articles, auxiliaries, conjunctions, and prepositions, that are more important for their part in the structure of the sentence than for their meaning. They indicate the function of other words in a sentence and the grammatical relationships between those words. Compare *lexical word*.

fused sentence (run-on) Two or more grammatically complete thoughts with no separating punctuation. See Chapter 13.

gender The classification of nouns and pronouns as masculine (*man, he*), feminine (*woman, she*), and neuter (*desk, it*). A few English nouns have special forms to indicate gender (*salesman, saleswoman; hero, heroine*).

genitive case The possessive case. See Chapter 27.

gerund A verbal that ends in *-ing* and is used as a noun. Gerunds may take complements, objects, and modifiers (*Graceful skating takes practice*). See **26g**.

helping verb See *auxiliary*.

idiom An expression established by usage and peculiar to a particular language. Many idioms have unusual grammatical constructions and make little sense if taken literally. Examples of English idioms are *by and large, catch a cold, lay hold of, look up an old friend*. See **23f**.

imperative See *mood*.

indefinite pronoun A pronoun, such as *anybody, anyone, someone*, that does not refer to a specific person or thing.

independent clause See *clause*.

independent element An expression that has no grammatical relation to other parts of the sentence. See *absolute*.

indicative See *mood*.

indirect object　See *object.*

indirect quotation　See *direct and indirect quotation.*

infinitive　A verbal usually consisting of *to* followed by the present form of the verb. With a few verbs *to* may be omitted (heard her *tell;* made it *work*). Infinitives can serve as nouns (*To swim* is to relax), as adjectives (I have nothing *to say*), or as adverbs (We were ready *to begin*). See **26g.**

inflection　Variation in the form of words to indicate case (*he, him*), gender (*he, she, it*), number (*mouse, mice*), tense (*walk, walked*), etc. **Declension** is the inflection of nouns and pronouns; **conjugation** is the inflection of verbs; and **comparison** is the inflection of adjectives and adverbs.

inflectional suffix　See *suffix.*

intensifier　A term applied to such modifiers as *much, so, too,* and *very,* which merely add emphasis to the words they modify. Words such as *actually, mighty, pretty,* and *really* often occur as vague intensifiers in colloquial English.

intensive pronoun　Any compound personal pronoun ending with *-self* used for emphasis. (I did it *myself.* The dean *himself* wrote the letter.)

interjection　A word or group of words that is grammatically independent and used to show mild, strong, or sudden emotion. (*Ych.* I hate caterpillars. *Say!* Let's go to a movie.)

intransitive verb　See *verb.*

inversion　A reversal of normal word order. (*Dejected, he left the witness stand. The verdict he clearly foresaw.*)

irregular verb　A verb that forms its past tense and past participle by a change in an internal vowel, or by some other individualized change (*begin, began, begun; do, did, done; fall, fell, fallen*), as opposed to the usual addition of *-d* or *-ed* to the basic form of so-called **regular verbs,** as in *walk, walked, walked.* See Chapter 29.

kernel sentence　A term used in some contemporary grammars to describe one of a limited number of basic sentence patterns from which all grammatical structures can be derived. See **26f.**

lexical word　Nouns, verbs, adjectives, and adverbs are sometimes termed lexical words, that is, words that carry most of the meaning in English, in contrast to *function words,* which indicate relationships among lexical words. Compare *function word.*

linking verb A verb that shows the relation between the subject of a sentence and a complement. (*He seems timid. The cake tastes sweet. She is my sister.*) The chief linking verbs are *be, become, appear, seem,* and the verbs pertaining to the senses (*look, smell, taste, sound, feel*). See Chapter 29.

main clause See *clause.*

mass noun Mass nouns name things not usually counted individually. They do not have plural forms. (Look at the *snow* on my hat.) See *noun* and **26a.**

misplaced modifier See *modifier.*

mixed construction A grammatical fault that consists of joining as a sentence two or more parts that do not fit in grammar or meaning. See Chapter 20.

modal auxiliary See *auxiliary.*

modification Describing or limiting the meaning of a word or group of words. Adjectives and adjective phrases or clauses modify nouns; adverbs and adverb phrases or clauses modify verbs, adjectives, or adverbs. See Chapter 28.

modifier A general term given to any word or word group that is used to limit, qualify, or otherwise describe the meaning of another word or word group. Adjectives, adverbs, prepositional and verbal phrases, and subordinate clauses are the usual modifiers in English. See Chapter 28 for adjectives and adverbs and Chapter 26 for various word groups as modifiers. For a discussion of misplaced modifiers, see Chapter 17.

mood The form of a verb used to show how the action is viewed by the speaker. English has three moods: (1) **indicative,** stating a fact or asking a question (The wheat *is* ripe. *Will* he *go?*); (2) **imperative,** expressing a command or a request (*Report* at once. Please *clear* your desk.); and (3) **subjunctive,** expressing doubt, wish, or condition contrary to fact (The grass looks as if it *were* dying. I wish she *were* more friendly.) See **29f.**

nominal A word or word group used as a noun. (The *blue* seems more suitable. *Eating that pie* will not be easy.) Compare *adjectival.* See Section **24a(1)**.

nominative case See *case.*

noncount noun See *mass noun* and *noun.*

nonfinite verb Infinitives, participles, and gerunds are nonfinite verbs. They cannot stand alone as main verbs in sentences or clauses, do not indicate person or number, and cannot by themselves make an assertion about a subject. See **26g.**

nonrestrictive modifier A modifying phrase or clause that is not essential to pointing out or identifying the person or thing modified.

> Smith, *who was watching the road*, saw the accident.
> The latest breakthrough, *reported last week*, has everyone talking.

See **32c**.

noun A word, like *man, horse, carrot, trip, theory*, or *capitalism*, that names a person, place, thing, quality, concept, or the like. Nouns usually form plurals by adding *-s*, and possessives by adding *'s*, and most frequently function as subjects and complements, although they also function in other ways. See **26a**.

Nouns are divided into various subclasses according to their meaning. The most common classes are the following:

Class	Meaning	Examples
common	general classes	*tiger, house, idea*
proper	specific names	*Chicago, Burma, Lee*
abstract	ideas, qualities	*liberty, love, emotion*
concrete	able to be sensed	*apple, noise, perfume*
collective	groups	*herd, bunch, jury*
count	able to be counted	*chicken, slice, book*
mass (or noncount)	not ordinarily counted (not used with *a, an*)	*salt, gold, equality*

noun clause A subordinate clause used as a noun. (*What I saw* was humiliating. I shall accept *whatever they offer*.) See **26h**.

noun marker See *adjectival*.

number The form of a noun, pronoun, verb, or demonstrative adjective to indicate one (singular) or more than one (plural).

object A general term for any word group or word that is affected by or receives action of a transitive verb or verbal, or of a preposition. A **direct object** receives the action of the verb. (I followed *him*. Keep *whatever you find*.) An **indirect object** indicates to or for whom or what something is done. (Give *me* the money.) The **object of a preposition** follows the preposition and is related to another part of the sentence by the preposition. (We rode across the *beach*.) See also *complement* and **26f** and **27b**.

object complement See *complement*.

objective case See *case*.

ordinal numbers Numbers such as *first, third, twentieth, sixty-fifth*, used to indicate order. Compare *cardinal numbers*.

parenthetical expression An inserted expression that interrupts the thought of a sentence. (His failure, *I suppose*, was his own fault. I shall arrive—*this will surprise you*—on Monday.)

participial phrase See *participle* and *phrase.*

participle A verbal used as an adjective. As an adjective, a participle can modify a noun or pronoun. The **present participle** ends in *-ing (running, seeing, trying)*. The **past participle** ends in *-d, -ed, -t, -n, -en,* or changes the vowel (*walked, lost, seen, rung*). Though a participle alone cannot make an assertion, it is derived from a verb and can take an object and be modified by an adverb (*swimming the river, completely beaten*). When accompanied by a form of the verb *to be* to create a verb phrase, the **present participle** is used to indicate the progressive tense—action continuing at the time indicated. (The dog *was chasing* a Frisbee.) When accompanied by a form of the verb *have* to create a verb phrase, the **past participle** is used to indicate the perfect tense—action completed before a given point in time. (The rain *has stopped*, and the sun *has come* out.) When combined with forms of the verb *to be*, the past participle indicates passive voice. (The sun *was covered* by the storm clouds.) See also **26g, 29a, 29e,** and Chapter 30.

parts of speech The classes into which words may be divided on the basis of meaning, form, and function. The traditional parts of speech are noun, pronoun, verb, adjective, adverb, preposition, conjunction, and interjection. See Chapter 26 and separate entries in this glossary.

passive voice See *voice.*

past participle See *participle.*

person The form of a pronoun and verb used to indicate the speaker (first person—*I am*); the person spoken to (second person—*you are*); or the person spoken about (third person—*she is*).

personal pronoun See *pronoun.*

phrase A group of related words lacking both subject and predicate and used as a single part of speech (see **26g**). Phrases may be classified as follows:

PREPOSITIONAL	We walked *across the street.*
PARTICIPIAL	The man *entering the room* is my father.
GERUND	*Washing windows* is tiresome work.
INFINITIVE	*To see the sunset* was a pleasure.
VERB	She *has been educated* in Europe.

plain form A term often used for the infinitive or dictionary form of a verb, as *run, stand, pounce.* See Chapter 29.

positive, positive degree See *comparison.*

possessive See *case.*

predicate The part of a sentence or clause that makes a statement about the subject. The *complete predicate* consists of the verb and its complements and modifiers. The *simple predicate* consists of only the verb and its auxiliaries. See **26f**.

predicate adjective An adjective serving as a subject complement. (We were *silent.*) See *complement.*

predicate noun A noun serving as a subject complement. (He was a *hero.*) See *complement.*

prefix One or more syllables, such as *a-, mis-, sub-,* or *un-,* that can be added at the beginning of a word or root to change or modify its meaning: *a* + moral = amoral; *mis* + print = misprint; *sub* + standard = substandard; *un* + zipped = unzipped. See **21d**.

preposition A word used to relate a noun or pronoun to some other word in the sentence. A preposition and its object form a **prepositional phrase.** (The sheep are *in* the meadow. He dodged *through* the traffic.) See **26e** and **26g**.

prepositional phrase See *phrase* and *preposition.*

present participle See *participle.*

principal clause A main or independent clause. See *clause.*

principal parts The three forms of a verb from which the various tenses are derived; the **present infinitive** (*join, go*), the **past tense** (*joined, went*), and the **past participle** (*joined, gone*). See Chapter 29.

progressive The form of the verb used to describe an action occurring, but not completed, at the time referred to. (I *am studying.* I *was studying.*) See Chapters 29 and 30.

pronoun A word used in place of a noun. The noun for which a pronoun stands is called its **antecedent** (see **26b** and **14b**). Pronouns are classified as follows:

PERSONAL	*I, you, he, she, it,* etc.
RELATIVE	*who, which, that* I am the person *who* lives here. We saw a barn *that* was burning.
INTERROGATIVE	*who, which, what* *Who* are you? *Which* is your book?

DEMONSTRATIVE	*this, that, these, those*
INDEFINITE	*one, any, each, anyone, somebody, all*, etc.
RECIPROCAL	*each other, one another*
INTENSIVE	*myself, yourself, herself,* etc. I *myself* was afraid. You *yourself* must decide.
REFLEXIVE	*myself, yourself, himself,* etc. I burned *myself.* You are deceiving *yourself.*

proper adjective See *adjective.*

proper noun See *noun.*

reciprocal pronoun See *pronoun.*

reflexive pronoun See *pronoun.*

register English can be described in terms of three registers—**formal, informal,** and **familiar**—which indicate the relationship between the writer, audience, and subject matter. See **22a** and *tone.*

regular verb See *irregular verb.*

relative clause A subordinate clause introduced by a relative pronoun. See *pronoun.*

relative pronoun See *pronoun.*

restrictive modifier A modifying phrase or clause that is essential to pointing out or identifying the person or thing modified. (People *who live in glass houses* shouldn't throw stones. The horse *that won the race* is a bay mare.) See **32c**.

run-on See *fused sentence.*

sentence A complete unit of thought containing a subject and a predicate. Sentences can be classified according to their form as **simple, compound, complex,** and **compound-complex.**

SIMPLE	They rested. [one main clause]
COMPOUND	They rested and we worked. [two main clauses]
COMPLEX	They rested while we worked. [one main clause, one subordinate clause]
COMPOUND-COMPLEX	They rested while we worked, but we could not finish. [two main clauses, one containing a subordinate clause]

sentence fragment A group of words capitalized and punctuated as a sentence but not containing both a subject and a finite verb. See Chapter 12.

simple predicate See *predicate.*

simple sentence See *sentence.*

simple subject See *subject.*

squinting modifier A word or phrase that can modify either a preceding word or a following word, thus confusing the reader. See **17d**.

subject The person or thing about which the predicate of a sentence or clause makes an assertion or asks a question. The **simple subject** is the word or word group with which the verb of the sentence agrees. The **complete subject** is the simple subject together with all its modifiers. In *The donkey that Jones keeps in the back yard brays all the time, donkey* is the simple subject, and *the donkey that Jones keeps in the back yard* is the complete subject. See **26f**.

subject complement See *complement.*

subjective See *case.*

subjunctive mood See *mood.*

subordinate clause, subordination See *clause.*

subordinator See *conjunction.*

substantive A word or group of words used as a noun. Substantives include pronouns, infinitives, gerunds, and noun clauses.

substantive clause A noun clause. See *clause.*

suffix An ending that modifies the meaning of the word to which it is attached. Suffixes may be **inflectional,** such as the *-s* added to nouns to form plurals (*rug, rugs*) or the *-ed* added to verbs to indicate past tense (*call, called*). Or they may be **derivational,** such as *-ful, -less,* or *-ize* (*hope, hopeful; home, homeless; union, union-ize*). Derivational suffixes often, though not always, change the part of speech to which they are added. See *inflection* and **21d**.

superlative See *comparison.*

syntax The part of grammar that describes the structure and function of meaningful word groups such as phrases, clauses, and sentences, as opposed to **morphology,** the part of grammar that describes the formation, function, and classification of words.

tag question A question that implies or confirms the expected answer, attached to the end of a statement. Tag questions typically consist of a pronoun and an auxiliary verb. The pronoun usually refers to the subject or implied subject of the sentence. (It's too early to go stand at the bus stop yet, *isn't it?* Let's order another cup of tea, *shall we?*)

tense Verbs show tense—the time of their action or state—by means of changes in form. Verbs have three basic tenses: **present** (the bus *stops*), **past** (the bus *stopped*), and **future** (the bus *will stop*). Verbs also show time relationships to other actions or events by means of the following forms: **simple** (the bus *stops*), **perfect** (the bus *has stopped*), **progressive** (the bus *is stopping*), and **perfect progressive** (the bus *has been stopping*). See Chapters 29 and 30.

tone The attitude, stance, or point of view writers express about their subject matter and their audience. Tone is created by means of vocabulary choice, sentence length and structure, verb tense and mood, and so forth. See **6g**, **22a**, and *register*.

transitive verb See *verb*.

verb A word, like *confide, raise, see*, which indicates action or asserts something (see **26c**). Verbs are inflected and combine with auxiliaries to form **verb phrases.** Verbs may be **transitive,** requiring an object (He *made* a report), or **intransitive,** not requiring an object (They *migrated*). Many can function both transitively and intransitively. (The wind *blew*. They *blew* the whistle.) **Linking verbs,** such as *be, become*, and *appear*, are followed by complements that refer to the subject. See Chapter 29.

verb complement See *complement*.

verb phrase See *phrase*.

verbal A word derived from a verb and able to take objects, complements, modifiers, and sometimes subjects but unable to stand as the main verb in a sentence. See *gerund, infinitive*, and *participle*. See also **26g**.

verbal phrase A phrase containing an infinitive, participle, or gerund. For examples, see *phrase*.

voice The form of the verb that shows whether the subject acts (**active voice**) or is acted upon (**passive voice**). Only transitive verbs can show voice. A transitive verb followed by an object is **active.** (They *bought* flowers.) In the **passive** the direct object is made into the subject. (The flowers *were bought*.) See **29e**.

word order The order of words in a sentence or smaller word group. Word order is one of the principal grammatical devices in English.

55 Glossary of Usage

Choosing the right word—or not choosing the wrong one—is one of the most difficult problems for writers. This glossary is intended to help you with some of the most commonly troublesome words and phrases. However, it is necessarily brief; you should keep a good college dictionary at hand and consult it both for words not listed here and for additional information about words that are listed.

For information about labels used in dictionaries, see Chapter 21. The following two labels are used in this glossary:

COLLOQUIAL Commonly used in speech but inappropriate in all but the most informal writing

NONSTANDARD Generally agreed not to be standard English

In addition to specifically labeled words, some words and phrases are included here because, although widely used, they are wordy or redundant (e.g., *but that, inside of, in the case of*); vague and overused (e.g., *contact, really*); or objected to by many readers (e.g., *center around, hopefully* meaning "it is hoped," *-wise* as a suffix). A few word pairs often confused (e.g., *imply, infer*) are included, but Section **23d** has a more extensive list of such pairs. See also **23f**.

a, an *A* is used before words beginning with a consonant sound, even when the sound is spelled with a vowel (*a dog, a European, a unicorn, a habit.*) *An* is used before words beginning with a vowel sound or a silent *h* (*an apple, an Indian, an hour, an uproar*).

accept, except To *accept* is to receive. To *except* is to exclude. As a preposition *except* means "with the exclusion of." (*He accepted the list from the chairman. The list excepted George from the slate of candidates. He asked why it included all except George.*)

actually Like *really*, frequently overworked as an intensifier.

adverse, averse These adjectives both mean "hostile" or "opposed." *Adverse*, however, means something is opposed to the subject; *averse* means the subject is opposed to something. (*Cats are averse to adverse weather such as rain.*)

advice, advise *Advice* is a noun; *advise* is a verb. (*Don't ask for my advice unless you really want me to advise you.*)

affect, effect As verbs, to *affect* is to influence, to *effect* is to bring about. *Effect* is more commonly used as a noun meaning "result." (*Recent tax reforms affect everyone. They are intended to effect a fairer distribution of taxes. The effects have yet to be felt.*)

aggravate, irritate Although the two words tend to be used interchangeably in informal conversation, the primary meaning of *aggravate* is "to make worse," whereas the primary meaning of *irritate* is "to exasperate, vex, or annoy." The distinction is useful and worth preserving. (*Scratching your poison ivy rash will only aggravate the itching and further irritate your mother, who told you to stay on the path and out of the underbrush.*)

agree to, agree with To *agree to* is to consent; to *agree with* means "to concur." (*I agree with Gail's opinion, and will therefore agree to the contract.*)

ain't A contraction of *am not*, extended to *is not, are not, has not, have not*. Though used in speech, *ain't* is strongly disapproved by the majority of speakers and writers.

a lot, alot The correct spelling is *a lot*; often considered to be colloquial.

all, all of Constructions with *all of* followed by a noun can frequently be made more concise by omitting the *of*; usually the *of* is retained before a pronoun or a proper noun; *all of Illinois*, but *all the money, all this confusion*.

allude, refer To *allude to* is to refer to indirectly; to *refer to* is to direct attention to. (*When he spoke of family difficulties, we knew he was alluding to his wife's illness even though he did not refer directly to that.*)

allusion, illusion An *allusion* is an indirect reference; an *illusion* is a false impression. (*He was making an allusion to magicians when he spoke of people who were adept at creating illusions.*)

already, all ready *Already* is an adverb meaning "previously" (*We had already left*) or "even now" (*We are already late*). In the phrase *all ready, all* modifies *ready*; the phrase means "completely prepared." (*We were all ready by eight o'clock.*)

alright, all right *All right* remains the only established spelling. *Alright* is labeled nonstandard in both the *New World* and *Random House* dictionaries, although *Webster's* lists it without a usage label.

also, likewise Not acceptable substitutes for *and*. (*We packed our clothes, our food, and* [not *also* or *likewise*] *our books.*)

altogether, all together *Altogether* means "wholly, completely"; *all together* means "in a group," "everyone assembled." (*She was altogether pleased with her new piano, which she played when we were all together for our reunion.*)

alumnus, alumna An *alumnus* (plural *alumni*) is a male graduate. An *alumna* (plural *alumnae*) is a female graduate. *Alumni* is now usually used for groups including both men and women.

among, between *Among* implies more than two persons or things; *between* implies only two. However, to express a reciprocal relationship, or the relationship of one thing to several other things, *between* is commonly used for more than two. (*She divided the toys among the three children. Jerry could choose between pie and cake for dessert. An agreement was reached between the four companies. The surveyors drove a stake at a point between three trees.*)

amount, number *Amount* refers to quantity of mass; *number* refers to countable objects. (*Large numbers of guests require a great amount of food.*)

an See *a, an.*

and etc. *Etc.* (Latin *et cetera*) means "and so forth." The redundant *and etc.* means literally "and and so forth."

and/or A legalism to which some readers object.

and which, and who Use only when *which* or *who* is introducing a clause that coordinates with an earlier clause introduced by *which* or *who.* (*Tina is a woman who has opinions and who often expresses them.*)

ante-, anti- *Ante-* means "before," as in *antedate. Anti-* means "against," as in *anti-American.* The hyphen is used after *anti* before capital letters, and before *i,* as in *anti-intellectual.*

any more, anymore Either spelling is correct. Meaning "now" or "nowadays," the expression is used only in negative contexts. (*He doesn't live here any more.*) Used in affirmative contexts, the expression is regional and should be avoided in writing. (*What's the matter with you anymore?*)

anyone, everyone, someone Not the same as *any one, every one, some one. Anyone* means "any person." (*He will talk to anyone who visits him.*) *Any one* means "any single person or thing." (*He will talk to any one of his neighbors at a time, but not more than one at a time.*)

anyplace Colloquial for *any place.*

anyway, any way, anyways *Anyway* means "nevertheless, no matter what else may be true." (*They're going to leave school anyway, no matter what we say.*) Do not confuse it with *any way.* (*I do not see any way to stop them.*) *Anyways* is a colloquial form of *anyway.*

apt See *liable.*

around Colloquial as used in *stay around* meaning "stay nearby" and in *come around to see me.* As a synonym for the preposition *about, around* is informal and objected to by some in writing; write *about one hundred* rather than *around one hundred.*

as In introducing adverbial clauses, *as* may mean either "when" or "because." Thus it is best avoided if there is any possibility of confusion. As a substitute for *that* or *whether* (*He didn't know as he could go*) or for *who* (*Those as want them can have them*), *as* is nonstandard. For confusion between *as* and *like*, see *like, as, as if.*

as...as, so...as In negative comparisons, some authorities prefer *not so...as* to *not as...as*, but both are generally considered acceptable.

as, like See *like, as.*

as to A wordy substitute for *about*. (*He questioned me about* [not *as to*] *my plans.*) At the beginning of sentences, *as to* is standard for emphasizing. (*As to teamwork, the more they practiced, the more successful they were.*)

at Wordy in such constructions as *"Where are you eating at?"* and *"Where is he at now?"*

athletics Plural in form, but often treated as singular in number. See **14a**.

awful, awfully In formal English *awful* means "inspiring awe" or "causing fear." Colloquially it is used to mean "very bad" or "unpleasant" (*an awful joke, an awful examination*). *Awfully* is colloquial as an intensifier (*awfully hard, awfully pretty*).

awhile, a while *Awhile* is an adverb and must modify a verb, an adjective, or another adverb. *A while* is an article with a noun. (*She said awhile ago that she would be gone for a while this afternoon.*)

bad, badly Often confused. *Bad* is an adjective and should be used only to modify nouns and as a predicate adjective after linking verbs. (*She had a bad cold and felt bad* [not *badly*].) *Badly* is an adverb. (*She hurt her leg badly* [not *bad*].) See Chapter 28.

basically An overworked intensifier meaning "actually" or "really."

being that, being as (how) Nonstandard substitutions for the appropriate subordinating conjunctions *as, because, since.*

beside, besides *Beside* is a preposition meaning "by the side of." *Besides* is an adverb or a preposition meaning "moreover" or "in addition to." (*He sat beside her. Besides, he had to wait for John.*)

better See *had better.*

between, among See *among, between.*

bring, take *Bring* should be used only for movement from a farther to a nearer location. *Take* is used for any other movement. (*You may take my raincoat, but don't forget to bring it back with the other things you have borrowed.*)

bunch Colloquial when used to mean a group of people or things (*a bunch of dishes, a bunch of money*). Used in writing to refer only to things growing or fastened together (*a bunch of bananas, a bunch of celery*).

bursted, bust, busted The principal parts of the verb are *burst, burst, burst. Bursted* is an old form of the past and past participle, which is no longer considered good usage. *Bust* and *busted* are nonstandard.

but, hardly, scarcely All are negative and should not be used with other negatives. (*She had only* [not *didn't have but*] *one hour. She had scarcely* [not *hadn't scarcely*] *finished. She could hardly* [not *couldn't hardly*] *see.*)

but however, but yet Redundant. Use *but, however,* or *yet* but not two together. (*I was ill, but* [not *but yet*] *I attended.*)

but that, but what Wordy equivalents of *that* as a conjunction or relative pronoun. (*I don't doubt that* [not *but that* or *but what*] *you are right.*)

can, may Informally *can* is used to indicate both ability (*I can drive a car*) and permission (*Can I use the car?*). In formal English, *may* is reserved by some for permission (*May I use the car?*). *May* is also used to indicate possibility. (*I can go to the movies, but I may not.*)

can't help but This expression is redundant. Use either *I can't help* (*wondering if she saw us*) or the more formal expression *I cannot but help* (*wondering if she saw us*).

case, in the case of Wordy and usually unnecessary. See Chapter 24.

censor, censure To *censor* means "to examine in order to delete or suppress objectionable material." *Censure* means "to reprimand or condemn."

center around, center about Common expressions, but objected to by many as illogical. Prefer *center on.* (*The debate centered on* [not *centered around* or *centered about*] *the rights of students.*)

character Wordy. *He had an illness of a serious character* means "He had a serious illness."

cite, site *Cite* is a verb meaning "to quote or mention"; *site* is a noun meaning "a particular place." (*I can cite the passage that refers to the site of the battle.*)

complected A colloquial or dialect equivalent of *complexioned* as in *light-complect-ed*. Prefer *light-* or *dark-complexioned* in writing.

complement, compliment *Complement* comes from "complete" and means "to add to"; to *compliment* means "to flatter." (*Let me compliment you on that tie. It certainly complements your suit.*)

complete See *unique*.

conscious, conscience *Conscious* is an adjective meaning "aware"; *conscience,* a noun, refers to one's sense of right and wrong. (*She was not conscious of her conscience.*)

consensus of opinion Redundant; omit *of opinion*. *Consensus* means "a general harmony of opinion."

considerable Standard as an adjective (*considerable success, a considerable crowd*). Colloquial as a noun. (*They lost considerable in the flood.*) Nonstandard as an adverb. (*They were considerable hurt in the accident.*)

contact Overused as a vague verb meaning "to meet, to talk with, to write," etc. Prefer a more specific word such as *interview, consult, write to, telephone*.

continual, continuous *Continual* means "frequently repeated." (*He was distracted by continual telephone calls.*) *Continuous* means "without interruption." (*We heard the continuous sound of the waves.*)

continue on Redundant; omit *on*.

convince, persuade Widely used interchangeably, but many careful writers *convince* people that something is so, but *persuade* them to do something. The distinction seems worth preserving.

could of Nonstandard for *could have*.

couple Colloquial when used to mean "a few" or "several." When used before a plural noun, it is nonstandard unless followed by *of*. (*We had a couple of* [not *couple*] *minutes.*)

credible, creditable, credulous Sometimes confused. *Credible* means "believable." (*Their story seemed credible to the jury.*) *Creditable* means "praiseworthy." (*You gave a creditable violin recital.*) *Credulous* means "inclined to believe on slight evidence." (*The credulous child really believed the moon was made of cheese.*)

criteria See *data*.

data, criteria, phenomena Historically *data* is a plural form, but the singular *datum* is now rare. *Data* is often treated as singular, but careful writing still often treats it as plural. (*These data* [not *this*] *are* [not *is*] *the most recent.*) *Criteria* and *phenomena* are plurals of the same kind for the singular forms *criterion* and *phenomenon*, and they take plural verbs.

deal Colloquial in the sense of *bargain* or *transaction (the best deal in town)*; of *secret arrangement* (*I made a deal with the gangsters*); and of *treatment* (*I had a rough deal from the dean*). Currently overworked as a slang term referring to any kind of arrangement or situation.

definite, definitely Colloquial as vague intensifiers. (*That suit is a definite bargain; it is definitely handsome.*) Prefer a more specific word.

differ from, differ with To *differ from* means "to be unlike." To *differ with* means "to disagree."

different from, different than *From* is idiomatic when a preposition is required; *than* introduces a clause. See **23f**.

discreet, discrete *Discreet* means "tactful" and comes from "discretion"; *discrete* means "separate and distinct." (*Her criticism of their behavior was discreet, but she observed that the police report showed four discrete instances of public disturbance.*)

disinterested, uninterested Now frequently used interchangeably to mean "having no interest." The distinction between the two, however, is real and valuable. *Uninterested* means "without interest"; *disinterested* means "impartial." (*Good judges are disinterested but not uninterested.*)

don't A contraction for *do not*, but not for *does not*. (*She doesn't* [not *don't*] *want a Saturday class.*)

doubt but what See *but that*.

due to Some writers object to *due to* as a preposition meaning "because of" or "owing to." (*The fair was postponed because of* [or *owing to*, not *due to*] *rain.*) Acceptable when used as an adjective. (*My failure was due to laziness.*)

due to the fact that Wordy for *because*.

each and every Unnecessarily wordy.

effect See *affect, effect*.

elicit, illicit *Elicit* is a verb meaning "to bring out or draw forth"; *illicit*, an adjective, means "illegal." (*The detective elicited a confession concerning an illicit drug sale.*)

elude, allude To *elude* means "to avoid or escape from"; to *allude* means "to refer to." (*I alluded to her elusive nature; she never seemed to be at home when I called.*)

emigrate, immigrate *Emigrate* means "to leave one's country or region" for the purpose of settling in another. *Immigrate* means "to settle in a foreign country," usually permanently. It may help you to remember the difference if you can recall that *emigrate* comes from a Latin word meaning "move *away from,*" and *immigrate* comes from a Latin word meaning "to move *into.*"

eminent, imminent *Eminent* means "distinguished"; *imminent* means "impending or about to occur." (*The arrival of the eminent guest was imminent.*)

ensure, insure, assure *Ensure* and *insure* both mean "to make certain." However, *insure* usually carries the connotation of protection from financial loss, as in an *insurance policy*. (*To ensure that we would always have transportation to work, we asked the agent to include replacement auto rental in the coverage when we insured our car.*) The primary meaning of *assure* is "to inform confidently," connoting a promise. (*The agent assured us that this extra coverage would not be expensive.*)

enthused, enthusiastic *Enthused* is a colloquial verb form used to mean "enthusiastic about." It should be avoided in formal writing.

equally as good The *as* is unnecessary. *Equally good* is more precise.

etc. See *and etc.*

everyday, every day *Every day* is an adjective (*every*) modifying a noun (*day*) to explain which day. *Everyday* is an adjective meaning "ordinary, commonplace, usual." (*Every day that he wore his comfortable everyday shoes to the office someone was sure to comment that he looked "down at the heel."*)

everyone, every one See *anyone.*

everywheres Nonstandard for *everywhere.*

except See *accept, except.*

expect Colloquial when used to mean "suppose" or "believe." (*I suppose* [not *expect*] *I should do the dishes now.*)

explicit, implicit *Explicit* means "fully expressed"; *implicit* means "unexpressed," although capable of being understood. (*Although he never explicitly said no, his disapproval was implicit in his tone of voice.*)

farther, further Some writers prefer to use *farther* to refer to distance and restrict *further* to mean "in addition." (*It was two miles farther to go the way you wished, but I wanted no further trouble.*) Dictionaries recognize the forms as interchangeable.

fewer, less *Fewer* refers to numbers, *less* to amounts, degree, or value. (*We sold fewer tickets than last year, but our expenses were less.*)

field Wordy and overworked. Say, for example, *in atomic energy* not *in the field of atomic energy.* See Chapter 24.

fine As an adjective to express approval (*a fine person*), *fine* is vague and overused. As an adverb meaning "well" (*works fine*), *fine* is colloquial.

flunk Colloquial; a conversational substitute for *fail.*

former, latter *Former* refers to the first-named of two; *latter* refers to the last-named of two. *First* and *last* are used to refer to one of a group of more than two.

function As a noun meaning "event" or "occasion," *function* is appropriate only when the event is formal (*a presidential function*). As a verb meaning "work," "operate," *function* is currently overused and jargonish. (*I work* [not *function*] *best after I've had a cup of coffee.*)

further See *farther, further.*

get A standard verb, but used colloquially in many idioms inappropriate in formal writing. (*Get wise to yourself. That whistling gets me. You can't get away with it.*)

good and Colloquial as a synonym for *very* (*good and hot, good and angry*).

good, well *Good* is colloquial as an adverb. (*The motor runs well* [not *good*].) *You look good* means "You look attractive, well dressed," or the like. *You look well* means "You look healthy."

graduate Either I *graduated from* college or I *was graduated from* college is acceptable, but I *graduated college* is nonstandard.

had better, had best Standard idioms for *ought* and *should*, which are more formal. (*You had better* [or *had best*] *plan carefully.*) More formally: *You ought to* [or *should*] *plan carefully. Better* alone (*You better plan carefully*) is colloquial.

had ought, hadn't ought Nonstandard for *ought* and *ought not.*

hang, hung The principal parts of the verb are *hang, hung, hung*, but when referring to death by hanging, formal English uses *hang, hanged, hanged.* (*We hung the pictures. The prisoners hanged themselves.*)

hardly See *but.*

have, of See *of, have.*

he or she See **14c** and **23c**.

himself See *myself*.

hisself Nonstandard for *himself*.

hopefully *Hopefully* means "in a hopeful manner." (*They waited hopefully for money.*) It is now widely used in the sense of "it is hoped." (*Hopefully, you can send me money.*) Many readers object to this use.

hung See *hang, hung*.

idea Often used vaguely for *intention, plan, purpose*, and other more exact words. Prefer a more exact choice. (*My intention* [not *idea*] *is to become an engineer. The theme* [not *idea*] *of the movie is that justice is colorblind.*)

ignorant, stupid The distinction is important. An *ignorant* child is one who has been taught very little; a *stupid* child is one who is unable to learn.

illusion See *allusion, illusion*.

immigrate See *emigrate, immigrate*.

implicit, explicit See *explicit, implicit*.

imply, infer To *imply* means "to suggest without stating"; to *infer* means "to draw a conclusion." Speakers *imply*; listeners *infer*. (*They implied that the price would increase; I inferred that I should buy the computer now.*)

in, into *In* indicates "inside, enclosed, within." *Into* is more exact when the meaning is "toward, from the outside in," although *in* is common in both meanings. (*I left the book in the room and went back into the room to get it.*)

in back of, in behind, in between Wordy for *back of, behind, between*.

incredible, incredulous Something that is *incredible* is "unbelievable"; someone who is *incredulous* is "unbelieving." (*I was incredulous—surely I could not have won such an incredible amount of money.*)

infer See *imply, infer*.

ingenious, ingenuous *Ingenious* means "clever"; *ingenuous* means "naive." (*Inventors are usually ingenious, but some are too ingenuous to know what their inventions are worth.*)

in regards to Nonstandard for *as regards* or *in regard to*.

inside of, outside of The *of* is unnecessary. (*He stayed inside* [not *inside of*] *the house.*)

in the case of, in the line of See *case.*

irregardless Nonstandard for *regardless.*

is when, is where, is because Faulty predications in such sentences as *A first down is when the football is advanced ten yards in four plays or fewer. A garage is where…; The reason is because…* (see **20a**).

its, it's The possessive pronoun *its* has no apostrophe. *It's* is a contraction of *it is.*

-ize The suffix *-ize* is one of several used to form verbs from nouns and adjectives (*hospitalize, criticize, sterilize*). Writers in government, business, and other institutions have often used it excessively and unnecessarily in such coinages as *finalize, concretize, permanize.* Such coinages are widely objected to; it is best to limit your use of *-ize* words to those that are well established and resist the temptation to coin new ones. See **23e**.

judicial, judicious A *judicial* decision is one reached by the court or a judge, but a *judicious* decision is one showing sound judgment.

kind, sort These are frequently treated as plural in such constructions as *these kind of books* and *those sort of dogs.* Preferred usage in both speech and writing requires singular or plural throughout the construction, as in *this kind of book* or *these kinds of books.*

kind of, sort of Colloquial when used to mean "somewhat," "rather." (*I was rather* [not *kind of*] *pleased.*)

kind of a, sort of a Omit the *a.*

later, latter *Later* refers to time, but *latter* refers to the second of two. (*Of the twins, Meg was born first. Peg, the latter, was born three minutes later.*)

latter See *former, later.*

lay, lie To *lay* means "to place, put down." (*Lay the book on the table.*) To *lie* means "to recline." (*The dog lies on the floor.*) See **29b**.

learn, teach To *learn* means "to gain knowledge"; to *teach* means "to give knowledge." (*We learn from experience; experience teaches us much.*)

leave, let To *leave* is to depart; to *let* is to permit or allow. (*We must leave now. Will you let us give you a ride home?*)

less See *fewer, less.*

let See *leave, let.*

liable, apt, likely Often used interchangeably. But careful writing reserves *liable* for "legally responsible," or "subject to," *likely* for "probably," and *apt* for "having an aptitude for." (*I am likely to drive carefully, for I am not an apt driver, and I know I am liable for any damages.*)

lie, lay See *lay, lie,* and see **29b**.

like, as, as if *Like* is a preposition; *as* and *as if* are conjunctions. Though *like* is often used as a conjunction in speech, writing preserves the distinction. (*He looks as if* [not *like*] *he were tired.*) Note that *as if* is followed by the subjunctive *were.*

likely See *liable.*

loose, lose *Loose* means "to free." *Lose* means "to be deprived of." (*She will lose the dog if she looses him from his leash.*)

lots, lots of, a lot of Colloquial for *much, many,* or *a great deal.* (*I had a great deal of* [not *lots of*] *money and bought many* [not *lots of* or *a lot of*] *cars.*) Note spelling: *alot* is incorrect.

mad Dictionaries recognize *mad* as a synonym for *angry,* or *very enthusiastic,* but some readers object to its use in these meanings.

manner Often unnecessary in phrases like *in a precise manner* where a single adverb (*precisely*) or a "with" phrase (*with precision*) would do.

may See *can, may.*

may of Nonstandard for *may have.*

maybe, may be *Maybe* means "perhaps"; *may be* is a verb form. Be careful to distinguish between the two.

media A plural form (singular *medium*) requiring a plural verb. (*The mass media are* [not *is*] *sometimes guilty of distorting the news.*)

might of Nonstandard for *might have.*

moral, morale *Moral* is usually used as an adjective meaning "concerned with what is good or evil" or "acting according to the norms of good behavior." Occasionally, the word is used as a noun, as in "the moral of the story." *Morale* is always a noun and means "state of mind with respect to confidence, cheerfulness, and so forth." (*The scouts began their hike with high morale, whistling and singing as they walked.*)

most Colloquial as a substitute for *almost* or *nearly*.

must of Nonstandard for *must have*.

myself, yourself, himself *Myself* is often used in speech as a substitute for *I* or *me* but is not standard in written English. Reserve *myself* for emphatic (*I myself will do the work)* or reflexive use *(I hurt myself)*. The same applies to the forms *yourself, himself, herself,* etc.

nohow Nonstandard for *not at all, in no way*.

none The indefinite pronoun *none* may take either a singular or a plural verb, depending on its context. (*None of the gold was stolen; None of the men were absent.*) See **14a**.

nothing like, nowhere near Colloquial for *not nearly*. (*I was not nearly* [not *nowhere near*] *as sick as you.*)

nowheres Nonstandard for *nowhere*.

number See *amount, number*.

of, have In speech the auxiliary *have* in such combinations as *could have, might have,* etc., sounds very much like *of,* leading some people to write *could of, might of,* etc. All such combinations with *of* are nonstandard. In writing be careful to use *have*.

off of, off from Wordy and colloquial. (*The paper slid off* [not *off of*] *the table.*)

OK, O.K., okay All are standard forms, but formal writing prefers a more exact word.

on account of Wordy for *because of*. Regional for *because*. (*She bought the car because* [not *on account of*] *she needed it.*)

outside of Colloquial for *except*. (*Nobody was there except* [not *outside of*] *Henry.*) See also *inside of*.

over with Colloquial for *ended, finished, completed*.

per Appropriate in business and technical writing (*per diem, per capita, feet per second, pounds per square inch*). *As per your request* is inappropriate. In ordinary writing prefer *a* or *an* (*ninety cents a dozen, twice a day*).

percent, percentage Both mean "rate per hundred." *Percent* (sometimes written *per cent*) is used with numbers (*fifty percent, 23 percent*). *Percentage* is used without numbers (*a small percentage*). Avoid using either as a synonym for *part*. (*A small part* [not *percentage*] *of the money was lost.*)

perfect See *unique*.

persuade See *convince, persuade*.

phenomena See *data*.

plan on Colloquial in such phrases as *plan on going, plan on seeing,* for *plan to go, plan to see*.

plenty Colloquial as an adverb meaning "very, amply." (*I was very* [not *plenty] angry.*) Note that as a noun meaning "enough, a large number," *plenty* must be followed by *of* (*I've had plenty of friends.*)

plus *Plus* is a preposition and, thus, part of a prepositional phrase containing its object. It means "with the addition of" or "increased by" and is most appropriately used in contexts referring to quantity. (*My scalloped potatoes plus your baked beans ought to be enough to serve everybody.*) Avoid the temptation to use *plus* as a substitute for the conjunction *and* or as a substitute for the adverb *besides.* Not *Mom plus my sisters met my plane* but *Mom and my sisters met my plane.* Not *I'm not going to get this paper finished by Friday. Plus I have a calculus test on Thursday afternoon* but *I'm not going to get this paper finished by Friday. Besides, I have a calculus test on Thursday afternoon.*

practical, practicable *Practical* means "useful, not theoretical." *Practicable* means "capable of being put into practice." (*Franklin was a practical statesman; his schemes were practicable.*)

precede, proceed *Precede* is a verb and means "to come before." *Proceed* is also a verb but means "to move on, to advance." (*You must precede me in the line-up for graduation or the sergeant-at-arms will not let us proceed onto the stage.*)

principal, principle As an adjective *principal* means "chief, main"; as a noun it means "leader, chief officer," or, in finance, "a capital sum, as distinguished from interest or profit." The noun *principle* means "fundamental truth" or "basic law or doctrine." (*What is my principal reason for being here? I am the principal of the local elementary school. That bank pays 5 percent interest on your principal. The textbook explained the underlying principle.*)

provided, providing Both are acceptable as subordinating conjunctions meaning "on the condition." (*I will move to Washington, providing* [or *provided] the salary is adequate.*)

raise, rise *Raise, raised, raised* is a transitive verb. (*They raised potatoes.*) *Rise, rose, risen* is intransitive. (*They rose at daybreak.*)

real Colloquial for *really* or *very* (*real cloudy, real economical*).

reason is because See *is when* and **20a**.

reason why Usually redundant. (*The reason* [not *reason why*] *we won is clear.*)

refer See *allude, refer.*

regarding, in regard to, with regard to Overused and wordy for *on, about,* or *concerning*. (*We have not decided on* [not *with regard to*] *your admission.*)

respectively, respectfully *Respectively* means "separately" or "individually"; *respectfully* means "full of respect." (*The participants in the debate were St. Lawrence High School and Delphi High School, respectively. The students respectfully stated their arguments.*)

right Colloquial or dialectal when used to mean "very" (*right fresh, right happy*). *Right along* and *right away* are colloquial for *continuously, immediately.*

rise, raise See *raise, rise.*

round See *unique.*

said *Said* in such phrases as *the said paragraph, the said person* occurs frequently in legal writing. Avoid the use in ordinary writing.

scarcely See *but, hardly, scarcely.*

set, sit Often confused. See **29b**.

shall, will, should, would *Will* is now commonly used for all persons (*I, you, he, she, it*) except in the first person for questions (*Shall I go?*) and in formal contexts (*We shall consider each of your reasons*). *Should* is used for all persons when condition or obligation is being expressed (*If he should stay...We should go*). *Would* is used for all persons to express a wish or customary action. (*Would that I had listened! I would ride the same bus every day.*)

should See *shall.*

should of Nonstandard for *should have.*

since, because The subordinating conjunction *because* always indicates cause. *Since* may indicate either cause or time. (*It has rained since yesterday. Since you need money, I'll lend you some.*) Be careful to avoid using *since* in sentences where it could indicate either cause or time and thus be ambiguous. In *since we moved, we have been working longer hours*, it is unclear whether *because we moved* or *from the time we moved* is meant.

sit, set See *set, sit.*

so *So* is a loose and often imprecise conjunction. Avoid using it excessively to join independent clauses. For clauses of purpose, *so that* is preferable. (*They left so that* [not *so*] *I could study.*) *Because* is preferable when cause is clearly intended. (*Because it began to rain, we left* [not *It began to rain, so we left*].)

some Colloquial and vague when used to mean "unusual, remarkable, exciting." (*That was some party. This is some car.*) In writing use a more specific word.

someone, some one See *anyone.*

sometime, some time Use one word in the sense of a time not specified; use two words in the sense of a period of time. (*Sometime we shall spend some time together.*)

somewheres Nonstandard for *somewhere.*

sort, sort of, sort of a See *kind, sort, kind of, sort of, kind of a.*

stationary, stationery *Stationary* means "not moving"; *stationery* is writing supplies.

straight See *unique.*

stupid See *ignorant, stupid.*

such a Colloquial and overused as a vague intensifier. (*It was a very* [not *such a*] *hot day.*)

supposed to Be careful to preserve the *d* in writing. (*He was supposed to* [not *suppose to*] *take out the trash.*)

sure Colloquial for *surely, certainly.* (*I was surely* [not *sure*] *sick.*)

sure and, try and Colloquial for *sure to, try to.*

take and Nonstandard in most uses. (*Lou slammed* [not *took and slammed*] *the book down.*)

teach, learn See *learn, teach.*

than, then Don't confuse these. *Than* is a conjunction (*younger than John*). *Then* is an adverb indicating time (*then, not now*).

that Colloquial when used as an adverb. (*She's that poor she can't buy food. I didn't like the book that much.*)

that, which, who *That* always introduces restrictive clauses: *which* and *who* may introduce either restrictive or nonrestrictive clauses. See **32c.** Some writers and editors prefer to limit *which* entirely to nonrestrictive clauses. (*This is the car that I bought yesterday. This car, which I bought yesterday, is very economical.*) Use *which* when referring to things or ideas. (*Liberty, which is cherished by all people, does not come without responsibility.*) Use *who* when referring to people. (*The veterinarian who treated my dog* [not *The veterinarian which treated my dog*] *stays open until six o'clock.*)

theirselves Nonstandard for *themselves.*

then, than See *than, then.*

there, their, they're Don't confuse these. *There* is an adverb or an expletive. (*He walks there. There are six.*) *Their* is a pronoun (*their rooms*). *They're* is a contraction for *they are.* (*They're very eager.*)

these kind, these sort See *kind, sort.*

this here, that there, these here, them there Nonstandard for *this, that, these, those.*

thusly Nonstandard for *thus.*

till, 'til, until *Till* and *until* are interchangeable spellings, both acceptable in formal English. However, note that *till* is not a shortened form or contraction of *until* and should never be spelled with an apostrophe. The shortened form, *'til*, is not commonly used in contemporary writing.

to, too, two Carefully check your spelling of these three homophones (words that have the same sound but different spellings and different word origins). *To* is a preposition. *Too* is an adverb meaning "also" (*She laughed too*) or "more than enough" (*You worked too hard*). In the sense of *indeed*, it is colloquial. (*She did too laugh.*) *Two* is an adjective. (*Two geese flew overhead.*)

toward, towards Both are correct, though *toward* is more common in the United States, *towards* in Britain.

try and See *sure and.*

type Colloquial for *type of.* (*This type of* [not *type*] *research is expensive.*) Often used, but usually in hyphenated compounds (*colonial-type architecture, tile-type floors, scholarly-type text*). Omit *type* from such expressions wherever possible.

uninterested See *disinterested, uninterested.*

unique Several adjectives such as *unique, perfect, round, straight,* and *complete* name qualities that do not vary in degree. Logically, therefore, they cannot be compared. Formal use requires *more nearly round, more nearly perfect,* and the like. The comparative and superlative forms, however, are widely used colloquially in such phrases as *the most unique house, most complete examination, most perfect day.* Their occurrence even in formal English is exemplified by the phrase *more perfect union* in the Constitution.

used to In writing, be careful to preserve the *d.* (*We used to* [not *use to*] *get up at six every morning.*)

used to could Nonstandard for *used to be able.*

wait on Colloquial when used to mean "wait for"; *wait on* means "to serve, attend." (*We waited for* [not *waited on*] *the clerk to wait on us.*)

well, good *Well* may function as an adjective (for example, when modifying the subject after a linking verb: *The baby doesn't feel well*) or as an adverb (when modifying a verb, adjective, or another adverb: *The baby slept well after she was well fed by her mother*). *Good* always functions as an adjective, modifying a noun or noun substitute. (*She allowed her mother to get a good night's sleep.*) See Chapter 28.

which, that See *that, which, who.*

who's, whose *Who's* is the contraction for *who is. Whose* is the possessive form of the pronoun *who.* (*Who's the person whose books are spread across the kitchen table?*)

-wise A suffix often needlessly attached to root words to mean "with regard to" or "concerning." Particularly in writing, standard usage strongly resists this form. Other more economical substitutes are preferable. Not *Careerwise, I think electronics is a good choice for me* but *I think electronics is a good career choice for me.* Not *Things are at a standstill, trafficwise* but *Traffic is at a standstill.* Standard usage does accept *-wise* to indicate direction in such words as *clockwise, crosswise, lengthwise.*

would of, should of Nonstandard forms of *would have* and *should have.* Not *We should of taken an umbrella* but *We should have taken an umbrella.*

you're, your *You're* is a contraction for *you are. Your* is the second-person possessive pronoun. (*You're not going to eat your other doughnut, are you?*)

you was Nonstandard for *you were.*

Index

To use the index, search first for the broad term you need, such as *Adjectives*. Under *Adjectives*, you will find a list of subheadings that will allow you to locate the specific information for which you are searching. For example, suppose you are trying to remember the difference between an adjective and an adverb. The subheading "and adverbs" will point you to the section of the handbook that discusses adjectives and adverbs together. The numbers in **boldface** refer you to Chapters 26 and 28, and more specifically to Sections **26d** and **28b**. The numbers in regular type are the page numbers. Use either the numbers and letters in the top corner of the pages to find Sections **26d** and **28b** or the page numbers to find the relevant discussion.

Revision and Proofreading Symbols

Symbol	Meaning	Chapter/Section	Symbol	Meaning	Chapter/Section
abbr	abbreviation	**44**	**ro** (also **fs**)	run-on sentence	**13**
adj/adv (also **ad**)	adjectives/adverbs	**28**		(fused sentence)	
agr	agreement	**14**	**shift**	shift	**16**
appr	appropriate langage	**22**	**sp**, (**sp**)	spelling, spell out	**25, 44**
awk (also **mix**)	awkward sentence; mixed	**20**	**sense** (also **ss**)	sentence sense	**26**
	construction		**subord** (also **sub**)	subordinating	**8b–d, 26e**
cap	capital letter	**40**		conjunction, clause	
case	case	**27**	**syl** (also **wd div**)	syllabication (word division)	**45**
coh	paragraph coherence	**6b, d**	**t** (also **vt**)	verb tense	**29d**
comp	comparison	**19**	**unn**	unnecessary	
coord	coordinating	**8a, 8d, 26e**	**var**	sentence variety	**11**
	conjunction, clause		**vb**	verb	**29–30**
cs	comma splice	**13**	**wd** (also **ww, d**)	word choice	**21-24**
dev	paragraph,	**6e**		(wrong word, diction)	
	idea development		**wd div**	word division	**45**
dgl mod	dangling modifier	**18**	**wdy**	wordy	**24a**
dict (also **d**)	dictionary, diction	**21–24**	**//**	parallelism	**9**
dir	directness	**24**	**. ? !**	period, question mark,	**31**
doc	documentation	**48, 50–52**		exclamation point	
eff sent	effective sentence	**8–11**	**; :**	semicolon, colon	**33, 34**
emph	emphasis	**10**	**— ( )**	dash and parentheses	**35**
exact	exact language	**23**	**" "**	quotation marks	**37**
frag	sentence fragment	**12**	**[ ] ...**	brackets, ellipsis marks	**38**
fs (also **ro**)	fused sentence (run-on)	**13**	**ital** ____	italics (underscore)	**39**
glos terms	glossary of grammatical	**54**	**'**	apostrophe	**41**
	terms		**-**	hyphen	**42**
glos use	glossary of usage	**55**			
gram	grammar	**26-30**	**∧** (caret)	insert	
hyph	hyphen	**42**	**g**	delete	
ital	italics	**39**	⌒	close up space	
jarg	jargon	**22d**	∿	transpose letter, word	
log	logic, fallacies	**7g**	lc /p	lower case a capital letter	
mix	mixed construction	**20b**	cap **d** UC	capitalize a letter,	
mpl mod (also **mm**)	misplaced modifier	**17**		make upper case	
num	numbers	**43**	# ∧	insert space	
om	omitted word, letter, etc.	**19a-c**	X	obvious error	
¶	new paragraph	**6**			
plan	planning	**2**			
pass	passive voice verb	**10f, 16a, 24a, 29e**			
punct (also **p**)	punctuation	**31-38**			
ref	pronoun reference	**15**			
redun (also **rep**)	redundant or repetitious	**24a**			
revise (also **rev**)	revision	**5**			

How to Use Your Handbook

Your *Prentice Hall Handbook* has been carefully designed so that you can easily use it as a reference source for questions about grammar, punctuation, mechanics, style, writing, and research strategies. Here are some suggestions to help you get the most out of your handbook when questions arise in your writing.

How to Find Information

You can look up your topic in one of four places:

- The **Table of Contents,** located at the front of the book

- The **Index,** located at the back of the book

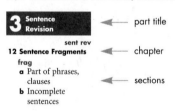

- The list of **Revision and Proofreading Symbols,** located at the end of the Index

frag	Unacceptable sentence fragment	**12**
symbol	meaning	section number

- The **Contents Overview,** located inside the front cover

  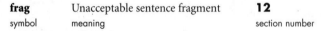

Then turn to the chapter covering your topic, which you can locate either by page number or by using the red circles at the top of each page. Each circle indicates the chapter number and section letter, and a correction symbol next to the circles tells you which topic is covered on the page.

How to Use Information

Once you have found the chapter covering your topic, read the rules and explanation. Rules will give you the basic information about your topic in a sentence or two. Explanations will give you a more detailed discussion of the rule you have just read.

Study the **examples.** Every rule is illustrated by an example. Examples of